Daniel

Windows®
Phone 8

UNLEASHED

SAMS | 800

Windows® Phone 8 Unleashed

ISBN-13: 978-0-672-33689-8
ISBN-10: 0-672-33689-8

Library of Congress Control Number: 2013936246

Printed in the United States of America

First Printing May 2013

Trademarks

All terms mentioned in this book that are known to be trademarks or service marks have been appropriately capitalized. Sams Publishing cannot attest to the accuracy of this information. Use of a term in this book should not be regarded as affecting the validity of any trademark or service mark.

Windows is a registered trademark of Microsoft Corporation.

Warning and Disclaimer

Every effort has been made to make this book as complete and as accurate as possible, but no warranty or fitness is implied. The information provided is on an "as is" basis. The author and the publisher shall have neither liability nor responsibility to any person or entity with respect to any loss or damages arising from the information contained in this book.

Bulk Sales

Sams Publishing offers excellent discounts on this book when ordered in quantity for bulk purchases or special sales. For more information, please contact

> **U.S. Corporate and Government Sales**
> 1-800-382-3419
> corpsales@pearsontechgroup.com

For sales outside the United States, please contact

> **International Sales**
> international@pearsoned.com

Editor-in-Chief
Greg Wiegand

Executive Editor
Neil Rowe

Development Editor
Mark Renfrow

Managing Editor
Sandra Schroeder

Senior Project Editor
Tonya Simpson

Copy Editor
Barbara Hacha

Indexer
Ken Johnson

Proofreader
Debbie Williams

Technical Editor
J. Boyd Nolan

Publishing Coordinator
Cindy Teeters

Book Designer
Anne Jones

Compositor
Jake McFarland

Contents at a Glance

Table of Contents

Part II   Essential Elements

Preface

Welcome to the second in the series of *Windows Phone Unleashed* titles. This book extends the previous book, *Windows Phone 7.5 Unleashed*, and provides new content covering the terrific new features of the Windows Phone 8 SDK. The Windows Phone 8 SDK builds upon the strong foundation of the previous SDK for creating XAML-based apps. If you read *Windows Phone 7.5 Unleashed*, you will find much of the content familiar. The content has, however, been updated across the board to cover changes in the 8.0 SDK, of which there are many. You also will find seven new chapters covering the new features of the 8.0 SDK.

Although the scope of this book remains squarely on building XAML-based apps, there have been some major changes to the other UI technologies supported by Windows Phone 8. The new SDK still enables you to build XNA UI apps for Windows Phone 7.1 devices, but support has been discontinued for Windows Phone 8 apps. And although Windows Phone 7.1 apps can be downloaded from the Windows Phone Marketplace and run on Windows Phone 8 devices, Windows Phone 7.1 apps cannot use the new features found in the 8.0 SDK. For high-performance games, Microsoft now encourages the use of Direct3D and C++ for native code, which was not available in Windows Phone 7.1. Although XNA is no longer directly supported for developing Windows Phone 8 apps, you can use third-party frameworks, such as MonoGame (www.monogame.net), to create XNA-based WP8 apps. However, this is outside the scope of this book.

As Microsoft continues to converge its various platforms, the Windows Phone SDK now contains some APIs that overlap with Windows 8's WinRT. Windows Phone does not inherit all these new APIs, and in fact, has its own new set of partially overlapping APIs known as WinPRT. No prizes for guessing what the 'P' stands for.

The environmental requirements for developing Windows Phone 8 apps are now restricted to Windows 8 x64 and Visual Studio 2012. And Windows Phone 8 apps do not run on older devices running Windows Phone 7.1. You can, however, develop Windows Phone 7.1 apps using the Windows Phone 8.0 SDK.

Scope of This Book

This book targets Windows Phone 8 (Apollo). Although you see some examples incorporating XNA for audio and media, this book's focus is squarely on XAML for Windows Phone. The book covers all main areas of the topic in a deep, yet easily comprehensible way, using practical examples with a real-world context. The goal is to provide you with concepts and techniques that will help you to design and develop well-engineered and robust Windows Phone apps.

Throughout this book you see a small number of techniques and custom code applied to make developing phone apps easier. It is not the intention to make what you will learn in the book harder to reach; on the contrary, the techniques are tried and tested approaches that, when they become familiar, will help you build more testable and maintainable apps that can be potentially ported to other platforms. The competition between apps on the Windows Phone platform has intensified as the number of apps in the Windows Phone Marketplace has increased dramatically. This competition not only brings with it a "long tail," where independent developers find evermore niche categories to create apps for, but also requires apps competing in the more popular categories to increase their feature sets. As apps become more complex, maintainability comes to the fore, and greater attention to managing complexity is required.

This book is not a book for those without at least some knowledge of XAML. Although there is considerable reference material for some essential XAML infrastructure, included within these chapters are advanced topics, such as the Model-View-ViewModel design pattern (MVVM). In fact, most sample apps follow the MVVM pattern. The concepts and techniques used throughout the book are described in Chapter 2, "Fundamental Concepts in Windows Phone Development." Do not worry if some of these approaches seem foreign to you; by the end of the book they will be second nature.

Wherever possible, you are provided with tips and techniques that go beyond the topic, and you will frequently find content not easily found elsewhere. A substantial amount of custom code is provided that extends the Windows Phone SDK to support real app scenarios.

Assumptions About the Reader

If you are an experienced developer who has basic experience in Silverlight, WPF, or Windows 8 XAML apps looking to transfer your skills to Windows Phone, then this book is for you. It is assumed that you are familiar with C#, XAML, and Visual Studio.

Book Structure

The book is divided into five parts:

▶ Part I, "Windows Phone App Development Fundamentals"

▶ Part II, "Essential Elements"

▶ Part III, "Windows Phone App Development"

▶ Part IV, "Building Data Driven Apps"

▶ Part V, "Multitasking"

Most chapters have sample apps. Chapter 2 is required reading to understand the techniques used throughout the book and the samples.

Some chapters, in particular Chapter 9, "Enriching the User Experience with the Windows Phone Toolkit Controls," are not intended to be read from beginning-to-end, but rather are intended as a reference that you may refer back to when you need to learn about a particular topic within the chapter.

Code Samples

To demonstrate each concept, this book contains more than 100 samples. The sample code for this book can be downloaded from www.informit.com/title/9780672336898.

All code is in C#. The project structure is divided into topic areas. To view a particular sample, you can run the main solution and select the sample page from the index (see Figure 1).

FIGURE 1   The sample code index page.

In the downloadable sample code are several solutions. In most cases, the Vaughan.WPUnleashed.sln is used. The code for some topics, however, has been placed into separate solutions because of technical constraints.

Much of the infrastructure code presented in the book has been consolidated into the Calcium open source project. You can find more information about the Calcium SDK at http://calciumsdk.net.

About the Author

Daniel Vaughan is cofounder of Outcoder, a Swiss software and consulting company dedicated to creating best-of-breed connected user experiences and leading-edge back-end solutions, using the Microsoft stack of technologies—in particular WPF, Windows 8, WinRT, Silverlight, and Windows Phone.

Daniel is a Microsoft MVP for Client Application Development, with commercial experience across a wide range of industries, including finance, e-commerce, and multimedia. Daniel is a Silverlight and WPF Insider, a member of the elite WPF Disciples group, a three-time CodeProject MVP, and is a member of the Microsoft Developer Guidance Advisory Council.

He is a technical advisory board member of PebbleAge, a Swiss finance company specializing in business process management.

He also is the creator of a number of open source projects, including Calcium and Clog.

Daniel blogs at http://danielvaughan.org, where he publishes articles and software prototypes. You also can catch Daniel on Twitter at @dbvaughan.

Daniel has a degree in Computer Science from UNE, where he received various awards, including twice the annual School of Mathematics, Statistics and Computer Science Prize, and the Thomas Arnold Burr Memorial Prize in Mathematics.

With his wife, Daniel runs the Windows Phone Experts group on LinkedIn at http://linkd.in/jnFoqE.

Originally from Australia and the UK, Daniel is based in Zurich, Switzerland, where he lives with his wife, Katka, and son Bertie.

Dedication

To my wonderful wife, Kateřina and my son, Bertie.

Acknowledgments

Katka Vaughan, for endless advice, proofreading, and formatting. Your contribution and unending patience made this book possible.

Peter Torr, for invaluable assistance on Microsoft forums.

Microsoft, for answering questions and building great tools.

The terrific team at Sams. Especially Neil Rowe, for guidance throughout the entire process. Technical editor J. Boyd Nolan, for going over my code with a fine-toothed comb.

The great folks at PebbleAge. In particular, Olivier Parchet and Christian Kobel for their encouragement and goodwill.

Inspiration and support (in no particular order):

Cliff Simpkins, John Papa, Davide Zordan, Jaime Rodriguez, Marlon Grech, Glenn Block, Charles Petzold, Josh Smith, Sacha Barber, David Anson, Peter O'Hanlon, Corrado Cavalli, Colin Eberhardt, René Schulte, Laurent Bugnion, Jeff Wilcox, Damian Mehers, Shawn Wildermuth, Sascha Corti, Rob Tiffany, Walt Ritscher, Michael Crump, Matteo Pagani, Atley Hunter, Ginny Caughey, my friends at Wintellect, Jeremy Likness, Steven Porter, Todd Fine, and Jeff Prosise.

We Want to Hear from You!

As the reader of this book, *you* are our most important critic and commentator. We value your opinion and want to know what we're doing right, what we could do better, what areas you'd like to see us publish in, and any other words of wisdom you're willing to pass our way.

We welcome your comments. You can email or write to let us know what you did or didn't like about this book—as well as what we can do to make our books better.

Please note that we cannot help you with technical problems related to the topic of this book.

When you write, please be sure to include this book's title and author as well as your name and email address. We will carefully review your comments and share them with the author and editors who worked on the book.

E-mail: feedback@samspublishing.com

Mail: Sams Publishing
        ATTN: Reader Feedback
        800 East 96th Street
        Indianapolis, IN 46240 USA

Reader Services

Visit our website and register this book at informit.com/register for convenient access to any updates, downloads, or errata that might be available for this book.

CHAPTER 1

Introduction to Windows Phone App Development

The mobile phone industry is highly competitive. After stiff competition from other mobile technologies, Microsoft has gone all out to reenter the mobile software market with a strong emphasis on software, hardware, and services. Windows Phone 8 builds on Windows Phone 7 and represents a clean break from the past. As a consequence Windows Mobile 6.5 applications are not compatible with Windows Phone.

Windows Phone provides developers with three powerful UI technologies for developing apps: XAML, XNA, and Direct3D. Although this book does not cover Direct3D, and the focus of this book is squarely on XAML-based apps, it would not be complete without some coverage of XNA because XNA APIs provide access to key features of the phone.

> **NOTE**
>
> XAML is a markup language, and variants of the technology exist in Silverlight, WPF, and even non-UI technologies such as Windows Workflow Foundation. If you are familiar with earlier version of the Windows Phone SDK; pre-Windows Phone 8, you may be wondering why the sudden emphasis on XAML as a UI technology. Where did Silverlight go? The answer is that it is still there, but it is no longer called Silverlight. The rendering technology underpinning XAML apps in Windows Phone is still firmly based on Silverlight, and Microsoft's shift away from Silverlight has resulted in the Silverlight technology in Windows Phone being rebranded as XAML plus .NET.

This chapter begins by guiding you through the installation of the Windows Phone development tools. Finally, it walks you through the creation of a first XAML base app for Windows Phone.

Installing the Windows Phone SDK

The Windows Phone SDK 8.0, includes all the software required to get you started building Windows Phone apps. It can be downloaded from the Windows Phone Dev Center site at http://dev.windowsphone.com.

NOTE

Unlike previous versions of the SDK, the Windows Phone SDK 8.0 requires Windows 8 64-bit (x64).

After you have downloaded and started the setup program, the setup automatically downloads and installs the required components. The SDK supports the development of XAML, XNA, and Direct3D apps. However, development of XNA apps is supported only for Windows Phone 7.1 apps. Although Windows Phone 8 devices can download and use Windows Phone 7.1 apps, those apps are unable to leverage the new features of the Windows Phone 8 SDK.

The developer tools include the following items:

- ▶ Visual Studio Express 2012
- ▶ The Windows Phone Emulator, which allows you to debug your applications on the desktop
- ▶ Microsoft Expression Blend for Windows Phone

NOTE

During installation, if you have Visual Studio 2012 already installed, the tools are integrated into the existing Visual Studio installation. If not, Visual Studio 2012 Express is installed.

Creating Your First XAML for Windows Phone App

This section walks through the creation of a simple XAML app using Visual Studio and looks at using the Windows Phone emulator to debug applications on the desktop.

To create an XAML-based project for Windows Phone, follow these steps:

1. From within Visual Studio 2012, select New Project from the File menu.

2. Select the Windows Phone node in the Installed Templates pane of the Add New Project dialog (see Figure 1.1).

3. Select Windows Phone App.

4. Provide the project with a name and location.

5. Click OK.

6. A dialog is presented allowing you to select either the 7.1 (Mango) or 8.0 (Apollo) platform. Select Windows Phone OS 8.0 and click OK.

FIGURE 1.1   Creating a new Windows Phone Application project using the Add New Project dialog.

The Windows Phone App template produces a project containing an App.xaml file, a MainPage.xaml, and their respective code-beside[1] files (see Figure 1.2).

> **NOTE**
>
> I prefer the Solution Explorer to be on the left in Visual Studio. This is different from the default layout, which positions the Solution Explorer on the right. You are free to configure the layout as you wish.

---

1. The term code-beside is analogous to code-behind, except that rather than the code-behind class being a subclass of the class generated from the markup file, the code-beside and the markup file are partial classes of the same class type.

TIP

The XAML design view within Visual Studio can take a few moments to render a page or control. To prevent the designer from automatically loading the design view, select Options from the Tools menu, locate the Text Editor/XAML/Miscellaneous node, and check the option Always Open Documents in Full XAML View.

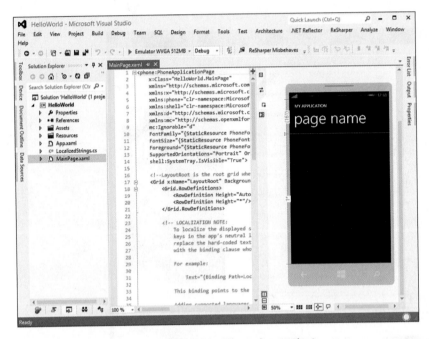

FIGURE 1.2   A newly created Windows Phone App project.

After the project has been created, it is ready to be run inside the emulator. Select Start Debugging from the Debug menu in Visual Studio or press F5 to launch the emulator and then the debugger. The first time the emulator starts, it presents a loading message and may take several seconds to initialize.

TIP

The Windows Phone emulator is a virtual machine containing the actual Windows Phone operating system (OS). Launching the emulator incurs a delay because the OS takes time to load. Leaving the emulator open between debugging sessions minimizes the initial startup delay.

The emulator contains a floating menu that allows you to close or minimize the emulator, change the orientation of the display, change the display size of the emulated device, and open the Additional Tools window (see Figure 1.3).

FIGURE 1.3   The Windows Phone emulator's floating menu.

The Close button shuts down the Windows Phone emulator. It is best to avoid using the Close button to end a debugging session for reasons set out in the previous tip.

The Minimize button works in the same manner as the Minimize button on a Windows desktop application. The emulator continues to run but is not visible on the desktop.

Rotate Orientation (Clockwise and Counter Clockwise) changes the display orientation from landscape to portrait or portrait to landscape. In Chapter 4, "Controlling Page Orientation," you see how to programmatically monitor and control the orientation of a page.

Fit to Screen scales the emulator display to fit about 80% of your smallest screen dimension.

Use the Show Resolution Settings item to display the Resolution Settings dialog, which is used to scale the display from 33% to 100%. The phone's screen has a pixel density of 262 DPI, which is more than twice as great as the default 96 DPI that Windows uses. This is why, at 100%, the emulator looks so large on the desktop.

When the emulator finishes loading, the newly created application launches, and the `MainPage` is displayed (see Figure 1.4).

FIGURE 1.4   A freshly created app running on the emulator.

A new Windows Phone App project starts out with a `PhoneApplicationPage` called `MainPage`, set to a `Portrait` orientation. `MainPage` is the default starting page for the application.

NOTE

You can change the display name of your app and other properties by modifying your app's WMAppManifest.xaml file, which is located in the Properties directory of the project (see Figure 1.5). You explore the various other tabs within the WMAppManifest.xml editor in subsequent chapters.

FIGURE 1.5   The project properties tab allows customization of the application's title.

The display name and icon fields are used to distinguish the application from others on the phone's App List (see Figure 1.6). You can reach the App List from the phone's start page, known as the Start Experience.

The Tile options, including the Title and Background Image fields, are applied when the app is pinned to the Start Experience.

You explore tiles in greater detail in Chapter 13, "Portraying Your App with Live Tiles."

FIGURE 1.6   The application's title is displayed on the App List.

Despite the debugger being detached from the emulator after a debugging session has ended, the app is still deployed to the emulator and can be relaunched from the App List. Closing the emulator, however, removes the app from the App List and, in fact, resets the state of the emulator. Therefore, customization of an app within the emulator persists only while the emulator is running and is lost when the emulator is closed.

The `Application` Class

XAML apps rely on an instance of the `System.Windows.Application` class to perform the startup activities of the app. Visual Studio's Windows Phone App template creates an `App` class that subclasses the `Application` class. The `App` class consists of an App.xaml.cs file (the code-beside) containing a partial class and an accompanying App.xaml XAML file. The App.xaml file allows for resources, such as styles, to be defined in XAML and used throughout your app (see Listing 1.1).

The `App` class derives from the `Application` class by using the `x:Class` attribute in the `Application` element of the App.xaml file.

LISTING 1.1   App.xaml

```
<Application
    x:Class="HelloWorld.App"
    xmlns="http://schemas.microsoft.com/winfx/2006/xaml/presentation"
    xmlns:x="http://schemas.microsoft.com/winfx/2006/xaml"
    xmlns:phone="clr-namespace:Microsoft.Phone.Controls;assembly=Microsoft.Phone"
```

```
xmlns:shell="clr-namespace:Microsoft.Phone.Shell;assembly=Microsoft.Phone">

    <!--Application Resources-->
    <Application.Resources>
<local:LocalizedStrings xmlns:local="clr-namespace:HelloWorld"
        x:Key="LocalizedStrings"/>
    </Application.Resources>

    <Application.ApplicationLifetimeObjects>
        <!--Required object that handles lifetime events for the application-->
        <shell:PhoneApplicationService
        Launching="Application_Launching" Closing="Application_Closing"
        Activated="Application_Activated"
        Deactivated="Application_Deactivated"/>
    </Application.ApplicationLifetimeObjects>

</Application>
```

Within App.xaml, the `PhoneApplicationService` is used to subscribe to application lifetime events. You look at lifetime events in greater detail in Chapter 3, "Understanding the Application Execution Model."

Event handlers for lifetime events are located in the `App` class. You use this class to perform tasks before the UI is shown. The App class creates the `PhoneApplicationFrame` instance, which plays host to the `MainPage`, and any other pages, at runtime. The `PhoneApplicationFrame` is analogous to a web browser in that it handles navigation to and from each `PhoneApplicationPage`.

The `App` class also includes an event handler for unhandled exceptions. If an exception is raised anywhere in the app, from any thread, and it is not handled, the `Application.UnhandledException` event is raised, affording your app the opportunity to log the error or warn the user that an error has occurred.

TIP

If there are multiple `Application` classes within a project, the desired `Application` class can be specified by selecting the Startup Object in the project's properties page. To open the properties page for a project, press Alt+Enter or right-click the project node in the Visual Studio Solution Explorer and select Properties.

Sometimes renaming a namespace can invalidate the Startup Object setting, which causes your app to silently fail during startup. If that happens, open the Properties tab and select a valid App class from the Startup Object drop-down list.

MainPage

The `MainPage` code-beside is shown in Listing 1.2. The using statement for `Microsoft.Phone.Controls` is particular to Windows Phone and contains controls such as the `PhoneApplicationPage`.

A commented region demonstrates how to initialize and populate the page's ApplicationBar control. I ordinarily delete that code because I leverage a custom application bar wrapper that supports data-binding. You learn about the application bar in Chapter 8, "Taming the Application Bar."

TIP

The using statements are placed in the code-beside file as a convenience, to save you time when writing code. It is a good practice to remove any unused using statements from a class because it decreases clutter and eliminates unnecessary dependencies, which can sometimes prevent compilation when linking class files across different projects, where the namespaces do not exist.

LISTING 1.2   MainPage.cs

```csharp
using System;
using System.Collections.Generic;
using System.Linq;
using System.Net;
using System.Windows;
using System.Windows.Controls;
using System.Windows.Navigation;
using Microsoft.Phone.Controls;
using Microsoft.Phone.Shell;
using HelloWorld.Resources;

namespace HelloWorld
{
    public partial class MainPage : PhoneApplicationPage
    {
        // Constructor
        public MainPage()
        {
            InitializeComponent();

            // Sample code to localize the ApplicationBar
            //BuildLocalizedApplicationBar();
        }

// Sample code for building a localized ApplicationBar
//private void BuildLocalizedApplicationBar()
```

```
//{
//    // Set the page's ApplicationBar to a new instance of ApplicationBar.
//    ApplicationBar = new ApplicationBar();

//    // Create a new button and set the text value to the localized string from
//    ➥AppResources.
//    ApplicationBarIconButton appBarButton = new ApplicationBarIconButton(new
Uri("/Assets/AppBar/appbar.add.rest.png", UriKind.Relative));
//    appBarButton.Text = AppResources.AppBarButtonText;
//    ApplicationBar.Buttons.Add(appBarButton);

//    // Create a new menu item with the localized string from AppResources.
//    ApplicationBarMenuItem appBarMenuItem = new
//    ➥ApplicationBarMenuItem(AppResources.AppBarMenuItemText);
//    ApplicationBar.MenuItems.Add(appBarMenuItem);
//}
    }
}
```

MainPage.xaml contains the initial layout, with a `Grid` as the root content, a child `StackPanel` containing the application title and page title, and another `Grid` to place the page's content (see Listing 1.3).

LISTING 1.3   MainPage.xaml

```
<phone:PhoneApplicationPage
    x:Class="HelloWorldXaml.MainPage"
    xmlns="http://schemas.microsoft.com/winfx/2006/xaml/presentation"
    xmlns:x="http://schemas.microsoft.com/winfx/2006/xaml"
    xmlns:phone="clr-namespace:Microsoft.Phone.Controls;assembly=Microsoft.Phone"
    xmlns:shell="clr-namespace:Microsoft.Phone.Shell;assembly=Microsoft.Phone"
    xmlns:d="http://schemas.microsoft.com/expression/blend/2008"
    xmlns:mc="http://schemas.openxmlformats.org/markup-compatibility/2006"
    FontFamily="{StaticResource PhoneFontFamilyNormal}"
    FontSize="{StaticResource PhoneFontSizeNormal}"
    Foreground="{StaticResource PhoneForegroundBrush}"
    SupportedOrientations="Portrait" Orientation="Portrait"
    mc:Ignorable="d" d:DesignWidth="480" d:DesignHeight="768"
    shell:SystemTray.IsVisible="True">

    <!--LayoutRoot contains the root grid where all other page content is placed-->
    <Grid x:Name="LayoutRoot" Background="Transparent">
        <Grid.RowDefinitions>
            <RowDefinition Height="Auto"/>
            <RowDefinition Height="*"/>
        </Grid.RowDefinitions>
```

```
<!--TitlePanel contains the name of the application and page title-->
<StackPanel x:Name="TitlePanel" Grid.Row="0" Margin="24,24,0,12">
    <TextBlock x:Name="ApplicationTitle"
            Text="MY APPLICATION"
            Style="{StaticResource PhoneTextNormalStyle}"/>
    <TextBlock x:Name="PageTitle" Text="page name" Margin="-3,-8,0,0"
            Style="{StaticResource PhoneTextTitle1Style}"/>
</StackPanel>

<!--ContentPanel - place additional content here-->
<Grid x:Name="ContentGrid" Grid.Row="1">
</Grid>
</Grid>

</phone:PhoneApplicationPage>
```

The `x:Class` attribute indicates the code-beside type, which in this case is the `HelloWorldXaml.MainPage` class.

The `mc:Ignorable="d"` attribute is used to instruct the compiler to ignore any elements or attributes that begin with `d:`. The two attributes `d:DesignHeight` and `d:DesignWidth` are used at design time by Visual Studio and Expression Blend to render the page using the specified dimensions. These attributes are for your benefit and do not influence the page at runtime.

Various text related properties are set in the `phone:PhoneApplicationPage` element, specifically the `FontFamily`, `FontSize`, and `Foreground` properties. These indicate the default appearance of text in an element such as a `TextBlock`, when not specified on the element itself. This is an example of parent-child property value inheritance, where the child control uses the closest ancestor's property value if it does not define its own.

Styles are set to predefined `StaticResources`, and colors vary according to what theme the user selected for the phone device, either light or dark and the selected accent color. For a complete list of predefined styles see http://bit.ly/cUmhGi.

Summary

This chapter began by guiding you through the installation of the Windows Phone development tools. It then walked you through the creation of a first XAML base app for Windows Phone. You saw how the `App` class is used to perform the startup activities of your app and enables you to define resources, such as styles, that can be used throughout your application.

CHAPTER 2

Fundamental Concepts in Windows Phone Development

This chapter provides an overview of some common pieces of phone infrastructure and describes various techniques that are useful when building Windows Phone apps.

This chapter begins with a look at the principal output of a Windows Phone Application project: the XAP file. The chapter discusses its composition and shows how to deploy a XAP file to a developer unlocked device.

The chapter then looks at the security capability model of the phone and at how this model is used to notify the user of any potential dangers before downloading an app from the Windows Phone Marketplace. You also look at using the Marketplace Test Kit to determine the capability requirements of your app.

Next, the chapter examines the threading model of XAML for Windows Phone and examines various performance considerations when creating animations or hiding and showing visual elements. You see how the Windows Phone frame rate counter works and learn how to interpret each reading shown on the display.

The chapter then looks at the Windows Phone Application Analysis tool. You see how to profile your app's performance and memory usage, improve the responsiveness of your app, and help ensure that your app passes the Windows Phone Marketplace certification requirements.

The chapter turns to the custom code and commonly used techniques that you see throughout the book and that underpin many of the examples in subsequent chapters.

It is not uncommon to have many pages in a Windows Phone app, and having a solid codebase that contains a common infrastructure and frequently used services can save a lot of time. In fact, with more than 100 example pages included in the downloadable sample code, creating the code for this book would have taken considerably longer without it.

The techniques demonstrated are tried and tested approaches that help you build more maintainable apps and, by the end of the book, will have become exceedingly familiar to you if they are not so already.

The overview of the custom infrastructure begins with an exposé of the Model-View-ViewModel pattern, and you see how it is applied in the downloadable sample code. You then examine how property change notification is implemented and see techniques for improving the traditional implementation of `INotifyPropertyChanged` so that it works effortlessly with multithreaded apps.

Next, the chapter looks at the commanding infrastructure used throughout the book and examines a custom `ICommand` that allows you to specify handlers for command evaluation and execution. There is also a brief overview of the argument validation system commonly used in the sample code to validate method arguments.

The chapter then explores a custom dialog service that enables you to ask the user a question from your viewmodel, while remaining compatible with unit testing.

Finally, the chapter shows how to consume Windows Communication Foundation (WCF) services that reside on the same machine as the emulator, and outlines important steps to enable several of the apps in the downloadable sample code.

Understanding the Role of XAP Files

The output of a Visual Studio project normally consists of a multitude of files, which may include assemblies, images, config files, manifest files, and so forth. XAP (pronounced *zap*) files contain project output that is bundled up, ready for deployment.

XAP files have been around since the early days of Silverlight 2 (beta 1) and allow developers to easily deploy an entire Silverlight application to a remote server. On the Windows Phone platform, they are used to deploy an app to the Windows Phone Marketplace or to a developer unlocked device.

A XAP file is a compressed zip file that contains your project assemblies and resources, along with two application manifest files: AppManifest.xml and WMAppManifest.xml, both of which are located in the Properties directory of the project.

NOTE

It is a certification requirement that the XAP file contains both an AppManifest.xml file and a WMAppManifest.xml file. Both of these files are automatically generated when creating a new Windows Phone application from within Visual Studio. In nearly all cases, AppManifest.xml does not require changes by you. WMAppManifest.xml, however, may require editing depending on the features supported by your app.

When publishing to the Windows Phone Marketplace, your app's XAP file is submitted as part of the publishing process.

To obtain the XAP file for your app, perform a build using a Release build configuration. You can then find the XAP file located in your app's Bin/Release directory.

> **NOTE**
>
> When submitting your application to the Windows Phone Marketplace, the XAP file that you submit must be built using a release configuration without debug information or it may fail the certification process.

> **NOTE**
>
> The maximum allowed size of the XAP package file for Windows Phone Marketplace certification is 225MB.

The Application Deployment Tool

XAP files allow you to circulate your app to developers that have a developer unlocked device. This is done using the Application Deployment tool that is installed along with the Windows Phone SDK. The tool allows you to navigate to select a XAP file and deploy it to a connected phone device (see Figure 2.1).

FIGURE 2.1   The Application Deployment tool.

If you have not encountered XAP files before, they will certainly become relevant when you want to publish your first app to the Windows Phone Marketplace.

The Windows Phone Capabilities Model

Microsoft recognizes that making the user experience on the phone the best it can be helps to secure greater adoption of the platform. To this end, users should never regret installing an app, and one way to ensure this is by using a security model that requires users to opt-in to certain functionality within the app, called capabilities.

A capability is a phone resource that when used by your app may bring with it privacy or security concerns, or it may incur a cost that the user should be made aware of. Examples of capabilities include the camera, geographic location services, microphone, and SMS.

Capabilities are a way of disclosing to the user what an app is potentially able to do. Your app's capabilities are displayed to potential users, those considering downloading the app from the Windows Phone Marketplace. It is at the user's discretion whether to download your app; if a user does not want an app to have access to, for example, the phone's camera, the user may decide not to download that app.

You define your app's capabilities in its WMAppManifest.xml file. When a new Windows Phone application is created, a subset of the available capabilities is included by default in the manifest file. The Windows Phone operating system grants security permissions to the application according to the capabilities listed in the manifest file. See http://bit.ly/Pj2YgE for a list of these capabilities.

When an app is submitted to the Windows Phone Marketplace, the XAP file is decompressed, validated, and repackaged. During this process the security capabilities of the app are discovered and written back to the WMAppManifest.xml file. As a result, if the manifest does not contain capabilities that are used by your app, these capabilities are inserted as part of the submission process.

NOTE

The capabilities specified in the WMAppManifest.xml file before submission are relevant only while debugging your app. By removing unnecessary capabilities from the manifest you ensure that no unintended capabilities have crept in during development.

Two capabilities, however, are exceptions to this process: ID_CAP_NETWORKING and ID_HW_FFCCAMERA.

If the ID_CAP_NETWORKING (networking) capability is removed from your app's manifest, it will not be reinserted during the submission process; this enables you to prevent all network activity from your app if you want.

If the ID_HW_FFCCAMERA (front facing camera) capability is specified in your manifest file, it is not automatically removed during the submission process.

NOTE

After submission to the Windows Phone Marketplace, and during the capability discovery process, the Microsoft Intermediate Language (MSIL) of the assemblies located in your XAP file are analyzed. If a phone API that requires a particular capability is detected, the capability is added to the WMAppManifest.xml file. This occurs even if your app never calls the code at runtime. It is therefore important to be mindful that referencing another assembly can inadvertently add security capabilities to your app if the other assembly uses an API that requires capabilities. The security capability detection mechanism is not clever enough to walk your MSIL to discover whether it is actually used; it merely identifies the presence of the API.

NOTE

To pass Windows Phone Marketplace certification, apps are not allowed to use P/Invoke or COM Interop.

Determining App Capabilities Using the Marketplace Test Kit

The Windows Phone SDK includes a tool for analyzing the capabilities required by your app. To analyze your app's capability requirements, perform the following steps:

1. Build the app using a Release configuration.

2. Right-click the Windows Phone app project's node in the Visual Studio Solution Explorer and select Open Store Test Kit (see Figure 2.2).

3. Click the Run Tests button to begin the analysis process.

NOTE

The Capabilities Validation test that is present for Windows Phone 7.1 apps is not available for apps that target Windows Phone 8.

NOTE

The Iconography and Screenshots automated tests fail if you have not specified any icons or screenshots for your app.

The Marketplace Test Kit offers numerous tests that can assist you in ensuring that your app is Marketplace ready. It can also save you time and the frustration caused by failing the Marketplace submission requirements.

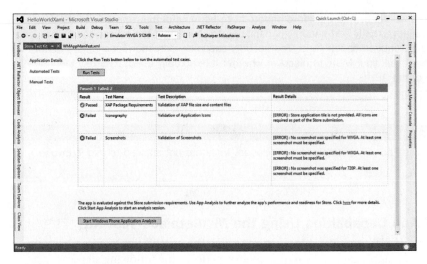

FIGURE 2.2   Store Test Kit.

The Threading Model for XAML-Based Graphics and Animation in Windows Phone

XAML apps use two threads for graphics and animation: a UI thread and a composition thread. The composition thread was introduced with the second release (7.5) of the Windows Phone OS. The first release of the OS had issues with performance around user input. A single UI thread had been largely acceptable for Silverlight for the desktop and browser because both generally rely on the mouse for input. The phone, however, relies on touch, which, as it turned out, needs to be substantially more reactive to user input. When using a mouse, a slight delay does not unduly affect the user's perception of your app, but when using touch, a slight delay can make the user feel like the device is broken. Thus, the composition thread was introduced in Windows Phone 7.5[1] to assist in rendering visuals by offloading some of the work traditionally done by the UI thread.

The UI thread is the main thread in Windows Phone XAML apps and handles user input, events, parsing, and creation of objects from XAML, and the initial drawing of all visuals.

The composition thread aides the UI thread in handling graphics and animation, freeing up the UI thread and making it more responsive to user input. Storyboard-driven animations that run on the composition thread are cached and handled by the device GPU in a process called autocaching.

---

1. The composition thread was also introduced to Silverlight for the browser with Silverlight 5 but still lacks the autocaching capabilities present in Windows Phone. Autocaching is described in a moment.

> **NOTE**
>
> Although the composition thread frees the UI thread in some situations, the key to writing responsive apps is still making sure that the UI thread is not overloaded or blocked by user code—in event handlers, for example. If you anticipate that a particular section of code will tie up the UI thread for a considerable amount of time, for more than, say, 50 milliseconds, use a background thread to perform the activity. The web service APIs, for example, are all designed to be used asynchronously so that they do not block the UI thread.
>
> The Windows Phone 8 SDK sees the inclusion of the new .NET async keyword that makes consuming asynchronous APIs far easier than it used to be.
>
> If you are not familiar with the various mechanisms for spawning background threads, do not be concerned; you see many examples throughout the book.

The composition thread is used for animations involving the `UIElement`'s `RenderTransform` and `Projection` properties. Typically these animations include the following from the `System.Windows.Media` namespace:

▶ `PlaneProjection`

▶ `RotateTransform`

▶ `ScaleTransform`

▶ `TranslateTransform`

> **NOTE**
>
> The composition thread is used only for scale transforms that are less than 50% of the original size. If the scale transform exceeds this amount, the UI thread performs the animation. In addition, the `UIElement.Opacity` and `UIElement.Clip` properties are handled by the composition thread. If an opacity mask or nonrectangular clip is used, however, the UI thread takes over.

Animations and Threads

The composition thread is ideal for handling storyboard animations because it is able to pass them to the device GPU for processing, even while the UI thread is busy. Code-driven animations, however, do not benefit from the composition thread because these kinds of animations are handled exclusively by the UI thread, frame by frame using a callback. They are, therefore, subject to slowdown depending on what else occupies the UI thread, and the animation will update only as fast as the frame rate of the UI thread.

Performance and Element Visibility

XAML-based apps provide two properties that allow you to hide or reveal UI elements: `UIElement.Visibility` and `UIElement.Opacity`—each of which has performance implications depending on how it is used.

The `UIElement.Visibility` property is handled by the UI thread. When an element's `Visibility` property is set to Collapsed, the visual tree must be redrawn. The upside is that when collapsed, the `UIElement` is not retained in visual memory, and thus decreases the amount of memory used by your app.

Conversely, controlling the visibility of an element using the `UIElement.Opacity` property allows the element to be bitmap cached; the element is stored as a simple bitmap image after the first render pass. Bitmap caching allows the rendering system to bypass the render phase for the cached element and to use the composition thread to display the bitmap instead, which can free up the UI thread considerably. By setting the opacity of a cached element to zero, you hide the element without requiring it to be redrawn later. This, however, does mean that unlike the `Visibility` property, the element is still retained in visual memory.

> **NOTE**
>
> Avoid manipulating the `UIElement.Opacity` property without enabling bitmap caching. Set the `UIElement.CacheMode` property to BitmapCache, as shown in the following example:
>
> `<Path CacheMode="BitmapCache" ... />`

Deciding Between Visibility and Opacity

Element opacity in conjunction with bitmap caching usually produces the best performance when hiding and revealing elements. There may be times, however, when the `UIElement.Visibility` property is better, and this is influenced by the number and complexity of the visual elements being rendered. In such cases it may require experimentation to determine the best approach.

Understanding the Frame Rate Counter

Developing for a mobile device requires particular attention to performance. Mobile devices have less computing power than desktop systems and are more susceptible to performance bottlenecks.

The Windows Phone SDK comes with a built-in control that allows you to monitor the performance of your app, including frames per second and memory usage.

By default, the frame rate counter is enabled in your app's App.xaml.cs file if a debugger is attached, as shown in the following excerpt:

```
if (System.Diagnostics.Debugger.IsAttached)
{
    // Display the current frame rate counters.
    Application.Current.Host.Settings.EnableFrameRateCounter = true;
    ...
}
```

> **NOTE**
>
> It is possible to enable or disable the frame rate counter programmatically at any time from your app.

The `EnableFrameRateCounter` property is somewhat of a misnomer because the control also reports a number of other UI metrics, such as texture memory usage, as shown in Figure 2.3.

FIGURE 2.3   The Frame Rate Counter.

Each field is updated periodically while the app is running. Table 2.1 describes each counter field.

TABLE 2.1   Frame Rate Counter Field Descriptions

Field	Description
Composition (Render) Thread Frame Rate (FPS)	The rate at which the screen is updated. It also represents how often supported animations driven by a storyboard are updated. This value should be as close to 60 as possible. Application performance begins to degrade when this value is below 30. The text in this counter is red when displaying a value below 30.
User Interface Thread Frame Rate (FPS)	The rate at which the UI thread is running. The UI thread drives input, per-frame callbacks, and any other drawing not handled by the composition thread. The larger this value, the more responsive your application should be. Typically this value should be above 20 to provide an acceptable response time to user input. The text in this counter is red when displaying a value below 15.
Texture Memory Usage	The video memory and system memory copies of textures being used in the application. This is not a general memory counter for the application but represents only memory that surfaces use.

Field	Description
Surface Counter	The number of explicit surfaces being passed to the GPU for processing. The biggest contributor to this number is automatic or developer-cached elements.
Intermediate Surface Counter	The number of implicit surfaces generated as a result of cached surfaces. These surfaces are created in between UI elements so that the application can accurately maintain the Z-order of elements in the UI.
Screen Fill Rate Counter	The number of pixels being painted per frame in terms of screens. A value of 1 represents 480×800 pixels. The recommended value is about 2.5. The text in this counter turns red when displaying a value higher than 3.

Source: MSDN: http://bit.ly/I8i02O

The frame rate counter is a valuable tool for identifying performance bottlenecks in your app. For more detailed performance metrics turn to the Application Analysis tool, discussed next.

The Windows Phone Application Analysis Tool

Not only is performance important in ensuring that your app provides an enjoyable experience for your users, but it is also important in a stricter sense: for meeting the certification requirements of the Windows Phone Marketplace. Marketplace certification includes a number of performance related criteria that your app must adhere to. The requirements are as follows:

▶ If an application performs an operation that causes the device to appear to be unresponsive for more than 3 seconds, such as downloading data over a network connection, the app must display a visual progress or busy indicator.

▶ An app must display the first screen within 5 seconds after launch. You see how to work around this requirement for slow loading apps by creating a splash screen, in Chapter 3, "Understanding the Application Execution Model."

▶ An app must be responsive to user input within 20 seconds after launch.

The Windows Phone Application Analysis tool comes with the Windows Phone SDK and is integrated into Visual Studio, allowing you to analyze and improve the performance of your apps. The tool profiles your app during runtime to gather either execution metrics or memory usage information.

Execution profiling may include method call counts and visual profiling, allowing you to view the frame rate of your app over time, while memory profiling allows you to analyze your app's memory usage.

To launch the tool select Start Windows Phone Application Analysis from the Debug menu in Visual Studio. You can select the profiling type, along with other advanced metrics, by expanding the Advanced Settings node, as shown in Figure 2.4.

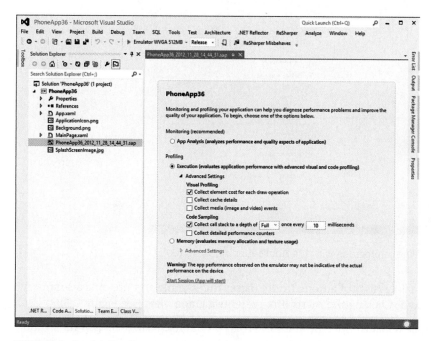

FIGURE 2.4   Configuring the Application Analysis settings.

To begin the profiling session, click the Start Session link.

Whenever the Application Analysis tool runs, it creates a .sap file in the root directory of your project. A .sap file is an XML file that contains the profiling information gathered during a profiling session and can later be opened by the profiling analysis tools built in to Visual Studio.

When done putting your app through its paces, click the End Session link, shown in Figure 2.5. You can, alternatively, use the device's hardware Back button to end the profiling session.

> **NOTE**
>
> Avoid disconnecting the phone device to end a profiling session, because this can lead to sampling errors. Instead, always use the End Session link or the hardware Back button.

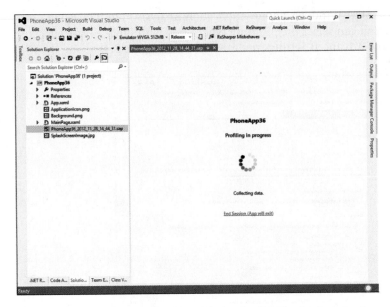

FIGURE 2.5   Profiling in progress with the Application Analysis tool.

Once stopped, the analysis tool automatically parses the .sap file and presents a summary of the analyzed data. Clicking the Alerts link presents a graph view (see Figure 2.6).

The .sap file can be reloaded into the analysis tools by double-clicking the .sap file in the Visual Studio Solution Explorer.

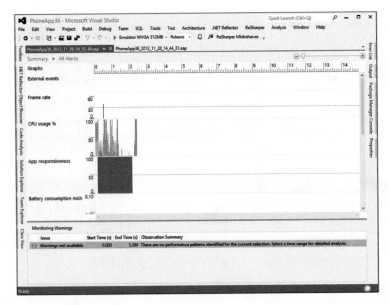

FIGURE 2.6   Viewing performance metrics in the Application Analysis tool.

Each section of the analysis tools view is discussed in the following sections.

External Events

External events indicate user events, such as UI input, or simulated network changes.

Frame Rate Graph

The Frame Rate graph displays the number of screen redraws (in frames per second) that the app completed at the particular point in the timeline.

> **NOTE**
>
> The Frame Rate graph shows nonzero values for periods in the timeline where the application was updating the display in some way. Therefore, areas that appear to have a zero frame rate indicate that no updating was taking place and not necessarily that your app was not able to render any frames.

> **NOTE**
>
> You should aim to have the frame rate value averaging between 30 and 60fps.

CPU Usage Graph

The CPU Usage graph displays the activity of various threads using different colors, as described in Table 2.2.

TABLE 2.2   CPU Graph Colors

Color	Thread	Notes
Green	UI Thread	Green shading indicates screen updates and touch input. You should aim to keep the UI thread to less than 50% of CPU usage.
Purple	App Threads	Purple indicates application activity that is not on the UI thread. Activity can be from the composition thread or from your apps background threads, such as those used from the `AppPool`.
Gray	System Threads	Gray indicates activity that is independent of your app, such as background agent activity.
White	Idle Threads	White indicates the available CPU percentage. The higher the idle thread percentage, the more responsive the app should be.

Memory Usage MB Graph

Memory Usage MB shows the amount of RAM being consumed by your app in megabytes, at any point along the timeline. This graph allows you to identify excessive memory usage.

Storyboards

Storyboards are displayed as an S flag on the timeline to indicate the occurrence of a storyboard event, and typically indicate the start of an animation. There are two kinds of flags: A red flag indicates a storyboard that is CPU bound; a purple flag indicates a storyboard that is not CPU bound.

Image Loads

When an image is loaded into memory, an I flag is displayed on the graph. Although JPG and PNG files might have a small size when stored in isolated storage, when displayed using an Image control for example, images are expanded into bitmaps and consume a lot more memory. Use the image load flag to identify places in your app where excessive memory consumption is taking place.

GC Events

When the CLR performs garbage collection, a G flag is displayed on the graph. Garbage collection reclaims memory and ordinarily decreases the value shown in the Memory Usage MB graph.

Viewing Detailed Profiling Information

Within the analysis tool, a region can be selected within the graph to view detailed performance warnings for that period. Much like Visual Studio's Error List view, the Performance Warnings view identifies three types of items: Information, Warning, and Error items (see Figure 2.7).

The Observation Summary provides advice on how to rectify each particular warning item.

The CPU Usage breadcrumb can also be expanded and allows you to view various other CPU-related metrics, such as a function call tree.

The Application Analysis tool provides detailed runtime performance metrics and allows you to identify the source of performance bottlenecks, enabling you to improve the responsiveness of your app and in turn the user experience for your app.

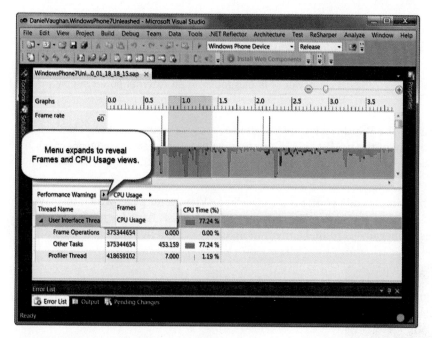

FIGURE 2.7   The Performance Warnings view.

Reading Device Information

The `Microsoft.Phone.Info.DeviceStatus` class is a static class used to retrieve information about the phone device, such as the device manufacturer, firmware version, and total memory available to your app.

Table 2.3 describes each property of the `DeviceStatus` class.

TABLE 2.3   `DeviceStatus` Properties

Name	Description
`ApplicationCurrentMemoryUsage`	The memory usage of the current application in bytes.
`ApplicationMemoryUsageLimit`	The maximum additional amount of memory, in bytes, that your application process can allocate.
`ApplicationPeakMemoryUsage`	The peak memory usage of the current application in bytes.
`DeviceFirmwareVersion`	The firmware version running on the device.
`DeviceHardwareVersion`	The hardware version running on the device.
`DeviceManufacturer`	The device manufacturer name.
`DeviceName`	The device name.
`DeviceTotalMemory`	The physical RAM size of the device in bytes.
`IsKeyboardDeployed`	If true the user has deployed the physical hardware keyboard of the device.

Name	Description
IsKeyboardPresent	If true the device contains a physical hardware keyboard.
PowerSource	Indicates if the device is currently running on battery power or is plugged in to an external power supply.

In the first release of the Windows Phone OS, the DeviceExtendedProperties class was used to retrieve many of the DeviceStatus property values. DeviceExtendedProperties has since been deprecated, and DeviceStatus takes its place for retrieving most device information.

The downloadable sample code contains a DeviceStatusView.xaml page, which displays each of the DeviceStatus properties. The memory related values have been converted from byte values to megabytes to make them more easily comprehendible (see Figure 2.8).

FIGURE 2.8   DeviceStatusView page.

Calculating Available Memory

Windows Phone 8 device manufacturers are obligated to produce phones that have at least 512MB of RAM.

NOTE

Although many phones have more than 512MB of RAM, be mindful of the minimum specification and aim to support the lowest common denominator. Do not assume your app will be running on a device with more than 512MB of RAM. Regardless of how much memory the device has, your app's memory is capped at either 150MB for lower memory phones or 300MB for higher memory phones. The ID_FUNCCAP_EXTEND_MEM capability can be added to your WMAppManifest.xml file to grant more memory to your app. See http://bit.ly/13o7Pmu for details.

To determine how much memory your app has to work with, use the DeviceStatus.ApplicationMemoryUsageLimit.

For example, if a particular task is estimated at costing an additional 10MB of memory, determining whether the task will exceed the memory usage limit can be calculated as follows:

```
long requiredBytesEstimate = 10 * 1048576; /* 1048576 bytes equals 1 megabyte. */
if (DeviceStatus.ApplicationMemoryUsageLimit
        >= DeviceStatus.ApplicationCurrentMemoryUsage + requiredBytesEstimate)
{
    /* Perform expensive task. */
}
```

> **NOTE**
>
> If your app attempts to allocate more memory than is available on the device, that is, it exceeds the value of DeviceStatus.ApplicationMemoryUsageLimit, the application terminates with an OutOfMemoryException.

In addition to foreground app memory constraints, background tasks are limited to 6MB of memory. Background tasks and their memory usage requirements are discussed in Chapter 32, "Conducting Background Activities with Scheduled Actions."

DeviceStatus **Events**

While DeviceStatus allows you to retrieve device information, it also includes the following two events:

▶ KeyboardDeployedChanged

▶ PowerSourceChanged

If the phone device has a hardware keyboard, such as a sliding keyboard, the KeyboardDeployedChanged event allows you to detect when the keyboard is extended.

You can subscribe to the KeyboardDeployedChanged event as shown:

```
DeviceStatus.KeyboardDeployedChanged += HandleKeyboardDeployedChanged;
```

The event handler can be used to determine whether the keyboard is deployed using the DeviceStatus class, as shown:

```csharp
void HandleKeyboardDeployedChanged(object sender, EventArgs e)
{
    bool keyboardDeployed = DeviceStatus.IsKeyboardDeployed;
...
}
```

PowerSourceChanged Event

When the phone device is connected to a user's computer, it may be a good time to perform some processor-intensive task that could potentially consume a lot of power, which would otherwise flatten the user's battery. The PowerSourceChangedEvent allows you to detect when the user attaches or detaches an external power supply.

The PowerSourceChanged event can be subscribed to as shown:

```csharp
DeviceStatus.PowerSourceChanged += HandlePowerSourceChanged;
```

The event handler can be used to retrieve the new PowerSource value from the DeviceStatus class, as shown:

```csharp
void HandlePowerSourceChanged(object sender, EventArgs e)
{
    PowerSource powerSource = DeviceStatus.PowerSource;
...
}
```

> **NOTE**
>
> The DeviceState.PowerSourceChanged event is not raised on the app's UI thread. All updates to visual elements must, therefore, be invoked on the UI thread, either directly by using the app's global Dispatcher or indirectly via a custom property change notification system, discussed later in this chapter.

> **NOTE**
>
> Avoid using DeviceState.PowerSource for determining whether to use the phone's network connection to transfer a substantial amount of data. See Chapter 27, "Communicating with Network Services," to learn how to monitor network connectivity and how to determine the type of network connection being used.

Applying the Model-View-ViewModel Pattern to a Windows Phone App

A dominant pattern that has emerged in XAML UI based technologies, in particular WPF and Silverlight, is the Model-View-ViewModel (MVVM) pattern. MVVM is an architectural pattern largely based on the Model-View-Controller (MVC) pattern, which, like the MVC pattern, serves to isolate the domain logic from the user interface logic. In addition, MVVM leverages the strong data binding capabilities of XAML based technologies, which allows loose coupling between the view and the viewmodel so that the viewmodel does not need to directly manipulate the view. This eliminates the need for almost all code-beside, which has a number of benefits, including freeing interactive designers from writing view specific code.

The following are the principal elements of the MVVM pattern:

- **Model**—The model is responsible for managing and delivering data.

- **View**—The view is responsible for displaying data. The view is ordinarily a UI element, and, in the case of XAML-based Windows Phone apps, it is a `UserControl` such as a `PhoneApplicationPage`.

- **ViewModel**—A bridge or intermediary between the model and the view, which commonly retrieves model objects and exposes them to the view. Often the viewmodel is designed to respond to commands that are bound to UI elements in the view. The viewmodel can be thought of as the model of the view.

With the release of the Windows Phone 7.1 SDK came Silverlight 4 and support for `ICommands`. The use of commands is discussed in the section "Using Commands" later in the chapter.

There are numerous benefits to using MVVM in your apps. MVVM can improve an app's testability because it is easier to test code from a unit test that does not rely on surfacing UI objects. Testing apps is discussed further in Chapter 24, "Unit Testing Apps."

Placing application interaction logic in a viewmodel also makes it easier to redesign your app while reducing the need to refactor interaction logic. Occasionally you may like to reuse some of your UI logic in different apps or, to a lesser extent, you might want to target different UI technologies, such as WPF, Silverlight, or Windows Store XAML applications. Decoupling interaction logic from any particular UI technology makes it easier to target multiple platforms.

Implementing the MVVM Pattern

There are two general approaches to MVVM viewmodel and view creation: view-first and viewmodel-first. The first approach sees the creation of the view before the viewmodel. Conversely, in the viewmodel-first approach, it is the viewmodel that creates the view. Both approaches have their pros and cons. Viewmodel-first potentially offers complete independence from the UI, allowing an app to be executed entirely without a UI; yet it suffers from various implementation challenges. View-first is far simpler to implement when page navigation is used, as is the case in a Silverlight for Windows Phone app.

This book uses the view-first approach exclusively.

MVVM in a XAML app relies on the assignment of a viewmodel to the view's `DataContext` property. There are a number of commonly used techniques for marrying a viewmodel to its view. Some offer a high degree of flexibility at the cost of greater complexity and decreased visibility. The technique employed throughout this book, and the one I find to be adequate in most cases, has the viewmodel instantiated in the view's constructor. In the following example a viewmodel is assigned to the view's `DataContext` property:

```
public partial class FooView : PhoneApplicationPage
{
    public FooView()
    {
        InitializeComponent();

        DataContext = new FooViewModel();
    }
...
}
```

With the `DataContext` set to the viewmodel, properties of the viewmodel can be used in data binding expression in the view's XAML.

ViewModelBase **Class**

Windows Phone apps often consist of many pages and, in turn, many viewmodels. It is useful to employ a viewmodel base class to share common infrastructure across all view-models in your app.

In the samples throughout this book, most viewmodels subclass a custom `ViewModelBase` class that provides, among other things, navigation support, error validation, state preservation, and property change notification (see Figure 2.9). Each of these capabilities is discussed alongside related topics in subsequent chapters.

`ViewModelBase` inherits from a custom `NotifyPropertyChangeBase` class, which provides for property change notification, discussed in the next section.

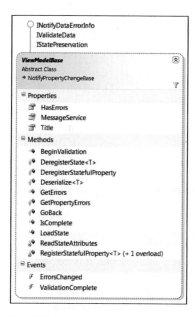

FIGURE 2.9   `ViewModelBase` class diagram.

Property Change Notification

A key aspect of MVVM related to data binding is property change notification. Property change notification allows a source object (for example, a viewmodel) to signal to a target `FrameworkElement` that a value needs updating in the UI.

There are two ways to implement change notification in a source class: either using dependency properties or by implementing the `INotifyPropertyChanged` interface, which is often referred to as just INPC.

> **NOTE**
>
> The use of dependency properties is not recommended for viewmodels because it requires that the viewmodel class inherit from `DependencyObject` and that all property updates occur on the UI thread. This can lead to a lot of thread-related plumbing code in the viewmodel and makes your code less portable because of dependence on the dependency property system.

Implementing `INotifyPropertyChanged`: The Traditional Approach

The `INotifyPropertyChanged` interface has a single event called `PropertyChanged`. The implementation of `INotifyPropertyChanged` ordinarily includes the following construct:

```
public event PropertyChangedEventHandler PropertyChanged;

protected virtual void OnPropertyChanged(
```

```
        [CallerMemberName] string propertyName = null)
{
    PropertyChangedEventHandler tempEvent = PropertyChanged;
    if (tempEvent != null)
    {
        tempEvent(this, new PropertyChangedEventArgs(propertyName));
    }
}
```

The `CallerMemberName` attribute is used by a new compiler feature that automatically passes the name of the calling member to the target method. No longer is it necessary in most cases to pass the name of a property as a loosely typed string.

> **NOTE**
>
> To determine whether the `PropertyChanged` event field has any subscribers, it is copied to a temporary local variable, which allows you to then test whether it is null in a thread-safe manner. Without first obtaining a copy, another thread could potentially unsubscribe from the event after the null check but before the event is raised, which would inadvertently lead to a `NullReferenceException` being thrown.
>
> An alternative that avoids the null check is to assign the event to an empty handler, as shown:
>
> ```
> public event PropertyChangingEventHandler PropertyChanging = delegate {};
> ```

A property is then able to signal to a subscriber of the event that a property value needs updating, like so:

```
string foo;

public string Foo
{
    get
    {
        return foo;
    }
    set
    {
        if (foo != value)
        {
            foo = value;
            OnPropertyChanged();
        }
    }
}
```

When setting a property that is the source property of a data binding, the update must occur on the UI thread or an `UnauthorizedAccessException` will ensue. Source properties can be set from non-UI threads using the application's `Dispatcher` as shown in the following excerpt:

```
Deployment.Current.Dispatcher.BeginInvoke(
    delegate
        {
            Foo = "bah";
        });
```

There are a number of reasons why peppering your code with `BeginInvoke` calls is not a good idea. First, it imposes an unnecessary threading model on your viewmodel code. Second, it can lead to code that need not be executed on the UI thread, creeping in to the delegate. And, third, it is pretty ugly and decreases the readability of your code.

The next section looks at extracting INPC into a reusable and UI thread friendly class.

Implementing `INotifyPropertyChanged`: **An Alternative Approach**

Although there is nothing manifestly wrong with adding the `OnPropertyChanged` method to every class that implements `INotifyPropertyChanged` (apart from violating the DRY principle), it makes sense to extract the change notification code into a reusable class, because this allows you to not only reduce boilerplate code but also to add other features to the event-raising code, such as improving support for multithreaded apps and implementing `INotifyPropertyChanging` (as well as `INotifyPropertyChanged`).

The WPUnleashed project in the downloadable sample code includes such a class, named `PropertyChangeNotifier`. The `ViewModelBase` class delegates change notification to a `PropertyChangeNotifier` instance.

Throughout this book you frequently see viewmodel properties (with backing fields) resembling the following:

```
string foo;

public string Foo
{
    get
    {
        return foo;
    }
    set
    {
        Assign(ref foo, value);
    }
}
```

Here, the name of the property, the current value, and the new value are passed to the base class's `Assign` method. The following excerpt shows the signature of the `Assign` method:

```
public AssignmentResult Assign<TField>(
        ref TField field,
        TField newValue,
        [CallerMemberName] string propertyName = "")
{
...
}
```

The `Assign` method updates the field value, while also offering the following advantages:

▶ The application's `Dispatcher` automatically raises the `PropertyChanged` event on the UI thread if called from a non-UI thread. This eliminates the need to add `Dispatcher.BeginInvoke` calls to a viewmodel to avoid cross-thread errors.

▶ The `Assign` method also raises a `PropertyChanging` event. `PropertyChangeNotifier` implements `INotifyPropertyChanging` interface as well as `INotifyPropertyChanged` and allows a subscriber to cancel an update if desired.

▶ `PropertyChangeNotifier` assists the viewmodel in remaining UI technology agnostic. That is, retrieving an application's `Dispatcher` in a Windows Phone app is done differently in a WPF application.

▶ `PropertyChangeNotifier` uses a weak reference to its owner, thereby preventing memory leaks from occurring when targets fail to unsubscribe from events.

▶ The single line `Assign` method reduces the amount of boilerplate code in properties.

The return value of the `Assign` method is an `AssignmentResult` enum value, whose values are described in the following list:

▶ **Success**—The assignment occurred and the field value now equals the new value.

▶ **Cancelled**—A subscriber to the `PropertyChanging` event cancelled the assignment. This relies on a custom extension to the `INotifyPropertyChanging` event.

▶ **AlreadyAssigned**—No assignment was made because the existing field value was already equal to the new value.

▶ **OwnerDisposed**—The `PropertyChangeNotifier` uses a weak reference to the object for which it is providing property changing monitoring. This value indicates that no assignment was performed because the owner object has been disposed.

Because property change notification is such a common requirement of model and viewmodel classes, for the sake of convenience a `NotifyPropertyChangeBase` class is also provided in the downloadable sample code. It leverages an instance of the `PropertyChangeNotifier`, and can be used as a base class for any class that needs `INotifyPropertyChanged` to be implemented.

In particular, the `ViewModelBase` class inherits from this class (see Figure 2.10).

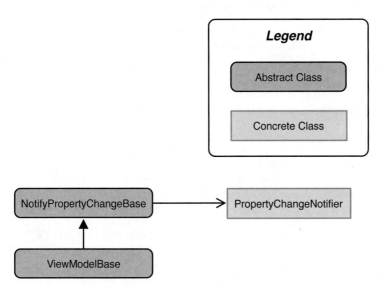

FIGURE 2.10 `ViewModelBase` inherits from `NotifyPropertyChangeBase`, which has a `PropertyChangeNotifier`.

The implementation details of the `PropertyChangeNotifier` are lengthy and are not included in this section. However, you can find an article already covering the topic at http://danielvaughan.org/post/Property-Change-Notification-using-a-Weak-Referencing-Strategy.aspx.

Before moving on to commanding, be assured that you do not need to use the property notification system presented here in your own projects. If you are happy using the traditional approach to INPC, that is perfectly fine. Be mindful, however, that a lot of the phone SDK APIs have events that do not always return on the UI thread, and you may need to rely more heavily on the `Dispatcher` to prevent cross-thread errors.

Using Commands

Windows Phone XAML apps support the ICommand interface for buttons and various other controls. Commands are useful because when exposed from a viewmodel they allow your view to bind to them just like other properties; when the user interacts with the visual element, the command is executed. This enables you to move your UI logic from event handlers to higher level classes.

The ICommand interface defines the following three members:

▶ CanExecute(object)—A method called by the commanding infrastructure, which automatically sets the enabled state of the target control

▶ Execute(object)—A method that performs the logic of the command

▶ CanExecuteChanged—An event that signals that the commanding infrastructure should reevaluate the executable state of the command by calling its CanExecute method

Within the downloadable sample code there is a default implementation of the ICommand interface called DelegateCommand<T>. This class has features such as object parameter type coercion, which, for example, enables you to use strings to represent enum values in binding expressions, which are automatically converted to the appropriate enum type.

In this book you commonly see commands defined as read-only fields exposed using a property get accessor, as this excerpt from the MediaViewModel in Chapter 7, "Employing Media and Web Elements," shows:

```
readonly DelegateCommand playCommand;

public ICommand PlayCommand
{
    get
    {
        return playCommand;
    }
}
```

Most often, you see commands instantiated in the viewmodels constructor.

The DelegateCommand constructor accepts an Action argument, which is invoked when the command is executed. In the following excerpt you see the instantiation of a command called playCommand that when executed sets a number of viewmodel properties:

```
public MediaViewModel()
{
    playCommand = new DelegateCommand(
```

```
        obj =>
        {
                PlayerState = PlayerState.Playing;
                CanPlay = false;
                CanPause = true;
        });
...
}
```

DelegateCommand along with its generic counterpart DelegateCommand<T> also allow you to specify an Action that is used to evaluate whether the command is able to be executed.

Ordinarily the built-in commanding infrastructure is supported only on buttons (ButtonBase) and a couple of specialized controls. Some extra capabilities are provided in the ICommand implementation that allow you to wire the command to any FrameworkElement, such as in the following example, which shows an Image element that when tapped causes an ICommand to be executed:

```
<Image Source="/Foo.png"
        c:Commanding.Command="{Binding ViewCommand}"
        c:Commanding.CommandParameter="{Binding FullScreen}" />
```

> **NOTE**
>
> The event used to trigger command execution can be specified by using the Commanding.Event attached property. In subsequent chapters you see several examples of using these custom commanding attached properties.

Argument Validation

The book sample code commonly uses a custom ArgumentValidator class to ensure that method arguments are not null or fall within a valid range. This allows a method to fail fast, rather than continuing and raising a more difficult to diagnose error.

You frequently see statements like the following at the beginning of a method:

```
string PerformSomeAction(string value)
{
    stringField = ArgumentValidator.AssertNotNull(value, "value");
...
}
```

Here, if value is null, then an ArgumentNullException is thrown. If not null, then the stringField field is set to the value in a fluent manner.

NOTE

Microsoft has a far more feature rich argument validation tool called Code Contracts, which integrates into Visual Studio and can provide static checking as well as runtime checking, along with documentation generation. See http://bit.ly/1OzWtK.

All the `ArgumentValidator` methods are fluent; they return the value passed to them so that they can be assigned to local variables or fields in a single statement.

The `ArgumentValidator.AssertNotNull` method is as follows:

```
public static T AssertNotNull<T>(T value, string parameterName) where T : class
{
    if (value == null)
    {
        throw new ArgumentNullException(parameterName);
    }

    return value;
}
```

`ArgumentValidator` contains various other assertion methods for strings and numeric values. Some are briefly discussed.

`ArgumentValidator` allows you to assert that an argument falls within a particular range. The following `AssertLessThan` method ensures that the value is less than a certain value:

```
public static double AssertLessThan(
    double comparisonValue, double value, string parameterName)
{
    if (value >= comparisonValue)
    {
        throw new ArgumentOutOfRangeException(
            "Parameter should be less than "
            + comparisonValue, parameterName);
    }
    return value;
}
```

This then allows you to validate that a numeric value is less than, for example, 1:

```
ArgumentValidator.AssertLessThan(1, value, "value");
```

Other methods, such as `AssertNotNullAndOfType`, allow you to raise an exception if an argument is null or not of the expected type, and `AssertNotNullOrWhiteSpace` accepts a string and raises an `ArgumentException` if `string.IsNullOrWhiteSpace(value)` returns true.

A Platform-Agnostic Dialog Service

Over the past few years, I have found myself doing a lot of cross-platform development, in particular Silverlight for the browser, WPF, and now Windows Phone development. Being able to abstract common tasks away from technology specific types, such as displaying simple dialogs, has made reusing code far easier. In addition, mocking things, which would otherwise cause a unit test to fail on a build server, such as displaying a message box, has proven invaluable.

In several places throughout the book you see the use of an `IMessageService`, which is used to display message dialogs to the user. The `ViewModelBase` class exposes the `IMessageService` as a `MessageService` property, and you see calls like the following:

```
MessageService.ShowMessage("Hi from Windows Phone!");
```

If you are itching to sink your teeth into more phone-specific content, feel free to skip this section and return to it later.

The `IMessageService` interface describes a class that is able to display messages to the user, and to ask the user questions (see Figure 2.11).

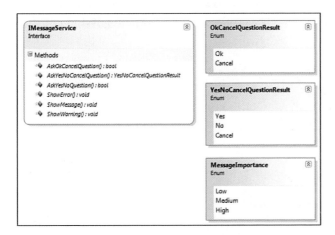

FIGURE 2.11   `IMessageService` class diagram.

There are various parameters for specifying captions and so forth, along with the capability to provide a message importance threshold value, so that the user can nominate to have messages filtered based on importance.

Differences exist between the built-in dialog related enums in the MessageBox APIs of Windows Phone and WPF. Hence, these types have been replaced with the technology-agnostic enum types shown in Figure 2.11.

The Windows Phone implementation of the `IMessageService` is done by extending a single class, the `MessageServiceBase` class, and by overriding two abstract methods: one called `ShowCustomDialog`, the other `AskQuestion` (see Figure 2.12).

FIGURE 2.12   `MessageService` extends `MessageServiceBase`.

The `ShowCustomDialog` method uses the `Dispatcher` to display the dialog on the UI thread (see Listing 2.1). Extension methods are used to convert the native Silverlight `MessageBoxButton` enum values and `MessageBoxResult` enum values to the technology-agnostic enum values.

LISTING 2.1   `MessageService` Class (excerpt)

```
public partial class MessageService : MessageServiceBase
{
    public override MessageResult ShowCustomDialog(
        string message,
        string caption,
        MessageButton messageButton,
        MessageImage messageImage,
        MessageImportance? importanceThreshold,
        string details)
    {
        /* If the importance threshold has been specified
         * and it's less than the minimum level required (the filter level)
         * then we don't show the message. */
        if (importanceThreshold.HasValue
                && importanceThreshold.Value < MinumumImportance)
        {
            return MessageResult.Ok;
        }

        if (Deployment.Current.Dispatcher.CheckAccess())
        {   /* We are on the UI thread,
```

```
                    and hence no need to invoke the call.*/
        var messageBoxResult = MessageBox.Show(message, caption,
            messageButton.TranslateToMessageBoxButton());
        return messageBoxResult.TranslateToMessageBoxResult();
    }
    MessageResult result = MessageResult.Ok;
    var context = new DispatcherSynchronizationContext(
        Deployment.Current.Dispatcher);
    context.Send(
        delegate
        {
          var messageBoxResult = MessageBox.Show(
                                    message, caption,

                            messageButton.TranslateToMessageBoxButton());
          result = messageBoxResult.TranslateToMessageBoxResult();
        }, null);

    return result;
    }


    /* Content omitted. */
}
```

The downloadable sample code also contains a `MockMessageService` class that inherits from `MessageService` and is designed to be used for unit testing purposes. It allows you to verify that code correctly displayed a message or asked a question. The absence of a mocking framework for Windows Phone makes it especially useful.

The `MessageService` can be used to display a message, or ask the user a question, from any viewmodel (see Figure 2.13).

You see how to use the `IMessageService` in greater detail in the next chapter.

FIGURE 2.13   Using the `MessageService` to display a message.

By using an interface based approach, it affords the opportunity to substitute the IMessageService implementation for a mock implementation, or to even change the behavior of the IMessageService entirely.

These classes are, of course, included in the downloadable sample code. Yet, they also reside in the CalciumSdk repository at http://calciumsdk.com, where you can always find the most up-to-date code, freely available for use in your projects.

Consuming Local Web Applications

Changes to the Windows Phone Emulator have made developing apps that communicate with web applications on the local machine more difficult to set up. Prior to Windows Phone 8, apps could rely on the emulator resolving localhost to the underlying host operating system IP address. This allowed you to rapidly set up a WCF project that could be readily consumed by your Windows Phone app.

In Windows Phone 8, the emulator is unable to resolve WCF services on the host machine without adding a URL reservation and adding a port exception to the Windows firewall.

Perform the following steps to allow a Windows Phone app to consume a service on the host machine:

1. Assuming that you are working with IIS Express for local development, use the Windows File Explorer to navigate to the IIS Express config files in C:\Users\ [Username]\My Documents\IISExpress\config

2. Open the applicationhost.config file. Update the physicalPath attribute to the path of the project on your computer. Add an http binding for your machine's name, as shown:

```
<site name="WPUnleashed.Web" id="22">
    <application path="/" applicationPool="Clr4IntegratedAppPool">
        <virtualDirectory path="/"
physicalPath="C:\Development\Source\WP8Unleashed\Source\MainExamples\Web" />
    </application>
    <bindings>
        <binding protocol="http" bindingInformation="*:27571:localhost" />
        <!-- Add the following: -->
        <binding protocol="http" bindingInformation="*:27571:YourMachineName" />
    </bindings>
</site>
```

3. To locate your machine name, from a command prompt type "HOSTNAME". Although not necessary, you can update your hosts file and use a different name if you want, which will allow your app to be debugged on other machines more easily.

4. Make a URL reservation by typing the following from an administrative command prompt:

```
netsh http add urlacl url=http://YourMachineName:27571/ user=everyone
```

This informs HTTP.SYS that it is okay to allow access to the URL.

To remove the reservation at a later stage, use the following:

```
netsh http delete urlacl url=http://YourMachineName:27571/
```

5. Allow IIS Express through the Windows Firewall. You can do this from the command line by typing:

```
netsh firewall add portopening TCP 27571 IISExpressWeb enable ALL
```

These steps must be completed for the main WPUnleashed.Web project in the downloadable sample code, and also for the Background Agents and Wallet samples seen later in the book.

NOTE

If you do not perform the steps to enable communication with WCF service on the local machine, several of the sample apps presented in this book that make use of local WCF services will not work.

To save time, Table 2.4 lists the path and port information for the projects in the downloadable sample code.

TABLE 2.4   Path and Ports for Sample Projects

Path	Port
`C:\[Path to Samples]\WP8Unleashed\Source\MainExamples\Web\`	27571
`C:\[Path to Samples]\WP8Unleashed\Source\Wallet\WalletWcfServices\`	14122
`C:\[Path to Samples]\WP8Unleashed\Source\BackgroundAgents\Web\`	60182

TIP

To locate the port that a Web project is using, open its properties page and select the Web tab.

Summary

This chapter provided an overview of some common pieces of phone infrastructure and described various techniques that are useful when building Windows Phone apps.

The chapter began with a discussion of the deployment and composition of XAP files. The security capability model of the phone was then discussed, and you learned how to use the Marketplace Test Kit to determine the capability requirements of your app.

The chapter examined the threading model of Windows Phone XAML apps, and you saw how the Windows Phone frame rate counter works.

You then learned about the Windows Phone Application Analysis tool and saw how to profile your app's performance and memory usage.

The chapter then turned to the custom code and commonly used techniques that you see used in subsequent chapters.

The overview of the custom infrastructure began with an exposé of the Model-View-ViewModel pattern, and you saw how it is applied in the downloadable sample code. How property change notification is implemented was discussed, and you saw techniques for improving the traditional implementation of `INotifyPropertyChanged` so that it works effortlessly with multithreaded apps.

The chapter then looked at the commanding infrastructure used throughout the book and gave a brief overview of the argument validation system commonly used in the sample code to validate method arguments.

The chapter explored a custom dialog service that enables you to ask the user a question from your viewmodel, while remaining compatible with unit testing.

Finally, the chapter showed how to consume WCF services that reside on the same machine as the emulator, and outlined important steps to enable several of the apps in the downloadable sample code.

CHAPTER 3

Understanding the Application Execution Model

Understanding the events within the life cycle of a Windows Phone application is critical to providing an optimal user experience on the phone. The phone's single application process model means that your app may be interrupted and terminated at any time. It is your responsibility to maintain the appearance of continuity across interruptions, to save your app's state whenever an interruption occurs, and, if necessary, restore the state when the user returns to your app.

While the Windows Phone OS includes support for *fast application switching*, where your app is kept in memory and its threads suspended, you still need to preserve the state of your app because there are no guarantees that an app will not be terminated if the device memory runs low.

Like localizability, app state preservation is an aspect of development that should not be deferred and is likely one of the biggest challenges you will face as a Windows Phone developer.

Traditionally, developers of Windows desktop applications have not needed to be overly concerned with persisting runtime state. A desktop application remains resident in memory when it is started. This is in stark contrast to Windows Phone apps, where an application may be stopped and started many times during a single session.

Seasoned ASP.NET developers who recall the days before AJAX may feel slightly more at home developing for Windows Phone, with ASP.NET's reliance on view state to overcome the transient nature of page state in which the lifespan of a web page is limited to the period before a postback occurs. This is not too dissimilar to the state model of the phone, although Windows Phone offers nothing like the view state system built into ASP.NET. For that you need to roll your own, and you see how to build an automated state preservation system in Chapter 28, "Preserving App State and Settings."

There is no doubt that the single application process model of the phone presents some challenge for developers, but it can also lead to better designed and more robust applications, with an emphasis on decoupling visual elements from their state so that it can be more readily preserved.

This chapter begins with an overview of the application execution model and examines the various application life cycle events, which are used to coordinate state persistence and restoration.

The chapter explores the new Windows Phone 8 feature: Fast App Resume, which promises to improve startup performance for dormant apps that are relaunched.

The chapter then looks at how to enable an app to run under the lock screen. You also look at page navigation and how to optimize the user experience by using a splash screen or a loading indicator.

Finally, the chapter delves into the sample application and looks at image caching, design-time data, and consuming a simple WCF service.

Exploring the Execution Model

The execution model of Windows Phone is designed to make the phone as responsive as possible and to maximize the battery life of the device. One way that this is achieved is by limiting the phone to a single running application. Multiple applications running in the background risk slowing the foreground application and may tie up the processor and cause the phone to consume more power.

> **NOTE**
>
> While the phone's execution model is limited to a single app being in execution at any time, Windows Phone allows the use of background tasks, which run periodically and are independent of your foreground app. These are explored in Chapter 32, "Conducting Background Activities with Scheduled Actions."

In addition to greater responsiveness and extended battery life, the execution model provides users with a consistent navigation experience between applications. On Windows Phone, users are able to launch applications from the App List screen or from a tile on the Start Experience. The hardware Back button allows users to navigate backward, through the pages of a running application or through the stack of previously running applications.

The goal of transient state preservation and restoration is to provide the user with a simulated multiple application experience, where it seems to the user that your application was left running in the background, even though it may have been terminated by the operating system.

Application State

There are two types of application state: persistent and transient. Persistent state exists when an application launches. It is saved to a private storage area called isolated storage and may include data such as configurable settings or files.

Transient state is discarded when an application is closed. It is stored at the application level in the `Microsoft.Phone.Shell.PhoneApplicationService.State` dictionary or at the page level in the `PhoneApplicationPage.State` dictionary.

There is a single `PhoneApplicationService` instance for the entire app, and its state dictionary should be used only by objects running in the context of the application as a whole. A unique state dictionary is created for each page in your app, and you should use it rather than the `PhoneApplicationService.State` dictionary whenever possible.

> **NOTE**
>
> The `PhoneApplicationPage.State` dictionary is accessible only during or after the `OnNavigatedTo` method is called, or during or before the `OnNavigatedFrom` method is called. If you attempt to access it too early or too late an exception is raised.
>
> The `PhoneApplicationPage.State` dictionary is limited to 2MB for each page and 4MB for the entire app. You should, therefore, not use it for storing a large amount of data.

Transient state may include results from web service calls or data from partially completed forms (see Figure 3.1).

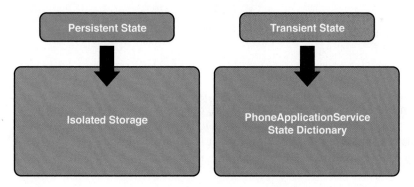

FIGURE 3.1   Persistent state and transient state storage locations.

Life Cycle Events

The `Microsoft.Phone.Shell.PhoneApplicationService` exposes four life cycle related CLR events, which provide an application with the opportunity to save or load state (see Figure 3.2).

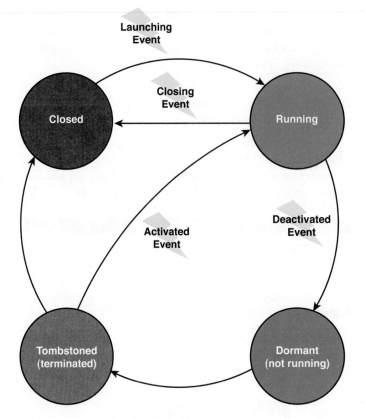

FIGURE 3.2   Application life cycle.

Launching Event

When a user selects an application from the App List screen, or from a tile on the Start Experience, or when the application is being debugged, the application moves from the stopped state, to the running state. This represents a cold start. Use the `Launching` event to restore any persistent state from isolated storage that is not page specific. This event occurs after the `App` class is instantiated, but before the main page of an application is created.

> **NOTE**
>
> The Windows Phone Certification Requirements state that an application must render the first screen within 5 seconds after launch and activation, and be fully responsive within 20 seconds. A splash screen can be used to offset startup delay. Later in this chapter you see how to create a splash screen for an application.

The `Launching` and `Activated` events are mutually exclusive. That is, exactly one of these two events occurs when the application is being started. Likewise, the `Deactivated` and

`Closing` events are also mutually exclusive; only one of these events occurs when the application is exiting.

Subscribing to Life Cycle Events Using the `PhoneApplicationService`

The `PhoneApplicationService` allows your app to be notified of the various life cycle events. The `PhoneApplicationService` is, by default, initialized in XAML by the application's `App` instance, as shown in the following example:

```
<Application.ApplicationLifetimeObjects>
    <!--Required object that handles lifetime events for the application-->
    <shell:PhoneApplicationService
        Launching="Application_Launching" Closing="Application_Closing"
        Activated="Application_Activated" Deactivated="Application_Deactivated"/>
</Application.ApplicationLifetimeObjects>
```

The `PhoneApplicationService` is a singleton class, which exposes an instance of the class via a static property called `Current`. Code to handle the `Launching`, `Closing`, `Activated`, and `Deactivated` events can be placed in the `App` class, for which handlers are created when a new project is created, or directly in code by using the `Current` property of the `PhoneApplicationService`.

NOTE

Subscription to the `PhoneApplicationService.Activated` event must occur via the `App` class. If subscription to the event occurs in a UI element, the handler is not called. This is because the `PhoneApplicationService` itself subscribes to the `System.Windows.Application.Current`'s `Startup` event. When the application raises the `Startup` event, the `PhoneApplicationService` notifies the operating system that it is ready to receive execution model events (that is, `Launching`, `Closing`, `Activated`, and `Deactivated`). This causes the `PhoneApplicationService.Activated` event (or the `Launched` event in the case of a non-tombstoned application) to occur almost immediately. Therefore, subscription to the event after this point has no effect. Moreover, event subscription is lost when an application is tombstoned; the application has, after all, terminated at that point. Thus, subscription to the `Activated` or `Launching` events from, for example, the MainPage constructor, occurs after the event has already been raised.

There may be times when it is tempting to promote certain kinds of transient state to persistent state. When launching your app, however, the user should feel like he is not resuming your app, but rather that it is indeed a new instance, a clean slate.

Persistent state is stored in isolated storage, while transient state is stored in the `PhoneApplicationService.State` dictionary, which is an `IDictionary<string, object>` that is maintained while the application is tombstoned. The dictionary is abandoned when the application moves from the tombstoned state to the not running state.

Deactivation Event and Tombstoning

On entering the running state, an application must contend with being interrupted. Each interruption causes the `PhoneApplicationService.Deactivated` event to be raised. The app is then placed in a dormant state, where it remains in memory but its threads are suspended.

If an app is reactivated after being in the dormant state, there is no need for your app to restore its transient state, reducing its load time.

Detecting whether an app is returning from a dormant state can be achieved within the `PhoneApplicationService.Activated` event handler using the `IsApplicationInstancePreserved` property of the `ActivatedEventArgs`, as shown in the following excerpt:

```
void Application_Activated(object sender, ActivatedEventArgs e)
{
    if (e.IsApplicationInstancePreserved)
    {
        /* Application was placed in the dormant state. */
    }
    else
    {
        /* Application state should be restored manually. */
    }
}
```

When the device's memory usage reaches a minimum threshold, the operating system may decide to tombstone your app.

> **NOTE**
>
> When an application is tombstoned, it is terminated.

When tombstoned, the operating system is aware that the application may be reactivated. If an application moves from being tombstoned back to the running state, it will be from a cold start, and all objects must be instantiated and persistent and transient state needs to be restored. The only differences between the tombstoned state and the closed state are that when tombstoned, the operating system retains the transient state dictionary for the app along with an identifier for the app, so that if activated, chooser and launcher events can be resubscribed. Launchers and choosers perform common tasks, such as sending email. You learn more about choosers and launchers in Chapter 14, "Leveraging Built-In Apps via Launchers and Choosers."

An application is deactivated when it is no longer the foreground application. The following is a list of causes for deactivation:

▶ The user presses the start button.

▶ The phone's lock screen is engaged without having enabled running under the lock screen. Enabling your app to run under the lock screen is discussed in the section "Running Under the Lock Screen" later in the chapter.

▶ A launcher or a chooser is shown.

▶ The user selects a toast notification, which launches another application.

Programmatically Exiting an App

Prior to Windows Phone 8, the only way to programmatically exit a XAML-based app was to raise and not handle an exception. It was an inelegant hack for a not-uncommon scenario.

In Windows Phone 8, however, the API includes a direct mechanism for terminating an app. It is achieved using the `Application` class's `Terminate` method, as demonstrated:

```
Application.Current.Terminate();
```

> **NOTE**
>
> Use the `Terminate` method only when the user is unable to make any useful forward progress. For example, if the user is presented with an End User License Agreement and declines it, the app may choose to terminate. Or if the app requires the user to log in and the user cannot provide valid credentials, the app may display a message and then terminate. You should not use this method to provide a general exit mechanism.

> **CAUTION**
>
> The `Terminate` method does not raise any application life cycle events. Before you call this method, you must save the state of the app.

Saving Transient State

The `Deactivated` event provides an application with the opportunity to save its transient and persistent state.

> **NOTE**
>
> Saving the transient state of a `PhoneApplicationPage` should be performed in its `OnNavigatedFrom` method, as you see later in the chapter.

The goal is to enable restoration of the application to its prior state before being tombstoned. It should be assumed, however, that when the `Deactivated` event occurs, that the application is going to be closed, moving to the closed state. The user may, after all, opt not to resume the application, or may use the Start Experience to re-launch the application, rather than using the hardware Back button to return to the application. Moreover, if the user launches many other apps, your app may get bumped off the end of the Back button application stack.

The Visual Studio new project templates place an empty handler for the Deactivated event in the App class. See the following excerpt:

```
void Application_Deactivated(object sender, DeactivatedEventArgs e)
{
    /* Save transient state like so:
     * PhoneApplicationService.Current.State["DataContractKey"]
     *         = DataContract;
     */

    /* Save persistent state like so:
     * IsolatedStorageSettings.ApplicationSettings["Key"] = someObject; */
}
```

You can also subscribe to the Deactivated event elsewhere, in the following manner:

```
PhoneApplicationService.Current.Deactivated += OnDeactivated;

void OnDeactivated(object o, DeactivatedEventArgs args)
{
//...
}
```

CAUTION

The operating system gives an app 10 seconds when the PhoneApplicationService.Closing event occurs, before it is forcibly terminated. If the time required to save your app's state exceeds this amount, its state should be saved periodically, and perhaps incrementally, while it is running.

NOTE

The Windows Phone emulator terminates an application if it takes longer than 10 seconds to display its first visual. Therefore, when debugging an Activated or Launched event, if this time is exceeded the application exits and the debugger detaches before any UI elements can be shown.

Transient State Requirements

All objects to be stored in the PhoneApplicationService.State property must meet one of the following requirements:

▶ It is a primitive type.

▶ It is a known serializable reference type including `decimal`, `string`, or `DateTime`, with a matching `System.Convert.ToString` method signature.

▶ It is capable of being serialized using a `DataContractSerializer`. To achieve this, it must be decorated with a `System.Runtime.Serialization.DataContract` attribute. Each property or field intended for serialization must be decorated with the `DataMember` attribute, and in turn each serializable property or field type must be decorated with the `DataContract` attribute.

Storing an application's transient state can be difficult because objects containing state often have event subscriptions to or from other objects that are not serialized. Also, types from third-party libraries are usually not decorated with the `DataContract` attribute, preventing serialization.

To avoid difficulties in serializing objects, keep classes that you intend to serialize as simple as possible, without dependencies on third-party classes. A design pattern that is commonly used for this situation is the Memento Pattern. For more information, see http://en.wikipedia.org/wiki/Memento_pattern.

Restoring Transient State

When an app transitions from being tombstoned or dormant back to the running state, the `PhoneApplicationService.Activated` event is raised. This provides an opportunity to restore the transient and persistent state of the app.

> **NOTE**
>
> Restoring the transient state of a `PhoneApplicationPage` should be performed in its `OnNavigatedTo` method, as you see later in the chapter.

Restoring the transient state involves taking the user to the point where she was when the `Deactivated` event occurred, and may involve restoring the positions of UI elements, repopulating viewmodel properties, and so on. The goal is to provide the user with a seamless experience, and to emulate a multiple application environment, in which the application appears as though it was left running in the background.

The following code demonstrates handling of the `PhoneApplicationService.Activated` event, to restore transient and persistent state:

```
void Application_Activated(object sender, ActivatedEventArgs e)
{
    /* Restore persistent state like so: */
    someObject = IsolatedStorageSettings.ApplicationSettings["Key"];

    /* Restore transient state like so: */
    DataContract = PhoneApplicationService.Current.State["DataContractKey"];
}
```

Saving Persistent State

Persistent state is usually stored whenever transient state is stored. In addition, your app should save its persistent state when it is closing, by subscription to the `PhoneApplicationService.Closing` event. Persistent state may include files or application settings, as shown in the following excerpt from the `App` class:

```
void Application_Closing(object sender, ClosingEventArgs e)
{
    System.IO.IsolatedStorage
        .IsolatedStorageSettings.ApplicationSettings["someObject Key"]
            = someObject;
}
```

> **NOTE**
>
> Transient state should not be retained when the `Closing` event occurs.

> **NOTE**
>
> Windows Phone 8 offers an alternative storage API present in the `Windows.Storage` namespace. You explore this new API in Chapter 28.

Implementing Fast App Resume

Fast App Switching (FAS) is a feature that places an app in a suspended state when the user navigates away from it. The app's state is preserved in memory. If the user returns to the app by tapping the hardware Back button or by using the task switcher, the app instance resumes. Because the app is preserved in memory, the app is returned to the same state it was when the user navigated away.

By default, if the app is suspended and the user relaunches the app by tapping on the app name in the app list or tapping the app's primary Tile, the suspended instance of the app is terminated and a new instance of the app is created. This process is slower than resuming a suspended app.

Windows Phone 8 introduces a new feature called Fast App Resume that gives apps the capability to request that user actions that would typically relaunch the app, such as tapping the app's primary tile, instead resume the suspended app instance, if one exists.

Enabling Fast App Resume

Enabling Fast App Resume requires a modification to your app's WMAppManifest.xml file. Add the ActivationPolicy attribute to the DefaultTask element and set the value to Resume, as demonstrated in the following example:

```
<DefaultTask Name="_default" NavigationPage="MainPage.xaml"
             ActivationPolicy="Resume" />
```

If `ActivationPolicy` is not specified, the default value of Replace is used.

Optimizing the Resume Experience

Fast App Resume in your app should be implemented in a manner that ensures a predictable experience for the user. The behavior of your app when it is resumed should depend on the entry point of your app when it was initially launched from a cold start and the entry point when it was resumed.

There are two kinds of entry points. Primary entry points occur via a primary tile on the Start Experience or an app link in the App List or Games hub. Secondary entry points occur via a deep link from a secondary tile, a toast notification, or from an extensibility point such as a protocol handler.

The Windows Phone OS maintains a navigation history for your app. When the user taps the hardware Back button, the OS navigates back through the stack of previously visited pages. With Fast App Resume the OS attempts to navigate to a URI within your app. If the URI is different from the current page of the app, a new page instance is created and placed on the navigation back stack. If the URI is identical to the app's current location, no new page is created and the app's current page is displayed.

If the entry point is your app's primary tile, for example, the URI is your app's main landing page. When an app is resumed via a primary entry point, it can respond in one of the following two ways:

▶ It can start fresh by clearing the back stack and navigating to the app's main landing page. If the user navigates backward from the resumed app, because there are no pages in the history the app will exit, returning the user to the Start Experience or the previous app.

▶ It can resume as if nothing happened by canceling navigation to the requested URI. In this case, the user arrives on the page that he last viewed and the back stack from the previous session remains intact.

Although it is possible to resume as if nothing happened whenever the user launches your app from a primary entry point, after a few minutes of inactivity it is better to start fresh. The user may no longer be mindful of the app's presence in the background and will expect that relaunching the app starts a new instance. In the sample for this section, you see how to detect and expire a Fast App Resume in this scenario.

Implementing Fast App Resume gets more complicated when the user launches or resumes an app from a secondary entry point. For example, if the user launches the app via its primary tile and then taps the hardware Start button, the app is deactivated and waits to be resumed. If the user then navigates to the Photo hub and relaunches the app from the picture viewer, the app should resume by clearing the back stack and navigating to the requested deep link URI.

Table 3.1 shows the recommended behavior for resuming via a primary or secondary launch point after being launched from either a primary or secondary entry point.

TABLE 3.1   Fast App Resume Recommended Resume Behavior

Launched From	Resumed From		
	Primary Launch Point Before 5 Minutes	**Primary Launch Point After 5 Minutes**	**Secondary Launch Point**
Primary Launch Point	Resume unchanged	Clear back stack and arrive at home page	Clear back stack and arrive at deep link URI
Secondary Launch Point	Clear back stack and arrive at home page	Clear back stack and arrive at home page	Clear back stack and arrive at deep link URI

An appropriate place for detecting and coordinating Fast App Resume is in your project's `App` class. The `App` class in the WPUnleashed.Examples project, in the downloadable sample code, responds to the various Fast App Resume scenarios.

When the sample app is deactivated, the `App` class records the time of deactivation in the app's isolated storage settings. When the app is activated, a field is set to the result of the `HasFastResumeExpired` method, which is shown in Listing 3.1.

Although it is not absolutely necessary for the purposes of Fast App Resume to store the deactivation time in isolated storage, it does allow the value to be used for other purposes in which tombstoning may occur.

LISTING 3.1   `App.HasFastResumeExpired` Method

```
bool HasFastResumeExpired()
{
    DateTimeOffset lastDeactivated;

    if (settings.Contains(DeactivationTimeKey))
    {
        lastDeactivated = (DateTimeOffset)settings[DeactivationTimeKey];
    }

    TimeSpan duration = DateTimeOffset.Now.Subtract(lastDeactivated);

    return TimeSpan.FromSeconds(duration.TotalSeconds)
            > fastResumeExpiryTime;
}
```

You saw earlier that an app can be launched or resumed via a primary or secondary entry point. The App class uses a custom enum named SessionType to record if the app is navigating to the app's home page via a primary entry point or to a deep link URI via a secondary entry point. SessionType can be either None, Home, or DeepLink.

Each time a navigation event is raised, the App class's RootFrame_Navigating handler determines the SessionType using the NavigatingCancelEventArgs object's Uri property (see Listing 3.2). If the session type has not been recorded and the navigation mode is set to New, it indicates that the app is launching. When the navigation mode is equal to Reset, a Fast App Resume is underway.

During a Fast App Resume, if the current page URI is not the same as the requested URI, the root frame's Navigating event is raised twice; once for the page that was displayed before deactivation and once for the requested URI. If the current page URI is the same as the requested URI, the Navigating event is raised only once for the page that was displayed before deactivation.

LISTING 3.2   App.RootFrame_Navigating Method

```
void RootFrame_Navigating(object sender, NavigatingCancelEventArgs e)
{
    string url = e.Uri.ToString();

    if (sessionType == SessionType.None && e.NavigationMode == NavigationMode.New)
    {
        /* App is launching. */

        if (url.Contains("?"))
        {
            sessionType = SessionType.DeepLink;
        }
        else if (url.Contains("/MainPage.xaml"))
        {
            sessionType = SessionType.Home;
        }
    }

    if (e.NavigationMode == NavigationMode.Reset)
    {
        /* The current navigation is the result of a Fast App Resume.
         * If so the URI is different from the current page URI
         * then another navigation will follow. */
        lastNavigationWasReset = true;
    }
    else if (e.NavigationMode == NavigationMode.New && lastNavigationWasReset)
    {
```

```
                /* This block will run once if the previous navigation
                 * was the result of a Fast App Resume. */
        lastNavigationWasReset = false;

        if (url.Contains("?"))
        {
                /* We reach this point if a secondary entry point was used,
                 * such as via the secondary tile
                 * created in FastAppResumeViewModel.cs */

            sessionType = SessionType.DeepLink;
            /* The page navigation stack will be cleared. */
        }
        else if (url.Contains("/MainPage.xaml"))
        {
            if (sessionType == SessionType.DeepLink)
            {
                /* When the app was previously launched via a deep link URI
                    * and relaunched via its primary tile,
                    * the back stack needs to be cleared. */
                sessionType = SessionType.Home;
            }
            else
            {
                if (!fastResumeExpired)
                {
                    /* The app was previously launched via its primary tile
                        * and relaunched via its primary tile.
                        * Cancel the navigation to resume. */
                    e.Cancel = true;
                    shouldClearJournal = false;
                }
            }
        }

        fastResumeExpired = false;
    }
}
```

The root frame's `Navigated` event is raised after its `Navigating` event, unless the `Cancel` property of the `NavigatingCancelEventArgs` is set to true.

The `RootFrame_Navigated` handler, shown in Listing 3.3, keeps track of whether the previous navigation was a result of a Fast App Resume, which is indicated when the `NavigationMode` property of the `NavigationEventArgs` is equal to Reset. If so, and the timeout period has not expired, the page navigation stack is cleared using the `RemoveBackEntry` method of the root frame.

LISTING 3.3 `App.RootFrame_Navigated` **Method**

```
void RootFrame_Navigated(object sender, NavigationEventArgs e)
{
    NavigationMode mode = e.NavigationMode;

    if (previousNavigationWasReset && mode == NavigationMode.New)
    {
        if (shouldClearJournal)
        {
            Debug.WriteLine("Clearing history.");

            /* Clear the entire page stack. */
            var rootFrame = (PhoneApplicationFrame)RootVisual;
            while (rootFrame.RemoveBackEntry() != null)
            {
                /* Nothing to do. */
            }
        }
        else
        {
            shouldClearJournal = true;
        }
    }
    else
    {
        previousNavigationWasReset = mode == NavigationMode.Reset;
    }
}
```

The FastAppResumeView.xaml page located in the FastAppResume directory, in the WPUnleashed.Examples project, allows you to try out the different Fast App Resume scenarios. A button on the view is bound to an `ICommand` named `CreateShellTileCommand` that places a secondary tile on the Start Experience (see Listing 3.4). Resuming the app from the secondary tile causes the page navigation stack to be cleared.

LISTING 3.4 `FastAppResumeViewModel` **Class**

```
public class FastAppResumeViewModel : ViewModelBase
{
    string tileUrl = "/FastAppResume/DeepLinkedView.xaml?DeepLink=true";
```

```csharp
public FastAppResumeViewModel()
{
    createShellTileCommand = new DelegateCommand(
        obj =>
        {
            if (!TileExists())
            {
                CreateTile();
            }
        },
        obj => !TileExists());
}

bool TileExists()
{
    ShellTile shellTile = ShellTile.ActiveTiles.FirstOrDefault(
        x => x.NavigationUri.ToString().Contains(tileUrl));

    return shellTile != null;
}

void CreateTile()
{
    StandardTileData tileData = new StandardTileData
        {
            Title = "Unleashed Secondary",
        };

    /* Pin the tile to Start Experience.
        * This causes a navigation event and deactivation of the app. */
    ShellTile.Create(new Uri(tileUrl, UriKind.Relative), tileData);
}

readonly DelegateCommand createShellTileCommand;

public ICommand CreateShellTileCommand
{
    get
    {
        return createShellTileCommand;
    }
}
}
```

Fast App Resume is an important new feature of the Windows Phone 8 OS that allows apps to forgo the usual startup penalty when being relaunched. Apps implementing this feature appear to start faster and give the impression of having better performance than apps that do not.

Running Under the Lock Screen

Users expect some kinds of apps to run under a locked screen. These apps include music players, mapping apps, stop watches, and so on.

In the first release of the Windows Phone OS, running under the lock screen was favorable to apps that wanted to avoid being tombstoned. These were apps that were slow to load or relied on complex state models. This was alleviated, however, with the introduction of fast application switching in Windows Phone 7.5. Now apps are placed in a dormant state and remain in memory.

> **NOTE**
>
> Running under the lock screen is not an alternative to implementing efficient transient state persistency. Recall that an app may still be tombstoned if the phone runs low on memory.

The following steps outline how to enable your app to run under the locked screen:

1. Set `PhoneApplicationService.Current.ApplicationIdleDetectionMode = IdleDetectionMode.Disabled`.

2. Detect when the lock screen is engaged, or disengaged, by handling the `PhoneApplicationFrame.Obscured` and `Unobscured` events, respectively.

3. When the lock screen is engaged your app should reduce its processing to a bare minimum to minimize CPU usage and thus battery consumption.

4. When the lock screen is disengaged your app should resume from where it left off.

5. Optionally, you should prompt the user to allow him or her to opt-in to running under the lock screen, and/or provide an options setting for enabling or disabling running under the lock screen.

> **TIP**
>
> To engage the lock screen within the Windows Phone emulator, press F12 on the computer keyboard twice. F12 emulates the power button on the phone. Pressing it once locks the phone and turns off the display; twice turns the display on again with the lock screen engaged. The mouse can be used to disengage the lock screen by sliding the lock screen up.
>
> To engage the lock screen when debugging on an actual device (or on the emulator), use the Simulation Dashboard, which can be opened by selecting Simulation Dashboard from the Tools menu in Visual Studio.

Lock Screen Management

I created a reusable class called LockScreenService that makes it easy to manage your app's lock screen policy. The class implements a custom ILockScreenService interface that has the following three properties:

▶ **RunningUnderLockScreen**—Gets a value indicating whether the app is running under the lock screen

▶ **RunningUnderLockScreenEnabled**—Allows you to set whether the app is allowed to run under the lock screen

▶ **UserPrompted**—Allows your app to remember whether the user has been prompted to allow running under the lock screen

At your app's first launch you query the UserPrompted property. If false, you present a dialog asking the user whether it is okay to run under the lock screen, and you set the RunningUnderLockScreenEnabled property accordingly. You subscribe to the PropertyChanged event of the LockScreenService, and when the RunningUnderLockScreen property changes, it indicates that the lock screen has been either engaged or disengaged. LockScreenService is a singleton and subclasses NotifyPropertyChangeBase for property change notification (see Listing 3.5). The private constructor attempts to retrieve the UserPrompted and RunningUnderLockScreenEnabled property values from isolated storage settings. It then subscribes to the PhoneApplicationFrame.Obscured and Unobscured events.

When the Obscured event is raised, the RunningUnderLockScreen property is set.

The LockScreenService class is located in the Shell directory of the WPUnleashed project.

LISTING 3.5   LockScreenService Class (excerpt)

```
public class LockScreenService : NotifyPropertyChangeBase, ILockScreenService
{
    static readonly string promptedKey
            = "UserPromptedToAllowRunningUnderLockScreen";
    static readonly string runningEnabledKey = "RunningUnderLockScreenEnabled";

    LockScreenService()
    {
        IsolatedStorageSettings settings
                = IsolatedStorageSettings.ApplicationSettings;
        bool prompted;
        if (settings.TryGetValue(promptedKey, out prompted))
        {
            UserPrompted = prompted;
        }

        bool enabledValue;
```

```
    if (settings.TryGetValue(runningEnabledKey, out enabledValue))
    {
        RunningUnderLockScreenEnabled = enabledValue;
    }


    var frame = (PhoneApplicationFrame)Application.Current.RootVisual;
    frame.Obscured += (o, args) => RunningUnderLockScreen = args.IsLocked;
    frame.Unobscured += (o, args) => RunningUnderLockScreen = false;
}
...
}
```

When either of the `UserPrompted` or `RunningUnderLockScreenEnabled` properties is set, its new value is saved to isolated storage settings using a `SaveSetting` method, as shown:

```
void SaveSetting(string key, object value)
{
    IsolatedStorageSettings settings
        = IsolatedStorageSettings.ApplicationSettings;
    settings[key] = value;
    settings.Save();
}
```

When the `RunningUnderLockScreenEnabled` property is enabled, the idle detection mode is disabled, which allows the app to run under the lock screen. If disabled, the app must be restarted or deactivated before the idle detection mode can be enabled or an `InvalidOperationException` is raised. This is a limitation of the phone OS. See the following excerpt:

```
public bool RunningUnderLockScreenEnabled
{
    get
    {
        return runningUnderLockScreenEnabled;
    }
    set
    {
        var result = Assign(ref runningUnderLockScreenEnabled, value);

        if (result == AssignmentResult.Success)
        {
            if (runningUnderLockScreenEnabled)
            {
                PhoneApplicationService.Current.ApplicationIdleDetectionMode
                    = IdleDetectionMode.Disabled;
            }
```

```
        /* Idle detection mode cannot be enabled
           until the application is restarted. */

        SaveSetting(runningEnabledKey, runningUnderLockScreenEnabled);
    }
  }
}
```

The `LockScreenView` page and its associated `LockScreenViewModel` class demonstrate the use of the `LockScreenService`, and are located in the ExecutionModel directory of the WPUnleashed.Examples project. The `LockScreenViewModel` uses the `MessageService` to ask the user whether she wants to opt-in to running under the lock screen. When the manager's `RunningUnderLockScreen` property changes, a string is written to the Visual Studio Output view (see Listing 3.6).

LISTING 3.6   `LockScreenViewModel` Class

```
public class LockScreenViewModel : ViewModelBase
{
    public LockScreenViewModel() : base("lock screen settings")
    {
        LockScreenService lockScreenService = LockScreenService.Instance;

        if (!lockScreenService.UserPrompted)
        {
            bool allow = MessageService.AskYesNoQuestion(
                "Is it OK to run under the phone's lock screen?");
            lockScreenService.RunningUnderLockScreenEnabled = allow;
            lockScreenService.UserPrompted = true;
        }

        lockScreenService.PropertyChanged
            += (o, args) =>
            {
                if (args.PropertyName == "RunningUnderLockScreen")
                {
                    Debug.WriteLine("RunningUnderLockScreen: "
                        + lockScreenService.RunningUnderLockScreen);
                }
            };
    }

    public bool RunningUnderLockScreenEnabled
    {
        get
        {
```

```
        return LockScreenService.Instance.RunningUnderLockScreenEnabled;
    }
    set
    {
        LockScreenService.Instance.RunningUnderLockScreenEnabled = value;
    }
  }
}
```

The `LockScreenView` XAML has a Windows Phone Toolkit `ToggleSwitch` control that is bound to the `RunningUnderLockScreenEnabled` viewmodel property, as shown in the following excerpt:

```
<StackPanel x:Name="ContentPanel">
    <toolkit:ToggleSwitch
        Header="run under lock screen"
        IsChecked="{Binding RunningUnderLockScreenEnabled, Mode=TwoWay}" />
</StackPanel>
```

Figure 3.3 shows the `ToggleSwitch` located on the LockScreenView page with the Run Under Lock Screen setting enabled.

FIGURE 3.3   LockScreenView page.

Running under the lock screen is the only way to allow your foreground app to run while the phone is idle. It should, however, be used with caution, because if an app continues to consume the device CPU, it may rapidly flatten the device battery.

Page Navigation

The navigation system in Windows Phone XAML apps is based on the Silverlight for the browser navigation model. The navigation class model looks a little different in the phone SDK however. Rather than Silverlight `Frame` and `Page` controls, Windows Phone apps use the subclasses `PhoneApplicationFrame` and the `PhoneApplicationPage` (see Figure 3.4).

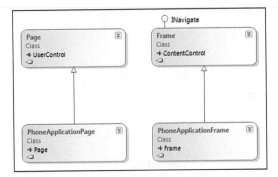

FIGURE 3.4   The `PhoneApplicationFrame` and `PhoneApplicationPage` classes are derived from the `Frame` and `Page` classes, respectively.

> **NOTE**
>
> `Frame` and `Page` must not be used directly in your app. They are prohibited because of underlying differences in the way the run-time environment interacts with the OS within the constrained environment of the phone.

Page navigation in Windows Phone works in much the same way as page navigation in a web browser. `PhoneApplicationFrame` is analogous to the web browser, coordinating page transitions within your app.

Figure 3.5 depicts the display elements of a Windows Phone app.

FIGURE 3.5   Display elements of a Windows Phone app.

The `PhoneApplicationFrame` is the host for `PhoneApplicationPages` and reserves space for the system tray and the application bar. The `PhoneApplicationPage` consumes all remaining space after the system tray and the application bar.

> **NOTE**
>
> There can be only one `PhoneApplicationFrame` for an application. Attempting to place a `PhoneApplicationFrame` within a `PhoneApplicationPage` causes the content to become infinitely nested at runtime because the page will be forced inside the frame, the frame inside the page, and so on.

Navigation Using Unmapped URIs

There are numerous ways of allowing the user to perform page navigation. This section looks at using `Buttons` with code-beside to open external URLs, and at `HyperlinkButtons`, which can rely solely on XAML. In subsequent chapters you explore other techniques to perform navigation including the use of commands and a custom navigation service.

Internal URIs

When navigating to `PhoneApplicationPages` within an application, URIs either must be relative to the root directory of the project and use the relative path syntax, as shown in the following excerpt:

```
Uri uri = new Uri("/DirectoryName/PageName.xaml", UriKind.Relative);
```

or they must use the relative component URI format, such as that used in the following example:

```
Uri uri = new Uri("/AssemblyName;component/PageName.xaml", UriKind.Relative);
```

The assembly name segment must be the name of an assembly that is locatable at runtime. The name of a project's output assembly can be found in the project properties editor by right-clicking the project node in the Solution Explorer and selecting Properties, or by pressing Alt+Enter.

The `HyperlinkButton` control can be used to allow the user to navigate directly to a page within your application, as shown:

```
<HyperlinkButton NavigateUri="/Directory/PageName.xaml" Content="Internal Page" />
```

External Navigation Using the Button Control

The `Button` control is a flexible way for determining user intent. A `Button` can be used for navigation by subscribing to its `Click` event, as shown in the following excerpt from the ProductDetailsView.xaml in the downloadable sample code:

```
<Button Click="Button_ExternalLink_Click"
```

```
Tag="{Binding Product.ExternalUrl}"
Content="External Page" />
```

The WebBrowserTask allows you to navigate to external URIs using the phone's built-in web browser Internet Explorer. This causes your app to be deactivated while the user views the page. You explore tasks in more detail in Chapter 14.

To provide the WebBrowserTask with the location of the web page, use the button's Tag property. The Click event handler, which initiates the WebBrowserTask, is shown in the following excerpt:

```
void Button_ExternalLink_Click(object sender, RoutedEventArgs e)
{
    FrameworkElement button = sender as FrameworkElement;
    if (button == null || button.Tag == null)
    {
        return;
    }
    WebBrowserTask task = new WebBrowserTask
    {
        Uri = new Uri(button.Tag.ToString(), UriKind.Absolute)
    };
    task.Show();
}
```

External Navigation Using the HyperlinkButton Control

The disadvantage of using a Button control for links to external content is that it does not provide the familiar look and feel of a hyperlink. The HyperlinkButton control provides an easier way for navigating to pages within an application. There is a trick to using the HyperlinkButton with external URIs. Set its TargetName property to _blank, as shown in the following example:

```
<HyperlinkButton TargetName="_blank" NavigateUri="http://create.msdn.com"
                 Content="http://create.msdn.com" />
```

> **NOTE**
>
> Failing to set the HyperlinkButton.TargetName to _blank, when using an external URI, raises the Frame.NavigationFailed event when the button is tapped.

Hosting Web Content Within an App

An alternative to using the phone's built-in Internet Explorer app is to host the content in a Microsoft.Phone.Controls.WebBrowser control.

The following excerpt from the WebBrowserView.xaml page, in the downloadable sample code, shows a `WebBrowser` placed within the main content grid of a page:

```
<Grid x:Name="ContentGrid" Grid.Row="1">
    <phone:WebBrowser Source="{Binding Url}"/>
</Grid>
```

Here the `Source` property of the `WebBrowser` is bound to the `Url` property of the view-model. The `WebBrowser` control is discussed in greater detail in Chapter 7, "Employing Media and Web Elements."

A dedicated web browser page can be used in your app to host all external content. To launch the dedicated web browser page, a relative URI can be constructed using the `Binding.StringFormat` property, as shown in the following excerpt:

```
<HyperlinkButton
    NavigateUri="{Binding ExternalUrl, StringFormat=/WebBrowser/\{0\}}"
    Content="External Page" />
```

Backslashes are used to escape the curly brackets in the `StringFormat` value.

The `StringFormat` property transforms the `HyperlinkButton`'s binding expression into the following:

```
string.Format("/WebBrowser/{0}", ExternalUrl);
```

URI mapping is used to pass the external URL as a query string parameter. This is explored further in a later section.

Passing Page Arguments Using Query Strings

Query strings allow for key value pairs to be embedded in a URL and passed to a page. Just like HTML web applications, Windows Phone apps use query string parameters for inter-page communication.

The `PhoneApplicationPage.NavigationContext` property, which is initialized after the page is created, is used to retrieve the query string. Its `QueryString` property is an `IDictionary` of string key and value pairs. The following excerpt from the WebBrowserView.xaml.cs, in the downloadable sample code, demonstrates how to retrieve a query string value:

```
protected overide void OnNavigatedTo(NavigationEventArgs e)
{
    base.OnNavigatedTo(e);

    string url;
    if (NavigationContext.QueryString.TryGetValue("url", out url)
        && url != null && url.ToLower() != "webbrowserview.xaml")
    {
```

```
        ViewModel.LoadPage(url);
    }
}
```

Navigation History Stack

The Windows Phone navigation infrastructure maintains a history of pages that have been loaded. Each time an app navigates to a different page, the current page's `OnNavigatedFrom` method is called and the page is placed on the history stack (see Figure 3.6).

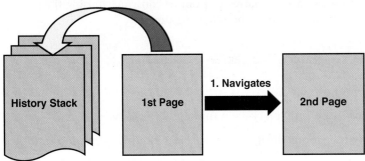

FIGURE 3.6 Pages are placed on the history stack.

While on the history stack, the page remains in memory unless the application is tombstoned or closed. This means that subscribing to the `PhoneApplicationService.Deactivated` event provides the page with the opportunity to save its transient state. It is, however, preferable to use the page's `OnNavigatedFrom` method for the saving of page state.

Using the `Deactivate` event to save page state runs the risk of slowing down deactivation when all pages on the history stack are saving their state simultaneously.

BEST PRACTICES

Use the `OnNavigatedFrom` and `OnNavigatedTo` methods of `PhoneApplicationPage` to save both transient and persistent state.

NOTE

Unlike Silverlight for the browser, in Windows Phone the page's `NavigationCacheMode` property is not assignable, and it is set to `Disabled` by default. This means that internal caching of pages does not occur, and when navigating to a page that does not exist on the history stack, the page is always instantiated.

Restoration of transient state should occur with the page's `OnNavigatedTo` method. The `OnNavigatedTo` method is called when the `PhoneApplicationFrame` navigates to the page. This is triggered by the following actions:

▶ Navigation to a specified page URI occurs using one of various navigation methods such as the `PhoneApplicationFrame.Navigate` method.

▶ The `NavigationService.GoBack` method is called.

▶ The user presses the hardware Back button.

▶ The page is the current page when the app moves from the tombstoned or dormant state to the running state.

▶ The page is the app's start page and the app is launched.

> **NOTE**
>
> When an application is activated, the frame navigates to the page that was active when the phone was dormant or tombstoned. The `NavigationContext.QueryString` is preserved, which means that there is no need to store this in the `PhoneApplicationService.State` dictionary.

URI Mapping

Relying on URIs that include the full path to each page in your app can make your app brittle and difficult to change the physical location of individual pages. If a page is moved, all references to that file must be updated. This can lead to maintainability issues as the size of the project grows.

The URI mapping system of Windows Phone apps allows requests for a URI to be routed to a different URI, and uses a single configuration point for the management of page URIs. Mapped URIs can be made shorter and are, thus, less subject to typographical errors. They also allow the exclusion of technology specific information, such as the .xaml page file extension, making it easier to retarget business logic for different platforms.

To use URI mapping, you must assign a `System.Windows.Navigation.UriMapper` instance to the `UriMapper` property of an app's `PhoneApplicationFrame`. This can be done in XAML, as shown in the following excerpt from the App.xaml file in the downloadable sample code:

```
<Application
    x:Class="DanielVaughan.WPUnleashed.Examples.App"
    xmlns="http://schemas.microsoft.com/winfx/2006/xaml/presentation"
    xmlns:x="http://schemas.microsoft.com/winfx/2006/xaml">

    <Application.RootVisual>
        <phone:PhoneApplicationFrame x:Name="RootFrame">
            <phone:PhoneApplicationFrame.UriMapper>
```

```
                      <navigation:UriMapper>
                        <navigation:UriMapper.UriMappings>
                          <navigation:UriMapping
                            Uri="/ProductDetails/{productId}"
              MappedUri="/Navigation/ProductDetailsView.xaml?productId={productId}" />
                            <navigation:UriMapping Uri="/WebBrowser/{url}"
                        MappedUri="/WebBrowser/WebBrowserView.xaml?url={url}" />
                        </navigation:UriMapper.UriMappings>
                      </navigation:UriMapper>
                </phone:PhoneApplicationFrame.UriMapper>
            </phone:PhoneApplicationFrame>
        </Application.RootVisual>


        <!-- Content omitted. -->
</Application>
```

The UriMapping class contains a Uri property and a MappedUri property. When navigation is requested from the Uri value, it is rerouted to the MappedUri property.

By using the curly brace syntax, as shown in the previous excerpt, a substring of the requested URI can be transplanted into the rerouted MappedUri value. This is especially useful when you want to target the same page using different URIs, and where the query string can be used to convey the action to be undertaken by the page.

In the previous excerpt you see a UriMapping for the ProductDetailsView page. The ProductDetailsView displays detailed information for a particular product, identified by a query string parameter. When navigating to the ProductDetails page, if the requested URL is /ProductDetails/2, this is rerouted to /Navigation/ProductDetailsView.xaml?productId=2.

If you were to request the ProductDetailsView page using the NavigationService, as shown in the following example, the request would be rerouted accordingly:

```
NavigationService.Source = new Uri("/ProductDetails/2", UriKind.Relative);
```

The product to be displayed can then be determined in the ProductsDetailsView by reading the productId query string parameter, as demonstrated in the following excerpt:

```
protected override void OnNavigatedTo(NavigationEventArgs e)
{
    base.OnNavigatedTo(e);
    string productIdString = NavigationContext.QueryString["productId"];
    int productId = int.Parse(productIdString);
    ViewModel.LoadProduct(productId);
}
```

You see later in this chapter how the viewmodel uses the product ID to retrieve the product information from a WCF service.

Navigation Using the `NavigationService`

The `PhoneApplicationPage` class exposes a public `NavigationService` property, which allows direct control over navigation.

NOTE

The `NavigationService` cannot be used to launch Internet Explorer to view an external URL. Instead, use either the `WebBrowserTask`, or open the page within the app using the `WebBrowserControl`. See the previous sections on external navigation using the `Button` and `HyperlinkButton` controls.

The `NavigationService.Navigate` method causes the frame to load the specified `PhoneApplicationPage`, like so:

```
NavigationService.Navigate(
    new Uri("/DirectoryName/PageName.xaml", UriKind.Relative));
```

The URI must be either a path relative to the project's root directory, as shown in the previous example, or a relative component URI, such as in the following example:

```
NavigationService.Navigate(
        new Uri("/AssemblyName;component/PageName.xaml", UriKind.Relative));
```

TIP

The `NavigationService` cannot be used within the constructor of the `PhoneApplicationPage` because it is assigned after the page's constructor has been called. Therefore, wait until the page's `OnNavigatedTo` method is called or the `Loaded` event has occurred before using the `NavigationService`.

The `NavigationService.Source` property allows you to retrieve the URI of the current page. Setting the `Source` property performs the same action as using the `Navigate` method; the frame loads the page at the specified URI. See the following example:

```
NavigationService.Source = new Uri(
        "/DirectoryName/PageName.xaml", UriKind.Relative);
```

Routing is also enabled for the `NavigationService`, which means that mapped URIs can be used instead of relative URIs.

If you examine the API of the `NavigationService`, you will likely wonder what the difference is between the `CurrentSource` property and the `Source` property. The answer is that the `CurrentSource` property does not change until navigation has completed. Conversely, the `Source` property changes as soon as navigation is initiated.

Backward Navigation

The NavigationService maintains the app's navigation history, via an internal Journal instance. This allows the GoBack method of the NavigationService to move to the previous page in the history stack.

> **NOTE**
>
> If the GoBack method is called, and the history stack is empty because the current page is the app's start page, then an InvalidOperationException is raised. To determine whether the NavigationService is able to go back, query its CanGoBack property.

Forward Navigation

Unlike Silverlight for the browser, the GoForward method of the NavigationService does not allow forward navigation and will raise an InvalidOperationException when called. Consequently, the CanGoForward property always returns false.

> **NOTE**
>
> Forward navigation using the NavigationService is not supported.

Handling Page Navigation

The PhoneApplicationPage extends the System.Windows.Controls.Page class, which has a number of virtual methods called when the page is brought into view or removed from view by the PhoneApplicationFrame (see Figure 3.7).

FIGURE 3.7   PhoneApplicationPage inherits page navigation methods.

The OnNavigatingFrom method is called before a page is removed from view by the PhoneApplicationFrame, and the OnNavigatedFrom method is called after navigation occurs. Conversely, the OnNavigatedTo method is called when the frame brings the page into view.

Canceling Navigation

The OnNavigatingFrom method offers the opportunity to cancel navigation using the NavigatingCancelEventArgs parameter.

NavigatingCancelEventArgs has the following properties:

▶ **NavigationMode**—An enum value that indicates the type of navigation. This value may be Back, Forward, New, or Refresh.

▶ **Uri**—The destination URI.

▶ **Cancel**—Setting this value to true cancels the navigation.

The NavigationCancelEventArgs class subclasses CancelEventArgs, which provides the Cancel property. By setting this property to true, the page can prevent the navigation from occurring, as shown in the following excerpt:

```
protected override void OnNavigatingFrom(
    System.Windows.Navigation.NavigatingCancelEventArgs e)
{
    base.OnNavigatingFrom(e);
    MessageBoxResult boxResult = MessageBox.Show(
        "Leave this page?", "Question", MessageBoxButton.OKCancel);
    if (boxResult != MessageBoxResult.OK)
    {
        e.Cancel = true;
    }
}
```

> **NOTE**
>
> You should not attempt to cancel navigation in the OnNavigatingFrom method when the hardware Back button is pressed. Instead, override the OnBackKeyPress method to cancel the back key, which prevents navigation.

Cross-Page Communication

After navigation has occurred, an opportunity remains for the previous page to interact with the current page from the previous page's OnNavigatedFrom method. This is achieved using the Content property of the NavigationEventArgs, which provides the destination PhoneApplicationPage object.

To see this in action, place a breakpoint in the OnNavigatedFrom method. When the breakpoint is hit, notice that the page being navigated to has already been instantiated and is provided in the Content property of the NavigationEventArgs (see Figure 3.8).

FIGURE 3.8   The `Content` property of the `NavigationEventArgs` contains the page being navigated to.

The `Uri` property of the `NavigationEventArgs` contains the URI of the destination page, including any query string that may be present.

Page Redirection

The `OnNavigatingFrom` method allows you to intercept a navigation event and to even cancel the navigation if needed. Additionally, there may be times when you want to redirect the user to a different URI based on some conditional logic.

The `NavigationService`, however, does not support overlapping navigation. That is, you are unable to cancel an existing navigation and immediately commence another.

You can, however, cancel navigation and schedule navigation to a different `Uri` using the page's `Dispatcher` property, as shown in the following excerpt:

```
protected override void OnNavigatingFrom(NavigatingCancelEventArgs e)
{
    if (e.Uri.ToString().Contains("RequestedUrl"))
    {
        e.Cancel = true;
        /* Perform the redirect on the UI thread. */
        Dispatcher.BeginInvoke(() => NavigationService.Navigate(
            new Uri("RedirectUrl", UriKind.Relative)));
    }

    base.OnNavigatingFrom(e);
}
```

By using the `Dispatcher` to invoke the lambda expression, which performs the call to the `NavigationService`, you allow the current navigation to complete first. This works because the UI thread can be thought of as a queue of prioritized delegates, all waiting in turn to be executed. After all the `Navigating` event handlers have been serviced, the delegate represented by the lambda expression will be taken of the queue and performed by the UI thread. This technique, of using the `Dispatcher` to enqueue an action, is also useful when working with some UI controls, whose event handlers may be called before the control is finished reacting to a user action.

Hardware Back Button

The hardware Back button is analogous to the Back button on a web browser. However, when the user presses the Back button, past the first page of a phone app, the app is closed. This is in contrast to the phone's hardware start button, which merely causes an app to be deactivated.

> **NOTE**
>
> The hardware Back button should not be used for application-specific behavior. It is only for navigation, and if used otherwise, may cause your app to fail Windows Phone Marketplace certification.

To determine whether navigation is occurring because the hardware Back button was pressed or the navigation was initiated by a call to `NavigationService.GoBack`, use the `NavigatingEventArgs.NavigationMode` property as shown:

```
protected override void OnNavigatedFrom(NavigationEventArgs e)
{
    base.OnNavigatedFrom(e);

    if (e.NavigationMode == NavigationMode.Back)
    {
        // Back button pressed.
    }
}
```

The back key button can also be canceled by overriding the `PhoneApplicationPage.OnBackKeyPress`, as shown in the following excerpt:

```
protected override void OnBackKeyPress(CancelEventArgs e)
{
    base.OnBackKeyPress(e);

    e.Cancel = true;
}
```

OnBackKeyPress is called before OnNavigatedFrom, and if the Back button is canceled, OnNavigatedFrom is not called at all.

NOTE

The Windows Phone Marketplace certification requirements forbid canceling the Back button in most cases. To maintain a consistent user experience, the Back button must only be used for backward navigation in the application. The following four certification requirements relate to use of the Back button:

▶ Pressing the Back button must return the application to the previous page or return to any previous page within the back stack.

▶ Pressing the Back button from the first screen of an application must close the application.

▶ If the current page displays a context menu or a dialog, the pressing of the Back button must close the menu or dialog and return the user to the screen where the context menu or dialog box was opened.

▶ For games, when the Back button is pressed during gameplay, the game can choose to present a pause context menu or dialog or navigate the user to the prior menu screen. Pressing the Back button again while in a paused context menu or dialog closes the menu or dialog.

For more information see section 5.2.4 of the Technical Certification Requirements at http://bit.ly/VpVxB7.

Creating an Application Splash Screen

Windows Phone App projects have baked-in support for application splash screens. To create a splash screen it is simply a matter of placing a JPG image called SplashScreenImage.jpg, with the dimensions of 480 by 800 pixels, in the root directory of your project. Ensure that its Build Action is set to Content (see Figure 3.9).

Using an image for a splash screen does not, however, prevent an application from being closed by the OS if the first page takes longer than 10 seconds to load. If your application's first page takes longer than this to load, it is best to overlay the content with a loading indicator and perform the time consuming initialization on a background thread. After loading is complete, the indicator can be dismissed.

The ProductsView and ProductsViewModel classes, located in the Navigation directory of the WPUnleashed.Examples project in the downloadable sample code, demonstrate this principle (see Figure 3.10).

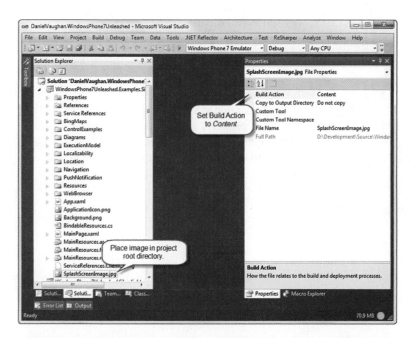

FIGURE 3.9   Creating an application splash screen.

FIGURE 3.10   A custom loading screen.

The ProductsView page uses a `StackPanel` to present an indeterminate progress bar to the user while the viewmodel is loading, as shown in the following excerpt:

```
<StackPanel Grid.Row="1"
            Visibility="{Binding Loaded,
            Converter={StaticResource BooleanToVisibilityConverter},
            ConverterParameter=Collapsed}"
            Height="150" >
```

```
<TextBlock Text="Loading..." Style="{StaticResource PhoneTextTitle2Style}"
        HorizontalAlignment="Center" Margin="20"/>
    <ProgressBar IsIndeterminate="True" />
</StackPanel>
```

The Visibility property of the StackPanel is assigned via a binding to the viewmodel's Loaded property. To convert the boolean Loaded property to a Visibility type, a custom IValueConverter called BooleanToVisibilityConverter is used (see Listing 3.7). The class is located in the ValueConverters directory of the WPUnleashed project, in the downloadable sample code.

LISTING 3.7   BooleanToVisibility Class

```
public class BooleanToVisibilityConverter : IValueConverter
{
    public object Convert(object value, Type targetType,
        object parameter, CultureInfo culture)
    {
        string paramValue = (string)parameter;

        if (value == null || (bool)value)
        {
            return paramValue == "Collapsed"
                ? Visibility.Collapsed : Visibility.Visible;
        }

        return paramValue == "Collapsed"
            ? Visibility.Visible : Visibility.Collapsed;
    }

    public object ConvertBack(object value, Type targetType,
        object parameter, CultureInfo culture)
    {
        string paramValue = (string)parameter;
        if (value == null || (Visibility)value == Visibility.Visible)
        {
            return paramValue != "Collapsed";
        }

        return paramValue == "Collapsed";
    }
}
```

The `ConverterParameter` attribute determines what value to assign to the `Visibility` property if the binding value is `true`. If the `Loaded` property of the viewmodel is `true`, then the `Visibility` property will set to `Visibility.Visible`.

To hide the rest of the content during loading, the same technique is employed for the main content control.

```
<StackPanel Grid.Row="1" Margin="10"
                Visibility="{Binding Loaded,
                    Converter={StaticResource BooleanToVisibilityConverter},
                    ConverterParameter=Visible}">
    <ScrollViewer>
        <!-- Content omitted. -->
        <ScrollViewer>
</StackPanel>
```

Here the `ConverterParameter` attribute is set to `Visible`, so that its `Visibility` is set to `Visible` when the viewmodel's `Loaded` property is `true` and `Collapsed` when it is `false`.

The code listings for the ProductsView page and associated files are provided in the following section.

Walking Through the Bookshop Sample Application

This chapter's sample app provides the beginnings of a simple data driven e-commerce app that demonstrates the use of navigation, transient and persistent state, image caching, and WCF services. It allows the user to select from a list of books, retrieved from a WCF service, and to view each item's details on a separate details page.

The `ProductsViewModel` class retrieves a list of `Product` objects from a WCF service. Each product has various properties such as a description, price, and an image URI.

The `ProductsViewModel` saves and restores its own transient state consisting of the list of products it retrieves from the WCF service (see Listing 3.8).

The code for this section resides in the Navigation directory of the WPUnleashed. Examples project in the downloadable sample code.

The viewmodel's constructor determines whether transient state exists for itself. If so, it restores the list of `Products` or else it requests the list of products from the WCF using the `BookshopServiceClient`. The call occurs asynchronously, and the products list is populated after the call completes.

The `ViewModelBase` class subclasses the `NotifyPropertyChangeBase` class, which implements `INotifyPropertyChanged`. The source for `NotifyPropertyChangeBase` is located in the downloadable sample code, and was discussed in Chapter 2, "Fundamental Concepts in Windows Phone Development."

LISTING 3.8   `ProductsViewModel` Class (excerpt)

```
public class ProductsViewModel : ViewModelBase
{
    readonly IDictionary<string, object> transientStateDictionary;
    const string transientStateKey = "ProductsViewModel_Products";

    public ProductsViewModel(
        IDictionary<string, object> transientStateDictionary)
    {
        this.transientStateDictionary = ArgumentValidator.AssertNotNull(
                transientStateDictionary, "transientStateDictionary");

        LoadTransientState();
        if (products != null)
        {
            return;
        }

        BookshopServiceClient client = new BookshopServiceClient();
        client.GetProductsCompleted += (sender, args) =>
        {
            if (args.Error != null)
            {
                MessageService.ShowError("Unable to retrieve products.");
                return;
            }

            Products = args.Result;
            Loaded = true;
        };
        client.GetProductsAsync();
    }

    ObservableCollection<Product> products;

    public ObservableCollection<Product> Products
    {
        get
        {
            return products;
        }
        private set
        {
```

```
            Assign(ref products, value);
        }
    }
    bool loaded;

    public bool Loaded
    {
        get
        {
            return loaded;
        }
        private set
        {
            Assign(ref loaded, value);
        }
    }

    public void SaveTransientState()
    {
        transientStateDictionary[transientStateKey] = products;
    }

    public void LoadTransientState()
    {
        object transientState;
        if (transientStateDictionary.TryGetValue(
                transientStateKey, out transientState))
        {
            products = transientState as ObservableCollection<Product>;
            if (products != null)
            {
                Loaded = true;
            }
        }
    }
}
```

Within the OnNavigatingTo method of the ProductsView page, a ProductsViewModel is instantiated and assigned to the page's DataContext. The ProductsViewModel is passed the transient state dictionary for the page (see Listing 3.9).

The OnNavigatingTo and OnNavigatedFrom methods are used to inform the viewmodel when to save its state.

LISTING 3.9   `ProductsView` Class

```
public partial class ProductsView : PhoneApplicationPage
{
    public ProductsView()
    {
        InitializeComponent();
    }

    ProductsViewModel ViewModel
    {
        get
        {
            return (ProductsViewModel)DataContext;
        }
    }

    bool loaded;

    protected override void OnNavigatedTo(NavigationEventArgs e)
    {
        Debug.WriteLine("ProductsView OnNavigatedTo");
        base.OnNavigatedTo(e);

        if (!loaded)
        {
            DataContext = new ProductsViewModel(State);
            loaded = true;
        }

        ViewModel.LoadTransientState();
    }

    protected override void OnNavigatedFrom(NavigationEventArgs e)
    {
        base.OnNavigatedFrom(e);
        Debug.WriteLine("ProductsView OnNavigatedFrom");
        ViewModel.SaveTransientState();
    }
}
```

Displaying the Product List

The list of products exposed by the `ProductsViewModel.Products` property is displayed using a `ListBox` control in the ProductsView page. The `ListBox`'s `ItemTemplate` has various controls that are used to display the details of each `Product`, as shown in the following excerpt:

```
<StackPanel Grid.Row="1" Margin="10"
            Visibility="{Binding Loaded,
                Converter={StaticResource BooleanToVisibilityConverter},
                ConverterParameter=Visible}">
    <ScrollViewer>
        <ListBox ItemsSource="{Binding Products}" Height="610">
            <ListBox.ItemTemplate>
                <DataTemplate>
                    <StackPanel Orientation="Horizontal">
                        <Image Source="{Binding SmallImageUri}"
                               MaxWidth="150" MaxHeight="150"
                               Margin="0,0,10,10" />
                        <StackPanel Margin="5">
                            <TextBlock Text="{Binding Title}"
                                       TextWrapping="Wrap" />
                            <TextBlock Text="{Binding Price,
                                             StringFormat=\{0:C\}}" />
                            <HyperlinkButton
                                NavigateUri="{Binding Id,
                                    StringFormat=/ProductDetails/\{0\}}"
                                Content="View Details"
                                HorizontalAlignment="Left" Margin="0,10,0,0" />
                        </StackPanel>
                    </StackPanel>
                </DataTemplate>
            </ListBox.ItemTemplate>
        </ListBox>
    </ScrollViewer>
</StackPanel>
```

An Image control displays a thumbnail of the product, using the SmallImageUri property of the Product.

A string format is used to convert the Price property, which is a double value, to a currency formatted string using the format {0:C}. Similarly, a link is provided for the product details page, using the format /ProductDetails/{0}, and the value of the Product's Id is substituted for the {0} placeholder. The UriMapping for this product details URI causes the application to reroute to the full URI of the ProductDetailsView.xaml page and includes the productId query string parameter.

Figure 3.11 shows the ProductsView displaying a list of books.

When the user presses the HyperlinkButton, he is directed to the ProductDetailsView.xaml page. This page displays the various properties of the product and includes a link for an external website, where the user can find more information about the product (see Figure 3.12).

FIGURE 3.11   Products View.

FIGURE 3.12   View a product's details.

When navigating to the `ProductDetailsView` the page attempts to retrieve the productId query string parameter from the `NavigationContext` (see Listing 3.10).

LISTING 3.10   `ProductDetailsView` Class (excerpt)

```
public partial class ProductDetailsView : PhoneApplicationPage
{
    public ProductDetailsView()
    {
        InitializeComponent();

        DataContext = new ProductDetailsViewModel(
            PhoneApplicationService.Current.State);     }
    ProductDetailsViewModel ViewModel
    {
        get
        {
            return (ProductDetailsViewModel)DataContext;
        }
    }

    protected override void OnNavigatedTo(NavigationEventArgs e)
    {       base.OnNavigatedTo(e);
        string productIdString = NavigationContext.QueryString["productId"];
        int productId = int.Parse(productIdString);
        ViewModel.LoadProduct(productId);
    }

    protected override void OnNavigatedFrom(NavigationEventArgs e)
    {       ViewModel.SaveTransientState();
        base.OnNavigatedFrom(e);
    }
}
```

The view then passes the parameter along to the `ProductDetailsViewModel` class, which handles the loading of the specified product (see Listing 3.11). The `LoadProduct` method first tests for the existence of the product in transient state. If not present, it retrieves the product using the service client.

LISTING 3.11   `ProductDetailsViewModel` Class (excerpt)

```
public class ProductDetailsViewModel : ViewModelBase
{
    const string transientStateKey = "ProductDetailsViewModel_Product";
    readonly IDictionary<string, object> transientStateDictionary;
    public ProductDetailsViewModel(
```

```csharp
    IDictionary<string, object> transientStateDictionary)
{
    this.transientStateDictionary = ArgumentValidator.AssertNotNull(
        transientStateDictionary, "transientStateDictionary");
}

public void LoadProduct(int productId)
{
    object transientState;
    if (PhoneApplicationService.Current.State.TryGetValue(
            transientStateKey, out transientState))
    {
        product = transientState as Product;
        if (product != null && product.Id == productId)
        {
            return;
        }
    }

    BookshopServiceClient client = new BookshopServiceClient();
    client.GetProductByIdCompleted += (sender, args) =>
    {
        if (args.Error != null)
        {
            throw args.Error;
        }
        Product = args.Result;
    };
    client.GetProductByIdAsync(productId);
}
Product product;

public Product Product
{
    get
    {
        return product;
    }
    /* Setter is not private to enable sample data.
     * See ProductDetailsViewSampleData.xaml */
    internal set
    {
        product = value;
        OnPropertyChanged("Product");
    }
}
```

```
    public void SaveTransientState()
    {
            transientStateDictionary[transientStateKey] = product;
    }
}
```

When navigating away from the page, the viewmodel's `SaveTransientState` method is called, which places the product in the state dictionary.

The ProductDetailsView.xaml page presents the product details via the viewmodel's `Product` property (see Listing 3.12).

LISTING 3.12   ProductDetailsView.xaml (excerpt)

```xaml
<StackPanel Grid.Row="1"
    Style="{StaticResource PageContentPanelStyle}"
    d:DataContext="{d:DesignData Source=ProductDetailsViewSampleData.xaml}">

    <TextBlock Text="{Binding Product.Title}" TextWrapping="Wrap"
            Style="{StaticResource PhoneTextTitle2Style}"/>
    <StackPanel Orientation="Horizontal">
        <Image Source="{Binding Product.LargeImageUri,
                Converter={StaticResource ImageCacheConverter}}"
                MaxWidth="250" MaxHeight="250" Margin="10,10,0,10" />
        <StackPanel>
            <TextBlock Text="{Binding Product.Author}" TextWrapping="Wrap"
                    Style="{StaticResource PhoneTextTitle3Style}"/>
            <TextBlock Text="{Binding Product.Price, StringFormat=\{0:C\}}"
                    Style="{StaticResource PhoneTextTitle3Style}"/>
            <StackPanel Orientation="Horizontal">
                <TextBlock Text="ISBN"
                        Style="{StaticResource PhoneTextTitle3Style}" />
                <TextBlock Text="{Binding Product.Isbn13}"
                        TextWrapping="Wrap"
                        Style="{StaticResource PhoneTextNormalStyle}" />
            </StackPanel>

            <HyperlinkButton
                NavigateUri="{Binding Product.ExternalUrl,
                        StringFormat=/WebBrowser/\{0\}}"
                Content="External Page"
                Margin="0,10,0,0" HorizontalAlignment="Left" />
        </StackPanel>
    </StackPanel>
    <TextBlock Text="{Binding Product.Description}"
            Margin="10,20,0,10" TextWrapping="Wrap" />
</StackPanel>
```

The `StackPanel` includes a `d:DataContext` attribute that defines a design-time data context object, discussed in the next section.

Design-Time Data

It can be difficult and time consuming constructing a page or control without knowing how the content will appear at runtime. The dimensions of images can disturb the layout, as can the length of text and text wrapping settings. The `d:DataContext` markup extension, which exists in the http://schemas.microsoft.com/expression/blend/2008 namespace, allows you to simulate the runtime `DataContext` of a control with a design-time object (see Figure 3.13).

FIGURE 3.13   The `d:DataContext` markup extension provides for design-time sample data.

Here a design-time instance of the `ProductDetailsViewModel` class presents some sample data to improve the design-time experience of the developer or designer.

The content `StackPanel` includes a `d:DataContext` attribute, which causes a `ProductDetailsViewModel` instance to be loaded from a sample data file, as shown in the following excerpt:

```
<StackPanel Grid.Row="1"
    Style="{StaticResource PageContentPanelStyle}"
    d:DataContext="{d:DesignData Source=ProductDetailsViewSampleData.xaml}">

    ...

</StackPanel>
```

You can see that the `d:DesignData` markup extension has its `Source` property set to the location of a sample data file, ProductDetailsViewSampleData.xaml. The sample data file defines the property values of the viewmodel (see Listing 3.13). The design-time environment of Visual Studio or Expression Blend instantiates the sample viewmodel at design-time.

LISTING 3.13   ProductDetailsViewSampleData.xaml

```
<local:ProductDetailsViewModel
        xmlns:local="clr-namespace:DanielVaughan.WPUnleashed
            .Examples.Navigation"
        xmlns="http://schemas.microsoft.com/winfx/2006/xaml/presentation"
        xmlns:BookshopServiceReference="clr-namespace:DanielVaughan
            .WPUnleashed.Examples.BookshopServiceReference">
    <local:ProductDetailsViewModel.Product>
        <BookshopServiceReference:Product
            Id="1"
            Title="Windows Phone 8 Unleashed"
            Author="Daniel Vaughan"
            Description="The complete guide to programming..."
            Price="37.79"
            Isbn10="0672336898"
            Isbn13="978-0672336898"
            SmallImageUri="/DanielVaughan.WPUnleashed
                .Examples;component/
                ➥Navigation/Images/Product01Small.jpg"
            LargeImageUri="/DanielVaughan.WPUnleashed
                .Examples;component/
                ➥Navigation/Images/Product01Large.jpg"
            ExternalUrl="
                http://www.amazon.com/Windows-Phone-Unleashed-
                ➥Daniel-Vaughan/dp/0672333481/"
        />
    </local:ProductDetailsViewModel.Product>
</local:ProductDetailsViewModel>
```

Notice the relative component URIs of the images. The design-time environment will fail to resolve the image location unless relative component URIs are used and the build action of the image is set to Resource.

Image Caching

While the viewmodel saves the result of the WCF service call, which allows the app to restore its state after being tombstoned, downloaded images are not saved in the state dictionary, but rather, the app relies on some custom image caching.

A custom `IValueConverter`, called `ImageCacheConverter`, is used to download the image from the specified image URI, as shown in the following excerpt:

```
<Image Source="{Binding Product.LargeImageUri,
        Converter={StaticResource ImageCacheConverter}}" />
```

By using the `ImageCacheConverter`, images can be downloaded once and stored in isolated storage for an arbitrary period. When that period has elapsed, the image is downloaded again. This allows the application to work offline (see Listing 3.14).

LISTING 3.14   `ImageCacheConverter` Class

```
public class ImageCacheConverter : IValueConverter
{
    public object Convert(object value, Type targetType,
        object parameter, CultureInfo culture)
    {
        if (EnvironmentValues.DesignTime)
        {
            return value;
        }

        string url = value as string;
        if (url != null)
        {
            try
            {
                return ImageCache.GetImage(new BitmapImage(new Uri(url)));
            }
            catch (IsolatedStorageException e)
            {
                Console.WriteLine(e);
                return value;
            }
        }

        BitmapImage bitmapImage = value as BitmapImage;
        if (bitmapImage != null)
        {
            return ImageCache.GetImage(bitmapImage);
        }
        return value;
    }

    public object ConvertBack(object value, Type targetType,
        object parameter, CultureInfo culture)
```

```
    {
        throw new NotImplementedException();
    }
}
```

The `ImageCacheConverter` can be used in conjunction with a URL or a `BitMapImage`. In the sample code, it is used with a URL, supplied by the product's `SmallImageUri` and `LargeImageUri` properties. The `ImageCache` class maintains a dictionary of URI keyed cached images. It stores the dictionary in isolated storage, and when an image is requested, it attempts to locate it in the dictionary. If found it checks to ensure that the image has not expired, and then returns the image.

Many thanks to Peter Nowak (http://winphonedev.de/) for his image cache code, which I have adapted, with his permission, for use in the downloadable sample code.

The `ImageCache` class, in the downloadable sample code, maintains a list of `ImageCacheItem` objects, which represent cached images. The `ImageCache.GetImage` method is used to retrieve an image from the cache. If the image is not located in the cache, it is scheduled to be downloaded by the static `ImageDownloader` class.

The `ImageDownloader` coordinates an asynchronous download of the image file. It uses an `HttpWebRequest` to retrieve the image from a remote server, and then stores the downloaded file in isolated storage. Once downloaded, the `Source` property of the original image is assigned, which means that, if it is present in the UI, the image will appear (see the `ImageDownloader` class, located in the Data/ImageCache directory of the WPUnleashed project, in the downloadable sample code for details).

Overview of the Sample Bookshop WCF Service

The Bookshop demo application includes a server-side component, which is used by both the `ProductsViewModel` and `ProductDetailsViewModel` classes, providing the application with a set of products to display. The server-side component is fairly arbitrary and is presented here merely for the sake of completeness.

The WCF service is called `BookshopService` and resides in the WPUnleashed.Web project of the downloadable sample code (see Listing 3.15).

LISTING 3.15   `BookshopService` Class

```
[AspNetCompatibilityRequirements(
    RequirementsMode = AspNetCompatibilityRequirementsMode.Allowed)]
public class BookshopService : IBookshopService
{
    public IEnumerable<Product> GetProducts()
    {
        return ProductManager.Products;
    }
```

```
public Product GetProductById(int productId)
{
    return ProductManager.GetProductById(productId);
}
}
```

The BookshopService exposes static methods of the ProductManager class, shown in
Listing 3.16. The ProductManager class creates an XDocument instance, using an XML file,
to populate a list of Products.

LISTING 3.16   ProductManager Class

```
public static class ProductManager
{
    static readonly List<Product> products = new List<Product>();

    public static IEnumerable<Product> Products
    {
        get
        {
            return products;
        }
    }

    static ProductManager()
    {
        string path = HttpContext.Current.Server.MapPath(
            "~/Services/Bookshop/Products.xml");
        XDocument document = XDocument.Load(path);
        foreach (XElement element in
            document.Element("Products").Elements("Product"))
        {
            var product = new Product(element);
            product.SmallImageUri
                = ServerUtility.ResolveServerUrl(product.SmallImageUri);
            product.LargeImageUri
                = ServerUtility.ResolveServerUrl(product.LargeImageUri);
            products.Add(product);
        }
    }

    public static Product GetProductById(int id)
    {
        if (id < 0 || id > products.Count)
        {
            throw new ArgumentOutOfRangeException("id");
```

```
        }
        return products[id - 1];
    }
}
```

The `Product` class contains the properties that are used to display each book's details, such as Title and Author. The `Product` class also knows how to populate itself from an `XElement`. The explicit casting operators of the `XElement` class make it easy to extract the values to the `Product` properties, as shown in the following excerpt from the `Product` class:

```
public Product(XElement element)
{
    if (element == null)
    {
        throw new ArgumentNullException("element");
    }
    Id = (int)element.Element("Id");
    Title = (string)element.Element("Title");
    Author = (string)element.Element("Author");
    Description = (string)element.Element("Description");
    SmallImageUri = (string)element.Element("SmallImageUri");
    LargeImageUri = (string)element.Element("LargeImageUri");
    Price = (double)element.Element("Price");
    Isbn10 = (string)element.Element("ISBN-10");
    Isbn13 = (string)element.Element("ISBN-13");
    ExternalUrl = (string)element.Element("ExternalUrl");
}
```

Summary

Maintaining the appearance of continuity after an application has been tombstoned is one of the key challenges facing Windows Phone developers.

There are two types of application state: persistent and transient. Persistent state exists across application launches and is saved using your app's private storage area. Transient state is discarded when an application is closed and is stored in the `Microsoft.Phone.Shell.PhoneApplicationService.State` dictionary.

Transient page state should be stored when the `Page.OnNavigatedFrom` method is called and restored when the `OnNavigatedTo` method is called. Transient application state can be stored when the `PhoneApplicationService.Deactivated` event occurs and restored when the `PhoneApplicationService.Activated` event occurs.

Persistent state should be saved when transient state is saved and also when the application is closing using the `PhoneApplicationService.Closing` event.

In this chapter you saw an overview of the application execution model and examined the various application life cycle events, which are used to coordinate state persistence and restoration.

The chapter then explored the new Windows Phone 8 feature, Fast App Resume, which promises to improve startup performance for dormant apps that are relaunched.

The chapter then looked at how to enable an app to run under the lock screen and then looked at page navigation and how to optimize the user experience by using a splash screen or a loading indicator.

Finally, the chapter delved into the sample application and discussed image caching, design-time data, and consuming a simple WCF service.

CHAPTER 4

Controlling Page Orientation

Pages in Windows Phone apps can support either the landscape or portrait orientation, or both. When creating a page that supports both orientations, it is prudent to define the UI in XAML in such a way that it produces the layout you want in either orientation without relying on code-beside. Fortunately, XAML's dynamic layout system makes it easy to build pages that can support both orientations. The Grid and StackPanel elements, for example, resize themselves to inhabit available space when the page orientation changes and the dimensions of the page change.

This chapter begins by exploring the properties and events that govern page orientation. You look at using a custom IValueConverter to hide and display page elements based on the page orientation and at setting the orientation of a page programmatically.

The chapter then looks at animating UI elements when the page orientation changes using the VisualStateManager and examines how to substitute an application's RootVisual with a custom PhoneApplicationFrame to animate the entire page when the orientation changes.

Finally, the chapter looks at animating page transition using the Windows Phone Toolkit.

Orientation and the PhoneApplicationPage Class

The PhoneApplicationPage class includes two orientation related properties: SupportedOrientations and Orientation.

The SupportedOrientations attribute allows you to restrict the orientation of the page and, if set to either Portrait or Landscape, prevent the orientation from being changed when the device is rotated. If the page is designed to support both portrait and landscape, set SupportedOrientation to PortraitOrLandscape, which allows the orientation to be switched automatically when the device is rotated.

The Orientation property indicates the actual orientation of the page and can be set only at design time. The Orientation property is discussed in greater detail later in the chapter.

When you create a new PhoneApplicationPage within Visual Studio, both SupportedOrientations and Orientation are set, by default, to Portrait in XAML.

OrientationChanged Event

Both the PhoneApplicationFrame and PhoneApplicationPage include an OrientationChanged event that allows you to detect when the orientation of the page changes. In addition, the PhoneApplicationPage includes an OnOrientationChanged virtual method. When the page orientation changes, the method is called, allowing you to update the UI, trigger animations, and so forth. See the following excerpt:

```
protected override void OnOrientationChanged(
                        OrientationChangedEventArgs e)
{
    base.OnOrientationChanged(e);
    /* Update UI, trigger animations etc. */
}
```

The OnOrientationChanged method is called before other OrientationChanged event handlers.

> **NOTE**
>
> The ActualWidth and ActualHeight of the page are not changed until after the OrientationChanged event has been raised.
>
> To change the size of a UI element based on the dimensions of the page after the orientation change occurs use the Dispatcher.

By using the Dispatcher to invoke layout changes, the correct height and width of the page can be determined after the OrientationChanged event has been handled, as shown in the following excerpt:

```
protected override void OnOrientationChanged(OrientationChangedEventArgs e)
{
    Debug.WriteLine("Orientation changed to " + e.Orientation.ToString("G"));

    Dispatcher.BeginInvoke(
        delegate
        {
            Debug.WriteLine(string.Format(
```

```
            "Using dispatcher: ActualWidth: {0}, ActualHeight: {1}",
            ActualWidth, ActualHeight));
    });

    Debug.WriteLine(string.Format(
        "Without dispatcher: ActualWidth: {0}, ActualHeight: {1}",
        ActualWidth, ActualHeight));

    base.OnOrientationChanged(e);
}
```

The following is the output when switching orientations:

```
Orientation changed to LandscapeLeft
Without dispatcher: ActualWidth: 0, ActualHeight: 0
Using dispatcher: ActualWidth: 800, ActualHeight: 480
Orientation changed to PortraitUp
Without dispatcher: ActualWidth: 800, ActualHeight: 480
Using dispatcher: ActualWidth: 480, ActualHeight: 800
```

The OrientionChanged event is always raised before the page is loaded. This explains the zero values for the ActualWidth and ActualHeight in the previous output. The Dispatcher allows the correct width and height values to be obtained because by the time each value is read, the page has already loaded and the properties are populated with the correct values.

The OrientationChangedEventArgs class contains an Orientation property, which is an enum of type PageOrientation, indicating the new page orientation. PageOrientation has the following values:

▶ Landscape

▶ LandscapeLeft

▶ LandscapeRight

▶ None

▶ Portrait

▶ PortraitDown

▶ PortraitUp

The only values you will ever see in the OrientationChangedEventArgs are, however, LandscapeLeft, LandscapeRight, and PortraitUp. These values indicate the location of the display in relation to the phone hardware buttons (see Figure 4.1).

| PortraitUp | LandscapeRight | PortraitDown (not supported) | LandscapeLeft |

FIGURE 4.1   Valid device orientations.

Although `PortraitDown` exists as an enum value, at the time of writing, no device supports this orientation, nor does the emulator.

To determine whether the `OrientationChangedEventArgs.Orientation` value is either landscape or portrait, the value can be ANDed with the `PageOrientation.Landscape` or `PageOrientation.Portrait` values, respectively. The `PageOrientationExtensions` class in the downloadable sample code includes two extension methods for performing this directly on a `PageOrientation` value (see Listing 4.1).

LISTING 4.1   `PageOrientationExtensions` Class

```
public static class PageOrientationExtensions
{
    public static bool IsLandscape(this PageOrientation pageOrientation)
    {
        return (pageOrientation & PageOrientation.Landscape) != 0;
    }

    public static bool IsPortrait(this PageOrientation pageOrientation)
    {
        return (pageOrientation & PageOrientation.Portrait) != 0;
    }
}
```

`PhoneApplicationPage` Orientation **Property**

The `PhoneApplicationPage` includes an `Orientation` dependency property, which is shown in the following excerpt (take note of the set accessor):

```
public PageOrientation Orientation
{
    get
    {
```

```
        return (PageOrientation)base.GetValue(OrientationProperty);
    }
    [EditorBrowsable(EditorBrowsableState.Never)]
    set
    {
        if (Frame.IsInDesignMode())
        {
            base.SetValue(OrientationProperty, value);
        }
    }
}
```

You see that changing the page orientation at runtime is not as straightforward as it might first appear. The Orientation property's set accessor has an effect only at design time and not at runtime. At runtime, the Orientation property indicates the physical orientation of the device, or the orientation of the emulator window. Setting the dependency property directly is also futile and has no effect on runtime page orientation either. A technique to set page orientation programmatically is discussed in the following section, "Setting Page Orientation at Runtime."

The Orientation property can be used in data binding expressions and allows you to adjust the layout depending on the availability of space. You can maximize space utilization by hiding or revealing content when the orientation changes. For example, when changing to a landscape orientation where horizontal space is more abundant, a TextBlock can be shown in the title section of an application. Conversely, in portrait mode, the TextBlock can be hidden to conserve space, as demonstrated by the following example:

```
<TextBlock Text="Application Title"
           Visibility="{Binding ElementName=Page, Path=Orientation,
           Converter={StaticResource PageOrientationToVisibilityConverter},
           ConverterParameter=Landscape}" />
```

You can see that the Orientation property of the PhoneApplicationPage is used to set the Visibility property of the TextBlock using a custom IValueConverter called PageOrientationToVisibilityConverter (see Listing 4.2), which is located in the WPUnleashed project in the downloadable sample code.

The converter's ConvertTo method translates the PageOrientation enum value to a System.Windows.Visibility enum value. The ConverterParameter from the previous excerpt indicates when to show the UIElement. If the PageOrientation value is a portrait orientation, for example, and the ConverterParameter is equal to Portrait, then Visibility.Visible will be returned.

LISTING 4.2   `PageOrientationToVisibilityConverter` **Class**

```
public class PageOrientationToVisibilityConverter .: IValueConverter
{
    public object Convert(object value, Type targetType,
        object parameter, CultureInfo culture)
    {
        var orientation = (PageOrientation)value;
        string showWhenOrientation
            = ArgumentValidator.AssertNotNullAndOfType<string>(
                parameter, "parameter").ToLower();

        if (showWhenOrientation != "portrait"
            && showWhenOrientation != "landscape")
        {
            throw new ArgumentException(
                "ConverterParameter must be either Portrait or Landscape.");
        }

        bool show;
        switch (orientation)
        {
            case PageOrientation.Portrait:
            case PageOrientation.PortraitDown:
            case PageOrientation.PortraitUp:
                show = showWhenOrientation == "portrait";
                break;
            case PageOrientation.Landscape:
            case PageOrientation.LandscapeLeft:
            case PageOrientation.LandscapeRight:
                show = showWhenOrientation == "landscape";
                break;
            default:
                throw new ArgumentException("Unknown orientation: "
                    + orientation);
        }

        return show ? Visibility.Visible : Visibility.Collapsed;
    }

    public object ConvertBack(object value, Type targetType,
        object parameter, CultureInfo culture)
    {
        throw new NotImplementedException();
    }
}
```

Setting Page Orientation at Runtime

As you saw in the previous section, the `Orientation` property of the `PhoneApplicationPage` class cannot be assigned at runtime. Another approach is required to change the page orientation. For this turn to the `SupportedOrientations` property, which is assignable at runtime.

To recap, the `SupportedOrientations` property defines the allowed orientation or orientations of the page, which can be `Portrait`, `Landscape`, or `PortraitOrLandscape`.

Setting the `SupportedOrientations` property to the desired orientation forces the page to be shown in that orientation. For example, if the page is being viewed in portrait orientation, and you want to change the page orientation to landscape, you can set the `SupportedOrientations` to `Landscape`, thereby restricting the allowed orientation to landscape and forcing the frame to change the orientation to landscape.

This technique is demonstrated in the `OrientationView` page in the downloadable sample code (see Figure 4.2).

FIGURE 4.2   Forcing the orientation of a page.

The `OrientationView` class's Switch Supported Orientation button alternates between the three `SupportedPageOrientation` values. This is performed in the button's `Tap` event handler, demonstrating how the orientation can be forcibly set by restricting the orientation, as shown in the following excerpt:

```
void Button_Tap(object sender, GestureEventArgs e)
{
    switch (SupportedOrientations)
    {
        case SupportedPageOrientation.Landscape:
            SupportedOrientations = SupportedPageOrientation.Portrait;
            break;
        case SupportedPageOrientation.Portrait:
            SupportedOrientations = SupportedPageOrientation.PortraitOrLandscape;
            break;
        default:
            SupportedOrientations = SupportedPageOrientation.Landscape;
            break;
    }
}
```

Animating Page Elements When the Page Orientation Changes

The VisualStateManager can be used to animate UIElements when the page orientation changes. This can be done by defining a set of VisualStateGroups corresponding to the PageOrientation values.

Each VisualStateGroup contains a collection of VisualState objects, each containing a collection of Storyboard objects that specify how an element's properties change when the control is placed in a particular visual state.

In Listing 4.3, you see how the LandscapeRight VisualState includes a set of DoubleAnimations, which move various TextBlocks on the page to new positions when the page orientation changes.

LISTING 4.3   OrientationView.xaml (excerpt)

```
<Grid x:Name="LayoutRoot">
    <VisualStateManager.VisualStateGroups>
        <VisualStateGroup x:Name="OrientationStates">
            <!--Portrait up is the default state-->
            <VisualState x:Name="PortraitUp">
                <Storyboard />
            </VisualState>

            <VisualState x:Name="LandscapeRight">
                <Storyboard>
                    <DoubleAnimation Storyboard.TargetName="topLeft"
                        Storyboard.TargetProperty="
                            (UIElement.RenderTransform).(TranslateTransform.X)"
                        To="650" />
                    <!-- Content omitted. -->
```

```
            </Storyboard>
          </VisualState>
          <!-- Content omitted. -->
        </VisualStateGroup>
    </VisualStateManager.VisualStateGroups>

    <!-- Content omitted. -->

    <Grid x:Name="ContentGrid" Grid.Row="1">
        <TextBlock Text="Top-left corner" x:Name="topLeft"
                HorizontalAlignment="Left" VerticalAlignment="Top">
        <TextBlock.RenderTransform>
            <TranslateTransform/>
        </TextBlock.RenderTransform>
        </TextBlock>
        <!-- Content omitted. -->
    </Grid>
</Grid>
```

We subscribe to `OrientationChanged` event within the view's constructor, as shown in the following excerpt:

```
OrientationChanged += (sender, args) => VisualStateManager.GoToState(
                            this, args.Orientation.ToString(), true);
```

When the `OrientationChanged` event is raised, the `VisualStateManager` is directed to the state identified by the `Orientation` property of the `OrientationChangedEventArgs` (see Figure 4.3).

FIGURE 4.3 `TextBlocks` are animated into position when page orientation changes.

Animating the Entire Page When Orientation Changes

While animating UIElements is performed within the page, to animate the page itself requires implementation of a custom PhoneApplicationFrame. This is achieved by subclassing the PhoneApplicationFrame class, and then subscribing to the frame's OrientationChanged event to initiate the animation.

To replace your application's standard PhoneApplicationFrame with a custom frame, modify the App class, either in XAML or in the code-beside, to use the custom frame as the application's RootVisual.

The following excerpt shows how the App.xaml file can be modified to use a custom PhoneApplicationFrame:

```
<Application.RootVisual>
    <unleashed:AnimateOrientationChangesFrame x:Name="RootFrame">
        <!-- Content omitted. -->
    </unleashed:AnimateOrientationChangesFrame>
</Application.RootVisual>
```

If the RootVisual is assigned in the App.xaml.cs file, as is the case by default, modify the InitializedPhoneApplication method to assign a custom frame, as shown in the following excerpt:

```
void InitializePhoneApplication()
{
    if (phoneApplicationInitialized)
    {
        return;
    }

    RootFrame = new AnimateOrientationChangesFrame();

    // Content omitted.
}
```

Microsoft's David Anson has written two custom PhoneApplicationFrames that perform rotation and fade animation when an orientation change occurs. With David's permission I have included them in the downloadable sample code.

The first is a frame that fades in content, called FadeOrientationChangesFrame. This class uses a WritableBitmap to create an image overlay, which animates the Opacity property of the image. By using a WritableBitmap to capture the screen, the performance of the transition is optimized and is unaffected by the page composition, that is, more controls won't risk slowing the animation.

The second frame, the AnimateOrientationChangesFrame, is less subtle and rotates the page when the orientation changes (see Figure 4.4).

FIGURE 4.4   The `AnimateOrientationChangesFrame` class rotates content when the page orientation changes.

To modify the default behavior of either the `FadeOrientationChangesFrame` or `AnimateOrientationChangesFrame`, use the `AnimationEnabled`, `Duration`, and `EasingFunction` properties.

`AnimationEnabled` allows you to turn off the animation at runtime.

The `Duration` property dictates how long the animation will take to complete, which if made too long—more than half a second—risks frustrating the user.

The `EasingFunction` property is used to control the speed of the animation. With easing, you can create a more realistic rate of acceleration and deceleration, such as when creating a bounce effect or to control other types of motion.

The following is a list of the various `IEasingFunction`s available in the Windows Phone FCL (Framework Class Library), located in the `System.Windows.Media.Animation` namespace of the System.Windows assembly:

▶ `BackEase`—Retracts the motion of an animation slightly before it begins to animate along the path.

▶ `BounceEase`—Creates an animated bouncing effect.

▶ `CircleEase`—Creates an animation that accelerates and/or decelerates using a circular function.

▶ `CubicEase`—Creates an animation that accelerates and/or decelerates using the formula f(t) = t3.

▶ `ElasticEase`—Creates an animation that resembles a spring oscillating back and forth until it comes to rest.

▶ `ExponentialEase`—Creates an animation that accelerates and/or decelerates using an exponential formula.

▶ `PowerEase`—Creates an animation that accelerates and/or decelerates using the formula f(t) = tp, where p is equal to the Power property.

▶ `QuadraticEase`—Creates an animation that accelerates and/or decelerates using the formula f(t) = t2. This is the default `IEasingFunction` of the `FadeOrientationChangesFrame` class.

▶ `QuarticEase`—Creates an animation that accelerates and/or decelerates using the formula f(t) = t4. This is the default `IEasingFunction` for the `AnimateOrientationChangesFrame` class.

▶ `QuinticEase`—Creates an animation that accelerates and/or decelerates using the formula f(t) = t5.

▶ `SineEase`—Creates an animation that accelerates and/or decelerates using a sine formula.

Windows Phone Toolkit Animated Page Transitions

Adding animated page transitions to your app can help it look more polished and, when used modestly, can increase the user's perception of the quality of your app.

The Windows Phone Toolkit includes a set of classes that make it easy to add animated page transitions. The Toolkit is discussed in depth in Chapter 9, "Enriching the User Experience with the Windows Phone Toolkit Controls."

Within the Toolkit, transitions are defined by assigning a transition effect represented by `TransitionElement` objects such as `TurnstileTransition` to various transition events. These events occur during navigation and indicate the direction of the navigation (see Figure 4.5).

Forward in navigation occurs when the page is first navigated to; *forward out* occurs when navigating to a new page. *Backward in* and *backward out* occur when a backward navigation takes place, such as when the user taps the hardware Back button.

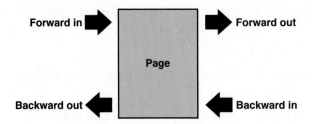

FIGURE 4.5   Transition navigation events.

Navigation events are married with `TransitionElements`. The Windows Phone Toolkit comes with the following five built-in `TransitionElements`:

▶ `RollTransition`

▶ RotateTransition

▶ SlideTransition

▶ SwivelTransition

▶ TurnstileTransition

In the next section you see how to add animated page transitions to an app, and how to specify the type of transition for each navigation event.

Using Windows Phone Toolkit Transitions

The following steps outline how to add page transitions to your app:

1. Add the Windows Phone Toolkit library to your project via NuGet by opening the package manager console. In Visual Studio select Tools/Library Package Manager/ Package Manager Console. At the PM prompt, enter the following command:

```
Install-Package WPtoolkit
```

If you receive an error message indicating that the wptoolkit package does not support Windows Phone version 8.0, you need to install the latest version of NuGet from www.nuget.org.

2. Replace the default `PhoneApplicationFrame` with a `TransitionFrame` from the Windows Phone Toolkit. To replace your app's standard `PhoneApplicationFrame`, modify the `App` class, either in XAML or in the code-beside, and set the custom frame as the application's `RootVisual`.

The following excerpt shows how the App.xaml file can be modified to use a Windows Phone Toolkit `TransitionFrame`:

```xml
<Application.RootVisual>
    <toolkit:TransitionFrame x:Name="RootFrame"
                             Navigated="RootFrame_Navigated"
                             Navigating="RootFrame_Navigating"
                             NavigationFailed="RootFrame_NavigationFailed">
        <!-- Content omitted. -->
    </toolkit:TransitionFrame>
    <!-- Content omitted. -->
</Application.RootVisual>
```

If the `RootVisual` is assigned in the App.xaml.cs file, as is the case by default, modify the `InitializedPhoneApplication` method to assign the `TransitionFrame`, as shown in the following excerpt:

```
void InitializePhoneApplication()
{
```

```
    if (phoneApplicationInitialized)
    {
        return;
    }

    RootFrame = new TransitionFrame();

    // Content omitted.
}
```

3. In the page that you want to add a transition effect, add the toolkit namespace definition as shown:

```
xmlns:toolkit="clr-namespace:Microsoft.Phone.Controls;
➡assembly=Microsoft.Phone.Controls.Toolkit"
```

4. Associate a transition with each navigation event by adding the `TransitionService.NavigationInTransition` and `NavigationOutTransition` attached properties to the page, as shown in the following excerpt:

```
<phone:PhoneApplicationPage
    ...
    xmlns:toolkit="clr-namespace:Microsoft.Phone.Controls;
    ➡assembly=Microsoft.Phone.Controls.Toolkit">

    <toolkit:TransitionService.NavigationInTransition>
        <toolkit:NavigationInTransition>
            <toolkit:NavigationInTransition.Backward>
                <toolkit:TurnstileTransition Mode="BackwardIn"/>
            </toolkit:NavigationInTransition.Backward>
            <toolkit:NavigationInTransition.Forward>
                <toolkit:TurnstileTransition Mode="ForwardIn"/>
            </toolkit:NavigationInTransition.Forward>
        </toolkit:NavigationInTransition>
    </toolkit:TransitionService.NavigationInTransition>
    <toolkit:TransitionService.NavigationOutTransition>
        <toolkit:NavigationOutTransition>
            <toolkit:NavigationOutTransition.Backward>
                <toolkit:TurnstileTransition Mode="BackwardOut"/>
            </toolkit:NavigationOutTransition.Backward>
            <toolkit:NavigationOutTransition.Forward>
                <toolkit:TurnstileTransition Mode="ForwardOut"/>
            </toolkit:NavigationOutTransition.Forward>
        </toolkit:NavigationOutTransition>
    </toolkit:TransitionService.NavigationOutTransition>
```

```
<!-- Content omitted. -->

</phone:PhoneApplicationPage>
```

At this point, a turnstile animation will be applied to the page when navigating to and from the page.

You can view the transition effect by uncommenting the `toolkit:TransitionFrame` element in the App.xaml file in the WPUnleashed.Examples project. Then launch the downloadable sample, and tap the TransitionPage1 page in the PageOrientation section.

Reusing the Transition Attached Properties

The transition attached properties are rather verbose, and adding them to every page in your app adds a substantial amount of duplication. Fortunately you can create a reusable style that can be applied to each page.

Listing 4.4 shows a style called `TransitionPageStyle`, whose `TargetType` is of `PhoneApplicationPage`. The transition properties are placed within the style, so that when the style is applied to a page, so too are the navigation transition properties.

LISTING 4.4   `TransitionPageStyle` in App.xaml

```
<Application.Resources>

    <Style x:Key="TransitionPageStyle" TargetType="phone:PhoneApplicationPage">
        <Setter Property="toolkit:TransitionService.NavigationInTransition">
            <Setter.Value>
                <toolkit:NavigationInTransition>
                    <toolkit:NavigationInTransition.Backward>
                        <toolkit:TurnstileTransition Mode="BackwardIn"/>
                    </toolkit:NavigationInTransition.Backward>
                    <toolkit:NavigationInTransition.Forward>
                        <toolkit:TurnstileTransition Mode="ForwardIn"/>
                    </toolkit:NavigationInTransition.Forward>
                </toolkit:NavigationInTransition>
            </Setter.Value>
        </Setter>
        <Setter Property="toolkit:TransitionService.NavigationOutTransition">
            <Setter.Value>
                <toolkit:NavigationOutTransition>
                    <toolkit:NavigationOutTransition.Backward>
                        <toolkit:TurnstileTransition Mode="BackwardOut"/>
                    </toolkit:NavigationOutTransition.Backward>
                    <toolkit:NavigationOutTransition.Forward>
                        <toolkit:TurnstileTransition Mode="ForwardOut"/>
```

```
                        </toolkit:NavigationOutTransition.Forward>
                    </toolkit:NavigationOutTransition>
                </Setter.Value>
            </Setter>
        </Style>

    </Application.Resources>
```

The style can then be applied to each page in your app, like so:

```
<phone:PhoneApplicationPage
...
    Style="{StaticResource TransitionPageStyle}">
...
</phone:PhoneApplicationPage>
```

Windows Phone Toolkit transitions come with several out-of-the-box transitions that can immediately add pizzazz to your app.

Summary

This chapter began by exploring the properties and events that govern page orientation. The `PhoneApplicationPage.Orientation` property affects orientation only at design time. The `PhoneApplicationPage.SupportedOrientations` property is used to change the orientation at runtime.

The chapter then looked at using a custom `IValueConverter` to hide and display page elements depending on the page's orientation. You then saw how to animate page elements using the `VisualStateManager`, and how to substitute an application's `RootVisual` with a custom `PhoneApplicationFrame` to animate the entire page when the orientation changes.

Finally, the chapter looked at animating page transitions using the Windows Phone Toolkit.

CHAPTER 5

Using Content Controls, Items Controls, and Range Controls

The Windows Phone SDK provides an extraordinarily diverse and rich set of controls, from layout to media controls, form elements suitable for line of business applications, to even multiscale image support (a.k.a. deep zoom). This was made possible by leveraging the existing controls and platform maturity of Silverlight for the browser.

Yet, bringing Silverlight to the phone was no mean feat, and meant that the Microsoft Silverlight team faced the challenge of adapting an existing set of controls, designed for the most part with a web browser experience in mind, to the mobile platform, where it was necessary to contend with differences in display size and resolution, touch support, and so on. Fortunately Silverlight itself has been designed with a seemingly remarkable level of foresight, allowing many controls to be dropped in to the Windows Phone Framework Class Library (FCL) for XAML apps with only minor control template changes.

Accompanying this set of adapted controls are several new controls designed specifically for the phone, including the `Panorama` and `Pivot` (covered in Chapter 11, "Creating Expansive and Engaging Apps with the Pivot and Panorama").

Additionally, Microsoft provides a third set of controls, which are located in the Windows Phone Toolkit (covered in Chapter 9, "Enriching the User Experience with the Windows Phone Toolkit Controls"). It includes controls like the `ListPicker`, seen in some of the phone's built-in apps, which provide increased usability and behavior in harmony with the Windows Phone design philosophy.

This chapter begins by providing an overview of the elements available in the Windows Phone FCL. It then focuses on the three base control types: ContentControl, ItemsControl, and RangeBase. It examines the various subclasses of these controls, accompanied with practical examples. It looks at how ContentControls are able to host a single item of content and at the differences between the various button controls, including the HyperlinkButton, RepeatButton, and ToggleButton, and at how each is used. The chapter then ventures into some more advanced topics, such as binding CheckBox and RadioButton controls to viewmodel collections and shows how to bind to the ListBox.SelectedItems property, a feat not readily achievable with the Windows Phone SDK out-of-the-box!

Finally, the chapter explores the RangeBase controls: the Slider and ProgressBar and demonstrates how to provide feedback to a user during asynchronous activities carried out by a BackgroundWorker.

The majority of the source code for this chapter is located in the ControlExamples directory of the WPUnleashed.Examples project, in the downloadable sample code.

Control Type Taxonomy

Having a solid grasp of the class hierarchy of any library that you regularly use helps to improve your productivity and provides a good starting point to gaining a deeper understanding of how a framework is designed to work. It gives you a shortcut for determining what can and cannot be done with a particular type based on its inherited members and whether commonly named members from two different classes are from a shared superclass or have nothing to do with one another. In essence it allows you to better assess what you can achieve using the building blocks and how to avoid making poor design decisions. On that note, this section begins with an overview of the Windows Phone control class hierarchy.

The title of this part of the book is "Essential Elements," and we begin with the class FrameworkElement. The FrameworkElement provides a set of common APIs for objects that participate in XAML-based layout. FrameworkElement also defines members related to data binding, the visual tree, and object lifetime feature areas. It is also the superclass for most of the types presented in this part of the book (see Figure 5.1).

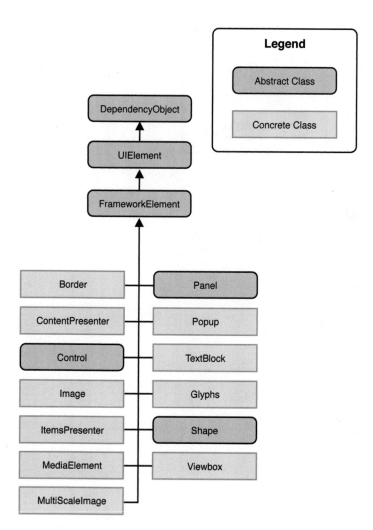

FIGURE 5.1   Top-level elements of the Windows Phone FCL for XAML apps.

The focus of this chapter is on types that derive from `Control` (see Figure 5.2), specifically `ContentControl`, `ItemsControl`, and `RangeBase` and their subclasses. The rest are explored in subsequent chapters.

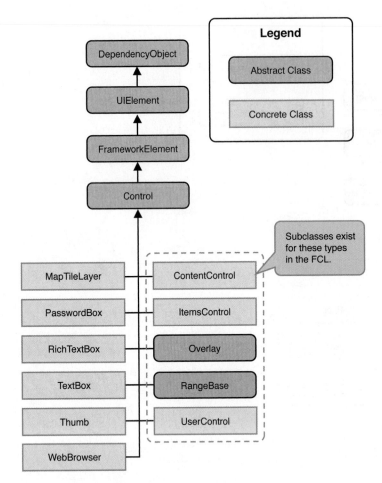

FIGURE 5.2   Control types within the FCL.

Identifying Controls Not Supported or Absent in Windows Phone

Some controls that are present in the Windows Phone SDK are not shown in the Visual Studio Toolbox or are not recommended for use due to platform differences or design constraints. These platform differences are mostly related to the phone's touch driven UI and reduced display size.

In addition, the following Silverlight controls do not exist in the Windows Phone FCL:

▶ `DataGrid`

▶ `DatePicker` (present in the Windows Phone Toolkit)

▶ `OpenFileDialog`

▶ `SaveFileDialog`

- ►   `Label`

- ►   `GridSplitter`

- ►   `TabControl`

- ►   `TreeView`

Some controls exist but are not supported. The following controls should not be used directly:

- ►   `Calendar`

- ►   `Frame`—Use the PhoneApplicationFrame instead.

- ►   `Page`—Use the PhoneApplicationPage instead.

- ►   `ScrollBar`—Used by the ScrollViewer.

Content Controls

Controls that are derived from `ContentControl` are able to host a single object. `ContentControls` include `Buttons`, `ListBoxItems`, and containers such as the `PhoneApplicationFrame` and the `ScrollViewer` control (see Figure 5.3).

This chapter does not cover the `Frame` and its derived classes. For information on the `Frame` class see Chapter 3, "Understanding the Application Execution Model." Nor does this chapter cover the `PanoramaItem` and `PivotItem` classes, which are discussed in Chapter 11.

`ContentControl` has a `Content` property, whose value can be of any type. The way content is presented in the UI, however, depends on its type and whether a `DataTemplate` is associated with the `ContentControl`. The following lists the three ways in which content is presented:

- ►   **UIElements**—If the object derives from `UIElement`, the object will be rendered.

- ►   **Non-UIElements**—If the object does not derive from `UIElement`, its `ToString` method is used to retrieve a textual representation of the object. If the `ToString` method has not been overridden, the result is the fully qualified class name of the object.

- ►   **Non-UIElements with an associated `DataTemplate`**—The `ContentControl.ContentTemplate` allows you to specify a `DataTemplate`, either as a `StaticResource` or inline, which is used to display an object. Data binding expressions within the `DataTemplate` are used to extract the object's property values and to render them.

To better understand the `Content` property, let's look at a commonly used `ContentControl`: the `Button` control. With a `Button`, you can set its `Content` property to a string, as shown:

```
<Button Content="Tap me!" />
```

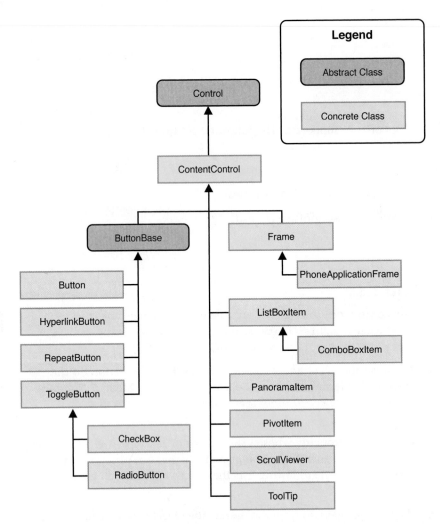

FIGURE 5.3   Content controls (excludes some mapping related types).

Unlike the TextBlock control, for example, the Button control does not have a Text property, yet by setting the Content property to a string, the Button displays the string.

Defining the Default Content Property

The Content property is the default property of the ContentControl. The ContentPropertyAttribute specifies which property of a class can be interpreted as the main content property when the class is parsed by a XAML processor. This means that when, for example, a TextBlock is placed as a nested element of a Button, the TextBlock is rendered within the button itself:

```
<Button>
    <TextBlock Text="Press me!" Foreground="Orange" />
</Button>
```

To further illustrate, the built-in control template for the `Button` control includes a `Border` that contains a `TemplateBinding` to the `Content` property of the `Button`, as shown in the following excerpt:

```
<Border>
    <ContentControl x:Name="ContentContainer"
                    ContentTemplate="{TemplateBinding ContentTemplate}"
                    Content="{TemplateBinding Content}" />
</Border>
```

When the `Button` is rendered using its built-in style, the `Content` value, whatever it may be, is placed within a `Border`.

If you examine the source code for the `ContentControl` using Reflector, you see that a `ContentPropertyAttribute` is used to indicate to the runtime that the `Content` property is the default property:

```
[ContentProperty("Content", true)]
public class ContentControl : Control
{ ... }
```

When creating your own custom controls, you can decorate a class with a `ContentPropertyAttribute` to specify a different default property.

Receiving Input with Buttons

In most Windows Phone XAML apps, buttons are the most commonly used element for receiving user input. Ordinarily, a button initiates an action when a user taps it. Unlike Silverlight for the browser, the minimum size of the `Button` has been increased, making it more amenable to touch. The shape is usually rectangular, and the standard layout allows for either text or an image to be displayed as content. `Buttons` support three visibility states: rest (the default state), pressed, and disabled. Unlike Silverlight for the browser, however, there is no visible focus state.

The inherited `FrameworkElement.HorizonalAlignment` and `VerticalAlignment` properties both default to `Stretch`. The `Button`'s `Horizontal` and `Vertical` size, therefore, depends on its parent's size; the bigger the parent `ContentControl` the bigger the button. By placing a `Button` in a `Grid`, the `Button` is free to expand to inhabit the entirety of the space provided by the `Grid` (see Figure 5.4).

If the parent `ContentControl` happens to be a `StackPanel`, the button will not expand farther than the space allowed. By default, the `StackPanel` arranges its child controls vertically. The `StackPanel` inhabits the entire width of its parent control, but only uses as much vertical space as it needs (see Figure 5.5).

FIGURE 5.4   By default a `Button` will expand to inhabit its parent.

FIGURE 5.5   `Button` conforms to the vertical size constraints afforded by the `StackPanel`.

To constrain the button size to the size of its content, set its `HorizontalAlignment` and `VerticalAlignment` properties to something other than `Stretch`. An effective way to do this is by using a style, as shown in the following example:

```
<Style x:Key="ButtonStyle" TargetType="ButtonBase">
    <Setter Property="HorizontalAlignment" Value="Left" />
    <Setter Property="VerticalAlignment" Value="Top" />
</Style>
```

The style can then be applied like so:

```
<Button Content="Press me!" Style="{StaticResource ButtonStyle}" />
```

Tap and Click Events

Since the release of the Windows Phone 7.1 SDK, the `Click` event of the `ButtonBase` class has been superseded by a `UIElement` event named `Tap`. The `Tap` event is designed for touch input, while the `Click` event relies on legacy code that handles mouse state.

> **NOTE**
>
> While the `ButtonBase` `Click` event is still present in the SDK, unless your UI code needs to be shared with Silverlight for the browser projects, use the `Tap` event.

The following is an example of a `UIElement.Tap` event handler.

```
void Button_Tap(object sender, System.Windows.Input.GestureEventArgs e)
{
...
}
```

> **NOTE**
>
> There is another public `GestureEventArgs` class residing in the Windows Phone Toolkit that is, unfortunately, located in the Microsoft.Phone.Controls namespace. If you are using the Windows Phone Toolkit, be mindful that the correct type needs to be specified or a runtime exception will be raised.
>
> Either use the namespace qualified type name, as shown in the previous example, or add a type alias to the top of your class file, like so:
>
> ```
> using GestureEventArgs = System.Windows.Input.GestureEventArgs;
> ```

Button Click Mode

If you need to use the `Button.Click` event, rather than the `Tap` event for whatever reason, you can tailor the type of user interaction that is required to raise the `Button`'s `Click` event using the `Button.ClickMode` property.

The following is a list of the three possible `ClickMode` values:

▶ **Press**—The `Click` event is raised as soon as the user touches the button.

▶ **Release**—The `Click` event is not raised until the user lifts his finger off the button. This is the default value.

▶ **Hover**—Has the same effect as `Press`. As there is currently no support for detecting when the user hovers over a control on a Windows Phone device, this value serves no purpose and exists to maintain compatibility with Silverlight for the browser.

Hyperlink Button

The `HyperlinkButton` allows you to embed hypertext links in a page.

As previously stated, all `UIElements` have a `Tap` event, which can be used to perform navigation within an event handler. Performing navigation in this manner, however, can be cumbersome, and the `HyperlinkButton` provides an easier way to navigate to pages within your app without having to subscribe to an event or use an `ICommand`.

The `HyperlinkButton` includes a `NavigateUri` property. When a user presses the `HyperlinkButton`, the button takes care of performing the navigation.

The default appearance of the `HyperlinkButton` does not resemble a button at all. In fact, the default style of a `HyperlinkButton` is underlined text, not unlike an HTML hyperlink.

For more information on using the `HyperlinkButton` and page navigation, see Chapter 3.

Repeat and Toggle Buttons

Neither the `RepeatButton` nor the `ToggleButton` controls are abstract. Yet both reside in the System.Windows.Controls.Primitives namespace, not in the System.Windows.Controls namespace, indicating that these two controls are not intended to be used in day-to-day page code.

Repeat Button

The `RepeatButton` behaves the same as the `Button` control; however, the `RepeatButton`'s `Tap` event is raised repeatedly while it is being pressed, whereas the `Button` control raises its `Tap` event once for each user press.

The `RepeatButton` is used as part of the `ScrollBar` control, which itself is part of the `ScrollViewer` control. Unlike Silverlight for the browser, however, which uses the `RepeatButton` to incrementally scroll content when pressed, the `RepeatButton` in the `ScrollBar` serves little purpose on the phone because the `ScrollBar` is for display purposes only.

The RepeatButton has two main properties:

▶ **Interval**—The duration between events, measured in milliseconds. The default value is 250 ms.

▶ **Delay**—The duration before the event is raised, measured in milliseconds. The default value is 250 ms.

The RepeatButton can be placed in XAML like so:

```
<RepeatButton Content="Press me!" Interval="200" Delay="500"
              Tap="RepeatButton_Tap" />
```

Sample Overview   An example for the RepeatButton control can be found in the ButtonExampleView page and the ButtonExampleViewModel in the downloadable sample code. The ButtonExampleView has a RepeatButton that is used to execute the RepeatCommand in the viewmodel, as shown:

```
<RepeatButton Content="{Binding RepeatCount}" Interval="200" Delay="500"
              Command="{Binding RepeatCommand}" />
```

The Content property of the RepeatButton is populated using a data binding to the RepeatCount property in the viewmodel:

```
int repeatCount;

public int RepeatCount
{
    get
    {
        return repeatCount;
    }
    private set
    {
        Assign(ref repeatCount, value);
    }
}
```

Tapping the RepeatButton causes the RepeatCommand to execute. The RepeatCommand is a public property of the viewmodel, defined as shown:

```
readonly DelegateCommand repeatCommand;

public ICommand RepeatCommand
{
    get
```

```
    {
        return repeatCommand;
    }
}
```

The `repeatCommand` is instantiated in the viewmodel constructor. When executed, the command increments the `RepeatCount` property, which updates the `RepeatButton`'s `Content` property:

```
public ButtonExampleViewModel() : base("Buttons")
{
    repeatCommand = new DelegateCommand(obj => RepeatCount++);
}
```

When the button is pressed and held, it causes the `RepeatCount` to increment periodically, which updates the content of the button (see Figure 5.6).

FIGURE 5.6   Pressing and holding the `RepeatButton` causes a counter to increment.

Toggle Button

The `ToggleButton` can visually represent two states: pressed or not pressed. When the user taps a `ToggleButton`, it switches state and stays in that state until tapped again. The `ToggleButton` is the base class for the `CheckBox` and `RadioButton` controls and, as such, is able to represent three states, which includes a third, indeterminate, state.

> **NOTE**
>
> The terms *pressed* and *not pressed* are more readily understandable when talking about the `ToggleButton`. The `ToggleButton`, however, contains an `IsChecked` property that is used to identify the state of the button. So checked and unchecked, pressed and not pressed are used interchangeably throughout this section.

Although the `ToggleButton` inherits the `Tap` event from the `UIElement` class, it has other events that are raised when the state of the button is changed.

The following shows how to create a `ToggleButton` in XAML:

```
<ToggleButton Content="ToggleButton"
```

```
Checked="ToggleButton_Checked"
Unchecked="ToggleButton_Unchecked" />
```

Depending on the state of the ToggleButton, one of two events: Checked or Unchecked, is raised when the user presses the ToggleButton.

Setting the ToggleButton.IsThreeState property to true allows the user to set the indeterminate state by tapping the button. If set to false, the only way to return to the indeterminate state is via code.

NOTE

The name of the ToggleButton.IsThreeState property can be confusing. Even though IsThreeState may be set to false, you can still set the indeterminate state in code. A better name might have been something like UserCanSetIndeterminateState.

The following is an example of a three-state ToggleButton:

```
<ToggleButton Content="ToggleButton" IsThreeState="True"
              Checked="ToggleButton_Checked"
              Unchecked="ToggleButton_Unchecked"
              Indeterminate="ToggleButton_Indeterminate" />
```

The ToggleButton.IsChecked property is a nullable Boolean, with true representing checked, false representing unchecked, and null representing its indeterminate state.

While the ToggleButton can be used to allow the user to cycle through three states, it makes little sense unless you are providing a custom template to visually represent the third indeterminate state. The CheckBox and RadioButton controls do provide a representation of each of the three states, as you see later in the chapter.

NOTE

The ToggleButton indeterminate state can be specified in XAML by setting the IsChecked property like so:

```
<ToggleButton Content="ToggleButton" IsChecked="{x:Null}" />
```

The Checked, Unchecked, and Indeterminate events detect when the button is tapped and has transitioned to a new state.

TIP

Rather than using the Checked, Unchecked, and Indeterminate events, use the Tap event to consolidate the logic for all three state changes. It is usually easier to handle all three state changes in the same place.

The state of the `ToggleButton` can be determined in a `Tap` event handler using the `ToggleButton.IsChecked` property, as shown in the following excerpt:

```
void ToggleButton_Tap(object sender, GestureEventArgs e)
{
    ToggleButton button = (ToggleButton)sender;
    Debug.WriteLine("IsChecked:"
        + (button.IsChecked.HasValue
                ? button.IsChecked.ToString() : "indeterminate"));
}
```

Radio Button

The `RadioButton` is a subclass of the `ToggleButton` class and offers the same events, such as `Checked`, `Unchecked`, and `Indeterminate`, and properties, such as `IsChecked`. A radio button is used to represent a set of related but mutually exclusive choices. The user taps on the radio button description text or glyph to select the control. Only one option from a particular group may be selected at a time.

`RadioButtons` that reside in the same container control automatically share the same group. In addition, the `RadioButton` has a `GroupName` property, which allows you to override the default behavior and to enforce mutual exclusivity explicitly by restricting those `RadioButtons` that share the same `GroupName` to no more than one being checked at a time. This is useful when multiple `RadioButtons` are placed in different containers but reside in the same logical group, or when multiple `RadioButtons` reside in the same container but reside in different logical groups. The `GroupName` property allows you to control the associations between the controls. Consider the following example:

```
<StackPanel>
    <RadioButton Content="RadioButton 1 (group 1)" GroupName="group1" />
    <RadioButton Content="RadioButton 2 (group 1)" GroupName="group1" />
    <RadioButton Content="RadioButton 3 (group 2)" GroupName="group2" />
    <RadioButton Content="RadioButton 4 (group 2)" GroupName="group2" />
</StackPanel>
```

By specifying the `GroupName`, you can have the `RadioButtons` reside in the same `ContentControl`, yet still operate as two distinct groups.

Data Binding Radio Button Controls to a ViewModel Collection

This example looks at data binding a `ListBox.ItemsSource` property to a collection of objects in a viewmodel, and you see how to represent each item in the collection as a `RadioButton` in the view. You also see how to synchronize the `IsChecked` property of a `RadioButton` with the `ListBoxItem.IsSelected` property.

The sample is located in the `ButtonExampleView` page and the `ButtonExampleViewModel` in the downloadable sample code. The viewmodel contains an `ObservableCollection` of a custom `DataItem` class, as shown:

```
readonly ObservableCollection<DataItem> radioItems
    = new ObservableCollection<DataItem>
    {
        new DataItem(0, "Item 1"),
        new DataItem(1, "Item 2"),
        new DataItem(2, "Item 3")
    };


public IEnumerable<DataItem> RadioItems
{
    get
    {
        return radioItems;
    }
}
```

The `DataItem` class is simply a container to hold an object value and an associated piece of text (see Listing 5.1).

Each `DataItem` object is represented as a `RadioButton` in the view. The `DataItem`'s `ToString` method override allows you to display the object easily in the view without requiring an explicit data binding path expression to the `DataItem.Text` property.

LISTING 5.1   `DataItem` Class

```
public class DataItem : NotifyPropertyChangeBase
{
    object itemValue;

    public object Value
    {
        get
        {
            return itemValue;
        }
        set
        {
            Assign(ref itemValue, value);
        }
    }

    object text;
    public object Text
    {
        get
        {
```

```
                return text;
        }
        set
        {
            Assign(ref text, value);
        }
    }

    public DataItem(object value, object text)
    {
        itemValue = ArgumentValidator.AssertNotNull(value, "value");
        this.text = ArgumentValidator.AssertNotNull(text, "text");
    }

    public override string ToString()
    {
        return text != null ? text.ToString() : base.ToString();
    }
}
```

The collection of `DataItem` objects is displayed in the `ButtonExampleView` using a `ListBox`. The `ListBox.ItemsSource` is bound to the collection, as shown in the following excerpt:

```
<ListBox ItemsSource="{Binding RadioItems}"
    SelectedItem="{Binding SelectedRadioItem, Mode=TwoWay}"
    ItemContainerStyle="{StaticResource RadioButtonListItemStyle}"/>
```

By binding to the `SelectedRadioItem` property, the viewmodel is able to monitor and even to set the `IsChecked` property of any or all of the `RadioButton` controls.

To display each item in the collection as a `RadioButton`, we use a custom `ItemContainerStyle` called `RadioButtonListItemStyle`, which is located in the phone:PhoneApplicationPage.Resources element of the ButtonExampleView.xaml page. This style defines the `ControlTemplate` for a `ListBoxItem`, as shown in the following excerpt:

```
<Style x:Key="RadioButtonListItemStyle" TargetType="ListBoxItem">
    <Setter Property="VerticalContentAlignment" Value="Top" />
    <Setter Property="Template">
        <Setter.Value>
            <ControlTemplate TargetType="ListBoxItem">
                <Grid Background="{TemplateBinding Background}">
                    <RadioButton Content="{TemplateBinding Content}"
                    IsChecked="{Binding Path=IsSelected,
                    RelativeSource={RelativeSource TemplatedParent},
                        Mode=TwoWay}" />
                </Grid>
```

```
            </ControlTemplate>
        </Setter.Value>
    </Setter>
</Style>
```

The `IsChecked` property is assigned using a binding to the `ListBoxItem.IsSelected` property. In addition, `BindingMode` is set to `TwoWay`, so that when the item is checked it will be selected in the `ListBox`. Conversely, when unchecked by the user or from code in the viewmodel, the items will be unselected in the `ListBox`.

The `Content` property of the `RadioButton` is assigned using a `TemplateBinding` to the `Content` property of the `ListBoxItem`. This causes the `DataItem` in the collection to be assigned to the `Content` property of the `RadioButton`. Because the `DataItem` does not derive from `UIElement`, the `RadioButton` renders the `DataItem` using the `ToString` method override of the `DataItem` class (see Figure 5.7).

FIGURE 5.7   The `DataItem` collection is displayed using `RadioButton` controls.

When a `RadioButton` is selected, it is assigned to the `SelectedRadioItem` property in the viewmodel.

Finally, the selected item is displayed using a `TextBlock`, as shown:

```
<TextBlock Text="{Binding SelectedRadioItem}"
        Style="{StaticResource ValueTextStyle}" />
```

Check Box

The `CheckBox` control is used to define a binary state and can be used in groups to display multiple choices from which the user can select one or more choices. A user can either tap a check box or the associated label text to select an option.

The `CheckBox` uses an alternative visual representation than its base class `ToggleButton` control, though it contains no new members.

`CheckBox` supports three visible states: rest, press, and disabled for both checked and unchecked settings. There is, however, no visible focus state. In addition to visible states, the `CheckBox` control is capable of representing three settings: checked, unchecked, or indeterminate, along with a disabled visual state for each (see Figure 5.8). The state of the `CheckBox` can be retrieved using its nullable Boolean `IsChecked` property.

FIGURE 5.8   The `CheckBox` control checked states.

The indeterminate state of the `CheckBox` is commonly used to show that the user has not set the state of the control, or that some data anomaly has been detected.

Sample Overview   An example for the `CheckBox` control can be found in the `ButtonExampleView` page and the `ButtonExampleViewModel`, in the downloadable sample code. The `ButtonExampleView` has a `CheckBox` that has a two-way data binding to the `Checked` property of the viewmodel, as shown:

```
<CheckBox Content="{Binding Checked}" IsChecked="{Binding Checked, Mode=TwoWay}"
    IsThreeState="True" />
```

The viewmodel's `Checked` property is a nullable Boolean:

```
bool? isChecked;

public bool? Checked
{
    get
    {
        return isChecked;
    }
    set
    {
        Assign(ref isChecked, value);
```

```
    }
}
```

When the user taps the `CheckBox`, it transitions to the next state and updates the view-model's `Checked` property (see Figure 5.9).

Three State CheckBox

✓ True

FIGURE 5.9   A `CheckBox` control, with its `IsChecked` property set to `true`.

Data Binding Check Boxes to a ViewModel Collection

This example looks at data binding a `ListBox.ItemsSource` property to a collection of objects in a viewmodel, and you see how to represent each item in the collection as a `CheckBox` in the view. You also see how to synchronize the `IsChecked` property of a `CheckBox` with the `ListBoxItem.IsSelected` property. Finally, you investigate how to bind to the `ListBox.SelectedItems` property, which is not readily achievable with the Windows Phone SDK out-of-the-box!

The sample for this section is located in the `ButtonExampleView` page and the `ButtonExampleViewModel`, in the downloadable sample code. Again, the viewmodel contains an `ObservableCollection` of a custom `DataItem` class:

```
readonly ObservableCollection<DataItem> checkBoxItems
    = new ObservableCollection<DataItem>
        {
            new DataItem(0, "Item 1"),
            new DataItem(1, "Item 2"),
            new DataItem(2, "Item 3")
        };

public IEnumerable<DataItem> CheckBoxItems
{
    get
    {
        return checkBoxItems;
    }
}
```

The collection of `DataItems` is displayed in the `ButtonExampleView` using a `ListBox`. Each `DataItem` is represented as a `CheckBox`. The `ListBox.ItemsSource` is data-bound to the collection, as shown in the following excerpt:

```
<ListBox ItemsSource="{Binding CheckBoxItems}"
         SelectionMode="Multiple"
         ItemContainerStyle="{StaticResource CheckBoxListItemStyle}"
         unleashed:SelectedItems.Items="{Binding SelectedCheckBoxItems}" />
```

To allow multiple `CheckBox` controls to be checked simultaneously, the
`ListBox.SelectionMode` property of the `ListBox` is set to `Multiple`.

We cannot bind to the `ListBox.SelectedItems` property because it is not a
`DependencyProperty`. As a workaround, the attached property
`SelectedItems.Items` is used to bind to the `SelectedCheckBoxItems` property of the viewmodel. The `SelectedItems.Items` attached property is discussed in the next section, "Data
Binding to `ListBox.SelectedItems`."

By binding to the `SelectedCheckBoxItems` property, you can monitor and set the
`IsChecked` property of any or all of the `CheckBox` controls in the view.

To display each item in the collection as a `CheckBox` you use a custom
`ItemContainerStyle` called `CheckBoxListItemStyle`, which is located in the
phone:PhoneApplicationPage.Resources element of the ButtonExampleView.xaml page.
This style defines the `ControlTemplate` for a `ListBoxItem`, as shown in the following
excerpt:

```
<Style x:Key="CheckBoxListItemStyle" TargetType="ListBoxItem">
    <Setter Property="VerticalContentAlignment" Value="Top" />
    <Setter Property="Template">
        <Setter.Value>
            <ControlTemplate TargetType="ListBoxItem">
                <Grid Background="{TemplateBinding Background}">
                    <CheckBox Content="{TemplateBinding Content}"
                    IsChecked="{Binding Path=IsSelected,
                    RelativeSource={RelativeSource TemplatedParent},
                    Mode=TwoWay}" />
                </Grid>
            </ControlTemplate>
        </Setter.Value>
    </Setter>
</Style>
```

The `IsChecked` property is assigned using a binding to the `ListBoxItem.IsSelected` property. In addition, the `BindingMode` is set to `TwoWay`, so that when the item is checked it
is selected in the `ListBox`. Conversely, when unchecked by the user or from code in the
viewmodel, the items will be unselected in the `ListBox`.

The `Content` property of the `CheckBox` is assigned using a `TemplateBinding` to the `Content`
property of the `ListBoxItem`. This causes the `DataItem` in the collection to be assigned
to the `Content` property of the `CheckBox`. Because the `DataItem` does not derive from

UIElement, the CheckBox renders the DataItem using the ToString method override of the DataItem class (see Figure 5.10).

FIGURE 5.10   DataItem collection is displayed using CheckBox controls.

When a CheckBox is checked or unchecked, it is added to or removed from the list of SelectedCheckBoxItems property in the viewmodel:

```
readonly ObservableCollection<DataItem> selectedCheckBoxItems
    = new ObservableCollection<DataItem>();

public ObservableCollection<DataItem> SelectedCheckBoxItems
{
    get
    {
        return selectedCheckBoxItems;
    }
}
```

Finally, the selected items are, again, displayed in a ListBox in the view. This time, however, they are displayed not with a CheckBox, but a TextBlock; as shown:

```
<ListBox ItemsSource="{Binding SelectedCheckBoxItems}">
    <ListBox.ItemTemplate>
        <DataTemplate>
```

```
            <TextBlock Text="{Binding}"
                Style="{StaticResource NormalTextStyle}" />
        </DataTemplate>
    </ListBox.ItemTemplate>
</ListBox>
```

> **NOTE**
>
> The `TextBlock.Text` data binding expression `{Binding}` indicates that value of the `Text` property is set to the result of calling the `ToString` method of the `DataItem`.

Data Binding to `ListBox.SelectedItems`

Recall that the previous example used the `SelectedItems.Items` attached property to enable data binding to the `SelectedItems` property of the `ListBox` control. We do this because the `ListBox.SelectedItems` property is not a `DependencyProperty`, which means it cannot be the target of a data binding.

The downloadable sample code contains a `SelectedItems` class, which enables data binding to the `ListBox.SelectedItems` property (see Listing 5.2).

The `SelectedItems` class contains two dependency properties: an `ItemsProperty` and a `SelectedItemsBehaviorProperty`. The `ItemsProperty` is used to specify the source property of the `DataContext` and is used to assign the selected items to the `ListBox`'s `DataContext`. When the `SelectionChanged` event of the `ListBox` is raised, the `DataContext`'s property is updated.

The `SelectedItemsBehavior` class contains the logic for updating the list of selected items, which also relies on the `DataContextChangedListener` class that raises an event when the `DataContext` of the `ListBox` changes. For more information on the `DataContextChangedListener`, see Chapter 26, "Validating User Input."

An instance of the `SelectedItemsBehavior` is associated with the `ListBox` using the `SelectedItemsBehaviorProperty`.

LISTING 5.2   `SelectedItems` Class

```csharp
public static class SelectedItems
{
    public static readonly DependencyProperty ItemsProperty
        = DependencyProperty.RegisterAttached(
            "Items",
            typeof(IList),
            typeof(SelectedItems),
            new PropertyMetadata(null, ItemsPropertyChanged));

    public static void SetItems(ListBox listBox, IList list)
    {
```

```
        listBox.SetValue(ItemsProperty, list);
    }


    public static IList GetItems(ListBox listBox)
    {
        return (IList)listBox.GetValue(ItemsProperty);
    }


    static readonly DependencyProperty SelectedItemsBehaviorProperty
        = DependencyProperty.RegisterAttached(
            "SelectedItemsBehavior",
            typeof(SelectedItemsBehavior),
            typeof(ListBox), null);
    static void ItemsPropertyChanged(
        DependencyObject d, DependencyPropertyChangedEventArgs e)
    {
        var target = d as ListBox;
        if (target != null)
        {
            GetOrCreateBehavior(target, (IList)e.NewValue);
        }
    }


    static SelectedItemsBehavior GetOrCreateBehavior(
        ListBox listBox, IList list)
    {
        var behavior = (SelectedItemsBehavior)listBox.GetValue(
                                        SelectedItemsBehaviorProperty);
        if (behavior == null)
        {
            behavior = new SelectedItemsBehavior(listBox, list);
            listBox.SetValue(SelectedItemsBehaviorProperty, behavior);
        }

        return behavior;
    }
    class SelectedItemsBehavior
    {
        readonly ListBox listBox;
        readonly IList sourceList;

        public SelectedItemsBehavior(ListBox listBox, IList sourceList)
        {
            this.listBox = ArgumentValidator.AssertNotNull(listBox, "listBox");
            this.sourceList = ArgumentValidator.AssertNotNull(
                                            sourceList, "sourceList");
```

```
        this.listBox.SelectionChanged += HandleSelectionChanged;
        DataContextChangedListener.Subscribe(
                        listBox, HandleDataContextChanged);
    }

    void HandleDataContextChanged(
        DependencyObject d, DependencyPropertyChangedEventArgs e)
    {
        UpdateList();
    }
    void HandleSelectionChanged(object sender, SelectionChangedEventArgs e)
    {
        UpdateList();
    }

    void UpdateList()
    {
        sourceList.Clear();

        foreach (object item in listBox.SelectedItems)
        {
            sourceList.Add(item);
        }
    }
  }
}
```

ToolTip

The ToolTip control is present in the Windows Phone FCL, yet it serves no real purpose because it is a control designed to work with a pointing device, such as a mouse, and relies on hovering the mouse over the control. Hover events, which ordinarily dictate when a ToolTip is displayed, do not exist in the realm of the phone, making the ToolTip redundant unless used in an unorthodox way.

Perhaps future displays will have the capability to sense finger display proximity. Then, no doubt, the ToolTip will make it to the Windows Phone platform.

Items Controls

Just as the ContentControl plays host to a single child control, the ItemsControl can have many children. Controls that can contain more than one child usually derive from the ItemsControl class; these include the ComboBox control and, most notably, the ListBox control (see Figure 5.11).

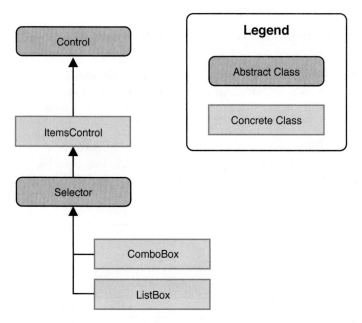

FIGURE 5.11   `ComboBox` and `ListBox` are derived from `ItemsControl`.

An `ItemsControl` allows you to populate its children either directly in XAML or in code using the `ItemsControl.Items` property, or indirectly using a data binding and the `ItemsControl.ItemsSource` property.

The `Selector` class extends the `ItemsControl` to provide the properties and events shown in Table 5.1.

TABLE 5.1   Selector Members

Name	Description
IsSynchronizedWithCurrentItem	Indicates that when the selected item in a collection changes, all the `Selector` controls that use the collection as their `ItemsSource` must be notified. This can be handy when you want to keep the selected item in several controls in synchronization without using code-beside or a secondary viewmodel property.
SelectedIndex	The zero based index of the selected item in the control.
SelectedItem	The content of the selected item in the control. If using the `ItemsSource` property, `SelectedItem` will resolve the object associated with the selected item's content, ordinarily its `DataContext`.
SelectionChanged	An event that is raised when the `SelectedItem` has changed.

ListBox

The ListBox is an items control, which means that you can populate it with items that contain text or other controls.

By default, the ListBox control allows the user to select a single item in the list. Multiple items can be selected if the ListBox.SelectionMode property is set to Multiple (see the previous section on the CheckBox control, where a ListBox was used to display a data bound collection).

The ListBox control contains a list of ListBoxItem controls. The ListBox control is a remarkably flexible control because it allows you to not only display ListBoxItems, but because the ListBoxItem control is a ContentControl any kind of object can be placed in a ListBox (see Figure 5.12).

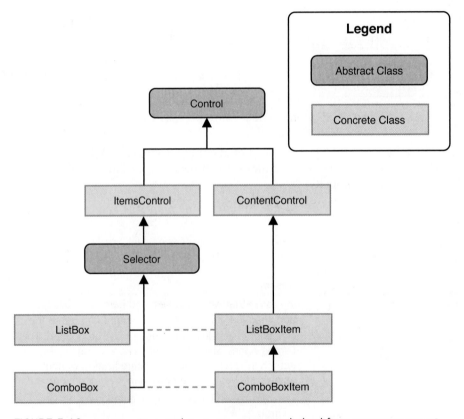

FIGURE 5.12   ListBoxItem and ComboBoxItem are derived from ContentControl.

In addition, it is unnecessary to wrap content in a ListBoxItem control, as shown in the following excerpt:

```
<ListBox>
    <ListBoxItem>
```

```
        <TextBlock Text="Item 1" Style="{StaticResource NormalTextStyle}" />
    </ListBoxItem>
    <ListBoxItem>
        <TextBlock Text="Item 2" Style="{StaticResource NormalTextStyle}" />
    </ListBoxItem>
</ListBox>
```

`ListBoxItems` are created implicitly for each element, making the previous excerpt equivalent to the following:

```
<ListBox>
    <TextBlock Text="Item 1" Style="{StaticResource NormalTextStyle}" />
    <TextBlock Text="Item 2" Style="{StaticResource NormalTextStyle}" />
</ListBox>
```

The example depicted in Figure 5.13 demonstrates that placing a `TextBlock`, implicitly or explicitly, in a `ListBoxItem` yields the same results.

FIGURE 5.13   `ListBox` with implicit and explicit `ListBoxItems`.

This works because the `ListBoxItem` `ControlTemplate` uses a `TemplateBinding` to the `Content` and `ContentTemplate` properties of the item control. When an item is being displayed, the `ControlTemplate` places it in a `ContentControl`, as this excerpt from the built-in `ListBoxItem` `ControlTemplate` shows:

```
<ControlTemplate TargetType="ListBoxItem">
    <Border x:Name="LayoutRoot">
        <ContentControl x:Name="ContentContainer"
                        ContentTemplate="{TemplateBinding ContentTemplate}"
                        Content="{TemplateBinding Content}" />
```

```
        </Border>
</ControlTemplate>
```

The `ListBox` control inherits the `Selector.SelectedItem` and `SelectedIndex` properties together with a `SelectionChanged` event, which allow you to detect when the user selects or deselects an item.

NOTE

The `SelectedItem` property is the value of the content item and not the `ListBoxItem` itself. It is the `Content` property of the `ListBoxItem` that is used to resolve the value.

For an example of how to consume the `ItemsSource` property using a data binding, see the previous sections on the `CheckBox` and `RadioButton` controls.

In addition to the selection related properties provided by the `Selector` class, the `ListBox` also provides a `SelectedItems` property, which can be used when using the multiple `SelectionMode`. The `SelectedItems` property is, however, not a `DependencyProperty`, and this means that it is not available for data binding. See the previous section on the `CheckBox` control for a solution.

ComboBox

Although the `ComboBox` control exists in the FCL, it is not suitable for use in most cases. The `ComboBox` has its origins in desktop UI and is more suited to a mouse-driven UI, where the user can rely on a high level of precision manipulating the control using a mouse. The `ComboBox` is not suited to touch input, and there are alternative superior controls, such as the `ListPicker` control provided in the Windows Phone Toolkit, which is examined in Chapter 9.

For this reason, the `ComboBox` does not appear in the Visual Studio Toolbox, and the built-in styles for the `ComboBox` do not reflect the light and dark themes of the phone.

Range Controls

The `RangeBase` control is an abstract class that represents a control that oversees a numeric value that falls between a minimum and a maximum value. Windows Phone provides three `RangeBase` controls: the `ProgressBar`, `ScrollBar`, and `Slider` (see Figure 5.14).

The `RangeBase` control provides various range related properties and events for monitoring its `Value` property (see Table 5.2).

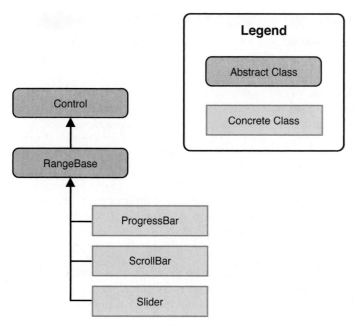

FIGURE 5.14 `RangeBase` controls.

TABLE 5.2 Properties of the `RangeBase` Class

Name	Description
Value	A `double` value that indicates the selected value within the control. This value should fall between the `Minimum` and `Maximum` values.
Minimum	A `double` value indicating the lower limit of the range. The default value is 0.0.
Maximum	A `double` value indicating the upper limit of the range. The default value is 10.0.
SmallChange	A `double` value that specifies by how much the `Value` property should be increased, or decreased, when the user performs a *small action*. The small action depends on the kind of control. `SmallChange` does not affect the user experience for the `ProgressBar`, `ScrollBar`, or the `Slider`, but is present for use in custom controls. The default value is 0.1.
LargeChange	A `double` value that specifies by how much the `Value` property should be increased, or decreased, when the user performs a *large action*. As with the `SmallChange` property, the large action depends on the kind of control. For example, when using a `Slider` control, a large action occurs when the user presses the `Slider`'s track. The default value is 1.0.
ValueChanged	A routed event that is raised when the `Value` property has changed. The data type is `RoutedPropertyChangedEventHandler<double>`.

NOTE

If the `Value` property is set to a value outside the range defined by the `Minimum` and `Maximum` properties, no `Exception` is raised. Instead the `Value` property is coerced and set to either the `Minimum` or `Maximum` value.

However, setting `Minimum`, `Maximum`, `Value`, `SmallChange`, or `LargeChange` to NaN, NegativeInfinity, or PositiveInfinity raises an `ArgumentException`. In addition, setting `SmallChange` or `LargeChange` to a value less than zero raises an `ArgumentException`.

ProgressBar

During time-consuming operations, it is important to provide an indication to the user that your application is busy, while still remaining responsive. The `ProgressBar` serves this purpose. It is not interactive; the user cannot modify it directly, and it is able to work in two modes: determinate and indeterminate.

Determinate mode allows you to display a value indicating the amount of work completed relative to the amount of work remaining, allowing the user to estimate how long the remainder of the operation will take. If the `IsIndeterminate` property is not specified, the control defaults to determinate.

Progress is displayed by setting the `Value` property of the control to the amount of work completed, and the `Maximum` property to the total amount of work to be performed. There is also a `Minimum` property that allows you to set a base point and can be useful when a portion of the work has already been completed.

The noninteractive nature of the control means that the `Value` property is updated from code, or via a data binding, while performing a background operation.

Alternatively, when progress of an operation cannot be monitored, or the total duration of an operation is unknown, the `ProgressBar`'s indeterminate mode can be engaged.

BEST PRACTICE

If the total amount of work required by an activity is known and progress can be periodically determined, avoid using an indeterminate `ProgressBar`. Use instead a determinate `ProgressBar`. Providing clear feedback about how long a user can expect to wait for completion of an operation improves the user's experience.

When using the indeterminate mode by setting the `IsIndeterminate` property to `true`, the control is displayed as a series of animated dots.

NOTE

In previous versions of the Windows Phone SDK, the ProgressBar had a performance issue. This issue has been resolved in the Windows Phone 8 SDK.

Progress Indicator

In the initial release of the Windows Phone OS, there was no way to control the native progress bar located in the status bar of the phone. Fortunately, since the release of Windows Phone 7.5, you can with the ProgressIndicator class.

ProgressIndicator is a subclass of the DependencyObject class and provides the following bindable properties:

- ▶ **IsIndeterminate**—A bool value that allows you to enable or disable the indeterminate state of the indicator.

- ▶ **IsVisible**—A bool value that allows you to show or hide the ProgressIndicator.

- ▶ **Text**—A string that is displayed beneath the indicator.

- ▶ **Value**—A double value between 0.0 and 1.0 that allows you to set the length of the progress bar when in determinate mode, that is, when IsIndeterminate is set to false.

> **NOTE**
>
> The default value of ProgressIndicator.IsVisible is false. You must set IsVisible to true, either explicitly or via a data binding for the control to be displayed.

A ProgressIndicator may be either defined in XAML or in code. The following example demonstrates adding a ProgressIndicator to a page's XAML file:

```
<phone:PhoneApplicationPage
...
    shell:SystemTray.IsVisible="True">

    <shell:SystemTray.ProgressIndicator>
        <shell:ProgressIndicator IsVisible="True"
                                 IsIndeterminate="False"
                                 Value="0.9"
                                 Text="{Binding Message}" />
    </shell:SystemTray.ProgressIndicator>
...
</phone:PhoneApplicationPage>
```

> **NOTE**
>
> SystemTray.IsVisible must be set to true for the ProgressIndicator to be displayed.

Adding a `ProgressIndicator` to a page must occur after the page has been initialized. This can be done by attaching the `ProgressIndicator` to the page within a `Loaded` event handler.

The `ProgressIndicator` instance may be retained as a field in the page and used directly, or data bindings can be established when the `ProgressIndicator` is instantiated, as demonstrated in Listing 5.3.

LISTING 5.3   Initializing a `ProgressIndicator` in Code

```
public partial class ExampleView : PhoneApplicationPage
{
    public ExampleView()
    {
        InitializeComponent();
        DataContext = new ExampleViewModel();
        Loaded += HandleLoaded;
    }

    void HandleLoaded(object sender, RoutedEventArgs e)
    {
        var progressIndicator = SystemTray.ProgressIndicator;
        if (progressIndicator != null)
        {
            return;
        }

        progressIndicator = new ProgressIndicator();

        SystemTray.SetProgressIndicator(this, progressIndicator);

        Binding binding = new Binding("Busy") { Source = ViewModel };
        BindingOperations.SetBinding(
            progressIndicator, ProgressIndicator.IsVisibleProperty, binding);

        binding = new Binding("Busy") { Source = ViewModel };
        BindingOperations.SetBinding(
            progressIndicator,
            ProgressIndicator.IsIndeterminateProperty,
            binding);

        binding = new Binding("Message") { Source = ViewModel };
        BindingOperations.SetBinding(
            progressIndicator, ProgressIndicator.TextProperty, binding);
    }
    ...
}
```

Chapter 29, "Storing App Data in a Local Database," uses the `ProgressIndicator` to display the progress of retrieving a live Twitter feed.

> ### BEST PRACTICE
>
> Performing time-consuming operations, such as downloads and database queries, on the UI thread is bad practice, as it locks the user interface making it unresponsive. Therefore, always perform any potentially long-running operation using a background thread.

Using a `BackgroundWorker` to Update the `ProgressBar`

The `BackgroundWorker` class allows you to run an operation on a separate, dedicated thread. When you want a responsive user interface and you must perform time-consuming operations, the `BackgroundWorker` class provides a convenient solution.

The `BackgroundWorker` class has events that are automatically raised on the UI thread, giving you the opportunity to update `UIElements` without risking cross-thread access exceptions. You can listen for events that report the progress of an operation and signal when the operation is completed. The following section uses a `BackgroundWorker` to perform an arbitrary time-consuming operation during which a `ProgressBar` is periodically notified of the progress.

`ProgressBar` and `BackgroundWorker` Sample Code

An example for the `ProgressBar` can be found in the `ControlExamplesView` page and the `ControlExamplesViewModel` class in the downloadable sample code.

The viewmodel contains a `BackgroundWorker` field. In the viewmodel's constructor, the `BackgroundWorker.WorkerReportsProgress` property is set to true. This causes the `BackgroundWorker` to raise an event when its `ReportProgress` method is called. We then subscribe to three events: the `DoWork` event, which is raised when the `RunWorkerAsync` method is called; the `ProgressChanged` event, which is called when the `BackgroundWorker` `ReportProgress` method is called; and the `RunWorkerCompleted`, which is raised when the `backgroundWorker_DoWork` method completes (see Listing 5.4).

LISTING 5.4   `ControlExamplesViewModel` Class (excerpt)

```
public class ControlExamplesViewModel : ViewModelBase
{
    readonly BackgroundWorker backgroundWorker = new BackgroundWorker();

    public ControlExamplesViewModel()
        : base("Controls")
    {
        backgroundWorker.WorkerReportsProgress = true;
        backgroundWorker.DoWork
            += new DoWorkEventHandler(backgroundWorker_DoWork);
        backgroundWorker.ProgressChanged
            += new ProgressChangedEventHandler(
```

```
                        backgroundWorker_ProgressChanged);
    backgroundWorker.RunWorkerCompleted
        += new RunWorkerCompletedEventHandler(
            backgroundWorker_RunWorkerCompleted);

    backgroundWorker.WorkerSupportsCancellation = true;
    cancelProgressCommand = new DelegateCommand(
        obj => backgroundWorker.CancelAsync());

    backgroundWorker.RunWorkerAsync();
    Message = "BackgroundWorker performing task.";
}
void backgroundWorker_ProgressChanged(
        object sender, ProgressChangedEventArgs e)
{
    ProgressPercent = e.ProgressPercentage;
}

void backgroundWorker_DoWork(object sender, DoWorkEventArgs e)
{
    BackgroundWorker worker = (BackgroundWorker)sender;
    for (int i = 0; i < 100; i++)
    {
        if (worker.CancellationPending)
        {
            e.Cancel = true;
            return;
        }
        Wait(300);
        worker.ReportProgress(i);
    }
}
void backgroundWorker_RunWorkerCompleted(
        object sender, RunWorkerCompletedEventArgs e)
{
    Message = e.Cancelled
        ? "Background worker cancelled."
        : "Background worker completed.";
}

int progressPercent;

public int ProgressPercent
{
    get
    {
```

```csharp
            return progressPercent;
        }
        private set
        {
            Assign(ref progressPercent, value);
        }
    }
    bool cancelProgress;
    DelegateCommand cancelProgressCommand;

    public ICommand CancelProgressCommand
    {
        get
        {
            return cancelProgressCommand;
        }
    }

    string message;

    public string Message
    {
        get
        {
            return message;
        }
        set
        {
            Assign(ref message, value);
        }
    }

    static readonly object waitLock = new object();

    static void Wait(int delayMs)
    {
        if (delayMs > 0)
        {
            lock (waitLock)
            {
                Monitor.Wait(waitLock, delayMs);
            }
        }
    }
}
```

While running, the worker thread repeatedly sleeps, using the viewmodel's `Wait` method, and then signals that the progress has changed.

> **NOTE**
>
> If the `BackgroundWorker.WorkerReportsUpdates` property is set to false and the `BackgroundWorker ReportProgress` method is called, an `InvalidOperationException` will be thrown.

The following excerpt shows the view's XAML for the relevant controls:

```
<TextBlock Text="ProgressBar" />
<ProgressBar Value="{Binding ProgressPercent}"
        Minimum="0" Maximum="100" />
<Button Content="Cancel Progress"
        Command="{Binding CancelProgressCommand}" />
<TextBlock Text="Message" />
<TextBlock Text="{Binding Message}" Height="80" />
```

On completion of the `backgroundWorker_DoWork` method, the `backgroundWorker_RunWorkerCompleted` method is called, and the viewmodel's `MessageProperty` is updated (see Figure 5.15).

FIGURE 5.15   Updating the UI using a `BackgroundWorker`.

The `BackgroundWorker` class also supports operation cancellation. By pressing the Cancel Progress button, the `CancelProgressCommand` is executed, which, in turn, calls the `backgroundWorker`'s `CancelAsync` method. This is then detected in the `backgroundWorker_DoWork` method, which sets the `Cancel` property of the `DoWorkEventArgs`.

Although cancelled, the `BackgroundWorker.RunWorkCompleted` event is still raised, and the `backgroundWorker_RunWorkerCompleted` handler is still called; however, the `RunWorkerCompletedEventArgs.Cancelled` property allows you to determine whether the operation was cancelled.

> **NOTE**
>
> The `NotifyPropertyChangeBase` class in the downloadable sample code, which is the base class of the `ViewModelBase` class, automatically raises `INotifyPropertyChanged.PropertyChanged` events on the UI thread (one of its many benefits). Therefore, you could achieve the same thing shown in the example by replacing the `BackgroundWorker` with a thread from, for example, the `ThreadPool`, and by including two Boolean `cancel` and `cancelled` fields. It would make for a simpler implementation with fewer event subscriptions.

Slider

The `Slider` is an interactive control that allows the user to set its `Value` property by dragging or pressing the `Slider` track. It is ideal for values that do not require a high level of precision, such as the volume setting for music in a game.

The following demonstrates how to define a `Slider` in XAML:

```
<Slider Value="5" Minimum="0" Maximum="100" LargeChange="20" />
```

The `Value`, `Minimum`, and `Maximum` properties are described in the previous section on the `RangeBase` control.

When the user taps the `Slider` track, the `Value` property is incremented or decremented by the value of the `LargeChange` property.

The default orientation of the `Slider` is horizontal. The orientation can be changed by setting the `Orientation` property to `Vertical`.

The `Slider` is an especially useful control on the Windows Phone platform, since the use of touch makes the slider easier to control than it would otherwise be with the mouse.

> **NOTE**
>
> The built-in `Slider` control is, however, somewhat cumbersome to use. The control template for the `Slider` was built for Silverlight for the Browser, where mice are better at hitting small targets. A number of custom templates are available on the Web that provide better usability. Dave Relyea, the lead developer of the Windows Phone Toolkit team, provides an improved `Slider` control. See http://bit.ly/b0YtQj for more information.

Further examples of the `Slider` control can be found throughout this book, such as in Chapter 14, "Leveraging Built-In Apps via Launchers and Choosers," and in Chapter 17, "Building Location Aware Apps."

BEST PRACTICE

Do not place a horizontal `Slider` control on a `Pivot` or `Panorama` control. Doing so may interfere with a user's ability to move between items, or it may prevent a user from manipulating the `Slider` without moving between `Panorama` or `Pivot` items. This also applies to other controls like the Bing Maps control, which rely on the user performing a drag gesture.

You learn more about the `Pivot` or `Panorama` in Chapter 11.

Note that you may see a `Slider` placed in a `Pivot` in the sample code. This has been done for the sake of convenience and should not be taken as guidance.

ScrollBar

`ScrollBar` is a control that has a sliding thumb whose position corresponds to a value. The `ScrollBar` class provides a `ViewportSize` property, which determines the amount of scrollable content that is visible and an `Orientation` property, which can be either `Horizontal` or `Vertical`.

It is rare to see the `ScrollBar` used directly. It is more commonly used within other controls such as the `ScrollViewer` or in custom controls.

Summary

This chapter began by providing an overview of the elements available in the Windows Phone FCL for XAML apps. It then focused on the three control types: `ContentControls`, `ItemsControls`, and `RangeControls`. It showed the various subclasses of these controls, accompanied with practical examples.

The chapter examined how `ContentControls` can host a single element and the differences between the various buttons such as the `HyperlinkButton`, `RepeatButton`, and `ToggleButton`. It also demonstrated how to bind `CheckBox` and `RadioButton` controls to viewmodel collections, and you saw how to bind to the `ListBox.SelectedItems` property, which is not readily achievable with the Windows Phone SDK out-of-the-box.

Finally, the chapter explored the `RangeBase` controls: the `Slider` and `ProgressBar`, and demonstrated how to provide feedback to a user during asynchronous activities carried out by a `BackgroundWorker`.

CHAPTER 6

Mastering Text Elements and Fonts

Text plays a key role in the design philosophy behind the Windows Phone UI. The Microsoft Design Language, previously known as Metro, is Microsoft's name for the design of the Windows 8 and Windows Phone UI. Microsoft Design Language, a.k.a. Modern UI, places emphasis on text as a primary design element. Microsoft Design Language is about content, readability, and clarity, and less about chrome (colored backgrounds, borders, and so on).

This chapter begins by looking at the various types used for displaying and entering text in a Windows Phone XAML app, in particular the `TextBlock`, `TextBox`, `PasswordBox`, and `RichTextBox`. It then explores each of these elements in greater depth, starting with the `TextBlock`, where you see how to create multiline text using `Run` and `LineBreak` objects. It then looks at font support, including the built-in fonts, and demonstrates techniques for providing custom fonts in your application using font embedding, or via a font data `Stream`. It also examines the Software Input Panel (SIP) and shows how to customize the onscreen keyboard using input scopes.

Also included in this chapter is a useful sample page that allows you to preview the various input scopes.

The chapter then looks at the `PasswordBox` and demonstrates how to bind the password string property to a view-model property. You then learn about the `RichTextBox`, which allows you to blend text and rich content such as hyperlinks, images, and other UI elements.

Finally, the chapter looks at the clipboard, and you see how to set the clipboard text and how to detect whether text is present on the clipboard.

Understanding Text Element Types

Within the Windows Phone Framework Class Library (FCL), there are some types, which, on first appearance, you could be forgiven for thinking that API similarities are the result of common ancestry. The `TextBlock` and `TextBox` elements, for example, have numerous similarly named text and font related properties, yet both have their own distinct API and their closest ancestor is `FrameworkElement` (see Figure 6.1).

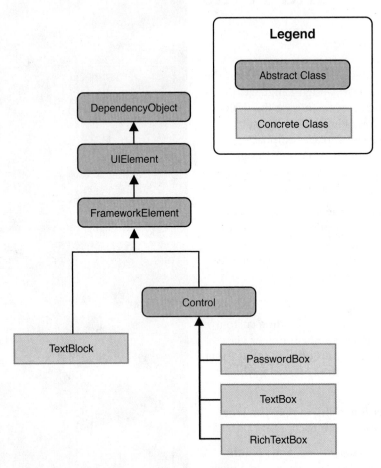

FIGURE 6.1   Text related framework elements.

The `TextBox` and `PasswordBox` are derived from the `System.Windows.Control` class. The `Control` class is the base class for UI elements that use a `ControlTemplate` to define their appearance. And while the `TextBlock` lives in the `System.Controls` namespace, it is not a `Control`, making it impossible to drastically change its appearance. Those familiar with WPF will know that WPF has the `Label` class, which is derived from `Control` and which fills this gap. There is, however, no such control in the Windows Phone SDK.

The similarities between the `TextBlock` and `TextBox` APIs do mean, however, that the elements can be styled in much the same manner; the characteristics of most font and layout related properties apply equally to all three text elements.

Displaying Text Using the `TextBlock`

The `TextBlock` is an essential element in most Windows Phone XAML apps. It represents a section of text and is normally used to label controls or control groups. The `TextBlock` supports word wrapping, so that long runs of text are not hidden when they exceed the width of the control. The following code shows how to create a `TextBlock` in XAML, using the built-in `PhoneTextNormalStyle`:

```
<TextBlock Text="Windows Phone 8 Unleashed"
    Style="{StaticResource PhoneTextNormalStyle}" />
```

Alternatively, the `TextBlock` also allows you to nest content within the `TextBlock` element, like so:

```
<TextBlock Style="{StaticResource LabelTextStyle}">
    Windows Phone 8 Unleashed
</TextBlock>
```

Using the `Run` and `LineBreak` Objects

In XAML, whitespace is interpreted in the same way as in XML. Whitespace is collapsed, leading and trailing whitespace is removed, and multiple lines are placed on the same line. The `LineBreak` class represents an explicit new line in a `TextBlock`. To create a multi-line `TextBlock`, use the `LineBreak` element within the content, as shown:

```
<TextBlock Style="{StaticResource LabelTextStyle}">
    You are reading<LineBreak />
    Windows Phone 8 Unleashed!
</TextBlock>
```

> **NOTE**
>
> The XML-like format of XAML does not allow you to use the greater than > or less than < symbols within XAML. This is because the symbols are interpreted as being part of an element. Instead, use the character entity references: `&gt;` and `&lt;`. These are translated to the greater than and less than characters at runtime.

`Run` elements can be embedded within the `TextBlock` content so that different font formatting can be applied to different parts of the text. `LineBreak` elements are generally used to delimit surrounding `Run` elements.

`LineBreak` and `Run` are derived from `System.Windows.Documents.Inline`. The `TextBlock` class contains a strongly typed `InlineCollection` called `Inlines`, which contains the items to be displayed (see Figure 6.2).

`Inlines` is the XAML content property of the `TextBlock` class. Thus, to specify items in the `TextBlock`, you specify various `Run` and `LineBreak` elements as child elements of the `TextBlock`.

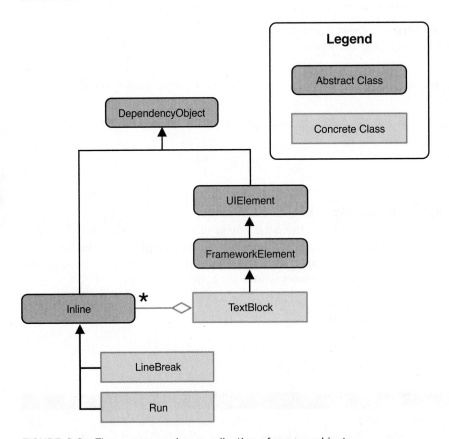

FIGURE 6.2   The `TextBlock` has a collection of `Inline` objects.

The following example shows how to display several strings of differing format in a `TextBlock` using `Run` elements separated with `LineBreak` elements.

```
<TextBlock>
    <Run Foreground="Blue" FontFamily="Courier New"
        FontSize="18">You are reading</Run><LineBreak/>
    <Run Foreground="Teal" FontFamily="Times New Roman"
```

```
            FontSize="24" FontStyle="Italic">Windows Phone 8 Unleashed!</Run>
</TextBlock>
```

The result is shown in Figure 6.3.

FIGURE 6.3   Using `Run` and `LineBreak` objects within a `TextBlock`.

> **NOTE**
>
> Unfortunately the `Run.Text` property is not a `DependencyProperty`, which prevents using data binding with the property. If you attempt to place a binding on the `Text` property in XAML, a difficult to diagnose error will be raised at runtime.
>
> A solution that allows you to display a mixture of static text and text populated via data bindings is to use multiple `TextBlock` elements within a `StackPanel`, with the `StackPanel` element's `Orientation` set to `Horizontal`.

> **NOTE**
>
> When attempting to provide different formatting for a contiguous string of text, in XAML, `Run` elements should be placed side by side without separating whitespace because even though they appear to be properly laid out in the Visual Studio designer, at runtime whitespace can appear between the `Run` elements.

`LineBreak` forces the text in each `Run` to display on a separate line. Without the `LineBreak`, the text in each `Run` would be displayed on the same line. This can cause the text to be clipped if it exceeds the `TextBlock` width or the width of the parent container.

To avoid the clipping without using a `LineBreak`, set the `TextBlock` `TextWrapping` to `Wrap`, like so:

```
<TextBlock TextWrapping="Wrap" />
```

Better still, create a reusable `Style` for your `TextBlock`, like so:

```
<Style x:Key="NormalTextStyle" TargetType="TextBlock"
        BasedOn="{StaticResource PhoneTextNormalStyle}">
    <Setter Property="TextWrapping" Value="Wrap" />
</Style>
```

The `Style` can be placed in the Resources element of your page or app.xaml file.

Multiline `TextBlock` Text

As you have seen, `TextBlock` supports multiline text, either by setting `TextWrapping` to `Wrap` or by using `LineBreak` instances within the content.

Two properties, `LineHeight` and `LineStackingStrategy`, affect how multiline text is displayed. `LineHeight` determines the height of every line of text in the `TextBlock`. If `LineHeight` is set to a smaller value than the `FontSize` property, it may cause text to be vertically cropped. Typically, you leave `LineHeight` unset and rely on the default text rendering, which calculates the line height using `FontSize` plus an internal padding value.

The `TextBlock` class's `LineStackingStrategy` property determines the algorithm that is used to calculate line height. The `LineStackingStrategy` is an enum value, which can be either `MaxHeight` or `BlockLineHeight`. `MaxHeight`, the default strategy, calculates line height using the maximum height of any character in the font, whereas `BlockLineHeight` calculates the line height using the *block* font design measure stored as a value in the font.

> **NOTE**
>
> If the `BlockLineHeight` strategy is used, line height is calculated using the default font for the `TextBlock` and the font size of any `Run` elements is ignored, which can cause text to be squashed together.

Controlling Font Properties

The `TextBlock` and `TextBox` classes rely on various font related dependency properties, which specify how text is displayed. The list of font related properties is presented in Table 6.1.

TABLE 6.1   Font Related Properties of the `TextBlock` and `TextBox` Classes

Property	Description
FontFamily	The preferred top-level font family for the text content. There are many built-in fonts to choose from. These are described in the following section "Built-In Fonts."

Property	Description
	Custom fonts can also be used by including them in your app's XAP file (see the following section "Font Embedding").
FontSize	The size of the font in pixels. The default value is 11 pixels. This value indicates the size of the text from top to bottom. If you specify a FontSize of, for example, 16, the text will have a height of 16 pixels. The size of the TextBlock, however, will usually exceed this amount by approximately 33%, due to an area of space that is set aside to prevent text from sitting too close to other text.
	The default font size of 11 pixels, which is more suited to Silverlight for the browser, is far too small to be used as the default font size on Windows Phone. The Windows Phone device display resolution is about 250% that of the conventional Windows desktop display resolution. It is, therefore, important to use the built-in set of text related styles, which have higher FontSize values. See http://bit.ly/xC8vgo for the list of built-in styles and theme resources.
FontSource	Allows a Stream containing font data to be used for rendering text. See the following section "Leveraging FontSource to Assign a Font Using a Stream."
FontStretch	OpenType fonts are able to be stretched or contracted by using this property. No fonts present on the phone, however, are OpenType, and setting this value has no effect for built-in fonts. The FontStretch value is obtained from one of the preset System.Windows.FontStretches properties, which include the following: ▶ Condensed ▶ Expanded ▶ ExtraCondensed ▶ ExtraExpanded ▶ Normal ▶ SemiCondensed ▶ SemiExpanded ▶ UltraCondensed ▶ UltraExpanded
FontStyle	Can be either Normal or Italic. The FontStyle value is obtained from one of the preset System.Windows.FontStyles properties.
FontWeight	The thickness or heaviness of the text. This value is retrieved from a set of presets in the System.Windows.FontWeights class. This property can be either Black, Bold, ExtraBlack, ExtraBold, ExtraLight, Light, Medium, Normal, SemiBold, or Thin. The default value is Normal. When setting a font to a variant that does not exist natively, such as Bold, rendering system simulates the font weight by drawing around the text.

BEST PRACTICE

Avoid using a font size less than 15 points. Text that is smaller than 15 points in size can be hard to read and is likely too small to be an adequate touch target.

When using colored fonts, use high-contrast colors at smaller point sizes to enhance readability. Test colors against both themes and all accent colors.

Understanding the Built-In Fonts

The Unicode font Segoe WP is the Windows Phone system font. It has kern pairing, which defines the distance between each character pair combination. It does not have font hinting. It is natively available in the following five styles:

▶ Regular

▶ Bold

▶ Semi-bold

▶ Semi-light

▶ Black

The standard fonts used by Windows Phone XAML apps all have at least native variants for bold and italic. The following example, located in the ControlExamplesView.xaml page in the downloadable sample code, displays the list of standard fonts used by Latin, Cyrillic, and Greek-based languages. A Run is used to display each font with the font name as example text. See the following excerpt:

```
<TextBlock>
    <Run FontFamily="Arial">Arial</Run><LineBreak />
    <Run FontFamily="Arial Black">Arial Black</Run><LineBreak />
    <Run FontFamily="Calibri">Calibri</Run><LineBreak />
    <Run FontFamily="Comic Sans MS">Comic Sans MS</Run><LineBreak />
    <Run FontFamily="Courier New">Courier New</Run><LineBreak />
    <Run FontFamily="Georgia">Georgia</Run><LineBreak />
    <Run FontFamily="Lucida Sans Unicode">Lucida Sans Unicode</Run><LineBreak />
    <Run FontFamily="Portable User Interface">Portable User Interface</Run>
        <LineBreak />
    <Run FontFamily="Segoe WP">Segoe WP</Run><LineBreak />
    <Run FontFamily="Segoe WP Black">Segoe WP Black</Run><LineBreak />
    <Run FontFamily="Segoe WP Bold">Segoe WP Bold</Run><LineBreak />
    <Run FontFamily="Segoe WP Light">Segoe WP Light</Run><LineBreak />
    <Run FontFamily="Segoe WP Semibold">Segoe WP Semibold</Run><LineBreak />
    <Run FontFamily="Segoe WP SemiLight">Segoe WP SemiLight</Run><LineBreak />
    <Run FontFamily="Tahoma">Tahoma</Run><LineBreak />
    <Run FontFamily="Times New Roman">Times New Roman</Run><LineBreak />
    <Run FontFamily="Trebuchet MS">Trebuchet MS</Run><LineBreak />
```

```
    <Run FontFamily="Verdana">Verdana</Run><LineBreak />
    <Run FontFamily="Webdings">Webdings</Run> (Webdings)
</TextBlock>
```

The result is shown in Figure 6.4.

FIGURE 6.4   Built-in font families.

The following East Asian languages are also supported:

▶ **Japanese**—Meiryo UI

▶ **Simplified Chinese**—Microsoft YaHei

▶ **Simplified Chinese**—SimSum. This font is included only on devices that have the Chinese (Simplified) display language.

▶ **Korean**—Malgun Gothic

TIP

Because the Segoe font is such an integral part of the Microsoft Design Language UI experience, use alternative fonts sparingly.

All fonts in the list of built-in fonts are free to use in your applications. There are, however, times when you may want to customize the font used to make your application stand out from the crowd. Fortunately, this is possible in Windows Phone using font embedding.

Using Third-Party Fonts via Font Embedding

Font embedding allows you to place a third-party font into your application. Numerous websites offer fonts for purchase, and some even offer free fonts.

NOTE

Like all media sourced from external sources, be sure that you are legally entitled to redistribute fonts that have been embedded in your application. Be aware that the licensing restrictions of some fonts allow you to create graphics with the font but not to redistribute the font itself.

To embed a font, include it in your Visual Studio project. Set the Build Action in the Visual Studio Properties pane to Content (see Figure 6.5). This causes the font file to be placed in the XAP file when the project is built.

FIGURE 6.5   For embedded fonts, set the file's Build Action to Content.

NOTE

The difference between the Content build action and the Resource build action is that the Resource option causes files to be placed in the project assembly, whereas Content files are not placed into an assembly but rather sit independently from the assembly inside the XAP file. This is important for performance reasons, because minimizing the assembly size causes it to load faster and ultimately improves the startup time of your app.

Embedding the font allows you to set the `FontFamily` of text controls by providing the path to the font file, as shown in the following example:

```
<TextBlock Text="Embedded Font"
           FontFamily="/ControlExamples/Fonts/orbitron-medium.ttf#Orbitron" />
```

Notice that the format for the path ends in a hash followed with the name of the font. This value allows the runtime environment to find the font within the font file, because some font files may contain more than one font. To determine the name of the font in Windows 7, double-click the font to open the Windows Font Preview tool (see Figure 6.6). For other operating systems, you might need to download a third-party font viewer.

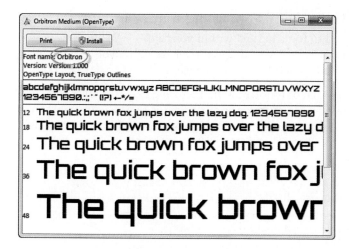

FIGURE 6.6   The Windows Font Preview tool indicates the name of the font.

Defining the `FontFamily` for each control used within your project is not a sound practice, because if the font is moved, or you later decide to use a different font, it will require updating the property across your project. Instead, define the `FontFamily` in the application's Resources and include a `Style` for `TextBlocks` that will use the `FontFamily` like so:

```
<Application.Resources>
    <FontFamily x:Key="EmbeddedFont">
        /ControlExamples/Fonts/orbitron-medium.ttf#Orbitron
    </FontFamily>
```

```
    <Style x:Key="EmbeddedTextStyle" TargetType="TextBlock"
            BasedOn="{StaticResource PhoneTextNormalStyle}">
        <Setter Property="FontFamily"
            Value="{StaticResource EmbeddedFont}" />
    </Style>
</Application.Resources>
```

It can then be used throughout your application in the following manner:

```
<TextBlock Text="Embedded font defined in app Resources
            Style="{StaticResource EmbeddedTextStyle}"/>
```

> **NOTE**
>
> The license terms of the Segoe WP fonts do not allow redistribution. This means packaging them within your application's XAP file is not allowed. Of course, you can still use the font in your app without embedding it.

Leveraging `FontSource` to Assign a Font Using a `Stream`

While font embedding is restricted to fonts located within your app's XAP file, the `FontSource` property of the `TextBlock`, `TextBox`, and `PasswordBox` allows you to download the font using an external data source, such as a cloud service.

The `FontSource` class requires a `Stream` of font data. The following example takes the same embedded font used in the previous example and provides it to a `TextBlock` object's `FontSource` property via a `Stream`, using the `Application.GetResourceStream` method as shown:

```
Uri fontUri = new Uri("ControlExamples/Fonts/orbitron-medium.ttf",
                                             UriKind.Relative);

StreamResourceInfo resourceInfo = Application.GetResourceStream(fontUri);
textBlockWithFontSource.FontSource = new FontSource(resourceInfo.Stream);
textBlockWithFontSource.FontFamily = new FontFamily("Orbitron");
```

The origin of the font file is arbitrary and could have just as easily been supplied via a web service.

Although this approach offers a great deal of flexibility, ordinarily it would be useful only for a highly specialized, perhaps font-related, app. If the font can be determined at development time, it is best to use embedding rather than the `FontSource` property to decrease the dependency on network services.

Receiving Input Using a `TextBox`

The Windows Phone SDK includes three controls designed for text entry: `TextBox`, `PasswordBox`, and `RichTextBox`. Text can be entered either by using the onscreen keyboard known as the Software Input Panel (SIP) or by using the hardware keyboard if the phone has one.

The `TextBox` control displays content as well as allowing the user to type or edit content. A `TextBox` can display text on a single line, or on multiple lines. A multiline `TextBox` wraps text to the width of the control.

Text is stored as a `System.String`, using the `TextBox.Text` property. The alignment of the text can be changed using the `TextAlignment` property. Text is displayed according to various font-related properties, shown earlier in Table 6.1.

Software Input Panel

The Software Input Panel (SIP) appears automatically when focus is set to an editable control unless the device has a hardware keyboard ready to receive input, such as when a sliding keyboard is in its extended position. When the control loses focus because the user taps outside the edit control, scrolls a list, or presses the hardware Back button, the SIP is closed by sliding down off the bottom of the screen. If a phone has a hardware keyboard, and it is deployed, the SIP closes automatically.

> **NOTE**
>
> To detect when the hardware keyboard is deployed, subscribe to the `Microsoft.Phone.Info.DeviceStatus.IsKeyboardDeployed` event, discussed in Chapter 2, "Fundamental Concepts in Windows Phone Development."

> **TIP**
>
> When using the emulator, a hardware keyboard can be simulated by pressing the PageUp button on your keyboard. The PageDown button disables the keyboard and reinstates the SIP.

Table 6.2 shows the 10 most commonly used context-specific SIP keyboard layouts. Input Scope is an `InputScopeNameValue` enumeration value described in the next section.

TABLE 6.2   SIP Keyboard Layouts

Keyboard	Input Scope	Keyboard Layout
Default	Default and other standard input scope values	Standard QWERTY/QWERTZ/AZERTY etc., depending on the phone locale setting
Text	Text	Standard layout with ASCII based emoticons

Keyboard	Input Scope	Keyboard Layout
Email Address	EmailSmtpAddress	Standard layout with .com and @ keys
Email Name or Address	EmailNameOrAddress	Standard layout with .com and @ key, and easy access to phone number layout
Phone Number	TelephoneNumber	Typical 12-key layout
Web Address	Url	Standard layout with .com key and customized Enter key
Maps	Maps	Standard layout with a customized Enter key
Search	Search	Semitransparent layout with a Search and .com key
SMS Address	NameOrPhoneNumber	Standard layout with easy access to phone number layout
Chat	Chat	Text input with emoticons

SIP Dimensions

The onscreen keyboard is 336 pixels tall in portrait view and 256 pixels tall in landscape view. The text suggestion window, which appears above the keyboard, is 65 pixels tall in both page orientations.

> **NOTE**
>
> It is your responsibility to ensure that the control, where text is being entered, is above the SIP and in view.

Although it is not possible to define your own keyboard types or modify existing ones, you can switch the keyboard scheme of the SIP by using the `TextBox.InputScope` property. `InputScope` is discussed again in a moment.

Opening the SIP Programmatically

The SIP appears whenever a `TextBox` or `PasswordBox` gains focus. The SIP can, therefore, be opened programmatically by calling the `Focus` method of the control.

In some circumstances, such as when the primary purpose of a page is to allow the user to enter one or two pieces of information, it make sense to open the SIP as soon as the page loads. This can be done by subscribing to the `PhoneApplicationPage.Loaded` event and calling the `Focus` method of the control, as shown in the following excerpt:

```
public partial class ExamplesView : PhoneApplicationPage
{
    public ExamplesView()
```

```
    {
        InitializeComponent();
        Loaded += new RoutedEventHandler(ExamplesView_Loaded);
    }

    void ExamplesView_Loaded(object sender, RoutedEventArgs e)
    {
        autoFocussedTextBox.Focus();
    }
}
```

BEST PRACTICE

Expand the SIP automatically only if the application page has no more than two editable controls and the first editable control is a single-line edit box. Likewise, do not automatically expand the SIP if the page has content or controls that would be obscured behind the keyboard.

Dismissing the SIP Programmatically

If the `TextBox` loses focus (the user taps the display outside the `TextBox`, for example) the SIP is closed. To dismiss the SIP programmatically, however, you must shift focus to another control on the page. An elegant way of achieving this, and one that does not rely on another arbitrary control, is to focus the main content container of your page.

The following example shows the main content `Grid` for a page. The `Grid` contains a single `TextBox` as shown:

```
<Grid x:Name="ContentGrid" Grid.Row="1"
      IsTabStop="True">
    <TextBox x:Name="TextBox_Input" KeyUp="TextBox_KeyUp" />
</Grid>
```

To allow the user to dismiss the SIP via the SIP Enter key, you can subscribe to the `TextBox.KeyUp` event. When the Enter key is detected, the SIP is dismissed by focusing the container. See the following excerpt:

```
void TextBox_KeyUp(object sender, KeyEventArgs e)
{
    if (e.Key == Key.Enter)
    {
        this.Focus();
    }
}
```

NOTE

Make sure that the control to which you are shifting focus has its `IsTabStop` property set to true. When `IsTabStop` is false, the control is unable to receive focus, and hence will not cause the SIP to be closed. Most controls use true as the default `IsTabStop` value.

Input Scope

The `InputScope` property determines the set of keys and layout provided on the SIP. This value allows you to provide the user with a specialized keyboard, particular to the data that is being entered.

The following code demonstrates how to change the default alphanumeric SIP to one containing telephone digits, suitable for allowing the user to enter a telephone number:

```
<TextBox InputScope="TelephoneNumber" />
```

The `InputScope` is specified using one of the values from the `InputScopeNameValue` enum (see Table 6.3).

Most of the `InputScopeNameValue` enum values are mapped to a particular keyboard layout from Table 6.2.

TABLE 6.3   `InputScopeNameValue` Enum Values

InputScope	InputScope	InputScope
AddressCity	EmailNameOrAddress	PersonalNamePrefix
AddressCountryName	EmailSmtpAddress	PersonalNameSuffix
AddressCountryShortName	EmailUserName	PersonalSurname
AddressStateOrProvince	EnumString*	PhraseList*
AddressStreet	FileName	PostalAddress
AlphanumericFullWidth	Levels	PostalCode
AlphanumericHalfWidth	FullFilePath	Private
ApplicationEnd	Hanja	RegularExpression*
Bopomofo	Hiragana	Search
Chat	KatakanaFullWidth	Srgs*
CurrencyAmount	KatakanaHalfWidth	TelephoneAreaCode
CurrencyAmountAndSymbol	LogOnName	TelephoneCountryCode
CurrencyChinese	Maps	TelephoneLocalNumber
Date	NameOrPhoneNumber	TelephoneNumber
DateDay	Number	Text
DateDayName	NumberFullWidth	Time
DateMonth	OneChar	TimeHour

InputScope	InputScope	InputScope
DateMonthName	Password	TimeMinorSec
DateYear	PersonalFullName	Url
Default	PersonalGivenName	Xml*
Digits	PersonalMiddleName	Yomi

At this time the value is not a valid InputScope. If used in XAML it will have no effect and the InputScope will fall back to the default value. Conversely, if set in code, an Exception is raised at runtime.

Word Prediction

Windows phone has built-in support for word prediction while the user is entering text into a TextBox. To enable this feature, set the InputScope to either Text or Chat, as shown in the following example:

```
<TextBox InputScope="Text" />
```

Intellisense Support for the InputScope Property

When populating the InputScope property in XAML, you will notice that there is no IntelliSense support. This makes selecting the InputScopeNameValue rather difficult, as there are quite a few of them. To regain IntelliSense, use the more verbose element syntax to specify the InputScope property, like so:

```
<TextBox>
    <TextBox.InputScope>
        <InputScope>
            <InputScopeName NameValue="TelephoneNumber" />
        </InputScope>
    </TextBox.InputScope>
</TextBox>
```

Input Scope Sample Overview

To provide you with an opportunity to explore the various SIP layouts, I have created a sample view that allows you to switch the InputScope for a TextBox at runtime. The sample is located in the ControlExampleView page and the ControlExampleViewModel class in the downloadable sample code.

The viewmodel exposes a list of InputScopeNameValues, shown in the following excerpt, which is consumed in the view via a data binding to a Windows Phone Toolkit ListPicker control. For more information on the Windows Phone Toolkit and the controls contained therein, see Chapter 9, "Enriching the User Experience with the Windows Phone Toolkit Controls."

```csharp
readonly IEnumerable<InputScopeNameValue> inputScopeNameValues
                    = EnumUtility.CreateEnumValueList<InputScopeNameValue>()
                        .OrderBy(nameValue => nameValue.ToString());

public IEnumerable<InputScopeNameValue> InputScopeNameValues
{
    get
    {
        return inputScopeNameValues;
    }
}
```

The `System.Enum.GetNames` method present in the .NET Desktop FCL is notably absent from the Windows Phone SDK. To retrieve the enum values as a list of strings, we retrieve its field values, using a custom class called `EnumUtility` (see Listing 6.1).

The `CreateEnumValueList<TEnum>` method uses reflection to extract the names of each enum value.

LISTING 6.1   `EnumUtility` Class

```csharp
public static class EnumUtility
{
    public static IEnumerable<TEnum> CreateEnumValueList<TEnum>()
    {
        Type enumType = typeof(TEnum);
        IEnumerable<FieldInfo> fieldInfos
            = enumType.GetFields().Where(x => enumType.Equals(x.FieldType));
        return fieldInfos.Select(
            fieldInfo => (TEnum)Enum.Parse(enumType, fieldInfo.Name,
            ➥true)).ToList();
    }
}
```

The viewmodel tracks the `InputScopeNameValue` that is selected by the user using a `ListPicker` control.

```csharp
InputScopeNameValue inputScopeNameValue = InputScopeNameValue.Default;

public InputScopeNameValue InputScopeNameValue
{
    get
    {
        return inputScopeNameValue;
    }
}
```

```
set
{
    Assign(ref inputScopeNameValue, value);
}
}
```

The view binds to the viewmodel properties in its TextBox and ListPicker controls, as shown:

```xml
<TextBlock Text="Single-line TextBox"
    Style="{StaticResource LabelTextStyle}" />
<TextBox InputScope="{Binding InputScopeNameValue,
    Converter={StaticResource InputScopeValueConverter}}" />

<toolkit:ListPicker Header="InputScope"
    ItemsSource="{Binding InputScopeNameValues}"
    SelectedItem="{Binding InputScopeNameValue, Mode=TwoWay}">
</toolkit:ListPicker>
```

Changing the ListPicker's selected item updates the viewmodel's InputScopeNameValue property. This, in turn, causes the TextBox.InputScope property to be updated.

A custom IValueConverter is used to convert the InputScopeNameValue property, which is an enum value, to an actual InputScope, which is a DependencyObject (see Listing 6.2).

LISTING 6.2   InputScopeValueConverter Class

```csharp
public class InputScopeValueConverter : IValueConverter
{
    public object Convert(
        object value, Type targetType, object parameter, CultureInfo culture)
    {
        if (value == null)
        {
            return null;
        }
        string scopeString = value.ToString();
        InputScope inputScope = new InputScope();
        var enumValue = (InputScopeNameValue)Enum.Parse(
            typeof(InputScopeNameValue), scopeString, true);
        inputScope.Names.Add(new InputScopeName { NameValue = enumValue });
        return inputScope;
    }
```

```
public object ConvertBack(
    object value, Type targetType, object parameter, CultureInfo culture)
{
    InputScope inputScope = value as InputScope;
    if (inputScope == null)
    {
        return null;
    }

    if (inputScope.Names.Count > 0)
    {
        InputScopeName scopeName = inputScope.Names[0] as InputScopeName;
        if (scopeName != null)
        {
            return scopeName.NameValue;
        }
    }
    return null;
}
}
```

The `InputScopeValueConverter` is defined as a resource in the view, as shown:

```
<phone:PhoneApplicationPage.Resources>
    <Examples:InputScopeValueConverter x:Key="InputScopeValueConverter" />
</phone:PhoneApplicationPage.Resources>
```

The view is initially presented with the Default `InputScope` selected. This is equivalent to leaving the `TextBox.InputScope` property unset.

Figure 6.7 depicts the view with a single-line and a multiline `TextBox` each with its `InputScope` property bound to the `InputScopeNameValue` viewmodel property.

FIGURE 6.7   Text entry sample view.

When either `TextBox` is selected, the SIP is displayed. See Figure 6.8, which shows the SIP displayed with the Default `InputScope`.

FIGURE 6.8   SIP displayed with default `InputScope`.

The Silverlight Toolkit `ListPicker` control is used to select the active `InputScope` (see Figure 6.9).

FIGURE 6.9   The Windows Phone Toolkit `ListPicker` control displays the list of `InputScopeNameValues`.

When an item is selected, the viewmodel's `InputScopeNameValue` property is updated, which causes the `InputScope` of both `TextBox` controls to be updated. In Figure 6.10, you see that by selecting the `TelephoneNumber` option, the SIP switches to a set of digits.

FIGURE 6.10   The SIP is displayed using the `TelephoneNumber` input scope.

Receiving Password Text Using a `PasswordBox`

`PasswordBox` works in much the same way as the `TextBox`, allowing the user to type or edit its contents. Each character entered into a `PasswordBox`, however, appears briefly, for two seconds or until another character is entered, whichever is shorter, and is then changed to an *obscurity character*. The obscurity character is a bullet character by default.

The obscurity character can be customized using the `PasswordChar` property. For example, to use a question mark instead of the default obscurity character, the following can be used:

```
<PasswordBox PasswordChar="?" />
```

The `PasswordBox` does not contain a `Text` property, but rather a `Password` property, which is used to retrieve (or set) the password string.

Likewise, there is no `TextChanged` event, but rather a `PasswordChanged` event, which can be used to monitor when the user has finished entering a password.

Rather than relying on the `PasswordChanged` event, the `PasswordBox.Password` property can be bound to a viewmodel property, like the one shown in the following excerpt:

```
string password;

public string Password
{
    get
    {
        return password;
    }
    set
    {
        Assign(ref password, value);
    }
}
```

A `TwoWay` binding expression allows the `PasswordBox` to update the viewmodel when the password text changes, as the following excerpt demonstrates:

```
<PasswordBox PasswordChar="?" Password="{Binding Password, Mode=TwoWay}" />
```

Displaying Rich Content Using a `RichTextBox`

`RichTextBox` is a control that enables you to intermingle rich content, including hyperlinks and inline images, with text. `UIElements` can also be embedded alongside other content, allowing you to display buttons and other interactive controls directly within the `RichTextBox` content.

Unlike Silverlight for the Browser, however, the `RichTextBox` control for Windows Phone is not editable. Its `IsReadOnly` property is always true and cannot be set to false.

> **NOTE**
>
> If you attempt to set `IsReadOnly` to true in XAML a `XamlParseException` is raised; when done in code, a `NotSupportedException` is raised.

`RichTextBox` contains a collection of `Paragraph` elements. Within a `Paragraph` object are placed text and various `Inline` elements. See the following example:

```
<RichTextBox>
    <Paragraph>
        Hi from <Underline><Bold>Windows Phone</Bold>!</Underline>
    </Paragraph>
    <Paragraph>
        Paragraph 2
```

```
        </Paragraph>
    </RichTextBox>
```

Although more verbose, creating a `RichTextBox` can also be done in code, as shown:

```
void CreateRichTextBox()
{
    RichTextBox richTextBox = new RichTextBox();

    /* Create a Run of plain text and some underlined bold text. */
    Run run1 = new Run {Text = "Hi from "};
    Underline underline = new Underline();
    Bold bold = new Bold();
    bold.Inlines.Add("Windows Phone");
    underline.Inlines.Add(bold);
    Run run2 = new Run {Text = "!"};

    /* Place the inlines in a paragraph. */
    Paragraph paragraph = new Paragraph();
    paragraph.Inlines.Add(run1);
    paragraph.Inlines.Add(underline);
    paragraph.Inlines.Add(run2);

    richTextBox.Blocks.Add(paragraph);

    ContentPanel.Children.Add(richTextBox);
}
```

Within each `Paragraph` can be placed the following `Inline` elements:

- ▶ Span
- ▶ Bold
- ▶ Italic
- ▶ Underline
- ▶ Hyperlink
- ▶ InlineUIContainer
- ▶ Run

`Span`, `Bold`, `Italic`, and `Underline` are able to nest other `Inline` elements.

The `Hyperlink` element is used to embed a hyperlink within paragraph content. It behaves in much the same way as a `HyperlinkButton`, and its `NavigateUri` property is assumed to be a relative URI to a page in the app. If the URI is external, the TargetName property must be set to _blank, as shown in the following excerpt:

```
<RichTextBox>
    <Paragraph>
        This is a
        <Hyperlink NavigateUri=http://danielvaughan.org
                   TargetName="_blank">Hyperlink</Hyperlink>.
    </Paragraph>
</RichTextBox>
```

To embed a UIElement within the RichTextBox use the InlineUIContainer. In the following example, an Image control is used to display an inline image, and a Button control is placed alongside:

```
<RichTextBox>
    <Paragraph>
        <InlineUIContainer>
            <Image Source="/Images/WindowsPhoneLogo.png"
                   Height="100" Width="100" />
        </InlineUIContainer>
        <InlineUIContainer>
            <Button>button</Button>
        </InlineUIContainer>
    </Paragraph>
</RichTextBox>
```

Formatting Text at Runtime

You can format text in a RichTextBox at the paragraph-level and inline-level at runtime. The following example shows how you can right-align the entire contents of the RichTextBox within a Button.Tap event handler:

```
void Button_Tap(object sender, System.Windows.Input.GestureEventArgs e)
{
    foreach (Block block in richTextBox1.Blocks)
    {
        block.TextAlignment = TextAlignment.Right;
    }
}
```

Figure 6.11 shows the contents of a RichTextBox after it has been right-aligned via a Button placed within the Paragraph.

The source for this section is located in the RichTextBoxView page in the ControlExamples directory of the WPUnleashed.Examples project in the downloadable sample code.

FIGURE 6.11   Tapping an inline `Button` causes the `Paragraph` to be right-aligned.

While the `RichTextBox` control for Windows Phone lacks the ability to be edited by the user, it does allow you to blend text and rich content in a way that is easier than, for example, nesting `TextBlocks` and other elements within a `StackPanel`.

Further Reading

An MSDN article that includes an overview of the `RichTextBox` content model is located at http://bit.ly/nmazA0.

Placing Text on the `Clipboard`

The static `System.Windows.Clipboard` class allows you to place text on the systemwide clipboard, or to detect whether any text exists on the clipboard.

> **NOTE**
>
> You cannot retrieve the clipboard text from a Windows Phone app, only set it. Calling the `GetText` method raises a `SecurityException`.

`Clipboard` contains the following three methods:

▶ `ContainsText()`—Queries the clipboard for the presence of text. Returns true if text is present; otherwise, false.

▶ `SetText(string text)`—Places text in the clipboard.

▶ `GetText()`—Raises a `SecurityException` on the Windows Phone platform.

Placing a Unicode string on the clipboard can be performed as shown:

```
Clipboard.SetText("foo");
```

The following example shows how to detect whether text is present on the clipboard:

```
bool clipBoardHasText = Clipboard.ContainsText();
```

If the `ContainsText` method returns true it indicates that the clipboard button will be visible when the SIP is displayed (see Figure 6.12).

FIGURE 6.12   Text on the clipboard causes the SIP to display the clipboard button.

Summary

This chapter began by looking at the various types used for displaying and entering text in a Windows Phone XAML app, in particular the `TextBlock`, `TextBox`, `PasswordBox`, and `RichTextBox`. It then explored each of these elements in greater depth, starting with the `TextBlock`, where it showed how to create multiline text using `Run` and `LineBreak` objects. It then looked at font support, including the built-in fonts, and demonstrated techniques for providing custom fonts in your application using font embedding, or the `FontSource` property using a `Stream`. It also examined the SIP, and how to customize the onscreen keyboard using input scopes.

Also included in this chapter was a useful sample page that allows you to preview the various input scopes.

The chapter then looked at the `PasswordBox` and demonstrated how to bind the password string property to a viewmodel property. We then examined the `RichTextBox`, which allows you to blend text and rich content such as hyperlinks, images, and other UI elements.

Finally, the chapter looked at the clipboard, and you learned how to set the clipboard text and how to detect whether text is present on the clipboard.

CHAPTER 7

Employing Media and Web Elements

The Windows Phone SDK provides a mature set of web and media-related elements. This chapter explores some of the most feature-rich controls present in the XAML toolbox.

This chapter is jam-packed full of examples and begins by looking in depth at the `Image` element. The `InkPresenter` is discussed, and you see how to create a simple sketch app.

The `MediaElement` is also discussed and you see how it is used to play audio and video files stored locally on the phone, or streamed over the Internet. This chapter also examines a sample app that provides you with a test bed for experimenting with the `MediaElement`'s main properties.

The chapter looks at leveraging XNA within your XAML-based app to play sound effects more efficiently and at using the new Windows Phone 8 Media Library extensions to add or remove music tracks to and from the Music+Videos Hub. It then explores Deep Zoom to see how the `MultiScaleImage` element is used to provide stunning visual experiences while making efficient use of your users' bandwidth. We delve into a sample client and server application that allows the user to select and manipulate a Deep Zoom image.

Finally, the chapter explores the `WebBrowser` control, and you see how to communicate to a web page from your Windows Phone app and vice versa. You also discover how to execute arbitrary JavaScript on a web page to modify CSS styles or to attach new behaviors, and how to store and browse offline content to decrease network usage.

Displaying Images with the `Image` Element

The `Image` is a `FrameworkElement` that makes it easy to display both local or remote images on the phone.

The `Image` element supports two image formats: PNG and JPEG, and displays indexed images with 1, 4, or 8 bit color-depth, or true color images with 24 or 32 bit color-depth.

The `Image.Source` property is used to set the URI of the image file location. This value can be either an absolute or relative URI. A URI can be used to specify a source file from a variety of locations, including the following:

▶ The current assembly

▶ A referenced assembly

▶ The XAP file

▶ An external network, such as an image on the Web

Relative URIs are the most common way to identify local images in Windows Phone apps. The following example demonstrates how to display an image called Book.jpg, which is located in the root directory of a project, and which has its Build Action set to Content:

```
<Image Source="/Book.jpg" />
```

> **NOTE**
>
> When the Build Action of an image file is set to Content, its path is relative to the root of the project. Conversely, when the Build Action is set to Resource, its path is relative to the directory in which it is located.

If the image were located in a subdirectory of the project—for example, a directory called *Images*, then the `Image` element would be as follows:

```
<Image Source="/Images/Book.jpg" />
```

The trailing slash is required when referring to images with a Build Action set to Content. If using a Build Action of Resource, a trailing slash cannot be used:

```
<Image Source="Images/BookAsResource.png" />
```

> **TIP**
>
> Avoid setting the Build Action of images to Resource. Instead use the Content Build Action because this will reduce the size of your project's assembly, thus reducing the time the CLR takes to load it.

One caveat, however, is that it takes longer for the CLR to fetch a file that is content than it does to fetch a file that is a resource. This is because the image file data becomes present in memory as soon as the assembly is loaded. So, the Content build action, while reducing the startup time of your app, may lead to some images being displayed after the rest of the UI has been displayed. This is especially important for background images, whose momentary absence will be glaringly evident. The general rule: If you need an image to be loaded immediately because it is the background for a page, for example, use the Resource Build Action; otherwise, use the Content Build Action.

An absolute URI, which targets an image in the same or another assembly, can be specified using the Relative Component URI scheme, as the following example demonstrates:

```
<Image Source="/AssemblyNameWithoutTheDllExtension;component/Images/Book.png" />
```

The URL of an image located on the Web can also be specified as shown:

```
<Image Source="http://www.example.com/Images/Book.jpg" />
```

> **TIP**
>
> Try to limit the number of images in your app. Even if your image happens to be a 30KB compressed JPEG image, at runtime that image becomes an uncompressed surface that may take several MBs of memory. In most cases an application must never consume more than 90MB of RAM, unless it has more than 256MB of total memory; otherwise, it will fail Windows Phone Marketplace certification.
>
> For more information on measuring the memory available to your app, see the section "Device Status," in Chapter 2, "Fundamental Concepts in Windows Phone Development."

Working examples for each of these cases are located in the MediaExamplesView.xaml page in the downloadable sample code.

There are numerous examples of using the `Image` control throughout this book; you see how to implement image localizability, image caching, and in Chapter 14, "Leveraging Built-In Apps via Launchers and Choosers," you see how to data bind the `Image.Source` property to a viewmodel property.

Image Sizing

The size of an image control either can be set explicitly using its `Width` and `Height` properties, or the image can depend on its container to determine its size. If the container is a simple container such as a `Canvas`, the `Image` will be displayed using the native dimensions defined in the image file. The `Image.Stretch` property is used to control the sizing behavior of the `Image` when its size differs from its native image size. The `Stretch` property is of type `System.Windows.Media.Stretch`, whose values are described in Table 7.1.

TABLE 7.1   `Stretch` Enum Values and Their Effect on `Image` Sizing

Name	Description
None	The image is displayed using its native dimensions.
Fill	The image is stretched to inhabit the entirety of the `Image` control, while not obeying the aspect ratio of the native image.
Uniform	The default value. The image is given the largest size available within the Image control, while still adhering to the aspect ratio of the native image.
UniformToFill	The aspect ratio of the native image is maintained. The native image is expanded to fill the Image control in both dimensions. This may result in the image being clipped.

The effects of each of these enum values on image sizing are depicted in Figure 7.1.

The source for this section is located on the MediaExamplesView.xaml page in the ControlExamples directory of the WPUnleashed.Examples project in the downloadable sample code.

FIGURE 7.1   The `Image.Stretch` property determines how an image is sized.

Providing a Drawing Surface with the `InkPresenter` Element

`InkPresenter` provides a primitive drawing surface to collect strokes or Bézier curves within a `Canvas` control. The `InkPresenter` is derived from the `Canvas` class and includes the addition of a single property called `Strokes`, which is a collection of `Stroke` objects. A `Stroke` represents a line segment and is composed of a collection of `StylusPoints`.

The behavior of the `InkPresenter` can be likened to that of a pen and paper. When the pen makes contact with the paper, you begin a `Stroke`. As the pen moves on the paper, the `Stroke` is constructed using `StylusPoints`. When the pen leaves the paper, the `Stroke` is complete.

The appearance of a `Stroke` can be defined by using its `DrawingAttributes` property. This includes its color, height, outline, and width (see Figure 7.2).

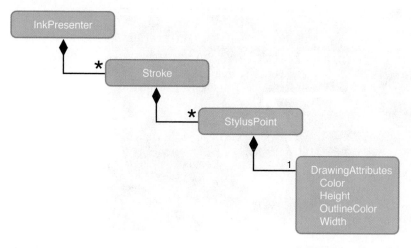

FIGURE 7.2   A `Stroke` consists of many `StylusPoint` objects.

The `InkPresenter` does not provide any specialized support for capturing touch input. Instead, `Strokes` are created either in code by subscribing to the various touch related events, which you see later in the section, or by defining a `StrokeCollection` directly in XAML, as shown:

```xml
<InkPresenter VerticalAlignment="Stretch">
    <InkPresenter.Strokes>
        <StrokeCollection>
            <Stroke>
                <Stroke.DrawingAttributes>
                    <DrawingAttributes Color="White"
                        OutlineColor="Yellow"
                        Width="20" Height="10" />
                </Stroke.DrawingAttributes>
                <Stroke.StylusPoints>
                    <StylusPoint X="118" Y="141" />

                    ...
                    <StylusPoint X="202" Y="383" />
                </Stroke.StylusPoints>
            </Stroke>
        </StrokeCollection>
```

```
        </InkPresenter.Strokes>
</InkPresenter>
```

In this excerpt, the single `Stroke` present in the `StrokeCollection` is styled using the `DrawingAttribute` element. The `OutlineColor` property is used to create a border around the `Stroke` (see Figure 7.3).

FIGURE 7.3   `InkPresenter` with a `StrokeCollection` defined in XAML.

Capturing User Input

The touch related events, `MouseLeftButtonDown`, `MouseMove`, and `MouseLeftButtonUp`, are used to collect and display strokes in the `InkPresenter` while the user interacts with the control. The following excerpt shows an `InkPresenter` with subscriptions to the three mouse events:

```
<Grid x:Name="ContentPanel" Grid.Row="1">
    <InkPresenter Strokes="{Binding Strokes}"
        VerticalAlignment="Stretch"
        Background="Black"
        MouseMove="InkPresenter_MouseMove"
        MouseLeftButtonDown="InkPresenter_MouseLeftButtonDown"
        MouseLeftButtonUp="InkPresenter_MouseLeftButtonUp" />
</Grid>
```

> **NOTE**
>
> The `Background` property of the `InkPresenter` must be assigned to register Mouse events.

Listing 7.1 shows how the mouse event handlers are used to add `Stroke` objects to the `InkPresenter` element's `Strokes` collection. When the user touches the display, the `MouseLeftButtonDown` event is raised; at that time a new `Stroke` is created and added to the `Strokes` collection. When the user moves her finger, the `MouseMove` event is raised and the handler adds new `StylusPoints` to the `Stroke`. The stylus points are accessed through the `MouseEventArgs` of both the `MouseLeftButtonDown` and `MouseMove` events. When the user lifts her finger off the display, the `MouseLeftButtonUp` handler completes the current `Stroke` by setting it to null.

LISTING 7.1   `InkPresenterView` Class—Non-MVVM (excerpt)

```
public partial class InkPresenterView : PhoneApplicationPage
{
    public InkPresenterView()
    {
        InitializeComponent();
    }

    readonly StrokeCollection strokes = new StrokeCollection();
    Stroke stroke;

    void InkPresenter_MouseLeftButtonDown(object sender, MouseButtonEventArgs e)
    {
        InkPresenter inkPresenter = (InkPresenter)sender;
        stroke = new Stroke();
        StylusPointCollection points
            = e.StylusDevice.GetStylusPoints(inkPresenter);
        stroke.StylusPoints.Add(points);
        stroke.DrawingAttributes.Color = Colors.White;
        strokes.Add(stroke);
        inkPresenter.Strokes = strokes;
    }

    void InkPresenter_MouseMove(object sender, MouseEventArgs e)
    {
        InkPresenter inkPresenter = (InkPresenter)sender;
        if (stroke != null)
        {
            stroke.StylusPoints.Add(e.StylusDevice.GetStylusPoints(inkPresenter));
        }
    }

    void InkPresenter_MouseLeftButtonUp(object sender, MouseButtonEventArgs e)
    {
        stroke = null;
    }
}
```

InkPresenter Sample Code

The sample for this section is a simple sketch page that allows the user to draw a picture, undo and redo sketch lines, and clear the page using an application bar menu item (see Figure 7.4). The code presented in this section elaborates on the previous example and takes a more MVVM-centric approach.

FIGURE 7.4　`InkPresenter` sample app.

The code for this sample is located in the `InkPresenterView` page and the `InkPresenterViewModel` class in the downloadable sample code.

An `InkPresenter` in the view is bound to the viewmodel's `StrokeCollection`. As the user interacts with the view, viewmodel commands populate the `StrokeCollection` with `Stroke` objects.

Each command is instantiated in the viewmodel's constructor. When executed, the `beginStrokeCommand` creates a new `Stroke` representing the beginning of a line drawn by the user. As the user moves a finger across the `InkPresenter`, the `setStrokePointCommand` is executed, which adds a new `StylusPoint` to the list of points for the current `Stroke`. Finally, when the user takes his finger off the display, the `endStrokeCommand` is executed setting the current `Stroke` to null (see Listing 7.2).

The viewmodel maintains a `Stack` of `Strokes`, called `undoneStrokes`, which contains strokes that have been undone by the user. The `undoCommand` pushes the last `Stroke` in the `StrokeCollection` onto `undoneStrokes` and then removes it from the `StrokesCollection`. Conversely, the `redoCommand` pops the top `Stroke` from `undoneStrokes` and places it back in the `StrokesCollection`.

LISTING 7.2   InkPresenterViewModel Class (excerpt)

```
public InkPresenterViewModel() : base("InkPresenter")
{
    beginStrokeCommand = new DelegateCommand<Point>(
        point =>
            {
                stroke = new Stroke();
                stroke.StylusPoints.Add(ConvertToStylusPoint(point));
                stroke.DrawingAttributes.Color = stylusColor;
                strokes.Add(stroke);
            });

    setStrokePointCommand = new DelegateCommand<Point>(
        point =>
            {
                if (stroke != null)
                {
                    stroke.StylusPoints.Add(ConvertToStylusPoint(point));
                }
            });
    endStrokeCommand = new DelegateCommand(obj => stroke = null);

    clearCommand = new DelegateCommand(obj => strokes.Clear());

    undoCommand = new DelegateCommand(
        delegate
            {
                if (strokes.Count > 0)
                {
                    undoneStrokes.Push(strokes.Last());
                    strokes.RemoveAt(strokes.Count - 1);
                }
            });

    redoCommand = new DelegateCommand(
        delegate
            {
                if (undoneStrokes.Count > 0)
                {
                    strokes.Add(undoneStrokes.Pop());
                }
            });
}
```

7

The `BeginStrokeCommand`, `SetStrokePointCommand`, and `EndStrokeCommand` are executed when the `InkPresenters` element's `MouseLeftButtonDown`, `MouseMove`, and `MouseLeftButtonUp` events are raised, respectively (see Listing 7.3).

LISTING 7.3   `InkPresenterView` Class

```
public partial class InkPresenterView : PhoneApplicationPage
{
    public InkPresenterView()
    {
        InitializeComponent();
        DataContext = new InkPresenterViewModel();
    }


    InkPresenterViewModel ViewModel
    {
        get
        {
            return (InkPresenterViewModel)DataContext;
        }
    }
    void InkPresenter_MouseMove(object sender, MouseEventArgs e)
    {
        InkPresenter inkPresenter = (InkPresenter)sender;
        ViewModel.SetStrokePointCommand.Execute(e.GetPosition(inkPresenter));
    }

    void InkPresenter_MouseLeftButtonDown(
            object sender, MouseButtonEventArgs e)
    {
        InkPresenter inkPresenter = (InkPresenter)sender;
        ViewModel.BeginStrokeCommand.Execute(e.GetPosition(inkPresenter));
    }

    void InkPresenter_MouseLeftButtonUp(object sender, MouseButtonEventArgs e)
    {
        ViewModel.EndStrokeCommand.Execute(null);
    }
}
```

The three commands `UndoCommand`, `RedoCommand`, and `ClearCommand` are executed via the custom `ApplicationBar` wrapper, named `AppBar`, in the view. The `AppBar` is discussed further in Chapter 8, "Taming the Application Bar."

```
<u:AppBar IsEnabled="True" IsVisible="True" IsMenuEnabled="True">
    <u:AppBarIconButton
```

```
        Command="{Binding UndoCommand}"
        Text="Undo"
        IconUri="/ControlExamples/Images/AppBarArrowUndo.png" />
    <u:AppBarIconButton
        Command="{Binding RedoCommand}"
        Text="Redo"
        IconUri="/ControlExamples/Images/AppBarArrowRedo.png" />
    <u:AppBar.MenuItems>
        <u:AppBarMenuItem
            Command="{Binding ClearCommand}"
            Text="Clear" />
    </u:AppBar.MenuItems>
</u:AppBar>
```

When the Undo or Redo buttons are pressed, the associated viewmodel command is executed. In addition, when the user taps the Clear button in the application bar menu the `ClearCommand` is executed, removing all items from the `StrokeCollection` in the viewmodel.

Playing Audio and Video with the `MediaElement`

`MediaElement` allows you to play audio and video from a file located in the app's XAP file, from isolated storage, or by streaming it from a remote location. `MediaElement` is a `FrameworkElement` that provides a rectangular region used for displaying video on its surface.

To show video content in your app, place the `MediaElement` markup where you want the video to be displayed, as shown in the following example:

```
<MediaElement Source="http://www.example.net/Video.wmv" />
```

After the `MediaElement` is loaded, it begins to download and play the content.

> **NOTE**
>
> The XNA `SoundEffect` class is better suited to playing short sound effects. There can be a slight delay when first playing a sound using the `MediaElement` class, which the `SoundEffect` class does not suffer from. The `SoundEffect` class also does not need to reside in your page's visual tree. See later in this chapter for an overview of the `SoundEffect` class.

The `Source` property indicates the location of the media file or stream and functions in the same manner as the `Image` element's `Source` property (see the previous "Displaying Images with the Image Element" section).

By default, the `MediaElement` begins playback as soon as it loads. To prevent this, set its `AutoPlay` property to `false`. Then playback will not occur until the `MediaElement`'s `Play` method is called. Two other methods provide playback control: `Pause` and `Stop`.

Controlling Audio Output

The `MediaElement` allows control of audio output, via its `IsMuted`, `Volume`, and `Balance` properties.

The `Volume` property, a `double` value with a range between 0 and 1, allows control of the audio volume level.

`Balance`, a `double` value with a range between –1 and 1, allows control over the output to the left or right speaker. Its default value, 0, represents the center balance.

Streaming Content

For content located on a remote server, the `DownloadProgress` property indicates the proportion of the download completed. The range of this property is between 0 and 1, inclusively. Multiply this value by 100 to calculate the percentage. When the `DownloadProgress` property is changed, the `DownloadProgressChanged` event is raised.

The `Position` property is used to seek to a location within a file or stream during playback. When a user skips to a location ahead of what has already been downloaded (for example, 5 minutes into a video), the `DownloadProgressOffset` property is set to this value.

The `BufferingProgress` property indicates the proportion of the stream that has been downloaded in relation to the minimum buffering time. This property also has a range between 0 and 1. When the value changes by more than 0.05, or a value of 1 is reached, the `BufferingProgressChanged` event is raised.

The buffering time is specified using the `BufferingTime` property, which has a default value of 5 seconds.

The `MediaElement` control has several read-only properties, such as the `BufferingProgress` property, which makes data binding to them difficult. Fortunately, there are events that provide the opportunity to update viewmodel or code-beside properties.

`MediaElement` Sample Code

The sample for this section is a media viewer page, which allows you to specify a URL to a media file and view and/or listen to the file. This sample demonstrates the main features of the `MediaElement` and gives you a test bed for exploring the `MediaElement`'s main properties and methods.

The sample code is located in the `MediaView` page and `MediaViewModel` class in the downloadable sample code.

The `MediaViewModel` class uses four commands to toggle the playback state of the `MediaElement` and to mute and unmute audio. When the `PlayCommand` is executed, it updates the PlayerState property, signaling to the view to begin playback. Likewise, the PauseCommand signals to the view that playback should be paused, as shown in the following excerpt:

```
public MediaViewModel() : base("Media View")
{
    playCommand = new DelegateCommand(
        obj =>
        {
                PlayerState = PlayerState.Playing;
                CanPlay = false;
                CanPause = true;
        });

    pauseCommand = new DelegateCommand(
        obj =>
        {
            PlayerState = PlayerState.Paused;
            CanPause = false;
            CanPlay = true;
        });

    muteCommand = new DelegateCommand(obj => Muted = true);

    unMuteCommand = new DelegateCommand(obj => Muted = false);
}
```

This example uses the PropertyChanged event of the viewmodel to signal that the MediaElement should pause or resume playback.

The MediaViewModel contains numerous properties that are consumed by the MediaElement in the view and that for the sake of brevity are not shown.

Much of the code in the view serves to update viewmodel properties when MediaElement events are raised. For example, when the DownloadProgressChanged event is raised, the viewmodel's DownloadProgress and DownloadProgressOffset properties are updated (see Listing 7.4).

LISTING 7.4   MediaView Class (excerpt)

```
public partial class MediaView : PhoneApplicationPage
{
    public MediaView()
    {
        InitializeComponent();
        MediaViewModel viewModel = new MediaViewModel();
        DataContext = viewModel;
```

```csharp
        viewModel.PropertyChanged += viewModel_PropertyChanged;
}


void viewModel_PropertyChanged(object sender, PropertyChangedEventArgs e)
{
    if (e.PropertyName == "PlayerState")
    {
        switch (ViewModel.PlayerState)
        {
            case PlayerState.Stopped:
                mediaElement.Stop();
                break;
            case PlayerState.Playing:
                mediaElement.Play();
                break;
            case PlayerState.Paused:
                mediaElement.Pause();
                break;
        }
    }
}


void mediaElement_DownloadProgressChanged(object sender, RoutedEventArgs e)
{
    MediaElement element = (MediaElement)sender;
    ViewModel.DownloadProgress = element.DownloadProgress;
    ViewModel.DownloadProgressOffset = element.DownloadProgressOffset;
}


void mediaElement_BufferingProgressChanged(
        object sender, RoutedEventArgs e)
{
    MediaElement element = (MediaElement)sender;
    ViewModel.BufferingProgress = element.BufferingProgress;
    ViewModel.DownloadProgressOffset = element.DownloadProgressOffset;
}
void mediaElement_MediaOpened(object sender, RoutedEventArgs e)
{
    MediaElement element = (MediaElement)sender;
    ViewModel.PlayLength = element.NaturalDuration.TimeSpan;
}


void mediaElement_CurrentStateChanged(object sender, RoutedEventArgs e)
{
    MediaElement element = (MediaElement)sender;
    ViewModel.MediaElementState = element.CurrentState;
```

```
        ViewModel.CanSeek = element.CanSeek;
        ViewModel.CanPause = element.CanPause;
    }


    void mediaElement_MediaFailed(object sender, ExceptionRoutedEventArgs e)
    {
        ViewModel.HandleMediaFailed(e.ErrorException);
    }
}
```

When a command, such as the `PlayCommand`, is executed via a button in the view, the viewmodel causes the `MediaElement` to play by updating its `PlayerState` property, which then raises the `PropertyChanged` event, handled in the view.

Various `MediaElement` properties are bound to the viewmodel, as shown:

```
<MediaElement x:Name="mediaElement" Grid.Row="1"
            DownloadProgressChanged="mediaElement_DownloadProgressChanged"
            BufferingProgressChanged="mediaElement_BufferingProgressChanged"
            Source="{Binding MediaUri, Mode=TwoWay}"
            Position="{Binding Position, Mode=TwoWay}"
            MediaOpened="mediaElement_MediaOpened"
            CurrentStateChanged="mediaElement_CurrentStateChanged"
            AutoPlay="{Binding AutoPlay}"
            BufferingTime="{Binding BufferingTime, Mode=TwoWay}"
            IsMuted="{Binding Muted}"
            Volume="{Binding Volume}"
            Balance="{Binding Balance}"
            MediaFailed="mediaElement_MediaFailed" />
```

Two viewmodel properties are employed to track and control the position of the current media file: `Position` and `SliderPosition`.

> **NOTE**
>
> Avoid placing a two-way data binding on the `MediaElement.Position` property to a source object that raises a `PropertyChanged` event. Doing so causes the `MediaElement` to stutter as it continually tries to return to the `Position` at the time when event was raised.

The view contains two sections. The upper section holds the `MediaElement`, and the lower holds various controls for modifying the `MediaElement` properties, for monitoring download progress, and so forth. There is a position `Slider` that tracks the position of the media and allows the user to seek to a different position. Moving the position `Slider` causes the download and buffer-related progress bars to provide feedback to the user (see Figure 7.5).

FIGURE 7.5   Playing a video in the `MediaView`.

The lower section of the view contains a `ScrollViewer`, allowing access, for example, to the autoplay `CheckBox` (see Listing 7.5).

LISTING 7.5   MediaView.xaml `ScrollViewer` (styling removed)

```
<ScrollViewer Height="400" Grid.Row="1"
        VerticalScrollBarVisibility="Visible">
    <StackPanel Margin="12,0,12,0">
        <TextBlock Text="Position" />
        <TextBlock Text="{Binding SliderPosition}" />
        <Slider Value="{Binding SliderPosition, Mode=TwoWay,
                    Converter={StaticResource TimespanToDoubleConverter}}"
            Maximum="{Binding PlayLength,
            Converter={StaticResource TimespanToDoubleConverter}}"
            IsEnabled="{Binding CanSeek}" />

        <TextBlock Text="{Binding MediaElementState}" />

        <TextBlock Text="{Binding Message}" />

        <TextBlock Text="Download Progress" />
        <ProgressBar Value="{Binding DownloadProgress}"
            Minimum="0" Maximum="1" />
```

```xaml
            <TextBlock Text="Download Progress Offset" />
            <ProgressBar Value="{Binding DownloadProgressOffset}"
                Minimum="0" Maximum="1" />

            <TextBlock Text="Buffer Progress" />
            <ProgressBar Value="{Binding BufferingProgress}"
                Minimum="0" Maximum="1" />

            <TextBlock Text="Volume" />
            <Slider Value="{Binding Volume, Mode=TwoWay}"
                Maximum="1" LargeChange=".1" />

            <TextBlock Text="Balance" />
            <Slider Value="{Binding Balance, Mode=TwoWay}"
                Minimum="-1"  Maximum="1" LargeChange=".1" />
            <TextBlock Text="Buffering Time" />
            <TextBlock Text="{Binding BufferingTime}" />
            <Slider Value="{Binding BufferingTime, Mode=TwoWay,
                Converter={StaticResource TimespanToDoubleConverter}}"
                Maximum="60000" LargeChange="10000" />
            <CheckBox IsChecked="{Binding AutoPlay, Mode=TwoWay}"
                Content="Auto Play" />
        </StackPanel>
</ScrollViewer>
```

An `AppBar` control is used in the sample page, which provides data binding and commanding support. A custom `AppBarToggleButton` allows the use of two commands in conjunction with a `Toggled` property, which allows one of the commands to be enabled depending on the value of the property. If the `Toggled` property is `false`, `Command1`, `Text1`, and `Icon1Uri` are used; if set to `true`, the second set is used. For more information regarding the `ApplicationBar`, and the custom `AppBar` control used here, see Chapter 8.

`PlayCommand` becomes active if the `CanPlay` property of the viewmodel is `true`; when the `CanPlay` property evaluates to false, the button text is replaced along with its icon, and the `PauseCommand` becomes active (see Listing 7.6).

LISTING 7.6   MediaView.xaml `AppBar`

```xaml
<u:AppBar IsEnabled="True"
        IsVisible="True"
        IsMenuEnabled="True">
    <u:AppBarToggleButton
        Command1="{Binding PauseCommand}"
        Text1="Pause"
        Icon1Uri="/ControlExamples/MediaView/Images/Pause.png"
```

```
                    Command2="{Binding PlayCommand}"
                    Text2="Play"
                    Icon2Uri="/ControlExamples/MediaView/Images/Play.png"
                    Toggled="{Binding CanPlay}" />
        <u:AppBarToggleButton
                    x:Name="button_Mute"
                    Command1="{Binding MuteCommand}"
                    Text1="Mute"
                    Icon1Uri="/ControlExamples/MediaView/Images/Speaker.png"
                    Command2="{Binding UnMuteCommand}"
                    Text2="Un-Mute"
                    Icon2Uri="/ControlExamples/MediaView/Images/Mute.png"
                    Toggled="{Binding Muted}" />
    </u:AppBar>
```

Tapping the mute button executes the `MuteCommand`, which updates the `Muted` property in the viewmodel, updating the `MediaElement` control via a data binding. When muted, the property changed event for the `Muted` property indicates to the `AppBarToggleButton` that `Command2`, `Text2`, and `Icon2Uri` should be used (see Figure 7.6).

FIGURE 7.6   Scrolling to the bottom of the view reveals the Balance, Buffering Time, and Auto Play settings.

XNA `SoundEffect` **Class**

Sometimes being a Windows Phone developer means being spoiled for choice. The XNA FCL contains various classes that you can harness in your XAML-based apps, and vice versa. One such class is the `SoundEffect` class, which is a lightweight class that allows you to specify an audio file and to play it from code without relying on, for example, the `MediaElement` control.

The `SoundEffect` class works well for short samples, where instant playback is required. `SoundEffect` provides support for controlling volume, panning, looping, and pitch of the audio, and even allows you to apply 3D audio effects. Be warned, however, that it is fussy about the format of the audio. I found that only PCM format wav files are supported. I recommend using a tool like GoldWave (www.goldwave.com/) to save all audio to a PCM format. For longer clips, it makes more sense to use a more space efficient format, such as MP3, but for this you need to use the `MediaElement` control.

To use the `SoundEffect` class, the Build Action of all audio files that you intend to be played must be set as Content.

A sound effect can be defined in your page code-beside, as demonstrated:

```
readonly SoundEffect footstepSoundEffect
    = SoundEffect.FromStream(TitleContainer.OpenStream("Audio/Footstep.wav"));
```

The `SoundEffect` can then be played like so:

```
FrameworkDispatcher.Update();
footstepSoundEffect.Play();
```

NOTE

Calling `FrameworkDispatcher.Update` regularly is necessary for the XNA infrastructure to function correctly and for fire and forget sound effects to function correctly. If not called, an `InvalidOperationException` will be thrown.

Configuring a XAML-based app to work correctly with the XNA framework is discussed in the following section.

Behind the scenes a `SoundEffectInstance` object is automatically created from the `SoundEffect` class as soon as the `Play` method is called. You can create multiple `SoundEffectInstance` objects and play them from a single `SoundEffect`. The benefit of using `SoundEffectInstances` is that these objects share the resources of their parent `SoundEffect`, and also that a `SoundEffect` object can be used to control all its `SoundEffectInstance` sounds. The `SoundEffect.MasterVolume` property, for example, can be used to modulate the volume of all child `SoundEffectInstances`.

Use the `CreateInstance` method of the `SoundEffect` class, to create a new `SoundEffectInstance`, as shown:

```
SoundEffectInstance instance = footStepSoundEffect.CreateInstance();
```

NOTE

A maximum of 16 `SoundEffectInstance` instances can be playing at one time, combined across all loaded `SoundEffect` objects. Attempting to play more than 16 has no effect.

NOTE

A `SoundEffect` continues to hold its memory resources throughout its lifetime. All `SoundEffectInstance` objects created from a `SoundEffect` share memory resources. When a `SoundEffect` object is destroyed, all `SoundEffectInstance` objects previously created by that `SoundEffect` will stop playing and become invalid.

Both the `SoundEffect` class and the `SoundEffectInstance` class implement `IDisposable`. When you are finished using an instance of either type, be sure to call its `Dispose` method to free valuable resources.

Harnessing the XNA Game Loop Via the `GameTimer` Class

In XNA, responding to user input, updating your app's state, and drawing content all happen periodically within the *game loop*. The game loop is the heart of every XNA game, and understanding it is fundamental to XNA development.

Unlike pure XNA games, which use the `Game` class for the game loop, hybrid apps rely on the `Microsoft.Xna.Framework.GameTimer`, which is unique to the phone.

In a pure XNA game, a `Game` class is used instead of an `Application` class. XNA games rely on overloading `Game` class methods that are specific to the game loop, such as `Update` and `Draw`, whereas hybrid apps (Windows Phone 7.1 apps that combine XNA and Silverlight) and apps that rely on XNA APIs, such as the sound effect API, use the `GameTimer` class instead. The `GameTimer` class offers various game loop events that correspond to methods of the same name in ordinary XNA games.

`GameTimer` has three events: `Draw`, `FrameAction`, and `Update`. When raised, the `Draw` and `Update` events deliver a `GameTimerEventArgs` object, which contains the same timing information as the `GameTime` object provided to the `Game.Update` and `Game.Draw` methods.

The `GameTimer` class extends the functionality around the game loop, going beyond the `Game` class by allowing you to create multiple `GameTimer` instances, each dedicated to drawing particular objects or sets of objects in your UI. The order in which the `Draw` event is raised for different `GameTimer` instances can be controlled using the `GameTimer.DrawOrder` property. `DrawOrder` indicates the order in which `Draw` events are called when more than one timer has the event raised at the same time. `GameTimer` objects with lower DrawOrder values have their event handlers called before those of GameTimer objects with higher values.

For example, the following excerpt shows three GameTimers. Each has a subscription to its Draw event, and each specifies a different DrawOrder value:

```
timer1.Draw += delegate { Debug.WriteLine("Timer 1"); };
timer1.DrawOrder = 10;

timer2.Draw += delegate { Debug.WriteLine("Timer 2"); };
timer2.DrawOrder = 100;

timer3.Draw += delegate { Debug.WriteLine("Timer 3"); };
timer3.DrawOrder = 1;
```

By specifying a lower DrawOrder value, the event handler of timer3 is called first, and timer2, having the highest DrawOrder, is called last. See the following output:

```
Timer 3
Timer 1
Timer 2
Timer 3
Timer 1
Timer 2
...
```

The other two GameTimer properties: GameTimer.UpdateOrder and FrameActionOrder, are analogous to the DrawOrder property yet pertain to the Update and FrameAction events, respectively.

Controlling the Interval Between Updates

The GameTimer.UpdateInterval property allows you to explicitly set the time between updates. By default this value is 333333 ticks or ~33 ms. A tick is the smallest unit of time, equal to 100 nanoseconds. This equates to 30 frames a second.

> **NOTE**
>
> Be careful when explicitly setting UpdateInterval. If set too short and the event handler consistently runs longer than the time interval set by UpdateInterval, game performance is adversely affected.

XNA Environment Initialization

When the Windows Phone XAML and XNA project template is used to create a Windows Phone 7.1 hybrid app, a region is generated within the App class for the purpose of initializing the XNA content manager and starting a GameTimer object. By default, a

ContentManager is exposed as a public property within your App class, allowing it to be consumed across your application. You can, however, create new instances of the ContentManager class if you want.

When instantiating a ContentManager, it must be passed an IServiceProvider that can later be used to retrieve an IGraphicsDeviceService. The App class implements IServiceProvider, and the IServiceProvider.GetService method implementation returns objects that reside in the ApplicationLifetimeObjects collection.

Because the App class implements the IServiceProvider interface, it is able to pass itself to the ContentManager constructor, providing the ContentManager access to an IGraphicsDeviceService, which, in this case, is a SharedGraphicsDeviceManager. See the following excerpt:

```
#region XNA application initialization

// Performs initialization of the XNA types required for the application.
void InitializeXnaApplication()
{
    // Create the ContentManager
    // so the application can load precompiled assets.
    ContentManager = new ContentManager(this, "Content");

    // Create a GameTimer to pump the XNA FrameworkDispatcher.
    GameTimer frameworkDispatcherTimer = new GameTimer();
    frameworkDispatcherTimer.FrameAction += FrameworkDispatcherFrameAction;
    frameworkDispatcherTimer.Start();
}


// An event handler that pumps the FrameworkDispatcher each frame.
// FrameworkDispatcher is required for a lot of the XNA events and
// for certain functionality such as SoundEffect playback.
void FrameworkDispatcherFrameAction(object sender, EventArgs e)
{
    FrameworkDispatcher.Update();
}

#endregion
```

The FrameworkDispatcher.Update method triggers event processing in the XNA framework. In a pure XNA app, it is automatically called whenever Game.Update is called. In XAML apps, however, the absence of a Game class means that we rely on a GameTimer instance to raise a manual call to FrameworkDispatcher.Update.

Saving Music to the Media Library

In Windows Phone 8 you can now add and remove music files from the user's music collection with the SaveSong and Delete methods that extend the MediaLibrary class. This allows you to create feature-rich music apps that tightly integrate with the phone's Music+Videos Hub.

This API is found in the Microsoft.Xna.Framework.Media.PhoneExtensions namespace in the assembly Microsoft.Xna.Framework.MediaLibraryExtensions.dll.

The sample for this section is located in the MediaLibrary directory of the WPUnleashed.Examples project, in the downloadable sample code.

To add a track to the media library, place the file in isolated storage and create an instance of the SongMetadata class to describe the attributes of the track. This includes album and artist details as well as album art. The following excerpt from the sample's MediaLibraryViewModel class saves a track's audio file and image to isolated storage. It then calls the MediaLibrary class's SaveSong method to add the track to the Music+Videos Hub, as shown:

```
void SaveSong()
{
    CopyAudioToStorage();

    Uri songUri = new Uri("MediaLibrary/Sample.wma", UriKind.Relative);
    Uri artUri = new Uri("MediaLibrary/Sample.jpg", UriKind.Relative);

    SongMetadata metadata = new SongMetadata
        {
            Name = "Unleashed Jingle",
            AlbumName = "Dev Hits 2013",
            AlbumArtUri = artUri
        };

    MediaLibrary mediaLibrary = new MediaLibrary();
    mediaLibrary.SaveSong(songUri, metadata, SaveSongOperation.CopyToLibrary);

    MessageService.ShowMessage("'Unleashed Jingle' is now located "
                    + "in the Music section of the Music+Pictures Hub.");
}
```

The SaveSong method accepts a SaveSongOperation argument that can be either CopyToLibrary or MoveToLibrary. MoveToLibrary deletes the file from isolated storage on completion, whereas CopyToLibrary leaves the source file in its current location.

After it is saved, the track appears in the Music+Videos Hub, as shown in Figure 7.7.

FIGURE 7.7   A track is added to the Music+Pictures Hub.

The `MediaLibrary` class allows you to retrieve the list of songs from the Music+Videos Hub and to delete items from the list. The following excerpt from the `MediaLibraryViewModel` retrieves a previously added track from the `Songs` collection using LINQ, and removes the song by calling the MediaLibrary class's `Delete` method:

```
void DeleteSong()
{
    MediaLibrary mediaLibrary = new MediaLibrary();
    Song savedSong = mediaLibrary.Songs.SingleOrDefault(
        song => song.Name == "Unleashed Jingle");

    if (savedSong == null)
    {
        MessageService.ShowMessage("Song not found.");
        return;
    }

    mediaLibrary.Delete(savedSong);
}
```

The `Delete` method presents a built-in confirmation dialog to the user before the item is physically removed from the media library. This prevents apps from indiscriminately deleting items and gives the user peace of mind.

The `Delete` method performs a cascading delete, so that if the song is the last song in the Album and the Album is the last Album for an Artist, the Album and Artist are also deleted from the media library.

Viewing High-Resolution Images with the `MultiScaleImage` Element

Providing web content optimized for mobile devices is an important challenge facing developers today. The high cost of data plans and relatively low connection speeds provided by many telcos mean phone app developers need to be mindful of techniques that can minimize network usage.

The `MultiScaleImage` class is one of the key elements of Silverlight's Deep Zoom technology. Deep Zoom allows an application to interactively view high-resolution images and to limit the download of image content to portions of an image that are being viewed on the screen and at a resolution appropriate to the scale of the image at the time.

Downloading only part of an image can vastly decrease the time it takes to present the initial view of the image, and it unlocks user exploration of high resolution images, which would otherwise consume too much bandwidth.

`MultiScaleImage` works well on the phone and is even more suited to the phone than to the browser or desktop because of Windows Phone's touch support, allowing the user to pinch to zoom, for example.

Potential uses of Deep Zoom technology include mapping, photo galleries, high-resolution images, and interactive ads.

`MultiScaleImage` is modeled after `MediaElement` and allows a user to open a multiresolution image or collection of images. Multiresolution images can be created using a free tool provided by Microsoft called the *Deep Zoom Composer*.

When a Deep Zoom image is first viewed, it is normally presented in its entirety scaled-up at a low resolution and allowing the user to drill down into the image. When drilling down, higher resolution subimages (or tiles) are retrieved, which blend with the larger and lower-resolution portion of the image.

> **NOTE**
>
> An image that is loaded by the `MultiScaleImage` control zooms out (expands) when first loaded. This behavior can be disabled by setting the `UseSprings` property to false.

As the user explores the image by panning and zooming, higher detail tile images are downloaded and blended in. This is like the interlacing feature of the GIF image format. At first the image appears to be fuzzy and blurry, but as more information is downloaded from the server, the image becomes more crisp. As a result, Deep Zoom images can be opened faster, regardless of file size, because they do not require a substantial part of the image to be downloaded before being displayed.

NOTE

Deep Zoom incurs an overall download penalty of approximately 33% in the worst-case scenario, which occurs if all the subimages are downloaded.

A compelling feature in Deep Zoom is that multiple images can be used to compose a scene, and they can be optimized individually while still maintaining the overall appearance of the image. Collections of images can also be manipulated programmatically.

Image Tiling

When exporting an image from Deep Zoom Composer at design-time, each image in the composition is partitioned (or sliced) into tiles. During the tiling process, an image pyramid is created of various resolutions. At the base of the pyramid sits the highest-resolution image, composed of multiple tiles, and at the top of the pyramid is a single tile, the lowest resolution image (see Figure 7.8).

FIGURE 7.8   Image tiling (image from MSDN).

The tiles produced by Deep Zoom Composer are supposed to be 256 by 256 pixels. I found, however, that the nominal tile size is 258 by 258 pixels. Each zoom level is scaled by a factor of two compared to the level above. However, most images won't come in multiples of 258 pixels, and the resulting tile sets will usually contain many tiles with fewer than 258 pixels in width or height.

Creating a Deep Zoom Image

To begin creating your own Deep Zoom image, download and install the Deep Zoom Composer from Microsoft.com at http://bit.ly/hwf8Wp.

The Deep Zoom Composer has a built-in user guide. To view it, within Deep Zoom Composer press F1, or select the User Guide menu item from the Help menu. The user guide provides a good overview of using the tool, as well as some more advanced concepts that are not covered here, such as creating panoramic images and image hotspots.

In the example for this chapter, I created a Deep Zoom image composed of two images: a wide shot, and a zoomed in close-up. To do this, I created a new project (select File, New Project) within Deep Zoom Composer. I then used the Add Image button, located on the Import tab, to insert the images.

Composing the Deep Zoom image involved resizing and positioning the close-up shot, so that it blended into to the wide shot (see Figure 7.9).

FIGURE 7.9   Composing a Deep Zoom image within Deep Zoom Composer.

When I was happy with the composition, I switched to the Export tab.

Various options exist for outputting the Deep Zoom image. For hosting on your own website, select the Silverlight Deep Zoom option button. The generated output includes Visual Studio projects that you probably will not need, so select an output location that is independent from your Windows Phone app (see Figure 7.10).

When the exporting process is complete, the Deep Zoom image files are located at \DeepZoomProjectSite\ClientBin\GeneratedImages in the output directory. This directory can be placed in a web application that will be accessible to your Windows Phone app.

The filename of the generated Deep Zoom image, and to which you point the `MultiScaleImage`, is dzc_output.xml. It contains references to other image definition files in subdirectories, along with image metadata.

FIGURE 7.10   Exporting a Deep Zoom image from Deep Zoom Composer.

Exploring the `MultiScaleImage` API

Before diving into the sample code for this section, let's look at some of the key features of the `MultiScaleImage` API.

Instantiating a `MultiScaleImage` can be done in XAML, as shown:

```
<MultiScaleImage Source="http://www.example.com/dzc_output.xml" />
```

Or in code:

```
MultiScaleImage multiScaleImage = new MultiScaleImage();
multiScaleImage.Source = new DeepZoomImageTileSource(
        new Uri("http://www.example.com/dzc_output.xml"));
```

`Source` Property

When set in XAML, the `Source` property of the `MultiScaleImage` indicates the URL of the Deep Zoom image definition file, an XML file containing image metadata, and paths to subimage definition files. The `Source` property type is, however, an abstract class called `MultiScaleTileSource`, with an abstract method `GetTileLayers`. This offers an extensibility point for generating dynamic Deep Zoom images, although that is beyond the scope of this book.

Logical and Element Coordinates

As you see, some properties and methods of the `MultiScaleImage` rely on logical coordinates rather than element coordinates. Logical coordinates (also known as normalized coordinates) are points whose X and Y axis values are between 0 and 1. The methods `ElementToLogicalPoint` and `LogicalToElementPoint` are used to convert to and from both coordinate types. For example, calling `ElementToLogicalPoint` with a touch `Point` at the center of the control, returns a `Point` with X and Y coordinates of 0.5. Conversely, calling `LogicalToElementPoint`, with a `Point(0.5, 0.5)` and where the control measures 200 by 200 pixels, returns a `Point` with X and Y coordinates of 100.

`SubImages` Property

The `SubImages` property provides access to a collection of `MultiScaleSubImage` objects, which is populated if the Deep Zoom image is composed of multiple images, rather than a single high-resolution image. This is useful if you want to programmatically move individual images around the screen, or filter your images.

`ViewportOrigin` and `ViewportWidth` Properties

The `ViewportOrigin` and `ViewportWidth` properties are both `Point` objects that use logical coordinates. They work in conjunction to determine the zoom level of the image and the visible area of the image. The `ViewportOrigin` specifies the position of the image and is the location of the top-left corner of the image, whereas the `ViewportWidth` is how wide the viewport window is relative to the entire image. In other words, `ViewportWidth` is the fraction of the width of the image that is visible. The following is a list of `ViewportWidth` values and their effects:

▶ `ViewportWidth = 1`—When equal to one, the entire image is displayed. This is the default value.

▶ `ViewportWidth < 1`—When less than 1, the image is zoomed in. The closer you get to zero, the more zoomed in the image appears. Zero is completely zoomed in and the user cannot see the image at all.

▶ `ViewportWidth > 1`—When greater than 1, the image is zoomed out, and the value indicates the number of times that the viewport is larger than the image.

The width of the viewport specifies by how much to zoom in or out of the image, but it does not specify where on the image the viewport is positioned. To specify the viewport position, use the `ViewportOrigin`.

`ZoomAboutLogicalPoint` Method

This method enables zooming and panning on the `MultiScaleImage`, relative to a specified logical coordinate. This method takes a `zoomIncrementFactor`, a double that indicates by how much to change the existing zoom level.

UseSprings **Property**

The UseSprings property is used to enable or disable the animations that occur transitioning to a new zoom level or panning, such as when ZoomAboutLogicalPoint is called. The default value is true.

AllowDownloading **Property**

The AllowDownloading property can be used to halt downloading of image data at any time. This can be useful for halting bandwidth usage when leaving a Wi-Fi connected area.

MotionFinished **Event**

The MotionFinished event is raised when a zoom or pan animation ends. This event can be used as an alternative to data binding to the ViewportOrigin and/or ViewportWidth properties because sometimes change events fail to be raised when using these properties.

Deep Zoom Viewer Sample Code

The sample code for this section is located in the DeepZoomView page and DeepZoomViewModel class, in the downloadable sample code.

The sample allows the selection of a Deep Zoom image, via a ListPicker control. The interface harnesses touch for zooming and panning of the MultiScaleImage control (see Figure 7.11).

For information on the ListPicker control, see Chapter 9, "Enriching the User Experience with the Windows Phone Toolkit Controls." For information on touch, see Chapter 12, "Processing Touch Input."

FIGURE 7.11   Selecting a Deep Zoom image to explore.

The view contains a grid with a `ListPicker`, which is data bound to an `ObservableCollection` of custom `DeepZoomSource` objects. Each `DeepZoomSource` holds the name and URL of a Deep Zoom image. When the user selects a different item from the `ListPicker`, the `SelectedItem` property of the `ListPicker` is updated, which updates the `DeepZoomSource` viewmodel property. See the following excerpt:

```
<Grid Grid.Row="1">
    <toolkit:ListPicker ItemsSource="{Binding DeepZoomSources}"
        SelectedItem="{Binding DeepZoomSource, Mode=TwoWay}">
        <toolkit:ListPicker.ItemTemplate>
            <DataTemplate>
                <TextBlock Text="{Binding Name}"
                Style="{StaticResource PhoneTextTitle2Style}"
                Foreground="{StaticResource PhoneContrastForegroundBrush}"
                Margin="12, 10, 12, 10" />
            </DataTemplate>
        </toolkit:ListPicker.ItemTemplate>
    </toolkit:ListPicker>
</Grid>
```

The `MultiScaleImage` is located in a second `Grid` and has its `Source` property bound to the `Url` property of the viewmodel's `DeepZoomSource` property. Thus, changing the item in the `ListPicker` switches the Deep Zoom image.

For the sake of simplicity, the logic for zooming and dragging is placed in the view code-beside. A Windows Phone Toolkit `GestureListener` is placed in the `Grid` as shown to monitor touch gestures, so that we can respond by zooming and dragging the `MultiScaleImage`:

```
<Grid x:Name="ContentPanel" Grid.Row="2">
    <toolkit:GestureService.GestureListener>
        <toolkit:GestureListener
        PinchStarted="OnPinchStarted"
        PinchDelta="OnPinchDelta"
        DragStarted="OnDragStarted"
        DragDelta="OnDragDelta" />
    </toolkit:GestureService.GestureListener>
    <MultiScaleImage x:Name="multiScaleImage"
        Source="{Binding DeepZoomSource.Url}" />
</Grid>
```

The view contains a method called `Zoom`, which uses the `MultiScaleImage.ZoomAboutLogicalPoint` to zoom in or out of the image. We constrain the zoom level to be greater than, or equal to, half the initial size of the image, as shown:

```
double zoomLevel = 1;
```

```
void Zoom(double level, Point point)
{
    const double minimumZoomLevel = 0.5;
    if (level < minimumZoomLevel)
    {
        level = minimumZoomLevel;
    }

    multiScaleImage.ZoomAboutLogicalPoint(
        level / zoomLevel, point.X, point.Y);

    zoomLevel = level;
}
```

When the user performs a pinch gesture, it is handled in the view by recording the current zoom level of the MultiScaleImage control. The center position of the touch gesture is determined relative to the MultiScaleImage. The center point is calculated automatically using the two touch points involved in the pinch gesture. We then convert this pixel location to a logical location, which results in a value between 0 and 1. See the following excerpt:

```
void OnPinchStarted(object sender, PinchStartedGestureEventArgs e)
{
    pinchStartLevel = zoomLevel;
    Point pinchStartPoint = e.GetPosition(multiScaleImage);
    pinchLogicalStartPoint
        = multiScaleImage.ElementToLogicalPoint(pinchStartPoint);
}
```

When the user moves his fingers together or apart, the OnPinchDelta handler is called. We then call the Zoom method, passing it the new zoom level and the gesture reference point, like so:

```
void OnPinchDelta(object sender, PinchGestureEventArgs e)
{
    Zoom(e.DistanceRatio * pinchStartLevel, pinchLogicalStartPoint);
}
```

To allow the user to drag the image, we respond to the DragStarted and DragDelta events of the Toolkit's GestureListener. This involves recording the touch location relative to the MultiScaleImage and the location of the top-left corner of the control, the ViewportOrigin:

```
void OnDragStarted(object sender, DragStartedGestureEventArgs e)
{
    dragStartPoint = e.GetPosition(multiScaleImage);
```

```
    dragStartViewportOrigin = multiScaleImage.ViewportOrigin;
}
```

As the user performs a drag motion, the `OnDragDelta` handler is called. Here we determine the relative distance from the initial touch point to the current touch location and reposition the `MultiScaleImage` using its `ViewportOrigin` property. The `ViewportWidth` property is a logical property with a value between 0 and 1:

```
void OnDragDelta(object sender, DragDeltaGestureEventArgs e)
{
    Point touchPoint = e.GetPosition(multiScaleImage);
    double visibleSize
        = multiScaleImage.ActualWidth / multiScaleImage.ViewportWidth;
    Point newPoint = dragStartViewportOrigin;
    newPoint.X += (dragStartPoint.X - touchPoint.X) / visibleSize;
    newPoint.Y += (dragStartPoint.Y - touchPoint.Y) / visibleSize;
    multiScaleImage.ViewportOrigin = newPoint;
}
```

The sample allows the user to zoom in via a double tap. To achieve this, we subscribe to the `DoubleTap` event of the Toolkit's `GestureListener`. In the handler, the location of the touch point relative to the `MultiScaleImage` is calculated. This point is then translated to a logical point, which acts as a reference point to perform the zoom. The zoom level is set to twice the existing zoom level, as shown:

```
void OnDoubleTap(object sender, GestureEventArgs e)
{
    Point tapPoint = e.GetPosition(multiScaleImage);
    Point logicalPoint = multiScaleImage.ElementToLogicalPoint(tapPoint);
    Zoom(zoomLevel * 2, logicalPoint);
}
```

Figure 7.12 shows the `MultiScaleImage` displaying the Deep Zoom image generated at the beginning of this section.

By performing a pinch gesture, or by double tapping, the user is able to zoom in to explore the image in greater detail (see Figure 7.13).

FIGURE 7.12   Viewing a Deep Zoom image from the sample app.

FIGURE 7.13   Zooming in on a composite Deep Zoom image.

Deep Zoom technology on the phone makes viewing high resolution imagery viable and allows you to leverage the built-in touch support of the phone to unlock exploration of visually rich content.

Displaying Web Content with the WebBrowser Element

Whereas the phone's built-in web browser can be launched from your app to view content on an external website, the WebBrowser control allows the user to view content directly from your app.

The WebBrowser control also allows you to host HTML content within your app, something the built-in web browser does not. It provides for static content loaded from a string or via a relative URI to a page located in isolated storage, or for live content from the Web, using an absolute URI. You can generate HTML and pass it to the WebBrowser control at runtime, and you can download content, save it to isolated storage, and display it later. The control responds to touch: a double tap zooms in, and the pinch gesture is also supported.

To have the WebBrowser load content, set the Source property of the URI to the location of the content as demonstrated in the following examples:

```
<phone:WebBrowser Source="http://www.example.com" />
<phone:WebBrowser Source="{Binding Url}" />
```

Alternatively, use the WebBrowser's Navigate method, as shown:

```
webBrowser.Navigate(
    new Uri("http://www.example.com", UriKind.Absolute));
```

The Navigate method has an overload that allows you to specify options for including posted form data and HTTP headers.

Loading a page from a string containing HTML is also possible using the NavigateToString method, as shown:

```
webBrowser.NavigateToString(
    "<html><head /><body>Windows Phone 8 Unleashed</body></html>");
```

The markup for the page loaded in the WebBrowser can be retrieved at runtime using the WebBrowser.SaveToString method.

Monitoring and Canceling Navigation

The WebBrowser control allows in-place navigation. Users may click on a link to change the page displayed in the control, and in addition, client-side JavaScript may assign the `window.location.href` property to navigate to a new location, which requires that the `WebBrowser.IsScriptEnabled` property be set to true.

Allowing the user free rein over navigation may not always be desirable, and you may want to monitor or even cancel the navigation of a web page programmatically. Fortunately, the `Navigating` event of the `WebBrowser` can be canceled. This is done by subscription to the event in code, or in XAML as shown:

```
<phone:WebBrowser Navigating="webBrowser_Navigating"/>
```

When the `WebBrowser` begins navigating to a new web page, the event is raised, at which time you can examine the URL and determine whether to allow the navigation:

```
void webBrowser_Navigating(object sender, NavigatingEventArgs e)
{
    if (e.Uri.ToString().IndexOf("www.example.com",
        StringComparison.CurrentCultureIgnoreCase) != -1)
    {
        e.Cancel = true;
    }
}
```

Communicating with a Web Page

The `WebBrowser.InvokeScript` method allows you to call JavaScript functions on a web page, and unlike Silverlight for the desktop, it is not restricted to scripts loaded from the same site as the XAP package. This method allows you to pass the JavaScript function an array of string parameters and is useful when you want to interact with the page, such as by highlighting text, changing the visibility of particular elements, or by adding behavior to a page through subscription to existing client-side events.

Conversely, a web page is able to send messages to your app using the client-side JavaScript method `window.external.Notify`, which raises the `WebBrowser.ScriptNotify` event, passing a single string argument.

The example for this section looks at both methods of communication. You see how to pass a string to your app via an HTML button and how to modify the content of a web page from your app.

The sample code for this section is located in the `WebBrowser` directory of the WPUnleashed.Examples project in the downloadable sample code, and includes the following files:

▶ Webpage.html

▶ WebBrowserWithScriptingView.xaml

▶ WebBrowserWithScriptingView.xaml.cs

We start by looking at the web page, which is loaded into the `WebBrowser` control at runtime (see Listing 7.7). This web page contains three key elements:

► A JavaScript function, called `Populate`, in its head element. We use `InvokeScript` to call this function from .NET.

► An HTML `div` element named `textDiv`, which is populated using the JavaScript `Populate` method.

► An HTML `input` button, which is used to send the content of the `textToSend` HTML text box to the Windows Phone app.

LISTING 7.7   Webpage.html

```html
<!DOCTYPE html PUBLIC "-//W3C//DTD XHTML 1.0 Transitional//EN"
 "http://www.w3.org/TR/xhtml1/DTD/xhtml1-transitional.dtd">
<html xmlns="http://www.w3.org/1999/xhtml">
<head>
    <meta name="mobileoptimized" content="480" />
    <title>Windows Phone 8 Unleashed</title>
    <style type="text/css"> h1 {color:red}
        div { margin-bottom: 30px; padding: 5px }
        div.received
        {
            border: thin solid #000000;
            font-size: x-large;
            font-weight: bold;
            color: Blue; }
    </style>
    <script type="text/javascript">
        function Populate(input) {
            textDiv.innerHTML = input;
            return true;
        }
    </script>
</head>
<body>
    <div>
        <input name="textToSend" type="text" value="Hi from Page!" />
        <br />
        <input type="button"
               value="Send to app"
               onclick="window.external.Notify(textToSend.value)"/>
    </div>
    <div>Value received from the app:
        <div id="textDiv" class="received" />
    </div>
```

```
        <a href="#dummy">A Link</a>
    </body>
</html>
```

The `PhoneApplicationPage`, `WebBrowserWithScriptingView.xaml`, contains a `WebBrowser` control with its `IsScriptEnabled` property set to `true`, as shown in the following excerpt:

```
<Grid x:Name="ContentGrid" Grid.Row="1">
    <Grid.RowDefinitions>
        <RowDefinition Height="Auto" />
        <RowDefinition Height="*" />
    </Grid.RowDefinitions>
    <StackPanel>
        <TextBox x:Name="textBox" Text="Hi from a!" />
        <Button Content="Send to Page"
                Click="Button_Click"
                Style="{StaticResource ButtonStyle}" />
    </StackPanel>
    <phone:WebBrowser x:Name="webBrowser"
        ScriptNotify="WebBrowser_ScriptNotify"
        IsScriptEnabled="True"   Grid.Row="1" />
</Grid>
```

By default, `IsScriptEnabled` is `false`.

The `PhoneApplicationPage` also contains a `TextBox` and a button that causes the content of the `TextBox` to be sent to the web page and placed into an HTML `div` element.

For the sake of simplicity, the logic for this example is placed in the XAML's code-beside file (see Listing 7.8). This file loads the web page, which is stored as content within the project and is tasked with calling the `WebBrowser`'s `InvokeScript` method when the Send to Page button is tapped, and with responding to the JavaScript `window.external.Notify` by displaying a message box.

LISTING 7.8   WebBrowserWithScriptingView.xaml.cs

```
public partial class WebBrowserWithScriptingView : PhoneApplicationPage
{
    public WebBrowserWithScriptingView()
    {
        InitializeComponent();
        DataContext = new WebBrowserWithScriptingViewModel();
    }

    void WebBrowser_ScriptNotify(object sender, NotifyEventArgs e)
    {
        MessageBox.Show(e.Value, "Received Value", MessageBoxButton.OK);
```

```csharp
    }

    protected override void OnNavigatedTo(NavigationEventArgs e)
    {
        base.OnNavigatedTo(e);

        StreamResourceInfo streamResourceInfo = Application.GetResourceStream(
            new Uri("WebBrowser/Webpage.html", UriKind.Relative));

        string html;
        using (StreamReader reader
                = new StreamReader(streamResourceInfo.Stream))
        {
            html = reader.ReadToEnd();
        }
        webBrowser.NavigateToString(html);
    }

    void Button_SendToPage_Tap(object sender,
    ➥System.Windows.Input.GestureEventArgs e)
    {
        webBrowser.InvokeScript("Populate", textBox.Text);
    }

    ...
}
```

The `PhoneApplicationPage` uses the `WebBrowser`'s `NavigateToString` method to push the loaded HTML into the control.

NOTE

Calls to `NavigateToString` must occur after the `WebBrowser` control is in the Visual Tree. Trying to call `NavigateToString` in your page constructor raises an `InvalidOperationException`.

Figure 7.14 shows that when a user taps the Send to Page button, the content of the `TextBox` control is sent to the web page.

Conversely, when the user taps the Send to App HTML button, the text located in the HTML input text control is sent to the app (see Figure 7.15).

FIGURE 7.14   Sending a string to a web page from a Windows Phone App.

FIGURE 7.15   Receiving a message from a web page within a Windows Phone app.

Injecting Web Page Behavior

On occasion you may want to invoke some JavaScript on a third-party web page, in which case relying on a named JavaScript function becomes impossible. Fortunately, JavaScript's `eval` function gives us the power to execute arbitrary JavaScript.

NOTE

Be aware that it is possible to override the JavaScript `eval` function, which may result in less than complete reliability for the technique presented in this section. Overriding `eval` is, however, rare, and web pages that do this do not comply with the ECMAScript 5 specification.

To demonstrate the execution of arbitrary JavaScript, another button has been added to the WebBrowserWithScriptingView.xaml page. Clicking the button causes a script to be invoked on the web page, which identifies all the hyperlinks on the page and attaches a client-side event handler to each anchor's `onclick` event, as shown in the following excerpt:

```
void Button_InjectScript_Tap(object sender, System.Windows.Input.GestureEventArgs e)
{
    webBrowser.InvokeScript("eval", evalScript);
}


const string evalScript
    = @"var anchors = document.getElementsByTagName('a');
    for(var i = 0; i < anchors.length; i++)
    {
        var anchor = anchors[i];
        anchor.attachEvent('onclick', function()
            {
                anchor.innerHTML = 'This text was changed by attaching'
                            + ' an event handler from the app!';
            });
    }";
```

This script executes client-side, after which, when the user clicks a link, the link's text is changed. It is a wacky example, yet we see that the `eval` function gives us the power to manipulate any part of the web page's Document Object Model (DOM). It could be used, for example, to highlight keywords on a web page or modify styles on a web page that you did not create.

Figure 7.16 shows the updated `PhoneApplication` page and the ordered steps for executing the JavaScript.

After the script is invoked, clicking the link causes an event handler to be called within the web page, where the style of the link is modified (see Figure 7.17).

FIGURE 7.16   Injecting web page behavior at runtime from .NET.

FIGURE 7.17   The anchor style is modified via an injected JavaScript event handler.

Storing and Browsing Content in Isolated Storage

There may be occasions where you want to allow an app to download content, perhaps modify it, and store it for later viewing. Fortunately the `WebBrowser` has built-in capability for browsing offline content located in isolated storage. There is, however, no automatic way to store such content. It is your responsibility to place whatever content needs to be available for offline browsing in isolated storage.

CAUTION

Content loaded from the network has cross-site restrictions, which ordinarily prevent a web page from communicating with sites other than its site-of-origin. Content loaded from isolated storage, or by using the `NavigateToString` method, however, has no such restrictions on cross-site access. Therefore, be mindful of unwittingly compromising the privacy of your users.

The example for this section looks at storing a web page and a referenced image in isolated storage and then directing a `WebBrowser` to read the content directly from isolated storage. The sample code for this section is located in the `WebBrowserIsolatedStorageView` page, in the downloadable sample code.

WebBrowserIsolatedStorageView

The `OnNavigatedTo` method of the `WebBrowserIsolatedStorageView` saves some example content to isolated storage. After the content has been stored, the `WebBrowser`'s `Base` property is assigned to the isolated storage directory containing the web page; this is then used by the `WebBrowser` to locate HTML content (see Listing 7.9).

The `Base` property should point to an isolated storage directory and is used by the `WebBrowser` to resolve relative references. This includes the `Uri Source` property and references to images within the HTML document.

LISTING 7.9 `WebBrowserIsolatedStorageView` Class

```
public partial class WebBrowserIsolatedStorageView : PhoneApplicationPage
{
    public WebBrowserIsolatedStorageView()
    {
        InitializeComponent();
    }

    protected override void OnNavigatedTo(NavigationEventArgs e)
    {
        base.OnNavigatedTo(e);
        SaveHtmlToIsolatedStorage();
        webBrowser.Base = "WebContent";
        webBrowser.Source = new Uri(@"Webpage.html", UriKind.Relative);
    }
```

```
...
}
```

When the `WebBrowser` attempts to load the URL Webpage.html, it uses the base directory of `WebContent` to load all relative content (see Figure 7.18).

FIGURE 7.18   Viewing a page from isolated storage.

Storing the Sample Web Content

Saving the web page and the image to isolated storage is done by retrieving the `IsolatedStorageFile` for the app and creating a directory called *WebContent* in which the content is placed. A simple document is written to a file in the directory, as shown in Listing 7.10.

LISTING 7.10   `SaveHtmlToIsolatedStorage` Method

```
void SaveHtmlToIsolatedStorage()
{
    using (IsolatedStorageFile isolatedStorageFile
        = IsolatedStorageFile.GetUserStoreForApplication())
    {
        if (!isolatedStorageFile.DirectoryExists("WebContent"))
        {
            isolatedStorageFile.CreateDirectory("WebContent");
        }

        using (IsolatedStorageFileStream isolatedStorageFileStream
            = isolatedStorageFile.OpenFile(
                @"WebContent\Webpage.html", FileMode.Create))
        {
```

```
        using (StreamWriter streamWriter
            = new StreamWriter(isolatedStorageFileStream))
        {
            streamWriter.Write(@"<html><head></head><body>
            <h2>Stored in Isolated Storage</h2>
            <p><img src=""Images/Book.jpg"" /></p>
                    </body></html>");
        }
    }

    if (!isolatedStorageFile.DirectoryExists("WebContent/Images"))
    {
        isolatedStorageFile.CreateDirectory("WebContent/Images");
    }

    StreamResourceInfo resourceInfo = Application.GetResourceStream(
        new Uri("WebBrowser/ImagePlacedInIsolatedStorage"
                + "/WP7Unleashed200x.jpg",
                UriKind.Relative));

    using (IsolatedStorageFileStream writeStream
        = new IsolatedStorageFileStream(
                @"WebContent/Images/Book.jpg",
                FileMode.Create, isolatedStorageFile))
    {
        CopyStreamBytes(resourceInfo.Stream, writeStream);
    }
}
}
```

The image, which is referenced by the `img` element in the HTML document, is a project item with its build action set to Content. This image file is first opened using the static method `GetResourceStream` of the `Application` class. It is then converted to a byte array and saved in isolated storage. For the sake of completeness, the `Stream` related methods are shown in Listing 7.11.

LISTING 7.11   `CopyStreamBytes` and `ReadStreamBytes` Methods

```
void CopyStreamBytes( \
    Stream fromStream, Stream toStream, bool closeToStream = true)
{
    if (toStream.CanWrite)
    {
        byte[] fileBytes = ReadStreamBytes(fromStream);
        toStream.Write(fileBytes, 0, fileBytes.Length);
        if (closeToStream)
```

```
        {
            toStream.Close();
        }
    }
}


byte[] ReadStreamBytes(Stream fileStream)
{
    /* Read the source file into a byte array. */
    byte[] bytes = new byte[fileStream.Length];
    int readLength = (int)fileStream.Length;
    int bytesRead = 0;
    while (readLength > 0)
    {
        /* Read may return anything from 0 to readLength. */
        int read = fileStream.Read(bytes, bytesRead, readLength);

        /* When no bytes left to read it is the end of the file. */
        if (read == 0)
        {
            break;
        }

        bytesRead += read;
        readLength -= read;
    }
    return bytes;
}
```

Summary

This chapter began by looking at the Image element, how to reference image files, and the effect on sizing by the Image.Stretch property. Setting Visual Studio's Build Action for a file to Resource means it will be located in the assembly, whereas setting it to Content means it will sit outside the assembly in the application's XAP file.

The chapter then explored the InkPresenter and demonstrated how to create a simple sketch app. You saw how the Background property of the InkPresenter must be assigned to register touch events.

It then moved to the MediaElement, and you saw how audio and video files can be played from the phone or streamed via the Internet. The XNA SoundEffect class is better suited to playing short sound effects. You saw how to use the new Windows Phone 8 Media Library extensions to add or remove music tracks to and from the Music+Videos Hub.

Deep Zoom and the `MultiScaleImage` element were discussed, including how they can be used to provide a stunning visual experience while making efficient use of your users' bandwidth. You saw how to allow the user to manipulate the Deep Zoom image using touch.

Finally, the chapter examined the `WebBrowser` control, and you saw how to communicate to a web page from a Windows Phone app and vice versa. You also saw how to execute arbitrary JavaScript on a web page to modify CSS styles or to attach new behaviors. You then looked at storing and browsing offline content to decrease network usage.

7

CHAPTER 8

Taming the Application Bar

The Windows Phone application bar provides a standard way of accessing common tasks within your app, and makes it easier for users to use your app by leveraging existing familiarity with a control that is used across all apps. Users are able to focus on content, rather than being distracted by having to learn an entirely new interface for each new app. The existence of the application bar also means that you as a developer do not have to reinvent the wheel every time you create a new app.

The application bar plays the same role as a combined toolbar and menu in a desktop or web application. It allows you to define a set of buttons and/or menu items that raise events when a user taps them.

This chapter explores the built-in application bar and its associated button and menu item classes. Most of this chapter is, however, devoted to a custom application bar, which is a wrapper for the built-in application bar and overcomes many of the built-in application bar's inherent limitations. The custom application bar improves on its built-in counterpart by providing support for data binding, commanding, toggle and hyperlink buttons, and controlling the visibility of menu items and buttons at runtime. Moreover, it is more compatible with design patterns like MVVM that rely on data binding.

Exploring the Built-In Application Bar

The phone's application bar API is somewhat of a conundrum. It has several serious limitations that make it difficult to work with, and considering that the application bar is such a fundamental element of most phone apps, it is odd that its API did not receive more care and attention during the development of the Windows Phone SDK.

The `ApplicationBar` class uses an interop wrapper to communicate with the phone's native application bar. The `ApplicationBar` is not a `UIElement`, nor is it a `DependencyObject`; in fact, it does not reside in the usual UI class hierarchy at all. Furthermore, at runtime, the `ApplicationBar` exists outside the visual tree of your root visual, making interaction with it awkward.

Several features to which experienced XAML developers have grown accustomed are also missing from the `ApplicationBar`, such as being able to control a button or menu item's visibility.

Using the `ApplicationBar`

Visual Studio provides you with a starting point by placing the markup for an `ApplicationBar` in a comment block when you create a new Windows Phone Portrait Page, a Windows Phone Landscape Page, and various Windows Phone projects using the Add New Item and New Project dialogs.

The `ApplicationBar` requires a namespace alias at the top of your page or control, as shown:

```
xmlns:shell="clr-namespace:Microsoft.Phone.Shell;assembly=Microsoft.Phone"
```

The markup for an `ApplicationBar` element is placed in the page's `phone:PhoneApplicationPage` element. Placed within it are `ApplicationBarIconButton` elements and a `MenuItems` element containing `ApplicationBarMenuItem`, as shown in the following example:

```xml
<phone:PhoneApplicationPage.ApplicationBar>
    <shell:ApplicationBar IsVisible="True" IsMenuEnabled="True">
        <shell:ApplicationBarIconButton
                    IconUri="/Images/appbar_button1.png"
                    Text="Button 1"/>
        <shell:ApplicationBarIconButton
                    IconUri="/Images/appbar_button2.png"
                    Text="Button 2"/>
        <shell:ApplicationBar.MenuItems>
            <shell:ApplicationBarMenuItem Text="MenuItem 1"/>
            <shell:ApplicationBarMenuItem Text="MenuItem 2"/>
        </shell:ApplicationBar.MenuItems>
    </shell:ApplicationBar>
</phone:PhoneApplicationPage.ApplicationBar>
```

NOTE

The application bar can contain up to four buttons and up to 50 menu items.

BEST PRACTICE

Avoid placing more than six menu items in the application bar. Doing so decreases the usability of your page, forcing the user to scroll down a long list to find the menu item that she is seeking.

When your `PhoneApplicationPage` is created, its `ApplicationBar` property is automatically assigned to the `ApplicationBar` instance if it exists.

The `ApplicationBar` consists of two collections of items, each with a corresponding `ApplicationBar` property: `Buttons` and `MenuItems`. The `Buttons` property is the `ApplicationBar`'s Content property, which means that in XAML any items located directly as child elements of the `ApplicationBar` element must be `ApplicationBarIconButtons` and are placed in the `ApplicationBar.Buttons` collection automatically.

Figure 8.1 shows an example of an application bar in its expanded state.

FIGURE 8.1   Expanding the application bar reveals its menu items.

To prevent the menu section from being expanded, set the `ApplicationBar.IsMenuEnabled` property to `false`. To hide the application bar entirely, set the `ApplicationBar.IsVisible` property to `false`.

Minimizing the Icon Button Tray

Since the release of Windows Phone 7.1 SDK, you have been able to minimize the application bar so that just the bar's ellipsis is shown. This is controlled by the `Mode` property of the `ApplicationBar`, which can be either Default or Minimized.

Application Bar and System Tray Dimensions

In portrait mode the height of the application bar is fixed at 72 pixels. In landscape mode its width is also fixed at 72 pixels. When minimized, the application bar's icon buttons are not shown, and the height of the icon button tray is reduced from 72 pixels to 30 pixels.

The system tray is 32 pixels high in portrait mode and 72 pixels wide in landscape mode. It always extends to the edge of the screen.

Modifying the Application Bar's Appearance

The `ApplicationBar`'s foreground (text and icon color) can be modified using its `ForegroundColor` property. By default this value is set to the PhoneForegroundColor application resource. For more information on built-in color styles, see http://bit.ly/xC8vgo.

The `Background` color property determines the background of the entire control. By default this value is set to the PhoneChromeColor application resource.

The `Opacity` property determines the level of transparency of the application bar's background. It does not affect the foreground, nor any icons present. Its value can range from 0 to 1, with 1 being completely opaque (the default value), and 0 being completely transparent.

The sample for this chapter, presented in a later section, provides a page to experiment with these properties.

Icon Button and Menu Item

The `ApplicationBarIconButton` and `ApplicationBarMenuItem` classes have many things in common. Apart from the `ApplicationBarIconButton` class's `IconUri` property, both `ApplicationBarIconButton` and `ApplicationBarMenuItem` classes contain the same set of identically named properties.

Both `ApplicationBarIconButton` and `ApplicationBarMenuItem` classes have a `Text` property, which is displayed on the application bar. At runtime the text for both menu items and icon buttons is transformed to lowercase to conform to the Microsoft Design Language aesthetic.

Icon button text is displayed beneath the icon when the user expands the application bar. If the length of the string exceeds 7 to 13 characters, depending on the width of the characters that make up the string, it is clipped.

Menu item text does not wrap and should be limited to 14 to 20 characters in length, depending on the width of the characters.

> **TIP**
>
> Many languages use different amounts of space to convey the same meaning. Therefore, when choosing menu item or button text, consider the different lengths of the text strings for the language your app will be in. Assume that an average of 30% more space will be required for any text. Depending on the language and the phrase, the localized string might even require twice as much space.

The `ApplicationBarIconButton.IconUri` is used to specify the location of the icon image. This value must be a relative URI, pointing to either a JPG or PNG image in the same project.

> **NOTE**
>
> When including an icon image in your project, be sure to set its build action to Content. Icon images must have a build action set to Content. If an image's build action is set to Resource, the image will not be resolved at runtime, and a default broken icon will be displayed in its place.

To disable a menu item or button, set its `IsEnabled` property to `false`.

Both `ApplicationBarIconButton` and `ApplicationBarMenuItem` have a `Click` event, allowing you to place a handler in your code-beside.

> **NOTE**
>
> If the `NavigationService` reports that navigation is in process, `Click` events will not be raised by your menu items or buttons. This prevents event handlers from interfering with your control or page during navigation, when it may be in an inconsistent state.

Icon Button Image

The Windows Phone SDK comes with a set of icons that you can use freely in your app. The default location of the icon images is C:\Program Files (x86)\Microsoft SDKs\ Windows Phone\v8.0\Icons\. Other free icon packs are also available online.

The icon image, for the `ApplicationBarIconButton`, should measure 48 by 48 pixels, but with a central area of 26 by 26 pixels. All content should be placed within a 26*26 square pixel area to ensure that it does not overlap the automatic circular button frame. Images that are other sizes will be scaled to fit, but image quality will be lower as a consequence.

> **NOTE**
>
> The circle displayed on each icon button is automatically generated by the application bar, and therefore should not be included in the source image.

The application bar automatically modifies the tone of your icon depending on the theme being used. This is to allow a single icon image to be used for both the light and dark phone themes.

Although icon button images can be either in PNG or JPG format, avoid using JPG, because this format does not support transparency and does not work well with the automatic tone conversion. All white pixels in a JPG image are replaced with the application bar's foreground color.

> **NOTE**
>
> The `ApplicationBarIconButton.IconUri` is limited to relative URIs. Relative component URIs are not supported, nor are images located on the Web. Attempting to use an absolute URI will cause an `ArgumentException` to be thrown at runtime.

Retrieving a Button or Menu Item at Runtime

Although the built-in application bar allows you to assign names to buttons and menu items in XAML using the `x:Name` attribute, the CLR runs into trouble resolving items by name at runtime. Consider the following example:

```xml
<phoneNavigation:PhoneApplicationPage.ApplicationBar>
    <shell:ApplicationBar>
        <shell:ApplicationBar.Buttons>
            <shell:ApplicationBarIconButton
                IconUri="/Images/Play.png"
                Click="OnPlayButtonClick" />
            <shell:ApplicationBarIconButton
                x:Name="PauseButton"
                IconUri="/Images/Pause.png"
                Click="OnPlayButtonClick"
                IsEnabled="True" />
        </shell:ApplicationBar.Buttons>
    </shell:ApplicationBar>
</phoneNavigation:PhoneApplicationPage.ApplicationBar>
```

When the `PlayButton` is tapped, it raises the `Click` event, calling the `OnPlayButtonClick` method:

```csharp
void PlayButtonClick(object sender, EventArgs e)
{
    PauseButton.IsEnabled = true; /* Fails, PauseButton is always null */
}
```

This, however, raises a `NullReferenceException` because the named `PauseButton` is always null. This occurs despite Visual Studio providing IntelliSense for the named item. Thus, you cannot refer to an `ApplicationBarIconButton` or an `ApplicationBarMenuItem` by name in the code-beside. Instead, the `ApplicationBar.Buttons` property must be used to resolve a button, as shown:

```
void PlayButtonClick(object sender, EventArgs e)
{
    ApplicationBar.Buttons[1].IsEnabled = true;
}
```

This example highlights an earlier point regarding difficulties associated with the `ApplicationBar` being outside the visual tree. It is an awkward class to develop with, and it has various limitations that make it a likely candidate for improvement in the future. In the meantime, however, I have created a wrapper for the class that behaves more as you would expect, yet possesses an almost identical API as the built-in `ApplicationBar`. The name of this custom wrapper class is `AppBar`, and it is the focus of the rest of this chapter.

Introducing the Custom `AppBar`

So far in this chapter we have examined the `ApplicationBar` and seen its limitations. This section examines a custom application bar called `AppBar`, which is an `ItemsControl` that wraps the built-in `ApplicationBar` class to provide support for data binding, button and menu item visibility, and commanding. `AppBar` also provides various extended buttons and menu items, such as a toggle button, which allows you to bind to multiple commands.

In this section you see how it is possible to bind to the various application bar, icon button, and menu item properties.

In Chapter 11, "Creating Expansive and Engaging Apps with the Pivot and Panorama," you see how to leverage some additional features of the `AppBar` to assign a different application bar for each `PivotItem` in a `Pivot` control.

`AppBar` and associated classes are available in the downloadable sample code but are maintained within the Calcium project at http://www.calciumsdk.com. I recommend downloading the maintained version.

`AppBar` **Buttons and Menu Items**

`AppBar` is accompanied by the following list of button and menu item controls:

▶ **`AppBarIconButton`**—Provides the same functionality as the built-in `ApplicationBarIconButton`, but with added support for data binding and commanding.

▶ **`AppBarMenuItem`**—Provides the same functionality as the built-in `ApplicationBarMenuItem`, but with added support for data binding and commanding.

▶ `AppBarToggleButton` and `AppBarToggleMenuItem`—Adds support for dual states, each containing a separate `Text` value, `Command`, `CommandParameter`, and in the case of the `AppBarToggleButton`, dual `IconUri` properties.

▶ `AppBarHyperlinkButton` and `AppBarHyperlinkMenuItem`—Allows you to launch a local or external URL directly from the button and provides a bindable `NavigateUri` property.

Button and Menu Item Visibility

`AppBar` brings some extended features, including the ability to show or hide a button or menu item using its `Visibility` property. This is not easily achievable with the built-in `ApplicationBar` class, because to hide an item in the application bar requires the item's removal from the `ApplicationBar`. `AppBar` takes care of this automatically by repopulating the application bar when the visibility of an item changes.

Sample Code

The sample code for this section is located in the `ApplicationBarView` and `ApplicationBarViewModel` classes in the downloadable sample code. This sample presents a simple interface for demonstrating various application bar properties. The following is a list of items demonstrated in the sample:

▶ Data binding `AppBar` menu items and buttons to viewmodel commands

▶ Modifying the foreground, background, and opacity of the application bar via data binding

▶ Using a toggle button within the `AppBar` to modify the `ApplicationBarIconButton`'s icon, text, and behavior based on a toggle state value

▶ Using a toggle menu item in the `AppBar` to modify the `ApplicationBarMenuItem`'s text and behavior based on a toggle state value

▶ Using the menu item's `Click` event

▶ Using a hyperlink button and menu item to navigate to internal and external URIs

The `ApplicationBarViewModel` class contains several commands that are used by the buttons and menu items in the view. These commands modify the state of the viewmodel, which in turn changes the application bar, system tray, and layout within the view.

The viewmodel's `Colors` property allows you to experiment with the background and foreground colors of the application bar. The `colors` collection is populated using reflection to obtain the `Color` values from the `System.Windows.Media.Colors` class, as shown:

```
static IEnumerable<Color> GetColors()
{
    /* Use reflection to get known colors. */
    Type colorsType = typeof(Colors);
```

```csharp
    PropertyInfo[] propertyInfos = colorsType.GetProperties(
        BindingFlags.Public | BindingFlags.Static);

    List<Color> knownColors = new List<Color>();
    foreach (PropertyInfo propertyInfo in propertyInfos)
    {
        try
        {
            Color color = (Color)propertyInfo.GetValue(null, null);
            knownColors.Add(color);
        }
        catch (Exception ex)
        {
            continue;
        }
    }
    return knownColors;
}

public void AddKnownColor(Color color)
{
    colors.Add(color);
}
```

The `AddKnownColor` method is used by the view to provide the viewmodel with some default colors, as shown in the following excerpt:

```csharp
public ApplicationBarView()
{
    InitializeComponent();
    ApplicationBarViewModel viewModel = new ApplicationBarViewModel();
    DataContext = viewModel;

    /* Let the viewmodel know what the foreground
     * and background colors are for the application bar. */
    Color foregroundColor = ((SolidColorBrush)Foreground).Color;
    Color backgroundColor = (Color)Resources["PhoneChromeColor"];
    viewModel.AddKnownColor(foregroundColor);
    viewModel.AddKnownColor(backgroundColor);
    viewModel.BackgroundColor = backgroundColor;
    viewModel.ForegroundColor = foregroundColor;
}
```

The `AppBar` is instantiated in the view via XAML (see Listing 8.1). Data bindings are used to set various properties of the `AppBar`.

The first `AppBarIconButton` executes the viewmodel's `SimpleCommand`.

The `AppBarToggleButton` uses the `Muted` property of the viewmodel to determine which command is active, and which text and icon to display. When the viewmodel's `Muted` property is `false`, it indicates that the button is not toggled, and `Text1` and `Icon1Uri` are displayed, and `Command1` becomes active. Conversely, when `Muted` is `true` it indicates that the button is toggled, and `Text2` and `Icon2Uri` are displayed. A second command can be specified if necessary. If a secondary property is not specified, then the control falls back to the primary (non-toggled property). For example, if `Text2` is not specified, and the `Toggled` property is `true`, then `Text1` is used.

`AppBarToggleMenuItem` works in the same manner as `AppBarToggleButton` but lacks the icon URI properties as the built-in application bar does not support icons in menu items.

An `AppBarHyperlinkButton` is used to navigate to an external URL. The `AppBarHyperlinkButton` uses a `WebBrowserTask` to launch the phone's built-in web browser. The `WebBrowserTask` is discussed further in Chapter 14, "Leveraging Built-In Apps via Launchers and Choosers."

An `AppBarHyperlinkMenuItem` is used to navigate to a relative URL to the main page of the phone app.

LISTING 8.1   ApplicationBarView.xaml `AppBar`

```
<u:AppBar IsVisible="{Binding ApplicationBarVisible}"
        IsMenuEnabled="{Binding MenuEnabled}"
        BarOpacity="{Binding BarOpacity}"
        BackgroundColor="{Binding BackgroundColor}"
        ForegroundColor="{Binding ForegroundColor}"
        Mode="{Binding Mode}">

    <u:AppBarIconButton
        Command="{Binding SimpleCommand}"
                        CommandParameter="Rewind"
        Text="Rewind"
        IconUri="/ControlExamples/MediaView/Images/Rewind.png"
        Visibility="{Binding FirstButtonVisible, Mode=TwoWay,
                Converter={StaticResource BooleanToVisibilityConverter}}"/>

    <u:AppBarToggleButton
        x:Name="button_Mute"
        Command1="{Binding ToggleMuteCommand}"
        Text1="Mute"
```

```
        Icon1Uri="/ControlExamples/MediaView/Images/Speaker.png"
        Text2="Un-Mute"
        Icon2Uri="/ControlExamples/MediaView/Images/Mute.png"
        Toggled="{Binding Muted}" />

    <u:AppBarHyperlinkButton
        IconUri="/ControlExamples/Images/appbar.upload.rest.png"
        Text="blog"
        NavigateUri="http://danielvaughan.org" />

    <u:AppBar.MenuItems>

        <u:AppBarMenuItem Text="MenuItem with Click Handler"
                          Click="AppBarMenuItem_Click" />

        <u:AppBarMenuItem Text="MenuItem with Command"
                          Command="{Binding SimpleCommand}"
                          CommandParameter="This custom AppBar rocks!" />

        <u:AppBarMenuItem Text="FullScreen"
                          Command="{Binding FullScreenCommand}"
                          CommandParameter="true" />

        <u:AppBarToggleMenuItem
            Command1="{Binding ToggleMuteCommand}"
            Text1="Mute"
            Text2="Unmute"
            Toggled="{Binding Muted}" />

        <u:AppBarHyperlinkMenuItem Text="Main Page"
                                   NavigateUri="/MainPage.xaml" />

    </u:AppBar.MenuItems>
</u:AppBar>
```

The `ApplicationBarView` page uses a `CheckBox` to toggle the `AppBar.IsMenuEnabled` property, a `Slider` for the `AppBar.BarOpacity` property, and two Windows Phone Toolkit `ListPicker` controls to change the background and foreground colors of the application bar (see Figure 8.2).

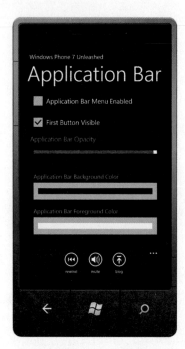

FIGURE 8.2　The sample application bar view.

Although `AppBar` menu items and icon buttons support `ICommands`, they also still support `Click` events. Tapping the first menu item causes an event hander to be called in the code-beside:

```
void AppBarMenuItem_Click(object sender, System.EventArgs e)
{
    ViewModel.Message = "Click event raised.";
}
```

> **NOTE**
>
> The `Click` event is raised regardless of whether a command has been specified for the button or menu item.

Disabling the Application Bar Menu

The view contains a check box that is bound to the viewmodel's `MenuEnabled` property:

```
<CheckBox IsChecked="{Binding MenuEnabled, Mode=TwoWay}"
        Content="Application Bar Menu Enabled" />
```

The AppBar IsMenuEnabled property is also bound to the viewmodel's MenuEnabled property, so that when the check box is checked or unchecked, the menu is enabled or disabled, respectively. By unchecking the check box, the application bar will not expand the menu when the expand button is tapped.

Minimizing the Icon Button Tray

Recall that the Mode property is used to minimize the application bar so that just the bar's ellipsis is shown.

In the sample, a custom IValueConverter called ApplicationBarModeToBooleanConverter converts the viewmodel's Mode property, which is of type ApplicationBarMode, to a Boolean value (see Listing 8.2).

LISTING 8.2   ApplicationBarModeToBooleanConverter Class

```
public class ApplicationBarModeToBooleanConverter : IValueConverter
{
    public object Convert(
        object value, Type targetType, object parameter, CultureInfo culture)
    {
        ApplicationBarMode mode = (ApplicationBarMode)value;
        return mode != ApplicationBarMode.Default;
    }

    public object ConvertBack(
        object value, Type targetType, object parameter, CultureInfo culture)
    {
        bool minimized = (bool)value;
        return minimized ? ApplicationBarMode.Minimized :
        ➥ApplicationBarMode.Default;
    }
}
```

The IValueConverter is defined as a page level resource.

The view contains a minimized CheckBox that is bound to the mode property, as shown:

```
<CheckBox IsChecked="{Binding Mode,
    Converter={StaticResource ApplicationBarModeToBooleanConverter}, Mode=TwoWay}"
    Content="minimized" />
```

The custom AppBar allows you to bind the Mode property of the application bar, which is demonstrated in the sample using the minimized button (see Figure 8.3).

FIGURE 8.3   Checking the minimized button causes the icon button tray to collapse.

Changing the Opacity of the Application Bar

To change the opacity of the application bar move the *application bar opacity* slider. The Slider is bound to the viewmodel's BarOpacity property, as shown:

```
<Slider Value="{Binding BarOpacity, Mode=TwoWay}"
        Maximum="1"
        LargeChange=".1" />
```

Changing the viewmodel's BarOpacity causes the AppBar.BarOpacity to be updated. Positioning the Slider all the way to the left causes the application bar background to be completely transparent.

Switching to Full-Screen

Switching to full-screen implies hiding the system tray and the application bar in its entirety. The early official Windows Phone architecture documents mention a supposed FullScreen property. Yet, in the final version of the SDK, no such property existed. No matter, because going full-screen involves simply hiding the system tray and the application bar. This is made rather easy by using the data binding capabilities of the custom AppBar class. Fortunately the system tray's visibility is specified using a Boolean attached property called SystemTray.IsVisible. As a consequence, in the view, we are able to data bind this property to a viewmodel property, like so:

```
shell:SystemTray.IsVisible="{Binding SystemTrayVisible}"
```

A menu item is used to execute a viewmodel command called `FullScreenCommand`, which sets the viewmodel's `SystemTrayVisible` and `ApplicationBarVisible` properties to `false`, effectively hiding both items (see Figure 8.4).

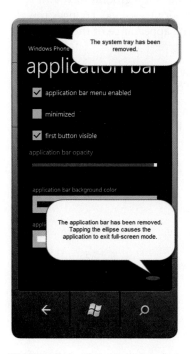

FIGURE 8.4   Full-screen mode is achieved by hiding the system tray and application bar.

A simple `Ellipse` element is provided to allow the user to return from full-screen mode. The ellipse markup makes use of the custom commanding infrastructure.

The `Ellipse` class does not provide a `Tap` event, and so a nondefault event `MouseLeftButtonUp` is specified using the `Commanding.Event` attached property, as shown:

```
<Ellipse dv:Commanding.Command="{Binding FullScreenCommand}"
         dv:Commanding.CommandParameter="false"
         dv:Commanding.Event="MouseLeftButtonUp"
         Visibility="{Binding ApplicationBarVisible,
             Converter={StaticResource BooleanToVisibilityConverter},
             ConverterParameter=Collapsed}"
         Fill="{StaticResource PhoneAccentBrush}"
         Width="50"
         Height="15"
         HorizontalAlignment="Right"
         VerticalAlignment="Bottom" />
```

The custom `BooleanToVisibilityConverter` is used to hide or show the ellipse depending on the value of the viewmodel's `ApplicationBarVisible` property.

Modifying the Application Bar's Foreground and Background Colors

Two Windows Phone Toolkit `ListPicker` controls are populated with a collection of colors, allowing you to try out variations of the application bar's foreground (text and icon) color and background color. Selecting a color from either `ListPicker` changes the corresponding viewmodel `Color` property, which changes the appearance of the application bar.

For more information on the Windows Phone Toolkit `ListPicker` control, see Chapter 9, "Enriching the User Experience with the Windows Phone Toolkit Controls."

A custom `IValueConverter` is used to convert to and from a `Color` value and a `SolidColorBrush`, allowing color bands to be rendered in the `ListPicker` (see Listing 8.3).

LISTING 8.3   `ColorToBrushConverter` Class

```
public class ColorToBrushConverter : IValueConverter
{
    public object Convert(
        object value, Type targetType, object parameter, CultureInfo culture)
    {
        if (value == null)
        {
            return null;
        }
        return new SolidColorBrush((Color)value);
    }

    public object ConvertBack(
        object value, Type targetType, object parameter, CultureInfo culture)
    {
        if (value == null)
        {
            return null;
        }
        return ((SolidColorBrush)value).Color;
    }
}
```

Each `ListPicker` is populated via a binding to the `Colors` property of the viewmodel. A `DataTemplate` defined as a page resource named `ColorPickerItemTemplate` determines how each `Color` is rendered within the `ListPicker`:

```
<phone:PhoneApplicationPage.Resources>
    <ValueConverters:ColorToBrushConverter x:Key="ColorToBrushConverter" />
```

```
<l:ApplicationBarModeToBooleanConverter
     x:Key="ApplicationBarModeToBooleanConverter" />

<DataTemplate x:Name="ColorPickerItemTemplate">
    <Rectangle
        Fill="{Binding .,
               Converter={StaticResource ColorToBrushConverter}}"
        Width="400" Height="20" Margin="0,10,0,10" />
</DataTemplate>
</phone:PhoneApplicationPage.Resources>
```

When the user selects a color, a property is updated in the viewmodel via the
`SelectedItem` property of the `ListPicker`, as shown:

```
<toolkit:ListPicker Header="application bar background color"
    ItemsSource="{Binding Colors}"
    SelectedItem="{Binding BackgroundColor, Mode=TwoWay}"
    ItemTemplate="{StaticResource ColorPickerItemTemplate}"
    FullModeItemTemplate="{StaticResource ColorPickerItemTemplate}" />
```

Customizing the Appearance of the System Tray

Unlike the `ApplicationBar`, the `SystemTray` class uses dependency properties, making it
compatible with the XAML data binding infrastructure. `SystemTray` has the following four
display-related properties:

▶ `BackgroundColor`

▶ `ForegroundColor`

▶ `Opacity`

▶ `IsVisible`

Each of these properties coincides with the `ApplicationBar` properties. In the sample, the
`SystemTray` is bound to the same viewmodel properties as the `AppBar`, as shown:

```
<phone:PhoneApplicationPage
...
    shell:SystemTray.IsVisible="{Binding SystemTrayVisible}"
    shell:SystemTray.BackgroundColor="{Binding BackgroundColor}"
    shell:SystemTray.ForegroundColor="{Binding ForegroundColor}"
    shell:SystemTray.Opacity="{Binding BarOpacity}">
...
</phone:PhoneApplicationPage>
```

Thus, when you alter the appearance of the application bar, the changes are also applied to the system tray.

Inside the `AppBar` Control

`AppBar` is a custom `ItemsControl` that wraps a `Microsoft.Phone.Shell.ApplicationBar`. As it is an `ItemsControl`, it enables you to add buttons and menu items to it, either in code or in XAML, in a manner not unlike the built-in `ApplicationBar`.

When the `AppBar` control is first loaded, it sets the host page's `ApplicationBar` to its own `ApplicationBar` field.

The `AppBar.Build` method is used to populate the `ApplicationBar` and is called in the following situations:

▶ When its `Loaded` event is raised

▶ When its collection of buttons or menu items changes

▶ When a button or menu item's visibility changes

The `Build` method calls the `BuildAux` method and prevents cycles from occurring while building is taking place, as shown:

```
bool building;

void Build()
{
    if (building)
    {
        return;
    }

    try
    {
        building = true;
        BuildAux();
    }

    finally
    {
        building = false;
    }
}
```

After requesting notification of button and menu item visibility changes, discussed in a moment, the `Build` method collects the members of its `ItemCollection` and, depending on their type, adds them to the `ApplicationBar`'s `Buttons` or `MenuItems` collection (see Listing 8.4).

LISTING 8.4   `AppBar.BuildAux` Method

```
void BuildAux()
{
    applicationBar.Buttons.Clear();
    applicationBar.MenuItems.Clear();

    foreach (FrameworkElement item in Items.OfType<FrameworkElement>())
    {
        RegisterForNotification("Visibility", item);
    }

    var buttonList = (from button in Items.Where(notUIElementOrVisibleFunc)
                                .OfType<IApplicationBarIconButtonProvider>()
                      select button.Button).ToList();

    if (buttonList.Count > 4)
    {
        buttonList = buttonList.Take(4).ToList();
    }

    applicationBar.Buttons.AddRange(buttonList);

    var menuItemList = (from item in Items.Where(notUIElementOrVisibleFunc)

                          .OfType<IApplicationBarMenuItemProvider>()
                        select item.MenuItem).ToList();

    applicationBar.MenuItems.AddRange(menuItemList);
}
```

Two classes, `AppBarIconButtonBase` and `AppBarMenuItemBase`, provide an extensibility point that allows you to create your own custom application bar buttons or menu items. If they do not suit your needs, however, you can opt to implement `IApplicationBarIconButtonProvider` and `IApplicationBarMenuItemProvider` instead.

The task of the custom `AppBar` items, such as the `AppBarIconButton` and the `AppBarMenuItem`, is to wrap an instance of the corresponding built-in `ApplicationBarIconButton` or `ApplicationBarMenuItem`, and to expose the wrapped item's properties as dependency properties.

Both `IApplicationBarIconButtonProvider` and `IApplicationBarMenuItemProvider` have a single property that is used to retrieve the actual `ApplicationBarIconButton` or `ApplicationBarMenuItem`.

During population of the `ApplicationBar`'s `Buttons` and `MenuItems` properties within the `AppBar.BuildAux` method, a `Func` named `notUIElementOrVisibleFunc` is used to determine the visibility of an item, as shown:

```
readonly Func<object, bool> notUIElementOrVisibleFunc
    = x =>
    {
        var element = x as UIElement;
        return element == null || element.Visibility == Visibility.Visible;
    };
```

Monitoring Item Visibility

No built-in event exists to monitor the `Visibility` property of `UIElements`. Therefore, to be notified when a button or menu item's visibility changes, we rely on an attached property and a custom `AppBar` method called `RegisterForNotification`, which uses a `Binding` to listen for button and menu item visibility changes. See the following excerpt:

```
void RegisterForNotification(
    string propertyName,
    FrameworkElement element)
{
    BindingExpression expression
        = element.GetBindingExpression(ItemVisibilityProperty);
    if (expression == null)
    {
        Binding binding = new Binding(propertyName) { Source = element };
        element.SetBinding(ItemVisibilityProperty, binding);
    }
}
```

Extending the Icon and Menu Item Base Classes

`AppBarHyperlinkButton` subclasses `AppBarIconButtonBase` to provide support for page navigation and navigation to external resources (see Listing 8.5).

When the base class's `Click` event is raised, the `PhoneApplicationFrame` navigates to the `NavigateUri` property. If the `Uri` is an external resource, the `WebBrowserTask` is used instead.

LISTING 8.5   `AppBarHyperlinkButton` Class

```
public class AppBarHyperlinkButton : AppBarIconButtonBase
{
    public static readonly DependencyProperty NavigateUriProperty
        = DependencyProperty.RegisterAttached(
            "NavigateUri",
            typeof(Uri),
```

```
        typeof(AppBarHyperlinkButton),
        null);

public Uri NavigateUri
{
    get
    {
        return (Uri)GetValue(NavigateUriProperty);
    }
    set
    {
        SetValue(NavigateUriProperty, value);
    }
}

protected override void OnClick(EventArgs e)
{
    base.OnClick(e);
    Navigate();
}

void Navigate()
{
    Uri uri = NavigateUri;
    if (uri == null)
    {
        return;
    }

    if (uri.IsAbsoluteUri)
    {
        WebBrowserTask task = new WebBrowserTask { Uri = uri };
        task.Show();
        return;
    }

    var frame = Application.Current.RootVisual as PhoneApplicationFrame;
    if (frame == null)
    {
        return;
    }

    frame.Navigate(uri);
}
}
```

Several `AppBar` items are in the downloadable sample code, which you are free to use in your own code. If you spend time using the built-in `ApplicationBar` I am certain you will appreciate the benefits of wrapping it in a more developer friendly class like the `AppBar`.

Summary

This chapter explored the built-in application bar and its associated button and menu item classes. The application bar can contain up to four icon buttons and up to 50 menu items. For reasons of usability, the number of menu items should be restricted to six or fewer.

This chapter was mostly devoted to a custom application bar, which is a wrapper for the built-in application bar, and which overcomes many of the built-in application bar's inherent limitations. The custom `AppBar` class improves on its built-in counterpart by providing support for data binding, `ICommands`, toggle buttons, hyperlink buttons, and controlling the visibility of menu items and buttons at runtime. Moreover, it is more compatible with design patterns like MVVM, which rely on data binding.

`AppBarToggleButton` and `AppBarToggleMenuItem` allow you to define two sets of properties that become active depending on the state of a bindable `Toggle` property. `AppBarHyperlinkButton` and `AppBarHyperlinkMenuItem` have a bindable `NavigateUri` property that allows you to navigate to a local or external URI.

CHAPTER 9

Enriching the User Experience with the Windows Phone Toolkit Controls

The Windows Phone Toolkit (henceforth referred to as just *Toolkit*) is a Microsoft open-source project that offers developers an additional set of components designed to match the rich user experience of Windows Phone and the Modern UI design aesthetic.

The Toolkit continues to enlarge Microsoft's offering beyond the official Phone Developer Tools. Over time, new components have been added to the Toolkit, and because the Toolkit has a shorter iteration cycle than the Windows Phone Developer Tools, it means that Microsoft is able to introduce new components more quickly and respond faster to the developer community.

One example of a control that benefited from the shorter release cycle is the progress bar control. After the first release of the `ProgressBar` as part of the FCL, it was found to be deficient in the area of performance, subsequently an alternative progress bar was introduced into the Toolkit. The performance issue has since been rectified in Windows Phone 8.

The downside of the Toolkit is that components may not necessarily undergo as much scrutiny before they are released, as those in the framework class library (FCL), and therefore may not be as polished as those that eventually make it into the FCL.

The Toolkit provides components that are fundamental to development on the platform. If you are doing Windows Phone development, you should be using it.

This chapter begins with a short getting started guide, which shows how to obtain and reference the Toolkit using NuGet. It then explores each Toolkit component.

This chapter is a long one. Do not feel obliged to read it from start to end. Feel free to skip through, and refer back to it when you need to.

Getting Started with the Toolkit

The Toolkit is hosted on CodePlex.com. CodePlex is a site dedicated to open-source software. Projects hosted on CodePlex must include source code. This means that, unlike the rest of the Windows Phone FCL, the toolkit source code is freely available and can even be modified by you under the MSPL license.

Add the Windows Phone Toolkit library to your project via NuGet by opening the package manager console. In Visual Studio, select Tools/Library Package Manager/Package Manager Console. At the PM prompt enter the following command:

Install-Package WPtoolkit

You can find more information about the Toolkit at http://phone.codeplex.com.

Downloadable from the Toolkit site are myriad examples that you may find worth exploring. The Toolkit and samples get updated frequently, so be sure to get the latest version from NuGet using the packager manager console command:

Update-Package WPtoolkit

This chapter also provides examples for each control, but often with a twist, and most examples seen here employ the MVVM pattern when demonstrating the functionality of each component.

To use components of the toolkit in XAML, add the following namespace definition to the top of your XAML file:

```
xmlns:toolkit="clr-namespace:
    Microsoft.Phone.Controls;assembly=Microsoft.Phone.Controls.Toolkit"
```

Subsequent sections look at each of the following components within the Toolkit (excluding those that have been described elsewhere in other chapters):

▶ ListPicker

▶ AutoCompleteBox

▶ ContextMenu

▶ DatePicker and TimePicker

▶ LoopingSelector

▶ Page transitions (presented in Chapter 4, "Controlling Page Orientation")

▶ TiltEffect

- ▶ ToggleSwitch
- ▶ WrapPanel
- ▶ GestureService (presented in Chapter 12, "Processing Touch Input")
- ▶ GestureListener (presented in Chapter 12)

In-Place Selection Using the `ListPicker`

Due to the relatively small screen size of the phone, it can be awkward displaying a large number of options to the user without resorting to the use of a second page. At development time, you may not know the number of options that will be displayed, making the choice of using an in-place selection mechanism such as a `ListBox` or a dedicated option selection page difficult. Moreover, navigating to a page to retrieve a response from a user is cumbersome and entails handling navigation events and so forth.

Fortunately, the `ListPicker` solves this problem by enabling the user to select from a list of options, either with an expandable in-place picker (if the number of items is small) or with a full-screen picker (if the number of items is large). The `ListPicker` allows you to tailor the number of items that can be displayed using the expandable picker, according to the design and space requirements of your UI.

`ListPicker` is an invaluable control for Windows Phone development. It is also highly customizable; through the use of custom data templates, you can change the way the in-place and full-screen pickers are displayed.

`ListPicker` is most appropriate where the user has several options, and where it makes sense to display only one option while the control does not have focus, such as on a settings page. Conversely, `ListPicker` is not appropriate for displaying long lists of data where the user is more likely to prefer viewing all options in place; scenarios such as the built-in People or Marketplace applications are better served by a `ListBox` or `LongListSelector`.

Display Modes

`ListPicker` is displayed in three modes: normal, expanded, and full screen.

When in normal mode, the `ListPicker` is inactive and does not have focus, and displays its selected item while hiding the rest.

In expanded mode, the `ListPicker` resizes itself to display all items. This works best when there are only a few items to display. Page content is positioned to accommodate the size of the expanded `ListPicker`, and then is repositioned when the `ListPicker` contracts when an item is selected (see Figure 9.1).

FIGURE 9.1   `ListPicker` in expanded mode.

When in full-screen mode, the `ListPicker` presents options using a pop-up, which hides the rest of the page content. Full-screen mode is appropriate when the number of options to choose from is large (see Figure 9.2).

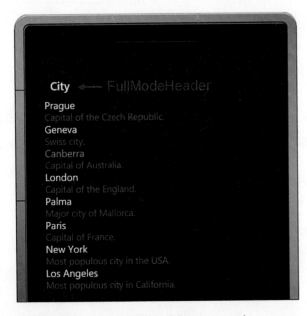

FIGURE 9.2   `ListPicker` in full-screen mode.

The `ListPicker.ItemCountThreshold` property determines the maximum number of items for which expanded mode is used. If the number of items exceeds this value, full-screen mode is used instead of expanded mode. `ItemCountThreshold` default value is five.

You can determine the current state of a `ListPicker` via its `ListPickerMode` property. `ListPickerMode` may be one of the following values:

- ▶ **Normal**—Only the selected value is visible.
- ▶ **Expanded**—The `ListPicker` is displaying all its items by expanding inline and displacing other page content.
- ▶ **Full**—A dedicated pop-up displays all items.

The `ListPicker` sample uses the MVVM pattern. The `ListPickerViewModel` creates and exposes a list of `City` objects, which is then presented using a `ListPicker` in the view.

The `City` class has a `Name` and a `Description` property (see Listing 9.1).

LISTING 9.1   `City` Class

```
public class City
{
    public string Name { get; private set; }
    public string Description { get; private set; }

    public City(string name, string description)
    {
        Name = name;
        Description = description;
    }
}
```

The viewmodel creates several `City` objects as shown:

```
readonly IEnumerable<City> cities = new List<City>
    {
        new City("Prague", "Capital of the Czech Republic."),
        /* Removed for brevity. */
        new City("Los Angeles", "Most populous city in California.")
    };


public IEnumerable<City> Cities
{
    get
    {
        return cities;
    }
}
```

6

The second task of the viewmodel is to keep track of the currently selected City, using a property named City.

The view contains a ListPicker whose ItemsSource property is bound to the viewmodel's Cities property. In addition, the ListPicker.SelectedItem property uses a two-way data binding to the City property, so that when the user selects an item in the ListPicker, the City property is set to the selected value. See the following excerpt:

```
<toolkit:ListPicker ItemsSource="{Binding Cities}"
            ItemCountThreshold="20"
            SelectedItem="{Binding City, Mode=TwoWay}"
            Header="city"
            FullModeHeader="city">
    <toolkit:ListPicker.FullModeItemTemplate>
        <DataTemplate>
            <StackPanel>
                <TextBlock Text="{Binding Name}"
                    FontSize="{StaticResource PhoneFontSizeNormal}" />
                <TextBlock Text="{Binding Description}"
                    FontSize="{StaticResource PhoneFontSizeSmall}"
                    Foreground="#ff666666" />
            </StackPanel>
        </DataTemplate>
    </toolkit:ListPicker.FullModeItemTemplate>
    <toolkit:ListPicker.ItemTemplate>
        <DataTemplate>
            <StackPanel>
                <TextBlock Text="{Binding Name}"
                    FontSize="{StaticResource PhoneFontSizeNormal}" />
                <TextBlock Text="{Binding Description}"
                    FontSize="{StaticResource PhoneFontSizeSmall}"
                    Foreground="#ff666666" />
            </StackPanel>
        </DataTemplate>
    </toolkit:ListPicker.ItemTemplate>
</toolkit:ListPicker>
```

You see that a custom DataTemplate is defined for both the Expanded and Full ListPickerMode values. If the ListPicker is populated with a list of strings (or objects whose ToString method affords an appropriate representation of the object), providing a custom DataTemplate for each of these modes is in most cases not necessary, because the built-in templates suffice.

The FullModeHeader property defines the content placed at the top of the item list when the ListPickerMode is equal to Full. The FullModeHeader property can be defined not only as a string, but also using a DataTemplate, much like the ItemTemplate and FullModeItemTemplate. The FullModeHeader property is not required (see Figure 9.3).

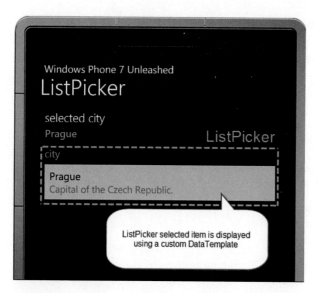

FIGURE 9.3   `ListPicker` with a custom `ItemTemplate`.

Suggesting Text with the `AutoCompleteBox`

The `AutoCompleteBox` displays suggestions in a drop-down list as the user enters text into a text box. The `AutoCompleteBox` control is composed of a `TextBox` and a `ListBox` that is made visible when the `TextBox` has focus.

The `TextBox` on which `AutoCompleteBox` relies is part of its default template. The `AutoCompleteBox` shares many of the `TextBox` control's characteristics, including a `Text` property, which allows you to set the text displayed.

Moreover, the `AutoCompleteBox` contains an `InputScope` property that allows you to set the keyboard shown on the software input panel (SIP). For more information on `InputScope`, see Chapter 6, "Mastering Text Elements and Fonts."

> **TIP**
>
> The `TextBox` control has built-in suggestion support using word completion when its `InputScope` is set to Text. If you do not need to customize the style or list of possible suggestions, the `TextBox` may be preferable.

The simplest way to have an `AutoCompleteBox` display suggestions is to assign it a predefined list of strings. Place an `AutoCompleteBox` on a page, like so:

```
<toolkit:AutoCompleteBox x:Name="autoCompleteBox" />
```

Then, set its `ItemsSource` property to the list, as shown:

```
List<string> suggestions = new List<string>
                         {
                             "Prague",
                             "Geneva",
                             "Canberra",
                             ...

                         };

autoCompleteBox.ItemsSource = cities;
```

When the user enters text into the `AutoCompleteBox`, list items that begin with the string are displayed as suggestions (see Figure 9.4).

FIGURE 9.4   `AutoCompleteBox` displays a list of suggestions as the user enters text.

Using `AutoCompleteBox` with MVVM

This section looks at controlling an `AutoCompleteBox` from a viewmodel. The example code for this section is located in the `AutoCompleteBoxView` and `AutoCompleteBoxViewModel` in the downloadable sample code.

`AutoCompleteBox` provides various ways for selecting the items to be displayed in the suggestion list. The `AutoCompleteBox.FilterMode` property allows you to specify how entered text is matched with items in the suggestion list. When a match occurs, the item is displayed in the selection list. If `AutoCompleteFilterMode` is not specified, the StartsWith filter mode is used, which is not a case-sensitive filter, where the returned items start with the entered text. Table 9.1 lists the `FilterMode` values.

TABLE 9.1   `AutoCompleteFilterMode` Enum Values

Enum Value	Description
`Contains`	Specifies a culture-sensitive, not case-sensitive filter where the returned items contain the specified text.
`ContainsCaseSensitive`	Specifies a culture-sensitive, case-sensitive filter where the returned items contain the specified text.
`ContainsOrdinal`	Specifies an ordinal, case-insensitive filter where the returned items contain the specified text.
`ContainsOrdinalCaseSensitive`	Specifies an ordinal, case-sensitive filter where the returned items contain the specified text.
`Custom`	Specifies that a custom filter is used. This mode is used when the `System.Windows.Controls.AutoCompleteBox.TextFilter` or `System.Windows.Controls.AutoCompleteBox.ItemFilter` properties are set. This filter mode is explored later in the chapter.
`Equals`	Specifies a culture-sensitive, not case-sensitive filter, where the returned items equal the specified text. The filter uses the `System.String.Equals(System.String,System.StringComparison)` method, specifying `System.StringComparer.CurrentCultureIgnoreCase` as the search comparison criteria.
`EqualsCaseSensitive`	Specifies a culture-sensitive, case-sensitive filter where the returned items equal the specified text. The filter uses the `System.String.Equals(System.String,System.StringComparison)` method, specifying `System.StringComparer.CurrentCulture` as the string comparison criteria.
`EqualsOrdinal`	Specifies an ordinal, not case-sensitive filter where the returned items equal the specified text. The filter uses the `System.String.Equals(System.String,System.StringComparison)` method, specifying `System.StringComparer.OrdinalIgnoreCase` as the string comparison criteria.

6

Enum Value	Description
EqualsOrdinalCaseSensitive	Specifies an ordinal, case-sensitive filter where the returned items equal the specified text. The filter uses the `System.String.Equals(System.String, System.StringComparison)` method, specifying `System.StringComparer.Ordinal` as the string comparison criteria.
None	Specifies that no filter is used. All items are returned.
StartsWith	This is the default `ItemFilter` value. Specifies a culture-sensitive, not case-sensitive filter where the returned items start with the specified text. The filter uses the `System.String.StartsWith(System.String, System.StringComparison)` method, specifying `System.StringComparer.CurrentCultureIgnoreCase` as the string comparison criteria.
StartsWithCaseSensitive	Specifies a culture-sensitive, case-sensitive filter where the returned items start with the specified text. The filter uses the `System.String.StartsWith(System.String, System.StringComparison)` method, specifying `System.StringComparer.CurrentCulture` as the string comparison criteria.
StartsWithOrdinal	Specifies an ordinal, not case-sensitive filter where the returned items start with the specified text. The filter uses the `System.String.StartsWith(System.String, System.StringComparison)` method, specifying `System.StringComparer.OrdinalIgnoreCase` as the string comparison criteria.
StartsWithOrdinalCaseSensitive	Specifies an ordinal, case-sensitive filter where the returned items start with the specified text. The filter uses the `System.String.StartsWith(System.String, System.StringComparison)` method, specifying `System.StringComparer.Ordinal` as the string comparison criteria.

To demonstrate the `FilterMode`, we place a `FilterMode` property in the viewmodel and then bind the `AutoCompleteBox.FilterMode` property to it. The viewmodel's `FilterMode` property is shown in the following excerpt:

```
AutoCompleteFilterMode filterMode;
```

```csharp
public AutoCompleteFilterMode FilterMode
{
    get
    {
        return filterMode;
    }
    set
    {
        Assign(ref filterMode, value);
    }
}
```

We bind the `ItemsSource` property of the `AutoCompleteBox` to the `Suggestions` property of the viewmodel. A two-way data binding is used to allow the `AutoCompleteBox` to update the `FilterMode` when a custom filter is supplied:

```xml
<toolkit:AutoCompleteBox ItemsSource="{Binding Suggestions}"
                FilterMode="{Binding FilterMode, Mode=TwoWay}" />
```

The viewmodel also exposes a list of available `FilterMode`s, as shown:

```csharp
readonly List<AutoCompleteFilterMode> filterModes
    = new List<AutoCompleteFilterMode>
            {
                AutoCompleteFilterMode.Contains,
                AutoCompleteFilterMode.ContainsCaseSensitive,
                /* Enum values removed for brevity. */
                AutoCompleteFilterMode.StartsWithOrdinalCaseSensitive,
            };

public IEnumerable<AutoCompleteFilterMode> FilterModes
{
    get
    {
        return filterModes;
    }
}
```

This list is used by a `ListPicker`, which enables the user to select the filter mode to use. The `ItemsSource` of the `ListPicker` is bound to the `FilterModes` property, and its `SelectedItem` property uses a two-way data binding to the viewmodel's `FilterMode` property:

```xml
<toolkit:ListPicker ItemsSource="{Binding FilterModes}"
                SelectedItem="{Binding FilterMode, Mode=TwoWay}" />
```

Selecting an alternative filter mode via the `ListPicker` changes the filtering behavior of the `AutoCompleteBox` (see Figure 9.5).

FIGURE 9.5   `AutoCompleteBox` with `FilterMode` set to `StartsWithCaseSensitive`.

Defining a Custom Filter Using the `ItemFilter` Property

If none of the predefined filters suit your needs, the `ItemFilter` property of the `AutoCompleteBox` allows you to define a custom method for determining whether a suggestion item matches the entered text. This works well in conjunction with the MVVM pattern, as you see in this section.

To add custom filtering to an `AutoCompleteBox`, you first create a method that conforms to the `AutoCompleteFilterPredicate` delegate, shown here:

```
bool AutoCompleteFilterPredicate<T>(string search, T item)
```

Your custom filter method must accept a search string (the text entered by the user) and an item from the list of suggestions (usually defined by the `ItemsSource` property of the `AutoCompleteBox`), and it must return a Boolean value indicating whether to display the item in the suggestion list.

The sample code located in the `AutoCompleteBoxViewModel` class contains a custom filter method called `FilterOnLastLetter`. This custom filter method determines whether the suggestion item ends with the entered text. See the following excerpt:

```
static bool FilterOnLastLetter(string enteredText, object suggestionItem)
{
    if (suggestionItem != null
        && suggestionItem.ToString().ToLower().EndsWith(enteredText))
    {
        return true;
    }

    return false;
}
```

To allow an `AutoCompleteBox` to use this method, a public property called `ItemFilter` is placed in the viewmodel. The `FilterOnLastLetter` is declared as a static method so that it can be assigned to the `itemFilter` field from outside the viewmodel's constructor, as shown:

```
AutoCompleteFilterPredicate<object> itemFilter = FilterOnLastLetter;

public AutoCompleteFilterPredicate<object> ItemFilter
{
    get
    {
        return itemFilter;
    }
    private set
    {
        Assign(ref itemFilter, value);
    }
}
```

With the `ItemFilter` property in place, the `AutoCompleteBox` is able to bind to the property like so:

```
<toolkit:AutoCompleteBox ItemsSource="{Binding Suggestions}"
                         FilterMode="{Binding FilterMode, Mode=TwoWay}"
                         ItemFilter="{Binding ItemFilter}" />
```

When a user enters text into the `AutoCompleteBox`, the custom filter method (`FilterOnLastLetter`) is called for each item in the data bound `Cities` property. Only those items ending with the entered text are displayed (see Figure 9.6).

FIGURE 9.6   An `AutoCompleteBox` with custom filtering.

> **NOTE**
>
> When using custom filtering, the `AutoCompleteBox.FilterMode` property is automatically set to Custom.

Dynamic Population of the Suggestion List

Until now you have looked at using only predefined suggestion lists. There are times, however, when you may want to change the contents of the suggestion list based on what the user has entered. One example is performing a web search for the entered text and using the search results as the suggestion list. The user enters some text, and you call a website to get a list of suggestions. Once the call completes you populate the `ItemsSource` property of the `AutoCompleteBox`. This entails an asynchronous operation, which means you need some way of telling the `AutoCompleteBox` to dispense with filtering until the result of the asynchronous call is obtained. Fortunately, the `AutoCompleteBox` contains a built-in mechanism for doing just this. By using the `AutoCompleteBox.Populating` event, you can safely coordinate the population of its suggestion list.

The following steps outline how to provide a dynamic list of suggestions as the user enters text.

1. Subscribe to the `Populating` event of the `AutoCompleteBox`.

2. When the event handler is called, set the `Cancel` property of the `PopulatingEventArgs` to true.

3. Populate the `ItemsSource` property of the `AutoCompleteBox`.

4. Call the `PopulateComplete` method of the `AutoCompleteBox` to signal that the `ItemsSource` property has been populated and can be filtered.

Let's walk through these steps. The `AutoCompleteBoxView`, in the downloadable sample code, contains an event handler for the `AutoCompleteBox` `Populating` event. When the handler is called, it cancels the event and calls the viewmodel's `Populate` method. When the viewmodel is finished retrieving the suggestions, perhaps from a web service, it calls the `AutoCompleteBox.PopulateComplete` method, which is provided as an `Action` parameter:

```csharp
void AutoCompleteBox_Populating(object sender, PopulatingEventArgs e)
{
    e.Cancel = true;
    AutoCompleteBox box = (AutoCompleteBox)sender;
    ViewModel.Populate(e.Parameter, box.PopulateComplete);
}
```

The `Populate` method is designed to show how the population of a list might take place, though it does not perform an asynchronous operation. All that is done is to replace the suggestion list with another. We could, however, be using Bing or Google, for example, to perform a search. See the following excerpt:

```csharp
public void Populate(string text, Action completeAction)
{
    Suggestions = new List<string>
                    {
                        "Daniel", "Sacha", "Marlon", "Pete",
                        "Josh", "Jaime", "Laurent", "Katka"
                    };
    if (completeAction != null)
    {
        completeAction();
    }
}
```

The specified `completeAction` eventually calls the `PopulateComplete` method of the `AutoCompleteBox`, at which point filtering is reengaged.

Upon setting the `FilterMode` of the `AutoCompleteBox` to Contains and entering a single character, the suggestion list is populated as shown in Figure 9.7.

FIGURE 9.7   The suggestion list is populated when the `AutoCompleteBox` text changes.

Styling the Suggestion List

`AutoCompleteBox` allows you to customize the presentation of suggestion items using its `ItemTemplate` property.

Sample code for this section is located in the `AutoCompleteBoxTemplatedView` and `AutoCompleteBoxTemplatedViewModel`.

So far a string has been used to represent suggestion items. This section uses a custom `SuggestionItem` class to demonstrate more complex data binding and styling features (see Listing 9.2).

LISTING 9.2   `SuggestionItem` Class

```
public class SuggestionItem
{
    public string Name { get; private set; }
    public string Description { get; private set; }

    public SuggestionItem(string name, string description)
    {
        Name = name;
```

```
        Description = description;
    }
}
```

Within the viewmodel is defined a list of `SuggestionItem` objects as shown:

```
IEnumerable<SuggestionItem> suggestions = new List<SuggestionItem>
    {
        new SuggestionItem("Prague", "Capital of the Czech Republic."),
        new SuggestionItem("Geneva", "Swiss city."),
        new SuggestionItem("Canberra", "Capital of Australia."),
        ...

    };
```

To have the `AutoCompleteBox` function correctly with a complex object, such as the custom `SuggestionItem` class, you need to inform it of which property to use for filtering. This is done using the `AutoCompleteBox.ValueMemberPath` property. The following excerpt shows how the `Name` property of the `SuggestionItem` class is designated as the filter property. You also see how a `DataTemplate` is used to present the `Name` and `Description` of each `SuggestionItem` object:

```
<toolkit:AutoCompleteBox
    ItemsSource="{Binding Suggestions}"
    ValueMemberPath="Name"
    FontFamily="{StaticResource PhoneFontFamilySemiBold}"
    FontSize="{StaticResource PhoneFontSizeSmall}"
    VerticalAlignment="Top">
    <toolkit:AutoCompleteBox.ItemTemplate>
        <DataTemplate>
            <StackPanel>
                <TextBlock Text="{Binding Name}"
                    FontSize="{StaticResource PhoneFontSizeNormal}" />
                <TextBlock Text="{Binding Description}"
                    FontSize="{StaticResource PhoneFontSizeSmall}"
                    Foreground="#ff666666" />
            </StackPanel>
        </DataTemplate>
    </toolkit:AutoCompleteBox.ItemTemplate>
</toolkit:AutoCompleteBox>
```

When the suggestion list is displayed, each `SuggestionItem` is presented using the `DataTemplate`, as shown in Figure 9.8.

9

FIGURE 9.8   A custom `ItemTemplate` displays each city's name and description.

TIP

If you want to programmatically collapse the suggestion list, set the
`AutoCompleteBox.IsDropDownOpen` property to false.

Data Binding and the `AutoCompleteBox.Text` Property

Populating the `Text` property of the `AutoCompleteBox` via a data binding can be problematic, since when a suggestion is chosen the binding is effectively removed and therefore
needs to be restored.

You can reapply a binding by subscribing to the `SelectionChanged` event of the
`AutoCompleteBox`.

```
void AutoCompleteBox_SelectionChanged(
            object sender, SelectionChangedEventArgs e)
{
    AutoCompleteBox autoCompleteBox = (AutoCompleteBox)sender;
    Dispatcher.BeginInvoke(delegate
    {
        Binding binding = new Binding("YourViewModelTextProperty");
```

```
            binding.Source = autoCompleteBox.DataContext;
            autoCompleteBox.SetBinding(AutoCompleteBox.TextProperty, binding);
        });
}
```

When the `AutoCompleteBox.IsTextCompletionEnabled` property is set to true, the `AutoCompleteBox.KeyUp` event can be used instead of the `SelectionChanged` event to ensure that the binding is restored regardless of whether a selection is made.

Displaying a `ContextMenu`

`ContextMenu` is an expanding menu control that is displayed when a host `FrameworkElement` is tapped and held. A `ContextMenu` can be added to any `FrameworkElement` using the `ContextMenuService.ContextMenu` attached property. The following excerpt shows a `Button` that has a context menu assigned to it, displaying three menu items:

```xml
<Button Margin="0,12" VerticalAlignment="Center" Padding="16"
        Content="Using Click Events">
    <toolkit:ContextMenuService.ContextMenu>
        <toolkit:ContextMenu>
            <toolkit:MenuItem
                Header="option 1"
                Click="MenuItem_Click"/>
            <toolkit:MenuItem
                Header="option 2"
                Click="MenuItem_Click"/>
            <toolkit:MenuItem
                Header="option 3"
                Click="MenuItem_Click"/>
        </toolkit:ContextMenu>
    </toolkit:ContextMenuService.ContextMenu>
</Button>
```

When the button is tapped and held, the page content is zoomed out and the list of menu items is displayed (see Figure 9.9).

In this example the event handler for each `MenuItem.Click` event is the same. The handler retrieves the `Header` text of the selected `MenuItem` and displays it in a `TextBlock`, like so:

```csharp
void MenuItem_Click(object sender, RoutedEventArgs e)
{
    TextBlock_LastSelectedMenuItem.Text = (string)((MenuItem)sender).Header;
}
```

FIGURE 9.9   A `Button` plays host to a `ContextMenu`.

By default, when shown, the `ContextMenu` reduces the scale of all other elements on the page, giving the context menu center stage. Internally the `ContextMenu` does this by creating a `WritableBitmap` containing an image of the page. A `ScaleTransform` is then applied to the `WritableBitmap`, which is placed above the page content but below `ContextMenu` host. This is a nice little trick, used often in the Toolkit. One downside of this approach, however, and one that you may become more aware of as you find yourself progressing with the `ContextMenu`, is that the snapshot taken of the page content captures buttons in their pressed state, which may or may not be what you want. Notice, in Figure 9.9, that the background of the button is white, which interferes with the highlighting of the menu items.

To prevent the background from being scaled when the context menu is shown, set the `ContextMenu.IsZoomEnabled` property to false, as shown:

```
<Button Margin="0,12" VerticalAlignment="Center" Padding="16"
        Content="Using IsZoomEnabled=false">
    <toolkit:ContextMenuService.ContextMenu>
        <toolkit:ContextMenu IsZoomEnabled="false">
            <toolkit:MenuItem Header="option 1" Click="MenuItem_Click"/>
            <toolkit:MenuItem Header="option 2" Click="MenuItem_Click"/>
            <toolkit:MenuItem Header="option 3" Click="MenuItem_Click"/>
        </toolkit:ContextMenu>
    </toolkit:ContextMenuService.ContextMenu>
</Button>
```

With `IsZoomEnabled` set to false, an image of the page content is not used, and the actual page elements are displayed and continue to show animation. Consequently, a button control is able to transition out of its pressed state when the menu is shown (see Figure 9.10).

FIGURE 9.10   Displaying a `ContextMenu` with `IsZoomEnabled` set to false.

`ContextMenu` **and MVVM**

So far you have seen the `ContextMenu` employed with hardwired `MenuItems` and `Click` events. This approach is adequate for simple apps. Yet, the `MenuItem` class supports `ICommands` out of the box. And, with this, you can bind a viewmodel's `ICommand` to a `MenuItem`, removing the need for `Click` event handlers in the code-beside.

To demonstrate, we bind a viewmodel command to a `MenuItem`, which displays a message to the user. The `ContextMenuViewModel` class, in the downloadable sample code, contains a `ShowMessageCommand` property, declared as shown:

```
readonly DelegateCommand showMessageCommand;

public ICommand ShowMessageCommand
{
    get
    {
```

```
        return showMessageCommand;
    }
}
```

The task of the `ShowMessageCommand` is to display a message using the custom
`IMessageService`. For more information regarding the `ImessageService`, see Chapter 2,
"Fundamental Concepts in Windows Phone Development." The `ShowMessageCommand` is
initialized within the viewmodel's constructor. When the command executes, it presents
the command parameter using the message service, as shown in the following excerpt:

```
public ContextMenuViewModel()
{
    showMessageCommand = new DelegateCommand(
        parameter =>
        {
            var messageService = Dependency.Resolve<IMessageService>();
            messageService.ShowMessage(parameter + " clicked!");
        });


    /* Content omitted. */
}
```

As with most examples in this book, the viewmodel is initialized and assigned to the
view's `DataContext` property like so:

```
public ContextMenuView()
{
    InitializeComponent();
    DataContext = new ContextMenuViewModel();
}
```

With the viewmodel and command in place, `MenuItems` are able to bind to the command
in the view XAML. In the following excerpt you see three `MenuItem` controls, each bound
to the `ShowMessageCommand`. The first uses a string as its command parameter. The second
and third use the `RelativeSource` markup extension to bind to their own `Header` properties. See the following excerpt:

```
<Button Margin="0,12" VerticalAlignment="Center" Padding="16"
    Content="Using ICommands">
    <toolkit:ContextMenuService.ContextMenu>
        <toolkit:ContextMenu>
            <toolkit:MenuItem
                Header="option 1"
                Command="{Binding ShowMessageCommand}"
                CommandParameter="option 1" />
            ...
```

```
        </toolkit:ContextMenu>
    </toolkit:ContextMenuService.ContextMenu>
</Button>
```

When a `MenuItem` is tapped, a message box is displayed with the `MenuItem`'s `Header` (see Figure 9.11).

FIGURE 9.11   Tapping a `MenuItem` causes a message box to be displayed.

Hosting a `ContextMenu` in a `ListBoxItem`

Sometimes the need arises to provide a context menu for dynamically generated elements, such as those presented using a data bound `ItemsControl`. The following example demonstrates how to host a context menu for each item in a `ListBox`.

The `ContextMenuViewModel` contains an `ObservableCollection` of strings, declared as shown:

```
readonly ObservableCollection<string> items
                = new ObservableCollection<string>();

public IEnumerable<string> Items
{
    get
```

```
    {
        return items;
    }
}
```

The `items` collection is populated within the viewmodel constructor. In addition, a new command, named `DeleteCommand`, is placed in the viewmodel. When the command is executed, it removes the item, passed as a command parameter, from the `items` collection. See the following excerpt:

```csharp
public ContextMenuViewModel()
{
    IEnumerable<string> temp = from int i in Enumerable.Range(1, 5)
                               select "Item " + i;
    foreach (var itemName in temp)
    {
        items.Add(itemName);
    }

    deleteCommand = new DelegateCommand<string>(
        itemName => items.Remove(itemName));

    /* Content omitted. */
}
```

A `ListBox` is placed on the page. Its `ItemTemplate` is defined, and a `TextBlock` is used to display each item in the list. The `TextBlock.Text` property is bound to the current item using the expression `{Binding}`. The `TextBlock` plays host to a `ContextMenu` onto which a single `MenuItem` is placed. Notice that the `MenuItem` is bound to the `DeleteCommand` using the `DataContext` property of the page. This is because the `DataContext` of the `MenuItem` is the string item and not the page, and therefore we specify the source explicitly using the `ElementName` binding property. See the following excerpt:

```xml
<ListBox ItemsSource="{Binding Items}" Height="200" Margin="12">
    <ListBox.ItemTemplate>
        <DataTemplate>
            <TextBlock Text="{Binding}" Margin="20">
        <toolkit:ContextMenuService.ContextMenu>
            <toolkit:ContextMenu IsZoomEnabled="false">
                <toolkit:MenuItem
                    Header="Delete"
                    Command="{Binding DataContext.DeleteCommand,
                                      ElementName=page}"
```

```
                    CommandParameter="{Binding}" />
            </toolkit:ContextMenu>
        </toolkit:ContextMenuService.ContextMenu>
            </TextBlock>
        </DataTemplate>
    </ListBox.ItemTemplate>
</ListBox>
```

Tapping and holding an item in the list causes the `ContextMenu` for that item to be displayed. The `DeleteCommand` accepts a single parameter, which is the item string (see Figure 9.12). When executed, the item is removed from the list as expected.

FIGURE 9.12   The `ListBoxItem` plays host to a `ContextMenu` with a delete button.

Selecting Date and Time Values with the `DatePicker` and `TimePicker`

Entering a date or time on the phone would be an otherwise cumbersome task if it relied solely on the phone SIP (Software Input Panel) or hardware keyboard. `DatePicker` and `TimePicker` conform to the language of the phone and provide an interface that makes selecting a date or time easy.

Both the `DatePicker` and `TimePicker` use a `TextBox` to display a date or time value (see Figure 9.13).

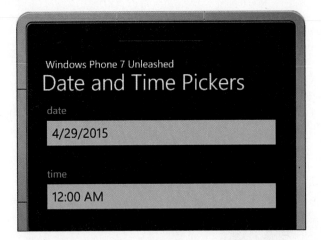

FIGURE 9.13   `DatePicker` and `TimePicker` controls.

When the user taps the `TextBox`, a form is presented that allows the user to specify the date or time using a set of infinitely scrollable controls (see Figure 9.14).

FIGURE 9.14   `DatePicker` while in selection mode.

The `DatePicker` and `TimePicker` inherit from the same base class, which is `DateTimePickerBase`. The `DateTimePickerBase` class contains a `Value` property of type nullable `DateTime`. The `DatePicker` and `TimePicker` share the same public API, which is provided entirely by the base class. The `DatePicker` deals with the date segment of the `DateTime` value; the `TimePicker`, the time segment.

There are two main differences between the `DatePicker` and `TimePicker`. The first is the string pattern used to present the `DataTime` value. The `DatePicker` presents the `DateTime` value using the short date pattern, such that a date value of 6/1/2015 1:45:30 PM is presented as 6/1/2015. Conversely, the `TimePicker` presents the `DateTime` value using the short time pattern, such that a date value of 6/1/2015 1:45:30 PM is presented as 1:45 PM. You look at customizing the value format for both controls in a later section.

The second difference is the type of the associated `PhoneApplicationPage` for each control. `DatePicker` and `TimePicker` each rely on a particular `PhoneApplicationPage` for allowing the user to select the `DateTime` value. When the user taps the `DatePicker`, the control navigates to the built-in `DatePickerPage`. Conversely, when the user taps the `TimePicker`, the control navigates to the built-in `TimePickerPage`.

Using the `DatePicker` and `TimePicker`

When building small and simple apps, you may choose to give your `DatePicker` or `TimePicker` a name and respond to its `ValueChanged` event in your page code-beside file. The following excerpt shows a `ValueChanged` event handler. `DateTimeValueChangedEventArgs` contains both the value before being modified by the user, and the value after being modified:

```
void DatePicker_ValueChanged(object sender, DateTimeValueChangedEventArgs e)
{
    DateTime? oldDataValue = e.OldDateTime;
    DateTime? newDateValue = e.NewDateTime;
}
```

Alternatively, you may choose to rely on data binding and bind your control to a view-model property, as shown:

```
<toolkit:DatePicker Value="{Binding Date, Mode=TwoWay}"
                    Header="date"
                    ValueChanged="DatePicker_ValueChanged" />
```

In either case, tapping the control navigates to a particular `PhoneApplicationPage`, allowing the user to set the `DateTime` value. The two pages, `DatePickerPage` and `TimePickerPage`, both rely on two icons that must be placed in your project. The icons are used to confirm or cancel the `DateTime` selection operation. Without these icons, the OK and Cancel `ApplicationBarIconButtons` are not displayed correctly (see Figure 9.15).

9

FIGURE 9.15   Without correct inclusion of PNG images, icon buttons are displayed using a broken icon.

For each `ApplicationBarIconButton` to be displayed correctly, images for the buttons must be placed in your project. The image icons should be placed in a directory called Toolkit.Content, in the root directory of your project. The images should be named ApplicationBar.Cancel.png and ApplicationBar.Check.png, and their Build Action should be set to Content (see Figure 9.16).

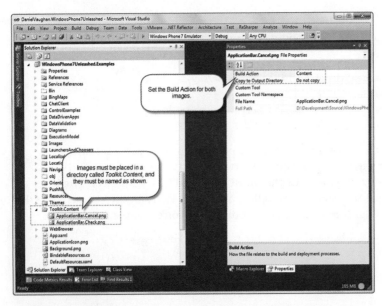

FIGURE 9.16   Set the icon image Build Action using the Properties pane.

Once in place, the images are automatically used by the `DatePicker` and `TimePicker`.

Adding a Control Header

Many of the Toolkit controls allow you to customize the title text displayed above the control using a `Header` property. In addition, the `HeaderTemplate` property allows you to customize how the `Header` content is displayed. The following example provides a custom header template for a `TimePicker`:

```
<toolkit:TimePicker Value="{Binding Time, Mode=TwoWay}"
        Header="time">
    <toolkit:TimePicker.HeaderTemplate>
        <DataTemplate>
            <Border BorderThickness="2" BorderBrush="Yellow" Padding="10">
                <TextBlock Text="{Binding}" />
            </Border>
        </DataTemplate>
    </toolkit:TimePicker.HeaderTemplate>
</toolkit:TimePicker>
```

The `DataTemplate` places the `Header` text in a `TextBlock`, which is wrapped in a yellow border (see Figure 9.17).

FIGURE 9.17   `TimePicker` with a custom `HeaderTemplate`.

Customizing the Value Format

The format of the `DateTime` value can be specified by setting the `DatePicker` or `TimePicker ValueStringFormat` property. For example, to present the `DateTime` value of a `TimePicker` using a long time format, the `ValueStringFormat` is set to {0:T}. Because curly brackets are treated as special characters in XAML, they must be escaped. This is done by prefixing {} to the format string, as shown in the following excerpt:

```
<toolkit:TimePicker x:Name="timePicker"
                    Value="{Binding Time, Mode=TwoWay}"
```

```
Header="time with custom format"
ValueStringFormat="{}{0:T}"/>
```

Alternatively, to set the format in the code-beside, you could use the following:

```
timePicker.ValueStringFormat = "{0:T}";
```

Figure 9.18 shows a `TimePicker` with the `ValueStringFormat` set to a long time format. You see that, unlike the default short time format, the seconds position is displayed.

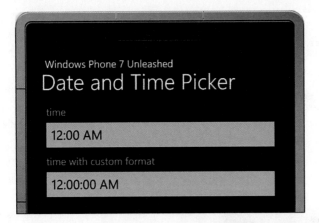

FIGURE 9.18   `TimePicker` with a custom format.

> **NOTE**
>
> By changing the `ValueStringFormat` and the `PickerPageUri` (discussed in the next section), you can effectively change a `DatePicker` into a `TimePicker`, and vice versa. This, however, would make little sense, yet it illustrates the similarity and the flexibility of both controls.

The `DateTimePickerBase.ValueString` property allows you to retrieve the string that is presented in the `TextBox` after the format has been applied.

Customizing the Full-Screen Picker Page

Both the `DatePicker` and `TimePicker` allow you to change the full-screen picker page using the `DateTimePickerBase.PickerPageUri` property. This property is normally specified using a component URI, with the assembly and path to the `PhoneApplicationPage`. In the following example a `DatePicker` uses a custom picker page, located in an Examples assembly:

```
<toolkit:DatePicker Value="{Binding Date, Mode=TwoWay}"
                    Header="date with custom picker"
                PickerPageUri="/Examples;component/CustomDatePickerView.xaml" />
```

The task of the picker page is to allow the user to select a `DateTime` value, and then to use the `NavigationService` to navigate back to the original page. A picker page must implement the `IDateTimePickerPage` interface. This interface consists of a single nullable `DateTime` property called `Value`.

A custom picker page called `CustomDatePickerView` is located in the ControlExamples/ WindowsPhoneToolkit/DateAndTimePickers directory in the downloadable sample code. The sample allows the user to select from an arbitrary list of `DateTime` values.

The viewmodel consists of a list of `DateTime` values that the user selects from, a single `DateTime` property that tracks the selected date, and a command that is used to set the selected date value from buttons in the view.

The list of dates is defined in the viewmodel like so:

```
readonly List<DateTime> dates = new List<DateTime>();

public IEnumerable<DateTime> Dates
{
    get
    {
        return dates;
    }
}
```

The list is populated with five `DateTime` values, within the viewmodel constructor:

```
for (int i = 1; i < 6; i++)
{
    dates.Add(DateTime.Now.AddYears(i));
}
```

Each `DateTime` value in the list is presented as a button in the view.

Within the viewmodel, a property called `Date` holds the selected date:

```
DateTime? date = DateTime.Now;

public DateTime? Date
{
    get
    {
        return date;
    }
```

```
    set
    {
        Assign(ref date, value);
    }
}
```

An `ICommand` is used to set the `Date` property via buttons in the view. The `ICommand` is shown in the following excerpt:

```
readonly DelegateCommand<DateTime?> setDateCommand;

public DelegateCommand<DateTime?> SetDateCommand
{
    get
    {
        return setDateCommand;
    }
}
```

The `setDateCommand` is initialized in the viewmodel constructor. The constructor accepts an `Action` parameter that is used during execution of the `SetDateCommand` to call the `NavigationService.GoBack` method, after a `DateTime` value has been selected by the user. The constructor is shown in full in the following excerpt:

```
public CustomDatePickerViewModel(Action completeAction)
{
    for (int i = 1; i < 6; i++)
    {
        dates.Add(DateTime.Now.AddYears(i));
    }

    setDateCommand = new DelegateCommand<DateTime?>(
        dateTime =>
            {
                if (dateTime == null)
                {
                    return;
                }

                Date = dateTime;

                if (completeAction != null)
                {
                    completeAction();
                }
            });
}
```

The custom picker view initializes its viewmodel, passing it a lambda expression, which allows the viewmodel to return to the calling page.

NOTE

As an alternative to passing the viewmodel a lambda expression, you may want to consider using a dedicated INavigationService for your app. Such a service is discussed in Chapter 29, "Storing App Data in a Local Database," and exists as part of the Calcium framework for Windows Phone http://calciumsdk.com.

Passing a reference to a page property, as shown in this example, causes the page to remain alive, ineligible for garbage collection, for the lifetime of the viewmodel. If the viewmodel does not share the same lifetime as the view, then a memory leak may ensue. In this example, the lifetime of the viewmodel is the same as the view's, and hence it is not an issue.

When the viewmodel determines that a DateTime value has been acquired, it invokes the specified Action, and the page with the DatePicker retrieves the DateTime value from the page's Value property (see Listing 9.3).

LISTING 9.3   CustomDatePickerView Class

```csharp
public partial class CustomDatePickerView
    : PhoneApplicationPage, IDateTimePickerPage
{
    public CustomDatePickerView()
    {
        InitializeComponent();
        DataContext = new CustomDatePickerViewModel(
            () => NavigationService.GoBack());
    }


    CustomDatePickerViewModel ViewModel
    {
        get
        {
            return (CustomDatePickerViewModel)DataContext;
        }
    }
    public DateTime? Value
    {
        get
        {
            return ViewModel.Date;
        }
```

```
    set
    {
        ViewModel.Date = value;
    }
  }
}
```

The XAML for the view contains a `ListBox` that is bound to the list of `DateTime` values. A `DataTemplate` is used to present each `DateTime` as a button. Each button is bound to the `SetDateCommand` of the viewmodel, as shown in the following excerpt:

```
<StackPanel x:Name="ContentPanel" Grid.Row="1">
    <ListBox ItemsSource="{Binding Dates}"
             SelectedItem="{Binding Date}">
        <ListBox.ItemTemplate>
            <DataTemplate>
                <Button Content="{Binding}"
                    Command="{Binding DataContext.SetDateCommand,
                    ElementName=page}"
                    CommandParameter="{Binding}" />
            </DataTemplate>
        </ListBox.ItemTemplate>
    </ListBox>
</StackPanel>
```

When visible, the custom picker page presents the five `DateTime` values, as shown in Figure 9.19.

FIGURE 9.19   The custom date/time picker page.

Providing Custom Looping Lists with the `LoopingSelector`

The previous section looked at the `DatePicker` and `TimePicker` controls, whose base class, `DateTimePickerBase`, relies on a simpler control called `LoopingSelector` to display date and time values.

`LoopingSelector` provides all the functionality for an infinitely looping list of values.

`LoopingSelector` is not intended to be used day-to-day like other controls presented in this chapter, and as a result it resides in the Microsoft.Phone.Controls.Primitives namespace. Nonetheless, it is a useful control.

To use the control you must define a data source, which can be any object that implements `ILoopingSelectorDataSource`. The `ILoopingSelectorDataSource` interface defines the following four members:

▶ `GetPrevious(object relativeTo)` method

▶ `GetNext(object relativeTo)` method

▶ `SelectedItem` property

▶ `SelectionChanged` event

`GetPrevious` and `GetNext` allow you to define the order of the data provided to the control. `SelectedItem` is used to keep track of the currently selected item in the control. The `SelectionChanged` event allows you to programmatically change the selected item in the control, which is normally done via the `SelectedItem` property.

To present a selectable list of numeric values to the user, we create an `ILoopingSelectorDataSource` called `NumericDataSource` (see Listing 9.4).

`NumericDataSource` allows you to define a range of integers using two properties: `Minimum` and `Maximum`.

LISTING 9.4   `NumericDataSource` Class

```
public class NumericDataSource : ILoopingSelectorDataSource
{
    public event EventHandler<SelectionChangedEventArgs> SelectionChanged;

    protected virtual void OnSelectionChanged(SelectionChangedEventArgs e)
    {
        EventHandler<SelectionChangedEventArgs> tempEvent = SelectionChanged;
        if (tempEvent != null)
        {
            tempEvent(this, e);
        }
    }
}
```

6

```csharp
public object GetNext(object relativeTo)
{
    int nextValue = (int)relativeTo + 1;

    return nextValue <= Maximum ? nextValue : Minimum;
}

public object GetPrevious(object relativeTo)
{
    int previousValue = (int)relativeTo - 1;

    return previousValue >= Minimum ? previousValue : Maximum;
}
int selectedItem = 1;

public object SelectedItem
{
    get
    {
        return selectedItem;
    }
    set
    {
        int newValue = (int)value;

        if (selectedItem == newValue)
        {
            return;
        }
        int oldValue = selectedItem;
        selectedItem = newValue;

        OnSelectionChanged(new SelectionChangedEventArgs(
                            new[] {oldValue}, new[] {newValue}));
    }
}

public int SelectedNumber
{
    get
    {
        return (int)SelectedItem;
    }
    set
    {
        SelectedItem = value;
    }
```

```
    }

    int minimum = 1;

    public int Minimum
    {
        get
        {
            return minimum;
        }
        set
        {
            minimum = value;
            if (selectedItem < minimum)
            {
                SelectedItem = value;
            }
        }
    }

    int maximum = 100;

    public int Maximum
    {
        get
        {
            return maximum;
        }
        set
        {
            maximum = value;

            if (selectedItem > maximum)
            {
                SelectedItem = value;
            }
        }
    }
}
```

To use the NumericDataSource, we expose an instance via a property in a viewmodel, like so:

```
NumericDataSource numericDataSource
  = new NumericDataSource { Minimum = 0, Maximum = 10, SelectedNumber = 5 };
```

```
public NumericDataSource NumericDataSource
{
    get
    {
        return numericDataSource;
    }
}
```

A `LoopingSelector` can be data bound to the `NumericDataSource` property in the view-model. Its `ItemTemplate` defines the appearance of each item retrieved from the data source. See the following example:

```
<toolkitPrimitives:LoopingSelector
    DataSource="{Binding NumericDataSource}"
    Margin="12" Width="200" Height="500" ItemSize="128,128">
    <toolkitPrimitives:LoopingSelector.ItemTemplate>
        <DataTemplate>
            <Grid>
                <TextBlock Text="{Binding}" FontSize="54"
                    FontFamily="{StaticResource PhoneFontFamilySemiBold}"
                    HorizontalAlignment="Center" VerticalAlignment="Center" />
            </Grid>
        </DataTemplate>
    </toolkitPrimitives:LoopingSelector.ItemTemplate>
</toolkitPrimitives:LoopingSelector>
```

It is critical to assign values to the `LoopingSelector` element's `Width`, `Height`, and `ItemSize` properties.

Figure 9.20 shows the `LoopingSelector` after it has gained focus.

FIGURE 9.20   `LoopingSelector` example.

`LoopingSelector` is a control ideally suited to the touch-centric environment of the phone.

Providing Touch Feedback with the `TiltEffect`

In an environment whose primary input method is touch, providing feedback when a user interacts with UI elements helps to engage the user and improves the perceived responsiveness of the UI. On the desktop, a pointer indicates the location of the mouse, and hover events are used to provide different states for interactive controls. On the phone, however, there is no mouse, and no way of knowing when a user's finger is above an element if screen contact is not made. The `TiltEffect` component provides feedback to the user when she taps and holds an element. It is simple to set up and has out-of-the-box support for many of the built-in controls (see Figure 9.21).

FIGURE 9.21   With the tilt effect enabled, a button tilts when it is tapped and held.

To use `TiltEffect` on your page, set the `IsTiltEnabled` attached property of the `TiltEffect` class to true within the `PhoneApplicationPage` element, like so:

```
<phone:PhoneApplicationPage
    ...
    toolkit:TiltEffect.IsTiltEnabled="True">
```

To prevent the tilt effect from being applied to a particular element on your page, set the `TiltEffect.SuppressTilt` attached property to True, as shown:

```
<Button Content="without tilt effect"
        toolkit:TiltEffect.SuppressTilt="True" />
```

Out of the box, `TiltEffect` supports two base control types: `ButtonBase` and `ListBoxItem`. The tilt effect is automatically applied to any classes deriving from `ButtonBase` or `ListBoxItem`, or indeed `ListBoxItem` itself.

Supporting Other Controls

Some controls may benefit from the tilt effect, yet may not necessarily derive from `ButtonBase` or `ListBoxItem`. To enable `TiltEffect` on an alternative `UIElement` type, such as on context menu items, add the element `Type` to the `TitleEffect`'s list of supported types via the `TiltEffect.TiltableItems` collection.

TIP

As `TiltEffect.TiltableItems` is a static property and global to your app, where possible populate it from a centralized location such as your `App` class, rather than in an ad hoc fashion from, for example, your page classes. This can help to reduce duplication, and allows you to manage type registrations in one location.

The following excerpt demonstrates how to add tilt effect support for the Toolkit's context menu `MenuItem` class:

```
public partial class App : Application
{

    public App()
    {
        /* Content omitted for clarity. */

        TiltEffect.TiltableItems.Add(typeof(MenuItem));
    }
//...
}
```

To enable the tilt effect on `MenuItem` elements, you must explicitly set the `IsTiltEnabled` attached property to true, as demonstrated in the following excerpt:

```
<Border Padding="10" BorderThickness="2" BorderBrush="White">
    <TextBlock Text="tilt effect applied to context menu" />
    <toolkit:ContextMenuService.ContextMenu>
        <toolkit:ContextMenu >
            <toolkit:MenuItem Header="item 1"
                toolkit:TiltEffect.IsTiltEnabled="true" />
            <toolkit:MenuItem Header="item 2"
                toolkit:TiltEffect.IsTiltEnabled="true" />
        </toolkit:ContextMenu>
```

```
        </toolkit:ContextMenuService.ContextMenu>
</Border>
```

> **NOTE**
>
> Regardless of whether the `TiltEffect.IsTiltEnabled` property is set to true, if the
> `TiltEffect.TiltableItems` collection does not contain the element type (or that of its
> ancestor), the tilt effect is *not* applied.

Applying the tilt effect to a context menu item causes it to be indented slightly (see
Figure 9.22).

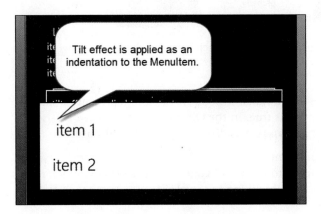

FIGURE 9.22   `TiltEffect` applied to a `MenuItem`.

Applied judiciously, `TiltEffect` can subtly enhance your UI, increasing its perceived
responsiveness and making it stand out from the crowd.

Providing a Boolean Option with the `ToggleSwitch`

`ToggleSwitch` enables the user to turn something on or off. It is much like the built-in
`CheckBox` control, yet more compatible with the modern UI design aesthetic of the phone.
`ToggleSwitch` presents a large, touch friendly switch that users can alternate between two
states (see Figure 9.23).

While `ToggleSwitch` does not inherit from any built-in button related controls, such
as `ButtonBase`, but rather from `ContentControl`, it behaves much like the built-in
`ToggleButton` control in the FCL of which the built-in `RadioButton` and `CheckBox` controls
are derived. In fact, internally the `ToggleSwitch` uses a `ToggleButton` to provide its
functionality.

FIGURE 9.23   `ToggleSwitch` can be localized and its switch color modified.

Using the `ToggleSwitch`

Like the `ToggleButton`, `ToggleSwitch` uses a nullable Boolean value to represent its state. In its On position, its `IsChecked` property is true. In the Off position, `IsChecked` is false. If the `IsChecked` property is `null`, the `ToggleSwitch` is displayed using its Off position.

You can use the `ToggleSwitch` by either binding its `IsChecked` property to a property in your viewmodel, or by responding to its `Checked` and `Unchecked` events in your code-beside. The later approach involves subscribing to the `ToggleSwitch.Checked` and `Unchecked` events, as shown:

```
<toolkit:ToggleSwitch
        Header="ToggleSwitch"
        IsChecked="true"
        Checked="ToggleSwitch_Checked"
        Unchecked="ToggleSwitch_Unchecked"/>
```

Both the `Checked` and `Unchecked` events are `RoutedEvents`. The following excerpt shows what event handlers for these events might look like:

```
void ToggleSwitch_Checked(object sender, RoutedEventArgs e)
{
    ToggleSwitch toggleSwitch = (ToggleSwitch)sender;
    bool? isChecked = toggleSwitch.IsChecked;
    /* Do something with value. */
    MessageBox.Show("Checked!");
}

void ToggleSwitch_Unchecked(object sender, RoutedEventArgs e)
{
```

```
    MessageBox.Show("Unchecked!");
}
```

`ToggleSwitch` allows customization of its header using its `Header` and `HeaderTemplate` properties. For more information on creating a custom header for the control, see the previous section "Adding a Control Header."

Binding the `ToggleSwitch` to a Viewmodel Property

Rather than placing UI logic in the code-beside, an alternative is to bind the `ToggleSwitch` to a viewmodel property. This is demonstrated in the `ToggleSwitchView` and `ToggleSwitchViewModel`, in the downloadable sample code.

The viewmodel contains a `ToggleOn` property, as shown:

```
bool? toggleOn;

public bool? ToggleOn
{
    get
    {
        return toggleOn;
    }
    set
    {
        Assign(ref toggleOn, value);
    }
}
```

Consuming this property in the view is a `ToggleSwitch`, whose `IsChecked` property has a two-way data binding to the `ToggleOn` property of the viewmodel:

```
<toolkit:ToggleSwitch
    Header="ToggleSwitch"
    IsChecked="{Binding ToggleOn, Mode=TwoWay}" />
```

Thus, when the user taps the `ToggleSwitch`, the `ToggleOn` property of the viewmodel is inverted.

Localizing the `ToggleSwitch`

Unlike controls located in the FCL, the Toolkit does not ship with localized resources. In the case of the `ToggleSwitch`, it is something to be mindful of because of the default `Header` values: Off and On, which must be localized if you want to support other languages.

You could take the Toolkit source code and provide a localized resource dictionary for each language you want to support. This, however, would leave you having to update each new version of the Toolkit with your custom dictionaries—not the best approach.

An alternative approach is to use a custom `IValueConverter` to populate the `Content` property of the `ToggleSwitch` based on the value of its `IsChecked` property. Depending on the value of its `IsChecked` property, we display a particular localized string from a resource dictionary (see Listing 9.5).

For more information on localizing Windows Phone apps, see Chapter 19, "Supporting Multiple Cultures and Languages."

LISTING 9.5   `LocalizedToggleSwitchConverter` Class

```
public class LocalizedToggleSwitchConverter : IValueConverter
{
    public object Convert(
        object value, Type targetType, object parameter, CultureInfo culture)
    {
        bool? toggleOn = (bool?)value;
        return toggleOn.HasValue && toggleOn.Value
                ? MainResources.ToggleSwitch_Checked
                : MainResources.ToggleSwitch_Unchecked;
    }

    public object ConvertBack(
        object value, Type targetType, object parameter, CultureInfo culture)
    {
        throw new NotImplementedException();
    }
}
```

The `IValueConverter` can be declared as an application resource by placing it in your app's App.xaml file or in a referenced `ResourceDictionary`. This allows it to be used throughout your app. Alternatively, it can be defined within your page, as shown:

```
<phone:PhoneApplicationPage.Resources>
    <e:LocalizedToggleSwitchConverter
        x:Name="LocalizedToggleSwitchConverter" />
</phone:PhoneApplicationPage.Resources>
```

Once in place, a `ToggleSwitch` can bind to the viewmodel value representing the checked state and use the `IValueConverter` to populate the `Content` property, as shown:

```
<toolkit:ToggleSwitch
    Header="Localizable ToggleSwitch"
    IsChecked="{Binding ToggleOn, Mode=TwoWay}"
```

```
Content="{Binding ToggleOn,
Converter={StaticResource LocalizedToggleSwitchConverter}}" />
```

Just as the `HeaderTemplate` property is used to customize how the control's header is displayed, the `ContentTemplate` is used to customize how the `Content` property is displayed.

Changing the Switch Color

By default, the `ToggleSwitch` control template presents the On state using the phone's theme color. You can explicitly set the `ToggleSwitch` color using its `SwitchForeground` property, as shown in the following excerpt:

```
<toolkit:ToggleSwitch
        Header="ToggleSwitch with custom switch color"
        IsChecked="true"
        SwitchForeground="Red"/>
```

In most cases, `ToggleSwitch` makes for a better choice than the standard `CheckBox` control. And after you start using it, it becomes almost as ubiquitous as the `Button` control.

Using Flexible Layouts with the `WrapPanel`

`WrapPanel` is a flexible container that is ideally suited to the limited display size of the phone because it allows your UI elements to use space more efficiently. The `WrapPanel` positions child elements sequentially, from left to right or from top to bottom. When elements extend beyond the panel edge, they are positioned in the next row or column. `WrapPanel` can operate in one of two layout modes. The `Orientation` property of the `WrapPanel` determines its layout mode, either Horizontal (the default value) or Vertical. Figure 9.24 portrays how the `WrapPanel` positions its children when using a horizontal orientation.

WrapPanel

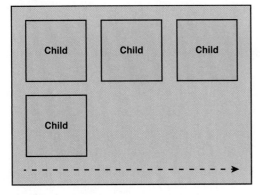

FIGURE 9.24 `WrapPanel` positions child elements sequentially from left to right (as shown), or from top to bottom.

Child Element Spacing

The `ItemHeight` and `ItemWidth` properties of the `WrapPanel` determine the amount of space that each child element is allocated. If the actual size of the element exceeds this amount, then the element is clipped.

Sample Overview

The `WrapPanel` sample is located within the ControlExamples/WindowsPhoneToolkit/ WrapPanel directory in the WPUnleashed.Examples project in the downloadable sample code.

The WrapPanelView.xaml presents two `WrapPanels`, one with the default horizontal orientation, the other with a vertical orientation. Each `WrapPanel` contains five `TextBox` child elements, as shown in the following excerpt:

```
<StackPanel x:Name="ContentPanel" Grid.Row="1">
    <TextBlock Text="horizontal wrap panel"
        Style="{StaticResource LabelTextIndentedStyle}" />
    <toolkit:WrapPanel ItemHeight="120" ItemWidth="120" Height="280"
            Background="DimGray">
        <TextBox Text="1" Background="Blue"
            Style="{StaticResource WrapPanelItem}" />
        <TextBox Text="2" Background="Red"
            Style="{StaticResource WrapPanelItem}" />
        <TextBox Text="3" Background="Orange"
            Style="{StaticResource WrapPanelItem}" />
        <TextBox Text="4" Background="Purple"
            Style="{StaticResource WrapPanelItem}" />
        <TextBox Text="5" Background="Green"
            Style="{StaticResource WrapPanelItem}" />
    </toolkit:WrapPanel>

    <TextBlock Text="vertical wrap panel"
        Style="{StaticResource LabelTextIndentedStyle}"
        Margin="12,30,0,0"/>
    <toolkit:WrapPanel Orientation="Vertical"
            ItemHeight="120" ItemWidth="120" Height="280"
            Background="DimGray">
        <TextBox Text="1" Background="Blue"
            Style="{StaticResource WrapPanelItem}" />
```

```
        <TextBox Text="2" Background="Red"
            Style="{StaticResource WrapPanelItem}" />
        <TextBox Text="3" Background="Orange"
            Style="{StaticResource WrapPanelItem}" />
        <TextBox Text="4" Background="Purple"
            Style="{StaticResource WrapPanelItem}" />
        <TextBox Text="5" Background="Green"
            Style="{StaticResource WrapPanelItem}" />
    </toolkit:WrapPanel>
</StackPanel>
```

Each `TextBox` is presented using a custom `ControlTemplate`, which places the `TextBox.Text` in a `TextBlock`. A `TextBox` was chosen because it allows you to create a template binding to its `Text` property. See the following excerpt:

```
<phone:PhoneApplicationPage.Resources>
    <Style x:Name="WrapPanelItem" TargetType="TextBox">
        <Setter Property="Width" Value="100" />
        <Setter Property="Height" Value="100" />
        <Setter Property="Template">
            <Setter.Value>
                <ControlTemplate TargetType="TextBox">
                    <Border Background="{TemplateBinding Background}">
                        <TextBlock Text="{TemplateBinding Text}"
                        VerticalAlignment="Center"
                        HorizontalAlignment="Center"
                        FontSize="50"
                        Foreground="White" />
                    </Border>
                </ControlTemplate>
            </Setter.Value>
        </Setter>
    </Style>
</phone:PhoneApplicationPage.Resources>
```

Each `TextBox` is presented as a `TextBlock` wrapped in a `Border`. The horizontal wrap panel illustrates how the child elements are displayed from left to right, and the vertical wrap panel illustrates the vertical layout (see Figure 9.25).

FIGURE 9.25   A vertical and horizontal `WrapPanel`.

Using a `WrapPanel` in Conjunction with a `ListBox`

`WrapPanel` is useful to present a list of items using XAML. However, using a `WrapPanel` to present a bound list of values located in a viewmodel can be best achieved by supplanting the `ItemsPanelTemplate` of a `ListBox` with a `WrapPanel`.

This technique is demonstrated in the downloadable sample code. The `WrapPanelViewModel` class contains a list of strings, representing the numbers 1 to 5, which we use as the source collection for a `ListBox` control. The list of strings is generated using the LINQ `Range` and `Select` methods. See the following excerpt:

```
readonly IEnumerable<string> items
    = Enumerable.Range(1, 5).Select(x => x.ToString());


public IEnumerable<string> Items
{
    get
    {
        return items;
    }
}
```

The view contains a ListsBox with its ItemsSource property bound to the viewmodel's Items property. We redefine the ItemsPanel of the ListBox and use a WrapPanel to host the child elements.

The ItemTemplate of the ListBox is also defined so that each item is presented in a TextBox, which is compatible with the custom WrapPanelItem template:

```
<ListBox ItemsSource="{Binding Items}">
    <ListBox.ItemsPanel>
        <ItemsPanelTemplate>
            <toolkit:WrapPanel
                ItemHeight="120" ItemWidth="120" Height="280"
                Background="DimGray"/>
        </ItemsPanelTemplate>
    </ListBox.ItemsPanel>
    <ListBox.ItemTemplate>
        <DataTemplate>
            <TextBox Text="{Binding}" Background="Blue"
            Style="{StaticResource WrapPanelItem}" />
        </DataTemplate>
    </ListBox.ItemTemplate>
</ListBox>
```

You see in Figure 9.26, that each item in the list is presented in a similar manner as the statically defined items presented earlier in this section.

FIGURE 9.26   A WrapPanel is used to display the items in a ListBox.

Another example of presenting a list of items using a `WrapPanel` in conjunction with a `ListBox` can be found in Chapter 11, "Creating Expansive and Engaging Apps with the Pivot and Panorama."

Summary

This chapter began with a short getting started guide that showed how to obtain and reference the Toolkit using NuGet. It then explored each Toolkit component starting with the `ListPicker`, which allows you to display a large number of options using an expandable or full-screen option picker. You saw how to bind a `ListPicker` to a viewmodel collection and how to customize the way items are displayed.

The chapter then looked at the `AutoCompleteBox`, which provides suggestions for the user in a drop-down list. You saw how to use the `AutoCompleteBox` from code-beside and via data binding to a viewmodel. You looked at dynamically changing the way the `AutoCompleteBox` filters items, at creating a custom filter, and at dynamic population of the suggestion list. How to overcome a limitation to allow binding from the `AutoCompleteBox.Text` property was also discussed.

The chapter looked at the `ContextMenu`, which is an expanding menu control that you can use to emulate the familiar right-click menu in Windows desktop applications. You saw how to consume the various `ContextMenu` events and how to use the `ContextMenu` in conjunction with the MVVM pattern. You also looked at hosting a `ContextMenu` in a `ListBoxItem`.

The `DatePicker` and `TimePicker`, which allow the user to select a date or time using infinitely scrollable lists, were discussed. You learned how to customize the `Value` format of the controls and how to create a custom full-screen picker page. You also learned how to use the lesser known `LoopingSelector` to allow the user to select a numeric value from an infinitely scrolling list.

The chapter then looked at the `TiltEffect` component, which allows you to add a subtle rotation effect to other controls when the user interacts with them, and which helps to engage the user and improve the perceived responsiveness of the UI. You also saw how to suppress the tilt effect on particular controls and how to add new control types to the list of tiltable control types.

The chapter then looked at the `ToggleSwitch`, which serves as a replacement for the `CheckBox` control in some scenarios. You saw how to respond to the `Checked` and `Unchecked` events of the `ToggleSwitch`, and at binding the `ToggleSwitch` to a viewmodel property. You looked at localizing the `ToggleSwitch` header text, allowing it to be used when the display language of the phone is not English, and also how to change the switch color using the `ToggleSwitch.SwitchForeground` property.

Finally, the chapter discussed the `WrapPanel`, which is a flexible container that positions items sequentially and is ideally suited to the limited display size of the phone. You learned how to use the `WrapPanel` in conjunction with a `ListBox`, to enable binding to a viewmodel collection.

CHAPTER 10

Creating Jump Lists with the Long List Selector

The LongListSelector is like a ListBox that allows you to group items together. It is effective for large lists, because it allows the user to more easily navigate through items by group.

LongListSelector supports full data and UI virtualization and can display flat lists and grouped lists. When using grouped lists, the user is able to jump between groups using a group picker interface, which overlays the list.

LongListSelector may be used in place of a ListBox for displaying flat lists. In fact, using the LongListSelector instead of the ListBox is recommended in Windows Phone 8.

LongListSelector was originally located in the Windows Phone Toolkit (formerly the Silverlight for Windows Phone Toolkit) but with the release of Windows Phone 8, the control has been made a first-class citizen of the Windows Phone SDK and resides alongside other controls, such as the ListBox, in the Windows Phone FCL (Framework Class Library).

This chapter begins with an overview of the visual structure of the LongListSelector. You then learn the basics of how to present flat and grouped lists using the control.

The chapter then dives into a sample app that allows the user to group a set of marketplace items. You see how to create a CustomGrouping class to allow the user to dynamically change the way the control groups items.

Finally, the chapter examines some more advanced features of the `LongListSelector` with another sample that demonstrates how to display a list of contacts with the `LongListSelector` using a grid layout.

The source code for this chapter is located in the ControlExamples/LongListSelector/ MarketplaceAppList directory of the WPUnleashed.Examples project, in the downloadable sample code.

Visual Structure of the Long List Selector

`LongListSelector` includes several regions that you may customize using `DataTemplates`. Each group item is presented between a group header and footer. The entire list is placed between a list header and footer (see Figure 10.1).

FIGURE 10.1   Visual structure of the `LongListSelector`.

When the group header is tapped, the `GroupItemsPanel` is presented, which allows the user to jump to a specific group. The `GroupItemsPanel` is discussed in greater detail later in the chapter.

Presenting Flat Lists

Presenting a list of nongrouped items is done by setting the LongListSelector's IsGroupingEnabled property to false, which is the default value. When presenting a flat list, there is little difference between a LongListSelector and a regular ListBox control, apart from the added header and footer of the LongListSelector.

To demonstrate how to display a flat list in a LongListSelector, we populate a LongListSelector with a list of custom City objects.

The FlatListViewModel in the downloadable sample code exposes a list of cities (see Listing 10.1).

LISTING 10.1   FlatListViewModel Class

```
public class FlatListViewModel : ViewModelBase
{
    readonly IEnumerable<City> cities = new List<City>
        {
            new City("Prague", "Capital of the Czech Republic."),
            new City("Geneva", "Swiss city."),
            new City("Canberra", "Capital of Australia."),
            new City("Palma", "Major city of Mallorca."),
            new City("New York", "Most populous city in the USA."),
        };

    public IEnumerable<City> Cities
    {
        get
        {
            return cities;
        }
    }
}
```

The view XAML uses a LongListSelector to display the list of cities. The LongListSelector.ItemsSource property is bound to the Cities property of the view-model. A header and footer are provided, and the ItemTemplate is responsible for presenting each City object. See the following excerpt:

```
<phone:LongListSelector ItemsSource="{Binding Cities}"
                    Background="Transparent">

    <phone:LongListSelector.ListHeader>
        <TextBlock Text="ListHeader"
            Style="{StaticResource PhoneTextTitle1Style}"/>
    </phone:LongListSelector.ListHeader>
```

```
    <phone:LongListSelector.ItemTemplate>
        <DataTemplate>
            <StackPanel Margin="{StaticResource PhoneMargin}">
                <TextBlock Text="{Binding Name}"
                    Style="{StaticResource PhoneTextLargeStyle}" />
                <TextBlock Text="{Binding Description}"
                    Style="{StaticResource PhoneTextNormalStyle}" />
            </StackPanel>
        </DataTemplate>
    </phone:LongListSelector.ItemTemplate>

    <phone:LongListSelector.ListFooter>
        <TextBlock Text="ListFooter"
            Style="{StaticResource PhoneTextTitle1Style}"/>
    </phone:LongListSelector.ListFooter>

</phone:LongListSelector>
```

In addition to the `ListHeader` and `ListFooter` properties, the `LongListSelector` also includes a `ListHeaderTemplate` and `ListFooterTemplate`, which are used to modify the way the header and footer content is presented (see Figure 10.2).

FIGURE 10.2   `LongListSelector` displaying a flat list of cities.

Presenting Grouped Lists

Presenting grouped, or composite, lists of items is where the `LongListSelector` shines. This section looks at two examples. The first example uses a `LongListSelector` to present a grouped list of Windows Phone Marketplace apps; the second example presents a grouped list of user contacts and demonstrates how to use a grid layout for the group items picker.

Marketplace App List Sample

The built-in Marketplace app presents apps in a flat list. This example groups a set of mock items using a `LongListSelector`.

The custom `MarketplaceApp` class defines an app as having a name, description, image, price, and marketplace category. The marketplace category and its price are used to group a list of randomly generated `MarketplaceApp` objects. First, the example briefly looks at the `MarketplaceApp` class and how to generate a list of `MarketplaceApp` objects; this will increase your understanding as you move further through the example.

`MarketplaceApp` defines an array of hard-coded categories and prices. The array of category names is called *categories*, and is defined as follows:

```
static readonly string[] categories
    = { "Games", "Photo", "Social", "Business", "Tools", "Travel" };
```

The array of prices is defined as shown:

```
static readonly double[] prices
    = { 0.99, 1.99, 2.99, 5.99 };
```

A category and price are randomly selected for each new `MarketplaceApp` using a `System.Random`.

The `MarketplaceApp` class includes a static method called `CreateRandomApp` that instantiates a `MarketplaceApp` and populates it with random data. The `LoremIpsumGenerator` class, borrowed from the Toolkit examples, produces random text. The `LoremIpsumGenerator` code is not covered in this book, but the code is available in the downloadable sample code for this book.

```
public static MarketplaceApp CreateRandomApp()
{
    string name = LoremIpsumGenerator.GetWords(
                    random.Next(1, 5),
                    LoremIpsumGenerator.Capitalization.AllWords);
    string description = LoremIpsumGenerator.GetParagraph(random.Next(3, 7));
    string category = categories[random.Next(6)];
    double price = prices[random.Next(4)];
    MarketplaceApp result = new MarketplaceApp(
```

```
        name, description, category, price,
        "/ControlExamples/LongListSelector/MarketplaceAppList
            /Images/MarketplaceAppIcon.png");
    return result;
}
```

To generate more than one `MarketplaceApp` object at a time, another static method called `CreateRandomApps` accepts an integer value and returns the specified number of instances. Although fairly arbitrary, this method is shown in the following excerpt because it is referred to later in this section:

```
public static IEnumerable<MarketplaceApp> CreateRandomApps(int numberToCreate)
{
    ArgumentValidator.AssertGreaterThan(0, numberToCreate, "numberToCreate");
    for (int i = 0; i < numberToCreate; i++)
    {
        yield return CreateRandomApp();
    }
}
```

The viewmodel for this sample is called `AppListViewModel`. It contains a list of grouped `MarketplaceApp` objects.

When presenting grouped items, the `LongListSelector` depends on each item in the source collection implementing `IEnumerable<TItem>`. You could, therefore, place each `MarketplaceApp` object in a `List<MarketplaceApp>`, and the `LongListSelector` would happily display them. However, doing so would not provide a means of displaying a group title for each group within the `LongListSelector`; you need a way to associate a name with each group. For this we turn to the `System.Linq.IGrouping` interface. The `IGrouping` interface has just what you need; it is `IEnumerable<TItem>` and contains a `Key` property that you can use as each group's title by binding to it in XAML (see Figure 10.3).

FIGURE 10.3   The `IGrouping<TKey, TElement>` interface extends `IEnumerable` interfaces.

The sample contains an implementation of IGrouping called CustomGrouping (see Listing 10.2). Rather than passing through a generic attribute for the IGrouping TKey attribute, the key type is defined as object to allow greater flexibility when switching collections within the viewmodel.

LISTING 10.2 CustomGrouping **Class**

```
public class CustomGrouping<TElement> : List<TElement>, IGrouping<object, TElement>
{
    readonly object key;

    public CustomGrouping(object key, IEnumerable<TElement> items)
    {
        this.key = ArgumentValidator.AssertNotNull(key, "key");
        AddRange(ArgumentValidator.AssertNotNull(items, "items"));
    }

    public object Key
    {
        get
        {
            return key;
        }
    }

    public bool HasItems
    {
        get
        {
            return items.Any();
        }
    }

    public override bool Equals(object obj)
    {
        var otherGrouping = obj as CustomGrouping<TElement>;
        return otherGrouping != null && Key.Equals(otherGrouping.Key);
    }

    public override int GetHashCode()
    {
        return Key.GetHashCode();
    }
}
```

10

The `AppListViewModel` contains a list of `CustomGrouping` objects, as shown:

```
IEnumerable<CustomGrouping<MarketplaceApp>> appGroupings;

public IEnumerable<CustomGrouping<MarketplaceApp>> AppGroupings
{
    get
    {
        return appGroupings;
    }
    private set
    {
        Assign(ref appGroupings, value);
    }
}
```

LINQ is used to populate `AppGroupings`. The `MarketplaceApp.CreateRandomApps` method generates many `MarketplaceApp` objects, which are then grouped by the `MarketplaceApp.Category` property, as shown:

```
void GroupByCategory()
{
    AppGroupings = (from app in MarketplaceApp.CreateRandomApps(appCount)
            group app by app.Category into grouping
            select new CustomGrouping<MarketplaceApp>(
                grouping.Key, grouping.AsEnumerable())).ToList();
}
```

> **NOTE**
>
> Conversion of the resulting `IEnumerable<T>` to a `List<T>` is done to avoid deferred execution, which would otherwise produce incorrect ordering and behavior.

The viewmodel allows the marketplace apps to be sorted either by category or by price. When sorted by price, the LINQ expression relies on the fact that the `CustomGrouping.Key` property is of type object, allowing you to reassign the `AppGrouping` property despite using the `MarketplaceApp.Price` property, which is of a different type to the `MarketplaceApp.Category`.

Grouping items by price is performed by the `GroupByPrice` method, as shown in the following excerpt:

```
void GroupByPrice()
{
    AppGroupings = (from app in MarketplaceApp.CreateRandomApps(appCount)
            group app by app.Price into grouping orderby grouping.Key
```

```
        select new CustomGrouping<MarketplaceApp>(
            grouping.Key, grouping.AsEnumerable())).ToList();
}
```

To allow the user to specify how items are grouped, the viewmodel includes a list of valid AppGroups:

```
readonly static IEnumerable<AppGroup> appGroups = new List<AppGroup>
                                    {
                                        AppGroup.Category,
                                        AppGroup.Price
                                    };

public IEnumerable<AppGroup> AppGroups
{
    get
    {
        return appGroups;
    }
}
```

How the items are grouped is determined by the viewmodel's GroupBy property. In the following excerpt, if the base class Assign method succeeds in setting the field value, then depending on the new value, the GroupByPrice or GroupByCategory method is called:

```
AppGroup groupBy = appGroups.First();

public AppGroup GroupBy
{
    get
    {
        return groupBy;
    }
    set
    {
        if (Assign(ref groupBy, value) == AssignmentResult.Success)
        {
            switch (value)
            {
                case AppGroup.Price:
                    GroupByPrice();
                    break;
                default:
                    GroupByCategory();
                    break;
            }
        }
```

```
        }


    }
}
```

For more information regarding the custom `ViewModelBase.Assign` method, see Chapter 2, "Fundamental Concepts in Windows Phone Development."

The view XAML contains a `ListPicker` that allows the user to switch how items are grouped. The `ListPicker`'s `ItemsSource` property is bound to the viewmodel's `AppGroups` property. The `ListPicker.SelectedItem` property has a *two way* data binding to the view-model's `GroupBy` property:

```
<toolkit:ListPicker
    Header="group by"
    ItemsSource="{Binding AppGroups}"
    SelectedItem="{Binding GroupBy, Mode=TwoWay}" />
```

When the user selects an item from the `ListPicker`, the viewmodel's `GroupBy` property is updated, which in turn calls one of the group by methods (see Figure 10.4).

FIGURE 10.4   The *group by* property is able to be changed via a `ListPicker`.

The `LongListSelector.ItemsSource` property is bound to the `AppGroupings` property of the viewmodel.

The LongListSelector includes a ListHeader, GroupHeaderTemplate, JumpListStyle, and an ItemTemplate. The ItemTemplate presents each MarketplaceApp object. See the following excerpt:

```
<phone:LongListSelector
        ItemsSource="{Binding AppGroupings}"
        IsGroupingEnabled="True"
        Grid.Row="1">
    <phone:LongListSelector.ListHeader>
        <TextBlock Text="latest apps"
                   Style="{StaticResource PhoneTextTitle1Style}"/>
    </phone:LongListSelector.ListHeader>

    <phone:LongListSelector.GroupHeaderTemplate>
        <DataTemplate>
            <Border Background="{StaticResource PhoneAccentBrush}"
                    Margin="{StaticResource PhoneTouchTargetOverhang}"
                    Padding="{StaticResource PhoneTouchTargetOverhang}">
                <TextBlock Text="{Binding Key}"
                           Style="{StaticResource PhoneTextTitle2Style}"/>
            </Border>
        </DataTemplate>
    </phone:LongListSelector.GroupHeaderTemplate>

    <phone:LongListSelector.JumpListStyle>
        <Style TargetType="phone:LongListSelector">
            <Setter Property="LayoutMode" Value="List" />
            <Setter Property="ItemTemplate">
                <Setter.Value>
                    <DataTemplate>
                        <Border Background="{StaticResource PhoneAccentBrush}"
                            Margin="{StaticResource PhoneTouchTargetOverhang}"
                            Padding="{StaticResource PhoneTouchTargetOverhang}">
                          <TextBlock Text="{Binding Key}"
                                Style="{StaticResource PhoneTextLargeStyle}"/>
                        </Border>
                    </DataTemplate>
                </Setter.Value>
            </Setter>
        </Style>
    </phone:LongListSelector.JumpListStyle>

    <phone:LongListSelector.ItemTemplate>
        <DataTemplate>
            <Grid Margin="{StaticResource PhoneTouchTargetOverhang}">
                <Grid.ColumnDefinitions>
```

10

```xml
                <ColumnDefinition Width="Auto"/>
                <ColumnDefinition Width="*"/>
            </Grid.ColumnDefinitions>
            <Image Source="{Binding ImageUrl}"
                   Width="110" Height="150"
                   VerticalAlignment="Top"/>
            <StackPanel Grid.Column="1" VerticalAlignment="Top">
                <TextBlock Text="{Binding Name}"
                           Style="{StaticResource PhoneTextLargeStyle}"
                    FontFamily="{StaticResource PhoneFontFamilySemiBold}"
                           TextWrapping="Wrap" Margin="12,-12,12,6" />
                <TextBlock Text="{Binding Description}"
                           Style="{StaticResource PhoneTextNormalStyle}"
                           TextWrapping="Wrap"
                    FontFamily="{StaticResource PhoneFontFamilySemiLight}"/>
            </StackPanel>
        </Grid>
    </DataTemplate>
  </phone:LongListSelector.ItemTemplate>
</phone:LongListSelector>
```

NOTE

When the `LongListSelector` resided in the Silverlight Toolkit, it included a
`GroupItemTemplate` property. This has since been superseded by the `JumpListStyle`
property.

When the user taps a group header, each grouping key is presented using the
`ItemTemplate` property of the long list selector's `JumpListStyle`. With *Category* selected as
the *group by* property, each category is presented, allowing the user to jump to a specific
category (see Figure 10.5).

With price selected as the *group by* property, the groups are presented from lowest to
highest (see Figure 10.6). Tapping on a price takes the user to the list of apps of that price.

FIGURE 10.5   `LongListSelector` displaying the group picker when grouped by category.

FIGURE 10.6   `LongListSelector` displaying the group picker when grouped by price.

Displaying a List of Contacts Using the `LongListSelector`

This second example looks at presenting a list of contacts, which represent people in a custom address book. This example illustrates some more advanced concepts, such as customizing the group picker using a custom `GroupItemsPanel`.

Each contact is represented by a custom `Contact` class. The `Contact` class includes the following properties:

- ▶ `Id`
- ▶ `FirstName`
- ▶ `LastName`
- ▶ `EmailAddress`
- ▶ `HomeNumber`
- ▶ `MobileNumber`
- ▶ `ImageUrl`

Like the `MarketplaceApp` class from the first example, the `Contact` class includes a static `GetRandomContacts` method that generates a specified number of `Contact` objects, randomly selected from a set of predefined names in the `RandomContactGenerator` class.

The viewmodel for this section, called `ContactListViewModel`, includes a list of grouped `Contact` objects called `ContactGroupings`; shown in the following excerpt:

```
IEnumerable<CustomGrouping<Contact>> contactGroupings;

public IEnumerable<CustomGrouping<Contact>> ContactGroupings
{
    get
    {
        return contactGroupings;
    }
    private set
    {
        Assign(ref contactGroupings, value);
    }
}
```

`ContactGroupings` is initialized in the viewmodel constructor. A constant, called `contactCount`, determines how many `Contact` objects are generated:

```
const int contactCount = 35;
```

LINQ is used within the viewmodel constructor to build the list of grouped contacts. We first use the Contact class to generate a list of random contacts, ordered by last name and then first name. The first letter of each contact's last name is used as the grouping key. The LINQ expression groups each contact by this key, creating a CustomGrouping object for each group. See the following excerpt:

```
List<CustomGrouping<Contact>> groupings
    = (from contact in Contact.GetRandomContacts(contactCount)
          orderby contact.LastName orderby contact.FirstName
          group contact by Char.ToLower(contact.LastName.First()) into grouping
          select new CustomGrouping<Contact>(
              grouping.Key, grouping.AsEnumerable())).ToList();
```

The result of this expression is a set of groups, one for each unique first character. At this point, however, the result does not contain groups for letters of the alphabet not present in the list. This is not what you want because the LongListSelector would be unable to display a list of all letters. To remedy this situation, create another set of groupings, one for each letter of the alphabet and each containing an empty list of contacts:

```
const string groupCharacters = "abcdefghijklmnopqrstuvwxyz";
List<Contact> emptyList = new List<Contact>();
var allGroupings = from character in groupCharacters
            where !groupings.Any(x => character.Equals(x.Key))
            select new CustomGrouping<Contact>(character, emptyList).ToList();
```

The two sets of groupings are then merged to create a single set of groupings, with each letter of the alphabet properly represented:

```
contactGroupings = groupings.Union(allGroupings).OrderBy(x => x.Key);
```

The LongListSelector in the view binds to the ContactGroupings property. Contact groups are presented in the same manner as were the MarketplaceApps in the previous section; the ItemTemplate specifies how each Contact object is presented.

This example differs from the Marketplace App List example in that the JumpListStyle uses a Grid LayoutMode rather than a List layout, which causes each group header to be placed side by side, and then dropped to a new line after they exceed the width of the container (see Listing 10.3). Pay particular attention to the LongListSelector.JumpListStyle, which is used to present each group when the LongListSelector is in the full-screen group selection mode.

NOTE

When the LongListSelector resided in the Silverlight Toolkit, customizing the layout of the group picker was achieved using the long list selector's GroupItemsPanel property. This property does not exist in the Windows Phone SDK. The long list selector's LayoutMode property is now used to either present items in a list or in a grid.

10

LISTING 10.3   Contacts `LongListSelector` (excerpt from LongListSelectorView.xaml)

```xaml
<phone:LongListSelector
    IsGroupingEnabled="True"
    Background="Transparent"
    ItemsSource="{Binding ContactGroupings}">

    <phone:LongListSelector.ListHeader>
        <TextBlock Text="ListHeader"
                   Style="{StaticResource PhoneTextTitle1Style}"/>
    </phone:LongListSelector.ListHeader>

    <phone:LongListSelector.GroupHeaderTemplate>
        <DataTemplate>
            <Border Background="Transparent">
                <Border Background="{StaticResource PhoneAccentBrush}"
                        Width="75" Height="75"
                        HorizontalAlignment="Left">
                    <TextBlock Text="{Binding Key}"
                               Foreground="{StaticResource PhoneForegroundBrush}"
                               Style="{StaticResource PhoneTextExtraLargeStyle}"
                               VerticalAlignment="Bottom" />
                </Border>
            </Border>
        </DataTemplate>
    </phone:LongListSelector.GroupHeaderTemplate>

    <phone:LongListSelector.ItemTemplate>
        <DataTemplate>
            <Grid Margin="{StaticResource PhoneTouchTargetOverhang}">
                <Grid.ColumnDefinitions>
                    <ColumnDefinition Width="Auto" />
                    <ColumnDefinition Width="*" />
                </Grid.ColumnDefinitions>
                <Image Source="{Binding ImageUrl}"
                       Width="110" Height="150"  VerticalAlignment="Top" />
                <StackPanel Grid.Column="1" VerticalAlignment="Top">
                    <TextBlock Text="{Binding FullName}"
                               Style="{StaticResource PhoneTextLargeStyle}"
                               FontFamily="{StaticResource PhoneFontFamilySemiBold}"
                               Margin="12,-12,12,6" />
                    <TextBlock Text="{Binding EmailAddress}"
                               Style="{StaticResource PhoneTextNormalStyle}"
                               TextWrapping="Wrap"
                               FontFamily="{StaticResource
                               ➥PhoneFontFamilySemiBold}" />
```

```xml
                <StackPanel Orientation="Horizontal">
                    <TextBlock Text="mobile"
                                    Style="{StaticResource PhoneTextSmallStyle}" />
                    <TextBlock Text="{Binding MobileNumber}"
                                    Style="{StaticResource PhoneTextSmallStyle}"
                        FontFamily="{StaticResource PhoneFontFamilySemiBold}" />
                </StackPanel>
                <StackPanel Orientation="Horizontal">
                    <TextBlock Text="home"
                                    Style="{StaticResource PhoneTextSmallStyle}" />
                    <TextBlock Text="{Binding HomeNumber}"
                            Style="{StaticResource PhoneTextSmallStyle}"
                            FontFamily="{StaticResource
                            ➥PhoneFontFamilySemiBold}" />
                </StackPanel>
            </StackPanel>
        </Grid>
    </DataTemplate>
</phone:LongListSelector.ItemTemplate>

<phone:LongListSelector.JumpListStyle>
    <Style TargetType="phone:LongListSelector">
        <Setter Property="GridCellSize"  Value="113,113"/>
        <Setter Property="LayoutMode" Value="Grid" />
        <Setter Property="ItemTemplate">
            <Setter.Value>
                <DataTemplate>

                    <Border
                        Background="{Binding
                            Converter={StaticResource BackgroundConverter}}"
                        Width="113" Height="113" Margin="6">
                        <TextBlock
                            Text="{Binding Key}"
                            FontFamily="{StaticResource
                            ➥PhoneFontFamilySemiBold}"
                            FontSize="48" Padding="6"
                            Foreground="{Binding
                                Converter={StaticResource ForegroundConverter}}"
                            VerticalAlignment="Center"/>
                    </Border>

                </DataTemplate>
            </Setter.Value>
        </Setter>
    </Style>
```

```
        </phone:LongListSelector.JumpListStyle>

    <phone:LongListSelector.GroupFooterTemplate>
        <DataTemplate>
            <Border Margin="{StaticResource PhoneTouchTargetOverhang}"
                    Padding="{StaticResource PhoneTouchTargetOverhang}">
                <TextBlock Text="Group Footer"
                           Style="{StaticResource PhoneTextExtraLargeStyle}" />
            </Border>
        </DataTemplate>
    </phone:LongListSelector.GroupFooterTemplate>

    <phone:LongListSelector.ListFooter>
        <TextBlock Text="ListFooter"
                   Style="{StaticResource PhoneTextTitle1Style}" />
    </phone:LongListSelector.ListFooter>

</phone:LongListSelector>
```

> **NOTE**
>
> When using the Grid `LayoutMode`, the `GridCellSize` property must be set or an Exception is raised at runtime.

Figure 10.7 shows the contacts list, presented with the `LongListSelector`.

When the user taps a group header, the `LongListSelector` presents all groups as a jump list. By examining the `JumpListStyle` in more detail, you see that each header is presented within a `Border`. The SDK's `JumpListItemBackgroundConverter`, which is declared as a page resource, changes the background of the `Border` depending on whether the group has any items in it. The foreground of the `TextBlock` is set using the `JumpListItemForegroundConverter` in the same manner.

Customizing the background and foreground colors of the group items can be achieved by using a custom `IValueConverter`. The sample includes an `IValueConverter` named `BooleanToBrushConverter`, which turns a Boolean value into one of two specified brushes (see Listing 10.4).

FIGURE 10.7   LongListSelector displaying the contacts list.

LISTING 10.4   BooleanToBrushConverter Class

```
public class BooleanToBrushConverter : IValueConverter
{
    public Brush BrushIfFalse { get; set; }
    public Brush BrushIfTrue { get; set; }

    public object Convert(
        object value, Type targetType, object parameter, CultureInfo culture)
    {
        return value != null && (bool)value ? BrushIfTrue : BrushIfFalse;
    }

    public object ConvertBack(
        object value, Type targetType, object parameter, CultureInfo culture)
    {
        throw new NotImplementedException("Only supports a one way binding");
    }
}
```

10

Define the `BooleanToBrushConverter` as a resource in the page resources, like so:

```
<phone:PhoneApplicationPage.Resources>
    <ValueConverters:BooleanToBrushConverter x:Name="BooleanToBrushConverter"
        BrushIfFalse="{StaticResource PhoneChromeBrush}"
        BrushIfTrue="{StaticResource PhoneAccentBrush}" />
</phone:PhoneApplicationPage.Resources>
```

Then amend the `Border` element from the `JumpListStyle` as shown:

```
<Border
    Background="{Binding HasItems,
            Converter={StaticResource BooleanToBrushConverter}}"
    Width="113" Height="113" Margin="6">
    <TextBlock
        Text="{Binding Key}"
        .../>
</Border>
```

Thus, when a `CustomGrouping HasItems` property evaluates to *true*, the `PhoneAccentBrush` is used for the header background; otherwise, the `PhoneChromeBrush` is used.

Figure 10.8 shows the `LongListSelector` presenting the `Contact` headers using the grid layout.

FIGURE 10.8   The jump list allows the user to jump to a group.

NOTE

The `LongListSelector` displays all groups regardless of whether they have any items in them. To hide empty groups, set the long list selector's `HideEmptyGroups` property to true.

Summary

This chapter began with an overview of the visual structure of the `LongListSelector`. You then learned the basics of how to present flat and grouped lists using the control.

The chapter then dove into a sample app that allows the user to group a set of marketplace items. You saw how to create a `CustomGrouping` class to allow the user to change the way the control groups items.

Finally, the chapter examined some more advanced features of the `LongListSelector` with another sample that demonstrates how to display a list of contacts with the `LongListSelector` using a grid layout.

CHAPTER 11

Creating Expansive and Engaging Apps with the Pivot and Panorama

In the past, Silverlight web or desktop applications that needed to present a large amount of information have usually done so by splitting the information across multiple pages. The Pivot and Panorama controls complement the existing page navigation infrastructure to provide the ability to present a large amount of information on a single page.

Pivot and Panorama are new controls and at the time of writing are unique to the phone. Both controls are fundamental to the visual user experience on the phone, and the phone's built-in apps use them extensively. You will, therefore, probably find yourself using them a lot, although they are not necessarily a suitable choice for every app.

This chapter begins by looking at both controls, their differences and similarities. It then looks at the anatomy of the Pivot and how to create a simple Pivot driven page. You see how to use the Pivot load events, allowing you to load content on demand. You explore a novel approach that allows you to associate a different application bar with each PivotItem using a custom AppBar control, which is not readily achievable with the built-in ApplicationBar! Putting it all together, you learn how to create a Pivot driven chat app, which is then augmented to demonstrate implicit PivotItem generation and data templating.

The second part of this chapter explores the Panorama. Again you look at the anatomy of the Panorama and discuss how to get the most out of the control. You learn how to create a simple bookshop app that uses a WCF service to retrieve a list of products displayed within a Panorama, and the chapter concludes by looking at some of the things to avoid when using a Pivot or Panorama.

`Pivot` and `Panorama` Differences and Similarities

The `Pivot` and `Panorama` are layout controls that help you display data in a unique way. They have several things in common. They both hold a number of horizontally arranged sections (items). They are visually similar; both show a segment of the offscreen content, have titles, and have section titles.

Both controls have built-in touch navigation. It is, therefore, not necessary to implement any special gesture functionality in your app, because it is already built in. The touch support allows the user to navigate left to right between the different sections using the pan and flick touch-gestures.

Horizontal navigation is cyclical; after navigating past the last section, the first section appears.

Also, both the `Pivot` and `Panorama` allow complete customization of the title and headers.

Both controls have many similarities, but they also have some fundamental differences, because each control is designed to serve a different purpose. The `Pivot` is designed to be more task oriented; it is about getting something done. It has greater emphasis on each individual section within the control, and section content is confined to the width of the layout screen, whereas the `Panorama` has sections that span over screen boundaries and is designed to entice the user to explore all sections.

> **TIP**
>
> A page with a `Pivot` is a suitable candidate for an application bar, whereas one with a `Panorama` is not. If your page needs an application bar, use a `Pivot` not a `Panorama`.

There are also performance differences between the two controls. When a `Panorama` loads, all `Panorama` items go through a render pass. Conversely, items within a `Pivot` are loaded incrementally for each neighboring item. Thus, the `Pivot` generally offers a faster start time.

> **TIP**
>
> Regardless of whether you use a `Pivot` or `Panorama`, try to limit the number of `Panorama` or `Pivot` items. Memory usage expands rapidly when there are a lot of views and images. Moreover, if the user navigates to another page, the current page stays in memory. Therefore, complex `Pivot` or `Panorama` pages will also remain in memory unless explicitly discarded.

Style Assumptions

`Panorama` and `Pivot` items are styled under the assumption that most of their content has a 12-pixel margin on the left and right. The built-in styles include this margin by default. Therefore, if you place a control into a `Pivot` or `Panorama` that has a margin of less than 12, it may make your interface layout look incorrect.

Introduction to the `Pivot` Control

The `Pivot` may be regarded as the tab control for the phone. The control places individual views horizontally next to each other and manages left and right navigation. Flicking or panning horizontally on the page cycles between pivot items.

Unlike the `Panorama`, where content may exceed screen boundaries, `Pivot` content is confined to the screen's width. Where the `Panorama` displays a few pixels of content of the next section, the `Pivot` does not, but instead relies on section titles to give the user an indication of neighboring sections.

The `Pivot` is designed to represent data or items of a similar type. For example, a `Pivot` can be used as activities for similar content around the same task flow. A good example of using a `Pivot` in this manner is the built-in Email app, which shows all emails in one view, flagged emails in another, unread email in another, and so on.

The `Pivot` plays host to a secondary control called a `PivotItem`. The `PivotItem` serves as a container that hosts other content and controls, such as grids, lists, and buttons.

> **BEST PRACTICE**
>
> Try to limit the number of `Pivot` items to seven. This ensures that users are able to visualize a mental map of the `Pivot` sections and to comprehend what is being presented.

Introduction to the `Panorama` Control

The `Panorama` is a wide horizontal canvas that spans over screen boundaries. The canvas is partitioned into several sections. The `Panorama` is designed to be a starting place and is normally used as the top layer to other pages. Ordinarily, page content is designed to fit within the confines of the phone display; the `Panorama`, however, offers a unique way to view controls and data by using the long horizontal canvas that extends beyond the confines of the display. Layered animations are used to smoothly pan content at different speeds, providing a parallax effect.

Like the `Pivot`, the `Panorama` also uses a secondary control called a `PanoramaItem`, which serves as a container that hosts other content and controls, such as grids, lists, and buttons.

As the `Panorama` is intended to coax the user to explore, it should show content that is interesting and specific to the user. The user should also not be overloaded with too much content; think *white space* and not *loads of data*. The `Panorama` should be thought of as a starting place, containing data and links that take the user to more detailed pages of content, pages that may include a `Pivot` for example. The user is then able to leave the exploratory style of the `Panorama` for the more focused style of the `Pivot`.

> **BEST PRACTICE**
>
> For the sake of usability and performance, try to limit the number of `Panorama` sections to four.

Unlike the `Pivot`, the `Panorama` is designed to be explorative; it is not about completing a task and should not show an application bar.

A page with a `Panorama` should offer a visually appealing experience. This can be achieved with an attractive background. A `Panorama` background can be either a single color or a background image. The image size should be 800 pixels high and 480 to 1000 pixels wide, depending on the number of sections to be displayed. It is possible to use an image with a width exceeding 1000 pixels, but more than 2000 pixels and the image will be clipped.

NOTE

An image with a height of less than 800 pixels is stretched to that height without constraining its proportions. This is important if you want to maintain the aspect ratio of your image.

`Pivot` and `Panorama` **Placement in the FCL**

`Pivot` and `Panorama` controls reside in the Microsoft.Phone.Controls assembly. Both the `Pivot` and the `Panorama` inherit from the `TemplatedItemsControl` (see Figure 11.1). The `TemplatedItemsControl`'s generic type parameter is specified as either a `PivotItem` for the `Pivot` class or a `PanoramaItem` by `Panorama` class.

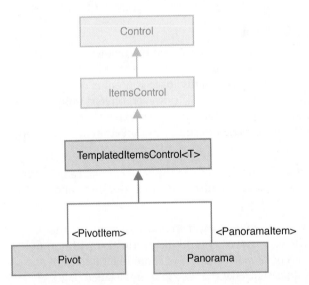

FIGURE 11.1   `Pivot` and `Panorama` inherit from `TemplatedItemsControl`.

The main role of the `TemplatedItemsControl` is the implicit creation of `PivotItems` and `PanoramaItems` when using the superclass `ItemsControl.ItemsSource` property to populate a `Pivot` or `Panorama`.

Performance Improvements in Windows Phone 8

In Windows Phone 8, the Pivot and Panorama controls have been removed from the SDK and are now located in the phone's read-only memory (ROM). They are still used the same way in your code, but at runtime the Windows Phone OS uses the classes from the ROM. This way your app can use a separate native input thread, which means a significant increase in the input responsiveness of these controls. The working set memory of the Panorama control has also been reduced.

Using the Pivot Control

The Pivot can be used for displaying combinations of controls, user controls, and even other pages. The Pivot plays host to individual pages of content called PivotItems. A PivotItem control is analogous to an individual tab and is responsible for displaying the content within a page. Only one PivotItem is displayed at a time. Flicking or panning left to right on the page, or tapping a PivotItem's header, advances to the next page of content.

The Pivot supports the following gestures and navigational effects:

▶ **Horizontal pan**—This is done by dragging a PivotItem or its header, from left to right, or right to left.

▶ **Horizontal flick**—This is done by a quick swipe, either left to right, or right to left.

▶ **Tap**—Tapping a PivotItem's header transitions to that PivotItem.

Placing a Pivot on a Page

The following items describe the ways in which to surface a Pivot on a page within Visual Studio:

▶ Using the Windows Phone Pivot Application template, which can be selected when creating a new project. This template generates a Windows Phone application project, with the main page prepopulated with a Pivot.

▶ Using the Windows Phone Pivot Page template from the Visual Studio Add New Item dialog.

▶ The Pivot control can be added to the Toolbox in Visual Studio and can then be dropped onto the design surface of your page or onto the XAML editor.

▶ The Pivot control can be simply added to an existing page by removing the title panel of a page and adding the Pivot XAML.

To use a Pivot on an existing page, remove the title panel on the page and add a Pivot element in XAML, like so:

```
<Grid x:Name="LayoutRoot" Background="Transparent">
```

```
<controls:Pivot Title="Windows Phone 8 Unleashed">
    <controls:PivotItem Header="first">
        <TextBlock Text="Lorem ipsum dolor sit amet, consectetur..."
            TextWrapping="Wrap"
            Style="{StaticResource PhoneTextSubtleStyle}"/>
    </controls:PivotItem>

    <controls:PivotItem Header="second">
        <TextBlock Text="Lorem ipsum dolor sit amet, consectetur..."
            TextWrapping="Wrap"
            Style="{StaticResource PhoneTextSubtleStyle}"/>
    </controls:PivotItem>

    <controls:PivotItem Header="third">
        <TextBlock Text="Lorem ipsum dolor sit amet, consectetur..."
            TextWrapping="Wrap"
            Style="{StaticResource PhoneTextSubtleStyle}"/>
    </controls:PivotItem>
</controls:Pivot>

</Grid>
```

The `Pivot` has Visual Studio design-time support. The Visual Studio designer automatically shifts to the active `PivotItem` when the cursor is placed with the `PivotItems` element in the XAML view.

When the app is launched, you see the result shown in Figure 11.2.

FIGURE 11.2   A page with a `Pivot` containing three `PivotItems`.

The usual page and application title panel should be omitted from any pages containing a `Pivot` or `Panorama`, because the `Pivot` and the `Panorama` take care of displaying that information.

Creating a Pivot Application with the Visual Studio New Project Dialog

The Visual Studio New Project dialog can also be used to generate an entire application along with a page surfacing a `Pivot` or `Panorama` control (see Figure 11.3).

FIGURE 11.3   Using the New Project dialog to create a Windows Phone pivot application.

The *Pivot Application* project template produces a `PhoneApplicationPage` (MainPage.xaml) containing a `Pivot`. The template produces a `Pivot` with two `PivotItems`, and each item contains a `ListBox`.

`Pivot` Anatomy

The `Pivot` is composed of two distinct sections: a header list and a `PivotItem` presenter (see Figure 11.4).

The `Pivot` headers are displayed using a `PivotHeadersControl`. The active `PivotItem` has its header highlighted. Inactive `PivotItems` have their headers displayed until the headers exceed the width of the control. If there are too few headers to take up the full width of the control, the headers do not loop, and each header is displayed only once.

`PivotItems` are displayed using an `ItemsPresenter`. `PivotItem` is a `ContentControl` playing host to a single item of content. A `ContentPresenter` is used to display the content of the `PivotItem`.

FIGURE 11.4   Anatomy of the `Pivot`.

Only `PivotItem` controls can be defined within the `Pivot` control. If you attempt
to place another element type directly within the `Pivot` control, in XAML, an
`InvalidOperationException` is thrown when the `Pivot` is initialized. This is contrary to
the official Microsoft documentation on MSDN, which states that an element other than a
`PivotItem` is implicitly wrapped into a `PivotItem` control.

The contents of a `PivotItem` control can either be specified in XAML, or added programmatically through the `PivotItem`'s `Content` property.

Setting the Active `PivotItem`

The `SelectedItem` or `SelectedIndex` can be used to shift to a particular `PivotItem`
within the `Pivot`. If the `Pivot` is populated using its `ItemsSource` property, then the
`SelectedItem` retrieves the data object rather than the actual `PivotItem` control.

> **NOTE**
>
> Setting a `Pivot`'s `SelectedIndex` before it has loaded raises an exception. This can be
> prevented by suppressing the `Exception` by wrapping the assignment in a try/catch block,
> or by performing the assignment in a `Loaded` event handler.

`Pivot` **Load Events**

`Pivot` raises various events to indicate when a `PivotItem` is being brought into view and when it is being moved out of view.

BEST PRACTICE

To improve the performance of your app, use the `LoadingPivotItem` event to load content on demand. One approach is to convert the content of each `PivotItem` into a `UserControl`. You can then subscribe to the `LoadingPivotItem` event on the `Pivot`, and then when the event is raised instantiate the `UserControl` and set it as the `PivotItem`'s content.

The `UnloadedPivotItem` event also provides the opportunity to clean up any unneeded resources.

When the user switches from one `PivotItem` to another, events are raised in the following order:

1. The `UnloadingPivotItem` event is raised for the first `PivotItem`.

2. The `LoadingPivotItem` event is raised for the second `PivotItem`.

3. The `UnloadedPivotItem` event is raised for the first `PivotItem`.

4. The `LoadedPivotItem` event is raised for the second `PivotItem`.

These events are not cancelable. That is, they are not designed to allow for preventing or returning the `Pivot` to the previously active `PivotItem`. It is possible, however, to queue a change back to the previously active `PivotItem`. Queuing an index change in one of the load event handlers has to be performed after the current `PivotItem` change has finished; otherwise, the `Pivot` will get out of sync. This can be done by using the `Dispatcher` to invoke the change, which means it occurs after the current UI thread task completes. The following example demonstrates how to use the `Dispatcher` to lock the `Pivot` to the first `PivotItem`:

```
void Pivot_LoadingPivotItem(object sender, PivotItemEventArgs e)
{
    Dispatcher.BeginInvoke(delegate { pivot.SelectedIndex = 0; });
}
```

Hosting Multiple Application Bars with the `Pivot`

Particular `PivotItems` within your `Pivot` may require differing capabilities with separate sets of application bar menu items and buttons. The ability to associate a different application bar with each `PivotItem` is not natively supported by the Windows Phone FCL. You can, however, achieve this by using the custom `AppBar` control (discussed in Chapter 8, "Taming the Application Bar").

This section looks at the relevant changes made to the AppBar that have been made to support this capability, and then at an example of creating a page containing a Pivot, whose items each contain an independent application bar that is swapped into place when the PivotItem becomes active.

Code has been added to the AppBar's Attach method, which detects whether the AppBar is located within a Pivot. This method is called when AppBar is first loaded and is shown in the following excerpt:

```
public void Attach()
{
    var page = this.GetVisualAncestors<PhoneApplicationPage>()
                                        .FirstOrDefault();

    var pivot = this.GetVisualAncestors<Pivot>().FirstOrDefault();
    if (pivot != null)
    {
        pivot.SelectionChanged -= pivot_SelectionChanged;
        pivot.SelectionChanged += pivot_SelectionChanged;
        UpdateApplicationBar(pivot);
    }
    else if (page != null)
    {
        page.ApplicationBar = applicationBar;
        Build();
    }
}
```

If the AppBar is located within a Pivot, each time a different PivotItem is displayed within the Pivot, the SelectionChanged event is raised, which in turn calls the UpdateApplicationBar method, shown here:

```
protected virtual void UpdateApplicationBar(Pivot pivot)
{
    var page = this.GetVisualAncestors<PhoneApplicationPage>()
                                        .FirstOrDefault();

    if (pivot == null || page == null)
    {
        return;
    }
    bool assignBar = false;

    if (pivot.SelectedItem == DataContext)
    {
        assignBar = true;
    }
```

```
else
{
    var frameworkElement = pivot.SelectedItem as FrameworkElement;
    if (frameworkElement != null
            && frameworkElement.DataContext == DataContext)
    {
        assignBar = true;
    }
}

if (assignBar)
{
    page.ApplicationBar = applicationBar;
    Build();
}
else if (page.ApplicationBar == applicationBar)
{
    page.ApplicationBar = null;
}
}
```

A custom extension method called GetVisualAncestors (located in the VisualTree class) is used to locate the parent page.

We then determine whether the AppBar is located in the currently selected PivotItem. This is done by either comparing the Pivot's SelectedItem or the DataContext of the SelectedItem with the DataContext of the AppBar. If equal, you know that the AppBar should be shown.

> **NOTE**
>
> When a Pivot's ItemsSource is used to populate the Pivot, PivotItems are generated implicitly, much like ListBoxItems are for the ListBox (see Chapter 5, "Using Content Controls, Items Controls, and Range Controls").

With these changes in place you can display a different application bar depending on the selected PivotItem. To demonstrate its use, the following example creates a simple messaging app that allows the user to send a message via one PivotItem and view received messages via another.

The example code for this section is located in the PivotView.xaml page and the PivotViewModel class in the downloadable sample code.

The PivotViewModel class bootstraps two other viewmodels: SendMessageViewModel and MessagesViewModel, both of which become the viewmodels for two different PivotItems in the PivotView page (see Listing 11.1).

LISTING 11.1   `PivotViewModel` Class

```csharp
public class PivotViewModel : ViewModelBase
{
    public PivotViewModel() : base("Pivot")
    {
        MockChatService chatService = new MockChatService();
        sendMessageViewModel = new SendMessageViewModel(chatService);
        messagesViewModel = new MessagesViewModel(chatService);
    }

    SendMessageViewModel sendMessageViewModel;

    public SendMessageViewModel SendMessageViewModel
    {
        get
        {
            return sendMessageViewModel;
        }
        private set
        {
            Assign(ref sendMessageViewModel, value);
        }
    }

    MessagesViewModel messagesViewModel;

    public MessagesViewModel MessagesViewModel
    {
        get
        {
            return messagesViewModel;
        }
        private set
        {
            Assign(ref messagesViewModel, value);
        }
    }
}
```

A class implementing the custom `IChatService` allows messages to be sent and received. The `MockChatService` class implements the custom `IChatService`, which has two members:

▶ **SendMessage**—A method that accepts a single string parameter and sends the message to all subscribers

▶ **MessageReceived**—An event that is raised when the chat service receives a message

For the purposes of the demonstration, a simple loopback implementation of the `IChatService` is used; when the `SendMessage` method is called, the `MessageReceived` event is raised.

The `SendMessageViewModel` uses the `IChatService` to send messages via the `SendCommand` (see Listing 11.2). When the `messageBody` field has been populated, the `IChatService.SendMessage` method is called.

LISTING 11.2   `SendMessageViewModel` Class

```
public class SendMessageViewModel : ViewModelBase
{
    public SendMessageViewModel(IChatService chatService) : base("Send")
    {
        ArgumentValidator.AssertNotNull(chatService, "chatService");

        sendCommand = new DelegateCommand(
            obj =>
            {
                if (!string.IsNullOrEmpty(messageBody))
                {
                    chatService.SendMessage(messageBody);
                    MessageBody = null;
                    Feedback = "Message sent";
                }
            });
    }

    string emailAddress = "John@example.com";

    public string EmailAddress
    {
        get
        {
            return emailAddress;
        }
        set
        {
            Assign(ref emailAddress, value);
        }
    }
    string messageBody = "Sample message";

    public string MessageBody
```

```
    {
        get
        {
            return messageBody;
        }
        set
        {
            Assign(ref messageBody, value);
        }
    }

    readonly DelegateCommand sendCommand;

    public ICommand SendCommand
    {
        get
        {
            return sendCommand;
        }
    }

    string feedback;

    public string Feedback
    {
        get
        {
            return feedback;
        }
        private set
        {
            Assign(ref feedback, value);
        }
    }
}
```

The purpose of the MessagesViewModel class is to listen for the MessageReceived event of the IChatService and to place incoming messages into an ObservableCollection, which is displayed in the view (see Listing 11.3). The RefreshCommand merely emulates a refresh by populating its Feedback property.

LISTING 11.3 MessagesViewModel Class

```
public class MessagesViewModel : ViewModelBase
{
    public MessagesViewModel(IChatService chatService): base("Received")
```

```
    {
        ArgumentValidator.AssertNotNull(chatService, "chatService");
        chatService.MessageReceived
            += (sender, args) =>
                {
                    if (args == null)
                    {
                        return;
                    }
                    messageItems.Add(new MessageItem(args.Message));
                    Feedback = "Message received.";
                };

        refreshCommand = new DelegateCommand(
            obj =>
            {
                Feedback = "Refresh command executed.";
            });
    }


ObservableCollection<MessageItem> messageItems
    = new ObservableCollection<MessageItem>();

public ObservableCollection<MessageItem> MessageItems
{
    get
    {
        return messageItems;
    }
    internal set
    {
        Assign(ref messageItems, value);
    }
}
string feedback;

public string Feedback
{
    get
    {
        return feedback;
    }
    private set
    {
        Assign(ref feedback, value);
    }
```

```
    }

    readonly DelegateCommand refreshCommand;

    public ICommand RefreshCommand
    {
        get
        {
            return refreshCommand;
        }
    }
}
```

The `PivotView` page instantiates the `PivotViewModel`, assigning it to its own `DataContext`:

```
public partial class PivotView : PhoneApplicationPage
{
    public PivotView()
    {
        InitializeComponent();
        DataContext = new PivotViewModel();
    }
}
```

The view's XAML contains a `Pivot` with two `PivotItems`: one for allowing the user to send messages using the `SendMessageViewModel`; the other for viewing received messages using the `MessagesViewModel`.

An independent `AppBar` is present in both `PivotItems`. The `PivotItem` showing the received messages allows the user to refresh the list using the viewmodel's `RefreshCommand` via its `AppBar`, while the `PivotItem` for sending a message allows the user to dispatch a message using a `SendCommand` via a different `AppBar`. Listing 11.4 shows an excerpt from the PivotView.xaml page containing the `Pivot`.

LISTING 11.4   PivotView.xaml (excerpt)

```xml
<Grid x:Name="LayoutRoot" Background="Transparent">

    <controls:Pivot x:Name="pivot"
            Title="Windows Phone 8 Unleashed">
        <controls:Pivot.Background>
            <ImageBrush ImageSource="../../../Images/PivotBackground.png"/>
        </controls:Pivot.Background>
        <controls:PivotItem DataContext="{Binding MessagesViewModel}"
                Header="{Binding Title}">
            <StackPanel>
```

```xml
                <u:AppBar>
                    <u:AppBarIconButton
                        Command="{Binding RefreshCommand}"
                        Text="Refresh"
                        IconUri="/Images/ApplicationBarIcons/AppBarRefresh.png" />
                </u:AppBar>
                <ListBox ItemsSource="{Binding MessageItems}">
                    <ListBox.ItemTemplate>
                        <DataTemplate>
                            <TextBlock Text="{Binding Body}"
                                Style="{StaticResource PhoneTextNormalStyle}" />
                        </DataTemplate>
                    </ListBox.ItemTemplate>
                </ListBox>
                <TextBlock Text="{Binding Feedback}"
                    Style="{StaticResource PhoneTextAccentStyle}"
                    Margin="12,30,12,0" />
            </StackPanel>
        </controls:PivotItem>
        <controls:PivotItem DataContext="{Binding SendMessageViewModel}"
                Header="{Binding Title}">
            <StackPanel>
                <u:AppBar>
                    <u:AppBarIconButton
                    Command="{Binding SendCommand}"
                    Text="Send"
                IconUri="/Images/ApplicationBarIcons/AppBarMessageSend.png"/>
                </u:AppBar>
                <TextBlock Text="user"
                    Style="{StaticResource PhoneTextTitle3Style}" />
                <TextBox InputScope="EmailSmtpAddress"
                    Text="{Binding EmailAddress, Mode=TwoWay}" />
                <TextBlock Text="message"
                    Style="{StaticResource PhoneTextTitle3Style}" />
                <TextBox Text="{Binding MessageBody, Mode=TwoWay}"
                    TextWrapping="Wrap"
                    Height="140" />
                <TextBlock Text="{Binding Feedback}"
                    Style="{StaticResource PhoneTextAccentStyle}"
                    Margin="12,30,12,0" />
            </StackPanel>
        </controls:PivotItem>
    </controls:Pivot>
</Grid>
```

An image is used as the background for the `Pivot`. It is usually recommended to set the Build Action of image files to Content so as to minimize the size of the assembly and thereby decrease your app's startup time. In the case of the `Pivot` and `Panorama`, this is not the case.

> **NOTE**
>
> If you use a background image in a `Pivot` or `Panorama` control, set its Build Action to Resource to ensure that it is shown as soon as the control is shown. When the Build Action is set to Content, it causes the image to be loaded asynchronously, and may leave your `Pivot` or `Panorama` momentarily sitting on a plain white or black background.

The `DataContext` of each `PivotItem` is set to a different property in the viewmodel. The `Header` for each `PivotItem` is then resolved to the `Title` property of the `ViewModelBase` class.

As an aside, while the `PivotItem.Header` property can be specified using either property attribute syntax, assigning it to a simple string; or property element syntax, assigning to a nested element, it can also be specified by using a `DataTemplate` defined at the `Pivot` element level, as shown in the following sample:

```
<controls:Pivot Title="Windows Phone 8 Unleashed">
    <controls:Pivot.HeaderTemplate>
        <DataTemplate>
            <TextBlock Text="{Binding Title}"
                    Style="{StaticResource PhoneTextTitle2Style}" />
        </DataTemplate>
    </controls:Pivot.HeaderTemplate>
    <controls:PivotItem DataContext="{Binding MessagesViewModel}">
        <!--Content omitted. -->
    </controls:PivotItem>
    <controls:PivotItem DataContext="{Binding SendMessageViewModel}">
        <!-- Content omitted. -->
    </controls:PivotItem>
</controls:Pivot>
```

Continuing with the example, when the Received `PivotItem` is active, the Refresh button allows the user to simulate refreshing the data source (see Figure 11.5).

Conversely, when the Send `PivotItem` is active, the user can enter a message and use the Send button to dispatch the message (see Figure 11.6).

FIGURE 11.5   Received view in the sample app.

FIGURE 11.6   Dispatching a message via the Send PivotItem.

When the Send button is tapped, the SendMessageViewModel's SendCommand is executed
and the message is passed to the IChatService using its SendMessage method. On
receipt, the chat service merely raises its MessageReceived event. Recall that the
MessagesViewModel subscribes to this event. When it is raised, the new message is added
to its MessageItems ObservableCollection, which causes the Received PivotItem to be
updated with the new message (see Figure 11.7).

FIGURE 11.7   The message is received and displayed on the Received `PivotItem`.

Populating a `Pivot` Via a Data Bound Collection

This second example looks at using a collection of viewmodels to dynamically populate a `Pivot` using a `DataTemplate`. The result of this example is the same as the previous example, except in this case the `PivotItems` are dynamically created based on their data type. This provides some added flexibility that can be useful in larger apps.

The example code for this section is located in the files DataboundPivotView.xaml, DataboundPivotView.xaml.cs, and DataboundPivotViewModel.cs in the downloadable sample code.

In this example the viewmodel has been changed from exposing two child viewmodel properties to a collection of viewmodels (see Listing 11.5).

LISTING 11.5   `DataboundPivotViewModel` Class

```
public class DataboundPivotViewModel : ViewModelBase
{
    public DataboundPivotViewModel() : base("Databound Pivot")
    {
        MockChatService chatService = new MockChatService();
        items.Add(new MessagesViewModel(chatService));
        items.Add(new SendMessageViewModel(chatService));
    }

    readonly ObservableCollection<ViewModelBase> items
        = new ObservableCollection<ViewModelBase>();

    public ObservableCollection<ViewModelBase> Items
    {
        get
```

```
        {
            return items;
        }
    }
}
```

By using this approach you can dynamically add and remove content via the main viewmodel. Depending on the data type of the viewmodel, a particular `DataTemplate` is resolved from the application's `Resources` collection. This is done using a custom `ContentControl` called `TypeTemplateSelector` (see Listing 11.6).

LISTING 11.6   `TypeTemplateSelector` Class

```
public class TypeTemplateSelector : ContentControl
{
    protected override void OnContentChanged(
                object oldContent, object newContent)
    {
        base.OnContentChanged(oldContent, newContent);
        if (newContent == null)
        {
            return;
        }
        Type newContentType = newContent.GetType();
        ContentTemplate = Application.Current.Resources[
            newContentType.Name + "Template"] as DataTemplate;
    }
}
```

The `TypeTemplateSelector` attempts to resolve the `DataTemplate` for the viewmodels by applying the naming convention *[data type]Template*. This simplifies our main view, whose XAML is shown in Listing 11.7.

LISTING 11.7   Data BoundPivotView.xaml (excerpt)

```
<Grid x:Name="LayoutRoot" Background="Transparent">

    <controls:Pivot Title="Windows Phone 8 Unleashed"
            ItemsSource="{Binding Items}">
        <controls:Pivot.Background>
            <ImageBrush ImageSource="../../../Images/PivotBackground.png"/>
        </controls:Pivot.Background>
        <controls:Pivot.HeaderTemplate>
            <DataTemplate>
                <TextBlock Text="{Binding Title}" />
            </DataTemplate>
```

```
            </controls:Pivot.HeaderTemplate>
            <controls:Pivot.ItemTemplate>
                <DataTemplate>
                    <p:TypeTemplateSelector Content="{Binding}"
                        VerticalAlignment="Top"
                        HorizontalAlignment="Left" />
                </DataTemplate>
            </controls:Pivot.ItemTemplate>
        </controls:Pivot>

</Grid>
```

The DataTemplates are placed in the application resources using the App.xaml file. Contained within the App.xaml file is the SendMessageViewModelTemplate, which is used to present the SendMessageViewModel, shown in the following excerpt:

```
<DataTemplate x:Key="SendMessageViewModelTemplate">
    <StackPanel Width="400">
        <u:AppBar>
            <u:AppBarIconButton
                Command="{Binding SendCommand}"
                Text="Send"
                IconUri="/Images/ApplicationBarIcons/AppBarMessageSend.png"/>
        </u:AppBar>
        <TextBlock Text="user"
            Style="{StaticResource PhoneTextTitle3Style}" />
        <TextBox InputScope="EmailSmtpAddress"
            Text="{Binding EmailAddress, Mode=TwoWay}" />
        <TextBlock Text="message"
            Style="{StaticResource PhoneTextTitle3Style}" />
        <TextBox Text="{Binding MessageBody, Mode=TwoWay}"
            TextWrapping="Wrap"
            Height="300" />
        <TextBlock Text="{Binding Feedback}"
            Style="{StaticResource PhoneTextAccentStyle}"
            Margin="12,30,12,0" />
    </StackPanel>
</DataTemplate>
```

In addition, the MessageViewModel is presented using the MessageViewModelTemplate:

```
<DataTemplate x:Key="MessagesViewModelTemplate">
    <StackPanel>
        <u:AppBar>
            <u:AppBarIconButton
                Command="{Binding RefreshCommand}"
```

```
                    Text="Refresh"
                IconUri="/Images/ApplicationBarIcons/AppBarRefresh.png"/>
            </u:AppBar>
            <ListBox ItemsSource="{Binding MessageItems}">
                <ListBox.ItemTemplate>
                    <DataTemplate>
                        <TextBlock Text="{Binding Body}"
                            Style="{StaticResource PhoneTextNormalStyle}"/>
                    </DataTemplate>
                </ListBox.ItemTemplate>
            </ListBox>
            <TextBlock Text="{Binding Feedback}"
                Style="{StaticResource PhoneTextAccentStyle}"
                Margin="12,30,12,0" />
        </StackPanel>
    </DataTemplate>
```

Using the Panorama Control

Working with the Panorama control is much like working with the Pivot. You can create a Panorama in the same way as a Pivot, either by using the built-in project or application template, or by manually adding the Panorama XAML to an existing page. The XAML for a Panorama usually looks something like this:

```
<controls:Panorama Title="an application">

    <controls:PanoramaItem Header="item1">
        <!-- Place content here. -->
    </controls:PanoramaItem>

    <controls:PanoramaItem Header="item2">
        <!-- Place content here. -->
    </controls:PanoramaItem>

</controls:Panorama>
```

The PanoramaItem controls host the panoramic content, and these represent the sections displayed within the control.

Panorama Anatomy

The Panorama is composed of three layers:

▶ Background layer

▶ Title layer

▶ Items layer

Each layer is contained within a `Grid` control that serves as the layout root for the `Panorama` control (see Figure 11.8).

FIGURE 11.8   The `Panorama` control anatomy.

Background Layer

The background represents the bottom layer of the `Panorama`, with sections sitting above. The background layer is represented by a `PanningBackgroundLayer` within the `Panorama` class. This layer is set with the `Background` property on the `Panorama` control.

You can set the background of the `Panorama` to an image using an `ImageBrush`. Alternatively, a color or gradient can be used by assigning the `Background` property to a `SolidColorBrush` or `GradientBrush`.

> **NOTE**
>
> You should not set a `Panorama` control's `Background` to null. If it is set to null, gesture response is unreliable. The `Background` is set to Transparent by default in the default template.

The background is stretched vertically to fill the height of the `Panorama`. The `ImageBrush` retains the width of the `ImageSource`, and the `GradientBrush` is stretched to fill the width of the items.

NOTE

The default template for the `Panorama` uses bitmap caching for the `Panorama`'s `Background` property. Clipping occurs for UI elements with bitmap caching enabled if they exceed 2000 by 2000 pixels. Therefore, restrict the size of your background image to less than this size.

Bitmap caching helps to improve performance by storing visual elements as bitmaps after the first time they are rendered. After an element has been cached as a bitmap, it no longer needs to be included as part of the render phase when the UI refreshes. This means less processing needs to be done, because just the cached bitmap is rendered. Cached bitmaps can take advantage of hardware acceleration using the phone's GPU, which has the potential of yielding significant performance improvements in some situations.

TIP

Avoid positioning the background according to the content position. The `Panorama` title moves at a different rate than its section titles, as the user moves across the `Panorama`.

Title Layer

The title layer is represented by a `PanningTitleLayer` within the `Panorama` class. This layer presents the title of the app and is assigned using the `Panorama.Title` property.

The `Panorama Title` can be specified as text; however, there is also a `TitleTemplate` property, which allows you to completely customize the appearance of the `Title`.

The vertical height of this layer remains constant and is unaffected by oversized content or the absence of content. The layer does not wrap back on itself but rather animates back to the starting position when you pan past the final section.

BEST PRACTICE

Avoid animating the `Panorama` title or dynamically changing its size after it has loaded. Doing so can interfere with the `Panorama`'s built-in animations.

Items Layer

The items layer is represented by a `PanningLayer` within the `Panorama` class. This layer contains the content of the `PanoramaItem` controls. A pan gesture causes this layer to move at the same rate. Therefore, the content beneath the finger at the beginning of the pan gesture remains beneath the finger until the finger leaves the display.

`PanoramaItem` Control

Each `PanoramaItem` control represents individual sections of content. The `PanoramaItem` is itself composed of two parts: a header part and a content part. Each part is contained within a `Grid` that serves as the layout root for the `PanoramaItem` control.

The contents of a `PanoramaItem` can either be specified in XAML, or added programmatically using its `Content` property.

The headers of all `PanoramaItems` can be uniformly customized by using the `Panorama`'s `HeaderTemplate` property. This works in the same manner as the example for the `Pivot` in the previous section.

You can hide a `PanoramaItem` by setting its `Visibility` property to Collapsed. This can be useful when you need to conceal an item before it has loaded some other resource.

> **TIP**
>
> As mentioned earlier in the chapter, when a `Panorama` loads, all `Panorama` items undergo a render pass. Thus, a `Panorama` with too many items may take a long time to load. Alternatively, to improve performance, where reducing the number of items is not an option, consider delay loading controls and content. Unlike the `Pivot`, however, the `Panorama` does not have load events (such as the `LoadingPivotItem` event), which further underscores the differences between the purpose and nature of the two controls. If you find that the `Panorama`'s performance is not up to scratch, it may indicate that your content is not suited to the `Panorama` and that a different control or approach is needed.

`PanoramaItem` Orientation

The `Orientation` property of the `PanoramaItem` affects how content is snapped into place during a pan gesture. The default value of the `Orientation` property is Vertical. By setting the property to `Horizontal`, the user is able to pan around the content without snapping a `PanoramaItem` into place. A horizontal orientation also allows for the content to be placed off the screen instead of being clipped. This reinforces the panoramic nature of the control.

Sample `Panorama` Application

The sample for this section makes use of the WCF Bookshop Service, which was detailed in Chapter 3, "Understanding the Application Execution Model." This service is used to retrieve a list of products and present them within a `Panorama`.

The code is located in the files PanoramaView.xaml, PanoramaView.xaml.cs, and PanoramaViewModel.cs in the downloadable sample code.

The viewmodel, for this example, exposes a collection of `Product` objects, which are retrieved from the Bookshop Service when the viewmodel is instantiated, and a single *featured* product, which is the first member of the collection (see Listing 11.8).

LISTING 11.8   `PanoramaViewModel` Class

```
public class PanoramaViewModel : ViewModelBase
{
    public PanoramaViewModel()
    {
```

```
        BookshopServiceClient client = new BookshopServiceClient();
        client.GetProductsCompleted
            += (sender, args) =>
                {
                    if (args.Error != null)
                    {
                        throw args.Error;
                    }

                    Products = args.Result;
                    FeaturedProduct = args.Result.FirstOrDefault();
                };
        client.GetProductsAsync();
    }


    ObservableCollection<Product> products;

    public ObservableCollection<Product> Products
    {
        get
        {
            return products;
        }
        private set
        {
            Assign(ref products, value);
        }
    }


    Product featuredProduct;
    public Product FeaturedProduct
    {
        get
        {
            return featuredProduct;
        }
        private set
        {
            Assign(ref featuredProduct, value);
        }
    }
}
```

The PanoramaView code-beside is used to instantiate an instance of the PanoramaViewModel, which is assigned to PanoramaView's DataContext (see Listing 11.9).

LISTING 11.9   `PanoramaView` Class

```
public partial class PanoramaView : PhoneApplicationPage
{
    public PanoramaView()
    {
        InitializeComponent();
        DataContext = new PanoramaViewModel();
    }
}
```

The view contains two `PanoramaItems`. The first displays the list of products and is titled Best Picks. A Windows Phone Toolkit `WrapPanel` control is used to display the Product images thumbs (see Listing 11.10). For more information on the `WrapPanel` control, see Chapter 9, "Enriching the User Experience with the Windows Phone Toolkit Controls."

The second `PanoramaItem` presents the details of the featured product; a larger image is displayed for the product, and a `HyperlinkButton` allows you to open the built-in web browser application.

LISTING 11.10   PanoramaView.xaml (excerpt)

```
<Grid x:Name="LayoutRoot" Background="Transparent">
    <controls:Panorama x:Name="Panorama"
        Title="Bookshop">
        <controls:Panorama.Background>
            <ImageBrush ImageSource="../../../Images/PanoramaBackground.png"/>
        </controls:Panorama.Background>

        <controls:PanoramaItem Header="Best Picks">
            <ListBox ItemsSource="{Binding Products}">
                <ListBox.ItemsPanel>
                    <ItemsPanelTemplate>
                        <toolkit:WrapPanel x:Name="wrapPanel"  />
                    </ItemsPanelTemplate>
                </ListBox.ItemsPanel>
                <ListBox.ItemTemplate>
                    <DataTemplate>
                        <Image Source="{Binding SmallImageUri}"
                            MaxWidth="150" MaxHeight="150"
                            Margin="10" />
                    </DataTemplate>
                </ListBox.ItemTemplate>
            </ListBox>
        </controls:PanoramaItem>


        <controls:PanoramaItem Header="Featured"
```

11

```xml
                    DataContext="{Binding FeaturedProduct}">
            <StackPanel>
                <TextBlock Text="{Binding Product.Title}"
                    TextWrapping="Wrap"
                    Style="{StaticResource PhoneTextTitle2Style}"/>
                <StackPanel Orientation="Horizontal">
                    <Image Source="{Binding LargeImageUri}"
                            MaxWidth="250" MaxHeight="250"
                            Margin="10,10,0,10"/>
                    <StackPanel>
                        <TextBlock Text="{Binding Author}"
                        TextWrapping="Wrap"
                        Style="{StaticResource PhoneTextTitle3Style}"/>
                        <TextBlock Text="{Binding Price,
                        Converter={StaticResource StringFormatConverter},
                        ConverterParameter=\{0:C\}}"
                        Style="{StaticResource PhoneTextTitle3Style}"/>
                        <StackPanel Orientation="Horizontal">
                            <TextBlock Text="ISBN"
                            Style="{StaticResource PhoneTextTitle3Style}"/>
                            <TextBlock Text="{Binding Isbn13}"
                            TextWrapping="Wrap"
                            Style="{StaticResource PhoneTextNormalStyle}"/>
                        </StackPanel>
                        <HyperlinkButton
                            NavigateUri="{Binding ExternalUrl}"
                            TargetName="_blank"
                            Content="External Page"
                            Margin="0,10,0,0"
                            HorizontalAlignment="Left" />
                    </StackPanel>
                </StackPanel>
            </StackPanel>
        </controls:PanoramaItem>

    </controls:Panorama>
</Grid>
```

Figure 11.9 shows the Panorama presenting the first PanoramaItem. Notice that the second PanoramaItem is partially displayed. This helps to improve the user's awareness of neighboring content.

FIGURE 11.9   The first `PanoramaItem` presents a list of `Products` in a `WrapPanel`.

Figure 11.10 shows the second `PanoramaItem` selected. Here the title and background have been scrolled horizontally.

FIGURE 11.10   The second `PanoramaItem` presents the featured product.

Things to Avoid When Using the `Panorama` and `Pivot`

The following is a list of things that should be avoided when using the `Pivot` and `Panorama`:

▶ Do not place a `Pivot` inside a `Panorama`, or nest `Pivots`.

▶ Do not attempt to use either the `Pivot` or `Panorama` for creating a wizard flow. The user sees the `Pivot` and `Panorama` as distinct areas of data, and not as a flow to be stepped through. For a wizard, use a page flow instead.

▶ Using a control that relies on horizontal touch gestures, such as a map control, inside a `Pivot` or `Panorama` is not recommended, as it interferes with horizontal navigation within the `Pivot` or `Panorama`.

▶ Avoid animating the `Panorama` title or section titles as they change position when the user moves across the control.

▶ Avoid dynamically changing the `Panorama` title.

▶ Do not override the horizontal pan and flick functionality of the controls because it may interfere with the built-in touch support.

▶ Keep to the recommended number of views, seven for the `Pivot` and four for the `Panorama`. The user should never lose his place inside the `Panorama`.

▶ Avoid making your `Panorama` overly complex, for example, where every link on the `Panorama` takes the user to a `Pivot`.

Windows Phone Toolkit Lockable Pivot

The Windows Phone Toolkit contains a `LockablePivot` control that allows a `PivotItem` to be locked in place so that navigation to other `PivotItems` is disabled. This allows you to host content, such as a `Slider` control, that would otherwise be unsuitable for a `Pivot` because of the `Pivot` control's reliance on horizontal panning gestures.

`LockablePivot` extends `Pivot` and provides a single public property named `IsLocked`. When set to true from your code, this property prevents navigation to other `PivotItems` and hides the adjacent pivot item names within the header.

Summary

This chapter began by looking at the differences and similarities of the `Pivot` and `Panorama`. You saw how the `Pivot` is designed to be used for completing a task, whereas the `Panorama` is designed to entice the user to explore.

The chapter then looked at the anatomy of the `Pivot` and how to create a simple `Pivot` driven page. You saw how to use the `Pivot` load events, allowing you to load content on demand, and you explored a novel approach that allows you to associate a different application bar with each `PivotItem` using a custom `AppBar` control. You then learned how to create a `Pivot` driven chat app, which was augmented to demonstrate implicit `PivotItem` generation and templating. By generating `PivotItems` by assigning the `Pivot.ItemsSource` property, the `Pivot` can be dynamically populated at runtime.

The second part of this chapter focused on the `Panorama`. You saw how to create a simple bookshop app that uses a WCF service to retrieve a list of products displayed within a `Panorama`.

Finally, the chapter concluded by looking at some things to avoid when using a `Pivot` or `Panorama`.

CHAPTER 12

Processing Touch Input

Windows Phone devices come equipped with capacitive touch screens that offer a smooth, accurate, multitouch enabled experience. By adding touch and gesture support to your apps, you can greatly enhance the user experience.

You can handle touch input in your XAML-based Windows Phone app in a number of ways, including

▶ Mouse events

▶ TouchPoint class

▶ Manipulation events

▶ UIElement gesture events

▶ Windows Phone Toolkit for gestures

Mouse events are an easy way to get basic touch support and detect simple, one-finger gestures, such as tap and double tap.

The TouchPoint class provides a low-level input system that you can use to respond to all touch activity in the UI. The TouchPoint class is used by the higher-level touch input systems.

Manipulation events are UIElement events used to handle more complex gestures, such as multitouch gestures and gestures that use inertia and velocity data.

UIElement and Toolkit gestures further consolidate the low-level touch API into a set of gesture-specific events and make it easy to handle complex single and multitouch gestures.

This chapter explores each of these four approaches in detail. The chapter presents an example app demonstrating how to move, resize, rotate, and animate a UIElement using gestures; and it concludes by looking at the best practices for optimizing your user inter-faces for touch input.

Handling Touch with Mouse Events

Mouse events can be used to detect a simple, one-finger gesture. Mouse event handlers can be quickly added to your app and provide an easy way to get basic touch support.

For more complex gestures, additional code is required to translate manipulation values to detect the actual gesture type. As you see in later sections of this chapter, there are easier higher-level APIs for handling more complex gestures.

In this chapter, the term *touch point* is used to describe the point of contact between a finger and the device screen.

The UIElement class includes the following mouse events:

- ▶ **MouseEnter**—Raised when a touch point enters the bounding area of a UIElement.

- ▶ **MouseLeave**—Raised when the user taps and moves his finger outside the bounding area of the UIElement.

- ▶ **MouseLeftButtonDown**—Raised when the user touches a UIElement.

- ▶ **MouseLeftButtonUp**—Raised when a touch point is removed from the screen while it is over a UIElement (or while a UIElement holds mouse capture).

- ▶ **MouseMove**—Raised when the coordinate position of the touch point changes while over a UIElement (or while a UIElement holds mouse capture).

- ▶ **MouseWheel**—This event is unutilized on a touch-driven UI.

The following example responds to the MouseLeftButtonDown, MouseLeftButtonUp, and MouseLeave events to change the background color of a Border control. See the following excerpt from the MouseEventsView.xaml file:

```
<Grid x:Name="ContentPanel" Grid.Row="1" Margin="12,0,12,0">
    <Border
        MouseLeftButtonDown="HandleLeftButtonDown"
        MouseLeftButtonUp="HandleLeftButtonUp"
        MouseLeave="HandleMouseLeave"
        Height="100"
        Width="200"
        Background="{StaticResource PhoneAccentBrush}" />
</Grid>
```

The event handlers in the code-beside change the color of the Border (see Listing 12.1).

LISTING 12.1 MouseEventsView Class

```
public partial class MouseEventsView : PhoneApplicationPage
{
    readonly SolidColorBrush dragBrush = new SolidColorBrush(Colors.Orange);
    readonly SolidColorBrush normalBrush;

    public MouseEventsView()
    {
        InitializeComponent();

        normalBrush = (SolidColorBrush)Resources["PhoneAccentBrush"];
    }

    void HandleLeftButtonDown(object sender, MouseButtonEventArgs e)
    {
        Border border = (Border)sender;
        border.Background = dragBrush;
    }

    void HandleLeftButtonUp(object sender, MouseButtonEventArgs e)
    {
        Border border = (Border)sender;
        border.Background = normalBrush;
    }

    void HandleMouseLeave(object sender, MouseEventArgs e)
    {
        Border border = (Border)sender;
        border.Background = normalBrush;
    }
}
```

The MouseButtonEventArgs class derives from MouseEventArgs. MouseEventArgs is a RoutedEvent, which is discussed in more detail later in this chapter.

Although mouse events provide a simple way to respond to touch in your app, they do not come equipped to support complex gestures or multitouch, nor do they provide any built-in means for ascertaining more detailed touch information, such as touch velocity. Fortunately, as you see later in the chapter, a number of alternative touch APIs do just that. For now, though, turn your attention to the Touch and TouchPoint classes that represent the low-level touch API.

Touch **and** TouchPoint **Classes**

The low-level interface for touch is the TouchPoint class. Unlike mouse events, the TouchPoint class is designed exclusively for touch without a pointing device in mind. A TouchPoint instance represents a finger touching the screen.

TouchPoint has four read-only properties, described in the following list:

▶ **Action**—Represents the type of manipulation and can have one of the three following values:

  ▶ **Down**—Indicates that the user has made contact with the screen.

  ▶ **Move**—Indicates that the touch point has changed position.

  ▶ **Up**—Indicates that the touch point has been removed.

▶ **Position**—Retrieves the X and Y coordinate position of the touch point, as a System.Windows.Point. This point is relative to the top-left corner of the element beneath the touch point.

▶ **Size**—This is supposed to get the rectangular area that is reported as the touch-point contact area. The value reported on Windows Phone, however, always has a width and height of 1, making it of no use on the phone.

▶ **TouchDevice**—Retrieves the specific device type that produced the touch point. This property allows you to retrieve the UIElement beneath the touch point via its TouchDevice.DirectlyOver property. The TouchDevice.Id property allows you to distinguish between fingers touching the display.

The Touch class is an application-level service used to register for touch events. It contains a single *public static* member, the FrameReported event. This event is global for your app and is raised whenever a touch event occurs.

To register for touch notifications, you subscribe to the Touch.FrameReported event like so:

```
Touch.FrameReported += HandleFrameReported;
```

A handler for the FrameReported event accepts a TouchFrameEventArgs argument, as shown:

```
void HandleFrameReported(object sender, TouchFrameEventArgs args)
{
.../* method body */
}
```

A *frame* is a time slice where one or more touch events have occurred. When the FrameReported event is raised, there may be up to four TouchPoint objects.

TouchFrameEventArgs contains four public members, which are described in the following list:

▶ **TimeStamp property**—An int value that indicates when the touch event occurred.

▶ **GetPrimaryTouchPoint(UIElement relativeTo)**—Retrieves the TouchPoint representing the first finger that touched the screen. A UIElement can be specified to make the TouchPoint object's Position property relative to that element. If a UIElement is not specified (it is *null*), the returned TouchPoint is relative to the top left of the page.

▶ **GetTouchPoints(UIElement relativeTo)**—Retrieves the collection of TouchPoints for the frame. The UIElement parameter works the same as the GetPrimaryTouchPoint. The parameter does not restrict the set of TouchPoints returned; all are returned and only the Position of each TouchPoint is affected.

▶ **SuspendMousePromotionUntilTouchUp()**—Prevents touch events from turning into mouse events. See the following section for a more detailed explanation.

Mouse Event Promotion

With the advent of Windows Phone, Silverlight transitioned from being a browser and desktop-only technology with a primarily mouse-driven UI, to a mobile device technology with a touch-driven UI.

To allow controls that were originally designed to work with mouse events to continue to function, the touch system was engineered so that touch events are automatically turned into (promoted to) mouse events. If a touch event is not suspended using the SuspendMousePromotionUntilTouchUp method, then mouse events are automatically raised.

> **NOTE**
>
> Promotion of a TouchPoint to a mouse event occurs only with the primary touch point.

To prevent a touch event from being promoted to a mouse event, call the SuspendMousePromotionUntilTouchUp within the FrameReported event handler, like so:

```
void HandleFrameReported(object sender, TouchFrameEventArgs e)
{
    TouchPoint primaryTouchPoint = e.GetPrimaryTouchPoint(null);
    if (primaryTouchPoint != null
        && primaryTouchPoint.Action == TouchAction.Down)
    {
        e.SuspendMousePromotionUntilTouchUp();
        /* custom code */
    }
}
```

NOTE

The `SuspendMousePromotionUntilTouchUp` method can be called only when the `TouchPoint.Action` property is equal to `TouchAction.Down`, or else an `InvalidOperationException` is raised.

In most cases, calling `SuspendMousePromotionUntilTouchUp` is something you should avoid, because doing so prevents the functioning of any controls that rely solely on mouse events and those that have not been built using the touch-specific API.

Handling the `Touch.FrameReported` Event

The following example shows how to change the color of a `Border` control by responding to the `Touch.FrameReported` event. Within the `TouchPointView` XAML file is a named `Border` control as shown:

```
<Grid x:Name="ContentPanel" Grid.Row="1" Margin="12,0,12,0">
    <Border x:Name="border"
        Height="100"
        Width="200"
        Background="{StaticResource PhoneAccentBrush}" />
</Grid>
```

The code-beside file, TouchPointView.xaml.cs, subscribes to the `Touch.FrameReported` event within the page constructor. The event handler retrieves the primary touch point, and if the `TouchPoint` is above the `Border`, the `Border` object's `Background` is switched (see Listing 12.2).

LISTING 12.2   `TouchPointView` Class

```
public partial class TouchPointView : PhoneApplicationPage
{
    readonly SolidColorBrush directlyOverBrush
                = new SolidColorBrush(Colors.Orange);
    readonly Brush normalBrush;

    public TouchPointView()
    {
        InitializeComponent();

        normalBrush = border.Background;

        Touch.FrameReported += HandleFrameReported;
    }

    void HandleFrameReported(object sender, TouchFrameEventArgs e)
    {
        TouchPoint primaryTouchPoint = e.GetPrimaryTouchPoint(null);
```

```
    if (primaryTouchPoint == null
        || primaryTouchPoint.TouchDevice.DirectlyOver != border)
    {
        return;
    }

    if (primaryTouchPoint.Action == TouchAction.Down)
    {           border.Background = directlyOverBrush;
    }
    else
    {
        border.Background = normalBrush;
    }
  }
}
```

Using the Touch and TouchPoint API provides you with the ability to respond to touch at a very low level. Subsequent sections of this chapter look at two higher-level abstractions of the Touch and TouchPoint APIs—namely, manipulation events and the Windows Phone Toolkit, beginning with manipulation events.

Manipulation Events

Manipulation events consolidate the touch activities of one or two fingers. Manipulation events combine individual touch point information, provided by the Touch.FrameReported event, and interpret them into a higher-level API with velocity, scaling, and translation information.

Moreover, unlike the Touch.FrameReported event, which provides touch notifications for your entire interface, a manipulation event is specific to the UIElement to which it is associated.

The manipulation events comprise three UIElement events, which are described in the following list:

▶ **ManipulationStarted**—Raised when the user touches the UIElement.

▶ **ManipulationDelta**—Raised when a second touch point is placed on the element, and when a touch input changes position. This event can occur multiple times during a manipulation. For example, if the user drags a finger across the screen, the ManipulationDelta event occurs multiple times during the finger's movement.

▶ **ManipulationCompleted**—Raised when the user's finger, or fingers, leaves the UIElement, and when any inertia applied to the element is complete.

These three events are routed events (they subclass the RoutedEvent class). In case you are not familiar with routed events, a RoutedEvent can be handled by an ancestor element in the visual tree. RoutedEvents *bubble* upwards through the visual tree, until they are either handled, indicated by the `Handled` property of the event arguments, or reach the root element of the visual tree. This means that you can subscribe to a manipulation event at, for example, the page level, and it gives you the opportunity to handle manipulation events for all elements in the page.

As you might expect, a manipulation begins with the `ManipulationStarted` event, followed by zero or more `ManipulationDelta` events, and then a single `ManipulationCompleted` event.

The event arguments for all three manipulation events have the following shared properties:

▶ `OriginalSource` **(provided by the** `RoutedEvent` **base class)**—This is the object that raised the manipulation event.

▶ `ManipulationContainer`—This is the topmost enabled `UIElement` being touched. Touch points on different `UIElements` provide a separate succession of manipulation events and are distinguished by the `ManipulationContainer` property. The `OriginalSource` and `ManipulationContainer` properties are in most cases the same. Internally, `ManipulationContainer` is assigned to the `OriginalSource` property when a manipulation event is raised.

▶ `ManipulationOrigin`—This property, of type `Point`, indicates the location of the touch point relative to the top-left corner of the `ManipulationContainer` element. If two touch points exist on the element, the `ManipulationOrigin` property indicates the middle position between the two points.

▶ `Handled`—A property of type `bool` that allows you to halt the bubbling of the routed event up the visual tree.

Handling Manipulation Events

When a manipulation begins, the `ManipulationStarted` event is raised. The event handler accepts a `ManipulationStartedEventArgs` parameter, as shown:

```
void HandleManipulationStarted(object sender, ManipulationStartedEventArgs e)
{
    /* method body */
}
```

Contrary to the low-level `TouchPoint` API, there is no need to store the ID of the touch point to track its motion. In fact, the manipulation events do not offer individual touch point information. If you need that information, the low-level `TouchPoint` API may be more suitable.

During manipulation, the `ManipulationDelta` event is raised when a touch point is added to the `ManipulationContainer` element, or when the position of a touch point on the element changes. The event handler accepts a `ManipulationDeltaEventArgs` parameter, as shown:

```
void HandleManipulationDelta(object sender, ManipulationDeltaEventArgs e)
{
    /* method body */
}
```

ManipulationDeltaEventArgs provides you with the most recent and the accumulated manipulation data. The following is a list of its properties, which have not yet been covered:

- ▶ **CumulativeManipulation**—Gets the accumulated changes of the current manipulation, as a ManipulationDelta instance. ManipulationDelta has the following two properties:

  - ▶ **Scale**—A Point indicating the horizontal and vertical scale amounts, relevant during multitouch manipulation.

  - ▶ **Translate**—A Point indicating the horizontal and vertical positional offset.

- ▶ **DeltaManipulation**—Gets the most recent changes of the current manipulation, as a ManipulationDelta.

- ▶ **IsInertial**—Gets whether the ManipulationDelta event was raised while a finger had contact with the element. In my experience the value of this property is always false during the ManipulationDelta event. This property is of more use during handling of the ManipulationCompleted event, as you soon see.

- ▶ **Velocities**—Gets the rates of the most recent changes to the manipulation. This property is of type ManipulationVelocities, which is a class with the following two properties:

  - ▶ **ExpansionVelocity**—Gets a Point representing the rate at which the manipulation was resized.

  - ▶ **LinearVelocity**—Gets a Point representing the speed of the linear motion.

Inertia is applied automatically to a manipulation and is based on the velocity of the manipulation. Both the ManipulationCompletedEventArgs and ManipulationStartedEventArgs classes contain a Complete method, which allows you to forcibly finish the manipulation event sequence, which raises the ManipulationComplete event and prevents the application of inertia.

The ManipulationComplete event handler accepts a ManipulationCompletedEventArgs parameter, as shown:

```
void HandleManipulationCompleted(
            object sender, ManipulationCompletedEventArgs e)
{
    /* method body */
}
```

ManipulationCompletedEventArgs provides you with the final velocities and overall manipulation data. The following is a list of its properties, which have not yet been covered:

▶ **FinalVelocities**—Gets the final expansion and linear velocities for the manipulation.

▶ **IsInertial**—Gets whether the ManipulationDelta event occurred while a finger has contact with the element.

▶ **IsInertial**—Gets whether the ManipulationDelta event was raised while a finger had contact with the element. If the manipulation consisted of a single touch point, it is indicative of a flick gesture.

▶ **TotalManipulation**—Gets a ManipulationDelta object containing two Points representing the total scale and translation values for the manipulation.

Manipulation Events Example

The following example illustrates how to move and scale a UIElement using the various manipulation events.

Within the ManipulationEventsView XAML file is a Border control, defined as shown:

```
<StackPanel x:Name="ContentPanel" Grid.Row="1" Margin="12,0,12,0">
    <Border
        Height="400"
        Width="400"
        Background="{StaticResource PhoneAccentBrush}"
        ManipulationStarted="HandleManipulationStarted"
        ManipulationDelta="HandleManipulationDelta"
        ManipulationCompleted="HandleManipulationCompleted">
        <TextBlock x:Name="TextBlock_Message" />
        <Border.RenderTransform>
            <CompositeTransform x:Name="compositeTransform"/>
        </Border.RenderTransform>
    </Border>
</StackPanel>
```

When the user touches the Border, the ManipulationStarted event is raised, calling the code-beside handler, which sets the background color of the Border. As the user moves her fingers, the ManipulationDelta event is raised repeatedly, each time the location and scale of the Border is adjusted using the CompositeTransform (see Listing 12.3).

LISTING 12.3   ManipulationEventsView Class

```
public partial class ManipulationEventsView : PhoneApplicationPage
{
    readonly SolidColorBrush startManipulationBrush
                        = new SolidColorBrush(Colors.Orange);
```

```
Brush normalBrush;

public ManipulationEventsView()
{
    InitializeComponent();
}

void HandleManipulationStarted(
        object sender, ManipulationStartedEventArgs e)
{
    Border border = (Border)sender;
    normalBrush = border.Background;
    border.Background = startManipulationBrush;
}
void HandleManipulationDelta(object sender, ManipulationDeltaEventArgs e)
{
    ...
    compositeTransform.TranslateX += e.DeltaManipulation.Translation.X;
    compositeTransform.TranslateY += e.DeltaManipulation.Translation.Y;

    if (e.DeltaManipulation.Scale.X > 0
        && e.DeltaManipulation.Scale.X > 0)
    {
        compositeTransform.ScaleX *= e.DeltaManipulation.Scale.X;
        compositeTransform.ScaleY *= e.DeltaManipulation.Scale.Y;
    }
}

void HandleManipulationCompleted(
            object sender, ManipulationCompletedEventArgs e)
{
    Border border = (Border)sender;
    border.Background = normalBrush;
    TextBlock_Message.Text = string.Empty;
    ...
}
...
}
```

Pinching or stretching the Border modifies the CompositeTransform scale values, which resizes the control. A tap and drag gesture modifies the CompositeTransform translation values, which repositions the control (see Figure 12.1).

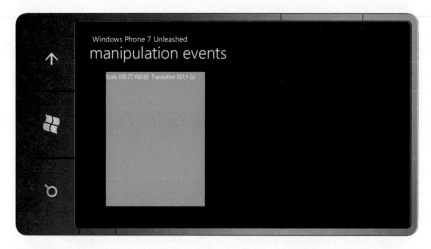

FIGURE 12.1   A `Border` is moved and resized in response to manipulation events.

`UIElement` Touch Gesture Events

Gestures are a high-level way of interpreting touch input data and include a set of common motions, such as tapping, flicking, and pinching. Controls, such as the `WebBrowser`, handle gestures such as the pinch gesture internally, allowing the user to pan and zoom in and out of content. By responding to gestures, you can provide a natural and immersive experience for your users.

Support for basic single touch gestures is incorporated into the Windows Phone SDK for XAML apps. Support for more complex gestures is provided by the Windows Phone Toolkit, discussed in the next section.

The sample code for this section is located in the UIElementTouchEventsView.xaml and UIElementTouchEventsView.xaml.cs files, in the Touch directory of the WPUnleashed. Examples project.

The `UIElement` class comes equipped to handle the following three touch gestures:

▶ Tap

▶ Double tap

▶ Hold

The `UIElement` includes three corresponding routed events: `Tap`, `DoubleTap`, and `Hold`.

The three tap events can be subscribed to in XAML, as the following excerpt demonstrates:

```
<Grid x:Name="ContentPanel" Grid.Row="1" Margin="12,0,12,0">
    <Border
```

```
        Tap="HandleTap"
        DoubleTap="HandleDoubleTap"
        Hold="HandleHold"
        Height="100"
        Width="200"
        Background="{StaticResource PhoneChromeBrush}">
        <TextBlock x:Name="textBlock"
                HorizontalAlignment="Center" VerticalAlignment="Center"
                Style="{StaticResource PhoneTextLargeStyle}"/>
    </Border>
</Grid>
```

Figure 12.2 shows the sample page responding to the double tap gesture.

FIGURE 12.2   `UIElementTouchEventsView` page.

Event handlers for all three events share the same signature and accept a
GestureEventArgs object. GestureEventArgs contains a Boolean Handled property,
which allows you to stop the event from continuing to bubble up the visual tree, and a
GetPosition method that allows you to retrieve the location coordinates of where the
touch occurred.

Each tap gesture supported by UIElement is examined in the following sections.

Tap Gesture

The simplest of all the gestures, a tap occurs when a finger touches the screen momen-
tarily (see Figure 12.3).

FIGURE 12.3   Tap gesture.

This gesture is analogous to a single-click performed with a mouse. The tap gesture can be broken down into the following two parts:

▶ Finger down provides touch indication.

▶ Finger up executes the action.

The `Tap` event is raised when the user performs a tap gesture. If the user's finger remains in contact with the display for longer than one second, the tap event is not raised.

An event handler for the `Tap` event is shown in the following excerpt:

```
void HandleTap(object sender, GestureEventArgs e)
{
    textBlock.Text = "tap";
}
```

Double Tap Gesture

The double tap gesture occurs when a finger quickly touches the screen twice (see Figure 12.4). This gesture is analogous to a double-click performed with a mouse.

The double tap is primarily designed to be used to toggle between the *in* and *out* zoom states of a control.

An event handler for the `DoubleTap` event is shown in the following excerpt:

```
void HandleDoubleTap(object sender, GestureEventArgs e)
{
    textBlock.Text = "double tap";
}
```

FIGURE 12.4   Double tap gesture.

Hold Gesture

The hold gesture is performed by touching the screen while continuing contact for a period of time (see Figure 12.5).

FIGURE 12.5   Hold gesture.

The `UIElement.Hold` event is raised when the user touches the screen for one second.

An event handler for the `Hold` event is shown in the following excerpt:

```
void HandleHold(object sender, GestureEventArgs e)
{
    textBlock.Text = "hold";
}
```

As an aside, the `UIElement` `Hold` event is used by the Windows Phone Toolkit's `ContextMenu` component. When used in this way, the hold gesture mimics the right-click of a mouse.

> **NOTE**
>
> `UIElement` and Windows Phone Toolkit gesture events (discussed in the next section) are raised only if the `UIElement` is detected beneath the touch point. Make sure that the `Background` property of the `UIElement` is not null. If a background is not defined, touch events pass through the host control, and gestures are not detected. To achieve a see-through background, while still maintaining gesture support, set the background property of the `UIElement` to Transparent.

Windows Phone Toolkit Gestures

Windows Phone Toolkit, introduced in Chapter 9, "Enriching the User Experience with the Windows Phone Toolkit Controls," abstracts low-level touch events and further consolidates touch event data into a set of events representing the various single and multitouch gesture types.

Toolkit gestures harness the `Touch.FrameReported` event (described in the previous section "Touch and `TouchPoint` Classes") to provide high-level gesture information.

Unless you require low-level touch point data, `UIElement` and Toolkit gestures are the recommended way to add single and multitouch capabilities to your apps.

> **NOTE**
>
> Some overlap exists between the `UIElement` touch gesture events and the Toolkit gestures API; both allow you to handle tap, double tap, and hold gestures.
>
> The first release of the Windows Phone SDK did not include baked-in support for these three gestures, and they were subsequently added with the 7.1 release of the SDK. In the meantime, the Toolkit had already included gesture support, so the presence of these gestures in the Toolkit remains as somewhat of a legacy feature. It is therefore recommended that you use the `UIElement` touch gesture events, rather than the Toolkit gesture API, for the tap, double tap, and hold gestures.

Getting Started with Toolkit Gestures

Unlike the other techniques seen in this chapter, Toolkit gestures are provided as a separate assembly, as part of the Windows Phone Toolkit package. To learn how to obtain the Toolkit, see Chapter 9.

The two main classes for working with Toolkit gestures are the `GestureService` and `GestureListener` classes. `GestureService` is used only to attach a `GestureListener` to a `UIElement`. Like manipulation events, Toolkit gestures are used in conjunction with a `UIElement`. Once attached, the `GestureListener` monitors the element for gestures that the element can support, such as tap, hold, pinch, and flick.

`GestureListener` allows you to specify handlers for each gesture type. The following example shows a `Border` control with subscriptions to these events via the attached `GestureListener`:

```
<Border Background="{StaticResource PhoneAccentBrush}">
    <toolkit:GestureService.GestureListener>
        <toolkit:GestureListener
            GestureBegin="HandleGestureBegin"
            GestureCompleted="HandleGestureCompleted"
            Tap="HandleTap"
            DoubleTap="HandleDoubleTap"
            Hold="HandleHold"
            DragStarted="HandleDragStarted"
            DragDelta="HandleDragDelta"
            DragCompleted="HandleDragCompleted"
            Flick="HandleFlick"
            PinchStarted="HandlePinchStarted"
            PinchDelta="HandlePinchDelta"
            PinchCompleted="HandlePinchCompleted">
        </toolkit:GestureListener>
    </toolkit:GestureService.GestureListener>
</Border>
```

The `GestureListener` class is designed for Silverlight's event-driven model. The class effectively wraps the low-level Silverlight touch mechanism to perform automatic conversion of the `Touch.FrameReported` events into unique events for each gesture type.

`GestureListener` Events in Detail

This section looks at each gesture and the events that correspond to each.

Tap Gesture

When a tap gesture is detected, the `GestureListener.Tap` event is raised. The event handler accepts a `GestureEventArgs` parameter, as shown:

```
void HandleTap(object sender, GestureEventArgs e)
```

```
{
    /* method body. */
}
```

The `GestureListener` events are quasi routed events. That is, they behave like routed events, yet their event arguments do not inherit from the `RoutedEvent` class. Like the `RoutedEventArgs` class, the `GestureEventArgs` includes an `OriginalSource` property that allows you to retrieve a reference to the object that raised the event, which may differ from the sender argument provided to the event handler.

The routing mechanism for gesture events also allows you to handle any or all of the gesture events at a higher level in the visual tree. For example, to listen for a `Tap` event that may occur in a child element, you can subscribe to the `Tap` event at the page level, like so:

```
<phone:PhoneApplicationPage
    x:Class="DanielVaughan.WPUnleashed.Examples.GesturesView"
    ... >
    <toolkit:GestureService.GestureListener>
        <toolkit:GestureListener Tap="HandleTapAtPageLevel" />
    </toolkit:GestureService.GestureListener>
    ...
</phone:PhoneApplicationPage>
```

The routing mechanism gives you the power to control whether an event should continue to bubble up the visual tree. Set the `GestureEventArgs.Handled` property to true to prevent the event from being handled at a higher level (in this case by the page level handler), as shown in the following example:

```
void HandleTap(object sender, GestureEventArgs e)
{
    e.Handled = true;
}
```

By setting the `Handled` property to true, the `HandleTapAtPageLevel` method is not called.

The `GestureEventArgs` class is the base class for other gesture event arguments, as shown later in this section.

Double Tap Gesture

When a double tap gesture is detected, the `GestureListener.DoubleTap` event is raised. The event handler accepts a `GestureEventArgs` parameter, as shown:

```
void HandleDoubleTap(object sender, GestureEventArgs e)
{
    /* method body. */
}
```

Hold Gesture

When a hold gesture is detected, the GestureListener.Hold event is raised. The handler accepts a GestureEventArgs parameter, as shown:

```
void HandleHold(object sender, GestureEventArgs e)
{
    /* method body. */
}
```

Drag Gesture

The drag gesture is performed by touching the screen and moving the finger in any direction while still in contact with the screen (see Figure 12.6).

FIGURE 12.6   Drag gesture.

The drag gesture is normally used to reorder items in a list or to reposition an element by direct manipulation.

The following three events are used to detect and coordinate activities during a drag gesture:

▶ **DragStarted**—Raised when the drag gesture begins, which is as soon as motion is detected following a touch event.

▶ **DragDelta**—Raised while a drag gesture is underway and the location of the touch point changes.

▶ **DragCompleted**—Raised on touch release after a drag, or when a second touch point is added.

When a drag gesture is detected, the GestureListener.DragStarted event is raised. The event handler accepts a DragStartedGestureEventArgs parameter, as shown:

```
void HandleDragStarted(object sender, DragStartedGestureEventArgs e)
{
    /* method body. */
}
```

DragStartedGestureEventArgs provides you with the initial direction of the drag gesture via its Direction property and can be either Horizontal or Vertical depending on the predominant direction.

As the user moves either finger during a drag gesture, the GestureListener.DragDelta event is raised. The event handler accepts a DragDeltaGestureEventArgs parameter, as shown:

```
void HandleDragDelta(object sender, DragDeltaGestureEventArgs e)
{
    /* method body. */
}
```

The DragDeltaGestureEventArgs parameter provides the difference between the current location of the touch point and its previous location. The DragDeltaGestureEventArgs has the following three properties:

▶ **Direction**—Provides the predominant direction of the drag gesture, either Horizontal or Vertical.

▶ **HorizontalChange**—The horizontal (x axis) difference in pixels between the current touch point location and the previous location. The value of this property is negative if the drag occurs from right to left.

▶ **VerticalChange**—The vertical (y axis) difference in pixels between the current touch point location and the previous location. The value of this property is negative if the drag occurs in an upward direction.

When the user completes the drag gesture by removing the touch points, the GestureListener.DragCompleted event is raised. This event provides the opportunity to conclude any activities that were being performed during the drag gesture. The handler accepts a DragCompletedGestureEventArgs parameter, as shown:

```
void HandleDragCompleted(object sender, DragCompletedGestureEventArgs e)
{
    /* method body. */
}
```

In addition to the data provided by the DragDeltaGestureEventArgs, the DragCompletedGestureEventArgs argument includes a VerticalVelocity property and a HorizontalVelocity property that measure the velocity of the drag. You may find that often both values are zero when the user stops the dragging motion before removing the touch point.

The example presented later in this section explores the drag gesture in greater detail and shows how the drag gesture can be used to change the location of UIElements on a page.

Flick Gesture

A flick gesture is performed by dragging a finger across the screen and lifting the finger without stopping (see Figure 12.7). A flick gesture normally moves content from one area to another.

FIGURE 12.7   Flick gesture.

When a flick gesture is detected, the GestureListener.Flick event is raised. The event handler accepts a FlickGestureEventArgs parameter, as shown:

```
void HandleFlick(object sender, FlickGestureEventArgs e)
{
    /* method body. */
}
```

FlickGestureEventsArgs provides you with the direction and velocity of the flick gesture via the following four properties:

▶ **Angle**—A double value, measured in degrees, indicating the angle of the flick. A downward flick results in an angle between 0 and 180 degrees; an upward flick in an angle between 180 and 360 degrees (see Figure 12.8). This value is calculated using the horizontal and vertical velocity of the flick.

▶ **Direction**—An Orientation value of either Horizontal or Vertical, indicating whether the flick was more horizontal than vertical, or vice versa.

▶ **HorizontalVelocity**—A double value indicating the horizontal (X) velocity of the flick.

▶ `VerticalVelocity`—A double value indicating the vertical (Y) velocity of the flick.

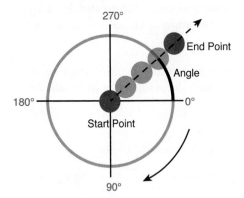

FIGURE 12.8   Origin of the `FlickGestureEventsArgs.Angle` property.

In the example code, presented later in this section, you see how to animate a `UIElement` in response to a flick gesture.

> **NOTE**
>
> Gesture events are not necessarily mutually exclusive. The `GestureListener.DragCompleted` event is raised along with the `GestureListener.Flick` event.

Pinch Gesture

A pinch gesture is performed by pressing two fingers on the screen and moving either or both fingers together (see Figure 12.9). A stretch gesture is performed by moving the fingers apart. Both gestures are detected using the `GestureListener.Pinch` event.

FIGURE 12.9   Pinch and stretch gestures.

The pinch gesture is the only multitouch gesture supported by the `GestureListener` and is typically used to zoom in or out of a page or element.

The following three events are used to detect and coordinate activities during a pinch gesture:

- ▶ `PinchStarted`—Raised when the pinch gesture begins, and occurring as soon as motion is detected when at least two fingers are touching the screen

- ▶ `PinchDelta`—Raised while a pinch gesture is underway and the location of either touch point changes

- ▶ `PinchCompleted`—Raised on touch release, of either touch points, after a pinch

When a pinch gesture is detected, the `GestureListener.PinchStarted` event is raised. The event handler accepts a `PinchStartedGestureEventArgs` parameter, as shown:

```
void HandlePinchStarted(object sender, PinchStartedGestureEventArgs e)
{
    /* method body. */
}
```

`PinchStartedGestureEventArgs` provides you with the direction and velocity of the pinch gesture via the following two properties:

- ▶ `Angle`—A double value, measured in degrees, indicating the angle from the first touch point, the first to make contact with the screen, to the second touch point (see Figure 12.10)

- ▶ `Distance`—A double value indicating the distance in pixels between the two touch points

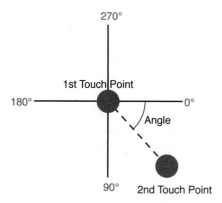

FIGURE 12.10   Determining the pinch angle.

As the user moves either finger during a pinch gesture, the GestureListener.PinchDelta event is raised. The handler accepts a PinchGestureEventArgs parameter, as shown:

```
void HandlePinchDelta(object sender, PinchGestureEventArgs e)
{
    /* method body. */
}
```

The PinchGestureEventArgs argument provides the distance and angle of the touch points compared to the original touch points that were registered when the pinch gesture began. PinchGestureEventArgs has the following two properties:

▶ **DistanceRatio**—Provides the ratio of the current distance between touch points divided by the original distance between the touch points

▶ **TotalAngleDelta**—Provides the difference between the angles of the current touch positions and the original touch positions

The PinchGestureEventArgs derives from MultiTouchGestureEventArgs, which also provides a GetPosition method that allows you to determine the position of the first or second touch point relative to a specified UIElement. The method accepts a UIElement and an int value indicating the index of a touch point, either 0 or 1.

When the user completes the pinch gesture by removing either or both touch points, the GestureListener.PinchCompleted event is raised. This event provides the opportunity to conclude any activities that were being performed during the pinch gesture, such as finalizing the locations of elements. The handler accepts a PinchStartedGestureEventArgs parameter, as shown:

```
void HandlePinchDelta(object sender, PinchGestureEventArgs e)
{
    /* method body. */
}
```

The PinchGestureEventArgs argument provides the same information as described for the GestureListener.PinchDelta event.

GestureBegin and GestureCompleted Events

In addition to the gesture-specific events, two events are raised before and after every gesture event. These are the GestureBegin and GestureCompleted events. Handlers for these events resemble the following:

```
void HandleGestureBegin(object sender, GestureEventArgs e)
{
    /* method body. */
}
```

```
}

void HandleGestureCompleted(object sender, GestureEventArgs e)
{
    /* method body. */
}
```

Gesture Sample Code

This section looks at the GesturesView page in the downloadable sample code and demonstrates the various events of the GestureListener class. You see how to move, rotate, and resize a UIElement using gestures. You also see how to provide an animation that responds to a flick gesture to send a UIElement hurtling across a page.

The view contains a Border. Within the Border we attach the GestureListener and subscribe to its various events:

```xml
<Grid x:Name="ContentPanel" Grid.Row="1" Margin="12,0,12,0">
    <TextBlock x:Name="messageBlock"
            Style="{StaticResource PhoneTextNormalStyle}"
            VerticalAlignment="Top" />
    <Button Content="reset" Click="Button_Click"
            VerticalAlignment="Bottom"
            HorizontalAlignment="Left" />
    <Border x:Name="border"
            Width="300" Height="200"
            BorderBrush="{StaticResource PhoneBorderBrush}"
            BorderThickness="4,32,4,4"
            Background="{StaticResource PhoneAccentBrush}"
            RenderTransformOrigin="0.5,0.5"
            Opacity=".8"
            CacheMode="BitmapCache">
        <Border.RenderTransform>
            <CompositeTransform x:Name="compositeTransform"/>
        </Border.RenderTransform>
        <toolkit:GestureService.GestureListener>
            <toolkit:GestureListener
                Tap="HandleTap"
                DoubleTap="HandleDoubleTap"
                Hold="HandleHold"
                DragStarted="HandleDragStarted"
                DragDelta="HandleDragDelta"
                DragCompleted="HandleDragCompleted"
                Flick="HandleFlick"
                PinchStarted="HandlePinchStarted"
                PinchDelta="HandlePinchDelta"
```

```
        PinchCompleted="HandlePinchCompleted">
      </toolkit:GestureListener>
    </toolkit:GestureService.GestureListener>
  </Border>
</Grid>
```

A `CompositeTransform` is used to change the position, size, and rotation of the `Border`.

The following sections walk through each gesture event and show how the `Border` control is manipulated in response.

Handling the `Tap`, `DoubleTap`, and `Hold` Events

When the user performs a tap gesture, the `HandleTap` method in the code-beside is called. This method resets the `CompositeTransform` translate values to 0, which returns the `Border` to its original location.

```
void HandleTap(object sender, GestureEventArgs e)
{
    compositeTransform.TranslateX = compositeTransform.TranslateY = 0;
}
```

When the user performs a double tap gesture, the `HandleDoubleTap` method is called, which resets the amount of scaling applied to the `Border`, returning it to its original size.

```
void HandleDoubleTap(object sender, GestureEventArgs e)
{
    compositeTransform.ScaleX = compositeTransform.ScaleY = 1;
}
```

When a hold gesture is performed, the `HandleHold` method is called. This, in turn, calls the `ResetPosition` method, resetting the size and location of the `Border`.

```
void HandleHold(object sender, GestureEventArgs e)
{
    ResetPosition();
}
```

```
void ResetPosition()
{
    compositeTransform.TranslateX = compositeTransform.TranslateY = 0;
    compositeTransform.ScaleX = compositeTransform.ScaleY = 1;
    compositeTransform.Rotation = 0;
}
```

Dragging the Border Control

When a drag gesture is performed, the HandleDragStarted method is called. This method changes the background of the Border, like so:

```
void HandleDragStarted(object sender, DragStartedGestureEventArgs e)
{
    border.Background = dragBrush;
}
```

An event handler for the DragDelta event moves the element by the drag amount, via the translation properties of the CompositeTransform:

```
void HandleDragDelta(object sender, DragDeltaGestureEventArgs e)
{
    compositeTransform.TranslateX += e.HorizontalChange;
    compositeTransform.TranslateY += e.VerticalChange;
}
```

When the drag gesture completes, the DragCompleted event handler resets the Border background:

```
void HandleDragCompleted(object sender, DragCompletedGestureEventArgs e)
{
    border.Background = normalBrush;
}
```

Rotating and Scaling in Response to a Pinch Gesture

When a pinch gesture is detected, the Pinch event handler records the amount of rotation applied to the element, along with the scale of the element:

```
double initialAngle;
double initialScale;

void HandlePinchStarted(object sender, PinchStartedGestureEventArgs e)
{
    border.Background = pinchBrush;

    initialAngle = compositeTransform.Rotation;
    initialScale = compositeTransform.ScaleX;
}
```

A change in the pinch gesture raises the PinchDelta event, at which point the level of rotation is applied to the CompositeTransform, and the element is scaled up or down using the PinchGestureEventArgs.DistanceRatio property:

```
void HandlePinchDelta(object sender, PinchGestureEventArgs e)
```

```
{
    compositeTransform.Rotation = initialAngle + e.TotalAngleDelta;
    compositeTransform.ScaleX
        = compositeTransform.ScaleY = initialScale * e.DistanceRatio;
}
```

The completion of a pinch gesture sees the border's background restored, as shown:

```
void HandlePinchCompleted(object sender, PinchGestureEventArgs e)
{
    border.Background = normalBrush;
}
```

Flick Gesture Animation

This section presents a technique for animating a UIElement in response to a flick gesture. When a flick occurs, we install a StoryBoard with a timeline animation, which performs a translation on the UIElement.

The detection of a flick gesture causes the Flick event handler, HandleFlick, to be called. This method calculates a destination point for the border control based on the velocity of the flick. It then creates an animation for the border using the custom AddTranslationAnimation. See the following excerpt:

```
const double brakeSpeed = 10;

void HandleFlick(object sender, FlickGestureEventArgs e)
{
    Point currentPoint = new Point(
        (double)compositeTransform.GetValue(
                    CompositeTransform.TranslateXProperty),
        (double)compositeTransform.GetValue(
                    CompositeTransform.TranslateYProperty));

    double toX = currentPoint.X + e.HorizontalVelocity / brakeSpeed;
    double toY = currentPoint.Y + e.VerticalVelocity / brakeSpeed;
    Point destinationPoint = new Point(toX, toY);

    var storyboard = new Storyboard { FillBehavior = FillBehavior.HoldEnd };

    AddTranslationAnimation(
        storyboard, border, currentPoint, destinationPoint,
        new Duration(TimeSpan.FromMilliseconds(500)),
        new CubicEase {EasingMode = EasingMode.EaseOut});

    storyboard.Begin();
}
```

The static method `AddTranslationAnimation` creates two `DoubleAnimation` objects: one for the horizontal axis, the other for the vertical axis. Each animation is assigned to the border's `CompositeTransform`, as shown:

```
static void AddTranslationAnimation(Storyboard storyboard,
    FrameworkElement targetElement,
    Point fromPoint,
    Point toPoint,
    Duration duration,
    IEasingFunction easingFunction)
{
    var xAnimation = new DoubleAnimation
                        {
                            From = fromPoint.X,
                            To = toPoint.X,
                            Duration = duration,
                            EasingFunction = easingFunction
                        };
    var yAnimation = new DoubleAnimation
                        {
                            From = fromPoint.Y,
                            To = toPoint.Y,
                            Duration = duration,
                            EasingFunction = easingFunction
                        };

    AddAnimation(
        storyboard,
        targetElement.RenderTransform,
        CompositeTransform.TranslateXProperty,
        xAnimation);

    AddAnimation(
        storyboard,
        targetElement.RenderTransform,
        CompositeTransform.TranslateYProperty,
        yAnimation);
}
```

The static method `AddAnimation` associates an animation `Timeline` with a `DependencyObject`, which in this case is the `Border` control:

```
static void AddAnimation(
    Storyboard storyboard,
    DependencyObject dependencyObject,
    DependencyProperty targetProperty,
```

```
    Timeline timeline)
{
    Storyboard.SetTarget(timeline, dependencyObject);
    Storyboard.SetTargetProperty(timeline, new PropertyPath(targetProperty));
    storyboard.Children.Add(timeline);
}
```

When launched, the GestureView page allows the user to flick the Border element across the page. A reset button exists to reset the position of the Border if it happens to leave the visible boundaries of the page (see Figure 12.11).

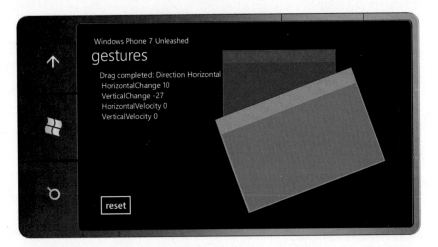

FIGURE 12.11   The Border can be moved, rotated, resized, and flicked in response to gesture events.

Toolkit gestures offer a high-level way of interpreting touch input data and make it easy to provide a natural and immersive experience for your users, without the bother of tracking low-level touch events.

Designing Touch-Friendly User Interfaces

The design and layout of your user interface influences how easy your app is to use with touch input. When designing your UI, it is important to ensure that page elements are big enough and far enough apart to be conducive to touch input. It is also important to consider the nature of mobile devices, and that your app may be used in conditions where touch precision is compromised, such as standing aboard a moving train. Adhering to the advice presented in this section helps you to ensure that your apps are touch friendly.

Three Components of Touch

Touch UI can be broken down into the following three components:

▶ **Touch target**—The area defined to accept touch input, which is not visible to the user

▶ **Touch element**—The visual indicator of the touch target, which is visible to the user

▶ **Touch control**—A touch target that is combined with a touch element that the user touches

The touch target can be larger than the touch element, but should never be smaller than it. The touch element should never be smaller than 60% of the touch target.

Sizing and Spacing Constraints

Providing adequate spacing between touch targets helps to prevent users from selecting the wrong touch control. Touch targets should not be smaller than 34 pixels (9 mm) square and should provide at least 8 pixels (2 mm) between touchable controls (see Figure 12.12).

FIGURE 12.12   Touch target sizing and spacing constraints.

In exceptional cases, controls can be smaller, but they should never be smaller than 26 pixels (7 mm) square.

It is recommend that some touch targets be made larger than 34 pixels (9 mm) when the touch target is a frequently touched control or the target resides close to the edge of the screen.

General Guidelines

The following is a list of some general guidelines when designing a touch-friendly interface:

▶ When designing your interface, you should allow all basic or common tasks to be completed using a single finger.

▶ Touch controls should respond to touch immediately. A touch control with even a slight lag, or one that seems slow when transitioning, has a negative impact on the user experience.

▶ Processing that would otherwise reduce the responsiveness of the UI should be performed on a background thread. If an operation takes a long time, consider providing incremental feedback.

▶ Try to use a gesture in the manner for which it was intended. For example, avoid using a gesture as a shortcut to a task.

Summary

This chapter began by looking at mouse events. Mouse events are an easy way to get basic touch support and allow you to detect simple, one-finger gestures such as tap and double tap.

The chapter examined the `TouchPoint` class and illustrated how it provides a low-level input system that you can use to respond to all touch activity in the UI.

The `UIElement` manipulation events also were discussed. Manipulation events are used to handle more complex gestures, such as multitouch gestures and gestures that use inertia and velocity data.

The chapter explored the gestures support for XAML-based apps in the Windows Phone SDK and the Windows Phone Toolkit, and you saw how they further consolidate the low-level touch API into a set of gesture-specific events and make it easy to handle complex single and multitouch gestures.

Finally, the chapter looked at the best practices for optimizing your user interfaces for touch input.

CHAPTER 13

Portraying Your App with Live Tiles

A live tile is a dynamic visual representation of your app that resides on the phone's Start Experience. Tiles serve not only as a shortcut to your app but they also provide a glimpse of your app's activities; providing feedback to the user even when your app is not running in the foreground. Each app on the phone can be associated with a single application tile and multiple secondary tiles.

This chapter begins with an overview of the different types of tile templates. You see how text and images are arranged in the flip, cycle, and iconic tile templates.

The chapter then explains how to update tiles programmatically from a foreground or background app.

Finally, the chapter explores the phone's lock screen. You see how to change the lock screen's background image and how your app's primary tile can be used to provide notification text and other content for the lock screen.

Getting Started with Live Tiles

When discussing live tiles (also known as shell tiles) it is important to recognize the distinction between primary and secondary tiles. An app can have at most one primary tile, which can be pinned to the Start Experience by the user. In addition, an app can place multiple secondary tiles on the Start Experience, which can deep-link back to a specific area within the app. A primary tile is defined statically in the app's WMAppManifest.xml file, whereas secondary tiles are created dynamically within code.

NOTE

It is at the user's discretion to pin an app to the Start Experience. You should not, therefore, rely on the presence of a particular tile on the Start Experience.

Windows Phone 8 supports three tile templates: flip, iconic, and cycle. The tile template determines the layout and composition of the tile and the behavior of the tile when it is pinned to the Start Experience.

To configure the template used by your app, open the WMAppManifest.xml file in Visual Studio. The Application UI tab includes a Tile Template drop-down list that allows you to select the template used by your app's primary tile (see Figure 13.1).

The Tile Template drop-down list box contains the following three items, corresponding to the flip, cycle, and iconic tile templates, respectively:

▶ TemplateFlip

▶ TemplateCycle

▶ TemplateIconic

You explore each of the three templates, and see their differences, later in the chapter.

The size of a shell tile is customizable by the phone user. By tapping and holding a tile, the user is able to resize a tile to be either small or medium sized, and if enabled in your app, to a wide size that spans across an entire row on the Start Experience.

NOTE

If you intend to support large tiles, be sure to check the *Support for Large Tiles* check box, which is not checked by default. If left in its default state, the user is prevented from resizing the tile to the large size.

Tile images must be in either JPG or PNG format. When you select a tile image from within the WMAppManifest UI, if the file does not already exist in your project, it is copied to your project's root directory. If the file is already included in your project prior to selecting it, it is referenced at its current location.

FIGURE 13.1   The WMAppManifest.xml file allows you to configure the primary tile.

> **NOTE**
>
> You cannot change the template used by your primary (default) tile programmatically. It is therefore important to carefully choose the template that your app uses before publishing it to the Windows Phone Marketplace. Once published, the only way to change the template is to issue an update for your app.
>
> This restriction, however, does not apply to secondary tiles, which can be added programmatically and which, like the primary tile, may use any of the three templates. Secondary tiles are discussed in greater detail in Chapter 32, "Conducting Background Activities with Scheduled Actions."

> **NOTE**
>
> Tiles use sound and animation; however, these are determined by the OS and are not extensible.

A tile can be updated from within your app while the app is in the foreground, from a background agent, from a scheduled notification, or by using a cloud service and push notifications.

A tile is updated using one of three classes depending on the tile template: `FlipTileData`, `CycleTileData`, or `IconicTileData`. We explore how to update a tile programmatically later in the chapter.

Tile Sizes and Resolutions

Tile dimensions vary according to the resolution of the device. In this chapter you see the layouts and dimensions of the various tile templates presented according to the WXGA resolution setting. On devices with WVGA or 720p displays, the Windows Phone OS automatically scales tiles so that they correctly inhabit the available space.

Windows Phone 8 supports three tile sizes: small, medium, and wide. The user can choose to display your app's primary or secondary tiles using any of the three sizes. It is therefore important to supply an image for each size. The image dimensions differ according to which tile template your app uses.

Introducing the Cycle Tile Template

The cycle template cycles between a maximum of nine images. This template is great for apps that work primarily with images, such as photography apps.

Unlike the iconic and flip templates when sized to be either medium or wide, the cycle template does not have a large portion devoted to text across the tile.

The cycle template allows you to define a small image for when the tile is in its small state, and up to nine additional images that are displayed, in sequence, when the tile is in its medium or wide state (see Figure 13.2).

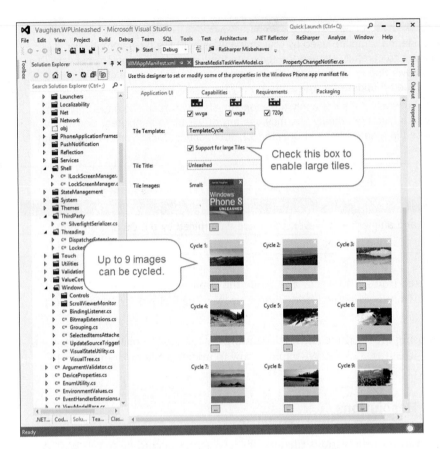

FIGURE 13.2   Configuring an app to use the cycle tile template.

NOTE

Cycle images can only have local URIs. A cycle image cannot be assigned a remote URI to an image on the cloud.

The information portrayed in a cycle template maps to the `CycleTileData` class, which is used to update any of the tile properties. Figure 13.3 shows the elements of the cycle tile template and the `CycleTileData` property name associated with each aspect of the cycle template.

The `Count` property of the `CycleTileData` class element is displayed on the badge region of the tile. `Count` must be a positive integer value between 0 and 99. If the value is 0 the badge is not displayed.

SmallBackgroundImage   Count   Title   CyclesImage (Up to 9 local image URIs)

FIGURE 13.3   Cycle tile template.

Figure 13.4 shows the size of each element within the cycle tile template.

FIGURE 13.4   Dimensions of elements within the cycle tile template.

You can edit the template properties outside of the WMAppManifest.xml designer by opening the WMAppManifest.xml file in a text editor. To do this, right-click the WMAppManifest.xml file in the Visual Studio Solution Explorer and select View Code.

The following excerpt shows the cycle template definition from a WMAppManifest.xml file:

```
<Tokens>
  <PrimaryToken TokenID="WPUnleashed.ExamplesToken" TaskName="_default">
    <TemplateCycle>
      <SmallImageURI IsRelative="true" IsResource="false">
          ApplicationIcon.png</SmallImageURI>
      <Title>Unleashed</Title>
      <Photo01ImageURI IsRelative="true" IsResource="false">
          Images\Tiles\Image01.png</Photo01ImageURI>
      ...
      <Photo09ImageURI IsRelative="true" IsResource="false">
          Images\Tiles\Image09.png</Photo09ImageURI>
      <Count>12</Count>
      <HasLarge>True</HasLarge>
      <DeviceLockImageURI IsRelative="true" IsResource="false">
      </DeviceLockImageURI>
    </TemplateCycle>
```

```
        </PrimaryToken>
</Tokens>
```

Each photo image URI element defines an image that is displayed in sequence.

The `DeviceLockImageURI` element is used to provide an icon for your app when it is set as a quick status app in the phone's lock screen settings. You look at creating and configuring a lock screen icon later in the chapter.

> **CAUTION**
>
> A downside of the cycle template is that when used in conjunction with the lock screen, a cycle tile does not provide the means to set the lock screen's notification text field. If you want to display images on your app's primary tile as well as enable text notifications on the lock screen, a better option may be the flip tile template.

Introducing the Flip Tile Template

The flip tile template is analogous to the Windows Phone 7 standard template. The flip tile template displays a tile with two sides; periodically changing from one side to the other. The flip tile template is able to cycle between two images, and, unlike the cycle tile template, provides a content region on the rear of the tile to display text.

The information portrayed in a flip template maps to the `FlipTileData` class, which is used to update any of the tile properties. Figure 13.5 shows the elements of the flip tile template and the `FlipTileData` property name associated with each aspect of the cycle template.

FIGURE 13.5   Flip tile template layout.

The background images of the tile can be assigned a local resource URI or a remote URI to an image on the cloud. By using a remote image, you have the opportunity to dynamically generate it on a remote server, giving you more control over information presented in the image but at the cost of bandwidth and power consumption.

The dimensions and coordinates of elements within the flip tile template match those of the cycle tile template, with the addition of the back content text (see Figure 13.6).

FIGURE 13.6   Flip tile template content position and dimensions.

The flip tile template allows you to display images and also provides a large area dedicated to text.

Introducing the Iconic Tile Template

The iconic tile template aligns itself with the Windows Phone aesthetic and design principles (see Figure 13.7). A monochromatic icon image is displayed prominently on the tile for all three sizes. Two icon images should be defined for the template. The icon images rely on transparency and both should be PNG images, not JPGs. Colored pixels within the image are ignored and areas of zero transparency take on the tile's color. JPG does not support transparency, so there is little point setting either of the icon images to a JPG file. Indeed, doing so results in an eye-catching square.

The medium tile size uses a single icon image, whereas the wide tile and the small tile share the small image. The icon image in the medium tile is scaled down and the tile's elements positioned correctly even when using the badge count, regardless of the size of the icon image. When using the small tile size, however, the image width may need tweaking to accommodate the badge count field.

FIGURE 13.7   Layout of the iconic tile template.

FIGURE 13.8   Element dimensions of the iconic tile template.

The iconic tile template does not allow you to display multicolored images, but its mono-chromatic look mirrors the design philosophy of the phone UI, which some users prefer.

Programmatically Updating Shell Tiles

Both primary and secondary tiles can be updated by your app, either while your app is running in the foreground or from a background agent. Observe the following example:

```
ShellTile tile = ShellTile.ActiveTiles.FirstOrDefault();
if (tile != null)
{
    IconicTileData tileData = new IconicTileData
        {
            BackgroundColor = Colors.Cyan
        };
    tile.Update(tileData);
}
```

Here the app uses the iconic tile template. The tile is retrieved from the static `ActiveTiles` collection of the `ShellTile` class. Regardless of whether the app is pinned to the Start

Experience, `ActiveTiles` always contains at least one tile: the app's primary tile. A tile is updated by creating an instance of a tile data class, which can be of type `IconicTileData`, `FlipTileData`, or `CycleTileData`, depending on the type of tile template you are using.

NOTE

You cannot update a tile using the `ShellTileData` class. Furthermore, you can update a tile using only the tile data class corresponding to the tile template. For example, when using the flip tile template, you can update only the tile using a `FlipTileData` object.

Tiles can be updated programmatically in your foreground app or from a background agent. In Chapter 32 you see how to programmatically create a secondary shell tile and how to update a shell tile using a background task. In Chapter 15, "Receiving Messages from the Cloud Using Push Notification," you see how to update a tile using push notification and a cloud service.

Controlling the Lock Screen's Background and Notification Area

Beginning with the Windows Phone 8 SDK, you have the opportunity to integrate your app with the phone's lock screen, which includes setting of the lock screen background image, posting notification text to the notification area, and displaying a numeric count field (see Figure 13.9). Apps that integrate with the phone's lock screen are known as live apps.

TIP

To view the lock screen when using the Windows Phone emulator, press F12 twice. Pressing F12 once simulates locking the device via the power button. Pressing F12 again brings up the lock screen.

Three parts of the lock screen can potentially be modified by your app. Changing the lock screen background image is achieved using the phone SDK's lock screen API. Setting of the lock screen's notification text and count field is done via your app's primary tile.

To enable modification of the lock screen, you need to add extension elements to the app's WMAppManifest.xml file. In the Visual Studio Solution Explorer, expand Properties, right-click WMAppManifest.xml, click View Code. If not already present, insert an `Extensions` element immediately after the `Tokens` element in the WMAppManifest.xml file. Observe the following excerpt, which shows the extensions elements for the various lock screen related features:

```
<Extensions>
  <Extension ExtensionName="LockScreen_Background"
      ConsumerID="{111DFF24-AA15-4A96-8006-2BFF8122084F}"
      TaskID="_default" />
  <Extension ExtensionName="LockScreen_Notification_IconCount"
      ConsumerID="{111DFF24-AA15-4A96-8006-2BFF8122084F}"
      TaskID="_default" />
  <Extension ExtensionName="LockScreen_Notification_TextField"
      ConsumerID="{111DFF24-AA15-4A96-8006-2BFF8122084F}"
      TaskID="_default" />
</Extensions>
```

FIGURE 13.9   Lock screen background and notification area.

If you plan to change the lock screen's background image, include the LockScreen_
Background extension. If you plan to include your tile's Count on the lock screen,
include the LockScreen_Notification_IconCount extension. Include the LockScreen_
Notification_TextField extension if you plan to include notification text on the lock
screen.

> **NOTE**
>
> Include only the `Extension` elements that you want to support. This avoids unnecessarily cluttering the lock screen's setting page and avoids misleading the user about your app's capabilities.

Setting the Lock Screen's Background Image

The Windows Phone OS applies tight control over which, if any, of the lock screen's fields an app can modify. The user must grant permission to an app to allow it to change the lock screen background image. The user can do this either by appointing your app as the lock screen background image provider in the phone's settings (see Figure 13.10) or by accepting a confirmation dialog the first time your app attempts to change the lock screen's background image.

FIGURE 13.10   The phone's lock screen settings page.

The `SetBackgroundAsync` method of the custom `LockScreenService` class demonstrates how to set the background image to an image located either in private storage or in the XAP package (see Listing 13.1).

Setting of the lock screen background image requires that your app be the sole lock screen background image provider for the phone. The value of the `LockScreenManager` class's static `IsProvidedByCurrentApplication` property indicates whether the app is the provider. If it is not, the app must request to become the provider by calling

RequestAccessAsync. Being the provider allows the app to set the lock screen background image using the `LockScreen` class's `SetImageUri` method; passing in the URI of an image.

Prefixing the image URI with ms-appx:/// indicates that the image is located in the XAP, and prefixing it with ms-appdata:///Local/ indicates that the image is in local storage.

LISTING 13.1   `LockScreenService.SetBackgroundAsync` Method

```
public async Task<SetBackgroundResult> SetBackgroundAsync(
    string imagePath, ResourceLocation resourceLocation)
{
    bool isProvider = LockScreenManager.IsProvidedByCurrentApplication;
    if (!isProvider)
    {
        /* If the app has not been set as a provider in the phone's settings,
         * this call will prompt the user for permission.
         * Calling RequestAccessAsync from a background agent is not allowed. */
        LockScreenRequestResult requestResult
            = await LockScreenManager.RequestAccessAsync();

        isProvider = requestResult == LockScreenRequestResult.Granted;
    }


    if (isProvider)
    {
        /* The app is the active lock screen background provider. */

        /* The following code example shows the new URI schema.
         * ms-appdata points to the root of the local app data folder.
         * ms-appx points to the Local app install folder,
         * to reference resources bundled in the XAP package. */
        string schema = resourceLocation == ResourceLocation.XapContent
            ? "ms-appx:///" : "ms-appdata:///Local/";

        Uri uri = new Uri(schema + imagePath, UriKind.Absolute);

        LockScreen.SetImageUri(uri);

        return SetBackgroundResult.Success;
    }


    return SetBackgroundResult.UserDenied;
}
```

> **NOTE**
>
> Calling `LockScreenManager.RequestAccessAsync` without the `LockScreen_Background Extension` element present in the app's WMAppManifest.xml file raises an exception.

Setting the Lock Screen's Notification Text

Unlike the lock screen background image, the values for the lock screen's quick status and notification text are pulled from the app's primary tile.

When using a flip tile template, the notification text corresponds to the `WideBackContent` property of the `FlipTileData` object that is used to update the tile. When using the iconic tile template, the three lines of text in the notification area correspond to the `WideContent1`, `WideContent2`, and `WideContent3` properties of the `IconicTileData` object.

> **NOTE**
>
> The cycle tile template does not allow you to populate the notification area with text because the `CycleTileData` class does not contain a property that maps to the notification area text field.

Enabling your app to display notifications on the lock screen requires that the user select your app as the notification provider in the phone's lock screen settings. Unlike the lock screen background image, there is no built-in confirmation dialog for enabling text notifications, and no way to request permission from your app.

The `SetNotification` method of the custom `LockScreenService` class, shown in Listing 13.2, retrieves the primary tile for the app. There is no API for determining the type of tile being used, so it attempts to update the tile using each type of tile data. The method is deemed successful as soon as an `ArgumentException` is not raised during the call to `ShellTile.Update`.

LISTING 13.2 `LockScreenService.SetNotification` Method

```
public void SetNotification(
    string line1, int? count = null,
    string line2 = null, string line3 = null)
{
    ShellTile tile = ShellTile.ActiveTiles.First();

    var iconicTileData = new IconicTileData
                            {
                                WideContent1 = line1,
                                WideContent2 = line2,
                                WideContent3 = line3,
                                Count = count
                            };
```

```csharp
try
{
    tile.Update(iconicTileData);
}
catch (ArgumentException)
{
    var data = new FlipTileData
                    {
                        WideBackContent = string.Format(
                                "{0} {1} {2}", line1, line2, line3),
                        Count = count
                    };

    try
    {
        tile.Update(data);
    }
    catch (ArgumentException ex)
    {
        var cycleTileData = new CycleTileData {Count = count};

        try
        {
            tile.Update(cycleTileData);
        }
        catch (ArgumentException)
        {
            throw new Exception("Unable to set notification text. "
            + "Tile must be either flip or iconic.", ex);
        }
    }
}
}
```

CAUTION

When updating a tile, the tile data object replaces all of its content. Keep this in mind when you are attempting to update a single field—for example, the tile's Count property—because you may unintentionally clear the tile and lock screen's notification text.

The source code for this section is located in the LockScreen directory of the WPUnleashed.Examples project in the downloadable sample code. The LockScreenContentViewModel class uses the custom lock screen service to set the notification text, count field, and background image of the lock screen, as shown in the following excerpt:

```
async void SetLockScreen()
{
    ILockScreenService lockScreenService =
                        Dependency.Resolve<ILockScreenService>();

    lockScreenService.SetNotification(
        "Text set at " + DateTime.Now.ToShortTimeString(), ++countField);

    SetBackgroundResult result = await lockScreenService.SetBackgroundAsync(
        "Images/LockScreenBackground.png", ResourceLocation.XapContent);

    if (result == SetBackgroundResult.Success)
    {
        MessageService.ShowMessage(
            "Lock screen background and notification text set.");
    }
}
```

When trying out the sample, be sure to grant access to the sample app in the phone's lock screen settings.

Creating a Lock Screen Icon

A lock screen icon identifies your app at the bottom of the lock screen and is displayed next to the value of your app's primary tile's Count property.

To include an icon for your app, begin by creating a 30×30 pixel PNG image. Like the icon present in the iconic tile template, the image should contain only white pixels with areas of transparency.

> **NOTE**
>
> If the Count property of your app's primary tile is less than 1, the icon and the Count value are not displayed.

Declare the icon in the WMAppManifest.xml file by updating the DeviceLockImageURI element, which is a child of the PrimaryToken's template element. Add the full path to your image file and set the IsResource attribute to false and IsRelative to true, as shown in the following excerpt:

```
<Tokens>
  <PrimaryToken TokenID="WPUnleashed.ExamplesToken" TaskName="_default">
    <TemplateFlip>

      ...


      <DeviceLockImageURI IsRelative="true" IsResource="false">
          Images\LockScreenIcon.png</DeviceLockImageURI>
```

```
    ...
    </TemplateFlip>
  </PrimaryToken>
</Tokens>
```

It is at the user's discretion whether to allow your app to display its primary tile's Count value on the lock screen. The user does this by selecting your app as a quick status provider in the phone's settings (see Figure 13.11).

FIGURE 13.11   Apps that provide a *quick status* have their Count property displayed.

Integrating your app with the phone's lock screen is yet another great way to enrich the user experience and to bring your app to prominence.

Summary

This chapter began with an overview of the different types of tile templates. You saw how text and images are arranged in the flip, cycle, and iconic tile templates.

The chapter then explained how to update tiles programmatically from a foreground or background app.

Finally, the chapter explored the phone's lock screen. You saw how to change the lock screen's background image and how your app's primary tile can be used to provide notification text and other content for the lock screen.

CHAPTER 14

Leveraging Built-In Apps via Launchers and Choosers

Windows Phone apps execute within a sandbox and lack direct access to phone services such as email and messaging. Launchers and choosers allow your app to reach outside the sandbox in a safe and system-friendly way to give indirect access to a set of built-in system applications.

Launchers and choosers are fundamental to Windows Phone development. They enable users to perform common tasks in the same way across all apps, providing a consistent user experience.

This chapter begins by looking at the two types of tasks: launchers and choosers. It then explores the execution model of choosers, the internal workings of event subscriptions that span across application lifetimes. It then examines each launcher and chooser in detail.

Finally, the chapter examines how to programmatically retrieve contact and appointment information in a read-only manner.

Many launchers and choosers are presented in this chapter, so do not think that you need to absorb them all at once. You may want to skim over them, just to get a feel for what is on offer, and then refer back to this chapter when you are implementing a particular launcher or chooser in your app.

API Overview

The launcher and chooser API is located in the Microsoft. Phone.Tasks namespace of the Microsoft.Phone.dll assembly.

Launchers and choosers share two characteristics. First, all contain a `Show` method, which initiates an associated system app. Second, all cause your app to be deactivated when the `Show` method is called. For more information on deactivation, see Chapter 3, "Understanding the Application Execution Model."

Both launchers and choosers use an internal API, and there is little or no capability for custom launchers or choosers. In addition, nearly all are sealed classes, meaning that extending the existing implementations is not possible. The one exception is the `MediaPlayerLauncher` task, although subclassing it would serve little to no purpose because it has no virtual or protected members.

Launchers are a set of classes that do not return data to your application; they are fire and forget. Launchers, in general, do not share a common base class or interface.

Conversely, choosers derive from the `ChooserBase<TTaskEventArgs>` class, which contains a `Completed` event that is raised when the user either completes a task, such as selecting an image with the `PhotoChooserTask`, or when the user cancels the task, either explicitly within the system app or by using the hardware Back button.

The generic parameter `TTaskEventArgs` of the `ChooserBase` class specifies the type passed to the event handler for the `Completed` event.

> **NOTE**
>
> When your app is activated, after being deactivated by calling the `Show` method of a chooser, the chooser's `Completed` event is raised. This occurs even if the user takes a detour to another app or to the Start Experience (home screen), and then returns to your application via the hardware Back button.

The Windows Phone launchers and choosers available for your application are listed in Table 14.1.

TABLE 14.1   Launchers and Choosers

Launcher	Chooser
BingMapsDirectionsTask	AddressChooserTask
BingMapsTask	CameraCaptureTask
ConnectionSettingsTask	EmailAddressChooserTask
MapDownloaderTask*	GameInviteTask
MapsTask*	PhoneNumberChooserTask
MapsDirectionsTask*	PhotoChooserTask
EmailComposeTask	SaveContactTask
MarketplaceDetailTask	SaveEmailAddressTask
MarketplaceHubTask	SavePhoneNumberTask
MarketplaceReviewTask	SaveRingtoneTask

Launcher	Chooser
MarketplaceSearchTask	
MediaPlayerLauncher	
PhoneCallTask	
SaveAppointmentTask	
SearchTask	
ShareLinkTask	
ShareMediaTask	
ShareStatusTask	
SmsComposeTask	
WebBrowserTask	

* Discussed in Chapter 18, "Incorporating Map-Based Positioning."

Choosers and the Application Execution Model

Recall from Chapter 3 that when tombstoned, your app is terminated, and therefore all regular CLR event subscriptions are discarded. Choosers use a subscription model that relies on CLR events, and using a chooser can lead to your app being tombstoned. To contend with this, the chooser infrastructure has some interesting plumbing that allows it to survive tombstoning and to reinstate subscriptions to the ChooserBase.Completed event when an app is reactivated.

Internal Workings of the ChooserBase.Completed Event

When subscription to the ChooserBase.Completed event occurs, the location of the subscription, in particular the class name and method name, is used as an identifier for the event subscription. This information is serialized to your app's transient state, allowing it to survive application termination. When the system application associated with the chooser completes, your app is restarted, and the OS signals that a chooser has completed by invoking a static method. When the event subscription occurs again in your class, the subscription identifier is re-created and compared with the list of subscription identifiers for that chooser. If there is a match, the event handler in your class is called.

> **NOTE**
>
> Subscribing to the Completed event causes the event to be raised.

To understand this further, consider the following code:

```
readonly SaveEmailAddressTask saveEmailAddressTask
    = new SaveEmailAddressTask();

public SomeViewModel()
{
    /* Step 2. */
    saveEmailAddressTask.Completed += saveEmailAddressTask_Completed;
    /* Step 4. */
    Debug.WriteLine("Constructor.");
}

public void ShowLauncher()
{
    /* Step 1. */
    saveEmailAddressTask.Show();
}

void saveEmailAddressTask_Completed(object sender, TaskEventArgs e)
{
    /* Step 3. */
    Debug.WriteLine("Task Completed.");
}
```

Subscription to the `SaveEmailAddressTask.Completed` event is performed in the view-model's constructor. When the `Show` method of the `saveEmailAddressTask` is called (step 1) the user app is deactivated. Presuming that the app is tombstoned, when the system app completes and the user app is restarted and activated, the viewmodel's constructor is called again (step 2). When the event subscription occurs this time, however, the `Completed` event is raised and the event handler is called (step 3). When the event handler returns, the code in the constructor resumes (step 4).

> **BEST PRACTICE**
>
> When subscribing to the `Completed` event of a chooser, declare the chooser at the class level and subscribe to the event within the class constructor.

Launchers and Choosers in Detail

The following sections cover each launcher and chooser class in detail. There is some repetition in the structure of several of the sections, but each is intended to be self-contained to allow you to look up a particular launcher or chooser when needed.

The examples presented in this chapter show tasks used directly from within view-model classes. Chapter 24, "Unit Testing Apps," looks at techniques for removing the dependency on the Windows Phone FCL (Framework Class Library) for XAML apps, which allows your code to be more portable across other platforms.

Retrieve Driving Directions Using the `BingMapsDirectionsTask`

The Bing Maps directions task launches the built-in Maps application and displays driving directions between two points. A start and an end point can be specified using the task's `Start` and `End` properties, which are of type `LabeledMapLocation`. If only one location is specified, the user's current location is used in place of the unspecified location.

> **NOTE**
>
> At least one of the `Start` or `End` properties must be specified, or an `InvalidOperationException` is thrown when you call the `BingMapsDirectionsTask.Show` method.

Both `Start` and `End` properties allow you to specify a string label and geographic coordinates indicating the latitude and longitude of the location. If you omit the geographic coordinates, the Maps application searches for the label string.

The following example demonstrates how to launch the Maps application to search for two locations.

```
BingMapsDirectionsTask bingMapsDirectionsTask
                            = new BingMapsDirectionsTask();
...
bingMapsDirectionsTask.Start = new LabeledMapLocation("geneva", null);
bingMapsDirectionsTask.End = new LabeledMapLocation("london", null);
bingMapsDirectionsTask.Show();
```

To specify geographic coordinates, insert a using statement for System.Device.Location at the top of your class. A `GeoCoordinate` can then be passed to the task as shown:

```
GeoCoordinate geoCoordinate = new GeoCoordinate(46.25829, 6.20966);
bingMapsDirectionsTask.Start
                    = new LabeledMapLocation("Geneva", geoCoordinate);
bingMapsDirectionsTask.Show();
```

By specifying the geographic coordinates, the Maps application places a label at the location using the supplied text.

The sample for this section allows the user to enter the start and end search terms, and to launch the `BingMapsDirectionsTask` via an application bar button.

The sample can be found in the LaunchersAndChoosers/BingMaps directory of the WPUnleashed.Examples project.

The BingMapsDirectionsTaskViewModel class contains two string properties, which are used as search terms for a BingMapsDirectionsTask (see Listing 14.1).

An ICommand, named SearchCommand, initializes the BingMapsDirectionsTask and calls its Show method.

LISTING 14.1   BingMapsDirectionsTaskViewModel Class

```csharp
public class BingMapsDirectionsTaskViewModel : ViewModelBase
{
    readonly BingMapsDirectionsTask bingMapsDirectionsTask
                                    = new BingMapsDirectionsTask();

    public BingMapsDirectionsTaskViewModel() : base("get directions")
    {
        searchCommand = new DelegateCommand(arg => ShowTask());
    }

    void ShowTask()
    {
        bingMapsDirectionsTask.Start
                        = new LabeledMapLocation(startLocation, null);
        bingMapsDirectionsTask.End
                        = new LabeledMapLocation(endLocation, null);
        bingMapsDirectionsTask.Show();
    }

    readonly DelegateCommand searchCommand;

    public ICommand SearchCommand
    {
        get
        {
            return searchCommand;
        }
    }

    string startLocation;

    public string StartLocation
    {
        get
        {
            return startLocation;
        }
        set
```

```
        {
            Assign(ref startLocation, value);
        }
    }
    string endLocation;

    public string EndLocation
    {
        get
        {
            return endLocation;
        }
        set
        {
            Assign(ref endLocation, value);
        }
    }
}
```

The `BingMapsDirectionsTaskView` page contains two `TextBox` controls that are bound to the viewmodel string properties, as shown:

```xml
<StackPanel x:Name="ContentPanel" Grid.Row="1">
    <TextBlock Text="start location"
                    Style="{StaticResource LabelTextStyle}" />
    <TextBox Text="{Binding StartLocation, Mode=TwoWay}" />

    <TextBlock Text="end location"
                    Style="{StaticResource LabelTextStyle}" />
    <TextBox Text="{Binding EndLocation, Mode=TwoWay}" />
</StackPanel>
```

In addition, the view contains an `AppBarIconButton` that is used to execute the viewmodel's `SearchCommand`. See the following excerpt:

```xml
<u:AppBar>
    <u:AppBarIconButton
        Command="{Binding SearchCommand}"
        Text="Search"
        IconUri="/LaunchersAndChoosers/BingMaps/Images/AppBarSearch.png" />
</u:AppBar>
```

Figure 14.1 shows the view before launching the Bing Maps directions task.

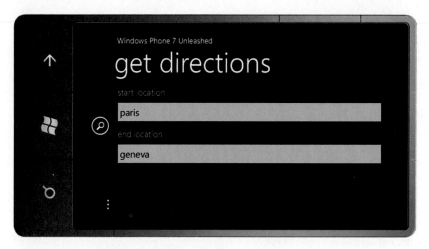

FIGURE 14.1   `BingMapsDirectionsTaskView` page.

Tapping the Search button launches the built-in Maps application (see Figure 14.2).

FIGURE 14.2   Built-in Maps application.

The Bing Maps directions task is a simple way to launch the built-in Maps application. Chapter 18, "Incorporating Map-Based Positioning," shows how to build similar capabilities directly into your app, allowing you to completely customize how direction information is presented.

Displaying a Location on a Map Using the `BingMapsTask`

The Bing Maps task allows you to launch the built-in Maps application centered at the location specified by the `BingMapsTask.Center` property, which is of type `GeoCoordinate`. If not specified the map is centered at the user's current location. If provided, the `Center` property is ignored and the `BingMapsTask.SearchTerm` property is used to search for matching locations. The best match is then tagged on the map.

To use the `BingMapsTask` to search for a location, define it as a field in your class and set its `SearchTerm` property, as demonstrated:

```
BingMapsTask bingMapsTask = new BingMapsTask();
...
bingMapsTask.SearchTerm = "prague";
bingMapsTask.Show();
```

The following example demonstrates how to specify a geographic location:

```
bingMapsTask.Center = new GeoCoordinate(50.08021, 14.416983);
bingMapsTask.Show();
```

A sample for the `BingMapsTask` can be found in the LaunchersAndChoosers/BingMaps directory of the WPUnleashed.Examples project. The sample is almost identical to the previous `BingMapsDirectionsTask` sample.

Navigating to a Connection Setting Page Using the `ConnectionSettingsTask`

The connection settings task allows you to launch a settings page for a specified set of network connection related settings.

The `ConnectionSettingsType` property of the `ConnectionSettingsTask` class allows you to display the settings dialog using one of the following four `ConnectionSettingsType` values:

- ▶ `AirplaneMode`
- ▶ `Bluetooth`
- ▶ `Cellular`
- ▶ `WiFi`

To display the Wi-Fi settings dialog, for example, use the following:

```
ConnectionSettingsTask task = new ConnectionSettingsTask();
task.ConnectionSettingsType = ConnectionSettingsType.WiFi;
task.Show();
```

The four built-in settings pages available to the `ConnectionSettingsTask` are shown in Figure 14.3.

FIGURE 14.3   Connection settings pages.

The sample for the `ConnectionSettingsTask` allows you to select one of the `ConnectionSettingsType` values from a Windows Phone Toolkit `ListPicker` control (see Figure 14.4). Tapping the Settings button in the application bar executes an `ICommand` in the viewmodel, which initializes and calls the `Show` method of the `ConnectionSettingsTask`.

FIGURE 14.4   `ConnectionSettingsTaskView` page.

Selecting an Email Address with the `EmailAddressChooserTask`

The email address chooser task launches the Windows Phone Contacts application and allows the user to select a contact. When the user completes the task, the `Completed` event is raised, and the event handler receives an `EmailResult` object that exposes a string containing the selected contact's email address.

> **NOTE**
>
> To query the user's contact list, without requiring the user to select a contact, use the `Contacts` class, which is described later in this chapter.

The `EmailAddressChooserTask` should be defined as a field in your class, like so:

```
readonly EmailAddressChooserTask emailAddressChooserTask
                            = new EmailAddressChooserTask();
```

Subscribe to the `EmailAddressChooserTask.Completed` event within your class constructor, as shown:

```
emailAddressChooserTask.Completed
    += new EventHandler<EmailResult>(HandleEmailAddressChooserTaskCompleted);
```

Use the `Show` method of the `EmailAddressChooserTask` to launch the built-in Contacts app. When the task completes, the handler receives an `EmailResult` object, as shown:

```
void HandleEmailAddressChooserTaskCompleted(object sender, EmailResult e)
{
    if (e.TaskResult == TaskResult.OK)
    {
        ToAddress = e.Email;
    }
    else if (e.Error != null)
    {
        Message = "Unable to choose email address. " + e.ToString();
    }
    else if (e.TaskResult == TaskResult.Cancel)
    {
        Message = "Cancelled";
    }
}
```

Sample Overview

Example code for the `EmailComposeTask` can be found in the `EmailViewModel` in the downloadable sample code. The `EmailView` allows the user to select the recipient and to launch a new `EmailComposeTask` via a button (see Figure 14.5).

The viewmodel contains a public property of type `ICommand` called `ChooseRecipientCommand`. The view's Choose Email button is bound to the command.

FIGURE 14.5   The `EmailView` page.

When the `ChooseRecipientCommand` is executed, the `Show` method of the `emailAddressChooserTask` is called. This behavior is defined in the viewmodel constructor, as shown:

```
public EmailViewModel() : base("Email")
{
    emailAddressChooserTask.Completed
                            += HandleEmailAddressChooserTaskCompleted;

    chooseRecipientCommand = new DelegateCommand(
        obj => emailAddressChooserTask.Show());
...
}
```

When the `EmailAddressChooserTask.Show` method is called, the built-in Contacts application is launched (see Figure 14.6).

FIGURE 14.6   The Windows Phone Contacts application.

The result returned by the Contacts app is used by an `EmailComposeTask`, which is presented in the next section.

Preparing an Email with the `EmailComposeTask`

The `EmailComposeTask` launches the Windows Phone Email application, which displays a page allowing the user to create a new email.

> **NOTE**
>
> The email is not sent until it is initiated by the user.

You can optionally specify recipients, a message subject, and a message body, which are prepopulated in the new email, as shown in the following excerpt:

```
EmailComposeTask task = new EmailComposeTask
                        {
                            To = "name1@example.com",
                            Cc = "name2@example.com",
                            Subject = "Windows Phone",
                            Body = "Hi from Windows Phone!"
                        };
task.Show();
```

Multiple recipients in the `To` and `Cc` properties can be specified by delimiting the address with a semicolon character.

Sample Overview

Example code for the `EmailComposeTask` can be found in the `EmailViewModel` in the downloadable sample code. The `EmailView` allows the user to select the recipient and to launch a new `EmailComposeTask` via a button (shown previously in Figure 14.5).

The view's Compose Email button is bound to a viewmodel command called `ComposeCommand`.

When executed, the `ComposeCommand` creates a new `EmailComposeTask` and sets its `To` property to the text supplied by the `EmailAddressChooserTask`. This behavior is defined in the `EmailViewModel` constructor, as shown:

```
public EmailViewModel() : base("Email")
{
...
    composeCommand = new DelegateCommand(
        delegate
            {
                EmailComposeTask emailComposeTask
                    = new EmailComposeTask
                        {
```

```
                              To = toAddress,
                              Subject = "Windows Phone Unleashed",
                              Body = "Hi from Windows Phone!"
                          };
                emailComposeTask.Show();
            });
}
```

When the `EmailComposeTask.Show` method is called, the built-in Email application is launched. If the user has multiple email accounts defined on the device, the Email application prompts the user to select which account to use. The user is then presented with a new email message, prepopulated with the `To`, `Cc`, `Subject`, and `Body` properties of the `EmailComposeTask`.

Saving a Contact's Email Using the `SaveEmailAddressTask`

The `SaveEmailAddressTask` is a chooser that allows the user to save a specified email address using the built-in Contacts application. An email address can be saved to an existing contact or to a new contact. `SaveEmailAddressTask` does not return data, but its `Completed` event can be handled to determine whether the task was completed correctly.

The `SaveEmailAddressTask` should be defined as a field in your class, like so:

```
readonly SaveEmailAddressTask saveEmailAddressTask
                              = new SaveEmailAddressTask();
```

Subscribe to the `SaveEmailAddressTask.Completed` event within your class constructor, as shown:

```
saveEmailAddressTask.Completed += HandleSaveEmailAddressTaskCompleted;
```

Use the `Show` method of the `SaveEmailAddressTask` to launch the built-in Contacts app. When the task completes the handler receives a `TaskEventArgs` object, as shown:

```
void HandleSaveEmailAddressTaskCompleted(object sender, TaskEventArgs e)
{
    if (e.Error != null)
    {
        Message = "Unable to save the email address. " + e.Error;
        return;
    }

    if (e.TaskResult == TaskResult.OK)
    {
        Message = "Email address saved";
    }
    else if (e.TaskResult == TaskResult.Cancel)
```

```
    {
        Message = "Cancelled";
    }
}
```

Sample Overview

Example code for the `SaveEmailAddressTask` can be found in the `SaveEmailAddressViewModel` in the downloadable sample code.

The `SaveEmailAddressView` page allows the user to enter an email address and then to initiate the `SaveEmailAddressTask` using a button (see Figure 14.7).

FIGURE 14.7   `SaveEmailAddressView` page.

The view's Email Address `TextBlock` has a two-way binding to the viewmodel's `EmailAddress` property, as shown:

```
<TextBox Text="{Binding EmailAddress, Mode=TwoWay}"
         InputScope="EmailSmtpAddress" />
```

The `InputScope` property of the `TextBox` causes the onscreen keyboard to be displayed with a set of keys suitable for typing an email address. For more information on `InputScopes`, see Chapter 6, "Mastering Text Elements and Fonts."

To initiate the `SaveEmailAddressTask`, the viewmodel contains a public property called `SaveCommand`:

```
readonly DelegateCommand saveCommand;
```

```
public ICommand SaveCommand
{
    get
    {
        return saveCommand;
    }
}
```

When the `saveCommand` is executed, the `Show` method of the `saveEmailAddressTask` is called. This behavior is defined in the viewmodel's construct, as shown in the following excerpt:

```
public SaveEmailAddressViewModel() : base("Save Email Address")
{
    saveEmailAddressTask.Completed += saveEmailAddressTask_Completed;

    saveCommand = new DelegateCommand(
        delegate
            {
                Message = string.Empty;
                saveEmailAddressTask.Email = emailAddress;
                saveEmailAddressTask.Show();
            });
}
```

The view's Save button is bound to the `SaveCommand`, as shown:

```
<Button Command="{Binding SaveCommand}"
        Content="Save" />
```

When the `saveEmailAddressTask.Show` method is called, the built-in Contacts application is launched (see Figure 14.8).

When the user selects either an existing contact or the new contact option, the Edit Email page is displayed (see Figure 14.9).

If the user selects an existing contact, when the Save icon button is tapped, the Edit Phone Contact page is displayed (see Figure 14.10).

FIGURE 14.8   The Contacts application allows the user to select an existing contact or create a new one.

FIGURE 14.9   Edit Email page.

Alternatively, if the user opts to create a new contact, the New Contact page is displayed.

After the contact information is saved using the disk icon, the sample application is activated, and the `HandleSaveEmailAddressTaskCompleted` handler is called.

FIGURE 14.10 Edit Phone Contact page.

Navigating to an App on the Marketplace with the `MarketplaceDetailTask`

The Marketplace detail task is used to launch the built-in Marketplace app, which shows the details page for a product specified by a unique identifier that you provide. If an identifier is not specified, the details page for the current application is shown.

The following code demonstrates how to launch the `MarketplaceDetailTask`:

```
MarketplaceDetailTask task
    = new MarketplaceDetailTask
        {
            ContentIdentifier = "<ID>",
            //ContentType = MarketplaceContentType.Applications
        };
task.Show();
```

The `MarketplaceDetailTask` has two properties: `ContentIdentifier` and `ContentType`. The `ContentIdentifier` is the unique product identifier for an app. When an application is published on the Windows Phone Marketplace it is assigned a unique identifier, which is located in a `ProductID` attribute of the WMAppManifest.xml file. This identifier can be used to launch the `MarketplaceDetailsTask` from other apps.

If the `ContentIdentifier` is specified, the value must be a valid product identifier. If the identifier has an invalid format, a `FormatException` is raised. The identifier format is 32 digits separated by hyphens and enclosed in braces, as shown in the following example:

```
{45dc3711-8af7-42bf-a749-6c491f2b427f}
```

As an aside, this format can be achieved using a `Guid`, by calling its `ToString` method with "B" as the format argument, as shown:

```
string productId = guid.ToString("B");
```

Retrieving Your Application's Product ID at Runtime

Although the `ContentIdentifier` is not required to launch the `MarketplaceDetailTask` for the current app, it is required to launch the details page for a different app. This value can be read at runtime by retrieving the WMAppManifest.xml file using the `Application.GetResourceStream` method, and then by extracting the value using the System.Xml.Linq API, as shown in the following excerpt:

```
public string GetProductId()
{
    Uri uri = new Uri("WMAppManifest.xml", UriKind.Relative);
    StreamResourceInfo info
        = Application.GetResourceStream(uri);
    XElement manifestElement = XElement.Load(info.Stream);
    XElement appElement = manifestElement.Element("App");
    XAttribute idAttribute
        = appElement.Attribute("ProductID");
    return idAttribute.Value;
}
```

Sample Overview

Example code for the `MarketplaceDetailTask` can be found in the `MarketplaceViewModel` in the downloadable sample code. The `MarketplaceView` page includes a `ListBox` to select content type for the `MarketplaceHubTask` and the `MarketplaceSearchTask`, both of which are discussed later in this chapter, and buttons for exercising the various tasks (see Figure 14.11).

FIGURE 14.11   `MarketplaceView` page.

The viewmodel contains a `DetailCommand` defined as follows:

```
readonly DelegateCommand detailCommand;

public ICommand DetailCommand
{
    get
    {
        return detailCommand;
    }
}
```

The `detailCommand` is instantiated in the `MarketplaceViewModel` constructor. When executed, the `detailCommand` creates a new `MarketplaceDetailTask` and calls its `Show` method. This behavior is defined in the viewmodel constructor, as shown:

```
public MarketplaceViewModel()
{
    detailCommand = new DelegateCommand(
            delegate
            {
                var task = new MarketplaceDetailTask();
                task.Show();
```

```
        });
// ...
}
```

The `MarketPlaceView` uses a button to execute the `DetailCommand` in the viewmodel:

```
<Button Command="{Binding DetailCommand}"
        Content="Marketplace Detail" />
```

Launching the Marketplace App with the `MarketplaceHubTask`

The Marketplace hub task is used to launch the built-in Marketplace app.

The marketplace category can be specified using the `ContentType` property of the `MarketplaceHubTask`. Set the `ContentType` property to a value from the `MarketplaceContentType` enumeration to launch the hub to a particular type of content, as shown in the following excerpt:

```
MarketplaceHubTask task
    = new MarketplaceHubTask
            {
                ContentType = MarketplaceContentType.Music
            };
task.Show();
```

`ContentType` allows you to specify one of two categories: Music or Applications.

> **NOTE**
>
> The only allowed value for the `ContentType` property is
> `MarketplaceContentType.Applications`, which is the default value if not supplied.
> If `MarketplaceContentType.Music` is used, an `ArgumentException` is raised.

Sample Overview

Example code for the `MarketplaceHubTask` can be found in the `MarketplaceViewModel` in the downloadable sample code.

The viewmodel contains an `ICommand` called `HubCommand`, which is instantiated in the `MarketplaceViewModel` constructor. A Windows Phone Toolkit `ListPicker` allows the user to select the marketplace content type.

When executed, the `hubCommand` creates a new `MarketplaceHubTask`, sets its `ContentType` property, and calls its `Show` method, like so:

```
public MarketplaceViewModel()
{
    hubCommand = new DelegateCommand(
```

14

```
        delegate
            {
                MarketplaceHubTask task = new MarketplaceHubTask();
                if (contentType.HasValue)
                {
                    task.ContentType = contentType.Value;
                }
                task.Show();
            });
// ...
}
```

Allowing the User to Review Your App Using the `MarketplaceReviewTask`

The Marketplace review task is used to launch the built-in Marketplace application. A review page allows the user to enter a text review for the current app and give it a rating out of five. The user can also see the average rating of the application by other users.

The `MarketplaceReviewTask` has no settable properties and is launched like so:

```
MarketplaceReviewTask task = new MarketplaceReviewTask();
task.Show();
```

Sample Overview

Example code for the `MarketplaceReviewTask` can be found in the `MarketplaceViewModel` in the downloadable sample code. The `MarketPlaceView` uses a button to execute an `ICommand` called `ReviewCommand` in the viewmodel.

The `reviewCommand` is instantiated in the `MarketplaceViewModel` constructor. When executed, the `reviewCommand` creates a new `MarketplaceReviewTask` and calls its `Show` method, like so:

```
public MarketplaceViewModel()
{
    reviewCommand = new DelegateCommand(
        delegate
            {
                MarketplaceReviewTask task = new MarketplaceReviewTask();
                task.Show();
            });
// ...
}
```

Searching the Marketplace with the `MarketplaceSearchTask`

The Marketplace search task is used to launch the built-in Marketplace app, which displays the search results for a specified search string.

The `MarketplaceSearchTask` class has two properties: `SearchTerms` and `ContentType`. `SearchTerms` is a string that contains one or more search terms. `ContentType` can be set to either `MarketplaceContentType.Applications` or `MarketplaceContentType.Music`. If not specified, `ContentType` defaults to `MarketplaceContentType.Applications`. The following excerpt demonstrates how to create and launch a `MarketplaceSearchTask`:

```
MarketplaceSearchTask task
    = new MarketplaceSearchTask
        {
            ContentType = MarketplaceContentType.Applications,
            SearchTerms = "puzzle"
        };
task.Show();
```

TIP

The Marketplace app is not shown on the emulator's App List page. It does, however, exist on the emulator, and it is not necessary to have an unlocked emulator to use it. By calling the `Show` method on the `MarketplaceSearchTask` in an app running on the emulator, it allows you to launch the Marketplace app search page and to browse search results using real data.

Sample Overview

Example code for the `MarketplaceSearchTask` can be found in the `MarketplaceViewModel` in the downloadable sample code.

The `MarketPlaceView` has a button that executes an `ICommand` named `SearchCommand` in the viewmodel. The `searchCommand` is instantiated in the `MarketplaceViewModel` constructor. When executed it creates a new `MarketplaceSearchTask`, sets its `SearchTerms` property with the text supplied by a `TextBox` in the view, sets its `ContentType` property, and finally calls its `Show` method, like so:

```
public MarketplaceViewModel()
{
    searchCommand = new DelegateCommand(
        delegate
            {
                MarketplaceSearchTask task = new MarketplaceSearchTask
                    {
                        /* SearchTerms can't be null or empty,
                         * or else an ArgumentException is thrown. */
                        SearchTerms = string.IsNullOrEmpty(searchTerms)
```

14

```
                                                              ? " " : searchTerms
                };
            if (contentType.HasValue)
            {
                task.ContentType = contentType.Value;
            }
            task.Show();
        });
// ...
}
```

Playing a Media File Using the `MediaPlayerLauncher`

The media player launcher is used to launch the built-in Media Player app to play a specified media file (see Figure 14.12).

FIGURE 14.12   Windows Phone Media Player application.

Media files can be stored either locally on the device or externally using an absolute `Uri`. If stored locally, the `MediaPlayerLauncher.Media` property must be assigned a relative `Uri` to the file location. Relative `Uri`s are used for files located in either isolated storage or in the app's XAP file.

Files downloaded from the Internet are placed in isolated storage, whereas files accompanying the app are placed into the app's XAP file during the build process.

The `MediaPlayerLauncher.Location` property allows you to specify where the content is located, either in the XAP, isolated storage, or on a remote server.

The `MediaPlayerLauncher.Location` property must be set to `MediaLocationType.Install` for media files located within the app's XAP file. For content located in isolated storage, `MediaLocationType.Data` should be used. If not specified, `MediaPlayerLauncher.Location` defaults to `MediaLocationType.Data`. For content located on a remote server, `MediaLocationType.None` is used along with an absolute `Uri`. If `MediaLocationType.None` is used in conjunction with a relative `Uri`, a `FileNotFoundException` is raised when the `MediaPlayerLauncher.Show` method is called.

You can optionally specify that one or more playback controls should be shown by the Media Player, by setting the `MediaPlayerLauncher.Controls` property using bitwise *OR* combinations of the `MediaPlaybackControls` enum values.

The following is the list of possible `MediaPlaybackControls` enum values:

▶ `All`—All controls. The equivalent of using *OR* to combine all the other members of the enumeration.

▶ `FastForward`—The fast-forward control.

▶ `None`—No controls are shown.

▶ `Pause`—The pause control.

▶ `Rewind`—The rewind control.

▶ `Skip`—The skip control.

▶ `Stop`—The stop control.

If not specified, the `MediaPlayerLauncher.Controls` property defaults to `MediaPlaybackControls.All`, and the rewind, pause, and fast-forward buttons are displayed by the Media Player app.

> **NOTE**
>
> Although it is possible to specify the Skip and Stop controls, the controls are not displayed, and it does not affect the Media Player app.

The following example shows how to use the `MediaPlayerLauncher` to play a local media file in the Media Player app, displaying a Pause and a Stop button:

```
MediaPlayerLauncher mediaPlayerLauncher
    = new MediaPlayerLauncher
        {
            Media = new Uri("LaunchersAndChoosers/Video.wmv",
            UriKind.Relative),
            Location = MediaLocationType.Install,
            Controls = MediaPlaybackControls.Pause |
            MediaPlaybackControls.Stop
        };
mediaPlayerLauncher.Show();
```

To specify a nonlocal media file, use an absolute `Uri`, as demonstrated in the following example:

```
MediaPlayerLauncher mediaPlayerLauncher
    = new MediaPlayerLauncher
        {
            Media = new Uri("http://www.example.com/Video.wmv",
                            UriKind.Absolute),
            Controls = MediaPlaybackControls.All
        };
mediaPlayerLauncher.Show();
```

Sample Overview

Example code for the `MediaPlayerLauncher` can be found in the `MediaPlayerLauncherViewModel`, in the downloadable sample code.

The `MediaPlayerLauncherView` page has a button that executes an `ICommand` named `SearchCommand` in the viewmodel.

When executed, the command instantiates a `MediaPlayerLauncher` and populates its `Controls` property with the `playbackControls` field, using a lambda expression (see Listing 14.2).

The lambda `Aggregate` extension method combines the values in the `IEnumerable` collection of `MediaPlaybackControls` enum flags by OR'ing each one with the previous result.

LISTING 14.2   `MediaPlayerLauncherViewModel` Class (excerpt)

```
public class MediaPlayerLauncherViewModel : ViewModelBase
{
    public MediaPlayerLauncherViewModel()
        : base("Media Player Launcher")
    {
        launchCommand = new DelegateCommand(
            delegate
            {
```

```csharp
        MediaPlayerLauncher mediaPlayerLauncher
            = new MediaPlayerLauncher
            {
                //Media = new Uri("http://example.com/Video.wmv",
                //                          UriKind.Absolute),
                Media = new Uri("LaunchersAndChoosers/Video.wmv",
                                          UriKind.Relative),
                Location = MediaLocationType.Install,
            };

        if (playbackControls.Count > 0)
        {
            mediaPlayerLauncher.Controls
                = playbackControls.Aggregate((a, b) => a | b);
        }

        mediaPlayerLauncher.Show();
    });
}

readonly List<MediaPlaybackControls> mediaPlaybackControls
    = new List<MediaPlaybackControls>
        {
            MediaPlaybackControls.FastForward,
            MediaPlaybackControls.Pause,
            MediaPlaybackControls.Rewind,
            /* Not used by Media Player. */
            //MediaPlaybackControls.Skip,
            //MediaPlaybackControls.Stop
        };
public IEnumerable<MediaPlaybackControls> AvailablePlaybackControls
{
    get
    {
        return mediaPlaybackControls;
    }
}

readonly ObservableCollection<MediaPlaybackControls> playbackControls
    = new ObservableCollection<MediaPlaybackControls>();

public ObservableCollection<MediaPlaybackControls> PlaybackControls
{
    get
    {
        return playbackControls;
```

14

```
        }
    }
...
}
```

The view presents the list of available playback controls in a `ListBox`. A custom attached property is used to provide quasi binding support for the `SelectedItems` property of the `ListBox`. This attached property is discussed further in the next section. See the following excerpt:

```xml
<StackPanel x:Name="ContentPanel" Grid.Row="1">
    <TextBlock Text="Media Player Controls:"
        Style="{StaticResource PhoneTextTitle2Style}" />
    <ListBox ItemsSource="{Binding AvailablePlaybackControls}"
        SelectionMode="Multiple"
        unleashed:SelectedItems.Items="{Binding PlaybackControls}"
        Margin="15">
    </ListBox>
    <Button Command="{Binding LaunchCommand}"
        Content="Launch Media Player" />
    <TextBlock Text="{Binding Message}"
        Style="{StaticResource PhoneTextMessageStyle}" />
</StackPanel>
```

Multiple items in the `ListBox` can be selected, and the Launch Media Player button initiates the `LaunchCommand` in the viewmodel (see Figure 14.13).

FIGURE 14.13   The media player launcher page.

Binding to the `ListBox.SelectedItems` Property

Unfortunately, the `ListBox.SelectedItems` property is not a `DependencyProperty`, which means it cannot be the target of a databinding. A custom attached property is included in the downloadable sample code that allows you to bind the `SelectedItems` property to a collection (see Listing 14.3).

The `SelectedItems` class contains two `DependencyProperty`s: an `ItemsProperty` and a `SelectedItemsBehaviorProperty`. `ItemsProperty` specifies the source property of the `DataContext` and is used to assign the selected items to the `ListBox`'s `DataContext`. When the `SelectionChanged` event of the `ListBox` is raised, the `DataContext`'s property is updated.

The `SelectedItemsBehavior` class contains the logic for updating the list of selected items, which also relies on the `DataContextChangedListener` class, which raises an event when the `DataContext` of the `ListBox` changes. For more information on the `DataContextChangedListener`, see Chapter 26, "Validating User Input."

An instance of the `SelectedItemsBehavior` is associated with the `ListBox` using the `SelectedItemsBehaviorProperty`.

LISTING 14.3   `SelectedItems` Class

```
public static class SelectedItems
{
    public static readonly DependencyProperty ItemsProperty
        = DependencyProperty.RegisterAttached(
            "Items",
            typeof(IList),
            typeof(SelectedItems),
            new PropertyMetadata(null, ItemsPropertyChanged));

    public static void SetItems(ListBox listBox, IList list)
    {
        listBox.SetValue(ItemsProperty, list);
    }

    public static IList GetItems(ListBox listBox)
    {
        return (IList)listBox.GetValue(ItemsProperty);
    }

    static readonly DependencyProperty SelectedItemsBehaviorProperty
        = DependencyProperty.RegisterAttached(
            "SelectedItemsBehavior",
            typeof(SelectedItemsBehavior),
            typeof(ListBox), null);

    static void ItemsPropertyChanged(
```

14

```csharp
        DependencyObject d, DependencyPropertyChangedEventArgs e)
{
    var target = d as ListBox;
    if (target != null)
    {
        GetOrCreateBehavior(target, (IList)e.NewValue);
    }
}
static SelectedItemsBehavior GetOrCreateBehavior(
    ListBox listBox, IList list)
{
    var behavior = (SelectedItemsBehavior)listBox.GetValue(
                                    SelectedItemsBehaviorProperty);
    if (behavior == null)
    {
        behavior = new SelectedItemsBehavior(listBox, list);
        listBox.SetValue(SelectedItemsBehaviorProperty, behavior);
    }

    return behavior;
}

class SelectedItemsBehavior
{
    readonly ListBox listBox;
    readonly IList sourceList;

    public SelectedItemsBehavior(ListBox listBox, IList sourceList)
    {
        this.listBox = ArgumentValidator.AssertNotNull(listBox, "listBox");
        this.sourceList = ArgumentValidator.AssertNotNull(
                                        sourceList, "sourceList");
        this.listBox.SelectionChanged += OnSelectionChanged;
        DataContextChangedListener.Subscribe(listBox, OnDataContextChanged);
    }

    void OnDataContextChanged(
        DependencyObject d, DependencyPropertyChangedEventArgs e)
    {
        UpdateList();
    }

    void OnSelectionChanged(object sender, SelectionChangedEventArgs e)
    {
        UpdateList();
    }
```

```
        void UpdateList()
        {
            sourceList.Clear();

            foreach (object item in listBox.SelectedItems)
            {
                sourceList.Add(item);
            }
        }
    }
}
```

Placing a Call with the `PhoneCallTask`

The phone call task is used to launch the built-in Phone app and displays the specified phone number and display name.

> **NOTE**
>
> The phone call is not placed until it is initiated by the user.

The following example demonstrates how to launch the phone call task:

```
PhoneCallTask phoneCallTask = new PhoneCallTask
                              {
                                  DisplayName = "Alan Turing",
                                  PhoneNumber = "882960"
                              };
phoneCallTask.Show();
```

If the `PhoneCallTask.PhoneNumber` is a null or empty string, calling the `PhoneCallTask.Show` method has no effect. If the `PhoneCallTask.PhoneNumber` has an invalid format, the Phone app prompts the user when the call is being made.

Sample Overview

Example code for the `PhoneCallTask` can be found in the `PhoneCallViewModel` in the downloadable sample code.

The `PhoneCallView` allows the user to enter a telephone number and place a call to that number when a button is tapped.

A Place Call button in the view is bound to the viewmodel's `CallCommand`.

The `callCommand` field is instantiated in the `PhoneCallViewModel` constructor. When executed, the `callCommand` creates a new `PhoneCallTask` and sets its `PhoneNumber` property with the text supplied by a `TextBox` in the view, as shown:

```csharp
public PhoneCallViewModel() : base("Phone Call Tasks")
{
    callCommand = new DelegateCommand(
        delegate
            {
                PhoneCallTask phoneCallTask = new PhoneCallTask
                                                {
                                                    DisplayName = "someone",
                                                    PhoneNumber = phoneNumber
                                                };
                phoneCallTask.Show();
            });
}
```

Figure 14.14 shows the PhoneCallView page.

FIGURE 14.14   PhoneCallView page.

When the PhoneCallTask.Show method is called, the Phone application is launched, which deactivates the sample application but leaves the sample app's UI visible in the background (see Figure 14.15).

FIGURE 14.15   The built-in Phone app is superimposed on the sample application.

Selecting a Phone Number with the `PhoneNumberChooserTask`

The phone number chooser task is used to launch the built-in Contacts application and allows the user to select a contact. A phone number for the contact is then returned to your app.

> **NOTE**
>
> To query the user's contact list without requiring the user to select a contact, use the `Contacts` class, described later in this chapter.

The `PhoneNumberChooserTask` should be defined as a field in your class, like so:

```
readonly PhoneNumberChooserTask phoneNumberChooserTask
                              = new PhoneNumberChooserTask();
```

Subscribe to the `PhoneNumberChooserTask.Completed` event within your class constructor, as shown:

```
PhoneNumberChooserTask.Completed
    += new EventHandler<PhoneNumberResult>(
                          HandlePhoneNumberChooserTaskCompleted);
```

Use the `Show` method of the `PhoneNumberChooserTask` to launch the built-in Contacts app. When the task completes the handler receives a `PhoneNumberResult` object, as shown:

```
void HandlePhoneNumberChooserTaskCompleted(object sender,
                          PhoneNumberResult e)
{
```

```
    if (e.TaskResult == TaskResult.OK)
    {
        PhoneNumber = e.PhoneNumber;
    }
    else if (e.Error != null)
    {
        Message = "Unable to choose number. " + e.ToString();
    }
    else if (e.TaskResult == TaskResult.Cancel)
    {
        Message = "Cancelled";
    }
}
```

Sample Overview

Example code for the `PhoneNumberChooserTask` can be found in the `PhoneCallViewModel` in the downloadable sample code. The `PhoneCallView` allows the user to populate the Phone Number `TextBox` by using a button that launches the `PhoneNumberChooserTask` (shown previously in Figure 14.14).

A button in the view is bound to a viewmodel `ICommand` property named `ChooseCommand`. The `chooseCommand` field is instantiated in the `PhoneCallViewModel` constructor. When executed, the command calls the `Show` method of the `PhoneNumberChooserTask`, as shown:

```
public PhoneCallViewModel() : base("Phone Call Tasks")
{
    phoneNumberChooserTask.Completed
                += HandlePhoneNumberChooserTaskCompleted;

    chooseCommand = new DelegateCommand(
                    obj => phoneNumberChooserTask.Show());
...
}
```

When the `Show` method is called, the Contacts application is launched (see Figure 14.16).

When the user selects a contact from the Contacts app, the sample app is activated, and the `Completed` event handler is called, which updates the `PhoneNumber` property in the viewmodel.

FIGURE 14.16   Windows Phone Contacts application.

Saving a Contact's Phone Number with the `SavePhoneNumberTask`

The save phone number task is used to launch the built-in Contacts app, allowing the user to save a specified phone number. This *chooser* does not return data, but you can handle the `Completed` event to determine whether the task was completed correctly.

`SavePhoneNumberTask` contains a single `PhoneNumber` property, which is passed to the Contacts application when the task's `Show` method is called.

The `SavePhoneNumberTask` should be defined as a field in your class, like so:

```
readonly SavePhoneNumberTask savePhoneNumberTask
                            = new SavePhoneNumberTask();
```

Subscribe to the `SavePhoneNumberTask.Completed` event within your class constructor, as shown:

```
savePhoneNumberTask.Completed
    += new EventHandler<TaskEventArgs>(HandleSavePhoneNumberTaskCompleted);
```

Use the `Show` method of the `SavePhoneNumberTask` to launch the built-in Contacts app. When the task completes the handler receives a `TaskEventArgs` object, as shown:

```
void HandleSavePhoneNumberTaskCompleted(object sender, TaskEventArgs e)
{
    if (e.Error != null)
    {
        Message = "Unable to save the phone number. " + e.Error;
        return;
    }
```

```
    if (e.TaskResult == TaskResult.OK)
    {
        Message = "Phone number saved";
    }
    else if (e.TaskResult == TaskResult.Cancel)
    {
        Message = "Cancelled";
    }
}
```

Sample Overview

Example code for the SavePhoneNumberTask can be found in the SavePhoneNumberViewModel in the downloadable sample code.

The SavePhoneNumberView page allows the user to enter a phone number into a TextBox and then to initiate the savePhoneNumberTask, using a button.

The button is bound to a viewmodel command named SaveCommand.

The TextBox is bound to the viewmodel's PhoneNumber property using a TwoWay data binding, as shown:

```
<TextBox Text="{Binding PhoneNumber, Mode=TwoWay}"
         InputScope="TelephoneNumber" />
```

The InputScope property of the TextBox causes the onscreen keyboard to be displayed with a set of keys suitable for typing a phone number. For more information on InputScopes, see Chapter 6.

When the SaveCommand is executed, the phoneNumber text is assigned to the task, and the task's Show method is called. See the following excerpt:

```
public SavePhoneNumberViewModel() : base("Save Phone Number")
{
    savePhoneNumberTask.Completed += savePhoneNumberTask_Completed;

    saveCommand = new DelegateCommand(
        delegate
            {
                Message = string.Empty;
                savePhoneNumberTask.PhoneNumber = phoneNumber;
                savePhoneNumberTask.Show();
            });
}
```

Figure 14.17 shows the custom SavePhoneNumberView page.

FIGURE 14.17   `SavePhoneNumberView` page.

When the `savePhoneNumberTask.Show` method is called, the Contacts application is launched (shown previously in Figure 14.8).

When the user selects either an existing contact, or the new contact option, the Edit Phone Number page is displayed (see Figure 14.18).

FIGURE 14.18   Edit Phone Number page.

When the Save icon button is pressed, if the user selected an existing contact, the Edit Phone Contact page, shown previously in Figure 14.10, is displayed.

Alternatively, if the user opts to create a new contact, the New Contact page is displayed.

Once the contact information has been stored, the sample application is activated, and the `Completed` handler is called.

Searching the Web with the `SearchTask`

The Search task is used to launch the built-in Search application and performs a search for the specified search string. The Search application presents search results for the following three categories:

▶ `Web`—The search query is used to perform a web search.

▶ `Local`—Geographic location is used to provide search results that are relevant to the user's location. For example, searching for the term *restaurant* presents a map with the location of nearby restaurants.

▶ `News`—The search query is used to perform a search of various news-related websites and blogs.

The `SearchTask` class has a single string property called `SearchQuery`.

> **NOTE**
>
> If the `SearchQuery` property is null or empty, calling the `SearchTask.Show` method has no effect.

The following excerpt demonstrates how to initiate a `SearchTask`:

```
SearchTask searchTask = new SearchTask { SearchQuery = "restaurant" };
searchTask.Show();
```

Sample Overview

Example code for the `SearchTask` can be found in the `SearchViewModel` in the downloadable sample code.

The `SearchView` allows the user to populate a `TextBox` with a search query. The `TextBox` has a two-way data binding to the viewmodel's `SearchQuery` property.

A button is used to execute an `ICommand` named `SearchCommand`, which initiates the `SearchTask`.

The `searchCommand` field is instantiated in the `SearchViewModel` constructor. When executed, the `searchCommand` creates a new `SearchTask` and sets its `SearchQuery` property to the text supplied by a `TextBox` in the view, as shown in the following excerpt:

```
public SearchViewModel()
{
    searchCommand = new DelegateCommand(
        delegate
            {
```

```
SearchTask searchTask = new SearchTask
                            {
                                SearchQuery = searchQuery
                            };
            searchTask.Show();
        });
}
```

Figure 14.19 shows the custom `SearchView` page.

FIGURE 14.19   The sample search page allows the user to enter a search query.

When the `SearchTask.Show` method is called, the built-in Search app is launched (see Figure 14.20).

FIGURE 14.20   The built-in Search app.

Sending Contacts a Link Using the `ShareLinkTask`

The share link task is used to enable the user to share a link on one or more social networks.

The `ShareLinkTask` allows you to specify a link URI, title, and message, as shown in the following excerpt:

```
ShareLinkTask task = new ShareLinkTask
    {
        LinkUri = new Uri("http://linkd.in/jnFoqE", UriKind.Absolute),
        Title = "Check out the Windows Phone Experts group.",
        Message = "Interested in Windows Phone development? "
                    + " Join the Windows Phone Experts group on Linked-In!"
    };

task.Show();
```

When the task's `Show` method is called, the built-in link sharing app is launched, allowing the user to select various social networks, such as Facebook, Twitter, and LinkedIn.

The sample for the `ShareLinkTask` is a page called `ShareLinkTaskView`, which allows the user to enter a URL, title, and message, and to launch the `ShareLinkTask` via an application bar button (see Figure 14.21).

FIGURE 14.21   `ShareLinkTaskView` page.

Allowing users to share links with their contacts is a great way to connect your app with a wider audience.

Posting a Status Update to Social Networks Using the `ShareStatusTask`

The share status task is used to enable the user to post a status update to one or more social networks. The `ShareStatusTask` contains a single `Status` property of type string. When the `Show` method is called, the `ShareStatusTask` presents the built-in message sharing app. See the following excerpt:

```
ShareStatusTask task = new ShareStatusTask();
task.Status = "I'm loving the new features of the Windows Phone API!";
task.Show();
```

The sample for the `ShareStatusTask` is a page called `ShareStatusTaskView`, which allows the user to enter some text and to launch the `ShareLinkTask` via an application bar button.

Preparing an SMS With the `SmsComposeTask`

The SMS compose task is used to launch the built-in Messaging app, allowing the user to create a new SMS message.

> **NOTE**
>
> The message is not sent until it is initiated by the user.

You can optionally specify recipients and a message body, which are prepopulated in the new message, as shown in the following excerpt:

```
SmsComposeTask smsComposeTask = new SmsComposeTask
                                {
                                    To = "885729",
                                    Body = "Hi from Windows Phone!"
                                };
smsComposeTask.Show();
```

Sample Overview

Example code for the `SmsComposeTask` can be found in the `SmsView` page and `SmsViewModel` classes in the downloadable sample code.

The `SmsView` allows the user to launch the built-in Messaging app when a button is tapped (see Figure 14.22).

FIGURE 14.22   The built-in Messaging app.

Navigating to a Web Page Using the `WebBrowserTask`

The web browser task is used to launch the built-in Web Browser app and optionally navigates the browser to a specified URL:

```
Uri uri = new Uri("http://msdn.microsoft.com", UriKind.RelativeOrAbsolute);
WebBrowserTask task = new WebBrowserTask { Uri = uri };
task.Show();
```

If the `Uri` results in a 404 HTTP standard response code (Not Found), no exception is raised; instead the Windows Phone Search application is launched.

Sample Overview

Example code for the `WebBrowserTask` can be found in the `LaunchWebBrowserViewModel` in the downloadable sample code.

The `LaunchWebBrowserView` page contains a `TextBox` in which the user can enter a URL and a Launch Web Browser `Button` (see Figure 14.23).

The view's `TextBox` has a `TwoWay` data binding to the viewmodel's `Url` property, as shown:

```
<TextBox Text="{Binding Url, Mode=TwoWay}" InputScope="Url" />
```

The `InputScope` property of the `TextBox` causes the onscreen keyboard to be displayed with a set of keys suitable for typing a URL. For more information on `InputScopes`, see Chapter 6.

FIGURE 14.23   Web Browser Launcher page.

A button is bound to an `ICommand` in the viewmodel named `LaunchCommand`. The command is instantiated in the viewmodel's constructor. When executed, `LaunchCommand` creates a new `WebBrowserTask` and sets its `Uri` property using the text supplied by a `TextBox` in the view. See the following excerpt:

```
public LaunchWebBrowserViewModel()
{
    launchCommand = new DelegateCommand(
        delegate
            {
                WebBrowserTask task = new WebBrowserTask { URL = url };
                task.Show();
            });
}
```

When the `WebBrowserTask.Show` method is called, the built-in Web Browser app is launched.

Selecting a Contact's Address Using the `AddressChooserTask`

The address chooser task is used to allow the user to provide your app with the street address of a contact. This task launches the built-in Contacts application so that the user can select a contact.

NOTE

To query the user's contact list without requiring the user to select a contact, use the `Contacts` class, described later in this chapter.

If the user completes the task, an event is raised and the task's `Completed` event handler receives an address in the result.

The sample for the `AddressChooserTask` consists of the `AddressChooserTaskView` page and `AddressChooserTaskViewModel` class.

The `AddressChooserTask` should be defined as a field in your class, like so:

```
readonly AddressChooserTask addressChooserTask = new AddressChooserTask();
```

Subscribe to the `AddressChooserTask.Completed` event within your class constructor, as shown:

```
addressChooserTask.Completed
                += new EventHandler<AddressResult>(HandleCompleted);
```

Use the `Show` method of the `AddressChooserTask` to launch the built-in Contacts application (see Figure 14.24).

FIGURE 14.24   Contacts application.

When the task completes, the handler receives an `AddressResult` object that contains the display name and address of the contact. See the following excerpt from the `AddressChooserTaskViewModel` class:

```
void HandleTaskCompleted(object sender, AddressResult e)
{
    if (e.Error != null)
    {
```

```
        MessageService.ShowError("Unable to retrieve address");
    }

    if (e.TaskResult != TaskResult.OK)
    {
        return;
    }

    DisplayName = e.DisplayName;
    Address = e.Address;
}
```

Saving a Contact to the Phone's Contact List Using the `SaveContactTask`

The save contact task is used to enable a user to save a contact to the phone's contact list. The `SaveContactTask` class contains 26 string properties such as `FirstName`, `Company`, and `Website`, which allow you to pass detailed information to the built-in Contacts app.

When the user finishes saving the contact, cancels out of the task, or an error occurs, the task's `Completed` event is raised.

The sample for the `SaveContactTask` consists of the `SaveContactTaskView` page and the `SaveContactTaskViewModel` class.

The `SaveContactTask` should be defined as a field in your class, like so:

```
readonly SaveContactTask saveContactTask = new SaveContactTask();
```

Subscribe to the `SaveContactTask.Completed` event within your class constructor, as shown:

```
saveContactTask.Completed
            += new EventHandler<SaveContactResult>(HandleCompleted);
```

The sample page allows the population of just some of the `SaveContactTask` properties (see Figure 14.25).

When the application bar button is tapped, the `Show` method of the `SaveContactTask` launches the built-in Contacts application.

When the task returns, the `Completed` event handler receives a `SaveContactResult` object that allows you to determine whether the task completed successfully. See the following excerpt:

```
void HandleTaskCompleted(object sender, SaveContactResult e)
{
    if (e.Error != null)
    {
        MessageService.ShowError("Unable to save contact.");
        return;
    }

    if (e.TaskResult == TaskResult.OK)
    {
        MessageService.ShowMessage("Contact saved.");
    }
}
```

FIGURE 14.25   SaveContactTaskView page.

Taking a Photo with the CameraCaptureTask

The camera capture task is a chooser that is used to launch the built-in Camera app. If the user completes the task by taking and confirming a photo, the Completed event is raised and the event handler receives a PhotoResult object, which exposes a stream containing the image data.

For information on working with photo image streams, see Chapter 20, "Extending the Windows Phone Picture Viewer."

The CameraCaptureTask should be defined as a field in your class, like so:

```
readonly CameraCaptureTask cameraCaptureTask
                            = new CameraCaptureTask();
```

Subscribe to the `CameraCaptureTask.Completed` event within your class constructor, as shown:

```
cameraCaptureTask.Completed
    += new EventHandler<PhotoResult>(HandleCameraCaptureTaskCompleted);
```

Use the `Show` method of the `CameraCaptureTask` to launch the built-in Camera app. When the task completes the handler receives a `PhotoResult` object, as shown:

```
void HandleCameraCaptureTaskCompleted(object sender, PhotoResult e)
{
    if (e.TaskResult == TaskResult.OK)
    {
        BitmapImage bitmapImage = new BitmapImage();
        bitmapImage.SetSource(e.ChosenPhoto);
        CapturedImage = bitmapImage;
    }
    else if (e.Error != null)
    {
        MessageService.ShowError("An error occurred. " + e.ToString());
    }
    else if (e.TaskResult == TaskResult.Cancel)
    {
        /* Cancelled. */
    }
}
```

Sample Overview

Example code for the `CameraCaptureTask` is located in the `CameraCaptureViewModel` in the downloadable sample code.

The view contains a button that is bound to a viewmodel `ICommand` property named `CaptureCommand`.

The `CameraCaptureView` allows the user to launch the `CameraCaptureTask` when she taps the button. When the `captureCommand` is executed, the `Show` method of the `cameraCaptureTask` is called, as shown in the following excerpt:

```
public CameraCaptureViewModel() : base("capture image")
{
    cameraCaptureTask.Completed += HandleCameraCaptureTaskCompleted;
    captureCommand = new DelegateCommand(obj => cameraCaptureTask.Show());
}
```

Calling the task's `Show` method launches the built-in Camera application (see Figure 14.26).

FIGURE 14.26   The built-in Camera application.

After the photo has been taken and accepted by the user, the task's `Completed` event handler is called, and a new `BitmapImage` is created using the `e.ChosenPhoto` image `Stream`. It is then assigned to the `CapturedImage` property of the viewmodel, as shown:

```
BitmapImage bitmapImage = new BitmapImage();
bitmapImage.SetSource(e.ChosenPhoto);
CapturedImage = bitmapImage;
```

An `Image` control in the view is used to display the image, as shown:

```
<Image Source="{Binding CapturedImage}" />
```

When the `CapturedImage` property is updated, the image is displayed in the view (see Figure 14.27).

FIGURE 14.27   The captured image is displayed on the `CameraCaptureView` page.

Inviting Game Players with the `GameInviteTask`

The game invite task is used to show a game invite screen that enables the user to invite players to a multiplayer game session that is in progress on a Windows Phone device. The invitation is sent asynchronously.

> **CAUTION**
>
> The game invite task works only when called from within a game that is approved for release on Xbox LIVE on Windows Phone.

When the user finishes sending the invite, cancels out of the task, or an error occurs, the task's `Completed` event is raised.

The `GameInviteTask` should be defined as a field in your class, like so:

```
readonly GameInviteTask gameInviteTask = new GameInviteTask();
```

Subscribe to the `GameInviteTask.Completed` event within your class constructor, as shown:

```
gameInviteTask.Completed += new EventHandler<TaskEventArgs>(HandleCompleted);
```

The `GameInviteTask` allows you to specify a unique session ID. The only information that another player needs to join an active game session is the session ID.

```
gameInviteTask.SessionId = "<session id>";
gameInviteTask.Show();
```

When the task's `Show` method is called, the built-in Game Invite app is launched, allowing the user to email recipients using either a gamer tag or an email address.

> **NOTE**
>
> Without a valid session ID, the Game Invite app is not able to send invitations.

The built-in Game Invite app is shown in Figure 14.28.

FIGURE 14.28   Built-in game invite page.

Selecting a Photo from the Photo Hub Using the `PhotoChooserTask`

The photo chooser task is used to launch the built-in Photo Picker app, which allows a user to select an image from isolated storage or, optionally, to take a photo using the device's camera.

The following is a list of the `PhotoChooserTask` properties:

- ▶ `PixelHeight`—The maximum height, in pixels, of the resulting image.

- ▶ `PixelWidth`—The maximum width, in pixels, of the resulting image.

- ▶ `ShowCamera`—If set to `true`, the user is presented with the option to use the device's camera to take a photo. A button is displayed on the first page of the Photo Picker app. If not specified, this value defaults to `false`.

The `PhotoChooserTask` should be defined as a field in your class, like so:

```
readonly PhotoChooserTask photoChooserTask = new PhotoChooserTask();
```

Subscribe to the `PhotoChooserTask.Completed` event within your class constructor, as shown:

```
PhotoChooserTask.Completed
    += new EventHandler<PhotoResult>(HandlePhotoChooserTaskCompleted);
```

Use the `Show` method of the `PhotoChooserTask` to launch the built-in Photo Picker app. When the task completes the handler receives a `PhotoResult` object, as shown:

```
void HandleTaskCompleted(object sender, PhotoResult e)
{
```

```
    if (e.TaskResult == TaskResult.OK)
    {
        BitmapImage bitmapImage = new BitmapImage();
        bitmapImage.SetSource(e.ChosenPhoto);
        CapturedImage = bitmapImage;
        ...
    }

    if (e.Error != null)
    {
        MessageService.ShowError("An error occurred. " + e.Error.ToString());
    }
}
```

When the task's Show method is called, the built-in Photo Picker app is launched, allowing the user to select or take a photo (see Figure 14.29).

FIGURE 14.29   The PhotoChooserTask.ShowCamera property determines whether the user is given the option to use the device's camera.

After an image has been selected by the user, it can be cropped to the aspect ratio specified by the PhotoChooserTask's PixelHeight and PixelWidth properties.

NOTE

If neither the `PixelHeight` nor `PixelWidth` is specified, the Photo Picker application skips the step that allows the user to crop the image.

The `PhotoChooserTask`'s `Completed` event is raised when an image has been selected or the user cancels out of the Photo Picker application. If the user completes the task of choosing an image, the `Completed` event is raised and the event handler receives a `PhotoResult` object that exposes a stream containing the image data. For information on working with image streams, see Chapter 20.

The properties of the `PhotoResult` class (a subclass of `TaskEventArgs`) are presented in the following list:

▶ **ChosenPhoto**—A `System.IO.Stream` for the selected image

▶ **OriginalFileName**—The path to the file in isolated storage

Sample Overview

The `PhotoChooserViewModel` class in the downloadable sample code demonstrates how to use the `PhotoChooserTask` (see Listing 14.4).

Subscription to the `PhotoChooserTask.Completed` event occurs in the class constructor. The `chooseCommand`'s execute handler assigns the task's various properties and calls its `Show` method. When the `Completed` event of the task is raised, a `BitmapImage` is created using the chosen image `Stream`.

LISTING 14.4 `PhotoChooserViewModel` Class (excerpt)

```
public class PhotoChooserViewModel : ViewModelBase
{
    readonly PhotoChooserTask task = new PhotoChooserTask();

    public PhotoChooserViewModel()
    {
        task.Completed += HandleTaskCompleted;
        chooseCommand = new DelegateCommand(
            delegate
                {
                    task.PixelWidth = pixelWidth;
                    task.PixelHeight = pixelHeight;
                    task.ShowCamera = showCamera;
                    task.Show();
                });
    }

    void HandleTaskCompleted(object sender, PhotoResult e)
    {
```

```
    if (e.TaskResult == TaskResult.OK)
    {
        BitmapImage bitmapImage = new BitmapImage();
        bitmapImage.SetSource(e.ChosenPhoto);
        CapturedImage = bitmapImage;
        PixelWidth = ImageWidth = bitmapImage.PixelWidth;
        PixelHeight = ImageHeight = bitmapImage.PixelHeight;
        OriginalFileName = e.OriginalFileName;
    }

    if (e.Error != null)
    {
        MessageService.ShowError("An error occurred. " + e.Error.ToString());
    }
  }
...
}
```

The `PhotoChooserView` is data bound to the `PhotoChooserViewModel`, which allows the user to affect the properties of the `PhotoChooserTask` when the viewmodel's `ChooseCommand` is executed. The `ChooseCommand` is executed when the Capture button is pressed. The user can change the aspect ratio of the image by modifying the Width and Height Ratio `sliders`.

A `PhotoChooserViewModel` instance is assigned to the view's `DataContext`, as shown in the following excerpt from the `PhotoChooserView` code-beside:

```
public PhotoChooserView()
{
    InitializeComponent();
    DataContext = new PhotoChooserViewModel();
}
```

The view uses data binding to populate its controls and to interact with the viewmodel. After the user chooses an image via the `PhotoChooserTask`, the `Image` control is populated via its data binding to the `CapturedImage` property of the `PhotoChooserViewModel`. The Capture button causes the execution of the `ChooseCommand` (see Listing 14.5).

LISTING 14.5   PhotoChooserView.xaml (excerpt)

```
<StackPanel x:Name="ContentPanel" Grid.Row="1">
    <TextBlock Text="{Binding PixelWidth, StringFormat='Width Ratio\: \{0\}'}"
               Style="{StaticResource PhoneTextNormalStyle}" />
    <Slider Value="{Binding PixelWidth, Mode=TwoWay}"
            Minimum="10" Maximum="200"  LargeChange="50" SmallChange="10"/>
    <TextBlock Text="{Binding PixelHeight, StringFormat='Height Ratio\: \{0\}'}"
```

```
                        Style="{StaticResource PhoneTextNormalStyle}" />
    <Slider Value="{Binding PixelHeight, Mode=TwoWay}"
            Minimum="10" Maximum="200" LargeChange="50" SmallChange="10"/>
    <CheckBox IsChecked="{Binding ShowCamera, Mode=TwoWay}"
              Content="Show Camera" />
    <Button Command="{Binding ChooseCommand}"
            Content="Choose" />
    <Image Source="{Binding CapturedImage}"
           Width="{Binding ImageWidth}" Height="{Binding ImageHeight}"
           HorizontalAlignment="Left" Margin="15,0,15,0" />
    <TextBlock Text="Path: "
               Style="{StaticResource PhoneTextSmallStyle}" />
    <TextBlock Text="{Binding OriginalFileName}"
               Style="{StaticResource PhoneTextSmallStyle}" TextWrapping="Wrap" />
</StackPanel>
```

The `PhotoChooserView` page is presented in Figure 14.30.

FIGURE 14.30   `PhotoChooserView` page.

The `PixelWidth` and `PixelHeight` properties of the `PhotoChooserTask` determine the maximum dimensions of the resulting image. The Photo Picker crop page presents the image with a selection overlay conforming to the aspect ratio `PixelWidth`/`PixelHeight`, which spans either the entire width or height of the image. When the user confirms the selection, the image is reduced to the size specified by `PixelWidth` and `PixelHeight` (see Figure 14.31).

FIGURE 14.31   The Photo Picker crop page.

When the user completes the `PhotoChooserTask`, the `PhotoChooserTask.Completed` event is handled by the `PhotoChooserViewModel.HandleTaskCompleted` method. A new `BitmapImage` is created using the resulting image stream, and it is assigned to the `CapturedImage` property of the viewmodel. The view is then automatically updated via the `Image` control's data binding (see Figure 14.32).

FIGURE 14.32   The chosen image is displayed in the view.

Sharing Images with Other Devices Using NFC or with Other Registered Phone Services

New to the Windows Phone 8 SDK is the `ShareMediaTask`, which allows you to pass an image to another device via NFC, or to another person using the phone's messaging app, or with another registered service on the phone such as OneNote.

To launch the `ShareMediaTask`, create a new instance of the task and set its `FilePath` property to the location of a file on the device, as shown:

```
ShareMediaTask shareMediaTask = new ShareMediaTask();
shareMediaTask.FilePath = fileName;
shareMediaTask.Show();
```

The `ShareMediaTask` works well in conjunction with other tasks, in particular the `CameraCaptureTask` and the `PhotoChooserTask`. This is demonstrated in the `ShareMediaTaskViewModel` in the WPUnleashed.Examples project of the downloadable sample code (see Listing 14.6).

The viewmodel contains a `PhotoChooserTask` that is initialized as a field of the class. When the `ShareCommand` is executed the `PhotoChooserTask` is shown. The `Completed` event handler uses the `PhotoResult` object's `OriginalFileName` property to launch a new `ShareMediaTask`.

LISTING 14.6   `ShareMediaTaskViewModel` Class

```
public class ShareMediaTaskViewModel : ViewModelBase
{
    readonly PhotoChooserTask photoChooserTask = new PhotoChooserTask();

    public ShareMediaTaskViewModel() : base("share image")
    {
        shareCommand = new DelegateCommand(arg => photoChooserTask.Show());

        photoChooserTask.Completed += HandlePhotoChooserTaskCompleted;
    }

    void HandlePhotoChooserTaskCompleted(object sender, PhotoResult e)
    {
        if (e.TaskResult == TaskResult.OK)
        {
            ShareMediaTask shareMediaTask = new ShareMediaTask();
            shareMediaTask.FilePath = e.OriginalFileName;
            shareMediaTask.Show();
        }
    }
}

    readonly DelegateCommand shareCommand;
```

```
public ICommand ShareCommand
{
    get
    {
        return shareCommand;
    }
}
}
```

When the `ShareMediaTask` is shown, the built-in Share Media app is displayed (see Figure 14.33).

FIGURE 14.33   The built-in Share Media app.

Creating a Ringtone with an Audio File Using the `SaveRingtoneTask`

The save ringtone task is used to launch the built-in Ringtones app, which enables the user to save an audio file to the system ringtones list and to optionally set it as the active ringtone on the device.

The ringtones list can be viewed by selecting the Ringtones + Sounds item on the phone's system settings page.

After the audio file is added to the list, the user can set it as the ringtone for individual contacts in the Contacts application.

When the user finishes saving the contact, cancels out of the task, or an error occurs, the task's `Completed` event is raised.

The `SaveRingtoneTask` should be defined as a field in your class, like so:

```
readonly SaveRingtoneTask saveRingtoneTask = new SaveRingtoneTask();
```

Subscribe to the `SaveRingtoneTask.Completed` event within your class constructor, as shown:

```
saveRingtoneTask.Completed
                += new EventHandler<TaskEventArgs>(HandleCompleted);
```

The `SaveRingtoneTask` allows you to specify a display name for the ringtone and the URI of the audio file. The audio file can be either located in isolated storage or within an assembly. Initialization and launching of the task is shown in the following excerpt:

```
saveRingtoneTask.DisplayName = displayName;
saveRingtoneTask.IsShareable = shareable;
saveRingtoneTask.Source = new Uri("appdata:/AudioFiles/Audio01.wma");
//saveRingtoneTask.Source = new Uri("isostore:/AudioFiles/Audio01.wma");
saveRingtoneTask.Show();
```

The appdata segment of the `Source Uri` value indicates that the file is located within the app's XAP file. In this case, the file is located in a project directory called AudioFiles.

> **NOTE**
>
> When using the appdata prefix, the file must have its Build Action set to Content; otherwise, it will be unresolvable.

Conversely, the isostore prefix indicates that the file is located in isolated storage. Files located in isolated storage must be placed there by your app.

Ringtone audio files must meet the following requirements:

▶ File must be of type MP3 or WMA.

▶ Files must be less than 1MB in size.

▶ Files must be less than 40 seconds in length.

▶ Files must not have digital rights management (DRM) protection.

When the task's `Show` method is called, the built-in Ringtone app is launched, allowing the user to edit the ringtone's display name and to optionally set the ringtone as the active ringtone.

The sample for the `SaveRingtoneTask` consists of the `SaveRingtoneTaskView` page and `SaveRingtoneTaskViewModel` class. The view allows the user to enter a display name for the ringtone and to launch the `SaveRingtoneTask` via an application bar button. The built-in Ringtone app is shown in Figure 14.34.

FIGURE 14.34   The built-in Ringtone app.

When the task returns control to your app, the `Completed` event handler is called. The `TaskEventArgs` object allows you to determine whether the user successfully saved the ringtone, as shown in the following excerpt:

```
void HandleTaskCompleted(object sender, TaskEventArgs e)
{
    if (e.Error != null)
    {
        MessageService.ShowError("Unable to save ringtone.");
        return;
    }

    if (e.TaskResult == TaskResult.OK)
    {
        MessageService.ShowMessage("Ringtone saved.");
    }
}
```

The save ringtone task is a great way to extend an audio app. You could have your app procure audio from third-party websites or from your own website.

Contacts and Appointments

While the three choosers: `AddressChooserTask`, `EmailAddressChooserTask`, and `PhoneNumberChooserTask` enable the user to select a contact, your app may also query the user's contact list without user intervention. Read-only access to the user's contacts and appointments can be achieved using the `Contacts` and `Appointment` classes, located in the Microsoft.Phone.UserData namespace.

Retrieving Contacts

The `Contacts` class allows you to search the user's contacts for a string. The search can be restricted to a single field of the `Contact` class, or to contacts that have been pinned to the phone's Start Experience (home screen). Searches are performed using one of the following `FilterKind` enumeration values:

▶ `None` (default value)

▶ `DisplayName`

▶ `EmailAddress`

▶ `PhoneNumber`

▶ `PinnedToStart`

To query the user's contact list, define a `Contacts` instance as a field in a class, as shown:

```
Contacts contacts;
```

Instantiate the `Contacts` object, subscribe to its `SearchCompleted` event, and then call `SearchAsync`, as shown in the following excerpt:

```
void SearchContacts()
{
    contacts = new Contacts();

    contacts.SearchCompleted += HandleSearchCompleted;
    contacts.SearchAsync("andrew", FilterKind.DisplayName, null);
}
```

NOTE

To access the user's contact list the ID_CAP_CONTACTS capability must be present in the WMAppManifest.xml file.

For more information on the phone's security capability model, see Chapter 2, "Fundamental Concepts in Windows Phone Development."

The `Contacts.SearchAsync` method allows the use of an empty search string when `FilterKind` is set to DisplayName, PinnedToStart, or None. An exception is raised if you attempt to search for an empty string in conjunction with a `FilterKind` value equal to EmailAddress or PhoneNumber.

When the search completes, the specified event handler receives a list of matching `Contact` objects. See the following excerpt:

```
void HandleSearchCompleted(object sender, ContactsSearchEventArgs e)
{
    if (e.Results == null)
    {
        return;
    }
    Contacts = e.Results;
}
```

The list of retrieved `Contact` objects can be further refined using LINQ.

Be mindful that when using LINQ, however, some users may have a lot of contacts, and it may be expensive to use LINQ to select a subset of the resulting `Contact` objects.

Internally, the contact list has various indexes placed on fields corresponding to the `FilterKind` enumeration, which may offer superior performance during retrieval. Therefore, favor the use of filters rather than LINQ wherever possible.

Windows Phone aggregates contacts from various social networking accounts, including Windows Live, Facebook, Twitter, and LinkedIn (and potentially more to come). To determine the accounts from which contacts are available, use the `Contacts` class's `Accounts` property.

Sample Contacts Page

The example for this section allows the user to enter a search string, select a `FilterKind` enumeration value, and perform a search against the user's contact list.

Within the `ContactsViewModel` class a `SearchText` property and a `FilterKind` property restrict the results of the call to `contacts.SearchAsync` (see Listing 14.7).

The list of available filter values is exposed by the viewmodel's `FilterKinds` property.

A `DelegateCommand` named `SearchCommand` calls the `SearchContacts` method when it is executed. When the `SearchCompleted` handler is called, a `Contacts` property is populated with the result.

LISTING 14.7   ContactsViewModel Class

```csharp
public class ContactsViewModel : ViewModelBase
{
    public ContactsViewModel() : base("search contacts")
    {
        searchCommand = new DelegateCommand(arg => SearchContacts());
    }

    Contacts contacts;

    void SearchContacts()
    {
        if (string.IsNullOrWhiteSpace(searchText)
                && (FilterKind == FilterKind.EmailAddress
                        || FilterKind == FilterKind.PhoneNumber))
        {
            MessageService.ShowMessage("Please enter the search text.");
            return;
        }

        contacts = new Contacts();

        contacts.SearchCompleted += HandleSearchCompleted;
        contacts.SearchAsync(searchText, FilterKind, null);
    }

    void HandleSearchCompleted(object sender, ContactsSearchEventArgs e)
    {
        if (e.Results == null)
        {
            return;
        }
        Contacts = e.Results;
    }

    IEnumerable<Contact> contactsList = new List<Contact>();
    public IEnumerable<Contact> Contacts
    {
        get
        {
            return contactsList;
        }
        private set
        {
            Assign(ref contactsList, value);
```

```
        }
    }

    readonly DelegateCommand searchCommand;

    public ICommand SearchCommand
    {
        get
        {
            return searchCommand;
        }
    }

    string searchText;

    public string SearchText
    {
        get
        {
            return searchText;
        }
        set
        {
            Assign(ref searchText, value);
        }
    }

    FilterKind filterKind = filterKinds.First();

    public FilterKind FilterKind
    {
        get
        {
            return filterKind;
        }
        set
        {
            Assign(ref filterKind, value);
        }
    }
    static readonly IEnumerable<FilterKind> filterKinds
        = EnumUtility.CreateEnumValueList<FilterKind>().OrderBy(x => x.ToString());

    public IEnumerable<FilterKind> FilterKinds
    {
        get
```

```
        {
            return filterKinds;
        }
    }
}
```

The view contains a `TextBox` that is bound to the viewmodel's `SearchText` property and a `ListPicker` whose `ItemsSource` property is bound to the `FilterKinds` viewmodel property (see Listing 14.8).

When the user selects an item in the `ListPicker`, the viewmodel's `FilterKind` property is updated.

Results are displayed using a `ListBox`, whose `ItemsSource` property is bound to the viewmodel's `Contacts` property. Each `Content` object is presented using a `TextBlock` to show its `DisplayName`, and a `ListBox` is used to display each of the contact's email addresses.

LISTING 14.8   ContactsView.xaml (excerpt)

```xml
<StackPanel x:Name="ContentPanel" Grid.Row="1">
    <TextBlock Text="search" Style="{StaticResource LabelTextStyle}" />
    <TextBox Text="{Binding SearchText, Mode=TwoWay}" />
    <toolkit:ListPicker
        ItemsSource="{Binding FilterKinds}"
        SelectedItem="{Binding FilterKind, Mode=TwoWay}"
        Header="filter" />
    <ListBox ItemsSource="{Binding Contacts}">
        <ListBox.ItemTemplate>
            <DataTemplate>
                <StackPanel Margin="0,0,0,20">
                    <TextBlock Text="{Binding DisplayName}"
                        Style="{StaticResource PhoneTextLargeStyle}" />
                    <ListBox ItemsSource="{Binding EmailAddresses}"
                        ScrollViewer.VerticalScrollBarVisibility="Disabled">
                        <ListBox.ItemTemplate>
                            <DataTemplate>
                                <StackPanel>
                                    <TextBlock Text="{Binding EmailAddress}"
                                        Style="{StaticResource
                                        ➥PhoneTextNormalStyle}" />
                                </StackPanel>
                            </DataTemplate>
                        </ListBox.ItemTemplate>
                    </ListBox>
                </StackPanel>
            </DataTemplate>
        </ListBox.ItemTemplate>
```

```
        </ListBox>
</StackPanel>
```

In addition, the view contains an `AppBarIconButton` that is bound to the viewmodel's `SearchCommand`, as shown:

```
<u:AppBar>
    <u:AppBarIconButton
                Command="{Binding SearchCommand}"
                Text="search"
                IconUri="/Images/ApplicationBarIcons/AppBarSearch.png" />
</u:AppBar>
```

When the user taps the application bar button, matching contacts are displayed at the bottom of the page (see Figure 14.35).

FIGURE 14.35   ContactsView page.

Storing Contacts in the Custom Contact Store

Beginning with Windows Phone 8, each Windows Phone app is provided with its own contact store. Your app can add or remove contacts from the store, and contacts that are present in the store are displayed in the phone's People Hub.

The contact store is retrieved by calling the `Windows.Phone.PersonalInformation.ContactStore` class's static `CreateOrOpenAsync` method. If the store does not exist, it is created the first time the method is called. To add a contact to the contact store, create a `StoredContact` instance and call its `SaveAsync` method, as demonstrated in the following example:

```
ContactStore store = await ContactStore.CreateOrOpenAsync();
StoredContact contact = new StoredContact(store)
```

```
{RemoteId = remoteId, GivenName = "Annie", FamilyName = "Easley"};
```

```
await contact.SaveAsync();
```

`ContactStore.CreateOrOpenAsync` has an overload that allows you to control the visibility of contacts within the store to other apps. The signature of the method is as follows:

CreateOrOpenAsync(ContactStoreSystemAccessMode access,
    ContactStoreApplicationAccessMode sharing)

The `ContactStoreSystemAccessMode` and `ContactStoreApplicationAccessMode` enumeration parameters specify the level of access the system and other apps have to your app's contact store. `ContactStoreSystemAccessMode` can be either `ReadOnly` or `ReadWrite`. `ReadOnly` indicates that only your app can modify your contacts. `ReadWrite` means that the phone can modify your contacts through its built-in contacts experience that can be reached via the People Hub.

`ContactStoreApplicationAccessMode` can be either `LimitedReadOnly` or `ReadOnly`. `LimitedReadOnly` means that other apps can read only the display name and the profile picture of your app's contacts, whereas `ReadOnly` allows other apps to read all the properties of your contacts.

The default settings are `ContactStoreSystemAccessMode.ReadOnly` and `ContactStoreApplicationAccessMode.LimitedReadOnly`.

`StoredContact` contains the following properties for storing a contact's personal details:

▶ `DisplayName`

▶ `DisplayPicture`

▶ `FamilyName`

▶ `GivenName`

▶ `HonorificPrefix`

▶ `HonorificSuffix`

▶ `Id`

▶ `RemoteId`

If not explicitly set in your code, the `DisplayName` property getter returns a concatenation of the following properties:

```
HonorificPrefix + GivenName + FamilyName + HonorificSuffix
```

The `Id` property is a read-only string that is assigned by the contact store when the contact is saved. `Id` can be used to retrieve a particular contact from the store, as shown in the following example:

```
ContactStore store = await ContactStore.CreateOrOpenAsync();
StoredContact contact = await store.FindContactByIdAsync(id);
```

The `RemoteId` property is also used to retrieve a contact. But, unlike the `Id` property, it is not read-only and can be set to a value that is known by your back-end system; such as a field in a database table. The following example demonstrates how to retrieve a contact using its remote ID:

```
ContactStore store = await ContactStore.CreateOrOpenAsync();
StoredContact contact = await store.FindContactByRemoteIdAsync(id);
```

The `DisplayPicture` property returns a `Windows.Storage.Streams.IRandomAccessStreamReference` to an image that is set either by the user via the People Hub or by your app using the `StoredContact` class's `SetDisplayPictureAsync` method, which is discussed later in the chapter.

If the data you want to associate with your contact does not fit into any of the `StoredContact` properties, the class also offers a property dictionary for storing any number of other pieces of information. The following excerpt demonstrates how to save an email address along with the `StoredContact` object:

```
IDictionary<string, object> properties = await contact.GetExtendedPropertiesAsync();
properties.Add(KnownContactProperties.Email, email);
```

The built-in `KnownContactProperties` class provides various strongly typed names of common contact properties. You can use the fields of the `KnownContactProperties` class for key values if you want the fields to be consistent with the phone's internal contact property names.

Property names, however, are not limited to those in the `KnownContactProperties` class. Indeed, you can supply any key value that you want, as demonstrated in the following excerpt:

```
properties.Add("Partner Name", "Mary");
```

To delete a contact from the store, either call `DeleteAsync` on an existing `StoredContact` object or use the `DeleteContactAsync` method, as shown in the following example:

```
ContactStore store = await ContactStore.CreateOrOpenAsync();
await store.DeleteContactAsync(id);
```

Now that you have looked at the essential operations of the contact store, the next section explores the sample for this section. The source code is located in the ContactsAndAppointments/CustomContactStore directory in the WPUnleashed.Example project of the downloadable sample code.

The sample contains two views: `ContactStoreView` and `ContactCreationView`, and two associated viewmodels: `ContactStoreViewModel` and `ContactCreationViewModel`.

14

ContactStoreViewModel loads the list of StoredContacts from the app's contact store. Each contact can be either deleted via a DeleteContactCommand or viewed in detail via a ViewContactCommand.

The Load method of the ContactStoreViewModel retrieves the list of contacts from the contact store (see Listing 14.9). The ContactQueryOptions class allows you to specify the known properties that you want returned using its DesiredFields property. In the current version of the Windows Phone SDK, however, the DesiredFields property appears to serve no purpose.

Use the OrderBy property of the ContactQueryOptions to specify the order of the results returned by the query. OrderBy is an enumeration value and can be either SystemDefault, FamilyNameGivenName, or GivenNameFamilyName.

> **NOTE**
>
> To provide a consistent user experience across different apps, use the default ordering (ContactQueryResultOrdering.SystemDefault) to order contact query results.

The ContactStoreViewModel class's Contacts property is set to the list returned by the store.

LISTING 14.9   ContactStoreViewModel.Load Method

```
public async void Load()
{
    ContactStore store = await ContactStore.CreateOrOpenAsync();

    /* These values are not used in the view, but merely demonstrates
     * how to load them as part of the query. */
    ContactQueryOptions options = new ContactQueryOptions();
    options.OrderBy = ContactQueryResultOrdering.SystemDefault;

    ContactQueryResult contactQuery = store.CreateContactQuery(options);
    IReadOnlyList<StoredContact> storedContacts
        = await contactQuery.GetContactsAsync();

    Contacts = storedContacts;
}
```

The ContactStoreViewModel class's DeleteContactCommand calls the DeleteContact method, which deletes the contact and reloads the contact list, as shown:

```
async void DeleteContact(StoredContact storedContact)
{
    ContactStore store = await ContactStore.CreateOrOpenAsync();
    await store.DeleteContactAsync(storedContact.Id);
```

```
    Load();
}
```

The `ContactStoreViewModel` class's `ViewContactCommand` calls the `ViewContact` method, which uses the viewmodel's base class method to navigate to the `ContactCreationView` page; passing it the ID of the `StoredContact` via a query string parameter, as shown:

```
void ViewContact(StoredContact storedContact)
{
    Navigate("/ContactsAndAppointments/CustomContactStore/"
        + "ContactCreationView.xaml?ContactId=" + storedContact.Id);
}
```

The `ContactStoreView` page uses a `ListBox` to display the list of contacts retrieved by the viewmodel (see Listing 14.10). An image displays a delete icon. The image element uses the custom commanding infrastructure to bind to the `DeleteContactCommand` in the viewmodel.

Tapping on the `TextBlock` containing the `DisplayName` of the `StoredContact`, executes the `ViewContactCommand`.

The use of the `bridge` resource allows the data template to reach outside of its data context to bind to properties of the `ContactStoreViewModel` instance.

An `AppBarHyperlinkButton` allows the user to create a new contact by navigating to the `ContactCreationView` without passing a contact ID.

LISTING 14.10   `ContactStoreView.xaml` (excerpt)

```
<u:AppBar>
    <u:AppBarHyperlinkButton
        NavigateUri="/ContactsAndAppointments/.../ContactCreationView.xaml"
                Text="new contact"
                IconUri="/ContactsAndAppointments/.../Images/Add.png" />
</u:AppBar>
...
<ListBox ItemsSource="{Binding Contacts}">
    <ListBox.ItemTemplate>
        <DataTemplate>
            <Grid d:DataContext="{d:DesignInstance p:StoredContact}"
                    Margin="0,0,0,20">
                <Grid.ColumnDefinitions>
                    <ColumnDefinition Width="Auto" />
                    <ColumnDefinition Width="*" />
                </Grid.ColumnDefinitions>
```

```
                <Image Source="/ContactsAndAppointments/.../Delete.png"
                        c:Commanding.Command="{Binding Content.DeleteContactCommand,
                                    Source={StaticResource bridge}}"
                        c:Commanding.CommandParameter="{Binding}" />

                <TextBlock Text="{Binding DisplayName}"
                        Style="{StaticResource PhoneTextLargeStyle}"
                        c:Commanding.Command="{Binding
                                        ➥Content.ViewContactCommand,
                                    Source={StaticResource bridge}}"
                        c:Commanding.CommandParameter="{Binding}"
                        Grid.Column="1" />
            </Grid>
        </DataTemplate>
    </ListBox.ItemTemplate>
</ListBox>
```

Figure 14.36 shows the ContactStoreView page with a number of contacts present in the app's contact store.

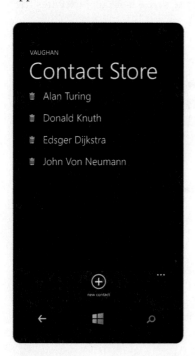

FIGURE 14.36   ContactStoreView page.

When the user taps a name in the list of contacts, the app navigates to the
`ContactCreationView` page, which passes the query string dictionary containing the
contact ID to the `ContactCreationViewModel` class, as shown:

```
protected override void OnNavigatedTo(NavigationEventArgs e)
{
    base.OnNavigatedTo(e);

    ViewModel.Load(NavigationContext.QueryString);
}
```

If a contact ID is not present in the query string, the viewmodel creates a new contact,
or else assumes its edit mode for an existing contact (see Listing 14.11) and retrieves and
copies the properties of the contact to matching viewmodel properties.

LISTING 14.11   `ContactCreationViewModel.Load` Method

```
public async void Load(IDictionary<string, string> queryString)
{
    string id;

    if (!queryString.TryGetValue("ContactId", out id))
    {
        return;
    }

    ContactStore store = await ContactStore.CreateOrOpenAsync();
    StoredContact contact = await store.FindContactByIdAsync(id);

    if (contact != null)
    {
        contactId = id;

        GivenName = contact.GivenName;
        FamilyName = contact.FamilyName;
        HonorificPrefix = contact.HonorificPrefix;

        IDictionary<string, object> extendedProperties
            = await contact.GetExtendedPropertiesAsync();

        object tempEmail;
        extendedProperties.TryGetValue(KnownContactProperties.Email, out tempEmail);
        EmailAddress = (string)tempEmail;

        object tempCodeName;
        extendedProperties.TryGetValue("CodeName", out tempCodeName);
```

```
        CodeName = (string)tempCodeName;
    }
}
```

The `ContactCreationViewModel` class contains a `SaveContactCommand` that calls the `SaveContact` method, shown in Listing 14.12. The various viewmodel properties are copied to a new or existing contact. The method retrieves an image resource, which becomes the contact's display picture. The contact is then saved and the page navigates back to the `ContactStoreView` page.

LISTING 14.12   `ContactCreationViewModel.Save` Method

```
async void SaveContact()
{
    ContactStore store = await ContactStore.CreateOrOpenAsync();

    StoredContact contact;

    if (string.IsNullOrEmpty(contactId))
    {
        contact = new StoredContact(store);
    }
    else
    {
        contact = await store.FindContactByIdAsync(contactId);
    }

    contact.GivenName = givenName;
    contact.FamilyName = familyName;
    contact.HonorificPrefix = honorificPrefix;

    IDictionary<string, object> extendedProperties
        = await contact.GetExtendedPropertiesAsync();
    extendedProperties[KnownContactProperties.Email] = emailAddress;
    extendedProperties["CodeName"] = codeName;

    Uri uri = new Uri("ContactsAndAppointments/CustomContactStore/Images/
                      ➥Contact.png",
                             UriKind.Relative);
    StreamResourceInfo resourceInfo = Application.GetResourceStream(uri);
    using (var stream = resourceInfo.Stream)
    {
        await contact.SetDisplayPictureAsync(stream.AsInputStream());
    }

    await contact.SaveAsync();
```

```
Navigate("/ContactsAndAppointments/CustomContactStore/ContactStoreView.xaml");
}
```

Figure 14.37 shows the `ContactCreationView` page. Tapping the save button adds or updates the contact in the app's contact store.

FIGURE 14.37   `ContactCreationView` page.

Detecting Changes in Stored Contacts

Sometimes contacts may be modified outside of your app. You can use the `ContactStore` change tracking API to retrieve a list of changes that have occurred to contacts since a previous point in time.

To establish the current revision number of the contact store, retrieve the value of the `ContactStore` object's `RevisionNumber` property. This is an unsigned `long` value that is updated whenever a contact is added or removed from the contact store, or whenever a contact is modified.

```
ContactStore store = await ContactStore.CreateOrOpenAsync();
ulong revisionCode = store.RevisionNumber;
```

You retrieve the list of changes since the last revision by calling the `ContactStore` class's `GetChangesAsync` method. Each change record includes the `Id` and `RemoteId` of the `StoredContact` and the type of change that occurred. See the following excerpt:

```
IReadOnlyList<ContactChangeRecord> changes =
➥await store.GetChangesAsync(revisionCode);
foreach (ContactChangeRecord change in changes)
{
    Debug.WriteLine("Record with ID {0} changed: {1}",
        change.Id, change.ChangeType);
}
```

The type of change is limited to one of three `ContactChangeType` enumeration values: `Created`, `Deleted`, or `Modified`.

Converting a Stored Contact to and from a vCard

vCard is a standard file format used for electronic business cards. The stored contact API allows you to convert a StoredContact to and from a vCard.

The ContactInformation class contains a ParseVcardAsnc method, which asynchronously converts an `IInputStream` of vCard data and then returns a populated `ContactInformation` object, as demonstrated by the following example:

```
ContactStore store = await ContactStore.CreateOrOpenAsync();
ContactInformation contactInformation
    = await ContactInformation.ParseVcardAsync(inputStream);
StoredContact contact = new StoredContact(store, contactInformation);
```

Conversely, a `StoredContact` object is converted to an `IInputStream` of vCard data using the `StoredContract` class's `ToVcardAsync` method, as shown:

```
ContactStore store = await ContactStore.CreateOrOpenAsync();
StoredContact contact = await store.FindContactByIdAsync(id);
IRandomAccessStream vcardStream = await contact.ToVcardAsync();
```

Being able to convert to and from the vCard format allows you to import and export contact information to and from other applications such as Microsoft Outlook.

Retrieving Appointments

The `Appointments` class allows you to retrieve appointments that fall between two specified dates.

> **NOTE**
>
> To access the user's appointments, the ID_CAP_APPOINTMENTS capability must be present in the WMAppManifest.xml file.
>
> For more information on the phone's security capability model, see Chapter 2.

To query the user's appointments, define an `Appointments` instance as a field in a class, as shown:

```
Appointments appointments;
```

Instantiate the `Appointments` object, subscribe to its `SearchCompleted` event, and then call `SearchAsync`. The following excerpt demonstrates the retrieval of appointments that fall within the next six months:

```
void SearchAppointments()
{
    appointments = new Appointments();

    appointments.SearchCompleted += HandleSearchCompleted;
    appointments.SearchAsync(DateTime.Now, DateTime.Now.AddMonths(6), null);
}
```

When the search completes, the specified event handler receives a list of matching `Appointment` objects. See the following excerpt:

```
void HandleSearchCompleted(object sender, AppointmentsSearchEventArgs e)
{
    if (e.Results == null)
    {
        return;
    }
    Appointments = e.Results;
}
```

To determine the accounts from which appointments are available, use the `Appointment` class's `Accounts` property.

Each appointment is represented by an `Appointment` object. The `Appointment` class provides various read-only properties, described in Table 14.2.

TABLE 14.2   `Appointment` Class Properties

Name	Description
Account	Gets the data source (for example, Windows Live) associated with this appointment
Attendees	Gets the list of attendees associated with this appointment
Details	Gets a detailed description of the appointment
EndTime	Gets the date and time that the appointment ends
IsAllDayEvent	Gets a value that indicates whether the appointment is an all-day event
IsPrivate	Gets a bool value that indicates whether the appointment is private

Name	Description
Location	Gets the location of the appointment
Organizer	Gets the organizer of the appointment
StartTime	Gets the date and time that the appointment starts
Status	Gets information about how to treat the block of time of this appointment, such as busy or out of the office
Subject	Gets the subject of the appointment

The `Appointments.SearchAsync` method is overloaded to allow you to restrict the retrieval of appointments from specific accounts. For example, to retrieve only those appointments associated with the user's Windows Live account, use the following:

```
Account account = appointments.Accounts.Where(
                        x => x.Name == "Windows Live").First();
appointments.SearchAsync(
    DateTime.Now, DateTime.Now.AddMonths(6), account, null);
```

Sample Appointments Page

The example for this section allows the user to retrieve the list of appointments for a specified period. The `AppointmentsViewModel` class, located in the downloadable sample code, contains a `StartTimeInclusive` property and an `EndTimeInclusive` property, which are used to specify the period (see Listing 14.13).

A `DelegateCommand` named `SearchCommand` calls the `SearchAppointments` method when it is executed. When the `SearchCompleted` handler is called, the `Appointments` property is populated with the result.

LISTING 14.13 `AppointmentsViewModel` Class

```
public class AppointmentsViewModel : ViewModelBase
{
    public AppointmentsViewModel() : base("appointments")
    {
        searchCommand = new DelegateCommand(arg => SearchAppointments());
    }

    Appointments appointments;

    void SearchAppointments()
    {
        appointments = new Appointments();
        appointments.SearchCompleted += HandleSearchCompleted;
        appointments.SearchAsync(startTimeInclusive, endTimeInclusive, null);
```

```
}
void HandleSearchCompleted(object sender, AppointmentsSearchEventArgs e)
{
    if (e.Results == null)
    {
        return;
    }
    Appointments = e.Results;
}


IEnumerable<Appointment> appointmentList = new List<Appointment>();

public IEnumerable<Appointment> Appointments
{
    get
    {
        return appointmentList;
    }
    private set
    {
        Assign(ref appointmentList, value);
    }
}
readonly DelegateCommand searchCommand;

public ICommand SearchCommand
{
    get
    {
        return searchCommand;
    }
}


DateTime startTimeInclusive = DateTime.Now.AddYears(-1);

public DateTime StartTimeInclusive
{
    get
    {
        return startTimeInclusive;
    }
    set
    {
        Assign(ref startTimeInclusive, value);
    }
}
```

```
DateTime endTimeInclusive = DateTime.Now.AddYears(1);

public DateTime EndTimeInclusive
{
    get
    {
        return endTimeInclusive;
    }
    set
    {
        Assign(ref endTimeInclusive, value);
    }
}
}
```

The view contains two Windows Phone Toolkit `ListPicker` controls that are bound to the viewmodel's `StartTimeInclusive` and `EndTimeInclusive` properties (see Listing 14.14).

Results are displayed using a `ListBox`, whose `ItemsSource` property is bound to the viewmodel's `Appointments` property. Each `Appointment` object is presented using a `TextBlock` to display its `StartTime`, `Subject`, and `Details` properties.

LISTING 14.14   AppointmentsView.xaml (excerpt)

```xml
<StackPanel x:Name="ContentPanel" Grid.Row="1">
    <toolkit:DatePicker Value="{Binding StartTimeInclusive, Mode=TwoWay}"
                        Header="start"/>
    <toolkit:DatePicker Value="{Binding EndTimeInclusive, Mode=TwoWay}"
                        Header="end"/>

    <ListBox ItemsSource="{Binding Appointments}">
        <ListBox.ItemTemplate>
            <DataTemplate>
                <StackPanel Margin="0,0,0,20">
                    <TextBlock Text="{Binding StartTime}"
                        Style="{StaticResource PhoneTextNormalStyle}" />
                    <TextBlock Text="{Binding Subject}"
                        Style="{StaticResource PhoneTextLargeStyle}" />
                    <TextBlock Text="{Binding Details}"
                        Style="{StaticResource PhoneTextNormalStyle}" />
                </StackPanel>
            </DataTemplate>
        </ListBox.ItemTemplate>
    </ListBox>
</StackPanel>
```

In addition, the view includes an AppBarIconButton that is bound to the viewmodel's SearchCommand, as shown:

```
<u:AppBar>
    <u:AppBarIconButton
                Command="{Binding SearchCommand}"
                Text="search"
                IconUri="/Images/ApplicationBarIcons/AppBarSearch.png" />
</u:AppBar>
```

When the user taps the application bar button, appointments that fall within the specified date range are displayed at the bottom of the page (see Figure 14.38).

FIGURE 14.38   AppointmentsView page.

By using the Appointments and Contacts classes, you are able to further integrate your app with the social networking features of the phone.

Saving an Appointment Using the SaveAppointmentTask

New to Windows Phone 8 is the SaveAppointmentTask, which allows you to save an appointment via the phone's built-in Calendar app.

`SaveAppointmentTask` contains various optional properties that allow you to prepopulate the appointment UI in the Calendar app when the task is shown. The following example demonstrates how to create a new appointment.

```
SaveAppointmentTask task = new SaveAppointmentTask
    {
        AppointmentStatus = AppointmentStatus.Busy,
        StartTime = DateTime.Now.AddDays(1),
        EndTime = DateTime.Now.AddDays(1).AddMinutes(15),
        IsAllDayEvent = false,
        Location = "Meeting room 10F",
        Reminder = Reminder.FifteenMinutes,
        Subject = "Project X planning meeting",
        Details = "Meeting to discuss Project X"
    };

task.Show();
```

`SaveAppointmentTask` has no `Completed` event; therefore, the only way to determine if the user completed the task, and did not cancel out of the task, is to query the appointment's collection after the task has been shown. Yet, because the user has the option to change any or all of the information in the appointment before it is added to the calendar, there is no way of knowing for certain if the appointment has been saved.

> **NOTE**
>
> All properties of the `SaveAppointmentTask` are optional. If, however, you attempt to show the task and the `EndTime` occurs before the `StartTime` property, an `InvalidOperationException` is raised.

The source code for this section resides in the ContactsAndAppointments directory of the WPUnleashed.Examples project, in the downloadable sample code. The `AppointmentCreationViewModel` class contains various properties that map to properties of the `SaveAppointmentTask` class. An appbar button in the view allows the user to launch the task, which then launches the built-in Calendar app.

Summary

This chapter began by looking at the two types of tasks: launchers and choosers. Launchers have no common base class, yet choosers all derive from `ChooserBase<TTaskEventArgs>`, which has a `Completed` event.

The chapter then explored the execution model of choosers and the internal workings of `ChooserBase.Completed` event subscriptions that span across application lifetimes. Each launcher and chooser was discussed in detail.

Finally, the chapter examined how to programmatically retrieve contact and appointment information in a read-only manner.

CHAPTER 15

Receiving Messages from the Cloud Using Push Notification

Push notification is a server to client, or cloud to phone, messaging system that allows notifications to be sent from the cloud to the phone and then displayed to the phone user. Notifications are one-way messages that are normally associated with a particular application and may be delivered both while the application is running and not running. The main purpose of the push notification system is to reduce the power consumption of the phone device, thereby increasing battery life.

This chapter begins with an overview of push notification, starting with the three types of push notifications: toast, tile, and raw notifications. The chapter examines the various types of channel errors that can occur during push notification and how the phone's battery level affects delivery of push notifications. Cloud service authentication using X.509 certificates is also discussed, as well as how to update an application tile without tile notifications using shell tile schedules.

Finally, the chapter explores a custom stock ticker sample app that allows the user to enter a stock symbol into the phone, after which a cloud service periodically notifies the phone of stock price variations.

Push Notifications Types

Windows Phone supports the following three types of push notifications:

▶ **Toast notification**—A systemwide notification that is shown for a few seconds at the top of the phone's display.

▶ **Tile notification**—Displays information using a tile on the Start Experience (home screen).

▶ **Raw notification**—Offers a completely flexible manner for delivering notifications to your running app. The OS does not display a raw notification, but rather the notification message is sent directly to your running app.

Benefits of Push Notification

The Microsoft Push Notification Service (MPNS) is designed to be resilient and to expose a persistent channel for sending notifications to Windows Phone devices.

Apart from some special cases, the Windows Phone platform does not allow multiple apps to be running at the same time.[1] The main reason is that, in most cases, it is not efficient to have background apps consuming device resources, such as maintaining an open connection and sending data over the wire. Network activity results in high power consumption and decreased battery life.

> **NOTE**
>
> By battery life I mean the amount of time a device runs before it requires a recharge. Conversely, battery lifespan means the total amount of time a battery lasts before it is discarded and replaced with a new battery.

Push notification reduces power consumption in several ways; most notably it uses a single shared network connection, eliminating the need for private persistent open connections. If an app needs to be running merely to receive updates from the cloud, a better approach is to use push notification. The push notification model has the following benefits:

▶ **Offline capability**—Windows Phone apps should be designed to be tolerant of interruptions as they may be deactivated or terminated at any time. Push notification allows the user to act on some information, even when your app is not running.

▶ **Notification aggregation**—Multiple notifications for different apps can be pushed at the same time.

▶ **Notification prioritization**—Notifications can be assigned a priority, which affects when the notification is delivered. This control allows a developer to assign lower priorities to those notifications that do not require immediate attention, thereby reducing the device's network activity.

▶ **Connection pooling**—It is more efficient to use a single shared network connection than to have each app owning its own connection.

---

1. Background tasks allow an app to run in the background periodically for short periods. For more information, see Chapter 32, "Conducting Background Activities with Scheduled Actions."

▶ **Small message size**—Notifications are designed to carry a small payload. This forces you to think carefully about what information is really necessary to be conveyed.

▶ **Deterministic behavior**—Tile and toast notifications use a well-defined format with a fixed set of data properties, which allows the OS to present them automatically.

▶ **Eliminates polling**—Apps that want to receive messages from a cloud service without the use of push notification must periodically poll the cloud service. Push notification eliminates the need for custom network communication code and for private persistent open connections.

Understanding Push Notification

Push notification relies on the MPNS to dispatch notifications to the phone. The process works like this:

1. A phone app requests subscription to the MPNS using a notification channel.

2. The MPNS returns a URI, where notifications can be sent.

3. The phone app forwards the URI to any third-party service (such as a web service created by you) that wants to send the phone app notifications (see Figure 15.1).

FIGURE 15.1   An app subscribes to the MPNS, which is then forwarded to a third-party server.

The Push Notification URI is the address of the MPNS plus an identifier for phone device. Having received the push notification URI, a third-party service is then able to send notifications to the phone, via the MPNS, as shown in Figure 15.2.

> **NOTE**
>
> The notification channel URI is not guaranteed to remain the same. Therefore, each time a phone app launches, it is expected to send its notification channel URI to its corresponding cloud service.

FIGURE 15.2   Your server sends a notification to the MPNS, which is then forwarded to the phone.

Notifications from the cloud service use a well-defined protocol for sending notifications to the MPNS. Subsequent sections of the chapter examine the protocol format for the various notification types.

> **NOTE**
>
> Microsoft does not offer a Service Level Agreement (SLA) for the delivery of push notifications.

Getting Started with Push Notification

The main CLR types used in push notification reside in the
`Microsoft.Phone.Notification` namespace.

To enable an application to use push notification, the ID_CAP_PUSH_NOTIFICATION
capability must be present in the WMAppManifest.xml file. Although not explicitly
required for push notification, the ID_CAP_NETWORKING capability is also required if
you want to notify a cloud service of the existence of an MNPS URI. Push notification is
useless in most cases without the latter capability.

The following excerpt shows the capabilities needed for push notification in the
WMAppManifest.xml file:

```
<Capabilities>
  <Capability Name="ID_CAP_NETWORKING" />
  <Capability Name="ID_CAP_PUSH_NOTIFICATION" />
</Capabilities>
```

For more information on application capabilities, see Chapter 2, "Fundamental Concepts
in Windows Phone Development."

> **NOTE**
>
> To pass certification for the Windows Phone marketplace, an app must provide the user
> with the ability to disable toast and tile notifications. The user must have the ability to
> perform this task from within the app.
>
> Furthermore, before calling either the `HttpNotificationChannel.BindtoShellToast` or
> `HttpNotificationChannel.BindToShellTile` methods for the first time, an application
> must explicitly ask the user for permission.
>
> These requirements give the user control over if and when push notification is used.

Subscribing to Push Notification

To subscribe to push notification within an app, we first attempt to retrieve an existing
`HttpNotificationChannel` by name.

```
channel = HttpNotificationChannel.Find("<a channel name>");
```

The `HttpNotificationChannel.Find` method does not raise an `Exception` and returns `null`
if the channel with the specified name is not found. If so, a new instance must be created.

The Push Notification sample in the downloadable code contains a class called
`PushNotificationSubscriber`, which manages subscription to the MPNS by wrapping a
notification channel. The main benefit of using a wrapper for the notification channel is
that if the `PushNotificationSubscriber` instance is unable to perform the subscription

to the MPNS, due to the absence of a network connection for example, it automatically retries.

If the channel cannot be found, a new channel is created as shown:

```
if (channel == null)
{
    channel = string.IsNullOrEmpty(serviceName)
        ? new HttpNotificationChannel(channelName)
        : new HttpNotificationChannel(channelName, serviceName);
}
```

The `HttpNotificationChannel` constructor has the following two overloads:

```
public HttpNotificationChannel(string channelName);
public HttpNotificationChannel(string channelName, string serviceName);
```

The `channelName` parameter is the name that the app uses to identify the notification channel instance. This allows an application to retrieve an existing channel by name using the static `HttpNotificationChannel.Find` method.

The `serviceName` parameter is the name of the cloud service to which the notification channel is associated. The `serviceName` parameter may be used to subscribe to an authenticated cloud service. For more information, see the section "Cloud Service Authentication" later in this chapter.

After you have obtained a channel instance, it can be opened like so:

```
channel.Open();
```

Binding to the Shell

For the OS to display toast and tile notifications, the channel must call the `BindToShellToast` and `BindToShellTile` methods, as demonstrated in the following excerpt:

```
/* Toast Notifications. */
if (!channel.IsShellToastBound)
{
    channel.BindToShellToast();
}

/* Tile Notifications. */
if (!channel.IsShellTileBound)
{
    channel.BindToShellTile();
}
```

To stop receiving toast and tile notifications, the channel provides the
UnbindToShellToast and UnbindToShellTile methods, respectively.

BEST PRACTICE

When creating an HttpNotificationChannel, avoid keeping it open if not subscribing
to its events. It is not necessary for the channel to be kept open for the shell to receive
either toast or tile notifications, and the channel itself consumes valuable resources.

HttpNotificationChannel implements IDisposable and can be safely disposed after
binding it to the shell, as shown in the following excerpt:

```
using (HttpNotificationChannel channel
        = new HttpNotificationChannel(channelName))
{
    channel.Open();
    channel.BindToShellTile();
    channel.BindToShellToast();
}
```

NOTE

Calling the Open method on a channel may immediately raise an Exception, most
commonly an InvalidOperationException, if the channel fails to establish a connection
with the MPNS.

After retrieving or creating a channel instance, you are able to subscribe to its various
events.

CAUTION

Be mindful that each Windows Phone device is limited to a total of 15 apps registered for
push notifications. If the user installs 15 apps that use push notifications and your app
is the 16th one installed, an InvalidOperationException (channel quota exceeded) is
raised if your app calls BindToShellTile or BindToShellToast.

HttpNotificationChannel **Events**

The following is a list of the HttpNotificationChannel events:

▶ **ChannelUriUpdated**—This event occurs when the push notification URI changes,
which can be at any time. If and when the URI changes, the new URI must be
forwarded to any cloud services that send push notifications to your app.

▶ **HttpNotificationReceived**—This event occurs when a raw notification is received.

▶ **ShellToastNotificationReceived**—This event occurs when a toast notification is received.

▶ **ErrorOccurred**—This event provides a handling mechanism for exceptions raised by the channel. The handler for this event receives a NotificationChannelErrorEventArgs object, which contains an ErrorCode property, an ErrorType property, and a Message property pertaining to the Exception that was raised.

Handling Channel Errors

When a channel error occurs, the NotificationChannelErrorEventArgs.ErrorType property can be used to determine the nature of the error, as the following excerpt demonstrates:

```
void HandleChannelErrorOccurred(
    object sender, NotificationChannelErrorEventArgs e)
{
    switch (e.ErrorType)
    {
        case ChannelErrorType.ChannelOpenFailed:
            // ...
            break;
        case ChannelErrorType.MessageBadContent:
            // ...
            break;
        case ChannelErrorType.NotificationRateTooHigh:
            // ...
            break;
        case ChannelErrorType.PayloadFormatError:
            // ...
            break;
        case ChannelErrorType.PowerLevelChanged:
            // ...
            break;
    }
}
```

The following list describes the NotificationChannelErrorEventArgs.ErrorType enumeration values:

▶ `ChannelOpenFailed`—Occurs when the push client is unable to establish a connection with the MPNS. Note that exceptions resulting from, for example, a channel already being open, are raised at the call to the `HttpNotificationChannel.Open` method.

▶ `MessageBadContent`—Occurs when using tile notifications and the `BackgroundImage` URI is pointing to a remote image, despite the `HttpNotificationChannel` not being bound to a list of URIs. Tile notifications are discussed later in the chapter.

▶ `NotificationRateTooHigh`—Occurs when the push notification client is unable to receive messages because the cloud service is sending too many messages at too high a rate.

▶ `PayloadFormatError`—Occurs when the XML payload format, or the HTTP header of the push notification, is syntactically invalid. When this error occurs, the `HttpNotificationChannel` is closed and the channel must be reopened.

▶ `PowerLevelChanged`—Occurs when the device's battery level changes significantly enough to trigger a change in the push client's power policy. This topic is discussed in the next section "Power Management and Push Notification."

Additional error information can be obtained by examining the `NotificationChannelErrorEventArgs.ErrorCode` property, which identifies the HRESULT of the `Exception`. The HRESULT is a coded numerical value that is assigned to some specific exceptions.

Power Management and Push Notification

Even though push notification assists in reducing the power consumption of the phone, maintaining any kind of network connection unfortunately expends more power than most other device functions. Therefore, when the phone's battery level is low, to help reduce power consumption, the phone progressively prevents certain types of notifications from being received by the device (see Figure 15.3).

When an `HttpNotificationChannel` raises its `ErrorOccured` event with an `ErrorType` value of `PowerLevelChanged`, it indicates that there is a change to the types of notifications that are to be delivered to the device.

The `NotificationChannelErrorEventArgs.ErrorAdditionalData` property can be used to obtain the `ChannelPowerLevel` enum value, as shown in the following excerpt:

```
void HandleChannelErrorOccurred(
        object sender, NotificationChannelErrorEventArgs e)
{
    switch (e.ErrorType)
    {
        case ChannelErrorType.PowerLevelChanged:
            if (e.ErrorAdditionalData == (int)ChannelPowerLevel.LowPowerLevel
                || e.ErrorAdditionalData
                        == (int)ChannelPowerLevel.CriticalLowPowerLevel)
            {
                /* Power level is too low. */
            }
            break;
    }
}
```

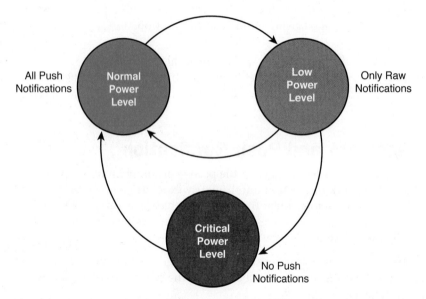

FIGURE 15.3   Device power states transition from a normal power level to low and to critically low.

The following list describes each of the ChannelPowerLevel enum values:

▶ **NormalPowerLevel**—The battery is not low. All push notification types are sent to the device.

▶ **LowPowerLevel**—The battery is low. Only raw notifications are sent to the device.

▶ **CriticalLowPowerLevel**—The battery is critically low. No push notifications of any type are sent to the device.

Sending Push Notifications

Sending a toast or tile push notification is done by creating an XML envelope containing the notification information, converting it to a byte array, and then sending it via an `HttpWebRequest` to the MPNS.

NOTE

When sending a push notification, only the HTTP POST method is allowed. Using any other method such as GET, PUT, CREATE, or DELETE results in a 405 MethodNotAllowed response. Moreover, a `ProtocolViolationException` results when writing to the request `Stream`.

For testing purposes, however, the HTTP GET method can be used, and results in a 200 OK response regardless.

An example of a push notification URL is http://sn1.notify.live.net/throttledthirdparty/ 01.00/AAGvdLTQzLGqRZ0FRZRVT1GBAgoOs1kPAQAAAAQOMDAwAAAAAAAAAAAAAAA.

The notification URL subscriber identifier, which is located after the final forward slash, does not need to resolve to an active subscription. This prevents a third party from fishing for an active subscription URL.

Raw notifications have more flexibility in their format; however, the process of sending a raw notification remains the same as that of tile and toast notifications. The following sections explore in detail how to send toast, tile, and raw notifications.

CAUTION

When sending a notification, the maximum size of a toast, tile, or raw notification body should not exceed 1KB. If this size is exceeded, a `System.Net.WebException` is raised, resulting from a 400 (Bad Request) response code returned from the MPNS.

For a complete list of MPNS response codes, see http://bit.ly/wd6SXy.

Toast Notifications

Toast notifications are systemwide action requests primarily designed for use with peer-to-peer communications. Toast notifications do not disrupt the user's workflow. They are, however, distracting and therefore should be used sparingly. Toast notifications are presented on the phone as a clickable overlay on the user's current screen even if the associated app is not running (see Figure 15.4). Toast notifications are, however, not displayed if the current app is the app that initiated the push notification subscription. If a user clicks a toast notification, the associated app is launched.

BEST PRACTICE

Toast notifications should be time critical and personally relevant to the user.

Assume that toast notifications are not enabled for your app, because they require the user to explicitly opt in to receive them.

FIGURE 15.4   Toast notifications are displayed as an overlay on the current application.

A toast notification consists of the application icon displayed at a reduced size and two text fields, one for a title, the other for the notification message.

Receiving a Toast Notification from Within an Application

The `HttpNotificationChannel.ShellToastNotificationReceived` event is used to receive toast notifications within your app, like so:

```
channel.ShellToastNotificationReceived +=
        channel_ShellToastNotificationReceived;
```

> **NOTE**
>
> Toast notifications are displayed only when your app is not running in the foreground. If your app is running in the foreground, the toast notification can still be received and handled in code.

When the `ShellToastNotificationReceived` event is raised, the handler receives a `NotificationEventArgs` object from which the relevant toast notification fields can be extracted, as shown:

```
void channel_ShellToastNotificationReceived(object sender,
                                NotificationEventArgs e)
```

```
{
    string text1 = e.Collection["wp:Text1"];
    string text2 = e.Collection["wp:Text2"];
    //...
}
```

Sending a Toast Notification

Toast notifications require an XML envelope for the notification information. Listing 15.1 demonstrates how the creation of an XML envelope is constructed and sent to the MPNS. An `HttpWebRequest` is created using the push notification subscription URL. The notification XML is converted to a byte array, and then it is written to the outgoing request `Stream`. After sending the request, the response is examined to ensure that it was correctly received by the MPNS.

> **NOTE**
>
> For more information on the `X-NotificationClass` request header, and setting a notification's priority level, see the upcoming section "Notification Classes."

LISTING 15.1   `PushNotifier` Class (excerpt)

```csharp
public PushNotificationSendResult SendToastNotification(
    string title, string message, string url, PushNotificationPriority priority)
{
    string priorityHeader;
    if (priority == PushNotificationPriority.RealTime)
    {
        priorityHeader = "2";
    }
    else if (priority == PushNotificationPriority.Priority)
    {
        priorityHeader = "12";
    }
    else
    {
        priorityHeader = "22";
    }

    /* Create the http message that will be sent
     * to the Microsoft hosted server. */
    HttpWebRequest request = (HttpWebRequest)WebRequest.Create(url);
    request.Method = "POST";
    request.ContentType = "text/xml";
    request.Headers = new WebHeaderCollection
```

```
                {
                    { "X-WindowsPhone-Target", "toast" },
                    { "X-NotificationClass", priorityHeader },
                    { "X-MessageID", Guid.NewGuid().ToString() }
                };

    /* The XML envelope contains the notification text. */
    string messageFormat = "<?xml version='1.0' encoding='utf-8'?>" +
                    "<wp:Notification xmlns:wp='WPNotification'>" +
                        "<wp:Toast>" +
                            "<wp:Text1>{0}</wp:Text1>" +
                            "<wp:Text2>{1}</wp:Text2>" +
                        "</wp:Toast>" +
                    "</wp:Notification>";
    /* Insert the message string. */
    string messageFormatted = string.Format(messageFormat, title, message);
    /* The message will be sent as a byte array. */
    byte[] messageBytes = Encoding.Default.GetBytes(messageFormatted);

    request.ContentLength = messageBytes.Length;

    using (Stream requestStream = request.GetRequestStream())
    {
        requestStream.Write(messageBytes, 0, messageBytes.Length);
    }

    /* Get the response after the message is sent. */
    HttpWebResponse response = (HttpWebResponse)request.GetResponse();
    string notificationStatus = response.Headers["X-NotificationStatus"];
    string deviceConnectionStatus
            = response.Headers["X-DeviceConnectionStatus"];
    string subscriptionStatus = response.Headers["X-SubscriptionStatus"];

    PushNotificationSendResult result = new PushNotificationSendResult(
        notificationStatus, deviceConnectionStatus, subscriptionStatus);

    Debug.WriteLine(result);
    return result;
}
```

An `HttpRequestHeader` named `WindowsPhone-Target` with the value toast is added to the request's `Headers` collection, indicating to the MPNS that it is a toast notification.

The XML format for a toast notification is shown in the following fragment:

```
<?xml version='1.0' encoding='utf-8'?>
```

```
<wp:Notification xmlns:wp='WPNotification'>
  <wp:Toast>
    <wp:Text1>WP Unleashed</wp:Text1>
    <wp:Text2>Toast example</wp:Text2> " +
  </wp:Toast>
</wp:Notification>
```

When the notification is displayed on the phone, the content of the `wp:Text1` element is placed in the title field of the notification overlay, while the content of the `wp:Text2` element is placed in the body field (see Figure 15.5).

FIGURE 15.5   Anatomy of a toast notification overlay

By default, the app icon is the ApplicationIcon.png file present in the root directory of the Windows Phone project. This can be customized from within the project's properties editor (see Figure 15.6).

Alternatively, the path to the image for the application icon can be modified manually within the WMAppManifest.xml file at the Deployment/App/IconPath element.

```
<IconPath IsRelative="true"
          IsResource="false">ApplicationIcon.png</IconPath>
```

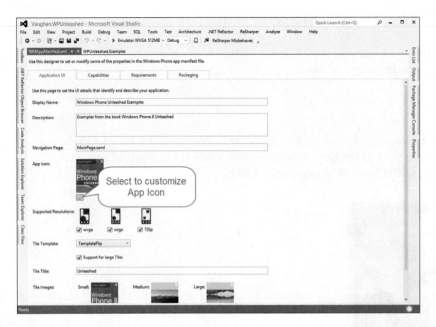

FIGURE 15.6   The application icon image can be set via the Application tab on the properties editor, within Visual Studio.

> **TIP**
>
> As you can see in Figure 15.5, it is wise to tailor the application icon so that it displays clearly at a small size when presented in a toast notification.

Tile Notifications

Tile notifications allow the application tile to be modified periodically, using a data driven template model, with a fixed set of data properties. Each property corresponds to a UI element, with each UI element having a fixed position on the tile. A tile notification can be used to communicate information sent from the cloud, such as updates from an email service, a social networking service, or a weather service.

It is at the user's discretion to pin an application to the Start Experience, and having the app pinned to the Start Experience is essential for receiving tile notifications.

When an application is pinned to the Start Experience, tile notifications are displayed regardless of whether the app is running.

The template for a tile notification consists of a standard three assignable data properties: a title property, a count property (also called a badge), and a background image property (see Figure 15.7). The three shell tile templates: flip, cycle, and iconic; provide additional updatable properties, which are described in Chapter 13, "Portraying Your App with Live Tiles." A cloud service may modify the content of an associated tile using tile notifications.

FIGURE 15.7   Anatomy of a standard tile notification.

Sending a Tile Notification

Sending a tile notification is done in the same manner as sending a toast notification; the differences are in the request headers and the format of the XML message (see Listing 15.2). As with toast notifications, we create an `HttpWebRequest`, build the message, convert the message to a byte array, and then write it to the request `Stream`. Finally, we verify that the notification was correctly received by the MPNS.

An `HttpRequestHeader` named `WindowsPhone-Target` with the value tile is added to the request's `Headers` collection, indicating to the MPNS that it is a tile notification.

LISTING 15.2   Sending a Tile Notification

```
public PushNotificationSendResult SendTileNotification(string title, int count,
    string imagePath, string url, PushNotificationPriority priority)
{
    string priorityHeader;
    if (priority == PushNotificationPriority.RealTime)
    {
        priorityHeader = "1";
    }
```

```csharp
else if (priority == PushNotificationPriority.Priority)
{
    priorityHeader = "11";
}
else
{
    priorityHeader = "21";
}

/* Create the http message that will be sent
 * to the Microsoft hosted server. */
HttpWebRequest request = (HttpWebRequest)WebRequest.Create(url);
request.Method = "POST";
request.ContentType = "text/xml";
request.Headers = new WebHeaderCollection
            {
                { "X-WindowsPhone-Target", "token" },
                { "X-NotificationClass", priorityHeader }
            };

/* The XML envelope contains the notification text. */
string messageFormat = "<?xml version='1.0' encoding='utf-8'?>" +
                    "<wp:Notification xmlns:wp='WPNotification'>" +
                        "<wp:Tile>" +
                            "<wp:BackgroundImage>{0}</wp:BackgroundImage>" +
                            "<wp:Count>{1}</wp:Count>" +
                            "<wp:Title>{2}</wp:Title>" +
                        "</wp:Tile>" +
                    "</wp:Notification>";
/* Insert the message string. */
string messageFormatted = string.Format(
    messageFormat, imagePath, count, title);
/* The message is sent as a byte array. */
byte[] messageBytes = Encoding.Default.GetBytes(messageFormatted);

request.ContentLength = messageBytes.Length;

using (Stream requestStream = request.GetRequestStream())
{
    requestStream.Write(messageBytes, 0, messageBytes.Length);
}

/* Get the response after the message is sent. */
HttpWebResponse response = (HttpWebResponse)request.GetResponse();
string notificationStatus = response.Headers["X-NotificationStatus"];
string subscriptionStatus = response.Headers["X-SubscriptionStatus"];
```

```
    string deviceConnectionStatus
            = response.Headers["X-DeviceConnectionStatus"];

    PushNotificationSendResult result = new PushNotificationSendResult(
        PushNotificationEnumConverter.ToNotificationStatus(notificationStatus),
        PushNotificationEnumConverter.ToDeviceConnectionStatus(
                                            deviceConnectionStatus),
        PushNotificationEnumConverter.ToSubscriptionStatus(subscriptionStatus)
        );
    Debug.WriteLine(result);
    return result;
}
```

The format for a tile notification is shown in the following fragment:

```
<?xml version="1.0" encoding="utf-8"?>
<wp:Notification xmlns:wp="WPNotification">
  <wp:Tile>
    <wp:BackgroundImage>
            ProjectSubdirectory/ExampleImage.png
    </wp:BackgroundImage>
    <wp:Count>
            An integer n, with 0 <= n <= 99
    </wp:Count>
    <wp:Title>Example Title</wp:Title>
  </wp:Tile>
</wp:Notification>
```

Additional properties can be appended within the wp:Tile element to update properties of a flip, cycle, and iconic tile.

When the notification is displayed on the phone, the content of the wp:BackgroundImage element specifies the URL of the tile's background image. This value can either be a local path within the project, or a remote URI such as www.example.com/ImageName.png.

CAUTION

A tile's background image size must not exceed 80KB. In addition, the download time for an image must not exceed 1 minute. If the image size is too large, or the download takes too long, the default image for the tile is used.

The wp:Title element denotes the title text to be displayed at the bottom of the tile.

> **NOTE**
>
> For information on how to create shell tiles or modify tile properties directly from your app, see Chapter 32, "Conducting Background Activities with Scheduled Actions."

> **TIP**
>
> Presenting too much information can slow down comprehension of a tile. Therefore, keep the style simple to improve clarity. When designing a background image for a tile, it is important to make different states easily recognizable.
>
> Do not presume that a background image will be placed on a particular screen color. Themes allow the phone's Start Experience color scheme to be modified. Therefore, when using PNG images as the tile image format, avoid using transparency if possible, as anti-aliasing may produce unintended discoloration around shape boundaries.

Updating an Application Tile Using a Shell Tile Schedule

You saw how to specify the background image of an application tile using push notification. There is, however, an alternative approach that lets you set the background image to a remote URI without using push notification, eliminating the need for a cloud service to issue tile notifications.

By using the `ShellTileSchedule` class the phone can be directed to periodically download an image from a remote server.

To create a schedule for a tile update, create a new instance of the `ShellTileSchedule` class and set the `RemoteImageUri` property, as shown in the following example:

```
string url = "http://www.example.com/ImageName.png";
ShellTileSchedule schedule = new ShellTileSchedule
{
    Interval = UpdateInterval.EveryHour,
    MaxUpdateCount = 10,
    Recurrence = UpdateRecurrence.Interval,
    RemoteImageUri = new Uri(url),
    StartTime = DateTime.Now
};
schedule.Start();
```

The following is a list of `ShellTileSchedule` properties that affect the download frequency:

- ▶ **Interval**—This property specifies the download frequency rate and is of type `Microsoft.Phone.Shell.UpdateInterval`. `UpdateInterval` is an enumeration with the following values:
    - ▶ EveryHour

▶ `EveryDay`

▶ `EveryWeek`

▶ `EveryMonth`

If the shortest frequency, `EveryHour`, does not offer a short enough interval, push notification or a background agent should be considered instead.

▶ `MaxUpdateCount`—This property defines the number of times the schedule runs. If this value is not set or set to a number less than 1, the schedule runs indefinitely. This value is ignored if `Recurrence` is set to `OneTime`.

▶ `Recurrence`—This property specifies whether the image is to be fetched periodically, or if retrieval of the image is to occur only once. The available values are `UpdateRecurrence.Interval` or `UpdateRecurrence.OneTime`.

▶ `RemoteImageUri`—This property is the fully qualified URI of the background image. It cannot point to a local image stored on the phone.

▶ `StartTime`—This property specifies the duration from the initial `ShellTileSchedule.Start` method call until the first time that the image is fetched. This property is used to delay the initial download of an image.

15

CAUTION

The same restrictions apply to images retrieved using a `ShellTileSchedule` as those in tile notifications. In particular, image size must not exceed 80KB, and the download time must not exceed 1 minute. If the image size is too large, or the download takes too long, not only is the default image used for the tile, but the tile schedule is also removed. The only way to reinstate a schedule is to rerun the schedule generation code.

Raw Notifications

Raw notifications are not displayed by the OS and are delivered directly to your running app, via an event. If your app is not running when a raw notification is received, the notification is discarded.

Sending a Raw Notification

Sending a raw notification differs from sending tile and toast notifications in that there is greater flexibility over the contents of the body of the notification.

Listing 15.3 demonstrates sending an object as part of a raw notification, using a `DataContractJsonSerializer`. As with tile and toast notifications, we create an `HttpWebRequest`, convert the content to a byte array, and then write it to the request `Stream`. Finally, we verify that the notification was correctly received by the MPNS.

LISTING 15.3   `PushNotifier` Class (excerpt)—Sending a Raw Notification

```
public PushNotificationSendResult SendRawNotification(
    object content, string url, PushNotificationPriority priority)
{
    string priorityHeader;
    if (priority == PushNotificationPriority.RealTime)
    {
        priorityHeader = "5";
    }
    else if (priority == PushNotificationPriority.Priority)
    {
        priorityHeader = "16";
    }
    else
    {
        priorityHeader = "26";
    }

    /* Create the http message that will be sent
     * to the Microsoft hosted server. */
    HttpWebRequest request = (HttpWebRequest)WebRequest.Create(url);
    /* HTTP POST is the only allowed method to send the notification. */
    request.Method = "POST";
    request.ContentType = "application/json; charset=utf-8";
    request.Headers = new WebHeaderCollection {
    { "X-MessageID", Guid.NewGuid().ToString()},
    { "X-NotificationClass", priorityHeader } };

    /* The message will be sent as a byte array. */
    byte[] contentBytes;
    var serializer = new DataContractJsonSerializer(content.GetType());

    using (MemoryStream stream = new MemoryStream())
    {
        serializer.WriteObject(stream, content);
        contentBytes = stream.ToArray();
    }
    request.ContentLength = contentBytes.Length;

    using (Stream requestStream = request.GetRequestStream())
    {
        requestStream.Write(contentBytes, 0, contentBytes.Length);
    }

    /* Get the response after the message is sent. */
```

```
HttpWebResponse response = (HttpWebResponse)request.GetResponse();
string notificationStatus = response.Headers["X-NotificationStatus"];
string subscriptionStatus = response.Headers["X-SubscriptionStatus"];
string deviceConnectionStatus
        = response.Headers["X-DeviceConnectionStatus"];

PushNotificationSendResult result = CreateSendResult(
    notificationStatus, deviceConnectionStatus, subscriptionStatus);

return result;
}
```

The use of the DataContractJsonSerializer is convenient because it allows you to serialize an entire object on the server in a format that is compatible with the phone. With
little effort the object can be rehydrated on the client. You could, however, use another
payload format, such as a string, as shown in the tile and toast notification examples.

TIP

The DataContractJsonSerializer type, as shown in this example, was chosen over
the more commonly used DataContractSerializer because JSON serialization is more
space efficient than XML, producing a payload of much smaller size. This is important
because the maximum body size for a toast, tile, or raw notification is 1KB.

The DataContractJsonSerializer approach relies on the content object's class being decorated with DataContract and DataMember attributes, as shown in the following example:

```
[DataContract]
public class StockQuote
{
    [DataMember]
    public string StockSymbol { get; set; }
    [DataMember]
    public double LastPrice { get; set; }

    [DataMember]
    public double ChangeInPrice { get; set; }
}
```

The DataContract and DataMember attributes provide the DataContractJsonSerializer
with the information it needs to serialize the StockQuote object. Neglecting to decorate a
property with a DataMember attribute causes that property to be ignored, and its value to
be absent when the object is deserialized in the client application.

Receiving a Raw Notification

To receive a raw notification in an app, subscribe to the
HttpNotificationChannel.HttpNotificationReceived event, as shown:

```
channel.HttpNotificationReceived += channel_HttpNotificationReceived;
...
void channel_HttpNotificationReceived(object sender,
                                           HttpNotificationEventArgs e)
{
...
}
```

When the HttpNotificationReceived event is raised, the handler receives an
HttpNotificationEventArgs object that contains a Notification property of type
HttpNotification. HttpNotification contains the following properties:

▶ **Body**—The payload for the notification. This is the main property of interest. It is a
Stream containing the raw notification data.

▶ **Channel**—The channel to which the notification arrived.

▶ **Headers**—The request headers that were supplied during the creation of the
notification.

The following excerpt from the PushNotificationViewModel class in the downloadable
sample code demonstrates how raw notification is handled on the phone, and in particular how the content object (in this case, a StockQuote) is rehydrated:

```
void subscriber_HttpNotificationReceived(
    object sender, HttpNotificationEventArgs e)
{
    Message = "Raw notification received.";
    Stream bodyStream = e.Notification.Body;

    if (bodyStream != null)
    {
        DataContractJsonSerializer serializer
                = new DataContractJsonSerializer(typeof(StockQuote));

        StockQuote = (StockQuote)serializer.ReadObject(bodyStream);
    }
}
```

A `DataContractJsonSerializer` reverses the serialization process by transforming the stream data back to a `StockQuote` object.

Identifying Notifications in an `HttpWebResponse`

Common to all push notification types is an optional custom header named `X-MessageID`, which can be added to the `HttpWebRequest.Headers` collection. Its purpose is to uniquely identify the notification message, and if present, the same value is able to be retrieved in the notification response. It must be a string that contains a universally unique identifier (UUID), as shown in the following excerpt:

```
request.Headers.Add("X-MessageID", "<UUID>");
```

At the time of writing, this header does not serve any purpose, because the resulting `HttpWebResponse` is retrieved using the original `HttpWebRequest`. It is, therefore, trivial to identify a notification based on an `HttpWebResponse`. In the future, however, this setting may be used in conjunction with an MPNS callback, to update the cloud service if a notification is impacted because of, for example, session expiry.

Notification Classes

Some kinds of notifications may be more time critical than others. For example, a notification indicating that tomorrow's weather forecast has changed may be less time critical than a notification about a traffic jam on your planned route home. The MPNS allows notifications to be assigned a batching interval, which works as a guide for the MPNS in determining when to deliver one or more notifications in a batch.

To inform the MPNS of the batching interval of a notification, a header named X-NotificationClass is added to the outgoing request. The batching interval is a string representation of an integer value. The set of valid priority values is determined by the kind of notification, be it a toast, tile, or raw notification.

When notifications are sent to the MPNS, they are placed in queues (see Figure 15.8). Each queue is serviced at different intervals according to its notification class. Accordingly, a queue for a lower notification class may be serviced more frequently than one with a higher notification class. For example, a raw notification with an X-NotificationClass of 3 means that the message is delivered by the MPNS immediately, a value of 13 means that the message is delivered within 450 seconds, and a value of 23 means the message is delivered within 900 seconds.

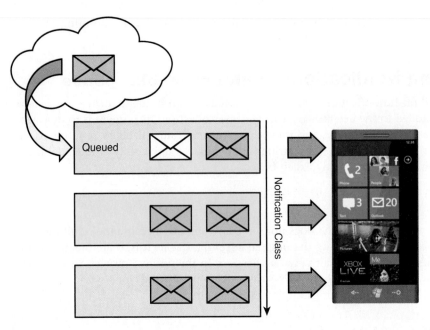

FIGURE 15.8   Notifications are queued and the notifications from each queue are periodically sent to the phone.

When sending a push notification, the X-NotificationClass may be omitted, in which case a default regular priority is used. Table 15.1 lists the push notification classes for each notification type.

TABLE 15.1   Push Notification Classes

Level	Description	Notification Class		
		Toast	Title	Raw
Real Time	Indicates that the toast notification is to be delivered as soon as possible.	2	1	3-10
Priority	Indicates that the toast notification is to be delivered at the next priority batch send. The interval is predefined. In most cases it is delivered within 450 seconds.	12	11	13-20
Regular	Indicates that the toast notification is to be delivered at the next regular batch interval. The interval is predefined, and it is longer than the priority interval. In most cases it is delivered within 900 seconds.	22	21	23-31

In the downloadable sample code, the notification class is represented as an enum called `PushNotificationPriority` and provides for strongly typed notification class values.

```
public enum PushNotificationPriority
{
    Regular,
    Priority,
    RealTime
}
```

Cloud Service Authentication

The Push Notification protocol enables a cloud service to send a notification to a phone application using a RESTful API. The cloud service can choose to operate as authenticated or unauthenticated by registering an X.509 certificate with the MPNS. An unauthenticated cloud service is limited to sending 500 notification requests a day for each subscription. Although in most cases this will suffice, having an authenticated cloud service removes this limitation, and an unlimited number of push notifications can be sent for the life of a subscription.

Authenticating a Cloud Service

To authenticate a cloud service, obtain an X.509 certificate issued by a Microsoft trusted root certificate authority. The certificate can then be registered on the Windows Phone Marketplace. The certificate is used to establish a Secure Sockets Layer (SSL) connection between the cloud service and the MPNS.

Creating a Notification Channel for an Authenticated Cloud Service

As mentioned earlier in this chapter, the HttpNotificationChannel has a constructor that accepts the fully qualified domain name (FQDN) of the cloud service certificate. The FQDN must match the registered certificate's subject name, which is the CN attribute. An example of a FQDN is www.example.com. Creating a channel using an FQDN is demonstrated in the following excerpt:

```
using (HttpNotificationChannel channel
        = new HttpNotificationChannel(channelName, "www.example.com"))
{
    channel.Open();
    channel.BindToShellEntryPoint();
    channel.BindToShellNotification();
}
```

Building a Stock Ticker Application

The main sample for this app demonstrates the three kinds of push notifications: tile, toast, and raw notifications. It is a stock ticker application that allows the user to enter a stock symbol into the phone, after which a cloud service periodically notifies the phone of stock price variations.

NOTE

When debugging using a phone device (not the emulator) a local WCF service is unreachable from the app. To allow a device to communicate with a local WCF service, configure Visual Studio to use IIS and use a machine name or external IP address in your WCF client configuration.

The server-side component of the sample application consists of a WCF service that allows the phone app to register itself to receive stock price update notifications. The server-side implementation retrieves stock price information periodically from Yahoo! Finance (see Figure 15.9).

FIGURE 15.9   The sample Stock Quoter application monitors stock prices according to stock symbol.

Input controls for the application include a text box, which allows the user to enter a stock symbol to be monitored, a Register button, and an Unregister button. Clicking the Register button causes the ViewModel's `RegisterForPushNotification` method to be called. This causes a `PushNotificationSubscriber` to be initialized and its events subscribed to, as shown in the following excerpt.

```
void Subscribe()
{
    if (subscriber == null)
    {
```

```
        InitializeSubscriber();
    }
    subscriber.Subscribe();
}


void InitializeSubscriber()
{
    subscriber = new PushNotificationSubscriber(
                        channelName, null, RegisterWithCloudService);
    subscriber.HttpNotificationReceived
                                += subscriber_HttpNotificationReceived;
    subscriber.ChannelUriUpdated += subscriber_ChannelUriUpdated;
    subscriber.ErrorOccurred += subscriber_ErrorOccurred;
}
```

A delegate is passed to the subscriber, which is used to notify the cloud service of the push notification URI after it is received from the MPNS.

As mentioned earlier in the chapter, the PushNotificationSubscriber handles the creation and opening of the HttpNotificationChannel (see Listing 15.4). When the Subscribe method is called, a channel is retrieved if it already exists; otherwise, a new channel is created. Subscription occurs to the channel's various events and the channel is opened. The channel then nominates itself to receive tile and toast notifications.

LISTING 15.4   PushNotificationSubscriber.Subscribe Method

```
public void Subscribe()
{
    try
    {
        channel = HttpNotificationChannel.Find(channelName);
        if (channel == null)
        {
            channel = string.IsNullOrEmpty(serviceName)
                ? new HttpNotificationChannel(channelName)
                : new HttpNotificationChannel(channelName, serviceName);
        }
        else
        {
            channel.UnbindToShellTile();
            channel.UnbindToShellToast();
            channel.Close();
            Subscribe();
            return;
        }
```

```
        UnsubscribeFromChannelEvents();
        SubscribeToChannelEvents();

        try
        {
            channel.Open();
        }
        catch (Exception ex)
        {
            channel.UnbindToShellTile();
            channel.UnbindToShellToast();
            channel.Close();
            WaitAndRetryChannelConnect();
            return;
        }

        /* Toast Notifications. */
        if (!channel.IsShellToastBound)
        {
            channel.BindToShellToast();
        }
        /* Tile Notifications. */
        if (!channel.IsShellTileBound)
        {
            channel.BindToShellTile();
        }

        if (channel.ChannelUri != null)
        {
            RegisterChannel(channel.ChannelUri);
        }
    }
    catch (Exception ex)
    {
        Debug.WriteLine("Unable to subscribe. " + ex.ToString());
        WaitAndRetryChannelConnect();
    }
}
```

If something goes wrong during the subscription phase, the subscriber waits 30 seconds and then tries again, as the following excerpt shows:

```
void WaitAndRetryChannelConnect()
{
    if (retryTimer == null)
    {
```

```
        /* Create a timer and have it fire once. */
        retryTimer = new Timer(o => Subscribe(), null, retryDueTimeMs,
            Timeout.Infinite);
    }
    else
    {
        /* The timer is changed to fire once after the period expires. */
        retryTimer.Change(retryDueTimeMs, Timeout.Infinite);
    }
}
```

PushNotificationSubscriber contains a field of type Action<string> named registerWithServer, whose task is to send the URI of the MPNS subscription to the StockQuoteService cloud service, along with the stock symbol for the stock that the user wants to monitor. By plugging in this behavior you can test the app without relying on the cloud service being present.

> **NOTE**
>
> The StockQuoteService implementation is for demonstration purposes only and lacks the capability to support multiple concurrent users. In supporting multiple users, it would be advisable to use a database to record each user's stock symbols, and to use a worker process to periodically query the database and to send notifications only when a price change occurs.

When the StockQuoteService.RegisterForStockQuoteNotifications method is called on the server, a Timer causes tile, toast, and raw notifications to be periodically sent to the subscriber (Listing 15.5).

The StockQuote result is provided by the StockQuoter class, discussed next.

LISTING 15.5   StockQuoteService Class

```
[AspNetCompatibilityRequirements(
    RequirementsMode = AspNetCompatibilityRequirementsMode.Allowed)]
[ServiceBehavior(InstanceContextMode = InstanceContextMode.Single)]
public class StockQuoteService : IStockQuoteService
{
    Timer timer;
    bool notify = true;
    int tilePushCount;
    string subscriptionUrl;
    string stockSymbol;
    StockQuote stockQuote;
    bool sendingNotifications;
    const int notificationPeriodMs = 30000;
```

```csharp
public void RegisterForStockQuoteNotifications(
    PushNotificationSubscriberId pushNotificationSubscriberId,
    string stockSymbol)
{
    subscriptionUrl = pushNotificationSubscriberId.PushNotificationUrl;
    this.stockSymbol = stockSymbol;
    notify = true;

    if (timer == null)
    {
        timer = new Timer(delegate
                    {
                        /* An exception must not be raised. */
                        try
                        {
                            NotifyWithStockQuote();
                        }
                        catch (Exception ex)
                        {
                            Debug.WriteLine("Unable to notify.", ex);
                        }
                    }, null,
            2000 /* 2000 MS = 5 seconds. */, notificationPeriodMs);
    }
}
void NotifyWithStockQuote()
{
    if (!notify || sendingNotifications)
    {
        return;
    }

    if (tilePushCount > 98)
    {
        tilePushCount = 0;
    }

    try
    {
        sendingNotifications = true;

        try
        {
            StockQuoter stockQuoter = new StockQuoter();
            stockQuote = stockQuoter.GetStockQuote(this.stockSymbol);
```

```
    }
catch (Exception ex)
{
    Debug.WriteLine("Unable to retrieve stock quote." + ex);
    return;
}

DateTime now = DateTime.Now;
Debug.WriteLine(
    "Sending notifications at " + now.ToLongTimeString());
PushNotifier notifier = new PushNotifier();

string background;
if (stockQuote.ChangeInPrice > 0)
{
    background = "PushNotification/Images/StockUp.png";
}
else if (stockQuote.ChangeInPrice < 0)
{
    background = "PushNotification/Images/StockDown.png";
}
else
{
    background = "PushNotification/Images/StockNone.png";
}

try
{
    notifier.SendTileNotification(
        stockQuote.ToString(),
        ++tilePushCount,
        background,
        subscriptionUrl,
        PushNotificationPriority.RealTime);
}
catch (Exception ex)
{
    Debug.WriteLine("Unable to send tile notifications:" + ex);
}

try
{
    notifier.SendToastNotification("Stock Quote",
                        stockQuote.ToString(),
                            subscriptionUrl,
                PushNotificationPriority.RealTime);
```

```
            }
            catch (Exception ex)
            {
                Debug.WriteLine("Unable to send toast notification:" + ex);
            }

            try
            {
                notifier.SendRawNotification(stockQuote,
                    subscriptionUrl, PushNotificationPriority.RealTime);
            }
            catch (Exception ex)
            {
                Debug.WriteLine("Unable to send raw notification: " + ex);
            }
        }
        finally
        {
            sendingNotifications = false;
        }
    }

    public void UnregisterForStockQuoteNotifications(
        PushNotificationSubscriberId pushNotificationSubscriberId)
    {
        notify = false;
        tilePushCount = 0;
    }
}
```

The GetStockQuote method creates an HttpWebRequest that is sent to the Yahoo! Finance
stock quote URL. This request produces a CSV (comma-separated values) file containing
the stock information of interest, including the price of the stock and the change in price
for the day. The following excerpt shows the GetStockQuote method:

```
public StockQuote GetStockQuote(string stockSymbol)
{
    string queryString = string.Format(
                    "s={0}&f=sl1p2d1t1c1hgvba", stockSymbol);
    string url = "http://download.finance.yahoo.com/d/quotes.csv?"
                + queryString;
    HttpWebRequest request = (HttpWebRequest)WebRequest.Create(url);

    string responseString;
    using (HttpWebResponse response
                    = (HttpWebResponse)request.GetResponse())
    {
```

```
        using (var reader = new StreamReader(
            response.GetResponseStream(), Encoding.ASCII))
        {
            responseString = reader.ReadLine();
        }
    }

    Debug.WriteLine("Stock Quote: " + responseString);

    var cells = responseString.Split(',');
    if (cells.Length < 3)
    {
        throw new Exception("Invalid response.");
    }
    if (cells[1].ToLower() == @"\na\")
    {
        throw new UnknownStockSymbolException(stockSymbol);
    }

    StockQuote stockQuote = new StockQuote();
    string changeInPrice = cells[2].Replace("\"", "").Replace("%", "");
    stockQuote.ChangeInPrice = double.Parse(changeInPrice,
        NumberStyles.AllowLeadingSign | NumberStyles.AllowDecimalPoint);
    stockQuote.LastPrice = double.Parse(cells[1].Replace("\"", ""));
    stockQuote.StockSymbol = cells[0].Replace("\"", "");
    return stockQuote;
}
```

The information that is sent back from Yahoo! Finance depends on the contents of the query string in the request URL. The format is like so:

```
http://finance.yahoo.com/d/quotes.csv?s=
                    <stock symbols separated by +>&f=<field identifiers>
```

For more information regarding the Yahoo! stock data format, see http://bit.ly/C5MPu.

The StockQuote class is a container for the information retrieved from Yahoo! Finance. It is decorated with DataContract and DataMember attributes so that it can be serialized for raw notifications, as shown in the following excerpt:

```
[Serializable]
[DataContract]
public class StockQuote
{
    [DataMember]
    public string StockSymbol { get; set; }
```

```csharp
    [DataMember]
    public double LastPrice { get; set; }

    [DataMember]
    public double ChangeInPrice { get; set; }

    public override string ToString()
    {
        return string.Format("{0} {1} {2}",
                       StockSymbol, LastPrice, ChangeInPrice);
    }
}
}
```

Sample App Notifications

The Stock Quoter app uses all three types of push notifications, which are described in the following sections.

Tile Notifications

Tile notifications are sent periodically from the StockQuoteService and are displayed as shown in Figure 15.7. The tile notification contains a Text1 data property equal to Stock Quote and a Text2 data property that is the result of calling the ToString method of the StockQuote object, which produces a combination of the stock symbol, the stock's last price, and its change in price.

Toast Notifications

Toast notifications are sent periodically from the StockQuoteService and are displayed as shown in Figure 15.4. The sample uses the title property of the tile notification to display the stock symbol, its price, and its change in price for the day. The count property is populated with an incrementing value, which is just for demonstration purposes.

Sample Background Images

For tile and raw notifications, the sample makes use of three images: StockUp.png, StockNone.png, and StockDown.png, located in the PushNotification/Images directory of the WPUnleashed.Examples project.

The logic for determining the background image for a tile notification is located server-side, as this excerpt from the StockQuoteService shows:

```csharp
string background;
if (stockQuote.ChangeInPrice > 0)
{
    background = "PushNotification/Images/StockUp.png";
}
else if (stockQuote.ChangeInPrice < 0)
{
```

```
    background = "PushNotification/Images/StockDown.png";
}
else
{
    background = "PushNotification/Images/StockNone.png";
}
```

Image paths are relative to the application project.

Raw Notifications

Raw notifications make use of the serialized StockQuote instance, as the following excerpt from the StockQuoteService class shows:

```
notifier.SendRawNotification(
    stockQuote, subscriptionUrl, PushNotificationPriority.RealTime);
```

The StockQuote instance is serialized to a byte array, which is then used as the content for the raw notification. For more information on the serialization process, see the previous section "Receiving a Raw Notification."

When a raw notification is received by the phone app and the StockQuote object is rehydrated in the PushNotificationViewModel class, the object is assigned to the viewmodel's StockQuote property.

The view displays the stock information via the viewmodel's StockQuote property, as shown in the following excerpt from the PushNotificationView.xaml file (style attributes have been removed for clarity):

```
<TextBlock Text="Price:" />
<TextBlock Text="{Binding StockQuote.LastPrice}" />
<TextBlock Text="Change:" />
<TextBlock Text="{Binding StockQuote.ChangeInPrice}" />
```

The stock direction image is presented using the viewmodel's StockPriceDirection property. When the StockQuote changes in the viewmodel, the StockPriceDirection property is reevaluated and a different image displayed in the view. The following excerpt shows the StockQuote property in the viewmodel:

```
StockQuote stockQuote;

public StockQuote StockQuote
{
    get
    {
        return stockQuote;
    }
    set
```

```
    {
        Assign(ref stockQuote, value);
        /* Set the direction so that the view
         * doesn't need to do any evaluation. */
        if (stockQuote == null || stockQuote.ChangeInPrice == 0)
        {
            StockPriceDirection = StockPriceDirection.None;
        }
        else if (stockQuote.ChangeInPrice > 0)
        {
            StockPriceDirection = StockPriceDirection.Up;
        }
        else
        {
            StockPriceDirection = StockPriceDirection.Down;
        }
    }
}
```

The view itself subscribes to the viewmodel's PropertyChanged event. When the
StockPriceDirection property changes, it determines what image should be displayed,
depending on its value.

```
void viewModel_PropertyChanged(object sender, PropertyChangedEventArgs e)
{
    if (e.PropertyName == "StockPriceDirection")
    {
        string url;
        switch (ViewModel.StockPriceDirection)
        {
            case StockPriceDirection.Down:
                url = "Images/StockDown.png";
                break;
            case StockPriceDirection.Up:
                url = "Images/StockUp.png";
                break;
            default:
                url = "Images/StockNone.png";
                break;
        }
        Image_StockQuote.Source = new BitmapImage(
            new Uri(url, UriKind.Relative));
    }
}
```

> **NOTE**
>
> Updating the UI based on a viewmodel property could be better orchestrated using the page's `VisualStateManager`. In Chapter 18, "Incorporating Map-Based Positioning," we discuss a custom `VisualStateUtility` class that allows you to bind the visual state of a UI element to a viewmodel property.

Opting Out of Stock Price Updates

The Stock Quoter application allows a user to unregister from receiving stock updates. By clicking the Unregister button, the viewmodel's `UnregisterPushNotification` method is called, which calls the `PushNotificationSubscriber` object's `Unsubscribe` method, as shown:

```csharp
public void UnregisterForPushNotification()
{
    try
    {
        Message = "Unregistering for notifications.";
        if (subscriber != null)
        {
            subscriber.Unsubscribe();
            subscriber.Dispose();
            subscriber = null;
        }
        Message = "Unregistered for notifications.";
    }
    catch (Exception ex)
    {
        Message = "Problem unregistering: " + ex.ToString();
    }

    if (channelUri != null)
    {
        try
        {
            UnregisterWithServer(channelUri.ToString());
        }
        catch (Exception ex)
        {
            Message = "Problem unregistering with server: " + ex.ToString();
        }
    }
}
```

When the `PushNotificationSubscriber` is disposed, its `Timer` and `HttpNotificationChannel` are also disposed. The cloud service is then notified that push notifications should no longer be sent.

Summary

This chapter looked at the advantages of push notification, and how it can be used to extend the battery life of the device.

The chapter began with an overview of push notification, starting with the three different types of push notifications: toast, tile, and raw notifications. The various types of channel errors that can occur during push notification were examined, and you saw how the phone's battery level affects delivery of push notifications. The chapter also looked at cloud service authentication using X.509 certificates, and at how to update an application tile without tile notifications using shell tile schedules.

Finally, the chapter explored a stock ticker sample app that allows the user to enter a stock symbol into the phone, after which a cloud service periodically notifies the phone of stock price variations.

CHAPTER 16

Sensing Motion and Attitude

Chapter 12, "Processing Touch Input," looked at touch input and gestures, which is ordinarily the first choice for user input in most Windows Phone apps. Yet the hardware of Windows Phone devices provides additional sensors that can be used for input, including an accelerometer, compass, and gyroscope, along with a combined virtual sensor called the motion sensor.

This chapter examines each sensor in detail, beginning with the accelerometer. You see how to process accelerometer readings, and how to simulate acceleration within the Windows Phone emulator. You learn how to apply data smoothing to accelerometer readings to decrease jittering of UI elements without sacrificing responsiveness. You also see how to calibrate the accelerometer and how to perform shake detection using the accelerometer.

The chapter then looks at the compass sensor and how to use the compass's magnetic heading to build a custom compass app that displays the heading using an arrow. How compass calibration is performed is also discussed.

The chapter then moves to the gyroscope sensor, and you see how to build a UI to display the angular rotation of the phone.

Finally, the chapter discusses the motion sensor, which is a virtual sensor that harnesses the other hardware sensors to improve accuracy and provide extended orientation and motion information.

Sensors Overview

All sensor classes derive from the class `SensorBase< TSensorReading>`, allowing you to work with what will become a familiar programming model. `SensorBase` ensures that sensors and readings are treated in the same way, a consistency that you will come to appreciate the more you work with sensors. The only variation occurs in the type of data that each sensor provides as a reading.

`SensorBase<TSensorReading>` has the following three properties:

- ▶ `CurrentValue`

- ▶ `IsDataValid`

- ▶ `TimeBetweenUpdates`

Windows Phone sensors use an event-based model for monitoring changes to sensor readings. When new data arrives from the sensor, the `SensorBase<TSensorReading>.CurrentValueChanged` event is raised, providing the ability to periodically process sensor readings. The type of reading depends on the type of sensor you are using. For example, the accelerometer uses an `AccelerometerReading`.

NOTE

The `CurrentValueChanged` event is not raised on the UI thread. It is, therefore, important to invoke any updates to the UI using a `Dispatcher`. This, however, poses no challenge if you choose to use the property change notification infrastructure present in the download-able sample code.

The interval between sensor readings can be set using the `TimeBetweenUpdates` property, which is of type `TimeSpan`. By default, this value is 17, 20, or 25 milliseconds, depending on the type of sensor. Setting the `TimeBetweenUpdates` to a value not supported by the sensor silently fails.

NOTE

If you require a specific value for the `TimeBetweenUpdates` interval, be sure to test the value of the property after it is set to ensure that the value was actually assigned.

The `CurrentValue` property holds the value of the most recent sensor reading taken. A good habit to get into is to make sure you check the `IsDataValid` property, which indicates whether the sensor's `CurrentValue` property contains valid data before retrieving the value from the `CurrentValue` property.

Two methods, `Start` and `Stop`, are used to start and stop acquisition of data from the sensor. Sensors consume native resources on the device and may unduly impact battery consumption if they are kept alive for longer than they are needed. It is therefore important to call `Start` only when sensor readings are needed, and to call `Stop` as soon as the new sensor readings are no longer needed.

`SensorBase<TSensorReading>` implements `IDisposable`. Calling `Dispose` on a sensor releases the managed and unmanaged resources used by the sensor. Obviously it is wise to dispose of sensors when they are not needed, such as when your app is deactivated; however, `SensorBase<T>` automatically subscribes to the `PhoneApplicationService.Closing` event, and when the event is raised, calls its own `Dispose` method. This means that, no matter what happens, resources related to the native sensor are correctly released when your app exits.

> **NOTE**
>
> The accelerometer, compass, motion, and gyroscope are limited to 10 instances of each type. If this number is exceeded, a `SensorFailedException` is raised when the sensor class's `Start` method is called. If this occurs, you can notify the user, providing this reason as a potential cause, and instruct the user to uninstall another app that uses the same sensor type.

The sensor classes available in the Windows Phone SDK reside in the Microsoft.Devices. Sensors namespace, and include the `Accelerometer`, `Compass`, `Gyroscope`, and `Motion` classes.

The following sections look at each sensor, beginning with the accelerometer.

Measuring Force with the Accelerometer

The accelerometer sensor measures the force applied to the device. The sensor detects the force of gravity along with any forces resulting from the movement of the phone. When the device is stationary, this force is equal to that of earth's gravity. Thus, when stationary, the accelerometer provides the position of the phone relative to the earth. When in the hands of a user, the accelerometer can be used to determine in which direction the user is moving the device, and when the phone is moved suddenly; while playing a game, for example, the force may exceed that of gravity.

The accelerometer is normally used for determining whether the phone is tilted. But it can also be used to allow the device to become the controller, such as steering a car in a game.

The accelerometer measures force in gravitational units (g's), where 1 g equals (by definition) 9.80665 m/s^2 (32.1740 ft/s^2).

Ideally, when stationary, accelerator readings range from −1 to 1. Slight variations introduced by differences in the earth's gravity around the world may take the value outside this range.[1]

Theoretically, if you dropped your phone, in free fall the phone's accelerometer should read 0.

---

1. *Gravity ranges at it is lowest in Mexico City (9.779 m/s^2) and highest in Oslo (Norway) and Helsinki (Finland) (9.819 m/s^2). Source: http://en.wikipedia.org/wiki/Gravity_of_Earth*

The accelerometer measures force in three directions. The acceleration value is represented as a three-dimensional vector, representing the dimension components X, Y, and Z axes (see Figure 16.1). The three-dimensional vector represents the direction from the point (0, 0, 0). For example, when the device is placed on a level surface with its screen facing upward, the Z-axis registers a value of –1 g. You can get a feel for the acceleration effects of tilting and flipping the phone using the sample page for this chapter, discussed in a moment.

Y is negative when this end points to the sky.

Z is negative when the front faces the sky.

X is negative when this end points to the sky.

X is positive when this end points to the sky.

Z is positive when the back faces the sky.

Y is positive when this end points to the sky.

FIGURE 16.1   Effects on axis values when facing upward.

Using the `Accelerometer` Class

`Accelerometer`, like the other sensor types, uses an event-based model for monitoring changes to sensor readings.

> **NOTE**
>
> Accelerometer contains a `ReadingChanged` event, which should not be used because it is a remnant of the first release of the Windows Phone OS and has been deprecated as of the 7.1 release of the SDK.

The event to use is the base class `SensorBase` event: `CurrentValueChanged`. Subscribing to the event can be done as follows:

```
var accelerometer = new Accelerometer();
accelerometer.CurrentValueChanged += HandleSensorValueChanged;
accelerometer.Start();
```

When the `CurrentValueChanged` event is raised, the event handler receives a `SensorReadingEventArgs<AccelerometerReading>` object, as shown:

```
void HandleSensorValueChanged(
    object sender, SensorReadingEventArgs<AccelerometerReading> e)
{
    ProcessReading(e.SensorReading);
}
```

`SensorReadingEventArgs` provides a reference to the `Accelerometer` via its single `Sensor` property. `AccelerometerReading` contains an `Acceleration` property, which is a `Microsoft.Xna.Framework.Vector3`. XAML apps do not have a type representing a three-dimensional vector baked into the SDK; thus, there is some crossover here, and `Vector3` is used throughout the phone sensor API.

Rather than relying on the XNA `Vector3` type in the sample code, a custom `ThreeDimensionalVector` class is used that has a markedly simpler implementation and uses properties rather than fields to access vector dimension values, which improves its compatibility with the XAMLdata binding infrastructure.

Simulating Acceleration with the Emulator

At times it may be difficult to test an app directly on a real device, such as when you are developing an app for a new version of the Windows Phone SDK that has not yet been rolled out to phone devices. Fortunately, the emulator has a tool for simulating the accelerometer, which can be accessed by clicking on the Additional Tools button of the emulator menu (see Figure 16.2).

FIGURE 16.2   Click the bottom arrow on the emulator menu to launch the Additional Tools window.

The Accelerometer tab of the Additional Tools window allows you to manipulate the position of the virtual device; moving the small red circle affects the reading taken by the `Accelerometer` class (see Figure 16.3).

> **NOTE**
>
> Within the emulator, the accelerometer is not subject to environmental effects, and readings taken within the emulator are perfectly stable.
>
> Although the emulator provides the means to test code that relies on the accelerometer, it is important to test your code on an actual device, to see how it behaves in real-world conditions.

FIGURE 16.3   The emulator's accelerometer simulator.

Smoothing Accelerometer Readings

The `Accelerometer`'s `CurrentValueChanged` event is raised, by default, 50 times a second and reflects the raw hardware sensor readings. Updating UI elements based on the raw values from the accelerometer can make elements appear jittery, much like the effects of Brownian motion under a microscope. You can allow your app to appear more stable by smoothing the readings received by the accelerometer through ignoring small changes in acceleration.

Some apps may benefit from some degree of smoothing, yet may need to react quickly to sudden fluctuations in reading values, such as games, which usually need input to be as direct as possible. This section looks at applying various data smoothing techniques to reduce jitter while also minimizing latency.

Much of the code and theory in this section is based on an article on the Windows Team Blog by Dave Edson at http://bit.ly/cXJ2EC. It is recommended that you take a look at the article to better understand the theory behind the smoothing algorithms employed in the sample code. The advantage of the sample code provided here is that you also have a number of other features included that you can take and use immediately in your own apps.

The example code for this section is located in the Devices/Sensors directory of the WPUnleashed project in the downloadable sample code.

In the example, a custom class called `EnhancedAccelerometer` is used in place of the built-in `Accelerometer`. The `EnhancedAccelerometer` class uses an `Accelerometer`, allowing the application of smoothing algorithms based on previous readings. `EnhancedAccelerometer` has a number of features that the `Accelerometer` does not, such as calibration support, shake detection, and data smoothing.

Like the `Accelerometer`, the `EnhancedAccelerometer` is `IDisposable`. When the `EnhancedAccelerometer` is disposed, it in turn disposes the built-in `Accelerometer`. So, too, `EnhancedAccelerometer` is started by calling its `Start` method, which instantiates an `Accelerometer`, subscribes to its `CurrentValueChanged` event, and starts the `Accelerometer` as shown:

```
public void Start()
{
    if (accelerometer == null)
    {
        lock (accelerometerLock)
        {
            if (accelerometer == null)
            {
                accelerometer = new Accelerometer();
                accelerometer.CurrentValueChanged
                                    += HandleSensorValueChanged;
                accelerometer.Start();
            }
        }
    }
}
```

`EnhancedAccelerometer` has a `Reading` property of type `EnhancedAccelerometerReading`, which not only supplies the raw value supplied by the `Accelerometer`, but also the following three smoothed reading values:

- ▶ `AverageAcceleration`

- ▶ `LowPassFilteredAcceleration`

▶ OptimallyFilteredAcceleration

Each value is the result of the application of a particular smoothing algorithm. The first, AverageAcceleration, has the highest latency (lag) of the three, while the other two attempt to combat the latency by responding to large reading variations immediately so that you get smoothing as well as responsiveness. These properties are examined in greater detail in the following sections.

AverageAcceleration

The AverageAcceleration property provides an average value of the last 25 readings. As stated, this approach has the highest latency; a large change in acceleration is less evident as the previous readings average it out. This approach may suit an app that requires input to be very steady—a spirit level app for example—but would not be suitable for a game that needs to respond quickly to user input.

LowPassFilteredAcceleration

The LowPassFilteredAcceleration property is calculated using the current reading and the previously calculated output. This approach has less latency than averaging, yet still does not respond to large changes in acceleration immediately.

The EnhancedAccelerometer.LowPassFilterCoefficient property allows you to adjust the level of smoothing applied to the output value. Each reading dimension value is calculated like so:

```
double newOutputValue = priorOutputValue
    + LowPassFilterCoefficient * (newInputValue - priorOutputValue);
```

By decreasing the LowPassFilterCoefficient, the more smoothing is applied.

OptimallyFilteredAcceleration

The OptimallyFilteredAcceleration property uses a low pass filter in conjunction with a threshold value, which causes the output value to be set to the raw reading immediately if the reading exceeds the threshold value. This approach eliminates the latency of the pure low pass approach for sharp changes in acceleration.

If the difference between a new reading and the previous output is greater than the noise threshold, the raw value is used, as shown in the following excerpt:

```
double ApplyLowPassFilterWithNoiseThreshold(
            double newInput, double previousOutput)
{
    double newOutputValue = newInput;
    if (Math.Abs(newInput - previousOutput) <= NoiseThreshold)
    {
        /* A simple low-pass filter. */
        newOutputValue = previousOutput
            + LowPassFilterCoefficient * (newInput - previousOutput);
```

```
    }
    return newOutputValue;
}
```

The noise threshold of the filter can be adjusted using the
`EnhancedAccelerometer.NoiseThreshold` property. Its default value is 0.05, and by
increasing the value you increase the level of acceleration needed to produce an immediate response.

Calibrating the Accelerometer

The built-in `Accelerometer` does not provide calibration support out of the box. Moreover,
there is no systemwide calibration setting that your app can update. It is up to your app
to have the user place the phone in a level position, calculate an offset value, and save the
offset value in isolated storage.

The custom `EnhancedAccelerometer` provides support for calibrating a device placed on a
level surface. It includes the following two calibration related methods:

▶ **bool** `CanCalibrate()`

▶ **bool** `Calibrate()`

`CanCalibrate` determines whether the device is stable enough for calibration to take place
and is determined by measuring the variation of the last several readings and whether the
current X, Y, and Z axes do not stray too far from the ideal level position. The level of
allowed variation can be specified using the `MaximumStabilityTiltDeltaAngle` property,
which is set to half a degree (0.5 * Math.PI / 180.0) by default.

The ideal level vector is (0,0,−1). The allowed variation from the ideal vector can be specified using the `EnhancedAccelerometer`'s `MaximumCalibrationTiltAngle` property, which is
set to 20 degrees (20.0 * Math.PI / 180.0) by default.

Sample Accelerometer View

The sample for this section is located in the Sensors/Accelerometer directory of
the WPUnleashed.Examples project in the downloadable sample code. It uses the
`EnhancedAccelerometer` via a custom `IAccelerometer` interface. This enables a mock accelerometer to be supplanted for testing purposes.

The `AccelerometerView` page presents four sliders for viewing the various readings from
the `EnhancedAccelerometer`. Its viewmodel, the `AccelerometerViewModel` class, contains
the following three commands:

▶ `StartCommand`

▶ `StopCommand`

▶ `CalibrateCommand`

StartCommand subscribes to the IAccelerometer.ReadingChanged event and calls the IAccelerometer's Start method, whereas StopCommand unsubscribes from the event and calls IAccelerometer's Stop method (see Listing 16.1).

CalibrateCommand uses the IAccelerometer.CanCalibrate method to determine whether the command can execute, which in turn sets the enabled state of the view's AppBar button.

LISTING 16.1   AccelerometerViewModel Constructor

```
public AccelerometerViewModel(IAccelerometer accelerometer) : base("accelerometer")
{
    startCommand = new DelegateCommand(
        obj =>
            {
                accelerometer.ReadingChanged -= HandleReadingChanged;
                accelerometer.ReadingChanged += HandleReadingChanged;
                accelerometer.Start();
            });

    stopCommand = new DelegateCommand(
        obj =>
            {
                accelerometer.ReadingChanged -= HandleReadingChanged;
                accelerometer.Stop();
            });

    calibrateCommand = new DelegateCommand(
        obj => MessageService.ShowMessage(accelerometer.Calibrate()
                                        ? "Successfully calibrated."
                                        : "Unable to calibrate."),
        obj => accelerometer.CanCalibrate());
}
```

When a new reading is received, the viewmodel's HandleReadingChanged handler sets the viewmodel's Reading property to the IAccelerometer's EnhancedAccelerometerReading, as shown:

```
void HandleReadingChanged(object sender, EventArgs e)
{
    IAccelerometer accelerometer = (IAccelerometer)sender;
    Reading = accelerometer.Reading;
    UpdateCommands();
}
```

The `UpdateCommands` method calls `calibrateCommand.RaiseCanExecuteChanged()`, which updates the enabled state of an `AppBar` button.

The view executes the viewmodel's `Start` command within the `OnNavigatedTo` method and the `Stop` command in the `OnNavigatedFrom` method, thus ensuring that the native `Accelerometer` is disposed when another page is shown or the app is deactivated (see Listing 16.2).

LISTING 16.2   `AccelerometerView` Class

```
public partial class AccelerometerView : PhoneApplicationPage
{
    public AccelerometerView()
    {
        InitializeComponent();

        DataContext = new AccelerometerViewModel(
            new EnhancedAccelerometer(new IsolatedStorageUtility()));
    }


    AccelerometerViewModel ViewModel
    {
        get
        {
            return (AccelerometerViewModel)DataContext;
        }
    }


    protected override void OnNavigatedTo(NavigationEventArgs e)
    {
        base.OnNavigatedTo(e);
        ViewModel.StartCommand.Execute(null);
    }


    protected override void OnNavigatedFrom(NavigationEventArgs e)
    {
        base.OnNavigatedFrom(e);
        ViewModel.StopCommand.Execute(null);
    }
}
```

16

The view's XAML contains a custom `AppBar` with an `AppBarIconButton` that is bound to the viewmodel's `CalibrateCommand`, as shown:

```xml
<u:AppBar>
    <u:AppBarIconButton
            Command="{Binding CalibrateCommand}"
            Text="Calibrate"
            IconUri="/Sensors/Accelerometer/Icons/Calibrate.png" />
</u:AppBar>
```

The view's main content panel contains several grids, each displaying a value from the `EnhancedAccelerometerReading`:

```xml
<Grid>
    <TextBlock Text="raw"
            Style="{StaticResource PhoneTextGroupHeaderStyle}" />
    <Slider Value="{Binding Reading.RawAcceleration.X,
            Converter={StaticResource SquashConverter}}"
            Style="{StaticResource SliderStyle}" Margin="0" />
    <Slider Value="{Binding Reading.RawAcceleration.Y,
            Converter={StaticResource SquashConverter}}"
            Style="{StaticResource SliderStyle}" Margin="0,30,0,0" />
    <Slider Value="{Binding Reading.RawAcceleration.Z,
            Converter={StaticResource SquashConverter}}"
            Style="{StaticResource SliderStyle}" Margin="0,60,0,0" />
    <TextBlock Text="{Binding Reading.RawAcceleration}"
            Margin="16,90,0,0" />
</Grid>
```

The `SquashConverter` is a custom `IValueConverter` that ensures the `Slider` always has a positive value that is within the range of 0 and 2, thus preventing binding failures.

The AccelerometerView page allows you to get a feel for the behavior of the accelerometer and to experiment with the various smoothing functions provided by the custom `EnhancedAccelerometer` (see Figure 16.4).

By placing your phone device face up on a flat surface, the calibrate button becomes enabled.

FIGURE 16.4   AccelerometerView page.

Shake Detection

The phone SDK does not come with any built-in support for detecting when the device is being shaken. This section extends the custom EnhancedAccelerometer to provide shake detection.

The EnhancedAccelerometer.IsShake method returns true if the difference between the current and previous acceleration readings exceeds a threshold value for two or more dimensional components, in which case, the movement is deemed a shake. Thanks to Mark Monster, http://bit.ly/9GMDJX, on which this code is based. See the following excerpt:

```
static bool IsShake(Vector3 currentAcceleration,
                    Vector3 previousAcceleration, double threshold)
{
    double deltaX = Math.Abs(previousAcceleration.X - currentAcceleration.X);
    double deltaY = Math.Abs(previousAcceleration.Y - currentAcceleration.Y);
    double deltaZ = Math.Abs(previousAcceleration.Z - currentAcceleration.Z);

    return deltaX > threshold && deltaY > threshold
            || deltaX > threshold && deltaZ > threshold
            || deltaY > threshold && deltaZ > threshold;
}
```

A `Shake` event has been added to the `IAccelerometer` interface. When a new reading is received from the `Accelerometer` within the `EnhancedAccelerometer`, the `DetectShake` method is called (see Listing 16.3). If a shake is detected, the `Shake` event is raised.

Two threshold properties control sensitivity during shake detection. Both threshold properties are of type double, representing the threshold in radians. The first, `ShakeThreshold`, is used to determine when a shake has begun; the second, `ShakeEndThreshold`, defines the maximum value of the acceleration delta, used for detecting when the device is no longer being shaken.

LISTING 16.3   `EnhancedAccelerometer.DetectShake` Method

```
void DetectShake(Vector3 acceleration)
{
    EventHandler tempEvent = Shake;

    if (tempEvent == null || !previousAcceleration.HasValue)
    {
        return;
    }

    Vector3 previousValue = previousAcceleration.Value;
    bool shakeDetected = IsShake(acceleration, previousValue, shakeThreshold);

    if (shakeDetected && !shaking && shakeCount > 0)
    {
        shaking = true;
        shakeCount = 0;
        OnShake(EventArgs.Empty);
    }
    else if (shakeDetected)
    {
        shakeCount++;
    }
    else if (!IsShake(acceleration, previousValue, shakeEndThreshold))
    {
        shakeCount = 0;
        shaking = false;
    }
}
```

The `AccelerometerViewModel` subscribes to the `IAccelerometer.Shake` event. When the event is raised, the viewmodel's `ShakeCount` property is incremented. `ShakeCount` is displayed using a `TextBlock`, as shown:

```
<TextBlock Text="{Binding ShakeCount, StringFormat='\{0\} shakes'}"
                Style="{StaticResource LabelTextStyle}"
```

```
Foreground="{StaticResource PhoneAccentBrush}"
HorizontalAlignment="Right" />
```

All Windows Phone devices are required to have an accelerometer, and the accelerometer API has been present since the first release of the phone SDK. It is, therefore, a staple piece of Windows Phone tech that offers a reliable way of enriching your app with movement sensing.

Measuring Direction with the Compass

The compass, also known as the magnetometer, is a Windows Phone required sensor that allows your app to determine which direction the phone is pointing—in particular, the offset from magnetic or geographic north.

The compass is useful in applications that use geographic location; for example, you may want to provide a compass arrow as a supplement for a mapping app. The compass also allows you to monitor raw magnetometer readings and to detect changes to magnetic forces around the device.

The sample code for this section creates a page that displays a compass arrow and the various compass readings, and you see how to allow the user to calibrate the compass.

The sample code for this section resides in the /Sensors/Compass/ directory of the WPUnleashed.Examples project in the downloadable sample code.

> **NOTE**
>
> The compass sensor is rather subject to interference. Bringing the device into close proximity of large metallic objects or other electronic devices, for example, a laptop, throws off the reading.

Using the Compass Sensor

The compass sensor is a required component of Windows Phone devices. In the first release of the Windows Phone OS (7.0), however, no API was provided for the compass, and some devices lacked the native drivers necessary to use the compass even when running the Windows Phone 7.5 OS (mango). If you are maintaining an app for a pre-mango device, it is therefore important to verify that the compass is supported before attempting to use it. For this, the static `Compass.IsSupported` property is used, as demonstrated in the `CompassViewModel` class (see Listing 16.4). The `Start` method of the `CompassViewModel` oversees the creation of the `Compass` instance.

The default value of the compass `TimeBetweenUpdates` property is 25 milliseconds, which on my test device was the minimum allowed value.

As with all sensor types, the `CurrentValueChanged` event is used to receive periodic updates from the sensor.

The `Calibrate` event allows your app to respond to when the phone is calibrating the sensor. Discussion of calibration continues later in this section.

> **NOTE**
>
> Calibration is an activity triggered by the OS; there is no `PerformCalibration` method that you can call to cause the device to begin calibration.

LISTING 16.4   `CompassViewModel.Start` Method (excerpt 1)

```
public void Start()
{
    if (!Compass.IsSupported)
    {
        MessageService.ShowMessage("Compass is not supported on this device.");
        return;
    }

    compass = new Compass();
    compass.TimeBetweenUpdates = TimeSpan.FromMilliseconds(updateIntervalMs);
    UpdateIntervalMs = (int)compass.TimeBetweenUpdates.TotalMilliseconds;

    compass.CurrentValueChanged += HandleCompassCurrentValueChanged;
    compass.Calibrate += HandleCompassCalibrate;
    compass.Start();
    ...
}
```

When the `CurrentValueChanged` event is raised, the event handler receives a `SensorReadingEventArgs<CompassReading>` object. `CompassReading` contains the five properties listed in Table 16.1.

TABLE 16.1   `CompassReading` Properties

Property Name	Description
HeadingAccuracy	A double value that indicates the level of accuracy of the reading in degrees.
MagneticHeading	A double value between 0 and 359 that is the difference between the earth's magnetic north and the direction of the phone device. This value is in degrees, and measured clockwise from the earth's magnetic north.
MagnetometerReading	The raw sensor readings provided as an XNA Vector3 struct.
Timestamp	A `DateTimeOffset` indicating the time when the sensor reading was taken.

Property Name	Description
TrueHeading	Similar to `MagneticHeading`, this property is a double value between 0 and 359 that indicates in degrees the direction of the device, measured clockwise from the earth's geographic north.

The handler for the `Compass` object's `CurrentValueChanged` event in the `CompassViewModel` extracts the values from the event arguments and assigns them to various viewmodel properties of the same name. XNA's `Vector3` data type is not amenable to data binding because it exposes its X, Y, and Z dimensions as public fields. Rather than use `Vector3`, a custom `ThreeDimensionalVector` object is created using the `Vector3` values, as shown in the following excerpt:

```
void HandleCompassCurrentValueChanged(
        object sender, SensorReadingEventArgs<CompassReading> e)
{
    MagneticHeading = e.SensorReading.MagneticHeading;
    TrueHeading = e.SensorReading.TrueHeading;
    HeadingAccuracy = e.SensorReading.HeadingAccuracy;
    Vector3 reading = e.SensorReading.MagnetometerReading;
    MagnetometerReading = new ThreeDimensionalVector(reading.X,
                                                     reading.Y,
                                                     reading.Z);

    SmoothedReading
        = readingSmoother.ProcessReading(e.SensorReading.MagneticHeading);
}
```

The raw sensor readings for `MagneticHeading` and `TrueHeading` are subject to slight variations in magnetic forces and, like the accelerometer, can make elements look unsteady when bound directly to the UI. A custom class, called `ReadingSmoother`, is used to dampen the stream of sensor reading values. I have abstracted the data smoothing code of the `EnhancedAccelerometer`, which was presented in the "Accelerometer" section of this chapter, into a new class called `ReadingSmoother`. The `ReadingSmoother` class uses the strategy pattern to allow you to change its filtering behavior via an `IFilterStrategy` interface provided to its constructor, as shown:

```
public ReadingSmoother(
        IFilterStrategy filterStrategy = null, int samplesCount = 25)
{
...
}
```

Listing 16.5 shows the `ReadingSmoother.ProcessReading` method. `ReadingSmoother` tracks the previous 25 values provided to it and uses the `IFilterStrategy` to smooth the data.

16

LISTING 16.5   `ReadingSmoother.ProcessReading` Method

```
public double ProcessReading(double rawValue)
{
    double result = rawValue;

    if (!initialized)
    {
        lock (initilizedLock)
        {
            if (!initialized)
            {
                /* Initialize buffer with first value. */
                sampleSum = rawValue * samplesCount;
                averageValue = rawValue;

                for (int i = 0; i < samplesCount; i++)
                {
                    sampleBuffer[i] = averageValue;
                }

                initialized = true;
            }
        }
    }


    double latestValue;
    if (filterStrategy != null)
    {
        latestValue = result = filterStrategy.ApplyFilter(rawValue, result);
    }
    else
    {
        latestValue = rawValue;
    }
    /* Increment circular buffer insertion index. */
    if (++sampleIndex >= samplesCount)
    {
        /* If at max length then wrap samples back
         * to the beginning position in the list. */
        sampleIndex = 0;
    }
    /* Add new and remove old at sampleIndex. */
    sampleSum += latestValue;
    sampleSum -= sampleBuffer[sampleIndex];
    sampleBuffer[sampleIndex] = latestValue;
```

```
    averageValue = sampleSum / samplesCount;

    /* Stability check */
    double deltaAcceleration = averageValue - latestValue;

    if (Math.Abs(deltaAcceleration) > StabilityDelta)
    {
        /* Unstable */
        deviceStableCount = 0;
    }
    else
    {
        if (deviceStableCount < samplesCount)
        {
            ++deviceStableCount;
        }
    }

    if (filterStrategy == null)
    {
        result = averageValue;
    }

    return result;
}
```

The `ReadingSmoother` instance is defined as a field of the viewmodel, like so:

```
readonly ReadingSmoother readingSmoother
            = new ReadingSmoother(new LowPassFilterStrategy());
```

`LowPassFilterStrategy` removes noise from the raw sensor values, while allowing fast changes of sufficient amplitude to be detected. See the `LowPassFilterStrategy` source in the downloadable sample code for more detail.

The content panel of the `CompassView` page displays the various viewmodel properties, including the current magnetic heading and the accuracy of the compass. In addition, the viewmodel's `SmoothedReading` is displayed using an arrow. The arrow is defined as a `Path` element. An enclosing `Canvas` uses a `RotateTransform`, which is bound to the `SmoothedReading` property, to rotate to the compass heading value. See the following excerpt:

```
<Canvas Width="280" Height="100">
    <Path Width="275" Height="95"
            Canvas.Left="0" Canvas.Top="0" Stretch="Fill"
```

```
            Fill="{StaticResource PhoneAccentBrush}"
            Data="** Arrow points omitted **">
        <Path.RenderTransform>
            <RotateTransform Angle="-90"
                             CenterX="140" CenterY="48" />
        </Path.RenderTransform>
    </Path>
    <Canvas.RenderTransform>
        <RotateTransform Angle="{Binding SmoothedReading,
                            Converter={StaticResource NegateConverter}}"
                            CenterX="140" CenterY="48" />
    </Canvas.RenderTransform>
</Canvas>
```

A custom IValueConverter, called NegateConverter, is used to negate the value so that the arrow's heading corresponds to north, rather than the offset value. The NegateConverter.Convert method is shown in the following excerpt:

```
public object Convert(
    object value, Type targetType, object parameter, CultureInfo culture)
{
    double degrees = (double)value;
    return -degrees;
}
```

Figure 16.5 shows the CompassView page with the heading arrow pointing to magnetic north. As the phone is rotated, the arrow maintains its heading.

FIGURE 16.5   CompassView page with arrow pointing to magnetic north.

The *compass orientation* value, shown in Figure 16.5, is determined by the accelerometer. This value is discussed in the following section.

Compass Orientation

The compass API uses a single axis to calculate the heading, depending on the orientation of the device. The device may be flat with its screen facing up, or it may be in an upright portrait position.

The `Compass` class does not provide the means to determine which orientation it is using; rather, you use an `Accelerometer` to tell you.

The viewmodel's `Start` method also includes the initialization of an `Accelerometer` (see Listing 16.6).

LISTING 16.6   `CompassViewModel.Start` Method (excerpt 2)

```
public void Start()
{
    ...
    accelerometer = new Accelerometer();
    accelerometer.CurrentValueChanged += HandleAccelerometerCurrentValueChanged;
    accelerometer.Start();
}
```

The orientation of the compass is represented using a custom enum called `CompassOrientation`. It has two values: Flat and Portrait. Listing 16.7 shows how the `Accelerometer`'s `CurrentValueChanged` event handler calculates the orientation of the device using the Y and Z dimensional components of the reading vector.

LISTING 16.7   `HandleAccelerometerCurrentValueChanged` Method

```
void HandleAccelerometerCurrentValueChanged(
        object sender, SensorReadingEventArgs<AccelerometerReading> e)
{
    Vector3 accelerationVector = e.SensorReading.Acceleration;

    bool usingNegativeZAxis = false;

    /* Determine the orientation of the device. */
    if (Math.Abs(accelerationVector.Z) < Math.Cos(Math.PI / 4)
        && accelerationVector.Y < Math.Sin(7 * Math.PI / 4))
    {
        usingNegativeZAxis = true;
    }

    CompassOrientation = usingNegativeZAxis
                            ? CompassOrientation.Portrait
```

16

```
                        : CompassOrientation.Flat;
}
```

Calibrating the Compass

Over time, the compass sensor can become inaccurate, and this is exacerbated if it is exposed to magnetic fields. Calibration of the device is performed by the user, by moving the phone repeatedly in a figure-eight pattern (see Figure 16.6). The `Compass.Calibrate` event is raised whenever the OS detects that the heading accuracy is worse than 20 degrees, at which point it is your app's responsibility to display a dialog to the user with instructions on how to perform the calibration motion.

The `CompassView` page includes a `StackPanel` with the calibration UI, consisting of an image with instructions for performing the figure-eight motion (see Listing 16.8).

As the user performs the calibration motion, the accuracy level is displayed in a `TextBlock` that is bound to the viewmodel's `HeadingAccuracy` property. When the user is satisfied that she has improved the accuracy of the sensor sufficiently, she taps a done button. The button is bound to the viewmodel's `ToggleCalibrationCommand`.

LISTING 16.8   Calibration UI XAML (excerpt from CompassView.xaml)

```xml
<StackPanel x:Name="stackPanel_Calibration" Visibility="Collapsed"
            Background="{StaticResource PhoneBackgroundBrush}">
    <Image Source="/Sensors/Compass/Images/CalibrateCompass.png"
           HorizontalAlignment="Center"/>
    <TextBlock TextWrapping="Wrap" TextAlignment="Center">
        The compass on your device needs to be calibrated.
        Hold the device in front of you and sweep it through
        a figure eight pattern as shown, until the calibration is complete.
    </TextBlock>
    <StackPanel Orientation="Horizontal" Margin="0,10"
                HorizontalAlignment="Center">
        <TextBlock Text="accuracy is "
                Style="{StaticResource LabelTextStyle}" />
        <TextBlock Text="{Binding HeadingAccuracy, StringFormat=\{0\}°}"
                Style="{StaticResource PhoneTextAccentStyle}"
                FontSize="{StaticResource PhoneFontSizeLarge}"/>
    </StackPanel>
    <Button Content="done"
            Command="{Binding ToggleCalibrationCommand}"
            HorizontalAlignment="Center" />
</StackPanel>
```

The `Calibrate` handler in the `CompassViewModel` sets its `VisualState` property to a custom enum value Calibrating, as shown:

```
void HandleCompassCalibrate(object sender, CalibrationEventArgs e)
{
    VisualState = VisualStateValue.Calibrating;
}
```

The visual state of the page is controlled using a custom `VisualStateUtility.VisualState` attached property, presented earlier in this chapter. The attached property is bound to the `VisualState` property of viewmodel, as shown:

```
<phone:PhoneApplicationPage
    ...
    u:VisualStateUtility.VisualState="{Binding VisualState}">
    ...
</phone:PhoneApplicationPage>
```

The Calibrating visual state affects the `Visibility` property of the calibration `StackPanel`, as shown:

```
<VisualState x:Name="Calibrating">
    <Storyboard>
        <ObjectAnimationUsingKeyFrames Duration="0"
                Storyboard.TargetProperty="Visibility"
                Storyboard.TargetName="stackPanel_Calibration">
            <DiscreteObjectKeyFrame KeyTime="0">
                <DiscreteObjectKeyFrame.Value>
                    <Visibility>Visible</Visibility>
                </DiscreteObjectKeyFrame.Value>
            </DiscreteObjectKeyFrame>
        </ObjectAnimationUsingKeyFrames>
    </Storyboard>
</VisualState>
```

The `ToggleCalibrationCommand` is initialized in the viewmodel constructor. When executed it changes the `VisualState` from Calibrating to NotCalibrating, and vice versa. This hides the calibration UI when the user taps the done button.

```
public CompassViewModel() : base("compass")
{
    toggleCalibrationCommand
                    = new DelegateCommand(obj => ToggleCalibration());
}

void ToggleCalibration()
{
    VisualState = VisualState == VisualStateValue.Calibrating
                ? VisualStateValue.NotCalibrating
```

```
                    : VisualStateValue.Calibrating;
}
```

Figure 16.6 shows the calibration UI after having performed the calibration, bringing the accuracy to five degrees.

FIGURE 16.6   CompassView page showing calibration instructions.

The compass sensor enables you to easily add heading information to your app, and to build specialized apps that can detect changes in magnetic forces around the device.

Sensing Rotation with the Gyroscope

The gyroscope is an optional hardware sensor that can sense rotation. Although the accelerometer is able to gauge the orientation of the phone when it is stationary, it is not able to sense rotation. If the device is in free fall, the accelerometer reading is theoretically zero. In contrast, the gyroscope measures the rate of rotation around a particular axis, so that while the device continues to be in rotation the reading is non-zero. The disadvantage, however, is that because the gyroscope measures rotational velocity, and not position, it is subject to drift.

The sample code for this section creates a page that displays raw readings from the gyroscope, as well as providing a visual representation of the angular rotation of the device.

The sample code for this section is located in the /Sensors/Gyroscope/ directory of the WPUnleashed.Examples project in the downloadable sample code.

Using the Gyroscope Sensor

The gyroscope sensor is not a required component of Windows Phone devices. It is therefore important to verify that it is supported before attempting to use it. For this, the static `Gyroscope.IsSupported` property is used, as demonstrated in the `GyroscopeViewModel` class (see Listing 16.9). The `Start` method of the `GyroscopeViewModel` oversees the creation of the `Gyroscope` instance.

The default value of the `Gyroscope`'s `TimeBetweenUpdates` property is 20 milliseconds, which on my test device was the minimum allowed value.

As with all sensor types, the `CurrentValueChanged` event is used to receive periodic updates from the sensor.

LISTING 16.9 `GyroscopeViewModel.Start` Method

```
public void Start()
{
    if (!Gyroscope.IsSupported)
    {
        MessageService.ShowMessage(
            "Gyroscope is not supported on this device.");
        return;
    }

    gyroscope = new Gyroscope();
    gyroscope.TimeBetweenUpdates = TimeSpan.FromMilliseconds(20);
    gyroscope.CurrentValueChanged += HandleGyroscopeCurrentValueChanged;
    gyroscope.Start();
}
```

When the `CurrentValueChanged` event is raised, the event handler receives a `SensorReadingEventArgs<GyroscopeReading>` object. `GyroscopeReading` contains two properties: a `Timestamp` property of type `DateTimeOffset`, which indicates when the sensor reading was taken, and a `RotationRate` property of type `Vector3`, which retrieves the rotational velocity around each axis of the device (X, Y, and Z) in radians per second.

The handler for the compass's `CurrentValueChanged` event in the `GyroscopeViewModel` converts the `RotationRate` property of the event arguments, which is of type `Vector3`, to a custom `ThreeDimensionalVector` instance and assigns it to the viewmodel's `RotationRate` property (see Listing 16.10).

The viewmodel tracks the angular rotation of the device by accumulating the value of each reading into a `ThreeDimensionalVector` called `cumulativeRotationRadians`. The amount of rotation since the last `CurrentValueChanged` event is calculated by multiplying the rotation rate by the time since the last event was raised. Put simply: (radians/second) * secondsSinceLastReading = radiansSinceLastReading.

LISTING 16.10 `HandleGyroscopeCurrentValueChanged` **Method**

```
void HandleGyroscopeCurrentValueChanged(
    object sender, SensorReadingEventArgs<GyroscopeReading> e)
{
    GyroscopeReading reading = e.SensorReading;
    Vector3 rate = reading.RotationRate;
    RotationRate = new ThreeDimensionalVector(rate.X, rate.Y, rate.Z);

    if (lastUpdateTime.Equals(DateTimeOffset.MinValue))
    {
        lastUpdateTime = e.SensorReading.Timestamp;
        cumulativeRotationRadians = rotationRate;
        return;
    }

    TimeSpan timeSinceLastUpdate = e.SensorReading.Timestamp - lastUpdateTime;

    cumulativeRotationRadians
                    += rotationRate * (timeSinceLastUpdate.TotalSeconds);
    CumulativeRotation = new RotationAngles(
        MathHelper.ToDegrees((float)cumulativeRotationRadians.X),
        MathHelper.ToDegrees((float)cumulativeRotationRadians.Y),
        MathHelper.ToDegrees((float)cumulativeRotationRadians.Z));

    lastUpdateTime = e.SensorReading.Timestamp;
}
```

The viewmodel's `CumulativeRotation` property is of type `RotationAngle`, a simple custom class with three read-only properties: X, Y, and Z, all of which are of type `double`.

As with most of the examples in this chapter, the page calls the viewmodel's `Start` method within its `OnNavigatedTo` method and calls the `Stop` method within its `OnNavigatedFrom` method.

The `Stop` method of the viewmodel disposes the `Gyroscope` instance, as shown:

```
public void Stop()
{
    if (gyroscope == null)
    {
        return;
    }
```

```
    gyroscope.Stop();
    gyroscope.CurrentValueChanged -= HandleGyroscopeCurrentValueChanged;
    gyroscope.Dispose();
    gyroscope = null;
}
```

The GyroscopeView page contains TextBlock elements that display both the raw reading values in radians/second and the accumulated angular rotation values in degrees.

The cumulative rotation values serve to rotate colored rectangles. As the device is rotated, a RotateTransform is applied to each rectangle, as shown:

```xml
<Canvas Width="400" Height="400" Margin="0,50,0,0">
    <Ellipse Width="400" Height="400" StrokeThickness="2"
                Stroke="{StaticResource PhoneSubtleBrush}" />
    <Rectangle Canvas.Left="195" Canvas.Top="0"
                Width="10" Height="200" Fill="Honeydew">
        <Rectangle.RenderTransform>
            <RotateTransform Angle="{Binding CumulativeRotation.X}"
                        CenterX="5" CenterY="200" />
        </Rectangle.RenderTransform>
    </Rectangle>
    <Rectangle Canvas.Left="195" Canvas.Top="0"
                Width="10" Height="200" Fill="Red">
        <Rectangle.RenderTransform>
            <RotateTransform Angle="{Binding CumulativeRotation.Y}"
                        CenterX="5" CenterY="200" />
        </Rectangle.RenderTransform>
    </Rectangle>
    <Rectangle Canvas.Left="195" Canvas.Top="0"
                Width="10" Height="200" Fill="Orange">
        <Rectangle.RenderTransform>
            <RotateTransform Angle="{Binding CumulativeRotation.Z}"
                        CenterX="5" CenterY="200" />
        </Rectangle.RenderTransform>
    </Rectangle>
</Canvas>
```

Figure 16.7 shows the GyroscopeView page with the rotation of the device across three dimensions indicated by the three colored lines.

FIGURE 16.7   GyroscopeView page.

You may notice, while running the sample, that the cumulative rotation drifts over time. This drift is indicative of the main disadvantage of the gyroscope; the gyroscope measures changes in angular rotation, and not the absolute angular rotation of the device. This is where the `Accelerometer` has an advantage, because it can provide the same rotational information without drift. In the case of the accelerometer, however, the magnitude of the signal is biased by gravity. This is not the case with the gyroscope.

The next section explores the `Motion` class, which promises to overcome the disadvantages of the individual sensors by unifying them into a single software virtual sensor.

Improving Sensor Accuracy with the Motion Sensor

The `Motion` class provides access to a virtual sensor. There is no dedicated motion sensor per se, rather the motion API combines the readings of the accelerometer, compass, and gyroscope to provide an enhanced API that overcomes the shortcomings of the individual sensors. The motion sensor provides the greatest accuracy of all the sensors, eliminating possible sensor inaccuracy issues that occur when relying on a single hardware sensor. For this reason, it is recommended that the motion sensor is used when available.

As mentioned in the previous section, the gyroscope is subject to drift. The motion API alleviates the drifting of the gyroscope by combing its readings with the compass and accelerometer readings.

Accelerometer readings include the force of gravity applied to the device as well as the force resulting from the motion of the device. The motion API separates the gravity vector from the device acceleration and provides you with the device's attitude, consisting of yaw, pitch, and roll.

The Motion API can use two different sensor modes: normal and enhanced. Normal mode uses the compass and the accelerometer sensor and is less accurate than enhanced mode, which uses the compass, the accelerometer, and the gyroscope (see Table 16.2).

TABLE 16.2   Motion Sensor Availability

Motion	Compass	Gyroscope	Accelerometer
✓ (enhanced mode)	✓	✓	✓
✓ (normal mode)	✓	✗	✓
✗	✗	✓	✓
✗	✗	✗	✓

If your app requires the accuracy of enhanced mode, you should verify that the device supports the gyroscope sensor. If the gyroscope is supported, enhanced mode is used automatically.

> **NOTE**
>
> Determining whether a device supports all the sensors required by your app happens before the app is deployed to the device. When a user views an app on Windows Phone Marketplace, a warning is issued if the user's device does not support a sensor that is used by the app.
>
> The Marketplace uses the compass sensor to determine whether the motion API is supported on a device. If a user views an app that uses the motion API and her device lacks a compass, a warning is displayed stating that the application requires a compass sensor.

Using the Motion Sensor

The sample code for this section follows the same pattern as the code for the gyroscope. The viewmodel's `Start` method first tests whether the motion sensor is supported, and then creates a new `Motion` instance, subscribes to its `CurrentValueChangedEvent`, and calls its `Start` method. See the following excerpt:

```
public void Start()
{
    if (!Motion.IsSupported)
    {
        MessageService.ShowMessage(
            "Motion is not supported on this device.");
```

```
      return;
   }

motion = new Motion();
double interval = motion.TimeBetweenUpdates.TotalMilliseconds;
motion.CurrentValueChanged += HandleMotionCurrentValueChanged;
motion.Start();
}
```

The `Motion` sensor's `TimeBetweenUpdates` property is, by default, set to 17 milliseconds.

When the `CurrentValueChanged` event is raised, a `SensorReadingEventArgs<MotionReading>` object is passed to your event handler. `MotionReading` reading contains the following properties:

▶ **Attitude** (of type `AttitudeReading`)—Gets the attitude (yaw, pitch, and roll) of the device, in radians

▶ **DeviceAcceleration** (of type `Vector3`)—Gets the linear acceleration of the device, in gravitational units

▶ **DeviceRotationRate** (of type `Vector3`)—Gets the rotational velocity of the device, in radians per second

▶ **Gravity** (of type `Vector3`)—Gets the gravity vector associated with the `Microsoft.Devices.Sensors.MotionReading`

▶ **Timestamp** (of type `DateTimeOffset`)—Gets the time at which the reading was calculated

The `Attitude` reading is useful in allowing you to determine the position of the device, which is broken down into pitch, roll, and yaw. Table 16.3 describes each of the `AttitudeReading` properties.

TABLE 16.3   `AttitudeReading` Struct Properties

Property Name	Description
Pitch	A float value indicating the vertical relationship in radians between the Y axis of the device and the horizon. See Figure 16.8 for a depiction of the X, Y, and Z dimensional components.
Roll	A float value indicating the vertical relationship in radians between the X axis of the device and the horizon.
Yaw	A float value indicating the direction of the device in radians.
Quaternion	An alternative representation of the attitude reading. The `Quaternion` data type is an XNA struct that defines a four-dimensional vector (x, y, z, w), which is used to represent the rotation of an object about the (x, y, z) vector by the angle theta, where w = cos(theta/2).

Property Name	Description
RotationMatrix	An alternative representation of the attitude reading using an XNA Matrix struct.
Timestamp	A `DateTimeOffset` value indicating when the reading was calculated.

The `CurrentValueChanged` handler, within the viewmodel, assigns the reading to various properties within the viewmodel. The reading's `DeviceAcceleration` and `DeviceRotationRate Vector3` properties are converted to a `ThreeDimensionalVector` using an extension method. See the following excerpt:

```
void HandleMotionCurrentValueChanged(
    object sender, SensorReadingEventArgs<MotionReading> e)
{
    MotionReading reading = e.SensorReading;
    AttitudeReading = reading.Attitude;
    DeviceAcceleration
                = reading.DeviceAcceleration.ToThreeDimensionalVector();
    DeviceRotationRate
                = reading.DeviceRotationRate.ToThreeDimensionalVector();
    Gravity = reading.Gravity.ToThreeDimensionalVector();
    AttitudeReading attitude = reading.Attitude;
    Attitude = new ThreeDimensionalVector(
                    attitude.Pitch, attitude.Roll, attitude.Yaw);
}
```

Within the view, the reading vector values are represented in the same manner as for the gyroscope; lines are rotated using a `RotateTransform` that is bound to the reading value. In this case, however, values are supplied in radians and must be converted to degrees. For this, a custom `IValueConverter` called `RadiansToDegreesConverter` is used (see Listing 16.11).

LISTING 16.11   RadiansToDegreesConverter Class

```
public class RadiansToDegreesConverter : IValueConverter
{
    public object Convert(
        object value, Type targetType, object parameter, CultureInfo culture)
    {
        float f = System.Convert.ToSingle(value);
        float result = MathHelper.ToDegrees(f);
        return result;
    }

    public object ConvertBack(
        object value, Type targetType, object parameter, CultureInfo culture)
```

```
    {
        float f = (float)value;
        float result = MathHelper.ToRadians(f);
        return result;
    }
}
```

A `ControlTemplate` is used to display the four `ThreeDimensionalVector` objects on the page. A `Rectangle` represents each vector component, and the `RadiansToDegreesConverter`, defined as page level resource, converts the source value to degrees for the `RotateTransform`. See the following excerpt:

```
<Rectangle Canvas.Left="195" Canvas.Top="0"
        Width="10" Height="200" Fill="Honeydew">
    <Rectangle.RenderTransform>
        <RotateTransform Angle="{Binding X,
            Converter={StaticResource RadiansToDegressConverter}}"
            CenterX="5" CenterY="200" />
    </Rectangle.RenderTransform>
</Rectangle>
```

Figure 16.8 shows the various readings displayed on the MotionView page. The attitude meter shows the pitch, roll, and yaw as the vector components X, Y, and Z, respectively. The other three reading types, acceleration, rotation rate, and gravity, are also displayed.

FIGURE 16.8   MotionView page.

The `Motion` class also includes a `Calibrate` event that indicates when the compass needs calibrating. This event provides your app with the opportunity to display the calibration dialog, as discussed previously in the "Measuring Direction with the Compass" section of this chapter.

Summary

This chapter examined each Windows Phone sensor in detail, beginning with the accelerometer. You saw how to process accelerometer readings, and how to simulate acceleration within the Windows Phone emulator. The chapter explored how to apply data smoothing to accelerometer readings to decrease jittering of UI elements without sacrificing responsiveness. You also learned how to calibrate the accelerometer, and how to perform shake detection using the accelerometer.

The chapter then looked at the compass sensor and explained how to use the compass's magnetic heading to build a custom compass app that displays the heading using an arrow. The chapter also discussed compass calibration.

The chapter then moved to the gyroscope sensor, and you saw how to build a UI to display the angular rotation of the phone.

Finally, the chapter examined the motion sensor, which is a virtual sensor that harnesses the hardware sensors to improve accuracy and provide extended orientation and motion information.

16

CHAPTER 17

Building Location Aware Apps

Geographic location has become one of the principal uses of smartphones, and for good reason. Smartphones are portable, they go with us nearly everywhere, and they offer the kind of processing power required to make displaying and interacting with complex maps possible.

The Windows Phone SDK provides an API that makes working with geographic location straightforward. The geographic location APIs on the phone abstract the location-sensing technologies and unburden the developer from having to know anything about the specific hardware in the device. Your app can specify a desired accuracy, either low or high, and the phone does the rest; it decides what location sensing components to use.

The .NET location API is consistent across platforms and can be used in much the same way in a phone app as it can in a desktop CLR application.

This chapter begins with an overview of the location sensing technologies available on Windows Phone and then dives into the location API. The chapter looks at monitoring location changes and at simulating location changes using both the emulator's location simulator and a custom class compatible with unit testing and testing on a physical device.

Finally, the chapter delves into the Reactive Extensions (Rx) and looks at sampling events to make rapidly firing position changes manageable.

Location Sensing Technologies

Windows Phone uses the following strategies to determine its geographic location:

▶ A-GPS

▶ Wi-Fi triangulation

▶ Cell tower triangulation

Each strategy has advantages and disadvantages, depending on environmental factors and power efficiency requirements (see Figure 17.1). The following sections discuss the pros and cons of each technology.

GPS

Highest accuracy.
Highest power consumption.
Slowest startup speed.
Doesn't work indoors.

Cell Towers

Low accuracy.
Low power consumption.
Fastest startup speed.
Doesn't work in the wilderness.

Microsoft Location Service

Wi-Fi

More accurate than cell tower,
  but less accurate than GPS.
Medium power consumption.
Medium startup speed.
Usually only works in urban areas.

FIGURE 17.1 Sensor technologies available to Windows Phone.

> **NOTE**
>
> The term *accuracy*, used frequently in this chapter, describes how close a location reading is to the true physical location.

A-GPS

Assisted Global Positioning System (A-GPS) is a satellite-based positioning system, which is generally the most accurate of the geo location methods available on the phone. The accuracy afforded by A-GPS, however, comes with a power penalty. It uses significantly more power than the other two sensing technologies. Because of this, it should be used only when an application needs a high level of accuracy.

GPS uses radio signals from satellites and does not perform as well in dense urban areas. In poor signal conditions, signals may suffer multipath errors; signals bounce off buildings or are weakened by passing through tree cover. Later in the chapter, you see how to reduce the effect of multipath errors by applying a movement threshold to signal readings.

A-GPS is an extension to GPS. It improves GPS's startup performance by using an assistance server to supply satellite orbital information to the device over the network. This is faster than acquiring the information from the satellite itself, which can also prove difficult in low signal conditions.

Cell Tower Triangulation

Cell tower location uses triangulation against multiple cell towers to pinpoint the phone's location based on the ping time from each tower. The distance from a single cell tower can be roughly determined by the time it takes for a phone to respond to a ping. The location of the cell towers combined with their ping times allows the phone's location to be pinpointed (see Figure 17.2).

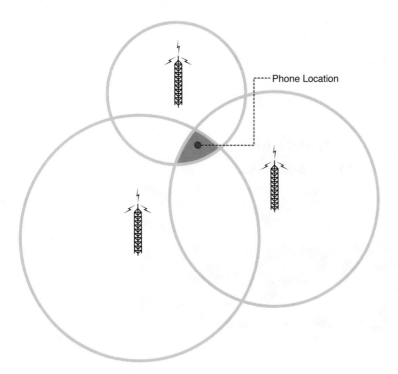

Phone Location

FIGURE 17.2   A phone's location can be pinpointed using cell tower triangulation.

Accuracy increases as more towers are included in the calculation.

Although cell tower triangulation uses less power than A-GPS, it is less accurate. Cell tower triangulation works best where there are more cell towers. Thus, areas such as city fringes or countryside may not provide an adequate level of accuracy. Unlike A-GPS, however, cell tower triangulation works indoors.

Wi-Fi Triangulation

Wi-Fi triangulation provides a middle ground between A-GPS and cell tower triangulation. Wi-Fi triangulation uses less power than GPS and can provide better accuracy than cell tower triangulation in some environments.

Wi-Fi location relies on a global location database of Wi-Fi networks and the ability of a phone device to detect Wi-Fi networks within its vicinity.

Wi-Fi triangulation works by detecting networks that are in range, measuring the signal strength of each network, and then triangulating the result using the Wi-Fi network location database.

> **NOTE**
>
> The Wi-Fi network location database is provided by the company Navizon; currently, no public API exists for accessing the data directly.

Geographic Location Architecture

The Windows Phone location architecture consists of three layers: a hardware layer, a native code layer, and a managed layer (see Figure 17.3).

FIGURE 17.3   Location architecture layers.

The hardware layer comprises the location related hardware components in the phone device, which includes a GPS receiver, a Wi-Fi interface, and a cellular radio. Each serves as a provider of location information with varying degrees of accuracy and power consumption.

The second layer, a native code layer, communicates directly with the hardware devices to determine the location of the device. The choice of hardware component, or combination of components, depends on the accuracy level requested by the app and the availability of data; there may not be any Wi-Fi networks in the vicinity, for example.

The native code layer also uses a Microsoft web service to provide location related information from a database.

Code cannot be written to directly interact with the native layer, nor the hardware layer. For this, a managed code layer exists, which provides a hardware agnostic API. Recall from Chapter 2, "Fundamental Concepts in Windows Phone Development," that P/Invoke is not allowed at all on the phone. All interoperation with location components on the phone must therefore be done via the managed layer.

Getting Started with Location

A new geographic location API is included with the Windows Phone 8 SDK. This WinPRT API supersedes the Windows Phone 7 .NET API that relies on the `GeoCoordinateWatcher` class. Although the .NET API is still supported, for new apps it is recommended that you use the new `Geolocator` class that is part of the new WinPRT API. The new WinPRT geo location API has many similarities with the .NET API.

The new geographic location API is located in the namespace `Windows.Devices.Geolocation`.

Geolocator Class

The `Geolocator` class can be used by your app to monitor the location of the phone. It contains events for monitoring hardware state changes and geographic position changes.

Retrieving the Current Location

`Geolocator` allows you to track the phone's location, using its `PositionChanged` event, and to retrieve the phone's current location using its `GetGeopositionAsync` method.

The `GetGeopositionAsync` method forgoes the need to subscribe to the `PositionChanged` event when all you need is a single reading. With `GetGeopositionAsync` you can use the await keyword to conveniently wait for the method to return the `Geoposition` result, as shown in the following example:

```
var geolocator = new Geolocator();
Geoposition geoposition = await geolocator.GetGeopositionAsync();
Geocoordinate geocoordinate = geoposition.Coordinate;
```

> **NOTE**
>
> When attempting to call the `Geolocator` object's `GetGeopositionAsync` method, if location is disabled in the phone's settings, an `UnauthorizedAccessException` is raised.

> **NOTE**
>
> The Coordinate property of the `Geoposition` class is of type `Windows.Devices.Geolocation.Geocoordinate`, which is not to be confused with the `System.Device.Location.GeoCoordinate` class. Notice the capital "C" in the latter type name.
>
> Other types, such as the `Geoposition` class, use the same casing pattern to indicate that they belong to the WinPRT API and not the .NET API.

The .NET GeoCoordinate type (and not the WinPRT Geocoordinate type) is used heavily by the phone's mapping API, which is explored in the next chapter. Converting between the two types is a matter of copying over the various property values. Listing 17.1 shows an extension method that is used to convert a WinPRT `Geocoordinate` into a .NET `GeoCoordinate`.

LISTING 17.1   `GeocoordinateExtensions.ToGeoCoordinate` Method

```
static class GeocoordinateExtensions
{
    public static GeoCoordinate ToGeoCoordinate(this Geocoordinate geocoordinate)
    {
        return new GeoCoordinate
            (
                geocoordinate.Latitude,
                geocoordinate.Longitude,
                geocoordinate.Altitude ?? Double.NaN,
                geocoordinate.Accuracy,
                geocoordinate.AltitudeAccuracy ?? Double.NaN,
                geocoordinate.Speed ?? Double.NaN,
                geocoordinate.Heading ?? Double.NaN);
    }
}
```

The `Geoposition` result of the `GetGeopositionAsync` method potentially represents a cached reading. Caching the reading saves the geo location infrastructure from having to engage hardware components. `GetGeopositionAsync` has a method overload that allows you to specify the maximum age of the cached reading and the maximum number of seconds that the OS should wait to get a location result before timing out and raising an exception.

It is recommended that you use the `GetGeopositionAsync` method when tracking is not required because it results in better battery life and, therefore, a better user experience.

DesiredAccuracy **Property**

`Geolocator` allows you to request a desired accuracy level via its `DesiredAccuracy` property, which can be set to either the default accuracy level, which lets the OS decide the accuracy level, or a high accuracy level, which causes the OS to prefer the accuracy of GPS. To create a `Geolocator` that uses the default accuracy setting, use the following:

```
Geolocator defaultAccuracyLocator = new Geolocator();
```

For high accuracy, set the `DesiredAccuracy` property like so:

```
Geolocator highAccuracyLocator
    = new Geolocator {DesiredAccuracy = PositionAccuracy.High};
```

The `PositionAccuracy` enum has the following two values:

► `Default`—Results in a power optimized (or low power) configuration at the probable cost of decreased accuracy. Moreover, the phone device favors the use of cell tower triangulation and Wi-Fi triangulation above GPS.

► `High`—Favors GPS when available at the cost of greater power usage and, thus, reduced battery life.

Use the default (power optimized) accuracy setting unless a higher level of accuracy is required. Using lower accuracy minimizes power consumption, thereby increasing battery life.

DesiredAccuracyInMeters **Property**

In addition to the `DesiredAccuracy` property, `Geolocator` includes a `DesiredAccuracyInMeters` property, which is not present in the older `GeoCoordinateWatcher` API. The `DesiredAccuracyInMeters` property is a nullable unsigned integer value that lets the OS choose the mechanism for geo location. Lower values cause the phone to prefer the accuracy of GPS.

Setting the `DesiredAccuracyInMeters` property to a non-null value overrides the `DesiredAccuracy` property.

MovementThreshold **Property**

In some environments, signal noise can cause a GPS device to register movement when there is no movement. This can be caused by surface reflection, which occurs when signals

17

bounce off walls or other structures, or by other environmental factors. It is also exacerbated by the absence of a GPS antenna on Windows Phone devices.

The `MovementThreshold` property of the `Geolocator` allows you to specify the minimum amount of movement required to register a change in position. When a change is registered, the `Geolocator`'s `PositionChanged` event is raised.

`MovementThreshold` is a `double` value, which indicates the distance in meters, relative to the last coordinate received. The `MovementThreshold` property allows position change notifications to be smoothed. If the value is set too low, the `PositionChanged` event may be raised too frequently, or when there is no actual change in location. Conversely, setting the value too high reduces the ability of the device to provide up-to-date location coordinates. A road navigation app, for example, with a `MovementThreshold` value set too high, may cause a user to miss a turn. Set too low, the application may provide continuous directions when the phone is, in fact, stationary.

> **TIP**
>
> Setting the `Geolocator.MovementThreshold` property to at least 20 helps to smooth out the signal, causing the `PositionChanged` event to be raised only when the location has changed significantly.

Monitoring Position Changes

The `Geolocator` class exposes the following two events:

- ▶ `PositionChanged`—This event is raised when a change in location is detected.

- ▶ `StatusChanged`—This event is raised when the underlying location service changes state; for example, when the location component is receiving data or when it has been disabled.

PositionChanged Event   The `PositionChanged` event is raised whenever a significant change is detected in the phone's location. How large the change needs to be is determined by the `Geolocator` object's `MovementThreshold` property.

The following code fragment demonstrates how to subscribe to the `PositionChanged` event:

```
geolocator.PositionChanged += HandlePositionChanged;
```

When the `PositionChanged` event is raised, the handler receives a `PositionChangedEventArgs` object that contains a `Geoposition` property, as shown:

```
void HandlePositionChanged(
    Geolocator sender, PositionChangedEventArgs e)
```

```
{
    Geoposition geoposition = e.Position;
    Geocoordinate geocoordinate = geoposition.Coordinate;
    CivicAddress civicAddress = geoposition.CivicAddress;
}
```

The `Position` property of the `PositionChangedEventArgs` is a `Geoposition` instance containing the following two properties:

▶ `Coordinate` (of type `Geocoordinate`)

▶ `CivicAddress` (of type `CivicAddress`

In the context of the geo location API, a *position* can be thought of as a location at a point in time. `Geocoordinate` includes a `Timestamp` property of type `DateTimeOffset`, which indicates when the reading was taken.

BEST PRACTICES

`Geolocator` leverages phone hardware that consumes power. Subscribe to its `PositionChanged` event only when it is needed by your app, and unsubscribe as soon as it is no longer needed. This reduces power consumption and increases the battery life of the phone.

`StatusChanged` **Event**   The status of the underlying geographic location component is indicated by the `Geolocator` object's `LocationStatus` property, which is of type `PositionStatus`. `PositionStatus` is an enum that contains the following values:

▶ `Disabled`—The location provider is disabled. No position updates occur.

▶ `Initializing`—The location provider is initializing. This status occurs, for example, when the GPS component is obtaining a fix.

▶ `NoData`—No location data is available from any location provider.

▶ `NotAvailable`—The Windows Sensor and Location Platform is not available on the device. The minimum Windows Phone hardware requirements preclude this status.

▶ `NotInitialized`—An operation to retrieve location has not yet been initialized. `LocationStatus` will have this value if the application has not yet called `GetGeopositionAsync` or registered an event handler for the `PositionChanged` event.

▶ `Ready`—A location provider is ready to supply new data. In this state, the `Geolocator` is able to raise its `PositionChanged` event.

The location provider transitions between these states, as depicted in Figure 17.4.

17

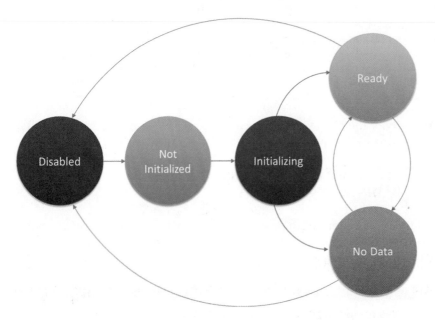

FIGURE 17.4   `Geolocator` transitions between `PositionStatus` values.

When the `Geolocator` object's `StatusChanged` event is raised, the handler receives a `StatusChangedEventArgs` object, as shown in the following excerpt:

```
void HandleStatusChanged(Geolocator sender, StatusChangedEventArgs args)
{
    PositionStatus status = args.Status;
    switch (status)
    {
            case PositionStatus.Disabled:
            // ...
            break;
            case PositionStatus.Initializing:
            // ...
            break;
            case PositionStatus.NoData:
            // ...
            break;
            case PositionStatus.NotInitialized:
            // ...
            break;
            case PositionStatus.Ready:
            // ...
            break;
    }
}
```

Background Location Tracking

In Windows Phone 7.5, apps that made use of location tracking were subject to events being lost when deactivated. When the app was dormant or tombstoned, `PositionChanged` event handlers would be discarded—lost forever, leaving the app without any knowledge of changes in location for the period before reactivation.

This has changed in Windows Phone 8, which allows only a single app to be in execution at any one time unless that app is a location tracking app, in which case it can continue to run in the background while a different app is running in the foreground.

To nominate your app as a location tracking app, add a `BackgroundExecution` element to the DefaultTask element in your project's WMAppManifest.xml file, as shown:

```
<DefaultTask Name="_default" NavigationPage="MainPage.xaml" >
    <BackgroundExecution>
        <ExecutionType Name="LocationTracking" />
    </BackgroundExecution >
</DefaultTask>
```

With this in place, your app will continue to run as long as it remains subscribed to a `Geolocator` object's `PositionChanged` event.

When your app is running in the background, it is important to stop all tasks not related to location tracking. To be notified when your app is running in the background, subscribe to the `RunningInBackground` event of the `PhoneApplicationService`. This can be done in your project's App.xaml file as shown:

```
<Application.ApplicationLifetimeObjects>

    <shell:PhoneApplicationService
        RunningInBackground="HandleRunningInBackground"
        ... />
</Application.ApplicationLifetimeObjects>
```

The event handler is placed in your App.xaml.cs file, like so:

```
void HandleRunningInBackground(object sender, RunningInBackgroundEventArgs e)
{
    /* Stop all tasks not related to location tracking. */
}
```

The `RunningInBackground` event enables your app to suspend unnecessary tasks, such as updating the UI.

17

> **NOTE**
>
> Only one location tracking app can be running in the background at any time. The most recently opened location tracking app takes precedence and causes any existing location tracking apps to be made dormant or tombstoned.

Although location tracking apps are currently the only type of app that can be enabled to run in the background, plan to see other types of background apps in the future.

Testing Apps That Use the `Geolocator`

The Windows Phone emulator includes a tool for simulating location tracking, which can be accessed by clicking the Additional Tools button on the emulator menu (this was shown in Figure 16.2), and then selecting the Location tab on the Additional Tools windows.

The location simulator works in two modes: a live mode that allows you to interact with the map to send location data to the emulator as soon as you click on the map and a play-back mode that causes the location simulator to step through a sequence of map points, which you enter by clicking on the map (see Figure 17.5).

Map points can be saved to a file and loaded again at a later time.

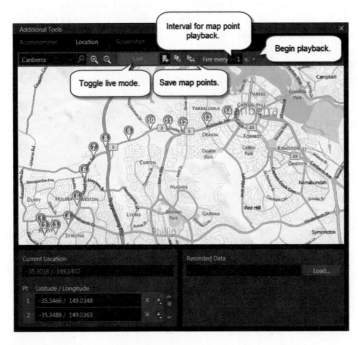

FIGURE 17.5   Location simulator.

> **NOTE**
>
> The Play button is enabled only when the Live button is toggled off.

When using the location simulator, any `Geolocator` instances in your app respond as though they are receiving actual location data, giving you the opportunity to test your app's geo location features.

Code-Driven Location Simulation

The Windows Phone emulator's location simulator is useful for testing your app while it is executing within the emulator. To test the geo location features of your app on a physical device or within a unit test requires a different code-driven approach.

This section demonstrates how to abstract the use of the Geolocator class so that it can be replaced by a testable mock class.

On first glance you might think that mocking the SDK's geo location API should be a simple affair. Many of the classes in the API are, however, sealed—including the `Geolocator` class. This makes mocking them awkward because they must be wrapped or accessed via custom proxy classes.

The `Geolocator` class implements an internal `IGeolocator` interface, which would make an excellent candidate for abstracting the duties of the `Geolocator` class. Unfortunately, `IGeolocator` is marked internal, putting it out of our reach.

So the downloadable sample code includes a custom `IGeoLocator` interface, which is almost identical to the SDK's `IGeolocator` interface (see Listing 17.2).

LISTING 17.2 `IGeoLocator` Interface

```
public interface IGeoLocator
{
    event EventHandler<PositionChangedProxyEventArgs> PositionChanged;
    event EventHandler<StatusChangedProxyEventArgs> StatusChanged;

    Task<GeopositionWrapper> GetGeoCoordinateAsync();

    Task<GeopositionWrapper> GetGeoCoordinateAsync(
        TimeSpan maximumAge, TimeSpan timeout);

    PositionAccuracy DesiredAccuracy { get; set; }
    PositionStatus LocationStatus { get; }
    double MovementThreshold { get; set; }
    uint ReportInterval { get; set; }

    void Start();
    void Stop();
}
```

17

A custom `GeolocatorProxy` class wraps the built-in `Geolocator` object. `GeolocatorProxy` implements the `IGeoLocator` interface (see Listing 17.3). `GeolocatorProxy` is designed to be used in place of the `Geolocator` class. It offers all the features of the built-in `Geolocator`, but can be swapped out during testing.

Although the built-in `Geolocator` class does not include methods for starting and stopping location tracking, implementations of the custom `IGeoLocator` interface do. `GeolocatorProxy` subscribes to its `Geolocator` events in the `Start` method and unsubscribes in the `Stop` method.

The `PositionChanged` and `StatusChanged` events of the built-in `Geolocator` class use a `TypedEventHandler<T>` as the delegate type rather than the familiar `EventHandler`. The appearance of the `TypedEventHandler` is new to the Windows Phone 8 SDK and several APIs, including the geo location API, make use of it. This proves troublesome when working with Reactive Extensions (Rx). Thus, the `GeolocatorProxy` exposes the events using the nongeneric `EventHandler` class. You look at the Rx later in this chapter.

One last obstacle to abstracting the geo location API is that some of the types in the SDK's geo location API do not provide the means for setting their members. These classes include, in particular, the `PositionChangedEventArgs`, `StatusChangedEventArgs`, and the `Geoposition` classes, which have been replaced with more flexible custom types to accommodate our mocking framework.

LISTING 17.3   `GeolocatorProxy` Class (Excerpt)

```
public sealed class GeolocatorProxy : IGeoLocator
{
    readonly Geolocator geolocator = new Geolocator();
...
    public uint ReportInterval
    {
        get
        {
            return geolocator.ReportInterval;
        }
        set
        {
            geolocator.ReportInterval = value;
        }
    }

    public void Start()
    {
        Stop();

        geolocator.PositionChanged += HandlePositionChanged;
        geolocator.StatusChanged += HandleStatusChanged;
    }
```

```
public void Stop()
{
    geolocator.PositionChanged -= HandlePositionChanged;
    geolocator.StatusChanged -= HandleStatusChanged;
}

public event EventHandler<PositionChangedProxyEventArgs> PositionChanged;

void OnPositionChanged(PositionChangedProxyEventArgs e)
{
    PositionChanged.Raise(this, e);
}

void HandlePositionChanged(Geolocator sender, PositionChangedEventArgs args)
{
    OnPositionChanged(new PositionChangedProxyEventArgs(
                    new GeopositionWrapper(args.Position)));
}
...
}
```

The custom MockGeoLocator mimics the behavior of the built-in Geolocator and allows you to supply a list of GeoCoordinate values that represent a predefined route and are analogous to the location simulator's map points.

In addition to the properties of the IGeoLocator interface, MockGeoLocator has the following three properties that allow you to tailor when the PositionChanged event is raised:

► **InitializationMs**—The time, in milliseconds, before transitioning the Status to the NoData state

► **FixDelayMs**—The time before the transitioning the Status from the NoData state to the Ready state

► **PositionChangedDelayMs**—The time interval, in milliseconds, between PositionChanged events

MockGeoLocator allows you to add waypoints to a list of GeoCoordinate values using its WayPoints property.

The MockGeoLocator.WalkPath method runs on a background thread and processes the waypoints sequentially (see Listing 17.4).

If there are no waypoints specified, the MockGeoLocator uses a default list of coordinates.

The first time WalkPath is called, the class simulates initialization by pausing for the duration specified by the InitializationMs value. It then updates its Status to Ready and iterates over the WayPoints collection, raising the PositionChanged event for each one.

17

LISTING 17.4 `MockGeoLocator.WalkPath` Method

```
void WalkPath()
{
    if (wayPoints.Count < 1)
    {
        List<GeoCoordinate> defaultWayPoints = GetDefaultCoordinates();
        wayPoints.AddRange(defaultWayPoints);
    }

    if (firstRun)
    {
        Status = PositionStatus.Initializing;
        Wait(InitializationMs);
    }

    Status = PositionStatus.NoData;
    Wait(FixDelayMs);

    GeoCoordinate coordinate = wayPoints.First();

    if (firstRun)
    {
        Position = new Position<GeoCoordinate>(
                            DateTimeOffset.Now, coordinate);
        firstRun = false;
    }
    Status = PositionStatus.Ready;
    Wait(PositionChangeDelayMs);
    int index = 1;

    while (started)
    {
        if (wayPoints != null && wayPoints.Count > index)
        {
            coordinate = wayPoints[index++];
        }
        SetPosition(coordinate);
        Wait(PositionChangeDelayMs);
    }
}
```

The `Wait` method uses the `Monitor` to block the background thread for the specified number of milliseconds (see Listing 17.5).

> **TIP**
>
> Using the `Monitor` to block the thread is preferable to calling `Thread.Sleep` because, unlike `Monitor.Wait`, `Thread.Sleep` cannot be unblocked.

LISTING 17.5 `Wait` Method

```
static readonly object waitLock = new object();

static void Wait(int delayMs)
{
    if (delayMs > 0)
    {
        lock (waitLock)
        {
            Monitor.Wait(waitLock, delayMs);
        }
    }
}
```

Both `MockGeoLocator` and the `GeolocatorProxy` implement `IGeoLocator`. This allows you to use either type without referring to a concrete implementation, which is demonstrated in the next section.

A Walkthrough of the Location Viewer Sample

The sample for this chapter includes a set of classes for monitoring location using either a `GeolocatorProxy` or a `MockGeoLocator`.

The sample code for this section is located in the GeographicLocation directory of the WPUnleashed.Examples project.

GeoLocationViewModel **Class**

The `GeoLocationViewModel.Start` method instantiates either the `GeolocatorProxy` or a `MockGeoLocator` depending on the value of the viewmodel's Boolean `useMockLocator` field (see Listing 17.6).

> **TIP**
>
> Rather than requiring the viewmodel to determine which `IGeoLocator` implementation it should use, Inversion of Control (IoC) could be employed to resolve the object. IoC is discussed in Chapter 24, "Unit Testing Apps."

The `Start` method subscribes to the `PositionChanged` and `StatusChanged` events of the `IGeoLocator`, and then calls the `IGeoLocator` object's `Start` method to begin receiving location notifications.

When the `PositionChanged` event is raised, the viewmodel's `GeoCoordinate` property is set to the current location.

LISTING 17.6   `GeoLocationViewModel.Start` Method (excerpt)

```
void Start()
{
    if (running)
    {
        return;
    }

    Running = true;
    CanStart = false;

    if (useMockLocator)
    {
        geoLocator = new MockGeoLocator();
    }
    else
    {
        geoLocator = new GeolocatorProxy
            {
                MovementThreshold = 20,
                DesiredAccuracy = PositionAccuracy.High,
                ReportInterval = 1000
            };
    }
...
    geoLocator.PositionChanged
        += (o, args) =>
            {
                GeoCoordinate coordinate = args.Position.GeoCoordinate;
                GeoCoordinate = coordinate;
                ResolveAddress(coordinate);
            };

    geoLocator.StatusChanged
        += (o, args) => PositionStatus = args.Status;


    geoLocator.Start();
}
```

The viewmodel contains two `DelegateCommands` that are used to start and stop position monitoring. The commands are initialized in the viewmodel constructor, as shown:

```
public GeoLocationViewModel()
{
    startCommand = new DelegateCommand(obj => Start(), arg => CanStart);
    stopCommand = new DelegateCommand(obj => Stop(), arg => Running);
    PropertyChanged += delegate { RefreshCommands(); };
}
```

Tapping the Stop button causes the viewmodel's `StopCommand` to execute, which calls the `Stop` method of the `geoLocator`. This prevents the `PositionChanged` event from being raised. The `Stop` method is shown in the following excerpt:

```
void Stop()
{
    if (!running || geoPositionWatcher == null)
    {
        return;
    }

    if (sampler != null)
    {
        sampler.Dispose();
        sampler = null;
    }

    geoPositionWatcher.Stop();
    Running = false;
    CanStart = true;
}
```

Displaying Location Using the `GeoLocationView` Page

The view has two buttons, which are bound to the viewmodel's `StartCommand` and `StopCommand` (see Listing 17.7).

The `GeoLocationView` contains several `TextBlock` elements that are bound to viewmodel properties.

A `Slider` is bound to the viewmodel's `SampleIntervalMs` property, allowing the user to control the sample frequency. The sampling feature is explored later in the chapter.

A Windows Phone Toolkit `ToggleSwitch` is bound to the viewmodel's `UseMockLocator` property and changes the `IGeoLocator` implementation that is used during tracking.

LISTING 17.7   `GeoLocationView` Page (excerpt showing main content panel)

```xml
<StackPanel Grid.Row="1" Margin="21,30,21,0">
    <StackPanel Grid.Row="1" Margin="21,0,21,0">
    <Grid>
        <Grid.RowDefinitions>
            <RowDefinition Height="60" />
            <RowDefinition Height="60" />
            <RowDefinition Height="*" />
        </Grid.RowDefinitions>
        <Grid.ColumnDefinitions>
            <ColumnDefinition />
            <ColumnDefinition />
        </Grid.ColumnDefinitions>
        <TextBlock Text="latitude"
                        Style="{StaticResource LatLongTitleStyle}"
                        VerticalAlignment="Center" />
        <TextBlock Text="{Binding GeoCoordinate.Latitude, StringFormat=\{0:F4\}}"
                        Style="{StaticResource LatLongStyle}"
                        Grid.Row="1"/>
        <TextBlock Text="longitude"
                        Style="{StaticResource LatLongTitleStyle}"
                        Grid.Column="1" VerticalAlignment="Center" />
        <TextBlock Text="{Binding GeoCoordinate.Longitude, StringFormat=\{0:F4\}}"
                        Style="{StaticResource LatLongStyle}"
                        Grid.Row="1" Grid.Column="1" />
    </Grid>

    <TextBlock Text="{Binding PositionStatus}"
                    Style="{StaticResource PhoneTextNormalStyle}"
                    Foreground="{StaticResource PhoneAccentBrush}"
                    Height="50" Margin="0" />
    <TextBlock Text="sample interval in milliseconds (0 for realtime)"
                Style="{StaticResource LabelTextStyle}"
                FontSize="{StaticResource PhoneFontSizeSmall}"/>
    <Slider Minimum="0"
            Maximum="10000"
            Value="{Binding SampleIntervalMs, Mode=TwoWay}"
            IsEnabled="{Binding CanStart}"
            LargeChange="1000" SmallChange="1000"/>
    <TextBlock Text="{Binding SampleIntervalMs}" Width="100" Height="50"
                HorizontalAlignment="Left"
                Style="{StaticResource PhoneTextNormalStyle}"/>

    <TextBlock Text="{Binding Message}" Height="50"
                Style="{StaticResource PhoneTextNormalStyle}"/>
```

```
<toolkit:ToggleSwitch Header="mock locator"
    IsChecked="{Binding UseMockLocator, Mode=TwoWay}"
    IsEnabled="{Binding CanStart}"/>

<StackPanel Orientation="Horizontal">
    <Button Content="Start"
            Command="{Binding StartCommand}"
            Margin="0,20,0,0" Width="150" HorizontalAlignment="Left"/>
    <Button Content="Stop"
            Command="{Binding StopCommand}"
            Margin="0,20,0,0" Width="150" HorizontalAlignment="Left"/>
</StackPanel>


</StackPanel>
```

Tapping the Start button causes the current location to be displayed whenever the `IGeoLocator` object's `PositionChanged` event is raised (see Figure 17.6).

The OS displays an indicator in the system tray when location tracking is engaged. In the sample this occurs when the mock locator is turned off.

FIGURE 17.6   `GeoLocationView` page.

Civic Address Resolution

`CivicAddressResolver` is supposed to be able to resolve a street address from a geographic coordinate. It has not, however, been fully implemented yet and is unable to resolve an address.

> **NOTE**
>
> In the 8.0 release of the Windows Phone OS, the `CivicAddressResolver` class has not been fully implemented.

In Chapter 18, "Incorporating Map-Based Positioning," you see how to use the Maps Geocode Service to resolve an address from a geo coordinate, and vice versa.

The `GeoLocationViewModel` class demonstrates how to use the `CivicAddressResolver`, but the `CivicAddressResolver.ResolveAddressCompleted` handler always receives an unknown address value.

Sampling the `PositionChanged` Event with Rx

If the built-in `Geolocator` class is assigned too low a `MovementThreshold` value, the event handler for the `Geolocator.PositionChanged` event may be raised more frequently than needed, which can potentially degrade the performance of your app. The Reactive Extensions (Rx) can eliminate this issue by modulating, or sampling, the event, restricting calls to the `PositionChanged` event handler to a certain number each second.

Rx is a managed library that has been included as part of the Windows Phone Framework Class Library (FCL). At its essence, Rx allows events to be treated as a data stream. Rx allows you to subscribe to this data stream and to manipulate and filter the data stream before it is handled by your app.

Rx can be thought of as LINQ to Events, and includes all the standard LINQ query operators. Rx provides a convenient mechanism for passing around event streams, which makes working with events easier. It uses the Dispose pattern and the `IDisposable` interface in conjunction with event subscriptions, and automatically unsubscribes from events, eliminating potential memory leaks.

If you are new to Rx, it is recommended that you learn more about it because it is an invaluable tool when working with an asynchronous programming model. Rx is being used evermore frequently by developers for asynchronous programming. The Windows Phone Toolkit team, for example, used Rx to write reliable, event-based asynchronous tests for many of the Toolkit components.

Getting Started with Rx for Windows Phone

Rx types reside in the Microsoft.Phone.Reactive namespace.

The key to using Rx is to understand the two principal interfaces: `IObserver` and `IObservable`. Rx's `IObservable` and `IObserver` are analogous to `IEnumerable` and `IEnumerator`, except for one key difference: They do not block.

Rx allows you to create an `IObservable` object from an event. In the following excerpt, an `IObservable` is created using the `IGeoLocator` instance's `PositionChanged` event:

```
IObservable<IEvent<PositionChangedProxyEventArgs>> observable
    = Observable.FromEvent<GeoPositionChangedProxyEventArgs>(
        ev => geoLocator.PositionChanged += ev,
        ev => geoLocator.PositionChanged -= ev);
```

By supplying both an add handler and a remove handler, the `PositionChanged` event is automatically unsubscribed after the `observable` instance is disposed.

When an `IObservable` has been acquired, you can limit the frequency of event notifications by using the `Sample` extension method for the `IObservable<T>` type, as shown in the following excerpt:

```
IObservable<IEvent<PositionChangedProxyEventArgs<T>>> sampled
    = observable.Sample(TimeSpan.FromMilliseconds(sampleIntervalMs));
```

The final step is to subscribe to the data stream. This is done by calling the `Subscribe` extension method, passing it a delegate. The following excerpt calls the `Subscribe` method and passes a lambda expression for the `PositionChanged` event handler:

```
sampled.Subscribe(
    args =>
        {
            GeopositionWrapper position = args.EventArgs.Position;
            Location = position.GeoCoordinate;
        });
```

If the `sampleIntervalMs` value is equal to 1000, the `PostionChanged` event handler is called, at most, once each second.

CAUTION

Using the `Subscribe` method results in an object that implements `IDisposable`. It is critical that the `Dispose` method be called on the object when it is no longer needed, because not doing so can lead to a memory leak. The event source (in this case the `IGeoLocator`) may keep the target (`GeoPositionSampler`) alive.

The downloadable sample code contains a class called `GeoLocatorSampler` that encapsulates this sampling functionality into a reusable class (see Listing 17.8).

GeoLocatorSampler wraps an IGeoLocator instance and allows you to sample the IGeoLocator.PositionChanged event. It implements INotifyPropertyChanged so that a UI element can bind to its Location property if needed.

GeoPositionSampler implements IDisposable so that when it is disposed, it disposes its Rx subscription object and unsubscribes from the watcher's StatusChanged event.

LISTING 17.8   GeoLocatorSampler Class (excerpt)

```
public class GeoLocatorSampler : NotifyPropertyChangeBase, IDisposable
{
    readonly IDisposable subscription;
    IGeoLocator geoLocator;

    public GeoLocatorSampler(IGeoLocator geoLocator, int sampleIntervalMs)
    {
        this.geoLocator = ArgumentValidator.AssertNotNull(geoLocator, "geoLocator");
        ArgumentValidator.AssertGreaterThanOrEqualTo(
                0, sampleIntervalMs, "sampleIntervalMs");

        IObservable<IEvent<PositionChangedProxyEventArgs>> sampled
            = Observable.FromEvent<PositionChangedProxyEventArgs>(
                ev => geoLocator.PositionChanged += ev,
                ev => geoLocator.PositionChanged -= ev)
                .Sample(TimeSpan.FromMilliseconds(sampleIntervalMs));

        subscription = sampled.Subscribe(
            args =>
                {
                    GeopositionWrapper position = args.EventArgs.Position;
                    Location = position.GeoCoordinate;
                });

        geoLocator.StatusChanged += HandleStatusChanged;
    }

    void HandleStatusChanged(
        object o, StatusChangedProxyEventArgs args)
    {
        Status = args.Status;
    }

    GeoCoordinate location;

    public GeoCoordinate Location
    {
        get
```

```
    {
        return location;
    }
    private set
    {
        Assign(ref location, value);
    }
}

PositionStatus status;

public PositionStatus Status
{
    get
    {
        return status;
    }
    set
    {
        Assign(ref status, value);
    }
}

...
}
```

The GeoLocatorSampler initialization has been incorporated into the
GeoLocationViewModel.Start method, as shown:

```
if (sampleIntervalMs > 0)
{
    sampler = new GeoLocatorSampler(
                geoLocator, sampleIntervalMs);

    sampler.PropertyChanged += (o, args) =>
                                {
                                    ResolveAddress(sampler.Location);
                                    GeoCoordinate = sampler.Location;
                                    PositionStatus = sampler.Status;
                                };
}
```

The GeoLocatorSampler constructor accepts an IGeoLocator (either a GeolocatorProxy or
a MockGeoLocator) and a sample interval in milliseconds.

The `GeoLocationView` page uses a `Slider` control to set the sample interval of the `GeoLocatorSampler` (see Figure 17.7).

FIGURE 17.7   A `Slider` control is used to set the sample interval.

Increasing the sample interval causes the latitude and longitude display values to be updated less frequently.

Sampling the `PositionChanged` event allows your app to respond periodically to location changes and can improve the behavior of your app when the `GeoLocator` object's movement threshold is set too low for the current conditions.

Summary

This chapter looked at the various location sensing technologies and how they compare in terms of power usage and accuracy. The chapter also explored how to monitor position changes using the `Geolocator` class, and how to simulate position changes using both the emulator's location simulator and a custom class that is compatible with unit testing and testing on a physical device.

Finally, the chapter demonstrated how Rx can be used to modulate, or restrict, the frequency of `PositionChanged` event handler calls.

CHAPTER 18

Incorporating Map-Based Positioning

Mapping capabilities are now an expected part of just about every smartphone, and, as you might expect, Windows Phone has a rich built-in Maps application that leverages Nokia mapping data as its principal mapping service. In addition to the built-in Maps app, the Windows Phone SDK includes a Map control, enabling you to incorporate mapping features into your own apps.

The new Windows Phone 8 Map control replaces the earlier Bing Maps control and allows the user to download maps from the built-in Maps app so that map data is available even when the phone does not have a data connection. The Bing Maps control is still supported in Windows Phone 8, but has been deprecated.

This chapter begins with an overview of the Map control and walks through the creation of a Map API key. You see how to programmatically manipulate the map view—in particular, how to pan and zoom, as well as how to adjust the pitch and heading of the map view. You look at using the new Geolocator API to pinpoint the phone's current location on the map.

The chapter then continues on from the previous chapter. You see how to track the phone's location on a map using the Geolocator class and the custom mock IGeoLocator implementation.

The chapter then examines the Route Query API and how to locate a route between two user-provided addresses. The chapter illustrates how to coordinate multiple asynchronous operations and how to create an asynchronous method using a task completion source. You also look at hiding and revealing page elements using a viewmodel's

`VisualState` property in conjunction with an attached property and a custom
`VisualStateUtility` class.

Finally, the chapter demonstrates how to present a list of itinerary items as an expandable
list. You look at allowing the user to download maps for offline viewing, and at launching
the built-in Maps app using the launcher API.

The majority of the source code for this chapter is located in the Mapping directory of the
WPUnleashed.Examples project in the Vaughan.WPUnleashed solution, in the downloadable sample code.

Getting Started with the Map Control

To use the Map control, begin by ensuring that the ID_Cap_Map capability is selected in
the project's WMAppManifest.xml file. Without the capability, an exception is raised at
runtime.

Adding a Map control to a page requires a namespace definition at the top of the page, as
shown:

```
xmlns:m="clr-namespace:Microsoft.Phone.Maps.Controls;
                        assembly=Microsoft.Phone.Maps"
```

An `m:Map` element can then be placed somewhere on your host page, like so:

```
<Grid x:Name="ContentPanel" Grid.Row="1" Margin="12,0,12,0">
    <m:Map Loaded="HandleMapLoaded" />
</Grid>
```

The `Map` control requires an API key to function in production. The `Map` object's `Loaded`
event is used to populate an application ID and an authentication token value, via the
static `ApplicationContext` property of the `MapsSettings` class, as shown:

```
void HandleMapLoaded(object sender, RoutedEventArgs e)
{
    MapsSettings.ApplicationContext.ApplicationId = "<applicationid>";
    MapsSettings.ApplicationContext.AuthenticationToken
                                    = "<authenticationtoken>";
}
```

You do not need the API keys during development of your app. The `Loaded` handler can be left in your code during development. Invalid `ApplicationId` and `AuthenticationToken` values do not affect or disable the `Map` control during development. Valid keys are required for production, however.

Obtaining an `ApplicationId` and `AuthenticationToken`

The earlier Windows Phone 7 Bing Maps control allowed you to obtain an API key and use it during development. This process has changed for the new Map control. You now obtain the API keys for your app, at the last minute, as part of the Windows Phone marketplace submission process.

The `ApplicationId` and `AuthenticationToken` values are specific to your app and are retrieved after you have provided a name for the app, at stage two of the marketplace submission process. On the Windows Phone Dev Center website, follow the Map services link and click Get Token. The new `ApplicationID` and `AuthenticationToken` are displayed on the same page. Copy and paste the values into the Map object's `Loaded` event handler. Rebuild your app with the new code, using a production build configuration, and upload the XAP.

> **NOTE**
>
> The `ApplicationId` and `AuthenticationToken` properties must be set after the first `Map` control has been loaded in your app. These values are retained by the mapping infrastructure for all subsequent maps. If you destroy all instances of the `Map` control in your app and then create a new instance, you have to set these properties again.

Overview of the Sample Map View

This chapter demonstrates the various features of the Map control using a sample `MapView` page. MapView.xaml contains a `Map` control, sliders to adjust the pitch and heading of the map, a list picker to select the cartographic mode of the map, and various application bar items that are discussed later in this chapter (see Figure 18.1).

18

FIGURE 18.1   MapView page.

The application bar icon buttons perform the tasks described in Table 18.1.

TABLE 18.1   MapView Application Bar Items

Button	Description
location	Zooms the map to the phone's current location
track	Begin or ends tracking of the phone's geographic location using an `IGeoLocator` implementation
route	Displays a search dialog, enabling the user to locate a path from one street address to another
Itinerary	Expands the itinerary view, which contains the route information present after a route search has completed

Adjusting for Low Light Conditions

The `Map` class's `ColorMode` property allows you to change the tonal palette of the map from a light palette, suitable for daytime viewing, to a dark pallet, suitable for night time viewing or low light conditions.

The dark mode/light mode menu item in the `MapView` page toggles the Map control's `ColorMode` property from light to dark. The Map control's `ColorMode` property is bound to the `MapViewModel`'s `MapColorMode`, as shown:

```
<m:Map x:Name="map"
    ...
    ColorMode="{Binding MapColorMode, Mode=TwoWay}"
    ...
</m:Map>
```

An `AppBarMenuItem` is bound to the viewmodel's `ToggleColorModeCommand`, like so:

```
<u:AppBarMenuItem
    x:Name="toggleColorModeMenuItem"
    Command="{Binding ToggleColorModeCommand}"
    Text="color mode placeholder" />
```

The command is initialized within the viewmodel's constructor. When executed, the command sets the viewmodel's `MapColorMode`, as shown:

```
toggleColorModeCommand = new DelegateCommand(
    obj => SetColorMode(mapColorMode == MapColorMode.Light
                        ? MapColorMode.Dark : MapColorMode.Light));
```

For more information on the `AppBarMenuItem` see Chapter 8, "Taming the Application Bar."

Changing Cartographic Modes

The Maps control can be viewed using one of the following four cartographic modes (represented by the `MapCartographicMode` enum):

▶ Aerial

▶ Hybrid

▶ Road

▶ Terrain

A cartographic mode represents a 2D projection of the Earth. You set the cartographic mode of a `Map` using its `CartographicMode` property.

The sample's `MapViewModel` class contains a `MapCartographicModes` property, which is an `IEnumerable<MapCartographicMode>`. The backing field for the property is populated using the custom `EnumUtility` class, which extracts each enum value and provides the viewmodel with an `IEnumerable` that is compatible with data-binding.

```
readonly IEnumerable<MapCartographicMode> mapCartographicModes
    = EnumUtility.CreateEnumValueList<MapCartographicMode>();
```

The `MapView` page uses a Windows Phone Toolkit `ListPicker` control, which is bound to the `MapCartographicModes` property, allowing the user to switch between modes. See the following excerpt:

```
<toolkit:ListPicker
    ItemsSource="{Binding MapCartographicModes}"
    SelectedItem="{Binding MapCartographicMode, Mode=TwoWay}"
    ExpansionMode="FullScreenOnly"
```

The `SelectedItem` property of the `ListPicker` is bound to the viewmodel's `MapCartographicMode` property. The Map control's `CartographicMode` property is also bound to the viewmodel's `MapCartographicMode` property, as shown:

```
<m:Map x:Name="map"
...
    CartographicMode="{Binding MapCartographicMode, Mode=TwoWay}"
    ...
>
</m:Map>
```

Changing the mode via the list picker causes the map to change modes.

Panning and Zooming the Map Control

The `Map` control's `Center` property is a `GeoCoordinate` that is used to retrieve and set the center location of the map view. The following example shows how to set the `Center` property of a `Map` control in XAML by providing the latitude and longitude (in that order):

```
<m:Map Center="45.8, 6.15" />
```

The `Center` property can also be data bound, as shown in the following example:

```
<m:Map Center="{Binding Center, Mode=TwoWay}" />
```

By using a `TwoWay` data binding, you can track the current center point of the map from your viewmodel.

Centering the Map to the Phone's Current Location

The sample's `MapViewModel` class contains a `GetLocation` method that uses the `Geolocator` class, which is new to Windows Phone 8, to retrieve the phone's current location (see Listing 18.1).

The GetPositionAsync method is an awaitable method that allows you to retrieve the phone's last known location without blocking the UI thread.

When attempting to call the Geolocator object's GetGeopositionAsync method, if location is disabled in the phone's settings, an UnauthorizedAccessException is raised.

For more information on location tracking and the Geolocator class, see Chapter 17, "Building Location Aware Apps."

LISTING 18.1   MapViewModel.GetLocation Method

```csharp
async Task<GeoCoordinate> GetLocation()
{
    var geolocator = new Geolocator();
    Geoposition geoposition;

    try
    {
        geoposition = await geolocator.GetGeopositionAsync();
    }
    catch (UnauthorizedAccessException)
    {
        MessageService.ShowMessage(
            "Location is disabled in the phone settings.");
        return center;
    }

    Geocoordinate geocoordinate = geoposition.Coordinate;
    return geocoordinate.ToGeoCoordinate();
}
```

The MapViewModel class sets its Center property to the value returned by the GetLocation method, as shown:

```csharp
async void CenterMapOnLocation()
{
    Center = await GetLocation();
    Location = center;
    ZoomLevel = 8;
}
```

MapView.xaml contains an AppBarIconButton that, when tapped, executes the viewmodel's CenterMapOnLocationCommand, which calls the CenterMapOnLocation method.

Setting the Viewable Area of the Map

An alternative way of setting the viewable area of the map is to use the Map control's SetView method. SetView accepts a LocationRectangle object, which specifies a rectangular region of the map.

The MapViewModel contains a LocationRectangle property that is applied to the map within the viewmodel's PropertyChanged event handler, as shown in the following excerpt:

```
public MapView()
{
    var viewModel = new MapViewModel(new RouteCalculator());

    viewModel.PropertyChanged += (sender, args) =>
        {
            switch (args.PropertyName)
            {
                ...
                case "LocationRectangle":
                    LocationRectangle rectangle = ViewModel.LocationRectangle;
                    if (rectangle != null)
                    {
                        map.SetView(ViewModel.LocationRectangle);
                    }
                    break;
            }
        };

    ...
}
```

Later in this chapter, you see how the Map control's SetView method is used to pan and zoom to an area of the map to display the shortest path between two points.

> **CAUTION**
>
> When the lifespan of the viewmodel exceeds that of the view, subscribing to a viewmodel's PropertyChanged event from the view can cause a memory leak. This is because the target of an event subscription (in this case the view) is kept alive by the garbage collector while the event source (the viewmodel) exists in memory. To prevent this, you may forgo the use of the PropertyChanged event in favor of an alternative approach, such as weak events, or a messaging system to communicate with the view, both of which are to be found in various MVVM frameworks including the Calcium SDK project.

The Map control's ZoomLevel property allows you to control the altitude of the viewpoint. This property ranges between 0 and 20, with 0 being completely zoomed out so that the entire map is visible, and 20 being zoomed in as close as possible. Unlike the old Bing Maps control, 20 is a hard limit. If you attempt to assign the zoom level to a higher value, an `ArgumentOutOfRangeException` is thrown. To demonstrate the `ZoomLevel` property of the Map control, the sample view uses a data-binding to the viewmodel's `ZoomLevel` property, as shown:

```
<m:Map x:Name="map"
    . . .
    ZoomLevel="{Binding ZoomLevel, Mode=TwoWay}"
    . . .
</m:Map>
```

As the user performs pinch and spread gestures, the viewmodel's `ZoomLevel` property is updated.

Adjusting Pitch and Heading

The Map controls `Pitch` and `Heading` properties that allow you to adjust the maps angle of inclination and the direction that the map is facing, respectively.

```
<m:Map
    . . .
    Heading="{Binding Heading, Mode=TwoWay}"
    Pitch="{Binding Pitch, Mode=TwoWay}"
    . . .
</m:Map>
```

`Pitch` represents the inclination in degrees and is a double value between 0 and 75.

`Heading` is also a double value and represents the rotational offset of the map in degrees. The value can be a negative or positive value.

Two slider controls on the `MapView` page control the pitch and heading of the map. The Pitch slider is a vertical slider that is bound to the viewmodel's `Pitch` property, as shown:

```
<Slider Value="{Binding Pitch, Mode=TwoWay}"
        Minimum="0" Maximum="75"
        Orientation="Vertical"
        . . . />
```

The Heading slider is bound to the viewmodel's `Heading` property.

Moving either slider updates the viewmodel, which updates the `Map` control.

18

Location Tracking

In Chapter 17 you saw how a `Geolocator` provides geographic location updates. In this section you see how the custom `IGeoLocator` (presented in that chapter) can be used to track the location of the phone using a Map control.

The `MapViewModel` class's `StartTracking` method instantiates either a `GeolocatorProxy` or a `MockGeoLocator`, depending on whether the class is executing within the emulator (see Listing 18.2).

When the `GeoLocatorSampler` object's `PropertyChanged` event is raised, the `Location`, `Center`, and `PositionStatus` properties are updated. Changing the `Center` property changes the visible center point of the `Map` control and pans the map to the new `GeoCoordinate`.

An `AppBarToggleButton` in the view is data-bound to the viewmodel's `ToggleTrackingCommand` property, as shown:

```
<u:AppBarToggleButton
        Icon1Uri="/Mapping/Images/Track.png"
        Icon2Uri="/Mapping/Images/TrackOff.png"
        Command1="{Binding ToggleTrackingCommand}"
        Text1="track"
        Text2="track off"
        Toggled="{Binding Tracking}" />
```

When executed, the command calls the `StartTracking` method of the viewmodel. The `StartTracking` method uses a Boolean tracking field to prevent tracking if it is already underway.

Before tracking can take place, the app prompts the user to confirm the use of location services. This is achieved by using the `ViewModelBase` class's `IMessageService`. If the `AskYesNoQuestion` method returns true, the location tracking is allowed to proceed.

> **NOTE**
>
> To pass the Windows Phone Marketplace Certification, your app must seek the user's consent to use location services. Additionally, you must provide an option in the settings page of your app to allow the user to disable location services.

For more information regarding the `IMessageService` see Chapter 2, "Fundamental Concepts in Windows Phone Development."

LISTING 18.2   `MapViewModel.StartTracking` Method

```
void StartTracking()
{
    if (tracking)
    {
```

```
        return;
    }

    /* Before using geo location, it is a certification requirement
     * that you seek permission from the user first. */
    bool canTrack = MessageService.AskYesNoQuestion(
        "Is it OK to use the geographic location system on your phone?");

    if (!canTrack)
    {
        return;
    }

    IGeoLocator geoLocator
        = EnvironmentValues.UsingEmulator
            ? new MockGeoLocator()
            : (IGeoLocator)new GeolocatorProxy()
                {
                    MovementThreshold = 20
                };

    sampler = new GeoLocatorSampler(geoLocator, 500);

    sampler.PropertyChanged
        += (o, args) =>
            {
                if (sampler.Location == null)
                {
                    return;
                }
                Location = sampler.Location;
                Center = location;
                PositionStatus = sampler.Status;
            };

    ZoomLevel = ZoomLevelForTracking;

    geoLocator.Start();

    Tracking = true;
}
```

During tracking, if the user taps the tracking AppBarToggleButton, the viewmodel's StopTracking method is called (see Listing 18.3). This halts tracking and disposes the GeoLocatorSampler to free resources.

LISTING 18.3   `MapViewModel.StopTracking` Method

```
void StopTracking()
{
    if (!tracking)
    {
        return;
    }

    Tracking = false;

    if (sampler != null)
    {
        sampler.Dispose();
        sampler = null;
    }
}
```

Tapping the Track button causes the `IGeoLocator` to begin raising events. The map center is moved to the location as reported by the `PositionChangedEventArgs`.

Overlaying Custom Map Content

Framework elements can be displayed within the `Map` control using map layers. Map layers allow you to control the location of the layer using `GeoCoordinates` and the z-index of layer content. You can add shapes, controls, and media such as images and even video to the map using map layers. Observe the following example:

```xml
<m:Map x:Name="map"
    ...>
    <m:Map.Layers>
        <m:MapLayer>
            <m:MapOverlay x:Name="currentLocationOverlay"
                PositionOrigin="0.5,0.5">
                <Ellipse Width="10" Height="10" Fill="Red" />
            </m:MapOverlay>
        </m:MapLayer>
    </m:Map.Layers>
</m:Map>
```

A red circle is placed on the map using a `MapOverlay`.

The `MapOverlay` object contains a `GeoCoordinate` property that allows you to position the content of the overlay anywhere on the map. Although the `GeoCoordinate` property is a `DependencyProperty`, it is not bindable in XAML.

To change the position of a `MapOverlay` according to a viewmodel property, create the binding in code, as demonstrated in the following excerpt from the MapView.xaml.cs class:

```
public MapView()
{
    ...
    MapLayer mapLayer = map.Layers.First();
    MapOverlay mapOverlay = mapLayer.First();
    mapOverlay.GeoCoordinate = viewModel.Location;

    /* Binding the Location property does not work in XAML.
     * We create the binding in code. */
    Binding binding = new Binding("Location") {Source = viewModel};
    BindingOperations.SetBinding(
        mapOverlay, MapOverlay.GeoCoordinateProperty, binding);

    AddMapShapes();
}
```

LINQ is used to retrieve the first `MapLayer` object, and then its first `MapOverlay` object. The location of the overlay is initialized to the viewmodel's `Location` property and then the binding is applied.

To add content to a map programmatically, see the following excerpt:

```
Rectangle rectangle = new Rectangle
    {
        Fill = new SolidColorBrush(Colors.Blue),
        Height = 10,
        Width = 10
    };

MapLayer mapLayer = new MapLayer();
MapOverlay mapOverlay = new MapOverlay
    {
        Content = rectangle,
        GeoCoordinate = new GeoCoordinate(47.5302, 8.5804)
    };

mapLayer.Add(mapOverlay);
map.Layers.Add(mapLayer);
```

A rectangle is placed in a `MapOverlay`, which is then placed in a `MapLayer`, and then into the Map. The rectangle can be seen in Figure 18.1.

Calculating and Displaying a Route

The new mapping infrastructure in the Windows Phone 8 SDK includes the capability to resolve the geographic coordinates of a street address and search for the shortest route between two points. This is a far cry from Windows Phone 7, which required you to deal directly with other third-party cloud services, such as the Bing Maps SOAP services that were covered in the first edition of this book.

This section looks at leveraging these new capabilities to allow the user to enter a start and an end location, which the app uses to locate the shortest path by road between the two points. This path is then displayed on the map and the itinerary placed in an expandable list box.

Calculating the Shortest Route Between Two Points

In the Windows Phone 8 SDK, two classes are fundamental in calculating a route: The `GeocodeQuery` class allows you to convert a street address to a `GeoCoordinate`, and the `RouteQuery` class finds the shortest path between two `GeoCoordinates`, with any number of way points in between.

The `GeocodeQuery` and `RouteQuery` class are located in the namespace `Microsoft.Phone.Maps.Services.GeocodeQuery`.

In the sample for this section, a custom class named `RouteCalculator` is used to calculate the route between two street addresses. The `RouteCalculator` class has a single method named `CalculateAsync` (see Listing 18.4).

The `GeocodeQuery` class has two required properties: `SearchTerm` and `GeoCoordinate`. `SearchTerm` allows you to specify the street address or geographic feature you would like to locate, and the `GeoCoordinate` property produces results closest to that coordinate.

`CalculateAsync` performs two Geocode Queries for its `fromAddress` and `toAddress` parameters.

`CalculateAsync` is designed to be consumed asynchronously and returns an awaitable `Task` object. Notice that the async keyword is not used in this case. For this method we take full control of the asynchrony by leveraging a `TaskCompletionSource` object. After each of the three asynchronous operations complete, if an exception was raised during the operation, or the operation was canceled, the `TaskCompletionSource` object is modified. This passes the error or cancellation back to the caller.

After the two geocode queries complete, a `RouteQuery` is initialized using the `GeoCoordinates` representing the `fromAddress` and the `toAddresses` parameters. If a route is returned, the result is assigned to the `TaskCompletionSource`.

> **CAUTION**
>
> At the time of writing, if you attempt to use the `GeocodeQuery` class to perform two queries at the same time, the `QueryCompletedEventArgs` is not correctly populated. This occurs even when using two different instances of the `GeocodeQuery` class. This prevents

you from using Rx, for example, to coordinate or 'Zip' more than one geocode operation at a time.

LISTING 18.4   RouteCalculator.CalculateAsync **Method**

```csharp
public Task<RouteCalculationResult> CalculateAsync(
    string fromAddress, string toAddress, GeoCoordinate hintCoordinate)
{
    ArgumentValidator.AssertNotNullOrEmpty(fromAddress, "fromAddress");
    ArgumentValidator.AssertNotNullOrEmpty(toAddress, "toAddress");
    ArgumentValidator.AssertNotNull(hintCoordinate, "hintCoordinate");

    var coordinates = new List<GeoCoordinate>();

    GeocodeQuery geocodeQuery = new GeocodeQuery
        {
            SearchTerm = fromAddress,
            GeoCoordinate = hintCoordinate
        };

    var source = new TaskCompletionSource<RouteCalculationResult>();

    geocodeQuery.QueryCompleted += delegate(
        object sender, QueryCompletedEventArgs<IList<MapLocation>> args)
        {
            if (args.Cancelled)
            {
                geocodeQuery.Dispose();
                source.SetCanceled();
                return;
            }

            if (args.Error != null)
            {
                geocodeQuery.Dispose();
                source.SetException(args.Error);
                return;
            }

            IList<MapLocation> mapLocations = args.Result;
            if (mapLocations == null)
            {
                geocodeQuery.Dispose();
                source.SetResult(null);
                return;
```

18

```
            }

        coordinates.Add(args.Result.First().GeoCoordinate);

        if (coordinates.Count < 2)
        {
            geocodeQuery.SearchTerm = toAddress;
            geocodeQuery.QueryAsync();
            return;
        }

        geocodeQuery.Dispose();

        var routeQuery = new RouteQuery
            {
                Waypoints = new List<GeoCoordinate>
                    {
                        coordinates[0],
                        coordinates[1]
                    }
            };

        routeQuery.QueryCompleted += delegate(
            object s, QueryCompletedEventArgs<Route> e)
                {
                    RouteCalculationResult result;
                    if (e.Error == null)
                    {
                        result = new RouteCalculationResult(e.Result);
                    }
                    else
                    {
                        var error = new RouteCalculationError(
                                        e.Error.Message, e.Error);
                        result = new RouteCalculationResult(null, error);
                    }

                    routeQuery.Dispose();

                    source.SetResult(result);
                };

        routeQuery.QueryAsync();
    };

geocodeQuery.QueryAsync();
```

```
        return source.Task;
}
```

Using the Route Calculator

The `MapViewModel` class contains two string properties: `FromAddress` and `ToAddress`, which are populated using two `TextBox` controls in the view.

When the viewmodel's `RouteSearchCommand` is executed, the viewmodel's `Message` property and a `Busy` Boolean flag are set, which are materialized using the `ProgressIndicator` of the page's System Tray, as shown:

```
<shell:SystemTray.ProgressIndicator>
    <shell:ProgressIndicator IsIndeterminate="{Binding Busy}"
                             IsVisible="{Binding Busy}"
                             Text="{Binding Message}" />
</shell:SystemTray.ProgressIndicator>
```

The `SearchRoute` method then awaits for the result of the `RouteCalculator` object's `CalculateAsync` method (see Listing 18.5).

The result of the route query is a `Route` object that contains a set of `RouteLeg` objects, with each containing a set of `RouteManeuver` objects. For each `RouteManeuver` object a custom `MapItineraryItem` is added to the viewmodel's `ItineryItems` collection.

Conveniently, the `Route` object also includes a `BoundingBox` property of type `LocationRectangle` that allows you to zoom and pan the map to display the route.

LISTING 18.5 `MapViewModel.SearchRoute` Method

```
async void SearchRoute()
{
    if (string.IsNullOrEmpty(fromAddress)
        || string.IsNullOrEmpty(toAddress))
    {
        return;
    }

    Message = "searching...";
    Busy = true;

    RouteCalculationResult calculationResult;

    try
    {
        HideItinerary();
```

18

```
        HideRouteSearch();

        calculationResult = await routeCalculator.CalculateAsync(
            fromAddress, toAddress, center);
    }
    catch (Exception ex)
    {
        MessageService.ShowError(
            "An error occurred while calculating the route.");
        return;
    }
    finally
    {
        Busy = false;
        Message = string.Empty;
    }

    Route route = calculationResult.Route;
    MapRoute = new MapRoute(route);

    var collection = new ObservableCollection<MapItineraryItem>();

    foreach (RouteLeg leg in route.Legs)
    {
        foreach (RouteManeuver maneuver in leg.Maneuvers)
        {
            collection.Add(new MapItineraryItem(maneuver));
        }
    }

    ItineraryItems = collection;
    LocationRectangle = route.BoundingBox;

    ShowItinerary();
}
```

Searching for a Route Using the View

The `MapView` page contains a `Border` control named RouteSearchView. This control is used to prompt the user for the origin (from) and destination (to) addresses (see Figure 18.2).

A visual state is used to hide and show the `Border`. When the `Border` is shown, it provides the user with the means to enter two addresses. When the user taps the Search button, the viewmodel's `SearchCommand` executes.

FIGURE 18.2   The RouteSearchView Border control allows the user to search for a route.

The following excerpt shows the RouteSearchView `Border`:

```xml
<Border x:Name="RouteSearchView"
        Height="160" Margin="0"
        Padding="8"
        RenderTransformOrigin="0.5,0.5"
        Width="480"
        Background="{StaticResource PhoneBackgroundBrush}"
        Grid.ColumnSpan="2">
    <Border.RenderTransform>
        <CompositeTransform TranslateY="-218"/>
    </Border.RenderTransform>
    <Grid>
        <Grid.RowDefinitions>
            <RowDefinition />
            <RowDefinition />
        </Grid.RowDefinitions>
        <Grid.ColumnDefinitions>
            <ColumnDefinition Width="50" />
            <ColumnDefinition Width="0.8*" />
            <ColumnDefinition Width="0.4*"/>
        </Grid.ColumnDefinitions>
        <TextBlock Text="from"
```

18

```
                        VerticalAlignment="Center" />
        <TextBox Text="{Binding FromAddress, Mode=TwoWay}"
                    Grid.Column="1"
                    Grid.ColumnSpan="2" />
        <TextBlock Text="to"
                    Grid.Row="1"
                    VerticalAlignment="Center" />
        <TextBox Text="{Binding ToAddress, Mode=TwoWay}"
                    Grid.Row="1"
                    Grid.Column="1" />
        <Button Command="{Binding RouteSearchCommand}"
                Content="search"
                Grid.Column="2"
                Grid.Row="1"  />
    </Grid>
</Border>
```

When the Search button is tapped, the RouteSearchView `Border` is hidden via the
`VisualState` property in the viewmodel.

Modifying Page Elements Using Visual States

The visibility of the search panel and itinerary list is controlled using visual states. The
visual state of either control is set via an associated string property in the viewmodel.
Using a visual state, rather than a Boolean property for visibility, affords greater flexibility
because you can create any number of visual state values, whereas a Boolean value allows
you just two. See the following viewmodel excerpt:

```
public const string ShowRouteSearchState = "ShowRouteSearch";
public const string HideRouteSearchState = "HideRouteSearch";
string routeSearchVisualState = HideRouteSearchState;
public const string ShowItineraryState = "ShowItinerary";
public const string HideItineraryState = "HideItinerary";
...

string visualState = HideItineraryState;

public string VisualState
{
    get
    {
        return visualState;
    }
    private set
    {
        Assign(ref visualState, value);
```

```
    }
}
```

Commands such as the `routeSearchToggleCommand` and the `itineraryToggleCommand` are used to switch the visual state properties. The commands are initialized in the viewmodel constructor, as shown:

```
public MapViewModel(IRouteCalculator routeCalculator)
{
    ...
    routeSearchToggleCommand = new DelegateCommand(
        obj => ToggleRouteSearchVisibility());
    itineraryToggleCommand = new DelegateCommand(
        obj => ToggleItineraryVisibility());

    ...
}
```

The toggle commands, such as the `RouteSearchToggleCommand`, each set a corresponding visual state property to an alternative state, as shown:

```
void ToggleRouteSearchVisibility()
{
    if (routeSearchVisualState == ShowRouteSearchState)
    {
        VisualState = routeSearchVisualState = HideRouteSearchState;
    }
    else
    {
        VisualState = routeSearchVisualState = ShowRouteSearchState;
    }
}
```

The `MapView` page contains various visual states that coincide with the viewmodel's `VisualState` properties (see Listing 18.6).

In the sample, the task of the `Storyboard` elements within the visual states is to either hide or reveal their associated target control or to update `AppBar` button and menu item text.

LISTING 18.6   MapView.xaml `VisualStateGroups` Excerpt

```
<Grid x:Name="LayoutRoot" Background="Transparent">
    ...
    <VisualStateManager.VisualStateGroups>
        <VisualStateGroup x:Name="RouteStates">
```

18

```
<VisualStateGroup.Transitions>
    <VisualTransition To="ShowRouteSearch" />
    <VisualTransition To="HideRouteSearch" />
</VisualStateGroup.Transitions>
<VisualState x:Name="ShowRouteSearch">
    <Storyboard>
        <DoubleAnimation
                Duration="0:0:0.3" To="20"
                Storyboard.TargetProperty=
        "(UIElement.RenderTransform).(CompositeTransform.TranslateY)"
                Storyboard.TargetName="RouteSearchView"
                d:IsOptimized="True">
            <DoubleAnimation.EasingFunction>
                <CircleEase EasingMode="EaseIn" />
            </DoubleAnimation.EasingFunction>
        </DoubleAnimation>
    </Storyboard>
</VisualState>
<VisualState x:Name="HideRouteSearch">
    <Storyboard>
        <DoubleAnimation
                Duration="0:0:0.3" To="-218"
                Storyboard.TargetProperty=
        "(UIElement.RenderTransform).(CompositeTransform.TranslateY)"
                Storyboard.TargetName="RouteSearchView"
                d:IsOptimized="True">  "
            <DoubleAnimation.EasingFunction>
                <CircleEase EasingMode="EaseOut" />
            </DoubleAnimation.EasingFunction>
        </DoubleAnimation>
    </Storyboard>
</VisualState>
</VisualStateGroup>
...
<VisualStateGroup x:Name="ColorModeStates">
    <VisualStateGroup.Transitions>
        <VisualTransition To="LightMode" />
        <VisualTransition To="DarkMode" />
    </VisualStateGroup.Transitions>
    <VisualState x:Name="LightMode">
        <Storyboard>
            <ObjectAnimationUsingKeyFrames
                    Storyboard.TargetProperty="Text"
                    Storyboard.TargetName="toggleColorModeMenuItem">
                <DiscreteObjectKeyFrame KeyTime="0" Value="dark mode"/>
            </ObjectAnimationUsingKeyFrames>
```

```
            </Storyboard>
        </VisualState>
        <VisualState x:Name="DarkMode">
            <Storyboard>
                <ObjectAnimationUsingKeyFrames
                        Storyboard.TargetProperty="Text"
                        Storyboard.TargetName="toggleColorModeMenuItem">
                    <DiscreteObjectKeyFrame KeyTime="0" Value="light mode"/>
                </ObjectAnimationUsingKeyFrames>
            </Storyboard>
        </VisualState>
    </VisualStateGroup>
    ...
    </VisualStateManager.VisualStateGroups>

</Grid>
```

When the `VisualState` of the viewmodel changes to ShowRouteSearch, for example, the `VisualStateManager` is directed to that state and the RouteSearchView `Border` control is brought into view. This is all orchestrated using a custom `VisualStateUtility` class and an attached property (see Listing 18.7).

The `VisualState` attached property can be placed on a `Control` element and automatically transitions the visual state of the control using the `VisualStateManager` according to the value of the attached property.

LISTING 18.7 `VisualStateUtility` Class

```csharp
public static class VisualStateUtility
{
    public static readonly DependencyProperty VisualStateProperty
        = DependencyProperty.RegisterAttached(
            "VisualState",
            typeof(string),
            typeof(VisualStateUtility),
            new PropertyMetadata(HandleVisualStateChanged));

    public static string GetVisualState(DependencyObject obj)
    {
        return (string)obj.GetValue(VisualStateProperty);
    }

    public static void SetVisualState(DependencyObject obj, string value)
    {
        obj.SetValue(VisualStateProperty, value);
    }
```

18

```
static void HandleVisualStateChanged(
    object sender, DependencyPropertyChangedEventArgs args)
{
    var control = sender as Control;
    if (control != null)
    {
        object newValue = args.NewValue;
        string stateName = newValue != null ? newValue.ToString() : null;

        if (stateName != null)
        {
            /* Call is invoked as to avoid missing
               * the initial state before the control has loaded. */
            Deployment.Current.Dispatcher.BeginInvoke(
                delegate
                    {
                        VisualStateManager.GoToState(control, stateName, true);
                    });
        }
    }
    else
    {
        throw new ArgumentException(
            "VisualState is only supported for Controls.");
    }
}
```

The attached property is set on the `phone:PhoneApplicationPage` element of the `MapView`
page, as shown:

```
<phone:PhoneApplicationPage
    ...
    u:VisualStateUtility.VisualState="{Binding VisualState}"
    ...>
```

When the viewmodel's `VisualState` property changes, the `HandleVisualStateChanged`
method of the `VisualStateUtility` class is called, which calls the built-in
`VisualStateManager.GoToState` method.

The advantage of this approach is that it becomes unnecessary to subscribe to viewmodel
property changed events from the page code-beside.

Displaying the Route and Itinerary

When a search completes successfully, the resulting route is displayed as a bending line on the map, connecting itinerary waypoints. A separate expandable view displays the detailed itinerary.

Recall that the `MapViewModel` class's `SearchRoute` method populates the list of `ItineraryItems` using the `RouteCalculationResult`, as shown in the following excerpt:

```
Route route = calculationResult.Route;
MapRoute = new MapRoute(route);

var collection = new ObservableCollection<MapItineraryItem>();

foreach (RouteLeg leg in route.Legs)
{
    foreach (RouteManeuver maneuver in leg.Maneuvers)
    {
        collection.Add(new MapItineraryItem(maneuver));
    }
}
```

The `MapView` presents the itinerary items in an expandable `ListBox`.

When a route is located, the map view is panned and zoomed to display the path and waypoints (see Figure 18.3).

FIGURE 18.3   The MapView page after a route search completes.

18

The `ListBox`'s `ItemsSource` property is bound to the `ItineraryItems` property in the viewmodel. Each custom `MapItineraryItem` has its `Text` and `DistanceString` property displayed within a `DataTemplate`, as shown in the following excerpt:

```
<Border x:Name="ItineraryView"
        VerticalAlignment="Bottom"
        Height="210"
        RenderTransformOrigin="0.5,0.5"
        Grid.Row="2"
        Grid.ColumnSpan="2">

    <ListBox ItemsSource="{Binding ItineraryItems}" Margin="0,10,0,70">
        <ListBox.ItemTemplate>
            <DataTemplate>
                <StackPanel Orientation="Horizontal" Margin="5,2.5">
                    <TextBlock
                        Text="{Binding Text}"
                        TextWrapping="Wrap"
                        Width="380"
                        FontWeight="Light" />
                    <TextBlock
                        Text="{Binding DistanceString}"
                        Margin="4,0,4,0"
                        FontWeight="Light"
                        Foreground="{StaticResource PhoneAccentBrush}" />
                </StackPanel>
            </DataTemplate>
        </ListBox.ItemTemplate>
    </ListBox>
</Border>
```

The parent `Border` control is used to hide or display the `ListBox` via a visual state defined by the `ItineraryVisualState` string property of the viewmodel. The itinerary button in the application bar executes the `ItineraryToggleCommand` in the viewmodel, which toggles the `VisualState` from `ShowItinerary` to `HideItinerary` and vice versa. The `ShowItinerary` state sets the height of the ItineraryView `Border` control so that it comes into view, whereas the `HideItinerary` state reduces the `Border`'s height so that it is hidden from view. When the `VisualState` is set to `ShowItinerary`, the list of itinerary items is presented.

Showing a Location with the Built-In Maps App

Often it is not necessary to go to the trouble of building a dedicated map view into your app. The built-in Maps app can be launched directly from your own app using the `MapsTask` launcher. Observe the following example:

```
MapsTask mapsTask = new MapsTask
    {
        Center = new GeoCoordinate(47.6204, -122.3493),
        ZoomLevel = 8,
        SearchTerm = "Caffe"
    };
mapsTask.Show();
```

The `MapsTask` class allows you to position the map view using its `Center` and `ZoomLevel` properties. You can also specify a search term that causes the map to display all matching search results on the map.

The sample's `MapViewModel` class demonstrates the `MapsTask` using a command named `ViewInMapsAppCommand` that is executed when the user taps an application bar menu item.

Showing Directions with the Built-In Maps App

In addition to displaying a single point using the built-in Maps app, you can also display a route. The `MapsDirectionsTask` class allows you to specify a start and end point for the route, as shown in the following example:

```
MapsDirectionsTask mapsDirectionsTask = new MapsDirectionsTask();

GeoCoordinate startCoordinate = new GeoCoordinate(47.635, -122.362);
mapsDirectionsTask.Start
            = new LabeledMapLocation("Start Point", startCoordinate);

GeoCoordinate endCoordinate = new GeoCoordinate(47.650, -122.349);
mapsDirectionsTask.End = new LabeledMapLocation("End Point", endCoordinate);

mapsDirectionsTask.Show();
```

18

> **NOTE**
>
> If you do not specify a `Start` value for the `MapsDirectionsTask`, the phone's current location is used.

If you provide a null `GeoCoordinate` to the `LabeledMapLocation`, for either the `Start` or `End` locations, the label parameter is used as a search term. For example, to display directions from the phone's current location to the Space Needle in Seattle, you could use the following:

```
MapsDirectionsTask mapsDirectionsTask = new MapsDirectionsTask();
mapsDirectionsTask.End = new LabeledMapLocation("Space Needle", null);
mapsDirectionsTask.Show();
```

Downloading Maps for Offline Use

New to Windows Phone 8 is the capability to download maps for offline use. The built-in Map app allows the user to download maps that are stored locally on the device. If the user has not pre-downloaded a map from the built-in Maps app, the Map control downloads map information as the user manipulates the control, which requires an active Internet connection.

You can launch the Map app to allow the user to select a map to download using the `MapDownloaderTask` launcher located in the `Microsoft.Phone.Tasks` namespace, as shown in the following example:

```
MapDownloaderTask mapDownloaderTask = new MapDownloaderTask();
mapDownloaderTask.Show();
```

The sample's `MapViewModel` contains a `DownloadMapCommand` that is executed via an application bar menu item. When the `MapDownloaderTask` is shown, the app is deactivated.

Summary

This chapter began with an overview of the `Map` control and walked through the creation of a Map API key pair. You saw how to programmatically manipulate the map view, in particular how to pan and zoom, as well as how to adjust the pitch and heading of the map view. You looked at using the new `Geolocator` API to pinpoint the phone's current location on the map.

The chapter then continued from the previous chapter. You saw how to track the phone's location on a map using the `Geolocator` class and the custom mock `IGeoLocator` implementation.

Next, the chapter examined the Route Query API and how to locate a route between two user-provided addresses. The chapter illustrated how to coordinate multiple asynchronous operations and how to create an asynchronous method using a task completion source. You also looked at hiding and revealing page elements using a viewmodel's `VisualState` property in conjunction with an attached property and a custom `VisualStateUtility` class.

Finally, the chapter demonstrated how to present a list of itinerary items as an expandable list. You looked at allowing the user to download maps for offline viewing and at launching the built-in Maps app using the launcher API.

CHAPTER 19

Supporting Multiple Cultures and Languages

IN THIS CHAPTER

▶ Using resx files

▶ Image localizability

▶ Updating localized strings and images at runtime

▶ Converting a byte stream to an image source

▶ Right-to-left support

Internationalization is the process of building an application so that it can be adapted for different languages and regions. The Windows Phone Marketplace provides the opportunity to market an app to people from all over the world. Reaching such a broad audience of users requires that your software can be translated and otherwise adapted at runtime to be linguistically and culturally relevant to whomever is using it. This is the realm of internationalization and this chapter looks at the techniques to make your app world-ready.

It is crucial to devise efficient strategies for internationalization from the beginning of an app's development. As development progresses, it becomes increasingly difficult to retrofit support for multiple cultures.

This chapter begins by describing the terminology around internationalization; it then walks you through techniques and examples showing how to provision for runtime language changes and image localizability in your Windows Phone XAML apps.

Finally, the chapter touches on right-to-left support in Windows Phone.

Terminology

The term *internationalization* is an umbrella term for the process of presenting an application in multiple languages. The terms *internationalization*, *globalization*, and *localization* are sometimes used interchangeably, yet they have different meanings.

Globalization describes engineering an application so that it does not have cultural preconceptions. For example, in the United States, dates are presented using the convention month/day/year, whereas in the United Kingdom and other countries, they are shown using the convention day/month/year. Fortunately, for developers working with .NET, Microsoft provides considerable infrastructure for provisioning for globalization.

Localizability describes the capacity of an application to have its resources replaced at runtime with culturally specific resources. Localization is the process of providing the sets of culturally specific resources. Such resources may include strings, icons, images, and sound files.

This chapter focuses on localizability.

The primary means for implementing localizability in Windows Phone XAML apps is through the use of resx files. Although the main ingredients exist in the Windows Phone SDK for localizability, there are techniques demonstrated in this chapter that improve compatibility with resx files and, in particular, enable them to be used with the XAML data-binding infrastructure. This allows the UI to respond to culture settings changes at runtime, something that the Windows Phone SDK does not provide out of the box.

Localizability Using Resx Files

Windows Phone apps follow the same hub and spoke model for localization that .NET desktop CLR applications do. Satellite assemblies provide culture-specific resources, while a main assembly contains a default set of resources that are used to fall back on. This process of producing the main assembly and satellite assemblies is done automatically at build time.

At runtime, the CLR selects the appropriate composite set of resources to use. The culture settings of a Windows Phone app and the language displayed are dependent on the culture settings of the phone itself.

Resx files have been employed to localize .NET applications since .NET 2.0 and Windows Forms. Resx files support the production of what is known as localized satellite assemblies. These are assemblies that are discovered at runtime and contain culture-specific resources.

In Silverlight browser applications, and desktop CLR projects, a major benefit of satellite assemblies is that they can be used to reduce the overall package size of an application. By storing culturally specific resources separately from the main assembly, culturally specific resources can be downloaded on demand. For example, if an application supports 10 languages, and each set of localized strings and images is 1MB, you can reduce the overall download size by 9MB (10MB–1MB = 9MB). In some scenarios this can prove to be critical, such as in Silverlight browser applications, where the proper use of bandwidth can play a large factor in an application's success. It is, however, largely irrelevant for Windows Phone apps, because the manner in which satellite assemblies are deployed to the phone, in particular the bundling of all assemblies into a single XAP file, including satellite assemblies, means that without the use of multiple resource projects, all satellite assemblies are deployed to the phone anyway; therefore, it does not reduce the overall footprint of an app. Moreover, the Windows Phone Marketplace requires each app to come complete with localized resources for all languages supported by the app. The topic of separate deployment of satellite assemblies, therefore, is not covered in this book.

Getting Started with Resx Files

The first step in enabling a project to support localizable resx files involves modification to your project's properties.

Enabling a project to support a particular culture has been made easier with the Windows Phone 8 SDK. No longer is it necessary to edit your app's project file in a text editor.

Select the project node in the Visual Studio Solution Explorer and press ALT+Enter. Then use the Supported Cultures section in the Application tab to select the languages that you intend to support.

Compiling your project with culturally specific resx files produces independent satellite assemblies located together within the resulting XAP file.

Working with Resx Files

To create a resx file, right-click a project node in the Solution Explorer and select Add and then New Item, or alternatively press Ctrl+Shift+A (see Figure 19.1).

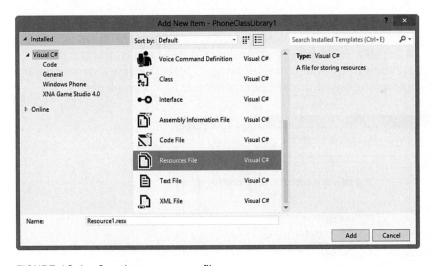

FIGURE 19.1   Creating a new resx file.

After the first default resource file has been created, enabling support for alternative languages is achieved by adding a new resource file for each additional language (see Figure 19.2) and by employing the following naming convention:

```
<Name of the default language resource file>.<Culture Name>.resx
```

FIGURE 19.2   By using different culture codes when naming resx files, Visual Studio generates satellite assemblies for specific cultures.

Names differ only by culture name, where the culture name has the following format:

```
<Lowercase two letter language code>-<Uppercase two letter region code>
```

If you are not specifying a region, use the following format:

```
<Lowercase two letter language code>
```

> **NOTE**
>
> The culture code present in the name of a resx file must match a `SupportedCultures` string within the project file. Otherwise, no satellite assembly is generated. This also applies when the region is defined with a wider scope without a locale in the `SupportedCultures` project element.

When editing a resx file, the resx editor allows the access modifier of the generated class to be set to internal or public (see Figure 19.3). Because the generated class will be the target of XAML data-binding expressions, it must be set to public because internal visibility prevents the data-binding infrastructure from resolving the class properties.

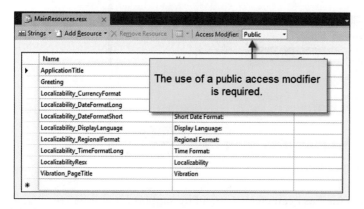

FIGURE 19.3   Setting the access modifier to public enables properties to be used in XAML binding expressions.

Although setting the access modifier to Public produces public properties, it unfortunately does not produce a public constructor. The resx file's generated designer class is left with an internal constructor, which prevents it from being used directly as a resource in a

XAML file. Furthermore, modifying the generated designer class is not a practical solution, because any changes to it are lost if the resx file is modified, causing the resx custom tool to run.

CAUTION

Unfortunately, the generated output of the `PublicResXFileCodeGenerator` (the tool that converts the resx file XML to a class) does not generate an extensibility point that is compatible with the XAML resource infrastructure. That is, it is not possible to include the generated output directly as an application resource via XAML. The generated class that it produces is not partial, and subclassing it breaks the ability to data bind to the static resource properties in the base class.

A solution is to use an intermediary class, whose task is to create an instance of the generated class and expose it as a public static property, thereby making it compatible with the data-binding infrastructure. This class, called `BindableResources`, is shown in Listing 19.1 and is available in the downloadable sample code.

LISTING 19.1   `BindableResources` Class

```
public class BindableResources
{
    static readonly BindableChangeNotifier<MainResources> resources
        = new BindableChangeNotifier<MainResources>(new MainResources());

    public static BindableChangeNotifier<MainResources> Resources
    {
        get
        {
            return resources;
        }
    }

    public static void RaiseNotifyPropertyChanged()
    {
        resources.RaisePropertyChanged();
    }
}
```

As new resx files are added to a project, they should also be added to the `BindableResources` class and exposed as static properties. For convenience, the default resources class, MainResources, is named `Resources`.

Although the approach presented here may at first appear complicated, it provides for change notification, allowing the data-binding infrastructure to be coerced into rereading the static properties of the localizable resources when the application culture changes.

> **NOTE**
>
> The Windows Phone 8 SDK now includes a `LocalizedStrings` class in the Windows Phone App project template, which resembles the `BindableResources` class that I originally demonstrated in the first edition of this book. What is still lacking from the SDK, however, is the dynamic update capability provided by the custom `BindableChangeNotifier` class, which is discussed later in the chapter.

The `BindableResources` class uses the `BindableChangeNotifier` to expose the localizable resources. When the culture is changed, the `BindableResources` class signals to each `BindableChangeNotifier` instance that the `PropertyChanged` event should be raised. After the event is raised, all data-bindings associated with the resources are refreshed.

The `BindableResources` class can be defined as a resource in an applicationwide resource file or directly in your app's App.xaml file, as shown in the following excerpt:

```
<Application ...>
    <Application.Resources>
        <local:BindableResources x:Key="BindableResources" />
    </Application.Resources>
</Application>
```

This allows an instance of the `BindableResources` proxy to be resolved in binding expressions, like so:

```
<TextBlock Text="{Binding Resources.Instance.ApplicationTitle,
        Source={StaticResource BindableResources}}" />
```

Here the `Source` property of the `Text` property's binding expression points to the `BindableResources` instance. The path accesses the `ApplicationTitle` resource string via the `Instance` property of the `BindableChangeNotifier`, which happens to be an instance of the resx generated designer class.

> **NOTE**
>
> Validation of binding expressions is performed at runtime. Unlike WPF, Windows Phone does not support the `x:Static` markup extension, which would otherwise provide the means to validate the binding expression at compile time.

Dynamic Localizability—Updating the UI When the Culture Changes

The Windows Phone XAML data-binding infrastructure relies on change notification to signal that a property in a data-binding expression should be reevaluated. Generated resource designer classes do not provide change notification. Simply exposing the generated resource class for data-binding does not allow the UI to be updated when a culture change occurs at runtime. Therefore, some other means is required to update the UI when the app's culture changes. This is the purpose of the custom `BindableChangeNotifier` class, shown in Listing 19.2. By using the `BindableChangeNotifier` class to wrap the resource's designer class, change notification can be surreptitiously added for all properties.

> **NOTE**
>
> If the desired `CurrentCulture` of the thread is set to the appropriate value before the UI is shown, refreshing the data-bindings is not required. If, however, the user is provided with the ability to change the language, after the UI is loaded, the `BindableChangeNotifier` or some other mechanism is necessary to refresh the data-bindings within the active view.

The `ResourceBase` class implements `System.ComponentModel.INotifyPropertyChanged` to signal to the data-binding infrastructure that properties should be reread (see Listing 19.2).

LISTING 19.2 `BindableChangeNotifier` Class

```csharp
public sealed class BindableChangeNotifier<T> : INotifyPropertyChanged
{
    public event PropertyChangedEventHandler PropertyChanged;

    static T instance;

    public T Instance
    {
        get
        {
            return instance;
        }
    }

    public BindableChangeNotifier(T observableObject)
    {
        instance = observableObject;
    }

    public void RaisePropertyChanged()
    {
        var temp = PropertyChanged;
        if (temp != null)
        {
            temp(this, new PropertyChangedEventArgs(string.Empty));
        }
    }
}
```

19

The `BindableChangeNotifier` class contains a public method called `RaisePropertyChanged`. By using `string.Empty` as the property name, it signals to the data-binding infrastructure that all source properties within the resources object should be reread. Thus, it is not necessary to raise the `PropertyChanged` event for each resource property.

Localizing Images Using Resx Files

The Resx Designer in Visual Studio 2012 has been improved and now provides better support for image files.

An image file can be added to a resx file by opening the resx file in design view and by selecting the Images item in the Resx Designer. You can then drag and drop an image file onto the Resx Designer surface.

An `Image` control can now be bound to a localized image, as shown in the following excerpt:

```
<Image Source="{Binding Resources.Instance.ImageResourceName,
    Source={StaticResource BindableResources},
    Converter={StaticResource BitmapImageConverter}}" />
```

As in the previous string resources example, the data-binding's `Source` property uses the `ResourceBindingWrapper BindableResources` instance defined in the app's resources. The data-binding's `Path` property is set to `Resources.Instance.ImageResourceName`, which is a `byte[]` property for the image.

Notice the use of the `BitmapImageConverter` in the previous excerpt. This `IValueConverter` is responsible for taking the image data in the form of a `byte[]` and converting it into an image (see Listing 19.3).

LISTING 19.3   `BitmapImageConverter` Class

```
public class BitmapImageConverter : IValueConverter
{
    public object Convert(object value, Type targetType,
        object parameter, System.Globalization.CultureInfo culture)
    {
        BitmapImage bitmapImage = new BitmapImage();
        using (MemoryStream stream = new MemoryStream(bytes))
        {
            stream.Seek(0, SeekOrigin.Begin);
            bitmapImage.SetSource(stream);
        }
        return bitmapImage;
    }
}
```

```
public object ConvertBack(object value, Type targetType,
    object parameter, System.Globalization.CultureInfo culture)
{
    throw new NotImplementedException();
}
}
```

The Resx Localizability Sample

The source code for this sample is located in the Localizability directory of the WPUnleashed.Examples project, in the downloadable sample code.

The sample for this chapter demonstrates how to leverage resource files to support multiple UI languages. The interface allows the user to set the application thread's culture value via a ListBox (see Figure 19.4). The interface includes fields to demonstrate the various culture-dependent data formats, such as currency, as well as demonstrating the use of a localizable image.

FIGURE 19.4   The Localizability sample demonstrates how to change the UI language at runtime.

19

Selecting a language endonym (name) changes the app's culture, and results in the image being replaced and the data format fields being updated to reflect the new selection.

> **NOTE**
>
> An *endonym* refers to the name of a language that is used by speakers of the language in the language itself.

> **BEST PRACTICE**
>
> Allow users to switch languages using endonyms. It makes little sense to display a pick list of languages and/or cultures, where the names are displayed in the current inter-face language. Odds are that if you are seeking to change the interface language, it is because you are having difficulty understanding it. If the interface language happens to be in Japanese, for example, and you are unable to read Japanese, being shown a list of languages to pick from in Japanese is not helpful. This is an all too common UI faux pas.

Controlling the UI Culture from the `LocalizabilityViewModel`

The viewmodel exposes a list of `CultureName` objects via its `SupportedCultures` property. The list of supported cultures is initialized as shown:

```
readonly List<CultureInfo> supportedCultures = new List<CultureInfo>
                              {
                                    new CultureInfo("en-US"),
                                    new CultureInfo("fr-FR"),
                                    new CultureInfo("ar-AE")
                              };
```

A method called `SetCulture` is used to change the `CurrentCulture` and `CurrentUICulture` of the UI thread, as shown in the following excerpt:

```
void SetCulture(CultureInfo cultureInfo)
{
    Thread.CurrentThread.CurrentCulture = cultureInfo;
    Thread.CurrentThread.CurrentUICulture = cultureInfo;

    BindableResources.RaiseNotifyPropertyChanged();
    Message = string.Empty;

    SetCurrentCultureValues();
}
```

`CurrentCulture` affects the formatting of currency values, dates, and so on, whereas `CurrentUICulture` determines the language and consequently the primary resource dictionary that is used by your app.

Not all culture names are supported in Windows Phone. Attempting to instantiate a `CultureInfo` class using an unsupported culture name raises a `PlatformNotSupportedException` (see Figure 19.5).

FIGURE 19.5   A `PlatformNotSupportedException` is raised if a specific culture name is not supported.

The viewmodel contains a `CurrentCulture` property that controls the active culture of the app. The `CurrentCulture` set accessor calls the `SetCulture` method if assignment succeeds. If a `PlatformNotSupportedException` is raised, the value falls back to the previous value. See the following excerpt:

```
CultureInfo currentCulture;

public CultureInfo CurrentCulture
{
    get
    {
        return currentCulture;
    }
    set
    {
        CultureInfo temp = currentCulture;
        AssignmentResult result
            = Assign(ref currentCulture, value);

        if (result == AssignmentResult.Success && value != null)
        {
            try
            {
```

```
                SetCulture(value);
            }
        catch (PlatformNotSupportedException)
        {
            CurrentCulture = temp;
            Message = "Platform not supported";
            return;
        }
    }
}
}
```

The viewmodel contains various properties that indicate the culture-specific date, time, and currency formatting. These properties are initialized in the SetCurrentCultureValues method, which is shown in the following excerpt:

```
void SetCurrentCultureValues()
{
    CultureInfo culture = Thread.CurrentThread.CurrentCulture;
    CultureInfo uiCulture = Thread.CurrentThread.CurrentUICulture;
    DisplayLanguage = uiCulture.DisplayName;
    RegionalFormat = culture.NativeName;
    DateTime date = DateTime.Now;

    try
    {
        DateFormatLong = culture.DateTimeFormat.LongDatePattern
                            + " " + date.ToString("D");
        DateFormatShort = culture.DateTimeFormat.ShortDatePattern
                            + " " + date.ToString("d");
        TimeFormat = culture.DateTimeFormat.LongTimePattern + " "
                            + date.ToString("T");
    }
    catch (IndexOutOfRangeException)
    {
        Message = "DateTimeFormat is not defined for culture.";
    }
    const int monetaryAmount = 123456789;
    CurrencyFormat = monetaryAmount.ToString("C");

    if (Equals(culture, supportedCultures[2]))
    {
        FlowDirection = FlowDirection.RightToLeft;
    }
    else
    {
```

```
        FlowDirection = FlowDirection.LeftToRight;
    }
}
```

Displaying Localized Text and Images Within the `LocalizabilityView` Page

The view's XAML file is entirely absent of literal strings. The `BindableResources` instance is used to retrieve all localized resource strings (see Listing 19.4).

A `ListBox` is bound to the viewmodel's `SupportedCultures` property. Selecting a value causes the current thread's `CurrentCulture` and `CurrentUICulture` to be set to a new `CultureInfo` instance. The `BindableResources.RaisePropertyChanged` method is then called to trigger an update of the UI. The `NativeName` property of the `CultureInfo` class displays the culture name's endonym.

The flag image is also bound to the `BindableResources`. The binding uses the `BitmapImageConverter`, which was presented earlier in this chapter, to transform the localized image bytes into a `BitmapImage`.

LISTING 19.4   LocalizabilityResxView.xaml (excerpt)

```xml
<Grid x:Name="LayoutRoot" Background="{StaticResource PhoneBackgroundBrush}">
    <Grid.RowDefinitions>
        <RowDefinition Height="140"/>
        <RowDefinition Height="*"/>
    </Grid.RowDefinitions>

    <Grid>
        <TextBlock x:Name="ApplicationName"
                   Text="{Binding Resources.Instance.ApplicationTitle,
                              Source={StaticResource BindableResources}}"
                   Style="{StaticResource PhoneTextNormalStyle}"/>
        <TextBlock x:Name="ListName"
                   Text="{Binding Resources.Instance.LocalizabilityResx,
                              Source={StaticResource BindableResources}}"
                   Style="{StaticResource PhoneTextTitle1Style}"
                   Margin="0,5,0,0"/>
    </Grid>

    <StackPanel Grid.Row="1" Margin="20">
        <ListBox ItemsSource="{Binding SupportedCultures}"
                 SelectedItem="{Binding CurrentCulture, Mode=TwoWay}">
            <ListBox.ItemTemplate>
                <DataTemplate>
                    <TextBlock Text="{Binding Path=NativeName}" />
                </DataTemplate>
```

19

```
      </ListBox.ItemTemplate>
</ListBox>

<!-- Flag and greeting. -->
<StackPanel Orientation="Horizontal">
    <Image Width="100" Height="100"
           Source="{Binding Resources.Instance.Flag,
                Source={StaticResource BindableResources},
                Converter={StaticResource BitmapImageConverter}}"
           Margin="5,5,20,5"/>
    <TextBlock Text="{Binding Resources.Instance.Greeting,
                  Source={StaticResource BindableResources}}"
               Style="{StaticResource PhoneTextLargeStyle}"
               VerticalAlignment="Center" Width="122" />
</StackPanel>

<!-- Culture details. -->
<StackPanel>
    <TextBlock
      Text="{Binding Resources.Instance.Localizability_DisplayLanguage,
                    Source={StaticResource BindableResources}}"
               Style="{StaticResource PhoneTextTitle3Style}" />
    <TextBlock Text="{Binding DisplayLanguage}"
               Style="{StaticResource PaddedTextStyle}" />
    <TextBlock
        Text="{Binding Source={StaticResource BindableResources},
                 Path=Resources.Instance.Localizability_RegionalFormat}"
        Style="{StaticResource PhoneTextTitle3Style}" />
    <TextBlock Text="{Binding RegionalFormat}"
               Style="{StaticResource PaddedTextStyle}" />
    <TextBlock
        Text="{Binding Source={StaticResource BindableResources},

        Path=Resources.Instance.Localizability_DateFormatLong}"
        Style="{StaticResource PhoneTextTitle3Style}" />
    <TextBlock Text="{Binding DateFormatLong}"
               Style="{StaticResource PaddedTextStyle}" />
    <TextBlock
        Text="{Binding Source={StaticResource BindableResources},
              Path=Resources.Instance.Localizability_DateFormatShort}"
        Style="{StaticResource PhoneTextTitle3Style}" />
    <TextBlock Text="{Binding DateFormatShort}"
               Style="{StaticResource PaddedTextStyle}" />
    <TextBlock
        Text="{Binding Source={StaticResource BindableResources},
        Path=Resources.Instance.Localizability_TimeFormatLong}"
```

```
                         Style="{StaticResource PhoneTextTitle3Style}" />
            <TextBlock Text="{Binding TimeFormat}"
                         Style="{StaticResource PaddedTextStyle}" Grid.Row="4" />
            <TextBlock
                Text="{Binding Source={StaticResource BindableResources},
                         Path=Resources.Instance.Localizability_CurrencyFormat}"
                         Style="{StaticResource PhoneTextTitle3Style}" />
            <TextBlock Text="{Binding CurrencyFormat}"
                         Style="{StaticResource PaddedTextStyle}" />
        </StackPanel>

        <TextBlock Text="{Binding Message}"
                     Foreground=" {StaticResource PhoneAccentBrush}"
                     Style="{StaticResource PhoneTextSubtleStyle}" />
    </StackPanel>
</Grid>
```

When a new culture is selected by the user, the flag and various string fields are updated, as shown in Figure 19.6.

FIGURE 19.6   Changing the UI language at runtime.

TIP

Consider in advance that translated strings may end up being longer or shorter in length than your intended design allows. Be generous when allocating space for text, and allow for as much as a 50% increase in length when the text is localized.

Data-binding expressions for localizable properties may be edited manually within Visual Studio's XAML editor or in the design view by selecting the property in the Properties pane (see Figure 19.7).

FIGURE 19.7   Selecting a resource property within Visual Studio.

Selecting the property in the property pane allows the data-binding expression's Source property to be set using the floating window. In Figure 19.8 you see that the binding's Source property is set to the resource with name BindableResources, which is defined at the application resources level within the App.xaml file.

FIGURE 19.8   Setting the Source value for a data-binding expression from within the designer.

Similarly, the data-binding's `Path` property can be set by expanding the Path tab in the floating window. Figure 19.9 shows that the `Text` property is bound to the `Greeting` string property.

FIGURE 19.9   Setting the `Path` value for a data-binding expression, from within the designer.

RTL Support

Right-to-left (RTL) support is used to display languages, such as Hebrew, which are right-aligned by default. Windows Phone XAML apps support RTL out of the box.

By setting the `FlowDirection` property on any `FrameworkElement` object, you can control whether text is presented from left to right (the default) or right to left. For example, a right-to-left flow direction can be applied to a `TextBlock` as shown:

```
<TextBlock FlowDirection="RightToLeft" />
```

Alternatively, a right-to-left flow direction can be applied to all elements on a page, like so:

```
<phone:PhoneApplicationPage
...
```

```
        FlowDirection="RightToLeft">
...
</phone:PhoneApplicationPage>
```

The `FlowDirection` property is bindable. The sample's `LocalizabilityViewModel`
class contains a `FlowDirection` property. The `FlowDirection` property of the
`LocalizabilityView` page is bound to this property. When switching to Arabic, the viewmodel changes the flow direction to right to left.

Figure 19.10 demonstrates the effect of a right-to-left flow direction on the sample page.

FIGURE 19.10   `LocalizabilityResxView` with right-to-left flow direction.

Summary

This chapter looked at how to use resx files to provide localizability for a Windows Phone
XAML app. The chapter explored techniques that allow resource designer classes to be
readily consumed by the data-binding infrastructure. You also saw how to provision for
runtime language changes, without requiring an application restart or the closing of a
view.

Finally, the chapter touched on using the `FrameworkElement.FlowDirection` property to
display text from right to left.

CHAPTER 20

Extending the Windows Phone Picture Viewer

The Windows Phone photo experience is a key aspect of the phone OS. These days, just about everyone who uses a smartphone wants to be able to alter and share photos with friends and family via social networks.

The Windows Phone picture viewer app displays local or online photos in a consistent way. You can reach the picture viewer on a Windows Phone by navigating to the Windows Phone Pictures Hub and then selecting any image. The picture viewer's menu is activated by tapping the three dots at the bottom of the page.

Whereas most of the built-in Windows Phone apps do not offer points of extensibility, the built-in picture viewer app is one exception.

With the picture viewer, it is possible to give users the capability to launch your app directly from the picture viewer itself, to provide extended image-processing capabilities, or to send an image to a third-party cloud service.

The picture viewer provides two extensibility points: photo extras applications and photo share applications.

Photo extras application extensibility allows you to integrate your photo altering app with the OS, giving users the capability to launch your app from the picture viewer, alter a photo, and save it back to the phone's picture library.

Photo share application extensibility allows you to integrate your photo upload app into the picture viewer application, giving users the capability to upload an image to a third-party service via your app.

This chapter begins by looking at photo Extras applications. You see how to add an app to the picture viewer's Extras menu and how to create an Extras application that traces the edges within an image and allows the user to save the image back to the phone's picture library.

Finally, this chapter looks at photo Share applications. You learn how to add an app to the picture viewer's Share menu and how to create a photo Share application that uploads images to a custom WCF service.

For developing Windows Phone apps, we are fortunate to have a number of technologies at our disposal. In Chapter 7, "Employing Media and Web Elements," you saw how an XNA API was used to play sound effects efficiently. In this chapter, you see how some of the picture and media capabilities are, again, provided by XNA APIs.

NOTE

Windows Phone supports either 16 or 32bpp (bits per pixel). By default Windows Phone apps use 16bpp, which can cause some images to appear to be of low quality. Gradients in particular are most subject to the apparent effects of low pixel density, and when using 16bpp, banding may be detected in some images.

To use 32bpp in your app, modify its WMAppManifest.xml file by adding a BitsPerPixel attribute to the App element, as shown in the following excerpt:

```
<App . . .

    BitsPerPixel="32">

</App>
```

Be aware that using 32bpp may impact the performance of your app, especially if you are rendering a lot of images in a list, for example. Where possible, apply dithering as preprocessing to image assets instead.

Creating a Photos Extras Application

The Extras menu of the built-in picture viewer app allows you to add a link to your app so that the user can quickly launch your app from within the picture viewer. This effectively allows you to extend the picture viewer with your own app.

An Extras application may be used to enhance an image's color, crop an image, convert an image to monochrome, or even read a photo's Exchangeable image file format (EXIF) information to display where the photo was taken on a map.

For an example of an app that reads EXIF data, see the Photo Location app on the Windows Phone Marketplace. (Full disclosure: The app is written by my wife.)

When users tap the three dots on the application bar in the picture viewer, they see a menu containing a link to the Extras menu (see Figure 20.1).

FIGURE 20.1   Users can activate a photo Extras application or a photo Share application.

Users selecting the Extras menu item see the list of apps that are registered as Extras applications (see Figure 20.2).

FIGURE 20.2   The sample Extras application displayed in the Extras menu.

When a user selects your app from the Extras menu, your app is launched, and it receives an identifier (a token) that is used to retrieve the image from the phone's image library.

Adding Your App to the Extras Menu

To indicate to the Windows Phone picture viewer that your app should be included in the Extras menu, the inclusion of an XML file called Extras.xml is required in the root of your XAP file.

To add the Extras.xml file to your project, follow these steps:

1. Right-click the name of your project in the Solution Explorer and select Add, New Item.

2. On the Add New Item page, select XML File; then name the file Extras.xml.

3. Select Add.

> **NOTE**
>
> Make sure that the Extras.xml file is set to Content. Contrary to the official documentation on MSDN, the Copy to Output Directory option should be set to Do Not Copy. You can do this via the Visual Studio Properties window after selecting the file in the Solution Explorer.

Edit the Extras.xml file so that it matches Listing 20.1.

LISTING 20.1   Extras.xml

```xml
<?xml version="1.0" encoding="utf-8" ?>
<Extras>
    <PhotosExtrasApplication>
        <Enabled>true</Enabled>
    </PhotosExtrasApplication>
</Extras>
```

When an app is installed on the phone, the OS scans the XAP file. When it discovers the Extras.xml file, it adds your app to the picture viewer's Extras menu.

An Edge-Tracing Extras Application

This section looks at building an Extras application that converts an image to a line drawing by tracing its edges, and then allows the user to save the image to the Saved Pictures folder in the Pictures Hub. The example app for this section is located in the WPUnleashed.ExtrasExample project in the downloadable sample code.

When your app is selected from the Extras menu, your app is launched, and the main page of your app has its query string populated with a string identifier named token. The token value is then used to retrieve the image from the phone's image library, as shown later in this section.

To hasten the pace of development and to enable testing of your app without deploying to a Windows Phone device, it is useful to feed your app with a dummy image so that it does not have to rely on the Pictures Hub.

In the following excerpt from MainPage.xaml.cs, you see how to detect whether the app is executing on the emulator using the `Microsoft.Devices.Environment.DeviceType` property. If so, substitute the image, which would otherwise be supplied by the picture viewer, with a sample image stored as an embedded resource.

Conversely, if not executing within the emulator, attempt to extract the token from the page's query string, as shown:

```
protected override void OnNavigatedTo(NavigationEventArgs e)
{
    base.OnNavigatedTo(e);

    /* Equivalent to: Environment.DeviceType == DeviceType.Emulator */
    if (EnvironmentValues.UsingEmulator)
    {
        ProcessTestImage();
    }
    else
    {
        string token;
        if (NavigationContext.QueryString.TryGetValue("token", out token))
        {
            ProcessImageUsingToken(token);
        }
        else
        {
            if (image.Source == null)
            {
                photoChooserTask.Show();
            }
        }
    }
}
```

When the query string does not contain a token, it indicates that the app has been launched from either the Start Experience (if the app has been pinned there), or from the Application List.

NOTE

It is a Windows Phone Marketplace certification requirement that if your Extras application is launched from the application list (not from the Extras menu) it must invoke the PhotoChooser task to allow the user to select an image or take a photo. Conversely, it is also a requirement that if your app is launched from the Extras menu, it should not require further image selection steps.

20

To retrieve an image from the phone's image library, we leverage the XNA framework—in particular, the `Microsoft.Xna.Framework.Media.MediaLibrary` class located in the Microsoft.Xna.Framework assembly.

The XNA `MediaLibrary` class is used to retrieve the image with the specified token. The `MediaLibrary` class implements `IDisposable`, and hence it is wrapped in a using statement, as shown in the following excerpt:

```
void ProcessImageUsingToken(string token)
{
    imageName = token;

    Picture picture;
    using (MediaLibrary mediaLibrary = new MediaLibrary())
    {
        picture = mediaLibrary.GetPictureFromToken(token);
    }
    Stream imageStream = picture.GetImage();
    ProcessImage(imageStream);
}
```

When the image `Stream` has been retrieved, the `ProcessImage` method is called, which creates a `BitmapImage` object. The `BitmapImage` is assigned to an `Image` control on the page (see Figure 20.3).

FIGURE 20.3   The sample Extras application.

The image is displayed until processing has completed. Then the `Image` control's `Source` property is assigned to the processed image in the `HandleEdgesFound` method.

The `ProcessImage` method creates a new `BitmapImage` object and passes it to the `BitmapUtility.FindEdgesUsingSobel` method (see Listing 20.2).

> **NOTE**
>
> The `CreateOptions` property of the `BitmapImage` class allows you to specify when the image is to be created. By default, the value is `BitmapCreationOptions.BackgroundCreation`, which causes the image to be created on a background thread and frees the UI thread from processing the image.
>
> Because we require the `BitmapImage` immediately, the `CreateOptions` property is explicitly set to `BitmapCreateOptions.None`.

The `saveCommand` is disabled by setting the `canSave` flag to false.

LISTING 20.2   `MainPage.ProcessImage` Method

```
void ProcessImage(Stream imageStream)
{
    BitmapImage sourceImage = new BitmapImage();
    sourceImage.CreateOptions = BitmapCreateOptions.None;
    sourceImage.SetSource(imageStream);
    image.Source = sourceImage;

    canSave = false;
    saveCommand.RaiseCanExecuteChanged();

    progressBar.Visibility = Visibility.Visible;
    BitmapUtility.FindEdgesUsingSobel(sourceImage, HandleEdgesFound);
}
```

The custom `BitmapUtility` class contains a `FindEdgesUsingSobel` method, which attempts to reduce an image to a line drawing by locating the distinct edges within the image. Unlike Silverlight for the browser, Windows Phone does not support `UIElement` pixel shader effects. You therefore must either switch to Direct3D, which supports pixel shaders, or resort to processing the image in code, which is unfortunately much slower than using a custom pixel shader.

To allow the app to remain responsive during processing, the image is processed asynchronously using a thread from the thread pool. When processing completes, the `resultAction` is invoked on the UI thread using the default `Dispatcher`, as shown:

```
public static void FindEdgesUsingSobel(BitmapSource bitmapSource,
    Action<ResultEventArgs<WriteableBitmap>> resultAction)
{
```

20

```
ArgumentValidator.AssertNotNull(bitmapSource, "bitmapSource");
ArgumentValidator.AssertNotNull(resultAction, "resultAction");

WriteableBitmap sourceBitmap = new WriteableBitmap(bitmapSource);
int[] sourcePixels = sourceBitmap.Pixels;
int imageWidth = bitmapSource.PixelWidth;
int imageHeight = bitmapSource.PixelHeight;

ThreadPool.QueueUserWorkItem(
    delegate
    {
        try
        {
            int[] resultPixels = FindEdgesUsingSobelCore(
                                    sourcePixels,
                                    imageWidth,
                                    imageHeight);
            Deployment.Current.Dispatcher.BeginInvoke(
                delegate
                {
                    WriteableBitmap resultBitmap
                        = new WriteableBitmap(bitmapSource);

                    for (int i = 0; i < resultPixels.Length; i++)
                    {
                        resultBitmap.Pixels[i] = resultPixels[i];
                    }

                    resultAction(new ResultEventArgs<WriteableBitmap>(
                                        resultBitmap));
                });

        }
        catch (Exception ex)
        {
            resultAction(new ResultEventArgs<WriteableBitmap>(null, ex));
        }
    });
}
```

The FindEdgesUsingSobelCore method is where the main processing takes place.
FindEdgesUsingSobelCore produces an int array representing the image pixels of the
traced image. On completion, these pixels are copied to a new WriteableBitmap and
returned to the caller via the resultAction.

A Sobel filter is implemented within the FindEdgesUsingSobelCore method. The method produces either white or black pixels, depending on a pixel's intensity and that of its neighbors. See the following excerpt:

```
static int[] FindEdgesUsingSobelCore(
    int[] sourcePixels, int imageWidth, int imageHeight)
{
    /* Sobel Matrices */
    int[,] gx = new[,] { { -1, 0, 1 }, { -2, 0, 2 }, { -1, 0, 1 } };
    int[,] gy = new[,] { { 1, 2, 1 }, { 0, 0, 0 }, { -1, -2, -1 } };

    int[] resultPixels = new int[sourcePixels.Length];

    for (int i = 1; i < imageHeight - 1; i++)
    {
        for (int j = 1; j < imageWidth - 1; j++)
        {
            float newX = 0;
            float newY = 0;
            float c;
            for (int hw = -1; hw < 2; hw++)
            {
                for (int wi = -1; wi < 2; wi++)
                {
                    int row = j + wi;
                    int column = i + hw;
                    int position = column * imageWidth + row;
                    int pixel = sourcePixels[position];
                    var bytes = BitConverter.GetBytes(pixel);
                    c = (bytes[0] + bytes[1] + bytes[2]) / 3;
                    int index0 = hw + 1;
                    int index1 = wi + 1;
                    newX += gx[index0, index1] * c;
                    newY += gy[index0, index1] * c;
                }
            }

            int resultPosition = i * imageWidth + j;
            int colorIntValue;

            if (newX * newX + newY * newY > 16384 /* 128 * 128 */)
            {
                colorIntValue = ToInt(Color.White);
            }
            else
            {
```

```
                colorIntValue = ToInt(Color.Black);
            }
            resultPixels[resultPosition] = colorIntValue;
        }
    }
    return resultPixels;
}
```

To produce either a black or white pixel, convert a `Microsoft.Xna.Framework.Color` value to an integer value by combining the A,R,G, and B byte color components, as shown:

```
static int ToInt(Color color)
{
    return (color.A << 24) | (color.R << 16)
            | (color.G << 8) | (color.B << 0);
}
```

When the asynchronous portion of the `FindEdgesUsingSobel` method completes, the resulting `WriteableBitmap` is passed back to the caller within an instance of the `ResultEventArgs`. The `ResultEventArgs` contains a generic `Result` property, which, in this case, holds the resulting `WriteableBitmap` and an `Error` property if something goes awry:

```
public class ResultEventArgs<T> : EventArgs
{
    public T Result { get; private set; }
    public Exception Error { get; private set; }

    public ResultEventArgs(T result, Exception error = null)
    {
        Result = result;
        Error = error;
    }
}
```

The `HandleEdgesFound` method within the `MainPage` class handles the result of the `FindEdgesUsingSobel` method. If no errors occurred during processing, the `WriteableBitmap` is assigned to the `Source` property of the `Image` control:

```
void HandleEdgesFound(ResultEventArgs<WriteableBitmap> obj)
{
    progressBar.Visibility = Visibility.Collapsed;

    if (obj.Error != null)
    {
        MessageBox.Show("Unable to find edges.");
        return;
```

```
    }
    image.Source = obj.Result;
    canSave = true;
    saveCommand.RaiseCanExecuteChanged();
}
```

When processing completes, the image is displayed (see Figure 20.4).

FIGURE 20.4   The sample Extras application after processing of the image is complete.

As mentioned earlier in this section, when debugging using the emulator, a dummy image is used. The location of this image is defined as a constant within the ProcessTestImage method, as shown:

```
void ProcessTestImage()
{
    const string testImageUrl = @"/DanielVaughan.WPUnleashed"
        + ".ExtrasExample;component/Images/TestImage.jpg";

    var imageUri = new Uri(testImageUrl, UriKind.Relative);

    using (Stream stream = Application.GetResourceStream(imageUri).Stream)
    {
        BitmapSource bitmapSource = new BitmapImage();
        bitmapSource.SetSource(stream);
```

20

```
        image.Source = bitmapSource;

        progressBar.Visibility = Visibility.Visible;
        BitmapUtility.FindEdgesUsingSobel(bitmapSource, HandleEdgesFound);
    }
}
```

When the app is launched from the Application List, rather than from the Extras menu, the app must use the PhotoChooserTask to allow the user to select an image. Accordingly, a PhotoChooserTask is defined as a field, and its Completed event is subscribed to in the page constructor, as shown:

```
readonly PhotoChooserTask photoChooserTask = new PhotoChooserTask();

public MainPage()
{
    InitializeComponent();
    ...
    photoChooserTask.Completed += HandlePhotoChooserTaskCompleted;
}
```

For more information on the PhotoChooserTask see Chapter 14, "Leveraging Built-In Apps via Launchers and Choosers."

The HandlePhotoChooserTaskCompleted method takes the resulting image Stream and, like the ProcessImageUsingToken method shown earlier, calls the ProcessImage method, as shown:

```
void HandlePhotoChooserTaskCompleted(object sender, PhotoResult e)
{
    if (e.TaskResult != TaskResult.OK)
    {
        return;
    }
    imageName = e.OriginalFileName;

    if (!string.IsNullOrWhiteSpace(imageName))
    {
        int index = imageName.LastIndexOf(@"\");
        if (index >= 0)
        {
            imageName = "Unleashed_" + imageName.Substring(index + 1);
        }
    }
    else
    {
```

```
        imageName = string.Format(
            "Unleashed_{0:yyyy-MM-dd-HH-mm-ss}.jpg", DateTime.Now);
    }
    Stream imageStream = e.ChosenPhoto;
    ProcessImage(imageStream);
}
```

The `imageName` field is constructed using the original filename of the image.

Saving the Image

After processing is complete, the user is provided with the means to save the image via an application bar icon button. The page contains an `ICommand` called `SaveCommand`, as shown:

```
readonly ICommand saveCommand;

public ICommand SaveCommand
{
    get
    {
        return saveCommand;
    }
}
```

The command is instantiated in the constructor and when executed calls the page's `SaveImage` method, which is shown in the following excerpt:

```
public MainPage()
{
    InitializeComponent();

    saveCommand = new DelegateCommand(obj => SaveImage());

    DataContext = this;

    photoChooserTask.Completed += HandlePhotoChooserTaskCompleted;
}
```

The `SaveImage` method retrieves the `WriteableBitmap` from the `Image` control and then uses the `WriteableBitmap` extension method `SaveJpeg` to write the image bytes to a `MemoryStream`. The `MemoryStream` is then passed to the `MediaLibrary.SavePicture` method, as shown:

```
void SaveImage()
{
    var writeableBitmap = (WriteableBitmap)image.Source;
```

20

```csharp
if (writeableBitmap == null)
{
    return;
}

const int jpegQuality = 90;

using (MemoryStream memoryStream = new MemoryStream())
{
    writeableBitmap.SaveJpeg(
        memoryStream,
        writeableBitmap.PixelWidth, // target width
        writeableBitmap.PixelHeight, // target height
        0, // orientation.
        jpegQuality);
    memoryStream.Seek(0, SeekOrigin.Begin);
    using (MediaLibrary mediaLibrary = new MediaLibrary())
    {
        Picture savedPicture
            = mediaLibrary.SavePicture(imageName, memoryStream);
    }
}

MessageBox.Show("Image saved to Saved Pictures.");
}
```

The `MediaLibrary.SavePicture` method requires that the specified image name is not null or an empty string. The `SavePicture` method has two overloads; one accepts a `Stream` of image bytes, the other a byte array representing the image. Both save the image to the Saved Pictures album in the Pictures Hub.

The XAML for the `MainPage` class contains an `AppBarIconButton` with a binding to the `SaveCommand` (see Listing 20.3). For more information on the custom `AppBarIconButton`, see Chapter 8, "Taming the Application Bar."

LISTING 20.3   Extras Example `MainPage` XAML (excerpt)

```xml
<Grid x:Name="LayoutRoot" Background="Transparent">
  <Grid.RowDefinitions>
    <RowDefinition Height="Auto"/>
    <RowDefinition Height="*"/>
  </Grid.RowDefinitions>

  <u:AppBar>
    <u:AppBarIconButton
```

```
                    x:Name="button_Save"
                    Command="{Binding SaveCommand}"
                    Text="Save"
                    IconUri="/Images/appbar.save.rest.png" />
    </u:AppBar>

    <StackPanel x:Name="TitlePanel" Grid.Row="0" Margin="12,17,0,28">
      <TextBlock Text="Windows Phone Unleashed"
                 Style="{StaticResource PhoneTextNormalStyle}"/>
      <TextBlock Text="extras" Margin="9,-7,0,0"
                 Style="{StaticResource PhoneTextTitle1Style}"/>
    </StackPanel>

    <Grid x:Name="ContentPanel" Grid.Row="1" Margin="12,0,12,0">
      <Image x:Name="image" />
      <ProgressBar x:Name="progressBar" IsIndeterminate="True" />
    </Grid>
  </Grid>
```

When the SaveImage method completes, a message is displayed informing the user that the image was successfully saved (see Figure 20.5).

FIGURE 20.5   The message box confirms that the image has been saved.

Share Menu Extensibility

The Share menu of the picture viewer functions in much the same way as the Extras menu. The Share menu enables users to select a particular app to transfer an image somewhere, such as via email or to a third-party service such as Twitter. When the Share menu is selected, a list of registered Share applications is presented (see Figure 20.6).

FIGURE 20.6   The picture viewer Share menu.

The title displayed in the Share menu is taken from your app's WMAppManifest.xml file. The screen displays the text *upload to*, followed by the App element's Title attribute. The length of the displayed title is limited to two lines and is truncated if it exceeds that number.

Although some services are available by default, you can extend the share picker with additional apps in a similar manner as the Extras menu.

Adding Your App to the Share Menu

To extend the share menu to include your photo share application, create a new file called E0F0E49A-3EB1-4970-B780-45DA41EC7C28.xml in the root directory of your main project. Rather than typing the name by hand, you may prefer to copy the XML file to your project from the downloadable sample code.

> **NOTE**
>
> Using the Visual Studio Properties window, make sure that the XML file build action is set to Content. Set the Copy to Output Directory option to Do Not Copy.

The existence of this file in the root of your XAP file indicates to the phone OS that your app participates as a Share application.

The awkwardly named XML file uses a GUID in its name. This appears to be an attempt to avoid collisions with other filenames. It is an unfortunate choice because it is unconventional and not in line with the Extras.xml filename.

A Simple Photo Upload Share Application

This section looks at building a photo Share application that takes an image and uploads it as a byte array to a WCF service. The example app is located in the WPUnleashed. ShareExample project in the downloadable sample code. The WCF service that the app communicates with is located in the WPUnleashed.Web project.

When your app is selected from the Share menu in the built-in picture viewer, your app is launched and the main page of your app has its query string populated with a string identifier named FileId. Extras applications use Token as their identifier; Share applications use FileId.

The FileId value is used to retrieve the image from the Pictures Hub in the same manner as an Extras application retrieves the image.

In the following excerpt from MainPage.xaml.cs, the code to detect whether the app is executing within the emulator has been abstracted to a custom class called EnvironmentValues, which provides for greater flexibility during testing and potentially increases the portability of your code.

If the code is executing within the emulator, we rely on a dummy image, or else the image is retrieved using the file ID provided in the page query string. If no file ID is present, the PhotoChooserTask is used to allow the user to select an image from the Pictures Hub:

```
protected override void OnNavigatedTo(NavigationEventArgs e)
{
    base.OnNavigatedTo(e);

    /* Equivalent to: Environment.DeviceType == DeviceType.Emulator */
    if (EnvironmentValues.UsingEmulator)
    {
        ProcessShareTestImage();
    }
    else
    {
        string fileId;
        if (NavigationContext.QueryString.TryGetValue("FileId", out fileId))
        {
            imageName = fileId;
            ProcessShareImage(fileId);
        }
        else
        {
            photoChooserTask.Show();
        }
```

```
        }
}
```

NOTE

It is a Windows Phone Marketplace certification requirement that if your Share application is launched from the application list (not from the Share menu), it must invoke the
PhotoChooser task to allow the user to select an image or take a photo. Conversely, it is
also a requirement that if your app is launched from the Share menu, no further image
selection steps should be required.

To determine whether your app has been launched from the Share menu in the Picture
Viewer, you can either test for the presence of the FileId query string parameter, as
demonstrated in the previous example, or test whether the query string contains an *Action*
parameter set to ShareContent, as shown in the following example:

```
string action;

NavigationContext.QueryString.TryGetValue("action", out action);

if (action == "ShareContent")
{
    /* Launched from Share menu. */
}
```

As with the Extras application in the previous section, Share applications rely on the
XNA `MediaLibrary` class for retrieving the selected image. The following using statements
should be included at the top of your page:

```
using System.IO;
using System.Windows.Media.Imaging;
using Microsoft.Phone.Tasks;
using Microsoft.Xna.Framework.Media;
```

The custom `ProcessShareImage` method uses the token provided in the query string to
retrieve the image from the phone's media library, as shown:

```
void ProcessShareImage(string token)
{
    MediaLibrary mediaLibrary = new MediaLibrary();
    Picture picture = mediaLibrary.GetPictureFromToken(token);
    SetImageStream(picture.GetImage());
}
```

The `SetImageStream` method takes the `Stream` returned from the `Picture.GetImage`
method and creates a new `BitmapImage`, which is then assigned to an `Image` control on the
page:

```
void SetImageStream(Stream imageStream)
{
    BitmapSource bitmapSource = new BitmapImage();
    bitmapSource.SetSource(imageStream);
    image.Source = bitmapSource;
}
```

When executing within the emulator, the ProcessShareTestImage takes a different approach and uses an image stored as a resource within the project. As stated previously, this facilitates development by removing the reliance on the Pictures Hub and is useful for testing purposes. See the following excerpt:

```
string testImageUrl = @"/DanielVaughan.WPUnleashed" +
                        ".ShareExample;component/Images/TestImage.jpg";
string imageName = "WPUnleashedTestImage";

void ProcessShareTestImage()
{
    var imageUri = new Uri(testImageUrl, UriKind.Relative);

    using (Stream stream = Application.GetResourceStream(imageUri).Stream)
    {
        SetImageStream(stream);
    }
}
```

So far, you have seen how the image is retrieved from the image library and displayed using an Image control. However, the real value of a photo Share application lies in its ability to send the image somewhere. In the sample, the image is sent to a web service located in the WPUnleashed.Web project.

An ICommand named UploadCommand is used to begin the upload and is initialized within the class constructor, like so:

```
public MainPage()
{
    InitializeComponent();

    uploadCommand = new DelegateCommand(obj => UploadImage());

    DataContext = this;

    client.UploadImageCompleted += HandleUploadImageCompleted;
    photoChooserTask.Completed += HandlePhotoChooserTaskCompleted;
}
```

20

The `uploadCommand` field is a `DelegateCommand` that calls the `UploadImage` method when the command is executed.

The `DataContext` of the page is set to the page itself. This enables you to easily bind to any commands within the page and acts as a quasi viewmodel.

After the command is executed and you have the image, you need to upload it somewhere. This chapter uses a simple web service called ImageUploadService that accepts a byte array representing an image and the name of the image.

The `ImageUploadService` with its single `UploadImage` method is shown in Listing 20.4.

LISTING 20.4   `ImageUploadService` Class

```
[ServiceContract(Namespace = "WPUnleashed")]
[AspNetCompatibilityRequirements(RequirementsMode
                            = AspNetCompatibilityRequirementsMode.Allowed)]
public class ImageUploadService
{
    [OperationContract]
    public void UploadImage(byte[] imageBytes, string name)
    {
        Debug.WriteLine(string.Format("Saving image {0}.", name));
        /* TODO: Save the image to a database or directory. */
    }
}
```

Ordinarily, the generated XML configuration for the WCF service would be adequate to send most objects over the wire. However, sending an image as a large byte array to the WCF service fails if the configuration is not modified. Specifically, the `maxArrayLength` and `maxReceivedMessageSize` need to be explicitly defined, as shown in the following excerpt:

```
<binding name="ImageUploadService.customBinding0">
  <binaryMessageEncoding>
    <readerQuotas
        maxArrayLength="2147483647" />
  </binaryMessageEncoding>
  <httpTransport
      maxReceivedMessageSize="2147483647" />
</binding>
```

To consume the WCF service from the Windows Phone app, a service reference is created by right-clicking the project node and selecting Add Service Reference (see Figure 20.7).

FIGURE 20.7   Adding a service reference for the custom `ImageUploadService`.

The app is then able to use the service via the generated service client, which is called
`ImageUploadServiceClient`. `UploadCommand` calls `UploadImage` when it is executed. The
`UploadImage` method retrieves the `BitmapImage` from the `Source` property of the `Image`
control and then uses it to create a `WriteableBitmap`. A `WriteableBitmap` is used because it
provides access to the image's pixels, whereas a `BitmapImage` does not.

After the image has been converted to a byte array using a custom extension method, the
bytes are sent to the WCF service, as shown:

```
void UploadImage()
{
    BitmapImage bitmapImage = (BitmapImage)image.Source;
    if (bitmapImage == null)
    {
        return;
    }

    WriteableBitmap writeableBitmap = new WriteableBitmap(bitmapImage);
    byte[] imageBytes = writeableBitmap.ToByteArray();

    try
    {
        SetProgressBarVisibility(true);
        client.UploadImageAsync(imageBytes, imageName);
    }
    catch (Exception)
    {
```

20

```
            SetProgressBarVisibility(false);
            throw;
        }
    }
}
```

To convert the `WriteableBitmap` to a `byte` array, we use a custom `BitmapExtensions` class that contains the `ToByteArray` method, shown in the next excerpt. The `WriteableBitmap` represents each pixel using an integer value. An integer contains four bytes, representing the red, green, blue, and alpha components of a pixel. The `ToByteArray` method splits the integer values into its consecutive bytes using the static `Buffer.BlockCopy` method, as shown:

```
public static byte[] ToByteArray(this WriteeableBitmap writeableBitmap)
{
    ArgumentValidator.AssertNotNull(writeableBitmap, "writeableBitmap");
    int[] pixels = writeableBitmap.Pixels;
    int arrayLength = pixels.Length * 4;
    byte[] result = new byte[arrayLength];
    Buffer.BlockCopy(pixels, 0, result, 0, arrayLength);
    return result;
}
```

The `MainPage` XAML file contains an `AppBarIconButton`, which, when tapped by the user, executes the `UploadCommand` in the code-beside. The image is displayed in an `Image` control. During the upload process, a `ProgressBar` is made visible to indicate that the image is being uploaded (see Listing 20.5).

LISTING 20.5   MainPage.xaml (excerpt)

```
<Grid x:Name="LayoutRoot" Background="Transparent">
    <Grid.RowDefinitions>
        <RowDefinition Height="Auto"/>
        <RowDefinition Height="*"/>
    </Grid.RowDefinitions>

    <u:AppBar>
      <u:AppBarIconButton
                x:Name="button_Upload"
                Command="{Binding UploadCommand}"
                Text="Upload"
                IconUri="/Images/appbar.upload.rest.png" />
    </u:AppBar>

    <StackPanel x:Name="TitlePanel" Grid.Row="0" Margin="12,17,0,28">
        <TextBlock Text="Windows Phone Unleashed"
                Style="{StaticResource PhoneTextNormalStyle}"/>
```

```
        <TextBlock Text="share" Margin="9,-7,0,0"
                    Style="{StaticResource PhoneTextTitle1Style}"/>
    </StackPanel>

    <Grid x:Name="ContentPanel" Grid.Row="1" Margin="12,0,12,0">
        <Image x:Name="image" />
        <ProgressBar x:Name="progressBar"
                        IsIndeterminate="True"
                        Visibility="Collapsed" />
    </Grid>
</Grid>
```

As soon as an image is selected by the user, it is displayed in the `Image` control. The user can then use the application bar icon button to upload the image to the WCF service (see Figure 20.8).

FIGURE 20.8   The sample photo share application.

When the WCF service client completes the image upload, the completed handler is called, as shown:

```
void HandleUploadImageCompleted(object sender, AsyncCompletedEventArgs e)
{
    SetProgressBarVisibility(false);
    if (e.Error != null)
```

```
    {
        MessageBox.Show("Error uploading image.");
        return;
    }
    MessageBox.Show("Image uploaded");
}
```

If the image bytes are successfully uploaded, a confirmation message is displayed (see Figure 20.9).

FIGURE 20.9   A message box confirms that the image was successfully uploaded.

Summary

This chapter began by looking at photo Extras applications. You saw how to add an application to the picture viewer's Extras menu and how to create an Extras application that traces the edges within an image and allows the user to save the image back to the phone's picture library.

Finally, this chapter looked at photo Share applications. You learned how to add an app to the picture viewer's Share menu, and how to create a photo Share application that uploads an image to a custom WCF service.

CHAPTER 21

Capturing Images and Video with the Camera

The camera has become an essential component of all mobile phones. Indeed, the manufacturing requirements for Windows Phone devices require them to have a camera with at least a 5 megapixel capability and an LED flash.

Most of the first-generation Windows Phone devices, however, did not have great cameras. New phones that have arrived since Windows Phone 7.5 (mango) have seen their cameras much improved, and mango brought with it programmatic access to both front- and rear-facing cameras, enabling scenarios such as video chat, image recognition, and augmented reality.

You saw in Chapter 14, "Leveraging Built-In Apps via Launchers and Choosers," how the `CameraCaptureTask` chooser can be used to launch the Windows Phone Camera app, allowing the user to take a photo and have it returned to your app. Although convenient in some scenarios, the `CameraCaptureTask` limits the capabilities of the capture process to that of the built-in camera app, which supports only photos and not video capture. By using the direct access camera APIs on the phone, you can control the camera directly from your app to capture both photos and video. The APIs allow you to control many aspects of the camera, including the flash, the hardware shutter button, and the autofocus mechanism.

The Windows Phone SDK includes two distinct APIs for the camera. The first is Windows Phone specific and centers on the `Microsoft.Devices.PhotoCamera` class. The second is the Silverlight webcam API.

The main difference between the webcam API and the `PhotoCamera` class is that the `PhotoCamera` allows you to make the camera perform autofocus, and to set the camera's flash mode, which the webcam API cannot.

Conversely, the webcam API allows you to capture video with audio and save it to isolated storage. The webcam API is platform agnostic, and code that uses the webcam API can also be used in Silverlight desktop and browser applications.

When deciding whether to use the `PhotoCamera` or the webcam API, you can make your decision based on the following criteria:

▶ If your app needs to take stills only, use `PhotoCamera`.

▶ If your app needs to capture audio and video, use the webcam API.

▶ If your app needs to be cross-platform and must support Silverlight for the browser, use the webcam API.

This chapter explores both approaches, beginning with `PhotoCamera`. You see how to capture still images and display live video using `PhotoCamera`, and you also look at leveraging the hardware shutter button and adding a live video effect.

The chapter then looks at the Silverlight webcam API and how to use it to capture audio and video and save it as an MP4 in isolated storage.

Finally, the chapter examines lenses, which are new to Windows Phone 8 and enable you to extend the phone's built-in camera experience.

> **NOTE**
>
> For the camera application to function, the Windows Phone application manifest, WMAppManifest.xml, must include a capability named ID_CAP_ISV_CAMERA. Without it, the application will not function correctly.
>
> The following capabilities element must be present in the WMAppManifest.xml file:
>
> `<Capability Name="ID_CAP_ISV_CAMERA" />`
>
> To use a device's front-facing camera, if it exists, you must add the ID_HW_FFCCAMERA capability, as shown:
>
> `<Capability Name=" ID_HW_FFCCAMERA" />`
>
> ID_HW_FFCCAMERA is not added automatically during the Windows Phone Marketplace capabilities detection process.
>
> If a particular camera capability is not present, an `InvalidOperationException` is raised when an attempt is made by your app to use the camera. Moreover, it may not be immediately apparent that the exception is due to the missing capability definition.

PhotoCamera

The advantage of the `PhotoCamera` class is that it gives control over the flash and autofocus when capturing images.

`PhotoCamera` is usually defined as a field in a page or viewmodel and then instantiated when needed. The device camera needs time to ready itself for use and cannot be used until it is initialized, indicated by an `Initialized` event. Initialization commences when the `PhotoCamera` is assigned to the source of a `VideoBrush`, using its `SetSource` method.

> **NOTE**
>
> Failure to call `VideoBrush.SetSource` with the `PhotoCamera` instance prevents the `Initialized` event from being raised.

The following example shows how to create and initialize a `PhotoCamera` using a `VideoBrush` within a `PhoneApplicationPage`:

```
PhotoCamera photoCamera;

protected override void OnNavigatedTo(NavigationEventArgs e)
{
    photoCamera = new PhotoCamera();
    photoCamera.Initialized += HandlePhotoCameraInitialized;

    videoBrush_Preview.SetSource(photoCamera);

    base.OnNavigatedTo(e);
}
```

The `Initialized` event allows the configuration of the camera. This may include setting the image resolution for captured images, setting the flash mode of the camera, and allowing subscription to the various `PhotoCamera` events, as demonstrated in the following excerpt:

```
void HandlePhotoCameraInitialized(
        object sender, CameraOperationCompletedEventArgs e)
{
    PhotoCamera camera = (PhotoCamera)sender;
    camera.Resolution = camera.AvailableResolutions.ElementAt(0);

    camera.AutoFocusCompleted += HandleAutoFocusCompleted;
    camera.CaptureCompleted += HandleCaptureCompleted;
    camera.CaptureThumbnailAvailable += HandleCaptureThumbnailAvailable;
    camera.CaptureImageAvailable += HandleCaptureImageAvailable;

    if (camera.IsFlashModeSupported(FlashMode.Auto))
    {
        FlashMode = FlashMode.Auto;
    }
}
```

Each of the events and the `PhotoCamera` properties are discussed in greater detail in the following section.

Building a `PhotoCamera` App

This section looks at using the `PhotoCamera` to create a custom camera app that allows the user to view live video from the camera and to take still image captures that are saved to the phone's media library. You look at performing post-processing of the `PhotoCamera`'s preview buffer to create a live video effect. In addition, this section looks at extending the app to provide a page that includes a list of photo thumbnails that link to images saved in the media library images.

The sample code for this section resides in the /Sensors/Camera directory of the WPUnleashed.Examples project in the downloadable sample code.

The section begins with the custom `PhotoCameraViewModel` class, which contains a `Start` and a `Stop` method that allows the `PhotoCamera` instance to be created on demand and disposed as soon as it is no longer required (see Listing 21.1).

Some phone devices support a front facing camera. The `Camera.IsCameraTypeSupported` method is used to determine whether a particular camera type is available on the device. Devices are required to have at least one camera, and by using the parameterless constructor of the `PhotoCamera` class, the primary (non-front facing) camera is used.

LISTING 21.1   `PhotoCameraViewModel` Class (excerpt)

```
public class PhotoCameraViewModel: ViewModelBase
{
    public PhotoCameraViewModel() : base("PhotoCamera")
    {
        /* Intentionally left blank. */
    }

    PhotoCamera photoCamera;

    public Camera Camera
    {
        get
        {
            return photoCamera;
        }
    }

    public void Start()
    {
        if (photoCamera != null)
        {
            return;
```

```
        }

        if (Camera.IsCameraTypeSupported(CameraType.FrontFacing))
        {
            photoCamera = new PhotoCamera(CameraType.FrontFacing);
        }
        else //if (PhotoCamera.IsCameraTypeSupported(CameraType.Primary))
        {
            photoCamera = new PhotoCamera(); /* Defaults to CameraType.Primary */
        }

        photoCamera.Initialized += HandlePhotoCameraInitialized;
    }
    ...
}
```

When the `PhotoCamera`'s `Initialized` event is raised, the `PhotoCamera` is ready for configuration, and the resolution and flash mode of the camera are set (see Listing 21.2). The first element of the camera's `AvailableResolutions` property indicates the lowest resolution that the camera supports. On my device, the available resolutions are 320×240, 640×480, 800×600, 1280×960, 1600×1200, 2048×1536, and 2592×1944.

When in operation, the `AutoFocusCompleted` event is raised indeterminately by the device itself whenever it decides to focus. The event is also raised following a call to the `PhotoCamera.Focus` method.

The `CaptureImageAvailable` and `CaptureThumbnailAvailable` events are raised after your code calls the camera's `CaptureImage` method, providing the opportunity to process the captured image and to save it to isolated storage, for example. In the sample, two things are performed when an image is captured: We handle the `CaptureImageAvailable` event to save the image to the phone's media library, and we handle the `CaptureThumbnailAvailable` event to save a thumbnail of the image to isolated storage.

The `CaptureCompleted` event is raised after the `CaptureImageAvailable` event, providing the opportunity to update the UI in response. In the sample app, we overlay the video stream with a custom focus indicator image when the user presses the hardware shutter button and hide the image when the `CaptureCompleted` event is raised.

LISTING 21.2 `PhotoCameraViewModel.HandlePhotoCameraInitialized` Method

```
void HandlePhotoCameraInitialized(
        object sender, CameraOperationCompletedEventArgs e)
{
    cameraInitialized = true;

    PhotoCamera camera = (PhotoCamera)sender;
    camera.Resolution = camera.AvailableResolutions.ElementAt(0);
```

```
    camera.AutoFocusCompleted += HandleAutoFocusCompleted;
    camera.CaptureImageAvailable += HandleCaptureImageAvailable;
    camera.CaptureThumbnailAvailable += HandleCaptureThumbnailAvailable;
    camera.CaptureCompleted += HandleCaptureCompleted;

    FlashModes = flashModes.Where(
                    mode => photoCamera.IsFlashModeSupported(mode)).ToList();

    if (camera.IsFlashModeSupported(FlashMode.Auto))
    {
        FlashMode = FlashMode.Auto;
    }

    CameraButtons.ShutterKeyPressed += HandleShutterKeyPressed;
    CameraButtons.ShutterKeyHalfPressed += HandleShutterKeyHalfPressed;
    CameraButtons.ShutterKeyReleased += HandleShutterKeyReleased;
}
```

The viewmodel contains a `FlashModes` property that is populated with a list of `FlashMode` enumeration values for which the camera supports. The potential `FlashMode` values are as follows:

▶ Auto

▶ Off

▶ On

▶ RedEyeReduction

`FlashMode.Auto` lets the device decide whether the flash is warranted. Bu using the Off and On values, you can force the camera to use or not use the flash. `FlashMode.RedEyeReduction` is the most commonly unsupported flash mode. With red eye reduction enabled, the camera performs a brief flash cycle before taking the photo, causing the subjects' pupils to close and thereby eliminating the red eye effect.

`PhotoCamera.IsFlashModeSupported` allows you to determine whether a particular flash mode is supported and should be used before setting the camera's `FlashMode`.

NOTE

Attempting to set the camera's `FlashMode` to an unsupported value does not raise an exception but rather silently defaults the `FlashMode` to Off, effectively disabling the flash.

The `CameraButtons` class is used to monitor the device's hardware camera button. The three events: `ShutterKeyPressed`, `ShutterKeyHalfPressed`, and `ShutterKeyReleased`, allow you to emulate the behavior of the phone's built-in camera app. `CameraButtons` is independent of the `PhotoCamera` and can also be used in conjunction with the Silverlight webcam API if you so choose.

`CameraButtons` does nothing apart from allowing you to monitor the pressed state of the phone's camera shutter button. It is up to you to subscribe to the `CameraButtons` events and to control camera behavior accordingly.

The `PhotoCameraViewModel` contains a `VisualState` property that determines the set of controls available in the view. The following excerpt shows that when the `CameraButtons.ShutterKeyHalfPressed` event is raised, the `PhotoCamera.Focus` method is called, which causes the device camera to attempt to automatically focus on the scene:

```
void HandleShutterKeyHalfPressed(object sender, EventArgs e)
{
    VisualState = VisualStateValue.Focussing;
    photoCamera.Focus();
}
```

When the user fully presses the hardware button, the `CameraButtons.ShutterKeyPressed` event is raised. The viewmodel's event handler calls the camera's `CaptureImage` method, which causes the camera to acquire the current frame as a still image and to raise the `PhotoCamera.CaptureImageAvailable` event.

Prior to calling `CaptureImage`, we take the opportunity to generate a filename (based on the current time), which is used for two image files: one stored in the phone's media library and the other a thumbnail representation stored in isolated storage. Generating the filename at this point is necessary because the order in which the two `PhotoCamera` events, `CaptureImageAvailable` and `CaptureThumbnailAvailable`, are raised is indeterminable. See the following excerpt:

```
volatile string fileName;

void HandleShutterKeyPressed(object sender, EventArgs e)
{
    fileName = string.Format(
                "Unleashed_{0:yyyy-MM-dd-HH-mm-ss}.jpg", DateTime.Now);
    photoCamera.CaptureImage();
}
```

The use of the volatile keyword prevents the CLR from caching the `fileName` value, so that all threads use the field's most recent value.

When the user releases the hardware camera button, the camera's `CancelFocus` method is called to halt any auto focusing that is underway, and the visual state is returned to `NotFocusing`, which hides the focus indicator image in the view. See the following excerpt:

```
void HandleShutterKeyReleased(object sender, EventArgs e)
{
    photoCamera.CancelFocus();

    VisualState = VisualStateValue.NotFocusing;
}
```

The `PhotoCamera.CaptureImage` method causes the `PhotoCamera` events `CaptureImageAvailable` and `CaptureThumbnailAvailable` to be raised on a non-UI thread. This means that event handler code must invoke any changes to UI elements on the UI thread. In the following excerpt, the viewmodel's `SaveImage` method is invoked using the current `Dispatcher` instance:

```
void HandleCaptureImageAvailable(object sender, ContentReadyEventArgs e)
{
    Deployment.Current.Dispatcher.BeginInvoke(
        () => SaveImage(e.ImageStream,
                        (int)photoCamera.Resolution.Width,
                        (int)photoCamera.Resolution.Height));
}
```

NOTE

After the `PhotoCamera.CaptureImage` method is called, subsequent calls must occur after the `CaptureCompleted` event has been raised; otherwise, an `InvalidOperationException` is thrown.

The viewmodel's `SaveImage` method uses the `Microsoft.Xna.Framework.Media.MediaLibrary` class to save the picture to the media library, making it available from the phone's Pictures Hub. The built-in `WritableBitmap.LoadJpeg` extension method is used to place the captured image into an `ObservableCollection`, which is bound to a `ListBox` in the view. See the following excerpt:

```
void SaveImage(Stream imageStream, int width, int height)
{
    ArgumentValidator.AssertNotNull(imageStream, "imageStream");

    var mediaLibrary = new MediaLibrary();
    mediaLibrary.SavePicture(fileName, imageStream);
    imageStream.Position = 0;

    var bitmap = new WriteableBitmap(width, height);
    bitmap.LoadJpeg(imageStream);

    CapturedImages.Add(bitmap);
}
```

The `HandleCaptureThumbnailAvailable` method saves the thumbnail of the image to isolated storage, allowing you to use the name to retrieve the image from the media library at a later time (see Listing 21.3). Building a page to view the thumbnails is discussed later in this chapter.

LISTING 21.3   `PhotoCameraViewModel.HandleCaptureThumbnailAvailable` Method

```csharp
void HandleCaptureThumbnailAvailable(object sender, ContentReadyEventArgs e)
{
    using (e.ImageStream)
    {
        /* Save thumbnail as JPEG to isolated storage. */
        using (IsolatedStorageFile storageFile
                    = IsolatedStorageFile.GetUserStoreForApplication())
        {
            if (!storageFile.DirectoryExists(imageDirectory))
            {
                storageFile.CreateDirectory(imageDirectory);
            }

            using (IsolatedStorageFileStream targetStream
                        = storageFile.OpenFile(
                            imageDirectory + "/" + fileName,
                            FileMode.Create, FileAccess.Write))
            {
                /* Initialize the buffer for 4KB disk pages. */
                byte[] readBuffer = new byte[4096];
                int bytesRead;

                /* Copy the thumbnail to isolated storage. */
                while ((bytesRead = e.ImageStream.Read(
                                    readBuffer, 0, readBuffer.Length)) > 0)
                {
                    targetStream.Write(readBuffer, 0, bytesRead);
                }
            }
        }
    }
}
```

The viewmodel's `Stop` method unsubscribes from the various `PhotoCamera` events and calls `Dispose` on the `PhotoCamera` instance to free all managed and unmanaged resources, as shown:

```
public void Stop()
{
    cameraInitialized = false;

    if (photoCamera == null)
    {
        return;
    }

    photoCamera.Initialized -= HandlePhotoCameraInitialized;
    photoCamera.AutoFocusCompleted -= HandleAutoFocusCompleted;
    photoCamera.CaptureCompleted -= HandleCaptureCompleted;
    photoCamera.CaptureThumbnailAvailable -= HandleCaptureThumbnailAvailable;
    photoCamera.CaptureImageAvailable -= HandleCaptureImageAvailable;

    CameraButtons.ShutterKeyPressed -= HandleShutterKeyPressed;
    CameraButtons.ShutterKeyHalfPressed -= HandleShutterKeyHalfPressed;
    CameraButtons.ShutterKeyReleased -= HandleShutterKeyReleased;

    photoCamera.Dispose();
    photoCamera = null;
}
```

The viewmodel is instantiated in the PhotoCameraView page (see Listing 21.4). The page's OnNavigatedTo method is used to call the Start method of the viewmodel, and the page's OnNavigatedFrom method calls the viewmodel's Stop method, thus ensuring that the PhotoCamera is disposed as soon as the user leaves the page.

> **NOTE**
>
> Although the approach taken in this section explicitly calls the Start and Stop methods of the viewmodel, it is feasible that this approach could be further abstracted by placing the infrastructure for handling navigation events in the ViewModelBase class. This is, however, outside the scope of this book. The Calcium SDK project (http://calciumsdk.com) has this infrastructure in place.

After the PhotoCamera has been instantiated by the viewmodel, it can be attached to a VideoBrush, which causes the initialization of the PhotoCamera.

LISTING 21.4   PhotoCameraView Class

```
public partial class PhotoCameraView : PhoneApplicationPage
{
    readonly PhotoCameraViewModel viewModel = new PhotoCameraViewModel();
```

21

```
public PhotoCameraView()
{
    InitializeComponent();

    DataContext = viewModel;
}

PhotoCameraViewModel ViewModel
{
    get
    {
        return (PhotoCameraViewModel)DataContext;
    }
}

protected override void OnNavigatedTo(NavigationEventArgs e)
{
    ViewModel.Start();
    videoBrush_Preview.SetSource(ViewModel.Camera);

    base.OnNavigatedTo(e);
}

protected override void OnNavigatedFrom(NavigationEventArgs e)
{
    ViewModel.Stop();
    base.OnNavigatedFrom(e);
}
}
```

The view contains a Rectangle whose Fill property is set to the VideoBrush connected to the viewmodel's PhotoCamera (see Listing 21.5).

The viewmodel contains an EffectImage property of type ImageSource. As you see in a moment, this image is used to display the video in grayscale.

An Image control is bound to the EffectImage property in the view, and a Windows Phone Toolkit ToggleSwitch is used to switch the effect on and off.

When the PhotoCamera is performing an automatic focus, the Image named image_Focus is made visible.

A ListBox is bound to the CapturedImages property of the viewmodel and displays each captured image as a thumbnail on the left side of the page.

A `ListPicker` control is bound to the list of `FlashModes` in the viewmodel. Selecting a flash mode causes the viewmodel's `FlashMode` property to be updated and, in turn, the `PhotoCamera.FlashMode`.

LISTING 21.5   `PhotoCameraView` Page (excerpt)

```xml
<Grid x:Name="LayoutRoot" Background="Transparent">

    <Rectangle Width="800" Height="480">
        <Rectangle.Fill>
            <VideoBrush x:Name="videoBrush_Preview" />
        </Rectangle.Fill>
    </Rectangle>

    <Image x:Name="image_Effect"
           Source="{Binding EffectImage}"
           Visibility="Collapsed" Stretch="Fill" Width="800" Height="480" />

    <Image x:Name="image_Focus" Source="/Sensors/Camera/Images/Focus.png"
           Margin="314, 197.5" Visibility="Collapsed"/>

    <ListBox ItemsSource="{Binding CapturedImages}">
        <ListBox.ItemTemplate>
            <DataTemplate>
                <Border BorderThickness="2,2,2,8" BorderBrush="White">
                    <Image Stretch="Uniform" Width="80" Source="{Binding}"/>
                </Border>
            </DataTemplate>
        </ListBox.ItemTemplate>
    </ListBox>

    <StackPanel Style="{StaticResource PageTitlePanelStyle}">
        <TextBlock Text="Windows Phone Unleashed"
                   Style="{StaticResource PhoneTextAppTitleStyle}" />
        <TextBlock Text="{Binding Title}"
                   Style="{StaticResource PhoneTextPageTitleStyle}"/>
    </StackPanel>

    <StackPanel Width="200"
                HorizontalAlignment="Right" VerticalAlignment="Bottom">
        <TextBlock Text="effect"
                   FontSize="{StaticResource PhoneFontSizeMediumLarge}"/>
        <toolkit:ToggleSwitch IsChecked="{Binding EffectEnabled, Mode=TwoWay}"
                   FontSize="{StaticResource PhoneFontSizeExtraLarge}" />

        <TextBlock Text="flash mode"
```

```
                FontSize="{StaticResource PhoneFontSizeMediumLarge}"/>
        <toolkit:ListPicker ItemsSource="{Binding FlashModes}"
                    SelectedItem="{Binding FlashMode, Mode=TwoWay}" />
    </StackPanel>
    <VisualStateManager.VisualStateGroups>
        <VisualStateGroup x:Name="FocusStates">
            <VisualState x:Name="Focussing">
                <Storyboard>
                    <ObjectAnimationUsingKeyFrames Duration="0"
                            Storyboard.TargetProperty="Visibility"
                            Storyboard.TargetName="image_Focus">
                        <DiscreteObjectKeyFrame KeyTime="0">
                            <DiscreteObjectKeyFrame.Value>
                                <Visibility>Visible</Visibility>
                            </DiscreteObjectKeyFrame.Value>
                        </DiscreteObjectKeyFrame>
                    </ObjectAnimationUsingKeyFrames>
                </Storyboard>
            </VisualState>
            ...
        </VisualStateGroup>
        <VisualStateGroup x:Name="EffectStates">
            ...
        </VisualStateGroup>
    </VisualStateManager.VisualStateGroups>
</Grid>
```

Apart from one of the `VisualStateGroup` elements, all have been omitted from the excerpt to reduce its length.

The `VisualStateGroup` is set according to the `VisualState` property of the view-model. When the `VisualState` of the viewmodel changes to Focusing, for example, the `VisualStateManager` is directed to that state. This is all orchestrated using the custom `VisualStateUtility` class and an attached property named `VisualState`. For more information on the `VisualStateUtility` class, see Chapter 18, "Incorporating Map-Based Positioning."

The attached property is set on the `phone:PhoneApplicationPage` element of the view, as shown:

```
u:VisualStateUtility.VisualState="{Binding VisualState}"
```

When the viewmodel's `VisualState` property changes, the `HandleVisualStateChanged` method of the `VisualStateUtility` class is called, which calls the built-in `VisualStateManager.GoToState` method.

Figure 21.1 shows the PhotoCameraView page with a number of still captures displayed on the left and the flash mode selected as Auto.

FIGURE 21.1   `PhotoCameraView` page.

The next section looks at enabling a grayscale effect for the video stream.

Adding a Video Effect

The viewmodel contains an `EffectEnabled` property to toggle the video effect on and off, shown in the following excerpt:

```
volatile bool effectEnabled;

public bool EffectEnabled
{
    get
    {
        return effectEnabled;
    }
    set
    {
        if (Assign(ref effectEnabled, value) == AssignmentResult.Success)
        {
            SetEffectState(value);
        }
    }
}
```

When the `EffectEnabled` property is set, the `SetEffectState` method is called, which assigns the `EffectImage` property to a new `WritableBitmap` and begins updating the `WritableBitmap` as new frames are received on another thread. See the following excerpt:

```
void SetEffectState(bool enabled)
{
    if (enabled)
    {
        EffectImage = new WriteableBitmap(
            (int)photoCamera.PreviewResolution.Width,
            (int)photoCamera.PreviewResolution.Height);

        effectThread = new Thread(ProcessEffectFrames);
        effectThread.Start();
    }

    VisualState = enabled ? VisualStateValue.EffectOn
                          : VisualStateValue.EffectOff;
}
```

Unlike Silverlight for the browser, Windows Phone XAML apps do not support custom pixel shaders. Consequently, image post-processing must be performed in custom code. This, unfortunately, does not provide for great performance, as you see when switching on the effect on your own phone device.

The viewmodel's ProcessEffectFrames method, as you saw, is called from a non-UI thread. Its task is to retrieve an array of pixels from the PhotoCamera. It then converts each pixel (represented as an int value) to grayscale and uses the UI thread, via the apps Dispatcher, to write the pixels to the effectImage (see Listing 21.6). An AutoResetEvent is used to prevent a new frame from being processed until the current frame has been written to the effect image.

The GetPreviewBufferArgb32 of the PhotoCamera class copies the current frame into a buffer array so that it can be further manipulated. We use this to retrieve the frame pixels.

LISTING 21.6   ProcessEffectFrames Method

```
readonly AutoResetEvent frameResetEvent = new AutoResetEvent(true);

void ProcessEffectFrames()
{
    try
    {
        while (effectEnabled)
        {
            frameResetEvent.WaitOne();

            int width = (int)photoCamera.PreviewResolution.Width;
            int height = (int)photoCamera.PreviewResolution.Height;
            int[] pixelArray = new int[width * height];
```

```
        photoCamera.GetPreviewBufferArgb32(pixelArray);

        int[] effectPixels = new int[pixelArray.Length];

        for (int i = 0; i < pixelArray.Length; i++)
        {
            effectPixels[i] = ConvertColorToGrayScale(pixelArray[i]);
        }

        Deployment.Current.Dispatcher.BeginInvoke(
            delegate
                {
                    /* Copy pixels to the WriteableBitmap. */
                    effectPixels.CopyTo(effectImage.Pixels, 0);

                    effectImage.Invalidate();
                    frameResetEvent.Set();
                });
    }
}
catch (Exception ex)
{
    Debug.WriteLine("Unable to process effect frames." + ex);
    EffectEnabled = false;
    frameResetEvent.Set();
}
}
```

Two other preview related `PhotoCamera` methods are not shown in the example: `GetPreviewBufferYCbCr` and `GetPreviewBufferY`. Both also copy the current frame from the camera, yet do so without transforming the pixels to 32-bit ARGB values. `GetPreviewBufferYCbCr` provides the frame expressed using the YCbCr color space, whereas `GetPreviewBufferY` copies only the luminance data.

By avoiding the conversion to ARGB, retrieving the preview can be done much faster. According to René Schulte (http://kodierer.blogspot.com/2011/05/why-is-y-in-windows-phone-mango-camera.html), `GetPreviewBufferYCbCr` not only excludes the alpha channel in the YCrCb buffer, but in addition the Cr and Cb color components are stored with reduced resolution, keeping the buffer size substantially smaller and making the method approximately four times faster than `GetPreviewBufferArgb32`. Extracting the color components and brightness when using the YCbCr methods requires some more effort, however, and is outside the scope of this book.

Converting a pixel to grayscale involves first extracting the ARGB color components, as performed by the viewmodel's ConvertColorToArgb method, shown in the following excerpt:

```
void ConvertColorToArgb(
        int color, out int alpha, out int red, out int green, out int blue)
{
    alpha = color >> 24;
    red = (color & 0x00ff0000) >> 16;
    green = (color & 0x0000ff00) >> 8;
    blue = (color & 0x000000ff);
}
```

The red, green, and blue components are averaged to provide the grayscale value, as shown:

```
int ConvertColorToGrayScale(int color)
{
    int alpha, red, green, blue;
    ConvertColorToArgb(color, out alpha, out red, out green, out blue);

    int average = (red + green + blue) / 3;
    red = green = blue = average;

    int result = ConvertArgbToColor(alpha, red, green, blue);
    return result;
}
```

Finally, the color components are converted back to a color value using the viewmodel's ConvertArgbToColor method, as shown:

```
int ConvertArgbToColor(int alpha, int red, int green, int blue)
{
    int result = ((alpha & 0xFF) << 24)
                    | ((red & 0xFF) << 16)
                    | ((green & 0xFF) << 8)
                    | (blue & 0xFF);
    return result;
}
```

Figure 21.2 shows the result of the video effect, with the video displayed in grayscale.

Using the PhotoCamera's preview buffer is a way to produce live video effects. It does, however, suffer from suboptimal performance when each frame is redrawn. For improved performance, we must wait until Windows Phone XAML apps support custom pixel shaders.

FIGURE 21.2 `PhotoCameraView` page showing grayscale video effect.

Viewing Thumbnails

Earlier in the chapter you saw that the `PhotoCamera.CaptureThumbnailAvailable` event can be used to save a thumbnail image to isolated storage. This section looks at materializing those thumbnails on a page so that the user can tap a thumbnail and retrieve its associated full-size image from the phone's media library, all from within your app.

Recall that within the `PhotoCameraViewModel`, when the user releases the hardware shutter button, the `PhotoCamera.CaptureImage` method is called, which raises the `PhotoCamera`'s `CaptureThumbnailAvailable` and `CaptureImageAvailable` events.

The `CaptureImageAvailable` handler saves the image to the media library, whereas the `CaptureThumbnailAvailable` handler saves the thumbnail version of the image to isolated storage. Both images share the same name, however, which allows the retrieval of the corresponding media library image using the name of the thumbnail image.

The `PhotoCameraViewModel` saves all full-size images to a default PhotoCameraImages directory in isolated storage. The task of the `ThumbnailsViewModel` is to provide the names of these image files to the `ThumbnailsView` page, via an `ObservableCollection` of custom `ImageInfo` objects.

The `ImageInfo` class has two properties, which identify the location of the thumbnail in isolated storage and the name of the media library image (see Listing 21.7).

LISTING 21.7 `ImageInfo` Class

```
public class ImageInfo
{
    public string MediaLibraryUrl { get; private set; }
    public Uri ThumbnailUri { get; private set; }
```

```
public ImageInfo(Uri thumbnailUri, string mediaLibraryUrl)
{
    ThumbnailUri = ArgumentValidator.AssertNotNull(
                        thumbnailUri, "thumbnailUri");
    MediaLibraryUrl = ArgumentValidator.AssertNotNullOrEmpty(
                        mediaLibraryUrl, "mediaLibraryUrl");
}
}
```

The `ThumbnailsViewModel.Populate` method creates an `ImageInfo` object for each JPG image it finds in the isolated storage directory (see Listing 21.8).

The viewmodel's `Populate` method is called in the `OnNavigatedTo` method of the `ThumbnailsView` page. This causes new images present in the directory to be detected immediately after returning from the `PhotoCameraView` page.

LISTING 21.8   `ThumbnailsViewModel.Populate` Method

```
public void Populate()
{
    string imageDirectory = PhotoCameraViewModel.ImageDirectory;

    ObservableCollection<ImageInfo> tempImages
                = new ObservableCollection<ImageInfo>();

    using (IsolatedStorageFile storageFile
                = IsolatedStorageFile.GetUserStoreForApplication())
    {
        string[] fileNames = storageFile.GetFileNames(
                                imageDirectory + @"\*.jpg");
        foreach (string fileName in fileNames)
        {
            ImageInfo info = new ImageInfo(
                new Uri(imageDirectory + "/" + fileName, UriKind.Relative),
                fileName);
            tempImages.Add(info);
        }
    }

    Images = tempImages;
}
```

The `ThumbnailsViewModel` contains a `ViewImageCommand`, whose task is to navigate to the `MediaLibraryImageView` page. The name of the image is provided as a querystring parameter, allowing the `MediaLibraryImageView` to retrieve the image from the phone's media library. See the following excerpt:

```
public ThumbnailsViewModel() : base("photos")
{
    viewImageCommand = new DelegateCommand<string>(ViewImage);
}

void ViewImage(string name)
{
    Navigate("/Sensors/Camera/MediaLibraryImageView.xaml?image=" + name);
}
```

Thumbnails are presented by binding to the viewmodel's `Images` property, as shown:

```
ObservableCollection<ImageInfo> images
                = new ObservableCollection<ImageInfo>();

public ObservableCollection<ImageInfo> Images
{
    get
    {
        return images;
    }
    private set
    {
        Assign(ref images, value);
    }
}
```

To convert a path to an image stored in isolated storage, a custom `IValueConverter` is used (see Listing 21.9).

> **NOTE**
>
> It would be useful if the URI prefix isostore, which is used when working with local databases, worked with the `Image.Source` property. This would make the custom `IValueConverter` unnecessary. Unfortunately, though, the isostore prefix does not work with images.

LISTING 21.9 `StringToImageConverter` Class

```
public class StringToImageConverter : IValueConverter
{
    public object Convert(
        object value, Type targetType, object parameter, CultureInfo culture)
    {
        if (value == null)
        {
```

```
        return null;
    }

    using (IsolatedStorageFile storageFile
                = IsolatedStorageFile.GetUserStoreForApplication())
    {
        using (IsolatedStorageFileStream stream
                = storageFile.OpenFile(value.ToString(), FileMode.Open))
        {
            BitmapImage image = new BitmapImage();
            image.SetSource(stream);
            return image;
        }
    }
}

public object ConvertBack(
    object value, Type targetType, object parameter, CultureInfo culture)
{
    throw new NotImplementedException();
}
}
```

Within the ThumbnailsView page, thumbnail images are presented using a ListBox in combination with a Windows Phone Toolkit WrapPanel, as shown in the following excerpt:

```
<Grid x:Name="ContentPanel" Grid.Row="1" Margin="12,0,12,0">
    <ListBox ItemsSource="{Binding Images}">
        <ListBox.ItemsPanel>
            <ItemsPanelTemplate>
                <toolkit:WrapPanel ItemHeight="150" ItemWidth="150" />
            </ItemsPanelTemplate>
        </ListBox.ItemsPanel>
        <ListBox.ItemTemplate>
            <DataTemplate>
                <Image Source="{Binding ThumbnailUri,
                    Converter={StaticResource StringToImageConverter}}"
                    c:Commanding.Command="{Binding Content.ViewImageCommand,
                    Source={StaticResource bridge}}"
                    c:Commanding.CommandParameter="{Binding MediaLibraryUrl}"
                    Width="120" Height="120" Margin="10" />
            </DataTemplate>
        </ListBox.ItemTemplate>
    </ListBox>
</Grid>
```

The data context of each `Image` control is an `ImageInfo` object.

To reach out of the `DataTemplate` and execute the viewmodel's `ViewImageCommand`, a `ContentControl` whose content is set to the page is defined as resource and serves as a bridge between items in the `DataTemplate` and the viewmodel. See the following excerpt:

```
<phone:PhoneApplicationPage.Resources>
    <ValueConverters:StringToImageConverter
                x:Name="StringToImageConverter" />
    <ContentControl x:Name="bridge"
                Content="{Binding Path=DataContext, ElementName=page}" />
</phone:PhoneApplicationPage.Resources>
```

The custom `Command` attached property (introduced in Chapter 2, "Fundamental Concepts in Windows Phone Development") is used to execute the `ViewImageCommand` when the user taps a thumbnail image. The path to the image in the media library is passed as the command parameter.

`ThumbnailsView` also contains an `AppBar` with a single `AppBarHyperlinkButton` that, when tapped, navigates to the `PhotoCameraView` page:

```
<u:AppBar>
    <u:AppBarHyperlinkButton
                NavigateUri="/Sensors/Camera/PhotoCameraView.xaml"
                Text="PhotoCameraView"
                IconUri="/Sensors/Camera/Icons/TakePhoto.png" />
</u:AppBar>
```

Figure 21.3 shows the ThumbnailsView page populated with several images.

FIGURE 21.3   `ThumbnailsView` page.

When the user taps a thumbnail image, the app is directed to the `MediaLibraryImageView` page. The name of the image to display is supplied as a querystring parameter. The `MediaLibraryImageViewModel` retrieves the specified image from the phone's media library and exposes it via its `Image` property. The viewmodel's `LoadImageCommand` calls its `LoadImage` method, in which the `Picture` object is retrieved from the media library (see Listing 21.10).

`Picture.GetImage` is used to retrieve a `Stream` object, which then becomes the source of a `BitmapImage`.

In addition, the `Title` property of the viewmodel is set to the name of the `Picture`, which is subsequently displayed in the view.

LISTING 21.10 `MediaLibraryImageViewModel.LoadImage` Method

```
void LoadImage(string name)
{
    MediaLibrary mediaLibrary = new MediaLibrary();
    Picture picture = mediaLibrary.SavedPictures.Where(
                                x => x.Name == name).FirstOrDefault();
    if (picture == null)
    {
        MessageService.ShowError(
            string.Format("The picture {0} was not found.", name));
        return;
    }

    BitmapImage bitmapImage;
    using (Stream stream = picture.GetImage())
    {
        bitmapImage = new BitmapImage();
        bitmapImage.SetSource(stream);
    }

    Image = bitmapImage;
    Title = name;
}
```

The view contains an `Image` that is bound to the viewmodel's `Image` property, as shown:

```
<Grid x:Name="ContentPanel" Grid.Row="1" Margin="12,0,12,0">
    <Image Source="{Binding Image}" />
</Grid>
```

As with most examples throughout this book, the page's title container includes a `TextBlock` that is bound to the `Title` property of the `ViewModelBase` class. By following this pattern, it provides the viewmodel the ability to change the title of the page. As you saw in the `LoadImage` method, the `Title` property is set to the name of the image. See the following excerpt:

```xml
<StackPanel Grid.Row="0" Style="{StaticResource PageTitlePanelStyle}">
    <TextBlock Text="Windows Phone Unleashed"
               Style="{StaticResource PhoneTextAppTitleStyle}" />
    <TextBlock Text="{Binding Title}"
               Style="{StaticResource PhoneTextPageTitleStyle}"
               FontSize="{StaticResource PhoneFontSizeMediumLarge}" />
</StackPanel>
```

Figure 21.4 shows the MediaLibraryImageView page displaying an image from the media library.

FIGURE 21.4   `MediaLibraryImageView` page.

By using the `PhotoCamera` class combined with the Media Library API, you can create a full-featured camera app. The `PhotoCamera` class is, however, not suitable for apps that need to capture audio and video. The next section explores the Silverlight webcam API and how it is used to save audio and video to isolated storage.

Using the Silverlight Webcam API

The Silverlight webcam API came to the phone with the Windows Phone 7.5 SDK release. If you already have code for processing audio and video using the `System.Windows.Media.CaptureSource` class, you will feel right at home. `CaptureSource` allows you to capture both audio and video, and when used in conjunction with a `FileSink` class, allows you to save video to isolated storage.

This section creates a simplified version of the Photo Camera page presented in the previous section. A page is created that allows the user to capture still images as well as video, and in both cases, you see how captured data is written to isolated storage.

The sample for this section includes a page named `CaptureSourceView` and its view-model `CaptureSourceViewModel`, both located in the /Sensors/Camera directory of the WPUnleashed.Examples project in the downloadable sample code.

To begin, the viewmodel contains a property named `CaptureSource`, which is of type `CaptureSource`. The `CaptureSource` class is analogous to the `PhotoCamera` class.

The `CaptureSource` backing field is initialized in the viewmodel's `Start` method (see Listing 21.11).

> **NOTE**
>
> In Windows Phone, `CaptureDeviceConfiguration.AllowedDeviceAccess` is always true, even if the app does not have the ID_CAP_ISV_CAMERA capability specified in its WMAppManifest.xml file.

In Listing 21.11, both the test for `AllowedDeviceAccess` and the subsequent call to `RequestDeviceAccess` exist to retain compatibility with Silverlight for the browser, which does not use a capabilities model, but instead requires that the user authorize the request to use the camera via a confirmation dialog.

A `CaptureSource` instance is initialized using static methods of the `System.Windows.Media.CaptureDeviceConfiguration` class, which connects the `CaptureSource` to the video and audio capture device classes.

> **NOTE**
>
> If your app does not have the ID_CAP_ISV_CAMERA capability, an exception is raised after the call to `CaptureSource.Start`.
>
> Wrapping the `Start` call in a try/catch block does not allow the ensuing `COMException` to be caught because the exception is raised at an indeterminate point after the `Start` call returns.

LISTING 21.11 `CaptureSourceViewModel.Start` Method

```
public void Start()
{
    Stop();

    if (CaptureDeviceConfiguration.AllowedDeviceAccess
            || CaptureDeviceConfiguration.RequestDeviceAccess())
    {
        captureSource = new CaptureSource
          {
              VideoCaptureDevice
                = CaptureDeviceConfiguration.GetDefaultVideoCaptureDevice(),
              AudioCaptureDevice
                = CaptureDeviceConfiguration.GetDefaultAudioCaptureDevice()
```

```
        };

        captureSource.CaptureImageCompleted += HandleCaptureImageCompleted;
        captureSource.CaptureFailed += HandleCaptureFailed;

        captureSource.Start();
        started = true;
        UpdateCommands();
    }
}
```

Specifying the image format, including the resolution of captured images, is done by
setting the `CaptureSource` object's `VideoCaptureDevice.DesiredFormat` property. To determine which formats are supported, the `VideoCaptureDevice.SupportedFormats` property
is used. On my device there are two supported formats, both with a resolution of 640 by
480, but one offering 32-bit color while the other offers 8-bit grayscale. The desired format
can be indicated using one of the supported formats, as shown:

```
captureSource.VideoCaptureDevice.DesiredFormat
    = captureSource.VideoCaptureDevice.SupportedFormats[1];
```

NOTE

Setting the `DesiredFormat` affects still image captures, and not captured video.

In addition, the audio format can be specified by setting the `DesiredFormat` property of
the `AudioCaptureDevice` to one of the supported formats, like so:

```
foreach (AudioFormat supportedFormat
                in captureSource.AudioCaptureDevice.SupportedFormats)
{
    if (supportedFormat.BitsPerSample > 16)
    {
        captureSource.AudioCaptureDevice.DesiredFormat = supportedFormat;
        break;
    }
}
```

CaptureSourceViewModel

The viewmodel contains the following three commands:

► `TakePhotoCommand`

► `ToggleVideoCaptureCommand`

► `PlayVideoCommand`

TakePhotoCommand uses the CaptureSource to save a still image to isolated storage. ToggleVideoCaptureCommand starts and stops the recording of video and initially causes the CaptureSource to be attached to a FileSink object so that a video file is written to isolated storage.

The commands are instantiated in the viewmodel constructor like so:

```
public CaptureSourceViewModel() : base("CaptureSource")
{
    takePhotoCommand
        = new DelegateCommand(obj => TakePhoto(), obj => started);

    toggleVideoCaptureCommand
        = new DelegateCommand(obj => ToggleCapturingVideo());

    playVideoCommand
        = new DelegateCommand(obj => PlayVideo(),
                              obj => !capturingVideo && IsVideoCaptured());
}
```

Whenever something takes place that may alter the executable state of a command, the viewmodel's UpdateCommands method is called, which is shown in the following excerpt:

```
void UpdateCommands()
{
    takePhotoCommand.RaiseCanExecuteChanged();
    playVideoCommand.RaiseCanExecuteChanged();
}
```

The viewmodel's TakePhoto method calls the CaptureImageAsync method of the CaptureSource object, as shown:

```
void TakePhoto()
{
    if (captureSource != null && captureSource.State == CaptureState.Started)
    {
        captureSource.CaptureImageAsync();
    }
}
```

CaptureImageAsync attempts to use the device camera to capture an image.

NOTE

If CaptureImageAsync is called without first calling the CaptureSource.Start method, an InvalidOperationException is raised.

The `CaptureSource.CaptureImageCompleted` event is raised if the call completes asynchronously, which does not necessarily mean that an image has been successfully acquired. If an error occurs during image capture, the `CaptureSource.CaptureFailed` event is raised.

> **NOTE**
>
> Although the resulting `CaptureImageCompletedEventArgs` has an `Error` property (inherited from its `AsyncCompletedEventArgs`), this property is never set; therefore, it cannot be used for error detection.

The resulting image is saved to the phone's photo hub using the `MediaLibrary` class (see Listing 21.12). The dimensions of the image are supplied by the event arguments. Just as the `PhotoCamera` example maintained a collection of captured images, so too does the `CaptureSourceViewModel`.

LISTING 21.12   `CaptureSourceViewModel.HandleCaptureImageCompleted` Method

```
void HandleCaptureImageCompleted(object sender, CaptureImageCompletedEventArgs e)
{
    if (e.Result != null)
    {
        Deployment.Current.Dispatcher.BeginInvoke(() =>
        {
            MediaLibrary mediaLibrary = new MediaLibrary();
            string imageName = string.Format(
                    "Unleashed_{0:yyyy-MM-dd-HH-mm-ss}.jpg", DateTime.Now);
            using (MemoryStream stream = new MemoryStream())
            {
                e.Result.SaveJpeg(
                    stream, e.Result.PixelWidth, e.Result.PixelHeight,
                    0, 100);
                stream.Position = 0;
                mediaLibrary.SavePicture(imageName, stream);
            }
            CapturedImages.Add(e.Result);
        });
    }
}
```

The `CaptureSource.State` property, which is an enum value of type `CaptureState`, indicates the state of the `CaptureSource` object and can be either Failed, Started, or Stopped.

Recording the audio and video of a `CaptureSource` instance requires the attachment of a `FileSink` (see Listing 21.13). The `FileSink` object is assigned the location of a file in isolated storage, to which it writes the video file in MP4 format.

> **NOTE**
>
> The `CaptureSource` object must be in a stopped state to attach or detach a `FileSink`.
> Attempting to set the `FileSink.CaptureSource` property while the `CaptureSource` object
> is in a Started state raises an `InvalidOperationException`.

Stopping the capture of video involves detaching the `FileSink` from the `CaptureSource`
object. Again, the `FileSink` can be removed only if the `CaptureSource` is not started;
`CaptureSource.State` must not equal `CaptureState.Started`.

LISTING 21.13 `CaptureSourceViewModel.ToggleCapturingVideo` Method

```
FileSink fileSink;

void ToggleCapturingVideo()
{
    if (!capturingVideo)
    {
        fileSink = new FileSink {IsolatedStorageFileName = videoFileName};

        captureSource.Stop();
        fileSink.CaptureSource = captureSource;
        captureSource.Start();
    }
    else
    {
        captureSource.Stop();
        fileSink.CaptureSource = null;
        captureSource.Start();
    }

    CapturingVideo = !capturingVideo;
    UpdateCommands();
}
```

After a video has been recorded to isolated storage, it can be played back using either a
`MediaPlayer` control within the app or via the `MediaPlayerLauncher`, as shown in the
following excerpt:

```
void PlayVideo()
{
    MediaPlayerLauncher mediaPlayerLauncher = new MediaPlayerLauncher
        {
            Media = new Uri(videoFileName, UriKind.Relative),
            Location = MediaLocationType.Data,
        };
```

```
        mediaPlayerLauncher.Show();
}
```

Displaying Video in the `CaptureSourceView`

As with the `PhotoCamera` example earlier in this chapter, the view displays video using a `VideoBrush`, which is defined as shown:

```
<Rectangle Width="780" Height="460" Margin="10">
    <Rectangle.Fill>
        <VideoBrush x:Name="videoBrush_Preview" />
    </Rectangle.Fill>
</Rectangle>
```

The `CaptureSourceViewModel.Start` method is called in the `OnNavigatedTo` method of the page. Once started, the `VideoBrush` has its source set to the viewmodel's `CaptureSource` property. See the following excerpt:

```
protected override void OnNavigatedTo(NavigationEventArgs e)
{
    base.OnNavigatedTo(e);
    Dispatcher.BeginInvoke(
        delegate
            {
                ViewModel.Start();
                videoBrush_Preview.SetSource(ViewModel.CaptureSource);
            });
}
```

The Dispatcher is used to push the `ViewModel.Start` call onto the work stack of the UI thread. This workaround, for what appears to be an issue with the `CaptureSource` class, prevents the `CaptureSource` from raising a `COMException` when the app is activated.

Unlike the `PhotoCamera`, no `Initialized` event is raised when the `CaptureSource` is attached to a `VideoBrush`.

Captured images overlay the video preview and are displayed using a `ListBox`, as shown:

```
<ListBox ItemsSource="{Binding CapturedImages}" Margin="12">
    <ListBox.ItemTemplate>
        <DataTemplate>
            <Border BorderThickness="2,2,2,8" BorderBrush="White" Margin="3">
                <Image Source="{Binding}" Stretch="Uniform" Width="80" />
            </Border>
        </DataTemplate>
    </ListBox.ItemTemplate>
</ListBox>
```

An `AppBar` contains buttons that are bound to the three viewmodel commands: `PlayVideoCommand`, `ToggleVideoCaptureCommand`, and `TakePhoneCommand`.

An `AppBarToggleButton` changes its icon depending on the value of the viewmodel's `CapturingVideo` property. See the following excerpt:

```
<u:AppBar>
    <u:AppBarIconButton
                Command="{Binding PlayVideoCommand}"
                Text="play video"
                IconUri="/Sensors/Camera/Icons/Play.png" />
    <u:AppBarToggleButton
                Command1="{Binding ToggleVideoCaptureCommand}"
                Text1="record video"
                Icon1Uri="/Sensors/Camera/Icons/Record.png"
                Text2="stop"
                Icon2Uri="/Sensors/Camera/Icons/Stop.png"
                Toggled="{Binding CapturingVideo}" />
    <u:AppBarIconButton
                Command="{Binding TakePhotoCommand}"
                Text="take photo"
                IconUri="/Sensors/Camera/Icons/TakePhoto.png" />
</u:AppBar>
```

Figure 21.5 shows the CaptureSourceView page with the three application bar buttons, allowing the user to take a still capture and to record and play back video.

`CaptureSource` is the recommended way for recording video to isolated storage; it offers exciting possibilities for creating rich multimedia apps.

FIGURE 21.5   `CaptureSourceView` page.

Extending the Camera Experience with a Lens

New to Windows Phone 8 is a type of camera app known as a lens. A lens is launched from the built-in camera app and provides a camera experience like that of the built-in camera app, but allows you to provide your own custom viewfinder and to extend and enhance the camera experience. A lens may provide a unique experience for viewing or editing photography, or it may be a gateway to an entirely different experience, such as a language translator that recognizes text and translates it to another language.

A lens is selected via the lenses button in the built-in camera app (see Figure 21.6).

FIGURE 21.6   Lens button navigates to the Lens Picker page.

The lens picker displays a list of installed lens apps and a link to the Marketplace, where the user may download other lens apps. When a user taps a lens in the lens picker, the corresponding app is launched via a deep link URI. The deep link URI targets the corresponding app and includes an *Action* querystring variable with the value ViewfinderLaunch to indicate that the app is to be launched as a lens.

Registering as a Lens

To register your app as a lens, you need to add an Extension element to the app's WMAppManifest.xml file. Open the WMAppManifest.xml file by right-clicking the file and selecting View Code. If not already present, add an Extensions element immediately after the Tokens element. Within the Extensions element add an Extension element, as shown:

```
<Extensions>
  <Extension ExtensionName="Camera_Capture_App"
             ConsumerID="{5B04B775-356B-4AA0-AAF8-6491FFEA5631}"
             TaskID="_default" />
</Extensions>
```

Once in place, your app is displayed on the lens picker page.

Tapping on your app's icon in the lens picker page launches your app to its main page.

To determine whether the launch is from the lens picker page, examine the query string of the URI that was used to launch your app. This can be done in a page's OnNavigatedTo method, as demonstrated in the following example:

```
protected override void OnNavigatedTo(NavigationEventArgs e)
{
    ...
    string action;
    if (NavigationContext.QueryString.TryGetValue("Action", out action)
            && action == "ViewfinderLaunch")
    {
        /* Launched from the lens picker. */
    }
}
```

To redirect to a particular page within your app, use a custom URI mapper. A URI mapper examines the requested URI for every navigation request and may redirect accordingly.

NOTE

Ordinarily you could place a URI mapping into your app's App.xaml file, but because the lens app deep link URI uses a query string, and the UriMapping class does not support mapping based on query strings, a custom URI mapper class is required.

Listing 21.14 shows a custom URI mapper named `UnleashedUriMapper`, which can be used in the same manner as the SDKs `UriMapper` class. In particular, the class allows you to define URI mappings in XAML in addition to providing mapping logic within the class itself.

The `UnleashedUriMapper` class's `MapUri` method attempts to locate a mapping from the `UriMappings` collections. In the case of the app being launched from the lens picker page, no such mapping is found, and the query string is used to redirect the app to the PhotoCameraView.xaml page.

LISTING 21.14   `UnleashedUriMapper` Class

```
[ContentProperty("UriMappings")]
public sealed class UnleashedUriMapper : UriMapperBase
{
    public Collection<UriMapping> UriMappings { get; private set; }

    public UnleashedUriMapper()
    {
        UriMappings = new Collection<UriMapping>();
    }

    public override Uri MapUri(Uri uri)
    {
        ArgumentValidator.AssertNotNull(uri, "uri");

        Collection<UriMapping> uriMappings = UriMappings;

        foreach (UriMapping mapping in uriMappings)
        {
            Uri mappedUri = mapping.MapUri(uri);

            if (mappedUri != null)
            {
                return mappedUri;
            }
        }

        string uriString = uri.ToString();

        if (uriString.Contains("?Action=ViewfinderLaunch"))
        {
            return new Uri("/Sensors/Camera/PhotoCameraView.xaml",
                    UriKind.Relative);
        }
```

```
        return uri;
    }
}
```

21

The `UnleashedUriMapper` is hooked up to the app's `PhoneApplicationFrame` in the App.xaml file, as shown:

```
<Application.RootVisual>
    <toolkit:TransitionFrame x:Name="RootFrame" ...>
        <phone:PhoneApplicationFrame.UriMapper>
            <local:UnleashedUriMapper>
                <local:UnleashedUriMapper.UriMappings>
                    ...
                </local:UnleashedUriMapper.UriMappings>
            </local:UnleashedUriMapper>
        </phone:PhoneApplicationFrame.UriMapper>

    </toolkit:TransitionFrame>
</Application.RootVisual>
```

Creating Lens Icons

The tile content that represents your app on the lens picker page is customized by creating three PNG images and placing them in the Assets directory of your Windows Phone App project. Each image is used depending on the phone's display resolution. An image that is 277×277 pixels is used for WXGA. An image that is 259×259 pixels is used for 720p. And an image that is 173×173 pixels is used when the resolution is WVGA. The three images must be named as follows:

▶ Lens.Screen-WXGA.png

▶ Lens.Screen-720p.png

▶ Lens.Screen-WVGA.png

Image color is ignored. The images are displayed so that transparent pixels are displayed using the tile background, and nontransparent pixels are displayed using the phone's foreground color (when using the phone's dark theme, for example; this is white).

Summary

This chapter explored two approaches for capturing still images and video. Beginning with `PhotoCamera`, you saw how to capture still images and display live video using the `PhotoCamera`'s preview buffer. You also looked at leveraging the phone's hardware shutter button and how to create a live video effect.

The chapter then looked at the Silverlight webcam API, specifically how to use the webcam API to capture audio and video and to save it as an MP4 in isolated storage.

Finally, the chapter examined lenses, which are new to Windows Phone 8 and allow you to extend the phone's built-in camera experience.

CHAPTER 22

Recording Audio with the Microphone

Every Windows Phone device is required to have a microphone. Without it, the phone would be no more than a smart camera.

This chapter looks at using the XNA microphone API to record audio. You have some fun with the microphone and create a helium voice app that allows the user to record audio and to modulate the pitch of the recorded audio during playback.

Recording Audio with the Microphone

The XNA `Microphone` class allows you to capture audio data from the phone's microphone. `Microphone` resides in the Microsoft.Xna.Framework.Audio namespace.

To use the `Microphone` class you need to create a `GameTimer` to pump the XNA `FrameworkDispatcher`. XNA components usually rely on initialization of the XNA environment before they can be used, and the `Microphone` class is no exception. Creating a `GameTimer` to pump the XNA `FrameworkDispatcher` normally involves adding some code to your `App` class that creates a `GameTimer` and subscribes to its `FrameAction` event. For more information on initializing the XNA environment, see Chapter 7, "Employing Media and Web Elements."

`Microphone` does not have a public constructor; an instance is retrieved using the static `Microphone.Default` property, as shown:

```
Microphone microphone = Microphone.Default;
```

`Microphone` uses an event driven approach to periodically deliver audio data while it is recording. The `Microphone.BufferReady` event is raised as soon as the `Microphone` instance's buffer is full. The size of the buffer is specified using the `Microphone.BufferDuration` property, like so:

```
microphone.BufferDuration = TimeSpan.FromSeconds(1);
```

The `Microphone.GetSampleSizeInBytes` can be used to determine the space requirements for reading the sample data when the `BufferReady` event is raised.

```
int sampleSizeInBytes
        = microphone.GetSampleSizeInBytes(microphone.BufferDuration);
```

This provides the opportunity to create a byte array for storing the sample bytes when the buffer has been filled:

```
byte[] buffer = new byte[sampleSizeInBytes];
```

The buffer can later be copied to a stream and saved in isolated storage, as shown:

```
void HandleBufferReady(object sender, EventArgs e)
{
    microphone.GetData(buffer);
    stream.Write(buffer, 0, buffer.Length);
}
```

The next section looks at putting this together to create a page that allows the user to record and play back audio.

Creating a Helium Voice App

They are a dime a dozen, and you may be surprised by just how simple it is to create a helium voice app, which can modulate the pitch of the user's voice. This section creates a page that allows the user to record audio, which is saved to isolated storage, and to play back the sample with the option to change the pitch of the playback using a slider.

The code for this section is located in the Sensors/Microphone directory of the WPUnleashed.Examples project in the downloadable sample code.

The `MicrophoneViewModel` class includes the following two commands:

▶ `ToggleRecordCommand`—Starts the microphone recording if not recording; otherwise, recording is stopped and the sample is saved to isolated storage.

▶ `PlayCommand`—Plays the previously saved sample, if it exists, from isolated storage.

MicrophoneViewModel initializes the default Microphone instance to a BufferDuration of 1 second. A byte array field is initialized using the microphone's sample size (see Listing 22.1).

LISTING 22.1   MicrophoneViewModel Class (excerpt)

```
public class MicrophoneViewModel : ViewModelBase
{
    readonly Microphone microphone = Microphone.Default;
    readonly byte[] buffer;
    const string fileName = "MicrophoneSample.bytes";
    MemoryStream stream = new MemoryStream();
    readonly object fileLock = new object();

    public MicrophoneViewModel() : base("microphone")
    {
        microphone.BufferDuration = TimeSpan.FromSeconds(1);
        microphone.BufferReady += HandleBufferReady;

        int sampleSizeInBytes = microphone.GetSampleSizeInBytes(
                                        microphone.BufferDuration);
        buffer = new byte[sampleSizeInBytes];

        toggleRecordCommand = new DelegateCommand(obj => ToggleRecording());
        playCommand = new DelegateCommand(obj => Play(), obj => !recording);
    }
    ...
}
```

Recording Audio

The viewmodel's ToggleRecording method either calls the StopRecording or StartRecording method, depending on the current recording state, as shown:

```
void ToggleRecording()
{
    if (recording)
    {
        StopRecording();
    }
    else
    {
        StartRecording();
    }
}
```

The viewmodel's `StartRecording` method instantiates a new `MemoryStream`, which is used to copy the sample data each time the `Microphone.BufferReady` event is raised. When the `Microphone` object is started, the `BufferReady` event is raised after 1 second of recording time. See the following excerpt:

```
void StartRecording()
{
    stream = new MemoryStream();
    microphone.Start();
    Recording = true;
    UpdateCommands();
}
```

The `UpdateCommands` method disables the play command if playback is in progress, as shown:

```
void UpdateCommands()
{
    playCommand.RaiseCanExecuteChanged();
}
```

The viewmodel's `StopRecording` method tests the state of the microphone. The `Microphone.Stop` method is not in the `StopRecording` method because doing so would prevent the last `BufferReady` event from being raised, which can cause the audio to be cut off. See the following excerpt:

```
void StopRecording()
{
    if (microphone.State != MicrophoneState.Stopped)
    {
        Recording = false;
        UpdateCommands();
    }
}
```

The stop request is, instead, dealt with in the viewmodel's `HandleBufferReady` method, in which the sample data is read into the buffer byte array and then written to a `MemoryStream`. If a stop recording request has been made at this point, the stream is flushed, the microphone stopped, and the `MemoryStream` is written to isolated storage; as shown:

```
void HandleBufferReady(object sender, EventArgs e)
{
    microphone.GetData(buffer);
    stream.Write(buffer, 0, buffer.Length);
```

```
    if (!recording)
    {
        stream.Flush();
        microphone.Stop();
        WriteFile(stream);
    }
}
```

Writing the sample to isolated storage involves retrieving an `IsolatedStorageFileStream` and writing the `MemoryStream` to it, as shown:

```
void WriteFile(MemoryStream memoryStream)
{
    lock (fileLock)
    {
        using (var isolatedStorageFile
                    = IsolatedStorageFile.GetUserStoreForApplication())
        {
            using (IsolatedStorageFileStream fileStream
                = isolatedStorageFile.OpenFile(fileName, FileMode.Create))
            {
                memoryStream.WriteTo(fileStream);
            }
        }
    }
}
```

Playback of the audio begins with the retrieval of the sample bytes from isolated storage, as shown:

```
void Play()
{
    byte[] bytes = null;

    lock (fileLock)
    {
        using (var userStore
                    = IsolatedStorageFile.GetUserStoreForApplication())
        {
            if (userStore.FileExists(fileName))
            {
                using (IsolatedStorageFileStream fileStream
                            = userStore.OpenFile(fileName,
                                                FileMode.Open,
                                                FileAccess.Read))
                {
```

```
                    bytes = new byte[fileStream.Length];
                    fileStream.Read(bytes, 0, bytes.Length);
                }
            }
        }
    }

    if (bytes != null)
    {
        PlayAudio(bytes);
    }
}
```

Playback

An XNA `SoundEffect` instance is used to play the sample bytes. The microphone's sample rate is used to match the sample rate of the `SoundEffect`. A `SoundEffectInstance` field is used to vary the pitch of the audio during playback. See the following excerpt:

```
SoundEffectInstance effectInstance;

void PlayAudio(byte[] audioBytes)
{
    if (audioBytes == null || audioBytes.Length == 0
        || effectInstance != null
        && effectInstance.State == SoundState.Playing)
    {
        return;
    }

    var soundEffect = new SoundEffect(audioBytes,
                                      microphone.SampleRate,
                                      AudioChannels.Mono);
    if (effectInstance != null)
    {
        effectInstance.Dispose();
    }
    effectInstance = soundEffect.CreateInstance();
    effectInstance.Pitch = (float)pitch;
    effectInstance.Play();
}
```

The `Pitch` property adjusts the playback of the `SoundEffectInstance` during playback, as shown:

```
double pitch;
```

```
public double Pitch
{
    get
    {
        return pitch;
    }
    set
    {
        Assign(ref pitch, value);
        if (effectInstance != null)
        {
            effectInstance.Pitch = (float)value;
        }
    }
}
```

MicrophoneView

The MicrophoneView page includes a custom AppBar definition, with buttons bound to the commands in the view. The first button is an AppBarToggleButton, which changes its icon according to the value of the viewmodel's Recording property. See the following excerpt:

```
<u:AppBar>
    <u:AppBarToggleButton
                Command1="{Binding ToggleRecordCommand}"
                Toggled="{Binding Recording}"
                Text1="Record"
                Text2="Stop"
                Icon1Uri="/Sensors/Microphone/Icons/Record.png"
                Icon2Uri="/Sensors/Microphone/Icons/StopRecording.png" />
    <u:AppBarIconButton
                Command="{Binding PlayCommand}"
                Text="Play"
                IconUri="/Sensors/Microphone/Icons/Play.png" />
</u:AppBar>
```

The main content panel includes a Slider that is bound to the viewmodel's Pitch property, as shown:

```
<StackPanel x:Name="ContentPanel" Grid.Row="1" Margin="12,0,12,0">
    <TextBlock Text="pitch"
                Style="{StaticResource LabelTextIndentedStyle}" />
    <Slider Value="{Binding Pitch, Mode=TwoWay}" Minimum="-1" Maximum="1" />
</StackPanel>
```

By moving the slider to the left, the pitch decreases during playback; by moving it to the right, the helium voice effect is achieved (see Figure 22.1).

FIGURE 22.1   `MicrophoneView` page with a `Slider` to control pitch.

The `Microphone` class provides an easy way to capture audio and provides interesting opportunities for adding voice-enabled services such as voice recognition and streaming communications.

Summary

This chapter began by looking at using the XNA microphone API to record audio. You had some fun with the microphone and created a helium voice app that allows the user to record audio and to modulate the pitch of the recorded audio during playback.

CHAPTER 23

Creating Speech Driven Experiences

Speech is a natural, efficient, and accurate way to interact with the phone. The new speech features of the Windows Phone 8 SDK allow you to create exciting speech driven experiences for your users and incorporate both speech recognition and speech synthesis, known as Text-to-Speech.

This chapter begins by exploring speech recognition. You see how to employ speech recognition using the SDK's ready-to-use grammars. You also see how to define simple list grammars, and then how to author an XML-based grammar. The sample for this section demonstrates how to create a voice-driven paint app, which allows the user to place shapes on a canvas using voice commands such as "Add blue circle."

The chapter then looks at how to override the built-in speech recognition GUI to create your own custom speech recognition UI, and at recognizing speech in other languages.

It then discusses voice commands and how they can be used to launch your app and to execute custom logic within your app. You learn how to create a Weather Voice app that leverages the Yahoo! Weather service to display weather information for a location spoken via a voice command.

Finally the chapter looks at Text-to-Speech, and you see how to customize the speaking voice of the phone's speech synthesizer. You look at creating a speech script using an XML definition, which allows you to set the language, gender, and intonation of sections of speech. You also look at how to employ bookmarks in your script to provide feedback to your code during speech synthesis.

The source code for this chapter can be found in the Vaughan.WPUnleashed solution, in the MainExamples directory of the downloadable sample code.

User Input with Speech Recognition

Windows Phone 8 includes several new features to support speech recognition, including a speech runtime, recognition APIs for programming the runtime, two ready-to-use grammars for dictation and web search, and a graphical user interface (GUI) that helps users discover and use speech recognition features.

Getting Started with Speech Recognition

To use speech recognition in your app, the WMAppManifest.xml file must include the following two capabilities:

▶ ID_CAP_SPEECH_RECOGNITION

▶ ID_CAP_MICROPHONE

To ensure that these capabilities are declared, open the WMAppManifest.xml file from the Properties directory of your project. In the Capabilities tab, ensure that the capabilities are checked.

In this section you look at using the default speech recognizer that allows you to quickly and easily recognize speech.

By default, the speech recognizer API uses a dictation grammar that relies on a Microsoft cloud service to perform speech recognition. Using the speech recognition API in your app is as simple as instantiating a `SpeechRecognizerUI` instance and calling its `RecognizeWithUIAsync` method, as shown in the following example:

```
SpeechRecognizerUI recognizer = new SpeechRecognizerUI();
SpeechRecognitionUIResult uiResult
    = await recognizer.RecognizeWithUIAsync();

if (uiResult.ResultStatus == SpeechRecognitionUIStatus.Succeeded)
{

    string recognitionText = uiResult.RecognitionResult.Text;
    // Do something with the recognized text.
}
```

When the `RecognizeWithUIAsync` is called, the `SpeechRecognizerUI` presents a dialog that prompts the user to speak to the device.

The `RecognizeWithUIAsync` method allows you to use the new asynchronous programming model of C#. The await keyword allows the containing method to wait for the asynchronous method to return without blocking the UI thread. You see a more complete example later in the chapter that demonstrates the use of the asynchronous feature.

> **TIP**
>
> The Windows Phone emulator is able to leverage the microphone of the host system. Thus, apps that use speech recognition and voice commands can be debugged using the Windows Phone Emulator with a microphone attached to your computer.

Overview of Recognition Grammars

Speech recognition relies on predefined grammars that determine valid speech input. Custom grammars allow you to limit the recognized words and phrases to those that make sense in the context of your app. Grammars allow you to improve the accuracy of speech recognition by limiting the set of recognizable phrases.

There are three types of grammars that can be used with the Windows Phone SDK:

▶ Ready-to-use grammars, which include a dictation grammar and a web search grammar; both of which rely on a Microsoft cloud service

▶ List grammars, which are lists of phrases that are defined programmatically by you

▶ XML grammars, which use a format defined by the Speech Recognition Grammar Specification (SRGS)

Dictation and Web Search Grammars

The ready-to-use grammars allow you to add speech recognition to your app without having to write a grammar. These grammars are not built-in per se; speech is sent to, and processed on, a Microsoft server. There are two ready-to-use grammars:

▶ A free-text dictation grammar that is supposed to recognize most words and phrases in a given language. This grammar is optimized to recognize short phrases.

▶ A web search grammar that is almost as general as the free-text dictation grammar but is optimized to recognize search phrases that people use when searching the web.

Both the ready-to-use grammars allow you to recognize free text; however, because they are large and operate via a cloud service, they do not offer the performance of a locally stored custom list grammar or SRGS grammar.

Phrase List Grammars

The simplest way to create your own custom grammar is by creating a phrase list grammar. Phrase list grammars (henceforth referred to as list grammars) are suited to simple recognition scenarios and are defined by creating an array of strings. Each string represents an individual spoken phrase that your app will accept. During speech recognition, the SpeechRecognizer attempts to match spoken input with any one of the strings in the array. If a match occurs, the operation is deemed successful.

SRGS Grammars

An SRGS grammar is defined as an XML file that conforms to the Speech Recognition Grammar Specification (SRGS). SRGS grammars provide more authoring capabilities than a list grammar does. In an SRGS grammar, phrases are composed using rules and semantic tags.

The type of grammar that you choose for your app depends on the complexity of the recognition required. List grammars are easy to define but do not offer the flexibility of XML grammars. The ready-to-use grammars, although being great for recognizing general speech, rely on a network connection and do not allow you to tailor the grammar for the context of your app. You may find that all three approaches will find a place in your app.

In the following sections you look at implementing each of the grammar types.

Recognizing Speech Using the Dictation and Web Search Grammars

The SpeechRecognizerUI uses the online dictation grammar by default if no grammar is added to its grammar set. In the following example, a SpeechRecognizerUI is created and its speech recognizer's RecognizeAsync method is called. The speech recognizer returns the recognized text in Result property of the SpeechRecognitionResult object, as shown:

```
SpeechRecognizerUI recognizerUI = new SpeechRecognizerUI();

SpeechRecognitionResult result;

try
{
    result = await recognizerUI.Recognizer.RecognizeAsync();
}
catch (Exception ex)
{
    // Handle unable to recognize speech...
    return;
}

string recognizedText = result.Text;
...
```

You can explicitly add the dictation, or a web search grammar, to a grammar set using the SpeechGrammarSet.AddGrammarFromPredefinedType, as shown:

```
SpeechRecognizerUI recognizerUI = new SpeechRecognizerUI();
recognizerUI.Recognizer.Grammars.AddGrammarFromPredefinedType(
    "WebSearch", SpeechPredefinedGrammar.WebSearch);
```

Unlike the dictation grammar, which is loaded by default, the web search grammar must be added to a speech recognizer's grammar set before starting recognition.

Recognizing Speech with Phrase List Grammars

Using a list grammar in your app requires the creation of a collection of strings that represent recognizable phrases, which is then passed to the SpeechRecognizer's grammar set, like so:

```
string[] numbers = {"one", "two", "three"};
SpeechRecognizerUI recognizerUI = new SpeechRecognizerUI();
SpeechGrammarSet grammarSet = recognizerUI.Recognizer.Grammars;
grammarSet.AddGrammarFromList("Numbers", numbers);
```

A speech recognizer is not limited to a single grammar. Multiple list grammars may be added to the same grammar set using successive calls to `AddGrammarFromList`. `AddGrammarFromList` accepts a key, which allows you to disable or enable the particular phrase list, and an `IEnumerable<string>` of phrases.

An instance of a speech recognizer has one grammar set. The speech recognizer loads its grammar set at the beginning of a recognition operation unless it has been preloaded. If its grammar set is empty, the speech recognizer falls back on the dictation grammar. You see how to preload a grammar later in the chapter.

> **NOTE**
>
> There are restrictions when combining types of grammars in a single grammar set. In the case of the dictation and web search grammars, no other grammar types can be added to the set. In other words, if a grammar set contains a dictation or web search grammar, it cannot contain any list grammars or SRGS grammars.

Create a Voice Paint App with a List Grammar

In the sample code for this section you see how to create a phrase list grammar that allows the user to use speech recognition to add colored shapes to a canvas. The sample code for this section is located in the Speech/VoicePaint/PhraseList directory of the WPUnleashed.Examples project in the downloadable sample code.

The `VoicePaintViewModel` class defines two list grammars. The first is defines the actions taken for the page

```
string[] actionPhrases = { "[add] circle", "[add] square", "clear" };
```

When you use a list grammar, the square brackets indicate that the word "add" in the previous excerpt is optional and may or may not be uttered by the user.

The second list grammar defines a set of colors:

```
string[] colorPhrases = { "red", "green", "blue" };
```

When navigating to the VoicePaintView.xaml page, the app asks the user for an action. If the user responds with an action that is either to add a circle or to add a square, the app prompts the user for the color of the new shape.

A `SpeechRecognizerUI` instance is created in the viewmodel's `GetSpeechRecognizerUI` method. This method adds the list grammars using the `AddGrammarFromList` method, as shown in the following excerpt:

```
SpeechRecognizerUI GetSpeechRecognizerUI()
{
    if (recognizerUI == null)
    {
        recognizerUI = new SpeechRecognizerUI();
        SpeechGrammarSet grammarSet = recognizerUI.Recognizer.Grammars;

        grammarSet.AddGrammarFromList(actionsKey, actionPhrases);
        grammarSet.AddGrammarFromList(colorsKey, colorPhrases);
    }

    return recognizerUI;
}
```

The viewmodel's `Prompt` method retrieves the `SpeechRecognizerUI` object and selectively enables the actions list grammar while disabling the colors list grammar. See Listing 23.1. This prevents the speech recognizer from recognizing phrases from the colors list grammar when it should expect a phrase from the actions grammar.

The `SpeechRecognizerUI` uses three built-in screens for guiding the user through the speech recognition process. The first is a listening screen, which requests speech input from the user. The second is a confirmation screen, which presents the recognized speech to the user and allows the user to confirm or discard it. If the speech input is matched with similar confidence to more than one phrase in the enabled grammars, the third screen, a disambiguation screen is displayed, which allows the user to decide the phrase. The disambiguation screen is capable of presenting up to 20 phrases from the enabled grammars.

NOTE

The disambiguation screen is not displayed when using the dictation or web search grammars.

The properties of the `SpeechRecognizerUI`'s Settings property affects if and how the built-in displays are presented.

The `ListenText` property of the `SpeechRecognizerUISettings` class is set to display an instructive message to the user on the built-in *listening* screen, to let him or her know what kind of information your app is expecting—for example, "Select a color." If you do not specify a value for this property, the text "Listening..." is displayed.

The `ExampleText` property allows you to provide one or more purely instructional examples to the user, such as "blue", or "Zurich Switzerland." If no value is specified, this portion of the listening screen is blank.

The `SpeechRecognizerUISettings` class also includes two other properties: `ReadoutEnabled` and `ShowConfirmation`.

`ReadoutEnabled` determines whether the phone speaks successfully recognized text back to the user from the built-in confirmation screen, and whether it speaks options from the built-in disambiguation screen. By default `ReadoutEnabled` is true; however, if TTS readout is disabled in the settings for speech on the phone, readout is disabled even if `ReadoutEnabled` is set to true.

`ShowConfirmation` determines whether the confirmation screen is displayed upon recognition of a phrase. The confirmation screen displays when a call to the `RecognizeWithUIAsync` method produces a successful recognition, and it shows the text of the recognized speech. By default `ShowConfirmation` is true. Set it to false to prevent it from being displayed, which also prevents reading out of recognized speech regardless of the `ReadoutEnabled` property.

If the disambiguation screen is presented, the phrases are read out to the user if fewer than five phrases are displayed, the `ReadoutEnabled` property is not set to false, and "Play audio confirmations" is enabled in the phone's speech settings.

A successful recognition is determined by the `ResultStatus` property of the `SpeechRecognitionUIResult` return value.

In the sample, when the viewmodel receives an action to add a shape, it then disables recognition of the action grammar and prompts the user for a color. See Listing 23.1.

LISTING 23.1   `VoicePaintViewModel.Prompt` Method

```
async void Prompt()
{
    SpeechRecognizerUI recognizer = GetSpeechRecognizerUI();
    recognizer.Recognizer.Grammars[actionsKey].Enabled = true;
    recognizer.Recognizer.Grammars[colorsKey].Enabled = false;

    recognizer.Settings.ListenText = "Say an action.";
    recognizer.Settings.ExampleText = " 'add circle', 'square', 'clear' ";

    SpeechRecognitionUIResult uiResult = await recognizer.RecognizeWithUIAsync();

    if (uiResult.ResultStatus == SpeechRecognitionUIStatus.Succeeded)
    {
        recognizer.Recognizer.Grammars[actionsKey].Enabled = false;
```

```
        string recognitionText = uiResult.RecognitionResult.Text;

        if (recognitionText == actionPhrases[0]) /* Add Circle */
        {
            Color outlineColor = await AskColor();
            AddShape(ShapeType.Circle, outlineColor);
        }
        else if (recognitionText == actionPhrases[1]) /* Add Square */
        {
            Color outlineColor = await AskColor();
            AddShape(ShapeType.Square, outlineColor);
        }
        else if (recognitionText == actionPhrases[2]) /* Clear */
        {
            ClearShapes();
        }
        else
        {
            throw new Exception("Unknown recognition response: " + recognitionText);
        }
    }
}
```

The `AskColor` method works in much the same way, as shown in Listing 23.2. The colors list grammar is enabled and the user is prompted for a color—either red, green, or blue. The color phrase is interpreted, and a `System.Windows.Media.Color` object is returned to the caller.

LISTING 23.2   `VoicePaintViewModel.AskColor` Method

```
async Task<Color> AskColor()
{
    SpeechRecognizerUI recognizer = GetSpeechRecognizerUI();
    recognizer.Recognizer.Grammars[colorsKey].Enabled = true;

    recognizer.Settings.ListenText = "What color would you like your shape to be?";
    recognizer.Settings.ExampleText = " 'red', 'green', 'blue' ";

    SpeechRecognitionUIResult uiResult = await recognizer.RecognizeWithUIAsync();

    if (uiResult.ResultStatus == SpeechRecognitionUIStatus.Succeeded)
    {
        string recognizedText = uiResult.RecognitionResult.Text;
        Color color;
        if (recognizedText == colorPhrases[0]) /* Red. */
        {
```

```
            color = Colors.Red;
        }
        else if (recognizedText == colorPhrases[1]) /* Green. */
        {
            color = Colors.Green;
        }
        else if (recognizedText == colorPhrases[2]) /* Blue. */
        {
            color = Colors.Blue;
        }
        else
        {
            throw new Exception("Unknown color response: " + recognizedText);
        }

        return color;
    }

    return Colors.White;
}
```

A custom abstract class named Shape serves as the base class for the Circle and Square classes. It contains two positional properties named Top and Left, two size properties named Width and Height, and an OutlineColor property that defines the color of the shapes border when displayed on a page.

Shape objects are stored in an ObservableDictionary<Shape> in the viewmodel. The AddShape method, shown in Listing 23.3, creates a new Shape of the specified ShapeType and positions it alongside the previous shape, offset by a small margin.

LISTING 23.3   VoicePaintViewModel.AddShape Method

```
void AddShape(ShapeType shapeType, Color outlineColor)
{
    double left = 0;
    double top = 0;

    Shape lastShape = shapes.LastOrDefault();
    if (lastShape != null)
    {
        left = lastShape.Left + 20;
        top = lastShape.Top + 20;
    }

    if (shapeType == ShapeType.Circle)
    {
```

```
            Circle circle = new Circle
                {
                    Left = left, Top = top, OutlineColor = outlineColor
                };
            Shapes.Add(circle);
        }
        else if (shapeType == ShapeType.Square)
        {
            Square square = new Square
                {
                    Left = left, Top = top, OutlineColor = outlineColor
                };
            Shapes.Add(square);
        }
    }
}
```

The view displays the shapes using an `ItemsControl` that is bound to the `Shapes`
`ObservableDictionary`. See Listing 23.4. Items are positioned absolutely using the `Shape`'s
`Top` and `Left` properties.

For seasoned WPF developers, you may be wondering why the `ItemsControl` does not
simply declare a `Canvas` in an `ItemsPanelTemplate`. Unfortunately, in XAML for Windows
Phone, the `ItemsControl` does not allow you to set the `ItemContainerStyle`, which would
otherwise allow us to correctly bind the `Canvas.Left` and `Canvas.Top` properties. Instead,
each shape is placed in its own `Canvas`.

The `DataTemplate` used to display each shape type is determined by the
`TypeTemplateSelector` (presented in Chapter 11, "Creating Expansive and Engaging Apps
with the Pivot and Panorama").

LISTING 23.4   `VoicePaintView.xaml` `ItemsControl` (excerpt)

```
<ItemsControl ItemsSource="{Binding Shapes}">
    <ItemsControl.ItemTemplate>
        <DataTemplate>
            <p:TypeTemplateSelector Content="{Binding}"
                            HorizontalAlignment="Left" VerticalAlignment="Top">
                <p:TypeTemplateSelector.Resources>
                    <DataTemplate x:Name="CircleTemplate">
                        <Canvas>
                            <Ellipse Width="{Binding Width}" Height="{Binding
                                                                    ➥Height}"
                                StrokeThickness="5"
                                Stroke="{Binding OutlineColor,
                                Converter={StaticResource ColorToBrushConverter}}"
                                d:DataContext="{d:DesignInstance l:Circle}"
                                Canvas.Left="{Binding Left}"
```

```
                              Canvas.Top="{Binding Top}" />
                      </Canvas>
                  </DataTemplate>
                  <DataTemplate x:Name="SquareTemplate">
                      <Canvas>
                          <Border Width="{Binding Width}" Height="{Binding
                                                              ➥Height}"
                              BorderBrush="{Binding OutlineColor,
                              Converter={StaticResource ColorToBrushConverter}}"
                              BorderThickness="5" CornerRadius="4"
                              d:DataContext="{d:DesignInstance l:Square}"
                              Canvas.Left="{Binding Left}"
                              Canvas.Top="{Binding Top}" />
                      </Canvas>
                  </DataTemplate>
              </p:TypeTemplateSelector.Resources>
          </p:TypeTemplateSelector>
      </DataTemplate>
    </ItemsControl.ItemTemplate>
</ItemsControl>
```

An `AppBarIconButton` is used to execute a command named `PromptCommand` in the view-model, which calls the viewmodel's `prompt` method and begins the speech recognition process:

```
<u:AppBar>
    <u:AppBarIconButton
            Command="{Binding PromptCommand}"
            Text="Begin"
            IconUri="/Speech/Images/TalkAppBarIcon.png" />
</u:AppBar>
```

BEST PRACTICE

The `SpeechRecognizerUI` class implements `IDisposable`. A `SpeechRecognizerUI` instance may retain native resources while it is being used by your app. It is, therefore, wise to dispose of your `SpeechRecognizerUI` object when the user navigates away from the page, as shown in the following excerpt:

```
public void CleanUp()
{
    if (recognizerUI != null)
    {
        recognizerUI.Dispose();
        recognizerUI = null;
```

```
        }
    }
}
```

Recognizing Speech with SRGS Grammars

In this section you look at creating an SRGS grammar file to augment the Voice Paint sample app from the previous section. By using an SRGS grammar, the user is able to add a shape to the canvas in a single step. You see how SRGS grammars give greater flexibility for composing phrases and for adding semantics to your grammars.

The sample for this section is located in the Speech/VoicePaint/Srgs directory of the WPUnleashed.Examples project in the downloadable sample code.

SRGS grammars have the following features:

▶ They allow combining of multiple phrase lists into a single grammar.

▶ They allow linking to other grammars.

▶ Weights can be assigned to words and phrases to increase or decrease the likelihood that a particular phrase will be detected.

▶ Optional words or phrases can be defined.

▶ Rules can be defined that help to filter out unanticipated speech.

▶ Semantic information can be embedded in a grammar to identify what was said without reparsing the recognized speech.

▶ Pronunciation can be specified either inline in a grammar or via a link to a lexicon.

When creating an SRGS grammar, the format must conform to that of the Speech Recognition Grammar Specification (SRGS) Version 1.0, located at http://bit.ly/SfqiXH.

SRGS grammars may either be defined in an XML document or provided as a string, and then loaded into a speech recognizer.

You now look at incorporating similar phrase list grammars from the previous section into a single SRGS grammar. See Listing 23.5.

The structure of the SRGS XML document has a root *grammar* element and a set of *rule* elements that allow you to combine sets of phrases within the grammar.

The *grammar* element contains the following four attributes:

▶ **version**—A required identifier that specifies the version of the SRGS specification.

▶ **xml:lang**—A required attribute that specifies the language for the content of the grammar.

▶ **root**—An optional attribute that specifies the name of the rule that is active when the grammar is loaded by the speech recognition engine. Rules that are not the root rule or that are not referenced by the root rule cannot be used for recognition. For this reason, the root rule often contains references to other rules that must be active when the grammar loads.

▶ **xmlns**—A required attribute that specifies the XML namespace.

Rule elements contain text or XML elements that define what users can say and the order in which speech fragments can be said. Every grammar must have at least one rule element.

The *rule* element may contain *item* elements and/or *ruleref* elements. Item elements specify words that a user might say, whereas *ruleref* elements reference other rules within the document or in another grammar.

Item elements may also contain *ruleref* elements and *tag* elements. *Tag* elements are used to embed semantic information in the grammar. We explore tag elements later in the chapter.

One-of elements define a set of alternative phrases that can possibly be matched to a phrase spoken by the user. Each alternative speech fragment must be enclosed within an item element.

In Listing 23.5, you see that the *ruleref* with the uri value of #Action indicates that when the speech recognizer encounters the element, it shall expect the user to either say "add" or "remove."

LISTING 23.5   Simple SRGS Voice Paint Grammar

```
<?xml version="1.0" encoding="utf-8" ?>
<grammar version="1.0" xml:lang="en-US" root="CoreCommands"
 xmlns="http://www.w3.org/2001/06/grammar">

  <rule id="CoreCommands" scope="public">
    <ruleref uri="#Action" />
    <item>a</item>
    <ruleref uri="#Color" />
    <ruleref uri="#Shape" />
  </rule>

  <rule id="Action">
    <one-of>
      <item>add</item>
      <item>remove</item>
    </one-of>
  </rule>

  <rule id="Color">
    <one-of>
      <item>red</item>
```

```
      <item>green</item>
      <item>blue</item>
    </one-of>
  </rule>

  <rule id="Shape">
    <one-of>
      <item>circle</item>
      <item>square</item>
    </one-of>
  </rule>

</grammar>
```

NOTE

Although version 1.0 of the SRGS supports EBNF (Extended Backus-Naur Form) notation, it is not supported by the Windows Phone SDK.

To use the grammar XML file, the sample viewmodel creates a new `SpeechRecognizerUI` object, passing it the location of the SRGS file. See Listing 23.6. The path to the file is constructed using the `Path` property current `InstalledLocation` object.

The `ShowConfirmation` property of the recognizer's settings is switched off. This prevents the confirmation dialog from being displayed after a phrase is recognized, which speeds up the process of selecting a shape. Setting the `ShowConfirmation` property to false also means, however, that the user does not have an opportunity to cancel the operation.

If a grammar set contains large or numerous grammars, the time it takes the speech recognizer to load its grammar set may delay the start of recognition. To prevent a delay, the grammar set can be preloaded using the speech recognizer's `PreloadGrammarsAsync` method before initiating a recognition operation.

LISTING 23.6   `VoicePaintSrgsViewModel.GetSpeechRecognizerUI` Method

```
async Task<SpeechRecognizerUI> GetSpeechRecognizerUI()
{
    if (recognizerUI == null)
    {
        recognizerUI = new SpeechRecognizerUI();

        string path = Path.Combine(Package.Current.InstalledLocation.Path,
                        @"Speech\VoicePaint\Srgs\VoicePaintGrammar.xml");
        Uri uri = new Uri(path, UriKind.Absolute);
```

```
    recognizerUI.Recognizer.Grammars.AddGrammarFromUri("CoreGrammar", uri);
    recognizerUI.Settings.ShowConfirmation = false;

    await recognizerUI.Recognizer.PreloadGrammarsAsync();
}

return recognizerUI;
}
```

> **NOTE**
>
> You may notice that in other examples, the ms-appx:// prefix is used to specify the root installation directory of the app, like so:
>
> `string path = "ms-appx:///Speech/VoicePaint/Srgs/VoicePaintGrammar.xml";`
>
> At the time of writing, however, the speech recognizer is unable to locate grammar files using the prefix, thus the `Package` class must be used instead.

Multiple SRGS grammars can be added to a grammar set using successive calls to `AddGrammarFromUri`. SRGS grammars may also be used alongside list grammars, in the same grammar set.

> **NOTE**
>
> The SRGS file must be a local file stored with your app. It cannot be a file located on the Internet.

Again the viewmodel's `Prompt` method is tasked with commencing speech recognition; see Listing 23.7.

The `TextConfidence` property of the `SpeechRecognitionResult` is used to determine how confident the `SpeechRecognizer` is of the result. It can be one of the following values:

▶ High

▶ Medium

▶ Low

▶ Rejected

A `Rejected` value indicates that the spoken phrase was not matched to any phrase in any active grammar. Depending on the action being undertaken in response to use speech input, you can decide whether to accept input that has low confidence in its accuracy.

If the recognition result fails to meet an adequate confidence level, the viewmodel's `Prompt` method loops by calling itself.

LISTING 23.7   `VoicePaintSrgsViewModel.Prompt` Method

```
async void Prompt()
{
    SpeechRecognizerUI recognizer = await GetSpeechRecognizerUI();

    recognizer.Settings.ListenText = "Say a core phrase.";
    recognizer.Settings.ExampleText
        = " 'add a red circle', 'remove a green square', 'add a blue square' ";

    SpeechRecognitionUIResult uiResult = await recognizer.RecognizeWithUIAsync();

    if (uiResult.ResultStatus == SpeechRecognitionUIStatus.Succeeded)
    {
        SpeechRecognitionResult result = uiResult.RecognitionResult;

        if (result.TextConfidence == SpeechRecognitionConfidence.Medium
            || result.TextConfidence == SpeechRecognitionConfidence.High)
        {
            PerformAction(result.Semantics);
        }
        else
        {
            MessageService.ShowMessage("Sorry, I'm not certain I understood.");
            Prompt();
        }
    }
}
```

The viewmodel's `PerformAction` method processes the output of the speech recognizer. It does this by using semantic information returned from the speech recognizer. Semantic information can be placed within the SRGS grammar.

The grammar that was presented earlier in the chapter, in Listing 23.5, has been adapted in Listing 23.8 to include semantic tags. These *tag* elements allow you to add semantic information to the speech recognition information, depending on the phrase that was spoken by the user.

Semantic tags allow you to avoid reinterpreting the recognized speech after it has been passed back to your code. It also makes it easier to process localized versions of your grammar, because semantic information can remain the same across all localized grammars.

To employ semantic tags in your grammar, add the tag-format attribute to the grammar element of the SRGS XML file.

The $ symbol, as shown in Listing 23.8, is used to populate a rule variable that is passed back to your code after the speech has been evaluated.

> **CAUTION**
>
> The semantic tag format shown in Listing 23.8 is Microsoft specific, and using it in your SRGS grammar may prevent it from being used outside of the Microsoft speech ecosystem. There is a different, non-Microsoft tag format that is specified using semantics/1.0 rather than semantics-ms/1.0. It is, however, somewhat more verbose. For example, when using the non-Microsoft-specific format, the Rule Variable is named "out". Conversely, when using the Microsoft-specific format, the Rule Variable is named "$".

LISTING 23.8   VoicePaintGrammar.xml

```xml
<?xml version="1.0" encoding="utf-8" ?>
<grammar version="1.0" xml:lang="en-US" root="CoreCommands"
 xmlns="http://www.w3.org/2001/06/grammar" tag-format="semantics-ms/1.0">

  <rule id="CoreCommands" scope="public">
    <ruleref uri="#Action" />
    <tag>$.Action=$Action;</tag>
    <item>a</item>
    <ruleref uri="#Color" />
    <tag>$.Color=$Color;</tag>
    <ruleref uri="#Shape" />
    <tag>$.Shape=$Shape;</tag>
  </rule>

  <rule id="Action">
    <one-of>
      <item>add<tag>$ = "add"</tag></item>
      <item>remove<tag>$ = "remove"</tag></item>
    </one-of>
  </rule>

  <rule id="Color">
    <one-of>
      <item>red<tag>$ = "red"</tag></item>
      <item>green<tag>$ = "green"</tag></item>
      <item>blue<tag>$ = "blue"</tag></item>
    </one-of>
  </rule>

  <rule id="Shape">
    <one-of>
      <item>circle<tag>$ = "circle"</tag></item>
      <item>square<tag>$ = "square"</tag></item>
```

```
      </one-of>
    </rule>

</grammar>
```

Recall that the viewmodel's `Prompt` method processes the recognized speech using its `PerformAction` method. The `SpeechRecognitionResult` object contains semantic information—in particular, the values of the rule variables—which give you a breakdown of the subphrases that were recognized.

The viewmodel's `PerformAction` method extracts the semantic information from the `SpeechRecognitionResult`'s `Semantics` dictionary property. Each piece of semantic information is stored using the rule variable name as a key. For example, the outcome of the *Action* rule in the SRGS grammar can be retrieved using `semantics["Action"]`; see Listing 23.9.

With these three pieces of information: action, color, and shape, the viewmodel is able to either add or remove the particular shape to or from the canvas.

LISTING 23.9   `VoicePaintSrgsViewModel.PerformAction` Method

```csharp
void PerformAction(IReadOnlyDictionary<string, SemanticProperty> semantics)
{
    string actionString = semantics["Action"].Value.ToString();
    string colorString = semantics["Color"].Value.ToString();
    string shapeString = semantics["Shape"].Value.ToString();

    ShapeType shapeType = (ShapeType)Enum.Parse(typeof(ShapeType), shapeString,
true);
    Color color = colorString == "red" ? Colors.Red : colorString
        == "green" ? Colors.Green : Colors.Blue;

    if (actionString == "add")
    {
        AddShape(shapeType, color);
    }
    else
    {
        Type type = shapeType == ShapeType.Square ? typeof(Square) : typeof(Circle);

        foreach (Shape shape in shapes.ToList())
        {
            if (shape.OutlineColor == color)
            {
                if (type.IsInstanceOfType(shape))
                {
                    shapes.Remove(shape);
```

```
                    break;
                }
            }
        }
    }
}
```

The view used for the SRGS is named VoicePaintView.xaml and is the same page that was used for the earlier list grammar sample.

Speech Recognizer Settings

In addition to the `SpeechRecognizerUI Settings` property, the `SpeechRecognizer` also provides a `Settings` property that allows you to adjust how it responds to the silence or the absence of recognizable input during speech recognition.

The `SpeechRecognizerSettings` class provides the following three properties:

InitialSilenceTimeout

`InitialSilenceTimeout` is a `Timespan` that represents the amount of time that the speech recognizer will remain waiting when all it hears is silence. If the speech recognizer does not detect recognizable speech before the interval expires, it finalizes the recognition operation. The default value is 5 seconds. In some cases, you may want to increase this value when you want to give the user more time to think about a response.

BabbleTimeout

`BabbleTimeout` is a `Timespan` representing the amount of time that the speech recognizer continues to listen while it receives only nonspeech input, such as background noise. Babble includes any speech that does not match any active rule in the grammars currently loaded and activated by the speech recognizer.

If the recognizer receives only nonspeech input for the duration of the `BabbleTimeout` value, it finalizes that recognition operation. The default setting is 0 seconds, which means that the feature is not activated by default. Set the property to a value greater than 0 to activate it.

EndSilenceTimeout

`EndSilenceTimeout` is a `Timespan` representing the amount of time that the speech recognizer waits to finalize the recognition operation, after speech has finished and only silence is being received as input. This timeout is reached when the speech recognizer has received speech input, but has not matched any of the rules in the active grammars. The default value is 150 milliseconds.

> **NOTE**
>
> `InitialSilenceTimeout`, `BabbleTimeout`, and `EndSilenceTimeout` have no effect when using the dictation or web search grammars.

The following excerpt demonstrates how to set the values of the
`SpeechRecognizerSettings` following the creation of a `SpeechRecognizerUI` instance:

```
async Task<SpeechRecognizerUI> GetSpeechRecognizerUI()
{
    if (recognizerUI == null)
    {
        recognizerUI = new SpeechRecognizerUI();
        SpeechRecognizer recognizer = recognizerUI.Recognizer;

        string path = Path.Combine(Package.Current.InstalledLocation.Path,
                        @"Speech\VoicePaint\Srgs\VoicePaintGrammar.xml");
        Uri uri = new Uri(path, UriKind.Absolute);

        recognizer.Grammars.AddGrammarFromUri("CoreGrammar", uri);

        SpeechRecognizerSettings settings = recognizer.Settings;
        settings.InitialSilenceTimeout = TimeSpan.FromSeconds(5.0);
        settings.BabbleTimeout = TimeSpan.FromSeconds(3.0);
        settings.EndSilenceTimeout = TimeSpan.FromSeconds(1.4);

        await recognizerUI.Recognizer.PreloadGrammarsAsync();
    }

    return recognizerUI;
}
```

`Timeout` settings pertain to a single instance of the `SpeechRecognizer` and persist
while the instance is active. A new instance of the `SpeechRecognizer` class or the
`SpeechRecognizerUI` class has its timeout values set to the default values.

Providing a Custom Speech Recognition UI

The listening, confirmation, and disambiguation screens provided by the
`SpeechRecognizerUI` may not suit your particular purposes and can be obtrusive under
some circumstances. Fortunately, you can replace this GUI with your own by working
directly with the `SpeechRecognizer` object rather than the `SpeechRecognizerUI`.

In this section you see how to assemble an interface that provides feedback to the user
during speech recognition. The sample code for this section is located in the Speech/
CustomUI directory of the WPUnleashed.Examples project in the downloadable sample
code.

We begin by looking at how to retrieve a `SpeechRecognizer` from a `SpeechRecognizerUI`
via its `Recognizer` property, as shown in Listing 23.10.

> **NOTE**
>
> Do not instantiate a `SpeechRecognizer` directly by using the new keyword. Rather, create a `SpeechRecognizerUI` object and retrieve its `SpeechRecognizer` from its `Recognizer` property.
>
> A `SpeechRecognizer` can be used for speech recognition only if it belongs to `SpeechRecognizerUI` object. This is because the `SpeechRecognizerUI` is responsible for presenting the user with a policy acceptance dialog that must be accepted by the user before speech recognition is allowed to take place. If your `SpeechRecognizer` has not been retrieved from a `SpeechRecognizerUI`, an `Exception` is raised when your app attempts to recognize speech. Curiously, however, when using the `SpeechRecognizer`, which *has* been retrieved from the `Recognizer` property, the policy acceptance dialog is not displayed.

The sample `RecognitionUIViewModel`'s `GetSpeechRecognizer` method creates a new `SpeechRecognizerUI` object and then subscribes to its various events (see Listing 23.10). The `AudioCaptureStateChanged` event provides notification when the recognizer begins listening for speech, at which point it is placed in a *Capturing* state. The `AudioCaptureStateChanged` event is also raised when the speech recognizer has finished capturing and is processing, and is placed in an *Inactive* state.

The `SpeechRecognizer`'s `AudioProblemOccurred` event is raised when there is an audio problem that could affect recognition accuracy.

The `SpeechRecognizer` in this example uses the default dictation grammar.

LISTING 23.10   `RecognitionUIViewModel.GetSpeechRecognizer` Class

```
SpeechRecognizerUI GetSpeechRecognizer()
{
    if (speechRecognizerUI == null)
    {
        speechRecognizerUI = new SpeechRecognizerUI();

        SpeechRecognizer speechRecognizer = speechRecognizerUI.Recognizer;

        speechRecognizer.AudioCaptureStateChanged
            += delegate(SpeechRecognizer sender,
                    SpeechRecognizerAudioCaptureStateChangedEventArgs args)
            {
                if (args.State == SpeechRecognizerAudioCaptureState.Capturing)
                {
                    Status = "Capturing";
                }
                else if (args.State == SpeechRecognizerAudioCaptureState.Inactive)
                {
                    Status = "Inactive";
```

```
                }
                else
                {
                    Status = string.Empty;
                }
            };

        speechRecognizer.AudioProblemOccurred
            += delegate(SpeechRecognizer sender,
                        SpeechAudioProblemOccurredEventArgs args)
            {
                Status = "Audio Problem Occurred.";
            };
    }

    return speechRecognizerUI;
}
```

The viewmodel's `Prompt` method retrieves the `SpeechRecognizerUI` and uses its `SpeechRecognizer` to perform the speech recognition (see Listing 23.11). The `SpeechRecognizer.RecognizeAsync` is analogous to the `SpeechRecognizerUI.RecognizerWithUIAsyc` method, but does not present the user with the built-in displays; all interaction must therefore be handled by custom code.

LISTING 23.11   `RecognitionUIViewModel.Prompt` Method

```
async void Prompt()
{
    SpeechRecognizerUI recognizer = GetSpeechRecognizer();

    SpeechRecognitionResult result;
    recognitionInProgress = true;

    try
    {
        result = await recognizer.Recognizer.RecognizeAsync();
    }
    catch (Exception ex)
    {
        Debug.WriteLine("Unable to recognize text. " + ex);
        return;
    }
    finally
    {
        recognitionInProgress = false;
```

```
        Status = string.Empty;
    }


    RecognizedText = recognizedText + "\n" + result.Text;
}
```

A `recognitionInProgress Boolean` field prevents the `PromptCommand` from being executed during speech recognition, which could otherwise lead to a race condition. The `AppBarIconButton` automatically toggles its enabled state, depending on the executable state of the `PromptCommand`.

The `PromptCommand` is initialized in the viewmodel's constructor, as shown:

```
public RecognitionUIViewModel() : base("Custom UI")
{
    promptCommand
        = new DelegateCommand(obj => Prompt(), o => !recognitionInProgress);
    PropertyChanged += delegate { UpdateCommands(); };
}
```

Replacing the GUI provided by the `SpeechRecognizerUI` can enable your app to streamline the recognition process, allowing you to customize the speech recognition experience to suit the purposes of your app. This also means abandoning the familiarity of the built-in speech recognition screens, and therefore should be done only if it makes sense for your app.

Recognizing Speech in Other Languages

The market for Windows Phone apps extends across many countries and regions. Supporting other languages is sometimes critical to effectively monetizing your app. Fortunately, the speech features of the Windows Phone SDK make it possible for you to provide speech capabilities for numerous languages.

In this section we look at selecting a language and region-specific speech recognizer to recognize speech in a non-English language.

The sample for this section is located in the Speech/NonEnglishRecognizer directory of the WPUnleashed.Examples project in the downloadable sample code.

Windows Phone 8 supports speech recognition and Text-to-Speech (TTS) for the languages and regions in Table 23.1.

TABLE 23.1   Speech Recognition Languages

en-US	ja-JP	zh-CN
de-DE	pl-PL	en-GB

zh-TW	pt-BR	es-MX
fr-FR	ru-RU	zh-HK
it-IT	en-IN	es-ES

A default speech recognizer language is selected automatically by the OS, depending on the language settings of the device. You can, however, substitute a different language by calling `SetRecognizer` on the `SpeechRecognizer` instance. A language-specific `SpeechRecognizerInformation` can be retrieved from the static `InstalledSpeechRecognizers.All` property, as shown in Listing 23.12.

LISTING 23.12   `NonEnglishViewModel.GetSpeechRecognizerUI` Method

```
SpeechRecognizerUI GetSpeechRecognizerUI()
{
    if (recognizerUI == null)
    {
        recognizerUI = new SpeechRecognizerUI();
        recognizerUI.Settings.ReadoutEnabled = true;

        IEnumerable<SpeechRecognizerInformation> frenchRecognizers
            = from recognizerInfo in InstalledSpeechRecognizers.All
                where recognizerInfo.Language == "fr-FR"
                select recognizerInfo;

        recognizerUI.Recognizer.SetRecognizer(frenchRecognizers.Single());


        /* Create a list grammar from the string array
         * and add it to the grammar set. */
        recognizerUI.Recognizer.Grammars.AddGrammarFromList(
                                        "frenchNumbers", frenchNumbers);
    }

    return recognizerUI;
}
```

In this example, a list grammar is used to define the set of words that the speech recognizer listens for. The viewmodel contains the following array of numbers in French:

```
readonly string[] frenchNumbers = { "un", "deux", "trois", "quatre", "cinq",
"six", "sept", "huit", "neuf", "dix" };
```

The use of a speech recognizer that has been initialized for a nondefault language remains the same. The `ListenText` and `ExampleText` properties of the recognizer's `Settings` should be set to strings in the applicable language. See Listing 23.13.

LISTING 23.13 `NonEnglishViewModel.Prompt` Method

```
async void Prompt()
{
    SpeechRecognizerUI recognizer = GetSpeechRecognizerUI();

    recognizer.Settings.ListenText = "Say a French number.";
    recognizer.Settings.ExampleText = " 'un', 'deux', 'trois', 'quatre' ";

    SpeechRecognitionUIResult uiResult = await recognizer.RecognizeWithUIAsync();

    if (uiResult.ResultStatus == SpeechRecognitionUIStatus.Succeeded)
    {
        RecognizedText = uiResult.RecognitionResult.Text;
    }
}
```

There is no limit placed on combining different languages in your app, which allows you to build rich, multilingual applications.

Launching Your App via Voice Commands

So far in this chapter we have seen how speech recognition can be harnessed within an app, while the app is in execution. The speech capabilities of Windows Phone also allow your app to subscribe to speech recognition services even when your app is not running in the foreground—or not running at all—using a feature known as voice commands. Voice commands allow users to both launch your app and execute actions within your app.

Voice-command functionality can be added to your app by performing the following steps:

1. Create a Voice Command Definition (VCD) file. This is an XML document that declares all the spoken commands that users can say to initiate actions when launching your app.

2. Add code to register the VCD file with the phone's voice-command system.

3. Add code to handle navigation and logic to execute commands.

In the sample for this section you see how to create a Weather Voice app that allows the user to request weather information for a particular location using voice commands. The app uses the Yahoo! Weather service to request the weather information for a specified location, which is then displayed on the phone.

The source code for this section is located in the Speech/VoiceCommands directory of the WPUnleashed.Examples project in the downloadable sample code.

We begin by looking at the placement and structure of VCD files. In the sample, the VoiceCommands.xml file defines the commands available to the entire WPUnleashed. Examples app.

To add a VCD file to your project, right-click the project node in the Solution Explorer and select Voice Command Definition from the Add New Item dialog. The VCD file is simply an XML file with its Build Action set to Content. There is no restriction on where the file can be located in your project.

Understanding the Structure of the VCD File

The structure of the VCD file has a root VoiceCommands element that contains zero or more CommandSet elements. See Listing 23.14.

The CommandSet element represents a group of commands that are activated when the value of the CommandPrefix element is spoken by the user. This allows you to group multiple phrases together.

The Example element determines the text that is displayed on the speech recognition dialog, which is displayed when the user taps and holds the phone's Windows button.

Each CommandSet is required to have at least one Command element, and each Command element is required to have at least one and a maximum of 10 ListenFor elements. ListenFor elements define the speech that activates a particular command. Square brackets within the ListenFor element indicate that the text is optional, whereas curly braces refer to another PhraseList within the document.

> **NOTE**
>
> A CommandSet cannot contain more than 25 command elements and a PhraseList element cannot contain more than 500 Item elements.

In Listing 23.14 the ShowWeather command is activated when the user says any of the following phrases:

- Weather for Zurich Switzerland
- Weather Zurich Switzerland
- Weather for London England
- Weather London England

Although commands themselves cannot be added programmatically to a CommandSet at run-time, the contents of a PhraseList can be replaced programmatically. You see how to achieve this later in the chapter.

The `Feedback` element defines the response to the user when the command is recognized. By using curly brace notation, such as {City}, the recognized phrase list value is placed into the response.

> **NOTE**
>
> A `PhraseList` reference in a `Feedback` element must match a corresponding reference in a `ListenFor` element in the same command.

When the voice command system recognizes a command, your app is launched and the URL specified by the `Target` attribute of the `Navigate` element is navigated to.

LISTING 23.14   VoiceCommands.xml

```xml
<?xml version="1.0" encoding="utf-8" ?>
<VoiceCommands xmlns="http://schemas.microsoft.com/voicecommands/1.0">
  <CommandSet xml:lang="en-us" Name="WeatherCommandSet">
    <CommandPrefix>Weather</CommandPrefix>
    <Example>Weather for Zurich Switzerland</Example>
    <Command Name="ShowWeather">
      <Example>Weather for Zurich Switzerland</Example>
      <ListenFor>[For] {City}</ListenFor>
      <Feedback>Showing weather for {City}</Feedback>
      <Navigate Target="Speech/VoiceCommands/VoiceCommandView.xaml"/>
    </Command>

    <PhraseList Label="City">
      <Item>Zurich Switzerland</Item>
      <Item>London England</Item>
      <!-- This phrase list is replaced programmatically
           in the VoiceCommandViewModel class. -->
    </PhraseList>
  </CommandSet>

  <!-- Other CommandSets for other languages -->

</VoiceCommands>
```

A wildcard token that recognizes any speech can be placed within the `ListenFor` element, as shown:

```xml
<ListenFor>Weather [for] {*}</ListenFor>
```

This allows you to define commands that register a partial match for a phrase.

Installing a VCD

Installation of a VCD is done programmatically and can be performed anywhere in your app, as demonstrated in the following example:

```
string path = "ms-appx:///Speech/VoiceCommands/VoiceCommands.xml";
Uri commandFileUri = new Uri(path, UriKind.Absolute);
await VoiceCommandService.InstallCommandSetsFromFileAsync(commandFileUri);
```

The ms-appx:/// prefix represents the install directory of the app. The VoiceCommandService InstallCommandSetsFromFileAsync method follows the asynchronous pattern, allowing you to wait for the method's completion without blocking the UI thread.

When the VCD has been installed, the user is then able to launch your app by tapping and holding the hardware Windows button on the device and by uttering a registered command for your app.

To verify that the VCD has been correctly installed, use the question mark (?) button to navigate to the "What Can I Say?" screen, as shown in Figure 23.1. If the VCD file has been installed correctly, your app is displayed on the "What Can I Say?" screen.

Tapping on your app's title brings up the list of commands defined in the VCD file.

FIGURE 23.1   The question mark button presents the "What Can I Say?" screen.

Command information is passed to your app using a query string appended to the command's Navigate Target URL attribute, as defined in the VCD.

The sample's VoiceCommandView page OnNavigatedTo method calls the viewmodel's Initialize method, passing it the navigation context's query string dictionary, like so:

```
protected override void OnNavigatedTo(NavigationEventArgs e)
{
    base.OnNavigatedTo(e);

    ViewModel.Initialize(NavigationContext.QueryString);
}
```

The `Initialize` method attempts to retrieve the weather command set. If the command set is not located, it indicates that the VCD has yet to be installed. See Listing 23.15. You look at retrieving a command set in a moment.

When the query string contains a 'voiceCommandName' key, it indicates that a voice command has been activated.

The text for the entire recognized phrase is included as the value of the 'reco' query string parameter. In addition, each phrase list value is provided as a parameter of the same name. Thus, the value of the *City* phrase list can be retrieved using the key 'City'.

LISTING 23.15   `VoiceCommandViewModel.Initialize` Method

```
public async Task Initialize(IDictionary<string, string> queryStringDictionary)
{
    VoiceCommandSet commandSet = GetWeatherCommandSet();

    if (commandSet == null)
    {
        const string path = "ms-appx:///Speech/VoiceCommands/VoiceCommands.xml";
        Uri commandFileUri = new Uri(path, UriKind.Absolute);
        await VoiceCommandService.InstallCommandSetsFromFileAsync(commandFileUri);

        commandSet = GetWeatherCommandSet();
        commandSet.UpdatePhraseListAsync("City", woeDictionary.Keys);
    }

    string voiceCommandName;
    if (queryStringDictionary.TryGetValue("voiceCommandName", out voiceCommandName)
        && voiceCommandName == "ShowWeather")
    {
        string city;
        if (queryStringDictionary.TryGetValue("City", out city))
        {
            UpdateWeather(city);
        }
    }
    else
    {
```

```
        SayWelcome();
    }
}
```

A command set defined in a VCD can be retrieved from the `InstalledCommandSets` property of the `VoiceCommandService`. In the following excerpt, LINQ is used to retrieve the weather command set via the viewmodel's `GetWeatherCommandSet` method:

```
VoiceCommandSet GetWeatherCommandSet()
{
    VoiceCommandSet commandSet
        = (from pair in VoiceCommandService.InstalledCommandSets
            where pair.Key == "WeatherCommandSet"
            select pair.Value).SingleOrDefault();
    return commandSet;
}
```

Having the city name allows the app to query the Yahoo! Weather web service. The web service uses a RESTful API and does not require a developer API key, so it should work out-of-the-box for you. The only piece of information needed by the web service is a weather location. This is specified using a Yahoo! WOEID (Where On Earth Identifier), which is a predefined number that maps to a physical place on the globe.

To query the web service, you perform an HTTP GET on the following address: http://weather.yahooapis.com/forecastrss?w=1234

1234 is replaced by a valid WOEID.

Temperature values are, by default, returned in degrees Fahrenheit. This can be switched to Celsius using the query string parameter and value "u=c".

You can look up WOEIDs for specific locations using various third-party websites, such as http://woeid.rosselliot.co.nz/lookup/ or http://sigizmund.info/woeidinfo/.

The sample Weather Voice app uses a small set of hard-coded locations. The viewmodel's `UpdateWeather` method uses a `WebClient` object and a dictionary of predefined WOEIDs and city names to query the Yahoo! Weather API. See Listing 23.16.

LISTING 23.16 `VoiceCommandViewModel.UpdateWeather` **Method**

```
async Task UpdateWeather(string city)
{
    CityName = city;

    string woeID;
    if (!woeDictionary.TryGetValue(city, out woeID))
    {
```

```
        MessageService.ShowMessage("Unknown city.");
        return;
    }

    Console.WriteLine(woeID);

    const string weatherUrl = "http://weather.yahooapis.com/forecastrss?u=c&w=";
    Uri uri = new Uri(weatherUrl + woeID, UriKind.Absolute);

    webClient.DownloadStringAsync(uri);
}
```

The `WebClient`'s `DownloadStringCompleted` event handler retrieves the weather information that is provided as an RSS document, as shown in the following excerpt:

```
void HandleWebClientDownloadStringCompleted(
    object sender, DownloadStringCompletedEventArgs e)
{
    if (e.Cancelled || e.Error != null)
    {
        MessageService.ShowWarning("Unable to retrieve weather information.");
        return;
    }

    string resultText = e.Result;

    UpdateFromRssResult(resultText);
}
```

The viewmodel's `UpdateFromRssResult` attempts to parse the RSS response. The RSS contains a lot of information, including forecast information, which is ignored in this sample. Only the current temperate and conditions are retrieved from the `yweather:condition` element. The following is an example of the pertinent element:

```
<yweather:condition  text="Partly Cloudy"  code="30"
                     temp="72"  date="Tue, 11 Sep 2012 3:50 pm CEST" />
```

Because the `condition` element is prefixed with the namespace *yweather*, to resolve the value using the `XDocument` API, the element must be combined with an `XNamespace` value, as shown in Listing 23.17.

LINQ is used to retrieve the weather information, and an anonymous type is created containing the value of the temperature and the weather description. The viewmodel's `Temperature` and `WeatherDescription` properties are updated.

LISTING 23.17 `VoiceCommandViewModel.UpdateFromRssResult` Method (excerpt)

```
async Task UpdateFromRssResult(string resultText)
{
    XDocument document = XDocument.Parse(resultText);

    XNamespace xNamespace = "http://xml.weather.yahoo.com/ns/rss/1.0";

    var weatherItem
        = (from condition in document.Descendants(xNamespace + "condition")
                    select new
                    {
                        Text = condition.Attribute("text").Value,
                        Temperature = condition.Attribute("temp").Value
                    }).SingleOrDefault();

    if (weatherItem != null)
    {
        WeatherDescription = weatherItem.Text;
        Temperature = weatherItem.Temperature + '\u2103';

        ...
    }
}
```

The VoiceCommandView.xml page contains three TextBlocks that display the city name, the temperature, and the weather description, as shown in the following excerpt:

```
<TextBlock Text="{Binding CityName, FallbackValue=Unknown}"
           Style="{StaticResource GridRowTextStyle}" />
<TextBlock Text="{Binding Temperature, FallbackValue=0°C}"
           Style="{StaticResource GridRowTextStyle}"
           FontSize="{StaticResource PhoneFontSizeHuge}"
           Grid.Row="1" />
<TextBlock Text="{Binding WeatherDescription, FallbackValue=Unknown}"
           Style="{StaticResource GridRowTextStyle}"
           VerticalAlignment="Top"
           Grid.Row="2"/>
```

After navigating to the VoiceCommandView.xaml page, the user is able to request the weather conditions from one of the predefined locations. Holding down the hardware Windows button and stating "Weather Zurich Switzerland" displays the page shown in Figure 23.2.

FIGURE 23.2   VoiceCommandView displays the weather conditions.

Updating a Phrase List Programmatically

The VCD file for the app contains only a couple of City phrases, which does not make for a very useful weather app.

To remedy the situation, the viewmodel contains a dictionary of WOEIDs keyed by city name, as shown in the following excerpt:

```
Dictionary<string, string> woeDictionary = new Dictionary<string, string>
    {
        {"Zurich Switzerland", "784794"},
        {"Canberra Australia", "1100968"},
        {"Bellevue Washington", "2362031"},
        {"London England", "44418"},
        {"Prague Czech Republic", "796597"},
        {"Bangkok Thailand", "1225448"},
        {"Paris France", "615702"},
        {"Moscow Russia", "2122265"},
        {"Madrid Spain", "766273"},
        {"New Delhi India", "2295019"},
    };
```

Rather than hardcoding the list of city names in the VCD file, city names are added programmatically by modifying the weather `VoiceCommandSet` object.

The viewmodel's `Initialize` method updates the phrase list by calling `UpdatePhraseListAsync` on the weather command set, as shown in the following excerpt:

```
commandSet.UpdatePhraseListAsync("City", woeDictionary.Keys);
```

`UpdatePhraseListAsync` expects the name of the phrase list, in this case *City*, and an `IEnumerable<string>` of new spoken phrases.

The capability to programmatically update a phrase list means that you are able to provide a single source of truth for the phrase list and affords you the option of retrieving phrase list data from the cloud.

Making the Phone Speak with Text-to-Speech

Providing spoken feedback to the user via Text-to-Speech (TTS) can give your app a modern and highly interactive feel. TTS complements the speech recognition components of the phone and can be used to prompt users for input, to confirm users' input, to read the passages of text, and many other tasks.

Getting Started with TTS

Like speech recognition, TTS also requires the ID_CAP_SPEECH_RECOGNITION capability. The capability must present in the WMAppManifest.xml file.

The `SpeechSynthesizer` class is the main class for achieving TTS. The class exists in the Windows.Phone.Speech.Synthesis namespace.

Out of the box, the speech synthesizer is able to speak using a default voice, as shown:

```
SpeechSynthesizer synthesizer = new SpeechSynthesizer();
synthesizer.SpeakTextAsync("Hi from Windows Phone!");
```

Selecting a Speaking Voice

The SDK's speech synthesizer is able to speak using a variety of languages, as spoken in a specific country or regions. See Table 23.1 for the list of speech supported country and region codes.

If no language is specified, the speech synthesizer uses a voice that matches the language that the user has selected in Settings/Speech page on the phone.

In addition to the language and region, the gender of the voice can be specified, effectively doubling the number of speaking voices available.

A speaking voice can be selected by locating a particular voice from the `InstalledVoices.All` collection, and then assigning it to the `SpeechSynthesizer` using its `SetVoice` method.

The following example creates an instance of a speech synthesizer and sets its language and gender. A LINQ query is used to retrieve a male English (Great Britain) speaking voice.

```
SpeechSynthesizer synthesizer = new SpeechSynthesizer();

VoiceInformation gbVoice = (from voice in InstalledVoices.All
                where voice.Language == "en-GB"
                && voice.Gender == VoiceGender.Male
                select voice).First();
synthesizer.SetVoice(gbVoice);
```

NOTE

The voice selection not only affects the character and intonation of the spoken words, but also, in some cases, what is said. For example, when using the U.S. English voice (en-US), the synthesizer knows that 32°C should be pronounced 32 degrees Celsius. The GB English voice fails to do to this and skips the °C altogether. The author's guess is that it is because the U.S. voice has had more effort spent on it.

Creating a Speech Synthesis Markup Language File

In addition to allowing TTS with strings, the speech synthesizer allows you to define speech using the Speech Synthesis Markup Language (SSML). SSML offers a powerful language for authoring TTS scripts.

The structure of an SSML document consists of a root *speak* element, which has an xml:lang attribute that determines the default speaking voice used. See Listing 23.18.

Voice elements define sections of speech that allow the speaking voice to be customized, including gender and language.

The stress and intonation of the speech can be modified using the prosody element, allowing you to vary the volume and pitch of a word or speech fragment. For more detailed information on the prosody element, see http://www.w3.org/TR/speech-synthesis/#edef_prosody.

Mark elements cause an event to be raised by the speech synthesizer when they are encountered during speech output. This can be useful if you need to synchronize some UI elements with points in the script.

LISTING 23.18   IntroductionSsml.xml

```xml
<?xml version="1.0" encoding="utf-8" ?>
<speak version="1.0" xmlns="http://www.w3.org/2001/10/synthesis" xml:lang="en-GB">

  <voice gender="female">
    Welcome to the Weather Voice sample.
  </voice>
```

```
<voice gender="male" xml:lang="en-US">
  To activate this sample hold down the hardware Windows button
  and say something like: <mark name="ExampleStart"/>
  <prosody volume="loud" pitch="-20Hz">Weather for Zurich Switzerland</prosody>.
  <mark name="ExampleEnd"/>
</voice>

<voice gender="female" xml:lang="fr-FR">
  J'espère que vous appréciez le livre!
</voice>

</speak>
```

The sample `VoiceCommandViewModel` class uses the script in Listing 23.18 to greet the user when the user navigates to the page. During synthesis, the `BookmarkReached` event is raised when a mark element is encountered. The `SpeakSsmlFromUriAsync` method loads the SSML file and outputs the spoken text, as shown in the following excerpt:

```
SpeechSynthesizer synthesizer = new SpeechSynthesizer();
synthesizer.BookmarkReached
    += delegate(SpeechSynthesizer sender, SpeechBookmarkReachedEventArgs args)
    {
        TextHighlighted = args.Bookmark == "ExampleStart";
    };
string path = "ms-appx:///Speech/VoiceCommands/IntroductionSsml.xml";
synthesizer.SpeakSsmlFromUriAsync(new System.Uri(path, UriKind.Absolute));
```

In addition to the `SpeakSsmlFromUriAsync` method, the `SpeechSynthesizer` is also able to speak a string of SSML that you provide as an argument to the `SpeakSsmlAsync` method.

The Boolean `TextHighlighted` property is used in the view to change the color of the example text from the SSML file. A custom `IValueConverter` named `BooleanToBrushConverter` (presented in Chapter 9, "Enriching the User Experience with the Windows Phone Toolkit Controls") converts the Boolean value of the property to a brush.

```
<TextBlock Foreground="{Binding TextHighlighted,
                Converter={StaticResource BooleanToBrushConverter}}">
            "Weather for Zurich Switzerland"</TextBlock>
```

The `BooleanToBrushConverter` is declared in the page resources as shown:

```
<phone:PhoneApplicationPage.Resources>
    <ValueConverters:BooleanToBrushConverter x:Name="BooleanToBrushConverter"
        BrushIfFalse="{StaticResource PhoneForegroundBrush}"
```

```
                    BrushIfTrue="{StaticResource PhoneAccentBrush}" />
</phone:PhoneApplicationPage.Resources>
```

When the speech synthesizer reaches the text "Weather for Zurich Switzerland," the same text is highlighted using the phone's accent color. See Figure 23.3.

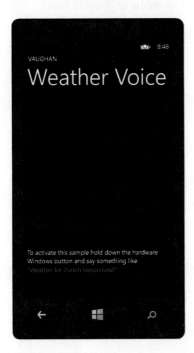

FIGURE 23.3   Example text is highlighted using a Mark element.

SSML gives you precise control over how text is spoken, including language, gender, and intonation; bookmarks enable you to coordinate and synchronize screen elements with your speech output.

Summary

This chapter began by exploring speech recognition. You saw how to employ speech recognition using the SDK's ready-to-use grammars. You also saw how to define simple list grammars, and then how to author an XML-based grammar. The sample for this section demonstrated how to create a voice-driven paint app, which allows the user to place shapes on a canvas using voice commands such as "Add blue circle."

The chapter then looked at how to override the built-in speech recognition GUI to create your own custom speech recognition UI and how to recognize speech in other languages.

It then looked at voice commands, and how they can be used to launch your app and to execute custom logic within your app. You learned how to create a Weather Voice app that leverages the Yahoo! Weather service to display weather information for a location spoken via a voice command.

Finally, the chapter looked at Text-to-Speech, and you saw how to customize the speaking voice of the phone's speech synthesizer. You looked at creating a speech script using an XML definition, which allows you to set the language, gender, and intonation of sections of speech. You also learned how to employ bookmarks in your script to provide feedback to your code during speech synthesis.

CHAPTER 24

Unit Testing Apps

Unit testing saves time and helps to find defects early in the development cycle. Unit tests become assets that provide assurance that further development or refactoring has not broken something. The more tests you create, the more confidence you have when adding features and fixing bugs. This is especially true if you are working with a team of developers.

Manual ad hoc testing becomes less effective as an app increases in size and complexity. Having a solid suite of unit tests can actually decrease the time it takes to get your app to the marketplace. This is because often an exorbitant amount of time is spent on ad hoc testing in the last stages of development before a release.

Another benefit of unit tests is that they can act as a tacit form of documentation. There is a distinct lack of code documentation in many software houses today. Unit tests can assist a developer in understanding how an app works, and unit tests are less susceptible than traditional system documentation to implementation drift, where design changes and feature creep can see the documentation of an app become outdated. Unit tests tend to fare better because they are verifiable. Relying solely on unit tests to document a system is, however, not wise. Unit tests should be considered production code, requiring their own adequate documentation.

For all its benefits, unit testing does have a cost. It takes time and skill to write effective unit tests. In your career, you may have experienced the reluctance of management to support unit testing because it is invariably seen as time stolen from writing product code. It is that old story: developers craft a product and then scramble in the last moments to iron out defects, producing fixes that frequently introduce new bugs. Unit testing can help to alleviate that last-minute scramble.

Some may also see unit tests as a liability because when there are substantial changes to an app, unit tests have to be rewritten. This cost is, however, usually overstated and can sometimes reflect unsound development practices.

Testing and patterns of testing vary, and divided opinion on the topic has spurred many a heated debate. This chapter is not about affirming one approach over another. The techniques and tools presented in this chapter should, however, make a worthy addition to your development toolbox.

Throughout this book you have seen the use of the Model-View-ViewModel (MVVM) pattern. MVVM comes into its own when combined with unit testing. In fact, it is one of the key motivations for using the pattern. MVVM allows you to separate UI technology-specific code so that it can be tested without a user interface (UI).

This chapter delves into the Windows Phone Toolkit Unit Test Framework (UTF). The chapter begins with a walk-through of the creation of a unit test project from scratch. You see how to create test classes and test methods, and get to know the tag expressions editor, which provides a useful mechanism for selecting which tests are to be run.

The UTF is then explored more deeply by creating a simple chat client app, in which you see how to verify a viewmodel before creating a user interface. Following the creation of the view, the test suite is extended to include code driven UI tests, where we manipulate the user interface, simulating button clicks and other user actions from a unit test. The chapter illustrates how to perform asynchronous testing and touches on the Microsoft Automation framework.

Some advanced topics, such as Inversion of Control (IoC) and mocking, are also discussed, and you learn how to use a custom IoC container.

Finally, we put it all together to see how to perform testing of trial applications and how to hide or reveal content based on a mock licensing service. You then look at a custom API for mocking launchers and choosers.

There is a lot to cover in this chapter, and the tools and techniques presented here can help spot unintended side effects, increase the robustness of code, assist in focusing the development effort, and perhaps, save you some time.

Automated Testing

By finding and guarding against defects, an automated test can save you many times the cost of creating it over the lifetime of a project. This chapter looks at three kinds of automated testing: unit testing, integration testing, and coded UI testing.

Unit Testing

A unit test verifies that a single unit of work, usually a class method, works correctly. Unit tests should generally avoid accessing the file system, database, or network resources.

Types requiring this kind of access ideally rely on an abstracted API and have the types used in production substituted with stubs or mock types during testing. Unit tests should execute rapidly and cause no side effects that affect other unit tests.

Integration Testing

Integration tests verify that multiple classes function correctly together. Integration occurs after unit testing. It involves testing groups of classes that have been unit tested.

Coded UI Testing

Coded UI tests simulate a user interacting with the application. These tests rely on an automation API to allow programmatic access to UI elements. For example, an automation object can be used to raise a button's `Tap` event.

There are other types of tests as well, including acceptance testing, performance testing, and stress testing. You often use different tools or extensions to your testing framework for these types of tests. Despite some tests not being formally unit tests, it's fine to use the existing unit testing framework and tools to perform other kinds of testing. The unit testing tools presented in this chapter are a good starting point for many other types of tests.

It is important to partition your tests by test type. For example, unit tests should execute quickly, and by grouping integration tests with unit tests, you risk slowing the execution of the group, which may make running the tests tedious, resulting in avoidance of unit testing altogether by you or another developer. Other test types, such as system tests, which test the entirety of your app, may rely on resources that are unavailable during a unit testing session. By including a system test with your unit tests, you may inadvertently prevent the test suite from passing.

Introduction to the Windows Phone Unit Test Framework

The API of the Windows Phone UTF is almost the same as the Silverlight Unit Test Framework for the browser. In fact, it is almost a superset of the Microsoft desktop CLR Unit Test Framework. This cross-screen compatibility means that you can run all your existing unit tests just as they are.

With Windows Phone 8, the unit testing story has been substantially improved. Unfortunately, however, tooling support for the Windows Phone UTF remains nonexistent. Unlike the Microsoft desktop UTF, there is no Visual Studio integration. This means you cannot run individual unit tests from Visual Studio as you might with a desktop application. Windows Phone test projects are Windows Phone XAML apps. Therefore, do not bother trying to create a new unit test from the Test menu in Visual Studio, because it is unsupported for Windows Phone.

Although tooling support is absent, all the metadata and assertions, discussed later in this chapter, are identical for both the desktop CLR and Windows Phone UTF. In addition, creating a unit test project is straightforward, as you see in the following section.

Creating a Test Project

Test projects are regular Windows Phone App projects with some small modifications. To create a test project, perform the following steps:

1. Add a new Windows Phone App project by selecting File/New/Project in Visual Studio, and select Windows Phone App from the Windows Phone node in the New Project dialog.

2. Click the ellipsis on the Package Manager Console to change the target project to the newly created test project (see Figure 24.1).

FIGURE 24.1   Click the ellipsis to change the target project.

3. From the Visual Studio Tools menu, select Library Package Manager/Package Manager Console.

4. Use NuGet to download the Windows Phone UTF by entering the following command into the Package Manager Console:

Install-Package WPToolkitTestFx

Note that if you receive an error indicating that the package is not compatible with WindowsPhone version 8.0, download the latest version of NuGet from http://www.nuget.org.

5. Modify the test project's MainPage constructor (in the MainPage.xaml.cs file) to match the following:

```
public MainPage()
{
    InitializeComponent();
    Content = UnitTestSystem.CreateTestPage();
}
```

6. Add a reference to the project that you intend to create unit tests for.

A test page instance is assigned to the `Content` property of the main page. Windows Phone does not allow the assignment of the `RootVisual` in the App.xaml.cs file. This is why the code to create the test page is placed in the `MainPage` class and not in the `App` class.

Creating a Test Class

To create a test class, add a new class to your test project. Then add the following two using statements to the top of the class:

```
using Microsoft.Phone.Testing;
using Microsoft.VisualStudio.TestTools.UnitTesting;
```

Test-related attributes and assertion types can be found within the namespace Microsoft. VisualStudio.TestTools.UnitTesting. Even if you have not used the Visual Studio UTF before, it is easy to pick up because the attribute names are fairly self-descriptive.

Tests consist of test classes and test methods. The UTF relies on metadata, provided by attributes, for identifying unit test classes and methods at runtime. To indicate that a class is a unit test class, decorate it with the `TestClassAttribute`, as shown in the following example:

```
[TestClass]
public class FirstTest : WorkItemTest
{
    [TestMethod]
    [Description("A first unit test.")]
    public void ShouldAlwaysPass()
    {
        Assert.IsTrue(true);
    }
}
```

To run the test, set the test project as the startup project by right-clicking the project node in the Visual Studio Solution Explorer and selecting Set as Startup Project. Then debug the solution by selecting Start Debugging from the Debug menu, or by pressing F5. When the app starts, the tag expressions editor is presented (see Figure 24.2).

The tag expressions editor allows you to run all or a subset of the tests. Tap the application bar's play button to commence testing.

When the test completes, a review page is presented in the test harness (see Figure 24.3).

The test harness enables you to drill down to see the details of each test method. The content of the test method's `Description` attribute is presented beneath the test method's name.

FIGURE 24.2   The tag expressions editor.

FIGURE 24.3   A passed unit test.

Tests run on a single thread and are executed within the Windows Phone sandboxed environment.

Tag Expressions

When you have a large number of tests, you need some way to execute just one or a subset of the tests. The UTF includes a tagging language, which allows you to create tag expressions that specify which tests should be run during a unit testing session.

Every test class and test method has an implicit set of tags, shown in the following list:

▶ Type or method name, for example, TestClass1, TestMethod1.

▶ Full type or method name, for example, TestClass1.TestMethod1.

▶ The priority specified by a `Priority` attribute if present. For further information on tag expressions and the `Priority` attribute, see the section "`Priority` Attribute" later in the chapter.

You can also explicitly assign a test class or test method with a tag, using the `Tag` attribute. The `Tag` attribute accepts a single string parameter, which is used to associate a test with a group of tests.

The following is an example of a test method decorated with a `Tag` attribute:

```
[TestMethod]
[Tag("UITest")]
public void AlwaysPass()
{
    Assert.IsTrue(true, "Test method intended to always pass.");
}
```

Multiple `Tag` attributes can be applied to any test class or method in your test suite. Tags can also be useful in selecting different kinds of tests to run.

When the testing session begins, you have the opportunity to enter a tag expression. To run the test method from the previous excerpt, or any other test methods with a matching attribute, you could enter `UITest` as the tag expression.

The tag expression syntax provides a set of operators to control test selection. The `!` (not) operator, for example, allows you to prevent those tests with a particular tag from being executed. A tag expression of `!UITest` causes all tests that do not have the tag `UITest` to be executed. A tag of `All-(UITest+IntegrationTest)` causes all tests that do not have the `UITest` or IntegrationTest tag to execute.

The tag expression syntax uses Extended Backus-Naur Form (EBNF). You can use the symbols presented in Table 24.1 in tag expressions.

TABLE 24.1   Tag Expression Symbols

Symbol	Description
All	Represents all test methods.
!	Compliment of two tag subexpressions.
-	Difference of two tag subexpressions.
*	Intersection of two tag subexpressions.
+	Union of two tag subexpressions.
( )	Parentheses allow you to group tag subexpressions.

Setting the Tag Expression Programmatically

To set the tag expression without using the UTF tag expressions editor, use the `TagExpression` property of the `UnitTestSettings` class, as shown in the following example:

```
public MainPage()
{
    InitializeComponent();

    UnitTestSettings settings = UnitTestSystem.CreateDefaultSettings();
    settings.TagExpression = "ChatClientUITests";

    Content = UnitTestSystem.CreateTestPage(settings);
}
```

> **NOTE**
>
> Unfortunately, the test harness does not allow you to programmatically change the Tag in the current version of the Windows Phone Toolkit UTF. Nonetheless, it is shown here in anticipation of a future release of the UTF.

Metadata and Assertions

As you have seen, attributes are used to identify test classes and methods. Attributes can also be used to provide other metadata information to the UTF. This section examines each of the UTF attributes in greater detail and provides descriptions of their usage, purpose, and effect on test execution.

TestClass Attribute

The `TestClass` attribute indicates that a class contains test methods.

`TestMethod` **Attribute**

The `TestMethod` attribute indicates that a method should be included in the suite of tests. The `Ignore` attribute can be used to temporarily exclude a test method from the suite of tests. Methods decorated with the `TestMethod` attribute should be public and have a void return type.

Metadata for Test Initialization and Cleanup

The UTF provides attributes that allow you to specify methods that should be run before and after test execution. You can provide methods that are executed once for each test assembly, once for each test class, and once for each test method. The order in which methods decorated with each particular attribute are run is presented in Figure 24.4.

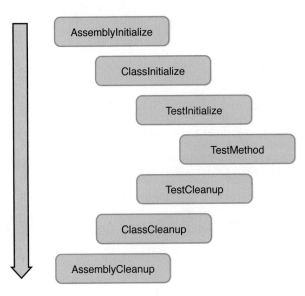

FIGURE 24.4   Test execution order is affected by initialization and cleanup metadata.

`AssemblyInitialize` **Attribute**

The `AssemblyInitialize` attribute identifies a method that contains code to be used before all tests in an assembly are run, and to allocate resources obtained by the assembly. A method decorated with the `AssemblyInitialize` attribute must be public and static, and have a `void` return type. The following demonstrates the use of the `AssemblyInitialize` attribute:

```
[AssemblyInitialize]
public static void AssemblyInitialize()
{
    /* Assembly initialization logic goes here. */
}
```

> **NOTE**
>
> The UTF runs a method that is marked with the `AssemblyInitialize` attribute only if that method is a member of a class that is marked with the `TestClass` attribute.

`AssemblyCleanup` **Attribute**

The `AssemblyCleanup` attribute is analogous to the `AssemblyInitialize` attribute but occurs at the end of the test run. As with the `AssemblyInitialize` attribute, a method decorated with this attribute should be located in a test class. The following shows an example of a method decorated with the `AssemblyCleanup` attribute:

```
[AssemblyCleanup]
public static void AssemblyCleanup()
{
    /* Assembly cleanup logic goes here. */
}
```

`ClassInitialize` **Attribute**

The `ClassInitialize` attribute provides the opportunity to run code before any of the tests in the test class have run, and to allocate resources to be used by the test class.

A method decorated with the `ClassInitialize` attribute must be public and static with a `void` return type. Only one method in a class may be decorated with this attribute.

The following shows an example of a method decorated with the `ClassInitialize` attribute:

```
[ClassInitialize]
public static void ClassInitialize()
{
    /* Class initialization logic goes here. */
}
```

`ClassCleanup` **Attribute**

The `ClassCleanup` attribute is analogous to the `ClassInitialize` attribute but occurs after all test methods have completed within the test class. The following shows an example of a method decorated with the `ClassCleanup` attribute:

```
[ClassCleanup]
public static void ClassCleanup()
{
    /* Class cleanup logic goes here. */
}
```

TestInitialize **Attribute**

The `TestInitialize` attribute is used to indicate that a method decorated with this attribute should be called before every test method within a test class. A method decorated with the `TestInitialize` attribute must be public and have a void return type. The following shows an example of a method decorated with the `TestInitialize` attribute:

```
[TestInitialize]
public void TestInitialize()
{
    /* Test initialization logic goes here. */
}
```

TIP

If more than one method is decorated with the `TestInitialize` attribute in a test class, it prevents the execution of all test methods. Furthermore, it does so silently. If you find that the debugger is failing to hit a break point in a test method, look for a duplication of the `TestInitialize` attribute.

TestCleanup **Attribute**

The `TestCleanup` attribute is useful for resetting the state of shared resources in between test methods, such as an object that is used by all tests within a test class.

```
[TestCleanup]
public void TestCleanup()
{
    /* Test cleanup logic goes here. */
}
```

Miscellaneous Metadata

The following attributes allow you to control various other aspects of test execution.

TestProperty **Attribute**

The `TestProperty` attribute allows arbitrary metadata to be associated with a test method. For example, you could use it to store the name of a test pass that this test covers by decorating the test method with `[TestProperty("TestPass", "Accessibility")]`. Unlike the Silverlight UTF for the browser and the Visual Studio desktop CLR unit testing tools, the Windows Phone UTF does not display `TestProperty` information within the test harness.

Ignore **Attribute**

The `Ignore` attribute can be used to temporarily exclude a specific test from execution. This can be useful for excluding a test that is blocking other tests from running. It allows you to retain compilation of the test, rather than merely commenting out the code.

> **NOTE**
>
> The number of tests listed in the unit test harness is unaffected by the Ignore attribute.

Description **Attribute**

The Description attribute is used on test methods and allows you to provide a string describing the purpose and/or behavior of the test method. The description is then presented beneath the title of the test result details screen on the phone. The following example demonstrates the use of the Description attribute:

```
[TestMethod]
[Description("An example test demonstrating the Description attribute.")]
public void ShouldAlwaysPass()
{
    Assert.IsTrue(true);
}
```

Timeout **Attribute**

The Timeout attribute allows you to specify an amount in milliseconds in which a test method must complete or the test method fails.

The following is an example of using the Timeout attribute to prevent an asynchronous test method from taking longer than 100 milliseconds to execute:

```
[TestMethod]
[Asynchronous]
[Timeout(100)]
public void ShouldFailDueToAsyncTestTimeout()
{
    EnqueueDelay(1000);
    EnqueueTestComplete();
}
```

This test method fails because the call to EnqueueDelay delays the completion of the test by 1000ms (1 second), and the Timeout attribute specifies that the test should take no longer than 100ms. The EnqueueDelay attribute and the other asynchronous related attributes are discussed later in this chapter.

Owner **Attribute**

The Owner attribute is used to specify the person responsible for maintaining, running, and/or debugging the test. This attribute accepts a single string parameter, indicating the name of the owner, as shown in the following example:

```
[TestMethod]
[Owner("Daniel Vaughan")]
public void ShouldAlwaysPass()
```

```
{
    Assert.IsTrue(true);
}
```

The value of the attribute is not displayed within the test harness of the current Windows Phone UTF.

`ExpectedException` **Attribute**

Verifying that your code produces a correct response to a known set of values is one thing; verifying that it responds appropriately when given bad input is another. This is called negative testing, and it allows you to verify that code behaves correctly even when exceptional conditions arise.

Ordinarily, if a test method raises an exception, the exception causes that test to fail. In a negative test, however, raising an exception may be the expected behavior. In that case the `ExpectedException` attribute can be used to indicate that if an exception of a particular type, with a particular message, is not thrown, the test should fail. The following example demonstrates the use of the `ExpectedException` attribute:

```
[TestMethod]
[ExpectedException(typeof(ArgumentException))]
public void ShouldFailDueToArgumentException()
{
    throw new ArgumentException("Invalid argument supplied.");
}
```

> **NOTE**
>
> The `TagAttribute`, `AsynchronousAttribute`, and `BugAttribute` are not available in the Microsoft desktop CLR test framework. Using any of them, therefore, means that your unit tests will not be compatible with the desktop CLR.

`Asynchronous` **Attribute**

The `Asynchronous` attribute informs the UTF that a test method should be considered to be in a running state until the `WorkItemTest.EnqueueTestComplete` method is called.

> **TIP**
>
> Use the `Asynchronous` attribute in combination with the `Timeout` attribute to prevent the test method from taking forever if it fails to call `EnqueueTestComplete`.

For more information on the `Asynchronous` attribute, see the section "Asynchronous Testing."

Bug **Attribute**

The Bug attribute allows you to associate a known bug with a unit test. Its key characteristic is that it reverses the result of a test, so you can first use it to demonstrate the existence of a bug, and after the bug is resolved, the Fixed property indicates that the test should pass. For example, if a method is able to reproduce a bug in the software, it may first look like this:

```
[Bug("TFS 123")]
[TestMethod]
public void ExerciseBuggyCode()
{
    Assert.IsTrue(false); /* Simulates some broken code. */
}
```

Consider the preceding test method. It passes because the Bug attribute's Fixed property is false by default.

When the issue is resolved, you can add the Fixed property to the Bug attribute, which removes the inversion behavior of the Bug attribute.

```
[Bug("TFS 123", Fixed = true)]
[TestMethod]
public void ExerciseBuggyCode()
{
    Assert.IsTrue(true); /* Simulates issue resolved. */
}
```

Priority **Attribute**

Contrary to first assumptions, the Priority attribute is not used by the test system. Its purpose can be defined by you. It is, however, added to the set of implicit expression tags. The attribute requires an integer constructor argument, which specifies the priority value. For example:

```
[TestMethod]
[Priority(1)]
public void AlwaysPass()
{
    Assert.IsTrue(true, "Test method intended to always pass.");
}
```

We can then use the tag expression Priority1 to execute this test method.

WorkItemTest: **The Base** TestClass **Type**

UTF test classes normally inherit from the WorkItemTest class. Although inheriting from this class is not strictly required, it does provide for some advanced features, such as asynchronous testing.

Asynchronous unit test methods are a key feature of the Windows Phone UTF, and one that is notably absent from the Microsoft UTF for the desktop CLR.

> **NOTE**
>
> By inheriting from WorkItemTest, you lose compatibility with the Desktop CLR Visual Studio UTF. Therefore, do not inherit from this class if you want to retain cross-screen compatibility and do not require advanced UI testing facilities, such as asynchronous tests.

Verifying Conditions with Assertions

Assertions are the cornerstone of UTF. The Assert class has a multitude of test related method overloads that allow you to ensure the validity of your app's state and behavior. The following is the core set of assertions used by most test classes:

▶ **AreEqual and AreNotEqual**—These methods rely on the Object.Equals method to determine object equality. There are various overloads for primitives, as well as reference types.

▶ **AreSame and AreNotSame**—Tests for whether two variables refer to the same object instance. These methods rely on the Object.ReferenceEquals method. There are various overloads for primitives, as well as reference types.

▶ **Fail**—Allows you to explicitly fail a test based on logic within the test method.

▶ **Inconclusive**—Allows you to explicitly set the outcome of a test to inconclusive.

▶ **IsTrue and IsFalse**—Verifies that a Boolean value is either true or false.

▶ **IsInstanceOfType and IsNotInstanceOfType**—Verifies that an object instance does or does not inherit from a specified type.

▶ **IsNull and IsNotNull**—Verifies that an object is, or is not, null.

If an Assert method fails, it raises a UnitTestAssertException, which is handled by the UTF infrastructure and is reported back to you as a test failure.

To complement the set methods provided by the Assert classes, there exists a CollectionAssert class, with methods particular to collections, and a StringAssert class, which provides assertions based on regular expressions.

Verifying Collection Conditions with `CollectionAssert`

The following is the list of collection assertions that enable you to verify the contents of collections:

▶ `AllItemsAreInstancesOfType`—Verifies that all items in a collection are, or inherit from, a specified type.

▶ `AllItemsAreNotNull`—Verifies that no item in the collection is null.

▶ `AllItemsAreUnique`—Verifies that a collection is a set; each item occurs only once.

▶ `AreEqual` and `AreNotEqual`—Verifies that two collections have the same number of items, and that each item in the first collection is equal to the item at the same index in the second collection.

▶ `AreEquivalent` and `AreNotEquivalent`—Verifies that two collections have the same number of items, and that each item in the first collection has an item that is equal to it in the second collection. This differs from `AreEqual` and `AreNotEqual` in that order does not matter.

▶ `Contains` and `DoesNotContain`—Verifies that a collection contains a specified item.

▶ `IsSubsetOf` and `IsNotSubsetOf`—Verifies that all items in one collection exist in another specified collection.

Verifying String Conditions with `StringAssert`

The `StringAssert` class provides various methods for verifying the contents of strings:

▶ `Contains`—Verifies that a string contains a specified substring.

▶ `Matches` and `DoesNotMatch`—Uses a regular expression to verify that the specified string matches, or does not match, a specified pattern.

▶ `StartsWith` and `EndsWith`—Verifies that a string starts or ends with a specified string.

Hiding the Expressions Editor

Sometimes you may want to execute your tests without having to interact with the UTF interface. It can be annoying to have to tap the Use Tag button to kick off the unit tests before the countdown timer reaches zero.

> **NOTE**
>
> Unfortunately, the test harness does not allow you to hide the tag expressions editor in the current version of the Windows Phone Toolkit UTF. Nonetheless, it is shown here in anticipation of a future release of the UTF.

To run the tests as soon as the test harness launches, you need to set the `StartRunImmediately` property of the `UnitTestSettings` instance. This is demonstrated in this excerpt from the MainPage.xaml.cs file in the downloadable sample code:

```
public MainPage()
{
    InitializeComponent();

    UnitTestSettings settings = UnitTestSystem.CreateDefaultSettings();
    settings.StartRunImmediately = true;

    Content = UnitTestSystem.CreateTestPage(settings);
}
```

Testing Multiple Assemblies

The current implementation of the UTF for Windows Phone does not support inclusion of tests from assemblies outside the test project; all tests must reside in the Windows Phone test project.

When this shortcoming is rectified, if you want to have a single project for testing and include other test assemblies, add assemblies to the `TestAssemblies` collection of the `UnitTestSettings` class, as shown:

```
UnitTestSettings settings = UnitTestSystem.CreateDefaultSettings();
settings.TestAssemblies.Add(typeof(TestClass1).Assembly);
settings.TestAssemblies.Add(typeof(TestClass2).Assembly);
UIElement testPage = UnitTestSystem.CreateTestPage(settings);
```

Testing Nonpublic Members

Sometimes you need to test classes and members that are not public but are internal to a project, such as during system testing, where you need to interact with UI elements directly. To have access to internal members, you must allow the test project access to the internal members of the main project. You do this by placing an `InternalsVisibleTo` attribute into the `AssemblyInfo` class of the main project, as shown:

```
[assembly: InternalsVisibleTo("WPUnleashed.Tests")]
```

The `InternalsVisibleTo` attribute accepts a single parameter, which is the name of the assembly. If the test project has a strong name, the full name of the assembly must be used, including its public key token.

Examples of the `InternalsVisibleTo` attribute are in the downloadable sample code.

A Testable Chat Client

This section explores a simple chat client app. First, a custom chat service that is used to send and receive messages is discussed. Next, you examine how to substitute types using mocking and look at mocking the chat service. You see how to test the functionality of a viewmodel without needing to create a view for it. Finally, you learn how to create coded UI tests using the UTF TestPanel in combination with the Microsoft Automation framework.

The code for this section is located in the `ChatClientView` and `ChatClientViewModel` classes in the downloadable sample code.

The chat client app relies on a chat service, represented by an `IChatService` interface. The `IChatService` specifies a method to send a message, presumably to a cloud service, and an event to indicate when the service receives a message. The interface is shown in the following excerpt:

```
public interface IChatService
{
    void SendMessage(string message);
    event EventHandler<ChatMessageEventArgs> MessageReceived;
}
```

A mock chat service is used during unit testing. Mock objects mimic the behavior of real objects in controlled ways. In this case, `MockChatService` acts as loopback; when the `SendMessage` method is called, the `MessageReceived` event is raised, as shown:

```
public class MockChatService : IChatService
{
    public bool MessageSent { get; private set; }
    public string LastMessage { get; private set; }

    public void SendMessage(string message)
    {
        MessageSent = true;
        LastMessage = message;
        OnMessageReceived(new ChatMessageEventArgs(message));
    }


    public event EventHandler<ChatMessageEventArgs> MessageReceived;

    public void OnMessageReceived(ChatMessageEventArgs e)
    {
        MessageReceived.Raise(this, e);
    }
}
```

The viewmodel for the chat client uses the chat service to send messages using a `SendCommand` (see Listing 24.1). When the `SendCommand` executes, the `IChatService.SendMessage` method receives the message.

The viewmodel subscribes to the `IChatService.MessageReceived` event. When a message is received, it is placed into an `ObservableCollection` of messages, which are then presented in the view.

LISTING 24.1   `ChatClientViewModel` Class (excerpt)

```
public class ChatClientViewModel : ViewModelBase
{
    readonly IChatService chatService;

    public ChatClientViewModel(IChatService chatService)
    {
        this.chatService = ArgumentValidator.AssertNotNull(
                                    chatService, "chatService");

        sendCommand = new DelegateCommand(
            delegate
            {
                if (string.IsNullOrEmpty(message))
                {
                    return;
                }
                chatService.SendMessage(message);
                Message = string.Empty;
            },
            delegate { return !string.IsNullOrEmpty(message); });

        chatService.MessageReceived
            += (sender, args) => messages.Add(args.Message);

        PropertyChanged += delegate { sendCommand.RaiseCanExecuteChanged(); };

        /* The rest of the constructor is shown later in the chapter. */
    }

    readonly ObservableCollection<string> messages
                = new ObservableCollection<string>();

    public ObservableCollection<string> Messages
    {
        get
        {
```

```
            return messages;
        }
    }

    string message;
    public string Message
    {
        get
        {
            return message;
        }
        set
        {
            Assign(ref message, value);
        }
    }

    readonly DelegateCommand sendCommand;

    public ICommand SendCommand
    {
        get
        {
            return sendCommand;
        }
    }

    /* The rest of the class is shown later in the chapter. */
}
```

With the infrastructure in place, you can set about creating some unit tests for the viewmodel.

NOTE

An alternative approach, known as Test Driven Development (TDD), sees the creation of the unit tests first. If you are willing to take an interface first approach, or have a tool such as Resharper that allows you to quickly generate class members, you may choose to create the unit tests before you implement the class that is the subject of the unit tests.

Listing 24.2 shows various test methods for verifying that the viewmodel is able to send a message correctly and that it is able to respond correctly when it receives a message from the chat service.

LISTING 24.2   Chat Client ViewModel Tests

```csharp
[TestClass]
public class ChatClientTests : WorkItemTest
{
    [TestMethod]
    public void ShouldSendMessage()
    {
        string testMessage = "Hello from unit test.";
        MockChatService chatService = new MockChatService();
        ChatClientViewModel viewModel = new ChatClientViewModel(chatService);
        viewModel.Message = testMessage;
        viewModel.SendCommand.Execute(null);
        Assert.AreEqual(chatService.LastMessage, testMessage);
    }


    [TestMethod]
    public void ShouldNotSendMessageIfEmpty()
    {
        MockChatService chatService = new MockChatService();
        ChatClientViewModel viewModel = new ChatClientViewModel(chatService);
        viewModel.Message = string.Empty;
        viewModel.SendCommand.Execute(null);
        Assert.IsFalse(chatService.MessageSent);
    }


    [TestMethod]
    public void CommandShouldBeDisabledIfMessageIfEmpty()
    {
        MockChatService chatService = new MockChatService();
        ChatClientViewModel viewModel = new ChatClientViewModel(chatService);
        viewModel.Message = string.Empty;
        Assert.IsFalse(viewModel.SendCommand.CanExecute(null));
    }
    [TestMethod]
    [Description(@"When the chat service receives a message,
        the client displays it.")]
    public void CommandShouldBeEnabledIfMessageNotEmpty()
    {
        MockChatService chatService = new MockChatService();
        ChatClientViewModel viewModel = new ChatClientViewModel(chatService);
        viewModel.Message = "Test";
        Assert.IsTrue(viewModel.SendCommand.CanExecute(null));
    }


    [TestMethod]
```

```
public void ShouldReceiveMessage()
{
    string testMessage = "Hello from unit test.";
    MockChatService chatService = new MockChatService();
    ChatClientViewModel viewModel = new ChatClientViewModel(chatService);
    chatService.OnMessageReceived(new ChatMessageEventArgs(testMessage));
    CollectionAssert.Contains(viewModel.Messages, testMessage);
}
}
```

The result of running the unit tests is shown in Figure 24.5.

FIGURE 24.5   Chat client test results.

Building the View

The view allows the user to send and receive messages via the viewmodel. The view consists of the following elements:

▶ A `TextBox` to allow the user to enter a message to send.

▶ An `AppBar`, which includes an `AppBarIconButton` to execute the viewmodel's `SendCommand`. For more information on the `AppBar`, see Chapter 8, "Taming the Application Bar."

▶ A `ListBox` to display all incoming messages.

The following excerpt shows the main content from the ChatClientView.xaml page:

```xml
<StackPanel Grid.Row="1"
        Style="{StaticResource PageContentPanelStyle}">
    <u:AppBar>
        <u:AppBarIconButton
        Command="{Binding SendCommand}"
        Text="Send"
        IconUri="/ChatClient/Images/AppBarMessageSend.png"
        x:Name="button_Send"
        AutomationProperties.AutomationId="button_Send" />
    </u:AppBar>

    <TextBox x:Name="textBlock_Message"
        Text="{Binding Message, Mode=TwoWay,
        UpdateSourceTrigger=Explicit}"
        TextWrapping="Wrap" AcceptsReturn="True"
        u2:UpdateSourceTriggerExtender.UpdateSourceOnTextChanged="True"/>
    <TextBlock Text="Messages" Style="{StaticResource LabelTextStyle}"/>
    <ListBox x:Name="listBox" ItemsSource="{Binding Messages}" Height="400">
        <ListBox.ItemTemplate>
            <DataTemplate>
                <TextBlock Text="{Binding}"
                    Style="{StaticResource NormalTextStyle}" />
            </DataTemplate>
        </ListBox.ItemTemplate>
    </ListBox>
</StackPanel>
```

The various input controls have been named. You see later in this chapter how the naming of elements allows you to directly manipulate them from a coded UI unit test.

> **TIP**
>
> If you are not creating coded UI tests, it is better to refrain from naming elements unless you need to refer to them in the code-beside. This helps to identify those elements that are referred to in the code-beside.

The view's code-beside (ChatClientView.xaml.cs) instantiates the viewmodel and supplies the viewmodel with an instance of the MockChatService, as shown in the following excerpt:

```csharp
public ChatClientView()
{
    InitializeComponent();
    DataContext = new ChatClientViewModel(new MockChatService());
}
```

Later in the chapter you see how to replace the `MockChatService` for a *real* chat service implementation using Inversion of Control.

The final result of the chat page is shown in Figure 24.6.

FIGURE 24.6   `ChatClientView` page

Code Driven UI Testing

A key benefit of the MVVM pattern is that it allows you to unit test an app without needing to display its UI. Sometimes, however, you may want to verify the behavior of the UI by emulating user interaction. This can be achieved using coded UI tests.

The advantage of coded UI tests is that they provide your app with a test environment that is closer to the real world; they allow you to simulate the tapping of buttons or entering of text while the app is running.

The downside of coded UI tests is that they are tightly coupled to the user interface, which is often the most likely thing to change over time. If the UI is modified, it can mean having to rewrite your coded UI tests.

Coded UI tests can be performed with the UTF by populating a test `Panel` control that can host `UIElements` during test execution. The `PresentationTest` class subclasses the `WorkItemTest` class and provides a `TestPanel` property that allows you to materialize the page or control that you want to test. Observe the following excerpt:

```
[TestClass]
public class ChatClientUITests : PresentationTest
{
    ChatClientView view;

    [TestInitialize]
    public void PreparePage()
    {
        view = new ChatClientView();
        TestPanel.Children.Add(view);
    }
...
}
```

Recall that the TestInitialize attribute causes the method to be called before each test method in the parent class. When the PreparePage method is called, it creates a new instance of the ChatClientView and places it into a container control within the test harness.

This section looks at the three test methods in the ChatClientUITests class.

The first test method simply verifies that the PhoneApplicationPage is presented in the TestPanel, as shown:

```
[TestMethod]
public void ShouldDisplayDefaultSize()
{
    Assert.IsTrue(view.ActualWidth > 0);
}
```

The ShouldDisplayDefaultSize method demonstrates that you are able to interact with the UI elements from code. In fact, while the tests are running, their actions are viewable within the test harness (see Figure 24.7).

To interact with controls on the page, give the test project access to the internal members of the main project. This is done by placing an InternalsVisibleTo attribute in the AssemblyInfo class of the main project, shown in the previous section "Testing Nonpublic Members."

When the InternalsVisibleTo is placed in the target project, IntelliSense is enabled for controls on the page.

FIGURE 24.7   A UI test in execution.

To test that the Send button is enabled when the message `TextBox` is populated, set the text and then perform an assert using the button, as shown in the following excerpt:

```
[TestMethod]
public void ButtonShouldBeEnabled()
{
    view.textBlock_Message.Text = "Test";
    Assert.IsTrue(view.button_Send.IsEnabled);
}
```

Asynchronous Testing

The UTF is designed to run tests on a single thread. The UI thread in Windows Phone XAML apps uses a message pump, and often calls to update properties or reactions to property changed events are driven forward using `Dispatcher` calls. The result is that a `UIElement` may not be in the state that you think it should be when you are performing an assertion. Fortunately the Windows Phone UTF compensates with some built-in asynchronous features.

The `Asynchronous` attribute tells the UTF to keep running the test until the test class's base method, `WorkItemTest.EnqueueTestComplete`, is called, or until an unhandled exception occurs. This allows you to spin off work to other threads, or queue work to happen on the UI thread, while keeping the test alive.

The `WorkItemTest.EnqueueCallback` method allows actions to be queued on the UI thread. This may include actions such as verifying the value of a `UIElement`'s property after a `PropertyChanged` event has been given the opportunity to propagate.

The following excerpt demonstrates how to use the `Asynchronous` attribute in combination with the `EnqueueCallback` method to set the text of a sample view's message box. It simulates a tap to the Send Message button and then verifies that the `ListBox` has been correctly populated:

```
[TestMethod]
[Asynchronous]
public void ButtonShouldSendMessage()
{
    view.textBlock_Message.Text = "Test";
    EnqueueCallback(() => ((IAppBarItem)view.button_Send).PerformClick());
    EnqueueCallback(() => Assert.IsTrue(view.listBox.Items.Count > 0));
    EnqueueTestComplete();
}
```

When the `textBlock_Message.Text` property is set, the Send button is not enabled until the viewmodel's `SendCommand` responds to the `Message` property's `PropertyChanged` event. After it has had a chance to respond, the command enables itself.

The `EnqueueCallback` method queues the `PerformClick` method, so that by the time it is called, the button is enabled. Similarly, verification that the `ListBox` has been populated must occur after the UI has responded to the new item in the `Messages` collection in the viewmodel.

The UTF is notified that all nonblocking activity has been completed by calling the base class's `WorkItemTest.EnqueueTestComplete` method.

Using Automation Peers to Manipulate UI Elements at Runtime

When performing code-driven UI testing, often you need to manipulate elements in ways that are not possible using the API of the elements themselves. The `Button` class, for example, does not have a `PerformTap` method to raise the `Tap` event. The built-in control classes are generally well encapsulated and are not designed to simulate interaction via code. For this we turn to the Microsoft UI Automation framework, which consists of a secondary API for manipulating UI elements from code. The Automation framework is designed for accessibility software, allowing third-party software to manipulate the UI on behalf of a user with a disability.

The Automation API is able to manipulate elements, such as a `Button`, using internal methods of the various built-in `FrameworkElement` types, which are ordinarily off-limits.

In this example, a button is placed on the `ChatClientView` page. When tapped, it sets the view's custom `ButtonClicked` property to true. The XAML for the button is as follows:

```
<Button x:Name="button_AutomationTest"
        Content="AutomationTestButton"
        Click="button_AutomationTest_Click" />
```

The code-beside for the view contains the event handler for the `Click` event of the button:

```
public bool ButtonClicked { get; private set; }

void button_AutomationTest_Click(object sender, RoutedEventArgs e)
{
    ButtonClicked = true;
}
```

An `AutomationPeer`, located in the System.Windows.Automation.Peers namespace, is used to verify that the button was indeed clicked. The `AutomationPeer` object is then used to retrieve an `IInvokeProvider` specific to the `Button` class, which allows you to invoke the button's `Click` event, shown in the following excerpt:

```
[TestMethod]
[Asynchronous]
public void DemonstrateButtonClick()
{
    AutomationPeer peer
            = FrameworkElementAutomationPeer.CreatePeerForElement(
                                            view.button_AutomationTest);
    IInvokeProvider provider
            = (IInvokeProvider)peer.GetPattern(PatternInterface.Invoke);
    provider.Invoke();

    EnqueueCallback(() => Assert.IsTrue(view.ButtonClicked));
    EnqueueTestComplete();
}
```

Behind the scenes, the `AutomationPeer` is calling an internal method of the `ButtonBase` named `AutomationButtonBaseClick`, which raises the button's `Click` event.

NOTE

The `ButtonAutomationPeer` raises the button's `Click` event and not its `Tap` event. Unfortunately, the `Tap` event is not supported by the Automation API in the current 8.0 release of the Windows Phone SDK.

Inversion of Control (IoC)

Windows Phone presents some interesting challenges for testing apps in various deployment scenarios. For example, a common requirement for phone apps is the need to behave differently depending on whether the app has been purchased or is in trial mode. Furthermore, the launcher and chooser API does not play well with unit tests because launchers and choosers cause the app to be deactivated. Hence, there is a need for some mechanism to alter the behavior of an app, depending on its deployment scenario, and to decouple and replace various phone-specific types so that code can be more easily tested. One way to achieve these things is by using Inversion of Control (IoC).

IoC encompasses two key concepts presented in this chapter: service location and dependency injection.

Service location allows you to associate a type, often an interface, with a concrete implementation of that type, so that when another component requests the first type, it is automatically delivered an instance of the associated type. This allows your code to be decoupled from any particular concrete implementation, which increases flexibility, and allows the behavior of your app to be modified, without having to change all references to a particular concrete implementation.

Dependency Injection (DI) assists in the creation of objects by automatically supplying known types to the objects constructor during instantiation.

Employing IoC in Windows Phone apps helps overcome the challenges brought on by the rigid infrastructure and numerous sealed classes that account for many of the key types in the SDK and that hinder both unit testing and ad hoc testing.

Numerous IoC frameworks have been designed for Silverlight for the browser and the desktop CLR. Previous versions of the Windows Phone OS, prior to Windows Phone 8, were based on the Microsoft .NET Compact Framework (.NET CF), which lacks the capability to generate Microsoft Intermediate Language (MSIL) and does not include the `Reflection.Emit` APIs, which is a key ingredient in generating types at runtime. This limitation meant that none of the well-known IoC projects, such as the Microsoft Patterns and Practices Unity framework, existed for the phone. This has changed in Windows Phone 8, which is no longer built on .NET CF.

Included in the sample code is an IoC container and DI framework that I have created, which is based on work by Ian Randall (http://microioc.codeplex.com/). It is a lightweight container that does not have all the features of other containers, but it is sufficient for most scenarios.

I leave it to you to discover and explore other third-party IoC containers.

Like much of the code presented in this book, these classes are present in the downloadable sample code. I recommend, however, that you procure the latest code from http://calciumsdk.com, where you are sure to have the most up-to-date version.

24

A Custom IoC Container and DI Framework

The custom `Dependency` class is a static class used to associate types or resolve instances of types at runtime. The `Dependency` class serves as a proxy to an instance of IoC container, allowing you to change the underlying IoC container implementation. It does this by leveraging the Microsoft.Practices.ServiceLocation API, which provides a container agnostic type resolution mechanism. The `Dependency` class also uses a custom `IDependencyRegistrar` to create type associations, something notably absent from the Microsoft.Practices.ServiceLocation API.

To use the `Dependency` class, an IoC container implementation must be specified.

Initialization of the IoC infrastructure should be performed as soon as possible before the app displays its UI. This helps prevent type resolution failures.

In the sample, located in the WPUnleashed.Examples project, the container initialization code is placed in the `App` class, as shown in the following excerpt:

```
void InitializeContainer()
{
    SimpleContainer container = new SimpleContainer();
    container.InitializeServiceLocator();

#if DEBUG
    Dependency.Register<ILicensingService>(new MockLicensingService
    {
        IsTrial = true
    });
    Dependency.Register<IMarketplaceDetailTaskAdapter>(
        new MockMarketplaceDetailTaskAdapter(
            () => Debug.WriteLine("Launching Marketplace Detail...")));
#else
    Dependency.Register<ILicensingService, LicensingService>();
    Dependency.Register<IMarketplaceDetailTaskAdapter,
                    MarketplaceDetailTaskAdapter>();
#endif
}
```

After the container is initialized, the `Dependency` class is used to register type associations. Creating a different set of type associations, depending on the build configuration, can be achieved using preprocessor directives. When using a DEBUG build configuration, mock implementations of the `ILicensingService` interface and the `IMarketplaceDetailTaskAdapter` interface are used. These types wrap and substitute the functionality provided by the built-in `MarketDetailTask` and `LicenseInformation` classes.

> **TIP**
>
> Rather than duplicating your type mappings across test and core projects, you may choose instead to create a dedicated class that includes type associations for each scenario you are covering: test, release, trial, and so on.

> **NOTE**
>
> This chapter demonstrates the use of manual mocking techniques and does not cover dynamic mocking using frameworks such as Moq. If you are not already familiar with mocking, I recommend exploring dynamic mocking because it offers advantages over manual mocking and can reduce the amount code that you need to write.

Testing Trial Conditions

Providing a trial version of your app may help to improve its monetization. If someone has the opportunity to try out your app, the user may be more likely to purchase it (assuming that it is any good). A usual requirement for an app employing a trial version is to provide the user with a link to buy the app within the app itself. In the following demonstration, you see how to display an application bar button when an app is in trial mode.

The `Microsoft.Phone.MarketPlace.LicenseInformation` class contains a single method called `IsTrial()`, which indicates whether your app has been purchased. When a user downloads the trial version of your app from the marketplace, this method returns true. On all other occasions, such as when debugging, this method returns false.

To ensure that an app functions correctly in both scenarios, you abstract the `LicenseInformation` class.

Abstracting the `LicenseInformation` Class

The downloadable sample code includes a custom `ILicenseService` interface, which contains a single property called `Trial`, indicating the trial state of the app. There are two implementations of this interface: one for testing and one for production.

The production implementation named `LicensingService` wraps a `LicenseInformation` instance, as shown in the following excerpt:

```
public class LicensingService : ILicensingService
{
    public bool Trial
    {
        get
        {
            LicenseInformation licenseInformation
                            = new LicenseInformation();
```

```
            return licenseInformation.IsTrial();
        }
    }
}
```

During development and testing, the LicensingService class is replaced by a MockLicensingService class, which allows you to change the value of its Trial property. See the following excerpt:

```
public class MockLicensingService : ILicensingService
{
    bool trial = true;

    public bool Trial
    {
        get
        {
            return trial;
        }
        set
        {
            trial = value;
        }
    }
}
```

The particular implementation that is used depends on the type association within the IoC container. When the project is built using a release configuration, LicensingService is used; otherwise, the MockLicensingService is used.

Within the ChatClientView page is a button whose visibility depends on a viewmodel property called BuyOptionVisible. See the following excerpt:

```
bool buyOptionVisible;

public bool BuyOptionVisible
{
    get
    {
        return buyOptionVisible;
    }
    private set
    {
        Assign(ref buyOptionVisible, value);
    }
}
```

In the viewmodel constructor, the value of the `buyOptionVisible` field is determined using the `ILicensingService`, which is resolved via the static `Dependency` method called `Resolve`:

```
var licensingService = Dependency.Resolve<ILicensingService>();
buyOptionVisible = licensingService.IsTrial;
```

An `AppBarMenuItem` is bound to the `BuyOptionVisible` property, as shown:

```
<u:AppBar.MenuItems>
    <u:AppBarMenuItem Text="Buy"
        Command="{Binding BuyCommand}"
        Visibility="{Binding BuyOptionVisible,
        Converter={StaticResource BooleanToVisibilityConverter}}" />
</u:AppBar.MenuItems>
```

A value converter is used to convert the Boolean value to a `Visibility` enum value.

When the user taps the button, the `BuyCommand` is executed. In the next section you see how the `BuyCommand` uses an abstracted `MarketPlaceDetailTask` to launch the built-in marketplace application on the phone.

Testing with Launchers and Choosers

Unit testing code that uses a launcher or chooser directly is a challenge because both types of tasks cause your app to be deactivated. No means to abstract launchers or choosers exists out-of-the-box; therefore, I have included in the downloadable sample code a set of classes that do just that.

Just as we abstracted the built-in `LicenseInformation` class in the previous section, here we do the same with the `MarketDetailTask`. The `MarketDetailTask` is a launcher which, when shown, takes the user to the built-in marketplace application. When showing the `MarketplaceDetailTask` during a debugging session, the native marketplace application displays an error because it expects an app with an id that has been officially published to the marketplace.

The main issue, however, is that when the `MarketplaceDetailTask` is shown, it deactivates the app. Thus, it makes sense to abstract the task as in the `LicenseInformation` class in the previous section.

The abstracted custom interface for the `MarketplaceDetailTask` is named `IMarketDetailTask` and contains a single method named `Show`. There are two implementations of this interface. The first, named `MarketplaceDetailTaskAdapter`, calls the `Show` method of a built-in `MarketplaceDetailTask` instance when its own `Show` method is called, as shown in the following excerpt:

```
public class MarketplaceDetailTaskAdapter : IMarketplaceDetailTask
{
```

```
public void Show()
{
    var marketplaceDetailTask = new MarketplaceDetailTask();
    marketplaceDetailTask.Show();
}
}
```

The unit test compatible implementation of the IMarketplaceDetailTask is called MockMarketplaceDetailTask and allows a specified Action to be invoked when the Show method is called:

```
public class MockMarketplaceDetailTask : IMarketplaceDetailTask
{
    readonly Action action;

    public MockMarketplaceDetailTask(Action action)
    {
        this.action = action;
    }

    public void Show()
    {
        if (action != null)
        {
            action();
        }
    }
}
```

The ChatClientViewModel class contains an ICommand named BuyCommand, which, when executed, retrieves the IMarketplaceDetailTask from the IoC container and calls its Show method. BuyCommand is initialized in the viewmodel's constructor, as shown:

```
buyCommand = new DelegateCommand(
    obj =>
    {
        var marketplaceDetailTask
            = Dependency.Resolve<IMarketplaceDetailTask>();
        marketplaceDetailTask.Show();
    });
```

When the BuyCommand is executed, it causes the IMarketDetailTask instance to be resolved using the static Dependency.Resolve method. Recall that a particular implementation of the IMarketDetailTask is registered according to the selected build configuration, as described in the earlier section "A Custom IoC Container and DI Framework." If the build is using a Release configuration, an instance of the `MarketplaceDetailTaskAdapter` is resolved, which, in turn, causes an instance of the built-in `MarketplaceDetailTask` to be shown. Conversely, if the build is using a Debug configuration, the `MockMarketplaceDetailTask` is used, which does not disrupt unit testing or any manual ad hoc testing.

Summary

This chapter explored the Windows Phone Toolkit Unit Testing Framework. The chapter began with a walk-through of the creation of a unit test project. You saw how to create test classes and test methods and looked at the tag expressions editor, which provides a useful mechanism for selecting which tests are to be run during a test session.

The chapter then examined the UTF in greater detail by creating a simple chat client app. You saw how to test a viewmodel's behavior before creating a UI and explored code driven UI testing. You also learned how to perform asynchronous testing and touched on the Microsoft Automation framework.

The chapter then examined some advanced topics, such as Inversion of Control and mocking and how to use a custom IoC container.

Finally, you saw how to perform testing of trial applications. You learned how to hide or reveal content based on a mock licensing service and examined a custom API for mocking launchers and choosers.

24

CHAPTER 25

Manage Payment Instruments Using Wallet Extensibility

The Wallet Hub is the home for all purchases on the device. It allows for contactless payments, deals, loyalty cards, in-app purchases, and credit and debit cards. Rather than having a list of individual apps that offer payment capabilities, the Wallet Hub provides an integrated and consistent account management experience that replaces your physical wallet in your pocket and also offers live updates on your accounts and access to nearby deals.

As a developer, you can create apps that integrate with the Wallet Hub. You can store, retrieve, and manipulate Wallet items from your app or use a background agent to keep your app's Wallet items up-to-date. You can interact with the user via status messages, and you can provide deep-links back to your app from the Wallet Hub to provide a more purposeful in-app experience.

This chapter begins with an overview of the Wallet Hub; its features and UI elements. You then look at storing payment instruments in the Wallet and at keeping them up-to-date using a background agent. You see how to leverage a WCF service using the new asynchronous await features of the .NET framework, and a workaround for a missing feature of the WCF service client code generation for Windows Phone.

The chapter then looks at storing membership cards, such as loyalty cards, in the Wallet Hub.

Finally, the chapter looks at placing deals in the Wallet. You see how to retrieve a list of deals from a WCF service and then how to allow the user to save a deal to the Wallet. You see how to dynamically present a relevant deal directly to the user using a background agent.

The source code for this section is located in the Wallet directory of the downloadable sample code.

Introducing the Wallet Hub

Launch the Wallet Hub by tapping its icon in the App list. The landing page for the Wallet Hub displays two lists (see Figure 25.1). On the left is a list of payment instruments and membership cards, and on the right is a list of deals. Think of the deals area as a folder containing coupons that you might have cut out of the newspaper, but now they are stored digitally.

From the application bar you can pin deals to the start experience or share them with other people. Deals can be found in web searches, in place cards, they can be handed from one person to another, and they can be part of what your app offers.

FIGURE 25.1   The Wallet Hub's landing page.

The Wallet Hub relies on apps for its content and is lit up with data coming from those apps and associated services. A user can access the Wallet and see a summary of this information from a multitude of sources.

As a place where financial information is stored, the Wallet Hub is designed to be secure. The user can provide a pin to prevent unauthorized access, and the Windows Phone OS prevents apps from accessing the Wallet items of other apps. Wallet items are accessible only by the app that put them there.

For certain types of Wallet items, the Windows Phone OS displays a confirmation dialog before the OS places them into the Wallet. This gives ultimate control of what goes into the Wallet, to the user, giving the user peace of mind.

The Wallet Hub allows the user to drill down into Wallet items. When a user taps a payment instrument or membership card, the Wallet displays a detail page for the item. If you pan over to transactions, your app can employ a background agent to retrieve the transaction history for the item. You see how to achieve this later in the chapter.

By adding Wallet functionality to your app, you can increase the reach of your app. Items can be added to the Wallet with your branded logo, making the brand visible from within the Wallet. In addition, deep-linking from the Wallet back to your app offers users an additional entry point to your app.

Apps that handle club memberships, loyalty cards, banking and financial transactions, and coupons are great candidates for Wallet integration. You can, however, think of other novel scenarios for integrating your app into the Wallet.

Required Capabilities for Wallet Integration

To use the Wallet API in your app, you must add the ID_CAP_WALLET capability to your app's WMAppManifest.xml file.

If you are using the payment instruments API, presented in the next section, you must also add the ID_CAP_WALLET_PAYMENTINSTRUMENTS capability.

If you are using Near Field Communication (NFC) for financial transactions (not covered in this chapter), the ID_CAP_WALLET_SECUREELEMENT capability must also be present.

> **NOTE**
>
> To submit an app to the marketplace that uses ID_CAP_WALLET_SECUREELEMENT or ID_CAP_WALLET_PAYMENTINSTRUMENTS, you must request that special permission be applied to your developer account. Visit the Windows Phone Dev Center, at https://dev.windowsphone.com/, for more information.

Storing Payment Instruments in the Wallet

Payment Instruments include banking cards, such as credit and debit cards, and financial payment services, which are capable of performing a financial transaction.

The following example demonstrates the creation of a PaymentInstrument object that represents a credit card:

```
var instrument = new PaymentInstrument(card.Id.ToString())
        {
            AccountNumber = "123456",
            CustomerName = "Alan Turing",
            ExpirationDate = DateTime.Now.AddMonths(3),
```

```
            DisplayName = "Unleashed Card",
            PaymentInstrumentKinds = PaymentInstrumentKinds.Credit
    };
```

Wallet items, such as the `PaymentInstrument` class and its super class `WalletTransactionItemBase`, have a multitude of optional properties for storing information such as address details, billing information, and financial transactions. You can choose to fill in as many or as few of those fields as you need. You can also create custom fields for storing other data if need be, which you look at later in the chapter.

Use the `AddWalletItemTask` class to add a payment instrument to the Wallet. The `AddWalletItemTask` follows the launchers and choosers model from Chapter 14, "Leveraging Built-In Apps via Launchers and Choosers."

The `AddWalletItemTask` resides in the Microsoft.Phone.Tasks namespace. As a general rule, if you are subscribing to a task's `Completed` event, the task should be instantiated as a field of your page or viewmodel, and its `Completed` event subscribed to in the constructor, as demonstrated in the following excerpt:

```
class CardViewModel : ViewModelBase
{
    readonly AddWalletItemTask addWalletItemTask = new AddWalletItemTask();
    ...

    public CardViewModel() : base("Card")
    {
        ...

        addWalletItemTask.Completed += HandleAddWalletItemTaskCompleted;
    }
...
}
```

With the `AddWalletItemTask` ready to go, the task's `Item` property is set to the instrument, and the task's `Show` method is called:

```
addWalletItemTask.Item = instrument;
addWalletItemTask.Show();
```

The `Show` method presents the user with a confirmation dialog, and the OS adds the payment instrument to the Wallet.

When the user completes or cancels out of the task, the `Completed` event is raised, and the event handler receives a `TaskResult` value indicating whether the item was successfully added to the Wallet.

The following excerpt demonstrates how to handle the `Completed` event:

```
void HandleAddWalletItemTaskCompleted(object sender, AddWalletItemResult e)
{
    if (e.TaskResult == TaskResult.OK)
    {
        MessageService.ShowMessage(
            e.Item.DisplayName + " was added to your wallet.");
    }
    else if (e.TaskResult == TaskResult.Cancel)
    {
        MessageService.ShowMessage("Cancelled");
    }

    Refresh();
}
```

In the following section, you see how these principles are applied to a simple banking app.

Overview of the Payment Instruments Sample App

The sample app for this section is a banking app that allows the user to retrieve a list of bank cards from a WCF service and to add the cards to the phone's Wallet.

NOTE

The sample for this chapter requires access to a locally deployed WCF service. Please see Chapter 2, "Fundamental Concepts in Windows Phone Development," for information on working with locally deployed WCF services.

The app has the following three views:

▶ MainPage.xaml

▶ CardView.xaml

▶ BillPayView.xaml

MainPage.xaml displays the user's cards and allows the user to tap on a card, which then navigates the app to the CardView.xaml page. The CardView.xaml page displays the card details and allows the user to add the card to, or remove the card from, the Wallet. In addition, the CardView.xaml page allows the user to reduce the card's available funds by performing a pretend purchase (see Figure 25.2).

25

FIGURE 25.2   The sample's CouponView.xaml page.

The BillPayView.xaml page allows the user to replenish a card's funds.

The sample app communicates with a WCF Service named BankService, which allows the user to retrieve a list of cards, make a credit card payment, get a list of transactions for a particular card, and to make purchases for credit and debit cards (see Listing 25.1).

The service uses two custom classes that represent a credit card and a debit card. The CreditCard and DebitCard classes both derive from the custom Card class.

The service uses the new awaitable asynchronous features of .NET. Each service method is decorated with an OperationContract attribute. The AsyncPattern property indicates that an operation is implemented asynchronously using either a Begin<methodName> and End<methodName> method pair in the service contract or, as demonstrated in the sample, the new async keyword combined with a Task return type.

LISTING 25.1   IBankService Interface

```
[ServiceContract]
[ServiceKnownType(typeof(CreditCard))]
[ServiceKnownType(typeof(DebitCard))]
public interface IBankService
{
    [OperationContract(AsyncPattern = true)]
    Task<IEnumerable<Card>> GetCards();
```

```
[OperationContract(AsyncPattern = true)]
Task<PerformPaymentResult> PerformPayment(CreditCard creditCard,
➥decimal amount);

[OperationContract(AsyncPattern = true)]
Task<IEnumerable<AccountTransaction>> GetCardTransactions(Guid cardId);

[OperationContract(AsyncPattern = true)]
Task<MakePurchaseResult> MakeCreditPurchase(CreditCard creditCard,
➥decimal amount);

[OperationContract(AsyncPattern = true)]
Task<MakePurchaseResult> MakeDebitPurchase(DebitCard debitCard, decimal amount);
}
```

The `MainPageViewModel` class retrieves the list of cards from the WCF service (see Listing 25.2).

The service reference code generation of the Windows Phone SDK does not, unfortunately, allow you to generate awaitable methods for asynchronous service methods (see Figure 25.3). Instead, you can use the `Task` class's `Factory` object to create an awaitable task, which then allows the method to populate the viewmodel's `Card` property without the use of an event handler.

The Factory class's `FromAsync` method requires access to the `BeginGetCards` and `EndGetCards` methods of the `IBankService`. These interface members are explicitly implemented in the service client. We therefore cast the `BankServiceClient` object to the `IBankService` interface to access the methods.

LISTING 25.2   `MainPageViewModel.Load` Method (Payment Instrument App)

```
public async void Load()
{
    var client = new BankServiceClient();
    var bankService = (IBankService)client;

    try
    {
        IEnumerable<Card> retrievedCards
            = await Task<IEnumerable<Card>>.Factory.FromAsync(
                bankService.BeginGetCards, bankService.EndGetCards, null);

        Cards = new ObservableCollection<Card>(retrievedCards);
    }
    catch (Exception ex)
    {
        Debug.WriteLine("Unable to retrieve cards." + ex);
```

```
        MessageService.ShowError("Unable to retrieve cards.");
    }
}
```

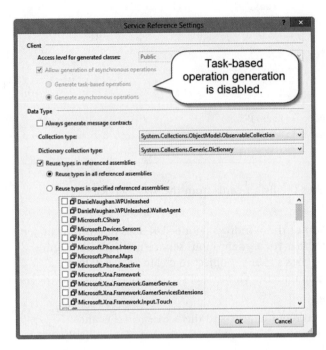

FIGURE 25.3   Windows Phone SDK does not allow for task-based operation generation.

The viewmodel retrieves the cards from the service and places them in an `ObservableCollection`, which is later materialized in the view.

On the server side, the WCF `BankService` sends back two dummy cards: a `CreditCard` and a `DebitCard` (see Listing 25.3). The async keyword means you no longer have to implement a `BeginX` and `EndX` method for the asynchronous service methods.

LISTING 25.3   `BankService` Class (excerpt)

```
public class BankService : IBankService
{
    readonly List<Card> cards = new List<Card>
        {
            new CreditCard
                {
                    Id = Guid.Parse("520E4521-A010-4155-9C61-0B31A0F59C8B"),
                    AccountNumber = "XXXX-XXXX-XXXX-1234",
                    CardName = "Unleashed Credit", CustomerName = "Alan Turing",
                    CreditLimit = 1000, AvailableCredit = 1000,
```

```
                    ExpirationDate = new DateTime(2014, 1, 1),
                    CultureName = "en-US"
                },
            new DebitCard
                {
                    Id = Guid.Parse("077C9304-9BD4-4527-8BB3-EED5F0A78284"),
                    AccountNumber = "XXXX-XXXX-XXXX-5432",
                    CardName = "Unleashed Debit", CustomerName = "Alan Turing",
                    Balance = 1000, ExpirationDate = new DateTime(2014, 1, 1),
                    CultureName = "en-GB"
                }
        };


    public async Task<IEnumerable<Card>> GetCards()
    {
        return cards;
    }
...
}
```

The custom `Card` class has several properties, including an `AccountNumber` property, a `CardName` property, a `CustomerName` property, and an `ExpirationDate` property.

MainPage.xaml displays the cards returned from the WCF service using a `ListBox`, as shown:

```
<ListBox ItemsSource="{Binding Cards}">
    <ListBox.ItemTemplate>
        <DataTemplate>
            <StackPanel
                    v:Commanding.Command="{Binding Content.ViewCardCommand,
                    Source={StaticResource bridge}}"
                    v:Commanding.CommandParameter="{Binding}"
                    Margin="12,10,0,10">
                <TextBlock Text="{Binding CardName}" />
                <TextBlock Text="{Binding AccountNumber}" />
            </StackPanel>
        </DataTemplate>
    </ListBox.ItemTemplate>
</ListBox>
```

The custom commanding infrastructure handles the `Tap` event of the `StackPanel`, which causes the command's `Execute` method to be called. The `DataTemplate` uses the `bridge` resource to resolve the viewmodel of the page, which is outside the scope of the `DataTemplate`. The bridge resource is a `ContentControl`, defined in the page resources as shown:

```
<phone:PhoneApplicationPage.Resources>
    <ContentControl x:Name="bridge"
                    Content="{Binding Path=DataContext, ElementName=page}" />
</phone:PhoneApplicationPage.Resources>
```

The `MainPageViewModel` class contains a `ViewCardCommand` property, so that when the user taps a card, the app navigates to the CardView.xaml page by using the viewmodel's custom `NavigationService`, as shown:

```
void ViewCard(Card card)
{
    Navigate("/CardView/CardView.xaml?CardId=" + card.Id);
}
```

The `CardView` page receives the ID of the card via a querystring parameter, which it then provides to the viewmodel's `Load` method (see Listing 25.4). The viewmodel parses the ID back to a Guid and, for the sake of simplicity, the `Card` is retrieved from the entire list of `Card` objects retrieved from the server.

The viewmodel's `Title` property is set to the `CardName` property of the `Card`.

LISTING 25.4   CardViewModel.Load Method

```
public async void Load(IDictionary<string, string> queryDictionary)
{
    string cardIdValue;
    if (!queryDictionary.TryGetValue("CardId", out cardIdValue))
    {
        Debug.WriteLine("Dictionary does not contain CardId key.");
        return;
    }

    Guid cardId;
    if (!Guid.TryParse(cardIdValue, out cardId))
    {
        throw new Exception("CardId cannot be passed.");
    }

    var bankService = (IBankService)new BankServiceClient();

    try
    {
        IEnumerable<Card> cards = await Task<IEnumerable<Card>>.Factory.FromAsync(
            bankService.BeginGetCards, bankService.EndGetCards, null);

        Card = cards.SingleOrDefault(c => c.Id == cardId);
```

```
        if (card != null)
        {
            Title = card.CardName;
        }
    }
    catch (Exception ex)
    {
        Debug.WriteLine("Unable to retrieve cards." + ex);
        MessageService.ShowError("Unable to retrieve cards.");
    }

    Refresh();
}
```

The `CardViewModel` class contains a `ToggleInWallet DelegateCommand` that adds a `PaymentInstrument` representing the `Card` to the Wallet. If an item already exists for the card, the command removes the item from the Wallet.

Detecting the presence of a card in the Wallet is done using the `Wallet` class's static `FindItem` method, as demonstrated in the following excerpt:

```
public bool InWallet
{
    get
    {
        return card != null && Wallet.FindItem(card.Id.ToString()) != null;
    }
}
```

The `CardViewModel`'s `AddToWallet` method constructs a `PaymentInstrument` using the card information (see Listing 25.5).

You can add custom properties to Wallet item objects. This allows you to add domain-specific information that is stored alongside a card.

In the sample, the culture name of the card is stored as a custom property, which allows the app to display currency values using the correct currency symbol and format. If the card is a `CreditCard` instance, its `DisplayCreditLimit` and `DisplayAvailableCredit` string properties are set using a `CultureInfo` object to produce the appropriate currency format.

The `PaymentInstrument` class's `Message` and `MessageNavigationUri` allow you to display some text alongside the payment instrument's logo in the Wallet. When the user taps the message in the Wallet, the Wallet navigates the user to a location in your app.

You must specify the `DisplayName` property of the Wallet item, along with logo images for each of its three logo properties. Your app may retrieve the image from the server or, as in the case of the sample, retrieve it locally from a *Content* resource in the app's main assembly.

The `NavigationUri` property of the payment instrument is used to launch your app when the user taps the Open App link in the instrument's About page in the Wallet.

LISTING 25.5   `CardViewModel.AddToWallet` Method

```
void AddToWallet()
{
    var instrument = new PaymentInstrument(card.Id.ToString())
        {
            AccountNumber = card.AccountNumber,
            CustomerName = card.CustomerName,
            ExpirationDate = card.ExpirationDate,
            DisplayName = card.CardName
        };

    /* The culture name is set as a custom wallet property. */
    var cultureCodeProperty = new CustomWalletProperty { Value = card.CultureName };
    instrument.CustomProperties.Add("CultureName", cultureCodeProperty);

    var cultureInfo = new CultureInfo(card.CultureName);

    var creditCard = card as CreditCard;
    DebitCard debitCard;

    if (creditCard != null)
    {
        instrument.PaymentInstrumentKinds = PaymentInstrumentKinds.Credit;

        instrument.DisplayCreditLimit
            = creditCard.CreditLimit.ToString("C", cultureInfo);
        instrument.DisplayAvailableCredit
            = creditCard.AvailableCredit.ToString("C", cultureInfo);

        /* Specify a message and a deep link URL that opens
         * the bill pay view from the Wallet. */
        instrument.Message = "Pay your credit card bill.";
        instrument.MessageNavigationUri = new Uri(
            "/BillPayView/BillPayView.xaml?CardId=" + card.Id, UriKind.Relative);
    }
    else if ((debitCard = card as DebitCard) != null)
    {
        instrument.PaymentInstrumentKinds = PaymentInstrumentKinds.Debit;

        instrument.DisplayBalance = debitCard.Balance.ToString("C", cultureInfo);
    }
    else
    {
```

```
      throw new Exception("Unknown card type: " + card.GetType());
    }


    /* Specify a logo that is displayed in the wallet. */
    var bitmapImage = new BitmapImage();
    var logoUri = new Uri("Assets/UnleashedBankIcon.png", UriKind.Relative);
    bitmapImage.SetSource(Application.GetResourceStream(logoUri).Stream);

    instrument.Logo99x99 = bitmapImage;
    instrument.Logo159x159 = bitmapImage;
    instrument.Logo336x336 = bitmapImage;

    /* Add a deep link so that when the app is launched from the Wallet item,
     * the card view page is shown instead of the main page. */
    instrument.NavigationUri = new Uri(
        "/CardView/CardView.xaml?CardId=" + card.Id, UriKind.Relative);

    addWalletItemTask.Item = instrument;
    addWalletItemTask.Show();
}
```

When the viewmodel calls the AddWalletItemTask object's Show method, the user is presented with a built-in confirmation dialog (see Figure 25.4).

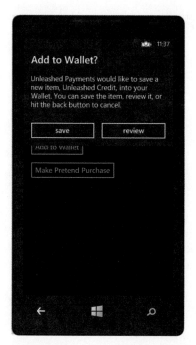

FIGURE 25.4   Adding an item to the Wallet presents a built-in confirmation dialog.

You remove an item from the Wallet using the `Wallet` class's static `Remove` method, as shown:

```
Wallet.Remove(card.Id.ToString());
```

Within the Wallet Hub, tapping a Wallet item displays the item's details (see Figure 25.5). If the item's `TransactionHistory IDictionary` has been populated, a pivot item listing all the transactions is included alongside the about pivot item.

The value of the payment instrument's `Message` property is displayed to the right of the logo. Tapping on the message navigates to the URI specified by the instrument's `MessageNavigationUri` property. This capability to link back to your app allows you to notify the user of important information each time the user visits the Wallet Hub. In the next section you look at updating the message using a background agent.

FIGURE 25.5   Viewing the Wallet item's details in the Wallet Hub.

The server-side `BankService` includes a `MakeCreditPurchase` method that deducts an amount from a specified credit card by reducing its `AvailableCredit` property (see Listing 25.6). The service method returns a `Success` result if the credit card is located and its available credit reduced.

LISTING 25.6   `BankService.MakeCreditPurchase` Method

```
public async Task<MakePurchaseResult> MakeCreditPurchase(
    CreditCard creditCard, decimal amount)
```

```
{
    CreditCard existingCard = (CreditCard)cards.Single(
                                card => card.Id == creditCard.Id);

    if (existingCard == null)
    {
        return MakePurchaseResult.NoSuchCard;
    }

    decimal newAvailableCredit = existingCard.AvailableCredit - amount;
    if (newAvailableCredit < 0)
    {
        return MakePurchaseResult.AmountExceedsAvailableFunds;
    }

    AccountTransaction transaction = new AccountTransaction(
                                "Purchase", "+" + amount, DateTime.Now);
    List<AccountTransaction> transactionList = GetTransactionList(creditCard.Id);
    transactionList.Add(transaction);

    existingCard.AvailableCredit = existingCard.AvailableCredit - amount;

    return MakePurchaseResult.Success;
}
```

The `BankingService` class also includes a `MakeDebitPurchase` method that behaves the same way as the `MakeCreditPurchase` method, but instead of reducing the available credit, it reduces the `DebitCard` object's `Balance`.

The `BankService` class maintains transaction history for each card by storing custom `AccountTransaction` objects in a `Dictionary`. When a caller requests the list of transactions for a particular card, and it is the first request, the service creates a new `List<AccountTransaction>` object as shown:

```
readonly Dictionary<Guid, List<AccountTransaction>> accountTransactions
                    = new Dictionary<Guid, List<AccountTransaction>>();

List<AccountTransaction> GetTransactionList(Guid cardId)
{
    List<AccountTransaction> result;

    if (!accountTransactions.TryGetValue(cardId, out result))
    {
        result = new List<AccountTransaction>();
        accountTransactions.Add(cardId, result);
    }
```

```
        return result;
}
```

The `CardViewModel` class calls either the WCF service's `MakeCreditPurchase` or `MakeDebitPurchase` method, depending on the card type, when a `MakePurchaseCommand` is executed (see Listing 25.7).

We create a `CultureInfo` object using the `CultureName` property of the card. A string representing the monetary amount of the purchase is constructed using the `CultureInfo` object, which ensures that the correct currency format and symbol are materialized.

LISTING 25.7   `CardViewModel.MakePurchaseCore` Method

```csharp
async Task MakePurchaseCore()
{
    var bankService = (IBankService)new BankServiceClient();
    MakePurchaseResult purchaseResult;

    CreditCard creditCard = card as CreditCard;
    if (creditCard != null)
    {
        purchaseResult = await Task<MakePurchaseResult>.Factory.FromAsync(
                            bankService.BeginMakeCreditPurchase,
                            bankService.EndMakeCreditPurchase,
                            creditCard, purchaseAmount, null);
    }
    else
    {
        purchaseResult = await Task<MakePurchaseResult>.Factory.FromAsync(
                            bankService.BeginMakeDebitPurchase,
                            bankService.EndMakeDebitPurchase,
                            (DebitCard)card, purchaseAmount, null);
    }

    string amountString = purchaseAmount.ToString(
                        "C", new CultureInfo(card.CultureName));

    if (purchaseResult == MakePurchaseResult.Success)
    {
        MessageService.ShowMessage("Purchase made for " + amountString);
    }
    else if (purchaseResult == MakePurchaseResult.AmountExceedsAvailableFunds)
    {
        MessageService.ShowMessage("Purchase amount exceeds available funds.");
    }
```

```
    else
    {
        MessageService.ShowError("Unable to perform purchase.");
    }
}
```

Relying on your foreground app to update a payment instrument can lead to out-of-date information in the Wallet. Fortunately, the Windows Phone SDK has tight integration with a specific type of background agent: the `WalletAgent`, which allows you to receive notification when the OS senses that a Wallet item may require updating or when a user taps the *Refresh* application bar menu item in the Wallet.

In the next section, you look at using a custom `WalletAgent` implementation to update a Wallet item's information from a cloud service.

Keeping Payment Instruments Up-To-Date with a Background Agent

Background agents allow your app to perform a task both while your app is running or not running. For more information on background agents, see Chapter 32, "Conducting Background Activities with Scheduled Actions."

Perform the following steps to create a Background Agent for your Wallet-enabled app:

1. Create a new Windows Phone Class Library project. Right-click the solution node in the Visual Studio Solution Explorer and select Add/New Project. Select the project type from the Windows Phone node in the Add New Project dialog.

2. Create a new class and add the following using statement to the top of the file:

```
using Microsoft.Phone.Wallet;
```

3. Make your class a subclass of `WalletAgent`.

4. Override the `WalletAgent` class's `OnRefreshData` method.

5. Add a reference to the class library from your main app project.

6. Modify the WMAppManifest.xml file of your main app project to include a `BackgroundServiceAgent` element that specifies your Wallet agent.

To modify the WMAppManifest.xml file in step 6, open the file in a text editor by right-clicking the WMAppManifest.xml file in the Visual Studio Solution Explorer and selecting View Code.

Listing 25.8 demonstrates how to nominate a `WalletAgent` in the WMAppManifest.xml file. The *Specifier* attribute indicates the type of background agent and must be equal to *WalletAgent*. The *Source* attribute is the name of the assembly where the agent resides. The *Type* attribute is the fully qualified type name of the agent.

LISTING 25.8   `WPUnleashed.PaymentInstrumentApp` **WMAppManifest.xml (excerpt)**

```xml
<Tasks>
  ...
  <ExtendedTask Name="BackgroundTask">
    <BackgroundServiceAgent Specifier="WalletAgent"
                            Name="WPUnleashed.WalletAgent"
                            Source="DanielVaughan.WPUnleashed.WalletAgent"
                            Type="DanielVaughan.WPUnleashed.UnleashedWalletAgent" />
  </ExtendedTask>
</Tasks>
```

The `WalletAgent` class's `OnRefreshData` method provides you with the opportunity to update Wallet items, including payment instruments, in the Wallet (see Listing 25.9). The `RefreshDataEventArgs` specifies the `WalletItem` objects that may require updating.

The `WalletAgent` for the Payment Instrument sample app iterates over the payment instruments and retrieves the transaction history for each instrument using the WCF service.

The method then retrieves the corresponding card from the server and updates either the `Balance` or `DisplayAvailableCredit` property, depending on the type of card. The agent uses the card's `CultureName` property to format the currency value.

LISTING 25.9   `UnleashedWalletAgent.OnRefreshData` **Method**

```csharp
protected override async void OnRefreshData(RefreshDataEventArgs args)
{
    /* Iterate through each wallet item that may require updating. */
    foreach (PaymentInstrument paymentInstrument
                in args.Items.OfType<PaymentInstrument>())
    {
        try
        {
            var bankService = (IBankService)new BankServiceClient();
            Guid cardId;

            if (!Guid.TryParse(paymentInstrument.Id, out cardId))
            {
                continue;
            }

            IEnumerable<AccountTransaction> transactions
                = await Task<IEnumerable<AccountTransaction>>.Factory.FromAsync(
                    bankService.BeginGetCardTransactions,
                    bankService.EndGetCardTransactions, cardId, null);
```

```csharp
if (transactions == null)
{
    continue;
}

paymentInstrument.TransactionHistory.Clear();
int count = 0;

foreach (AccountTransaction accountTransaction in transactions)
{
    WalletTransaction walletTransaction = new WalletTransaction
        {
            Description = accountTransaction.Description,
            DisplayAmount = accountTransaction.DisplayAmount,
            TransactionDate = accountTransaction.TransactionDate
        };

    string transactionKey = cardId.ToString() + DateTime.Now + count++;
paymentInstrument.TransactionHistory.Add(transactionKey, walletTransaction);
}

IEnumerable<Card> retrievedCards
                = await Task<IEnumerable<Card>>.Factory.FromAsync(
    bankService.BeginGetCards, bankService.EndGetCards, null);

Card cardFromServer = retrievedCards.SingleOrDefault(
    retrievedCard => retrievedCard.Id == cardId);

if (cardFromServer != null)
{
    CultureInfo cultureInfo = new
    ➥CultureInfo(cardFromServer.CultureName);

    if (paymentInstrument.PaymentInstrumentKinds
                            == PaymentInstrumentKinds.Credit)
    {
        var creditCard = (CreditCard)cardFromServer;
        paymentInstrument.DisplayAvailableCredit
            = creditCard.AvailableCredit.ToString("C", cultureInfo);
    }
    else if (paymentInstrument.PaymentInstrumentKinds
                            == PaymentInstrumentKinds.Debit)
    {
        var debitCard = (DebitCard)cardFromServer;
        paymentInstrument.DisplayBalance
                = debitCard.Balance.ToString("C", cultureInfo);
```

25

```
                }
            }

            await paymentInstrument.SaveAsync();
        }
        catch (Exception ex)
        {
            Debug.WriteLine("Unable to retrieve transaction history for card. + "
                          ➡ex);
        }
    }

    NotifyComplete();
}
```

For apps that provide banking-related capabilities, use payment instruments. For less payment-oriented scenarios, where you are handling things such as club memberships and loyalty cards, use the more general `WalletTransactionItem`. This is the topic of the next section.

Storing Membership Information in the Wallet

In the previous section you looked at storing payment instruments in the Wallet. The Wallet also allows you to save more general information that is not necessarily of a financial nature. Membership information for stores, clubs, libraries, and so forth can also be stored in the Wallet using the `WalletTransactionItem` class.

In the sample for this section you see how to add membership information for a fictitious *Unleashed Card*. An `IDealsAndMembershipService` in the `WalletWcfService` allows the user to log in and retrieve a custom `Member` object that contains the user's membership information. Later in the chapter you also see how the sample app uses the same service to retrieve coupons or deals that the user can save to the Wallet.

The source code for the app presented in this section is located in the Wallet\ DealsAndMembership directory of the downloadable sample code.

The custom `Member` class has the following string properties:

▶ Id

▶ Customer

▶ MembershipNumber

▶ PhoneNumber

▶ EmailAddress

For the sake of simplicity, the `DealsAndMembershipService` always returns the same member object when its `SignInWithToken` method is called. The method follows the awaitable asynchronous pattern, as shown in the following excerpt:

```
public async Task<Member> SignInWithToken(string signedInToken)
{
    Member member = new Member
        {
            CustomerName = "Anders Hejlsberg",
            EmailAddress = "anders@example.com",
            MembershipNumber = "123456789",
            PhoneNumber = "555 3342 1212",
            Id = "31415926"
        };

    return member;
}
```

> **NOTE**
>
> Normally you would use a database to store membership information in a production application. The `signedInToken` parameter used in the example is intended to represent a value that was sent to the client app after a previous successful login. It is not, however, used in the sample.

The `MembershipViewModel` class retrieves the user's membership information from the WCF service and allows the user to add the information to the Wallet. The viewmodel's `Load` method retrieves the `Member` object from the server, as shown in the following excerpt:

```
public async void Load()
{
    var service = (IDealsAndMembershipService)
                    new DealsAndMembershipServiceClient();

    try
    {
        Member = await Task<Member>.Factory.FromAsync(
            service.BeginSignInWithToken, service.EndSignInWithToken,
              string.Empty, null);

        OnPropertyChanged(() => InWallet);
    }
    catch (Exception ex)
    {
        Debug.WriteLine("Unable to sign in." + ex);
```

25

```
        MessageService.ShowError("Unable to sign in.");
    }
}
```

As in the previous payment instruments sample, the viewmodel's `AddToWallet` method saves the membership information to the Wallet using an `AddWalletItemTask` (see Listing 25.10).

The viewmodel uses a content resource to construct a `BitmapImage` for the Wallet item. The image is assigned to each of the `WalletTransactionItem` object's logo properties. A custom Wallet property stores the email address of the user.

> **TIP**
>
> To prevent automatic image scaling and provide the best logo image clarity possible, specify a different image for each of the three logo sizes.

LISTING 25.10   `MembershipViewModel.AddToWallet` Method

```
void AddToWallet()
{
    try
    {
        BitmapImage bitmapImage = new BitmapImage();
        Uri logoUri = new Uri("Assets/UnleashedCard.png", UriKind.Relative);
        bitmapImage.SetSource(Application.GetResourceStream(logoUri).Stream);

        WalletTransactionItem membershipItem = new WalletTransactionItem(itemName)
            {
                IssuerName = "Unleashed",
                DisplayName = "Unleashed Membership Card",
                CustomerName = member.CustomerName,
                AccountNumber = member.MembershipNumber,
                BillingPhone = member.PhoneNumber,
                IssuerWebsite = new Uri("http://example.com/"),
                DisplayAvailableBalance = "1000 points",
                /* An image must be defined for each logo size. */
                Logo99x99 = bitmapImage,
                Logo159x159 = bitmapImage,
                Logo336x336 = bitmapImage
            };

        membershipItem.IssuerPhone.Business = "123456789";
        membershipItem.CustomProperties.Add(
            "email", new CustomWalletProperty(member.EmailAddress));
```

```
            addWalletItemTask.Item = membershipItem;
            addWalletItemTask.Show();
        }
        catch (Exception ex)
        {
            Debug.WriteLine(ex);
            MessageService.ShowError(
                "An error occurred when saving your membership to the wallet.");
        }
    }
}
```

NOTE

The `WalletTransactionItem` ID, provided via the class constructor, must be unique for your app, or an `ArgumentOutOfRange` Exception is raised.

The main page of the sample DealsAndMembership app uses a `Pivot`. The first pivot item displays the user's membership information, and the second displays coupons available to the user.

The two viewmodels are defined as page resources in MainPage.xaml, like so:

```
<phone:PhoneApplicationPage.Resources>
    <WPUnleashed:MembershipViewModel x:Name="membershipViewModel" />
    <WPUnleashed:CouponsViewModel x:Name="couponsViewModel" />
</phone:PhoneApplicationPage.Resources>
```

Each `PivotItem` object's `DataContext` property is bound to its associated viewmodel resource. The first pivot item is bound to the `membershipViewModel` as shown:

```
<phone:PivotItem x:Name="memberPivotItem" Header="Member"
                    DataContext="{StaticResource membershipViewModel}">
    <StackPanel>
        <TextBlock Text="member name"
                        Style="{StaticResource LabelStyle}" />
        <TextBlock Text="{Binding Member.CustomerName}"
                        Style="{StaticResource ValueStyle}" />
        <TextBlock Text="phone number"
                        Style="{StaticResource LabelStyle}" />
        <TextBlock Text="{Binding Member.PhoneNumber}"
                        Style="{StaticResource ValueStyle}" />
        <TextBlock Text="email address"
                        Style="{StaticResource LabelStyle}" />
        <TextBlock Text="{Binding Member.EmailAddress}"
                        Style="{StaticResource ValueStyle}" />
```

25

```xml
        <Button Content="{Binding ToggleButtonText}"
                Command="{Binding ToggleInWalletCommand}" />
    </StackPanel>
</phone:PivotItem>
```

Tapping on the Add to Wallet button places the card in the Wallet. The card information is then viewable by tapping the item in the Wallet.

Using the `AddWalletItemTask`, you are able to add payment instruments and membership cards to the Wallet. In the next section you look at using the `Deal` class to add coupons to the Wallet Hub's Deals area.

Storing Deals in the Wallet

Deals are redeemable offers that the user can save to the Wallet and later present to a vendor for redemption.

To add a deal to the Wallet, create a new `Deal` object and call its `SaveAsync` method, as demonstrated:

```csharp
Deal deal = new Deal(coupon.Id)
    {
        DisplayName = "10% off!",
        Description = "Get 10% any item purchased.",
        IssuerName = "Unleashed",
        IssuerWebsite = new Uri("http://example.com"),
        IsUsed = false,
        MerchantName = "Unleashed",
        TermsAndConditions = "Valid at participating locations only.",
        Code = "123454321",
        ExpirationDate = DateTime.Now.AddMonths(3)
    };


await deal.SaveAsync();
```

> **NOTE**
>
> The `DisplayName` property must be set to a non-empty string before calling `SaveAsync`, or an exception is raised.

The sample app for this section retrieves a list of available coupons from a WCF service and displays them on a page. The user may select one of the coupons to view it in greater detail and to save it to the Wallet's Deals area.

The source code for this section is located in the Wallet\DealsAndMembership directory of the downloadable sample code.

The sample uses a custom class named `Coupon`. The `CouponsViewModel` retrieves the list of available coupons from the `DealsAndMembership` WCF service using the service's `GetCoupons` method.

For the sake of simplicity, the service declares a list of dummy coupons, like so:

```
readonly List<Coupon> coupons = new List<Coupon>
    {
        new Coupon
            {
                Id = "1",
                Title = "$25 Off!",
                Description = "$25 off your next purchase!",
                ExpirationDate = new DateTime(2013, 8, 1),
                Terms = "Valid at participating locations only.",
                Code = "3425167",
                Base64Image = GetBase64ImageCoupon()
            },          new Coupon { ... },
        new Coupon { ... },
        new Coupon { ... },
    };
```

The service retrieves a sample barcode image for each coupon from within the assembly. The service then converts the image to a base-64 encoded string (see Listing 25.11).

Base-64 encoding is a way of taking binary data and turning it into text so that it is easier to transmit. Sending the image encoded in Base-64 prevents the data from being misinterpreted during transmission because raw binary data may contain special control characters.

LISTING 25.11   `DealsAndMembershipService.GetBase64CouponImage` Method

```
static string GetBase64CouponImage()
{
    Assembly assembly = Assembly.GetExecutingAssembly();

    using (Stream stream = assembly.GetManifestResourceStream(
        "DanielVaughan.WPUnleashed.DealsAndMembershipService.Barcode.bmp"))
    {
        BinaryReader br = new BinaryReader(stream);
        byte[] bytes = br.ReadBytes((int)stream.Length);
        string result = Convert.ToBase64String(bytes);
        return result;
    }
}
```

The `CouponsViewModel` retrieves the list of available coupons from the service. The `CouponsViewModel.Load` method populates an `ObservableList` with the `Coupon` objects returned from the `DealsAndMembershipService`, as shown in the following excerpt:

```
public async void Load()
{
    var service = (IDealsAndMembershipService) new DealsAndMembershipServiceClient();

    try
    {
        Coupons = await Task<ObservableCollection<Coupon>>.Factory.FromAsync(
            service.BeginGetCoupons, service.EndGetCoupons, null);
    }
    catch (Exception ex)
    {
        Debug.WriteLine("Unable to retrieve coupons." + ex);
    }
}
```

The `CouponsViewModel` contains a `DelegateCommand<Coupon>` named `ViewCouponCommand` that uses the base class's `INavigationService` to navigate to the CouponView.xaml page, as shown:

```
void ViewCoupon(Coupon coupon)
{
    ArgumentValidator.AssertNotNull(coupon, "coupon");

    Navigate("/CouponView/CouponView.xaml?CouponId=" + coupon.Id);
}
```

The Deals pivot item on the MainPage.xaml displays each coupon within a `ListBox`. Tapping an item in the `ListBox` executes the viewmodel's `ViewCouponCommand` via the custom commanding infrastructure, as shown:

```
<phone:PivotItem Header="Deals"
                 DataContext="{StaticResource couponsViewModel}">
    <ListBox ItemsSource="{Binding Coupons}">
        <ListBox.ItemTemplate>
            <DataTemplate>
                <StackPanel Margin="12,20,0,0"
                    c:Commanding.Command="{Binding ViewCouponCommand,
                        Source={StaticResource couponsViewModel}}"
                    c:Commanding.CommandParameter="{Binding}">
                    <TextBlock Text="{Binding Title}"
                            Style="{StaticResource PhoneTextLargeStyle}" />
                    <TextBlock Text="{Binding Description}"
```

```
                    Style="{StaticResource PhoneTextSmallStyle}"
                    Foreground="{StaticResource PhoneSubtleBrush}" />
            </StackPanel>
          </DataTemplate>
        </ListBox.ItemTemplate>
      </ListBox>
    </phone:PivotItem>
```

The CouponView.xaml `OnNavigatedTo` method passes the query string dictionary containing the coupon ID to the `CouponViewModel`. The viewmodel's `Load` method retrieves the ID from the query string dictionary and uses it to retrieve the `Coupon` object from the WCF service. See the following excerpt:

```
public async void Load(IDictionary<string, string> parameters)
{
    string couponId;

    if (!parameters.TryGetValue("CouponId", out couponId))
    {
        return;
    }

    var service = (IDealsAndMembershipService)
                new DealsAndMembershipServiceClient();

    try
    {
        Coupon = await Task<Coupon>.Factory.FromAsync(
            service.BeginGetCoupon, service.EndGetCoupon, couponId, null);
    }
    catch (Exception ex)
    {
        Debug.WriteLine("Unable to retrieve coupon." + ex);
        MessageService.ShowError("Unable to retrieve coupon.");
    }

    Refresh();
}
```

The viewmodel converts the coupon's Base-64 image string to a `BitmapImage` and assigns it to the `Deal` object's `BarcodeImage` property. The `CouponViewModel.AddToWallet` method uses the `Base64ToImageConverter` to perform the conversion (see Listing 25.12). You look at this conversion process in more detail in a moment.

The `AddToWallet` method copies the coupon properties over to a new `Deal` object and saves it to the Wallet using the `Deal` class's `SaveAsync` method.

LISTING 25.12   `CouponViewModel.AddToWallet` **Method**

```
async Task AddToWallet()
{
    bool successful = true;

    try
    {
        BitmapImage barcodeImage
            = Base64ToImageConverter.ConvertToBitmapImage(
                    coupon.Base64Image);

        Deal deal = new Deal(coupon.Id)
            {
                BarcodeImage = barcodeImage,
                DisplayName = coupon.Title,
                Description = coupon.Description,
                IssuerName = "Unleashed",
                IssuerWebsite = new Uri("http://example.com"),
                IsUsed = false,
                MerchantName = "Unleashed",
                TermsAndConditions = coupon.Terms,
                Code = coupon.Code,
                ExpirationDate = coupon.ExpirationDate
            };

        await deal.SaveAsync();
    }
    catch (Exception ex)
    {
        successful = false;
        Debug.WriteLine(ex.ToString());
        MessageService.ShowError("Unable to add deal to wallet.");
    }

    if (successful)
    {
        MessageService.ShowMessage("Deal added to wallet.");
    }
}
```

The coupon's `Base64Image` is converted to a `BitmapImage` using the custom
`Base64ToImageConverter` class (see Listing 25.13). The static `ConvertToBitmapImage`
method accepts a string and converts it to a byte array, which is then used to create a
`Stream` to initialize a new `BitmapImage` object.

The `Base64ToImageConverter` is an `IValueConverter`, which the view also uses to display the coupon's barcode image.

LISTING 25.13   `Base64ToImageConverter` Class

```
public class Base64ToImageConverter : IValueConverter
{
    public object Convert(object value, Type targetType,
        object parameter, System.Globalization.CultureInfo culture)
    {
        if (value == null)
        {
            return null;
        }

        string base64String = value.ToString();
        return ConvertToBitmapImage(base64String);
    }

    public object ConvertBack(object value, Type targetType,
        object parameter, System.Globalization.CultureInfo culture)
    {
        throw new NotImplementedException();
    }

    public static BitmapImage ConvertToBitmapImage(string base64EncodedImage)
    {
        byte[] imageBytes = System.Convert.FromBase64String(base64EncodedImage);
        using (MemoryStream stream
                    = new MemoryStream(imageBytes, 0, imageBytes.Length))
        {
            BitmapImage bitmapImage = new BitmapImage();
            bitmapImage.SetSource(stream);
            return bitmapImage;
        }
    }
}
```

Figure 25.6 shows a deal displayed in the Wallet. The Wallet retains the barcode image and displays it whenever the user navigates to the deal.

FIGURE 25.6   Viewing a Deal in the Wallet Hub.

You remove a `Deal` from the Wallet in the same way as for other Wallet items: by calling the Wallet class's static `Remove` method with the string ID of the Wallet item, as shown:

```
Wallet.Remove(coupon.Id);
```

Keeping Deals and Membership Information Up-to-Date with a Background Agent

Use a background agent to keep membership information and deals associated with your app up-to-date. You can create a Wallet agent for membership and deals in the same manner as shown earlier in this chapter.

The sample app includes a declaration of the deals background agent in the WMAppManifest.xml file, shown in the following excerpt:

```
<Tasks>
  ...
  <ExtendedTask Name="BackgroundTask">
    <BackgroundServiceAgent
      Specifier="WalletAgent"
      Name="DealsAndMembershipAgent"
      Source="DanielVaughan.WPUnleashed.MembershipAgent"
      Type="DanielVaughan.WPUnleashed.DealsAndMembershipAgent" />
```

```
    </ExtendedTask>
</Tasks>
```

The sample's `DealsAndMembershipAgent` updates the Unleashed Membership card
(see Listing 25.14). It also retrieves a random coupon to display in the Wallet. The
`WalletTransactionItem` object's `MessageNavigationUri` property provides a deep link back
to the `CouponView` from the Wallet (see Listing 25.14.).

LISTING 25.14   `DealsAndMembershipAgent.OnRefreshData` Method

```
protected override async void OnRefreshData(RefreshDataEventArgs args)
{
    var service = (IDealsAndMembershipService) new DealsAndMembershipServiceClient();

    foreach (WalletTransactionItem card in args.Items.OfType<
                                            ➥WalletTransactionItem>())
    {
        try
        {
            int balanceRemaining = await Task<int>.Factory.FromAsync(
                service.BeginGetAvailableBalance,
                service.EndGetAvailableBalance, null);

            card.DisplayAvailableBalance = balanceRemaining + " points";

            Coupon coupon = await Task<Coupon>.Factory.FromAsync(
                service.BeginGetRandomCoupon,
                service.EndGetRandomCoupon, null);
            card.Message = "You might be interested in " + coupon.Description;
            card.MessageNavigationUri
                    = new Uri("/CouponView/CouponView.xaml?CouponId="
                                    + coupon.Id, UriKind.Relative);

            await card.SaveAsync();
        }
        catch (Exception ex)
        {
            Debug.Assert(false, "An error occurred during updating of a card. " +
                                ➥ex);
            continue;
        }
    }

    NotifyComplete();
}
```

The Open App link, on the deal's About page, navigates back to the sample app's CouponView page (see Figure 25.7). The available balance and the random deal is updated whenever the user taps the Refresh menu item in the application bar.

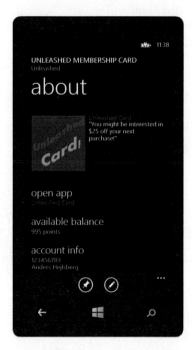

FIGURE 25.7   The Wallet's item detail page.

More and more businesses are using coupons to attract trade. Now Windows Phone has established coupons and deals as a core experience on the phone. Integrating Wallet capabilities for loyalty cards and deals offers you as a developer a great way to enrich your app.

Summary

This chapter began with an overview of the Wallet Hub—its features and UI elements. You then looked at storing payment instruments in the Wallet and at keeping them up-to-date using a background agent. You saw how to leverage a WCF service using the new asynchronous await features of the .NET framework, and learned a workaround for a missing feature of the WCF service client code generation for Windows Phone.

The chapter then looked at storing membership cards, such as loyalty cards, in the Wallet Hub.

Finally, the chapter looked at placing deals in the Wallet. You saw how to retrieve a list of deals from a WCF service and then saw how to allow the user to save a deal to the Wallet. You saw how to dynamically present a relevant deal directly to the user using a background agent.

CHAPTER 26

Validating User Input

Input validation is the process of validating input to an application before it is used. Most line-of-business applications rely on input validation to ensure that user input is correctly formatted, meaningful, safe to use, and that it properly conveys the intent of the user.

Input validation in a Windows Phone app may be purely client-side, or it can involve sending input to a web service for validation, which normally entails asynchronous processing.

Windows Phone XAML projects come equipped with support for input validation. There are, however, some crucial validation-related control styles missing from the SDK, which need to be put in place before visual indicators are displayed for validation errors.

This chapter begins by looking at the two types of input validation: syntactic and semantic, and then at the XAML data-binding system as it relates to input validation, its features, and its limitations.

The chapter then provides a walk-through for adding custom control styles for enabling visualization of data validation errors and shows how to create a custom error-validation summary control.

Finally, the chapter explores an alternative approach to validation, one that leverages a more recent set of APIs that allows for asynchronous and composite validation.

Defining Input Validation

Alexander Jung does a great job on his blog (http://ajdotnet.wordpress.com/2010/02/28/understanding-validation-in-silverlight/) of defining input validation.

He states that input validation involves ensuring that user input passes two types of validation: syntactic and semantic.

Syntactic Validation

Syntactic validation ensures that data entered by a user can be converted to the type required by the application. For example, when a user enters a date string into a `TextBox`, the input fails syntactic validation if it cannot be converted to a date.

In most cases, the XAML data-binding system attends to syntactic validation, coercing values to and from source property types.

> **NOTE**
>
> The XAML data-binding system performs syntactic validation before assigning a value to a property.

Semantic Validation

Unlike syntactic validation, semantic validation can occur after a value has been assigned. Semantic validation deals with more complex validation and usually encompasses the evaluation of business rules.

The following examples require semantic validation:

▶ Required fields.

▶ String length restrictions; for example, the length of a string input must not exceed 140 characters.

▶ Numeric range restrictions; for example, value must be greater than 0 but less than 100.

▶ Date range restrictions; for example, a date must occur in the future.

▶ Mutually dependent fields; for example, value A is required if value B has been provided.

▶ Distinguishing between absent and invalid fields. The application must be able to distinguish between when a user has chosen not to enter a field and when a field has been provided by the user, but it is an empty string, for example.

Input Validation Using Property Setters

The first validation system discussed in this chapter is the property setter validation system. This system has been with the phone since the first 7.0 release of the Windows Phone SDK and is part of Silverlight 3.

The XAML data-binding system provides validation support when assigning a value to the source of a data-binding expression. For example, when a `FrameworkElement` (the binding target) has a binding to a property in a viewmodel (the binding source) and the value in the `FrameworkElement` changes, validation occurs as the value is being assigned to the property in the viewmodel.

To enable property setter validation for an input control, set the binding's `NotifyOnValidationError` and `ValidatesOnExceptions` to true, as shown in the following example:

```
<TextBox Text="{Binding PropertyName, Mode=TwoWay,
         NotifyOnValidationError=True, ValidatesOnExceptions=True}" />
```

`ValidatesOnExceptions` enables property validation for the binding, and `NotifyOnValidationError` causes an event to be raised when a validation error occurs.

The XAML data-binding system performs the following three actions during assignment of a source object property:

▶ Conversion of the target `DependencyProperty` value using an `IValueConverter`. This occurs if the target's binding has its `ValueConverter` set.

▶ Type conversion of the result of step 1 to the source property type.

▶ Assignment of the result of step 2 to the source property, and detection and handling of exceptions raised in the source's property set accessor.

The validation and assignment of a source property is explored in greater detail in Figure 26.1, which is based on Alexander Jung's diagram at http://ajdotnet.wordpress.com/2010/02/28/understanding-validation-in-silverlight/.

The following list refers to numbered items in Figure 26.1 and describes each step performed by the data-binding system:

1. The change event is raised for the target's `DependencyProperty`. This event is subscribed to by the target's `BindingExpression` for the `DependencyProperty`. When the `FrameworkElement`'s property is changed, the `BindingExpression`'s `TargetPropertyChanged` method is called. The `BindingExpression` then calls its own `UpdateValue` method.

2. If there is a `ValueConverter` defined for the binding, its `ConvertBack` method is called. If an exception is raised in the `ConvertBack` method, it is not handled and must be handled by the `Application.UnhandledException` event handler, or the app exits.

3. An internal `IValueConverter`, called `DynamicValueConverter`, uses a `TypeConverter` to convert the target value to the source type. The `DynamicValueConverter` comes into play when, for example, a `TextBox.Text` string value needs to be converted to an `int` value. During conversion, noncritical `Exceptions` are treated as validation errors. Critical `Exceptions` are described in a later section.

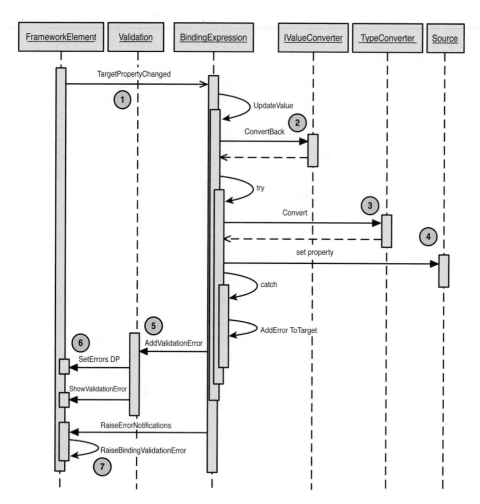

FIGURE 26.1 A change in a target property causes validation and assignment of its source property.

4. The property setter is called using the result from the `TypeConverter`. Again, if a noncritical exception is raised, it is treated as a validation error. Be mindful that if the property setter raises the `PropertyChanged` event, and an event handler throws an `Exception`, it results in a validation error.

5. The `BindingExpression` class uses the static `Validation` class to assign validation errors for the `FrameworkElement`.

6. The `Validation` class records validation information about a `FrameworkElement` using the `DependencyProperty`'s `Validation.ErrorsProperty` and `Validation.HasErrorProperty`. After the error has been set, the `FrameworkElement` is prompted to display the error. This is normally done by transitioning the `VisualState` of the control to an invalid state. We look at displaying validation errors, using `VisualState` and the `VisualStateManager`, later in this chapter.

7. If the binding has been set to notify of validation errors, discussed further in the following section, the `BindingValidationError` event is raised.

NOTE

`IValueConverters` are unable to participate in input validation because if an `IValueConverter` throws an exception, it is rethrown by the `BindingExpression`.

Validation Class

The static `Validation` class is used to determine whether a control has validation errors and to retrieve the errors if they exist. The `Validation` class has the methods `GetHasError` and `GetErrors` and provides two dependency properties for storing the validation information: `ErrorsProperty` and `HasErrorsProperty`.

Critical Exceptions

Most exceptions that occur during the assignment of a value to a source property are handled by the `BindingExpression` class. Several exception types, however, are deemed critical exceptions and are rethrown by the `BindingExpression`. The following is the list of critical exceptions:

▶ `OutOfMemoryException`

▶ `StackOverflowException`

▶ `AccessViolationException`

▶ `ThreadAbortException`

Binding Errors

Binding errors occur when a noncritical exception is raised after the `ConvertBack` method of the `ValueConverter` is called. The following is a list of the three types of binding errors that can occur when modifying the value of a target property:

▶ The user enters a value that fails to be converted to the source binding type (syntactic validation).

▶ An exception is raised within the property set accessor.

▶ The property does not have a set accessor and is, therefore, read-only.

NOTE

When a binding error occurs, the target, a `TextBox`, for example, retains the entered value, but the source property is not updated.

By default, the XAML data-binding infrastructure fails silently when a binding error occurs. The `NotifyOnValidationError` and the `ValidatesOnExceptions` binding properties allow you to provide the user with feedback when a value is incorrectly set.

`NotifyOnValidationError` Binding Property

With the `Binding.NotifyOnValidationError` property set to true, the data binding system raises a `BindingValidationError` event when a binding error occurs. The following example demonstrates enabling validation on a `TextBox` element:

```
<TextBox Text="{Binding ValidatedString2, Mode=TwoWay,
        NotifyOnValidationError=True, ValidatesOnExceptions=True}"
        Style="{StaticResource ValidatingTextBoxStyle}" />
```

The `BindingValidationError` is a `RoutedEvent`, allowing it to be handled by an ancestor element in the visual tree. `RoutedEvents` bubble upward through the visual tree until they are either handled, indicated by the `Handled` property of the event arguments, or they reach the root element of the visual tree. Subscription to the `BindingValidationError` event at the page level, therefore, provides the opportunity to handle validation errors for all elements in the page. We leverage this later in the chapter to create a validation summary control.

`ValidatesOnExceptions` Property

The `Binding` class's `NotifyOnValidationError` property works in unison with its `ValidatesOnExceptions` property. If the `ValidatesOnExceptions` property is not explicitly set to true and a binding error results from a noncritical exception being raised from a property accessor, the error is silently ignored. Furthermore, the `VisualState` of the `FrameworkElement` is not changed, and the `BindingValidationError` event is not raised.

Defining Validation Visual States in Windows Phone

When a binding error occurs, the data-binding system transitions the `VisualState` of the `FrameworkElement` to an invalid state. In Silverlight for the browser, various controls come ready to display validation errors. Unfortunately, those styles have not been incorporated into Windows Phone because the styles are not immediately transferable to the phone due to the reduced size of the phone display. Consequently, if you want to harness the existing validation infrastructure, you must replace the template for each control for which you intend to display validation errors.

Replacing a control's template can be done using Expression Blend. A copy can be made of the template, and error related `VisualStates` can then be modified.

> **NOTE**
>
> Microsoft Expression Blend is installed as part of the Windows Phone SDK. You can find more information about Expression Blend at http://www.microsoft.com/expression/.

To make a copy of a control's template, right-click a control within Expression Blend, select Edit Template, and then select Edit a Copy (see Figure 26.2).

FIGURE 26.2   Editing a copy of a control's template from within Expression Blend.

To allow the template to be reused across the entire app from any page, define the style at the application level (see Figure 26.3). This causes a style containing the template to be placed in the project's app.xaml file.

FIGURE 26.3   Defining the location of a new style in Expression Blend.

After the style has been created, a new Style element is placed in the App.xaml file. See the following excerpt:

```
<Style x:Key="ValidatingTextBoxStyle" TargetType="TextBox">
    . . .
</Style>
```

The States tab in Expression Blend allows you to define different ways of displaying the control, depending on its visual state. The control is placed into a named state by the `VisualStateManager`. To customize the way the control is displayed when a validation error occurs, select the InvalidUnfocused state (see Figure 26.4).

To modify the `TextBox` border so that it is displayed in a different manner when in the InvalidUnfocused state, select the yellow button next to the `BorderBrush` item in the Properties tab and choose Convert to Local Value.

FIGURE 26.4   Converting the `BorderBrush` to a local value.

Converting the `BorderBrush` to a local value allows the brush to be customized for the particular VisualState, and for its color to be set to one that better represents the state of the control when a validation error occurs.

Just as the `TextBox` style was made globally available by placing it in the app's resources, converting the new color to a resource enables its use in other styles (see Figure 26.5).

FIGURE 26.5   Creating a new color resource for the `BorderBrush` color.

When the color resource has been created, the template in the style resource contains a definition for the `InvalidUnfocused` state, with a reference to the `InvalidElementColor` resource, as shown in the following excerpt:

```
<VisualState x:Name="InvalidUnfocused">
    <Storyboard>
        <ColorAnimation Duration="0"
            To="{StaticResource InvalidElementColor}"
            Storyboard.TargetProperty
                ="(Border.BorderBrush).(SolidColorBrush.Color)"
            Storyboard.TargetName="EnabledBorder"
            d:IsOptimized="True"/>
    </Storyboard>
</VisualState>
```

Subsequently, whenever you want to display validation errors for a `TextBox`, the `Style` property of the `TextBox` is set to `ValidatingTextBoxStyle`, like so:

```
<TextBox Text="{Binding ValidatedString1, Mode=TwoWay,
        NotifyOnValidationError=True}"
        Style="{StaticResource ValidatingTextBoxStyle}" />
```

If a binding error occurs, the VisualState of the `TextBox` automatically transitions to the InvalidUnfocused state.

The following is an excerpt from the `ConventionalValidationViewModel` class in the downloadable sample code, which contains validation logic for the `ValidatedString1` property:

```
public string ValidatedString1
{
    get
    {
        return validatedString1;
    }
    set
    {
        if (string.IsNullOrEmpty(value))
        {
            throw new ArgumentException("Validated String 1 is required.");
        }
        validatedString1 = value;
    }
}
```

When a user removes all the text from the `TextBox` that is bound to this property, the property set accessor raises an `ArgumentException`. The exception is handled by the databinding system, and the `TextBox` is placed into the InvalidUnfocused state, which now provides visual indication that the value is invalid (see Figure 26.6).

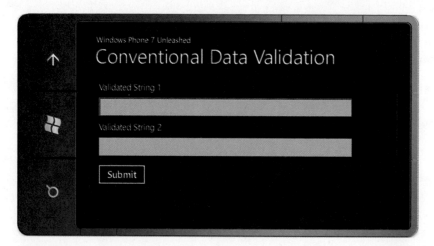

FIGURE 26.6   `ConventionalValidationView` page. A `TextBox` with a validation error is displayed with the custom `BorderBrush`.

This approach can be used to validate a variety of semantic rules. For example, data can be made to conform to a valid range. If the data falls outside a specified range, an exception can be thrown.

Custom validation logic can be applied to other control types as well. In some cases, however, it is necessary to provide a style for the InvalidFocused state as well as the InvalidUnfocused state. The InvalidUnfocused state is used in this example because, by default, the `TextBox.Text` property is set only when the `TextBox` loses focus.

Validating a `TextBox` as the User Types

The `BindingExpression` class's `UpdateSource` method forces the target property value to be assigned to its source property. This allows you to perform input validation while the user is entering text into a `TextBox`, rather than after the `TextBox` loses focus.

I have created a class called `UpdateSourceTriggerExtender`, which contains an attached property that is used to trigger an update of the binding source whenever the `TextBox`'s text changes.

When the attached property is placed on a `TextBox`, the `UpdateSourceTriggerExtender` class's `HandleUpdatePropertyChanged` method is called, which subscribes to the `TextBox.TextChanged` event (see Listing 26.1). When the text is changed the `BindingExpression` for the `TextProperty` is retrieved, and its `UpdateSource` method is called, which effectively pushes the `Text` string value to the source property.

The attached property can also be placed on a `PasswordBox`, in which case its `PasswordChanged` event is used to monitor for user input.

> **NOTE**
>
> The `TextBox.LostFocus` event is used to explicitly set the visual state of the `TextBox`. This is required because the XAML data-binding system does not place the `TextBox` into the correct visual state when it loses focus if the `Text` property has not changed, which is the case when you call `UpdateSource` on the `TextChanged` event.

LISTING 26.1   `UpdateSourceTriggerExtender` Class

```
public class UpdateSourceTriggerExtender
{
    public static readonly DependencyProperty UpdateSourceOnTextChanged
        = DependencyProperty.RegisterAttached(
            "UpdateSourceOnTextChanged", typeof(bool),
            typeof(UpdateSourceTriggerExtender),
            new PropertyMetadata(HandleUpdatePropertyChanged));

    public static bool GetUpdateSourceOnTextChanged(DependencyObject d)
    {
        return (bool)d.GetValue(UpdateSourceOnTextChanged);
```

```
    }

    public static void SetUpdateSourceOnTextChanged(
        DependencyObject d, bool value)
    {
        d.SetValue(UpdateSourceOnTextChanged, value);
    }
    static void HandleUpdatePropertyChanged(
        DependencyObject d, DependencyPropertyChangedEventArgs e)
    {
        TextBox textBox = d as TextBox;
        if (textBox != null)
        {
            if ((bool)e.OldValue)
            {
                textBox.TextChanged -= HandleTextBoxTextChanged;
                textBox.LostFocus -= HandleBoxLostFocus;
            }

            if ((bool)e.NewValue)
            {
                textBox.TextChanged += HandleTextBoxTextChanged;
                textBox.LostFocus += HandleBoxLostFocus;
            }
            return;
        }
        PasswordBox passwordBox = d as PasswordBox;
        if (passwordBox == null)
        {
            throw new Exception("UpdateSourceTrigger can only be used "
                                + "on a TextBox or PasswordBox.");
        }

        /* Wire up for password box. */
        if ((bool)e.OldValue)
        {
            passwordBox.PasswordChanged -= HandlePasswordBoxTextChanged;
            passwordBox.LostFocus -= HandleBoxLostFocus;
        }

        if ((bool)e.NewValue)
        {
            passwordBox.PasswordChanged += HandlePasswordBoxTextChanged;
            passwordBox.LostFocus += HandleBoxLostFocus;
        }
    }
```

```csharp
static void HandlePasswordBoxTextChanged(object sender, RoutedEventArgs e)
{
    UpdateSource((PasswordBox)sender, PasswordBox.PasswordProperty);
}

static void HandleTextBoxTextChanged(object sender, TextChangedEventArgs e)
{
    UpdateSource((TextBox)sender, TextBox.TextProperty);
}

static void UpdateSource(
    FrameworkElement element, DependencyProperty property)
{
    if (element == null)
    {
        return;
    }

    BindingExpression bindingExpression
            = element.GetBindingExpression(property);
    if (bindingExpression != null)
    {
        bindingExpression.UpdateSource();
    }
}
static void HandleBoxLostFocus(object sender, RoutedEventArgs e)
{
    /* This method prevents the control from being placed
     * into the valid state when it loses focus. */
    var control = sender as Control;
    if (control == null)
    {
        return;
    }
    bool hasError = Validation.GetHasError(control);
    if (hasError)
    {
        VisualStateManager.GoToState(control, "InvalidFocused", false);
    }
}
}
```

The following example demonstrates how the UpdateSourceTriggerExtender can be applied to a TextBox:

```
<TextBox Text="{Binding ValidatedString1, Mode=TwoWay,
                    UpdateSourceTrigger=Explicit,
                    NotifyOnValidationError=True,
                    ValidatesOnExceptions=True}"
          Style="{StaticResource ValidatingTextBoxStyle}"
          u:UpdateSourceTriggerExtender.UpdateSourceOnTextChanged="True" />
```

The `UpdateSourceTrigger` binding property determines when the source property is updated. It can be set to either Default or Explicit. Default causes the source property to be updated when the `TextBox` loses focus, and Explicit prevents the source from being updated until the binding's `UpdateSource` method is explicitly called.

As soon as the text changes, the source property named `ValidatedString1` is updated, which causes the input to be validated.

Performing Group Validation

Validating a series of input fields usually entails validating each field as the user leaves the field, and then checking for completeness and validity of all fields when the Submit button is tapped (see Figure 26.7).

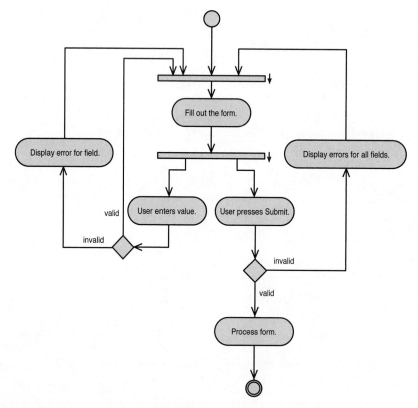

FIGURE 26.7   Form validation activity diagram.

The UpdateSource method of the BindingExpression class can be used to validate all controls on a form. As you saw in the preceding section, the UpdateSource method causes the target value to be reassigned to its source property. In other words, the value in the control is pushed to its data context, allowing the discovery of any input validation errors.

The following excerpt from ConventionalValidationView.xaml.cs in the downloadable sample code demonstrates how to validate all TextBox fields on a form:

```
void Button_Click(object sender, System.Windows.RoutedEventArgs e)
{
    IEnumerable<TextBox> children = ContentPanel.GetDescendents<TextBox>();
    foreach (TextBox textBox in children)
    {
        BindingExpression bindingExpression
            = textBox.GetBindingExpression(TextBox.TextProperty);
        if (bindingExpression != null)
        {
            bindingExpression.UpdateSource();
        }
    }
}
```

The custom GetDescendents extension method recursively retrieves all children, children's children, and so on, of a particular type for the specified FrameworkElement. The method is located in the VisualTree class in the downloadable sample code and is shown in the following excerpt:

```
public static IEnumerable<TChild> GetDescendents<TChild>(
    this FrameworkElement parent) where TChild : class
{
    ArgumentValidator.AssertNotNull(parent, "parent");

    int childCount = VisualTreeHelper.GetChildrenCount(parent);
    for (int i = 0; i < childCount; i++)
    {
        DependencyObject child = VisualTreeHelper.GetChild(parent, i);
        TChild candidate = child as TChild;
        if (candidate != null)
        {
            yield return candidate;
        }
        FrameworkElement element = child as FrameworkElement;
        if (element != null)
        {
            /* Could be improved with tail recursion. */
            IEnumerable<TChild> descendents
                    = element.GetDescendents<TChild>();
```

26

```
        foreach (TChild descendent in descendents)
        {
            yield return descendent;
        }
    }
  }
}
```

When the Submit button of the ConventionalValidationView page is tapped, all TextBoxes are retrieved and the UpdateSource method is called for each control's Text property binding. If any input validation errors are present, they are displayed in the UI (see Figure 26.8).

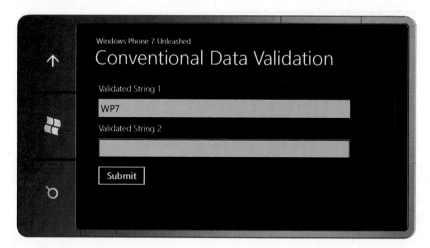

·FIGURE 26.8 ConventionalValidationView page. Tapping the Submit button causes all fields to be validated.

Displaying Error Details

Highlighting an invalid field indicates that the field needs attention, but it does not tell the user why. Feedback should be provided describing the nature of the error and how it can be corrected. In Silverlight for the browser, this is achieved using the ValidationSummary control. Unfortunately, no such control exists in the Windows Phone FCL. But that does not stop us from making our own!

A Custom ValidationSummary Control
Included in the downloadable sample code is a simple control for displaying all errors that occur on a page. It is named the same as its browser counterpart: ValidationSummary. When placed on a page, it retrieves the page and subscribes the page's BindingValidationError event during its Loaded event. When an unhandled validation

error occurs for any control on the page, the error is placed in an ObservableCollection and displayed in the view (see Listing 26.2).

LISTING 26.2   ValidationSummary Class (excerpt)

```
public partial class ValidationSummary : UserControl
{
    readonly ObservableCollection<object> errors
                    = new ObservableCollection<object>();

    readonly Dictionary<string, List<object>> errorLookup
                            = new Dictionary<string, List<object>>();
    const int lineHeight = 30;

    public IEnumerable<object> Errors
    {
        get
        {
            return errors;
        }
    }

    public ValidationSummary()
    {
        InitializeComponent();
        Loaded += HandleLoaded;
    }

    bool loaded;

    void HandleLoaded(object sender, System.Windows.RoutedEventArgs e)
    {
        if (loaded)
        {
            return;
        }
        loaded = true;

        Page page = this.GetVisualAncestors<Page>().FirstOrDefault();

        if (page == null)
        {
            throw new InvalidOperationException(
                        "Unable to locate parent page.");
        }
        page.BindingValidationError += HandleBindingValidationError;
```

```
    . . .
    }
    /// <summary>
    /// Performs property setter validation.
    /// </summary>
    void HandleBindingValidationError(
            object sender, ValidationErrorEventArgs e)
    {
        string content = e.Error.ErrorContent.ToString();

        if (e.Action == ValidationErrorEventAction.Added)
        {
            AddError(content);
        }
        else
        {
            RemoveError(content);
        }
    }

    void AddError(object error)
    {
        string content = error.ToString();

        if (!errors.Contains(content))
        {
            errors.Add(content);
        }
        MinHeight += lineHeight;
    }

    void RemoveError(object error)
    {
        string content = error.ToString();

        errors.Remove(content);
        MinHeight -= lineHeight;
    }
    . . .
}
```

The ValidationSummary control's XAML file contains a ListBox, whose ItemsSource has a data-binding to the Errors property (see Listing 26.3).

LISTING 26.3   `ValidationSummary` Control XAML

```xml
<UserControl x:Class="DanielVaughan.WPUnleashed.ValidationSummary"
            x:Name="control"
...
>
    <StackPanel x:Name="LayoutRoot"
            Background="{StaticResource PhoneBackgroundBrush}">
        <ListBox ItemsSource
                ="{Binding ElementName=control, Path=Errors}">
            <ListBox.ItemTemplate>
                <DataTemplate>
                    <TextBlock Text="{Binding}"
                        Style="{StaticResource PhoneTextSmallStyle}"
                        Height="30" />
                </DataTemplate>
            </ListBox.ItemTemplate>
        </ListBox>
    </StackPanel>
</UserControl>
```

As soon as the `BindingValidationError` event is raised in the host page, the `ObservableCollection` of errors is updated, and the user is provided with detailed feedback for each validation error (see Figure 26.9).

FIGURE 26.9   The `ValidationSummary` control displays validation errors as they occur.

Property Setter Validation Limitations

Although the Silverlight 3 property setter validation system is simple and easy to use, it has two significant limitations: mutually dependent property validation is cumbersome, and there is no support for asynchronous validation.

The Silverlight 3 property setter validation system allows you to validate one property at a time. Some properties, however, may be mutually dependent, with the value of one property altering the validity of another property.

One approach to solving this problem, while still using the property setter validation system, is to use a set of shadow properties that perform composite semantic validation. This approach, however, falls short because it adds undue complexity and often leads to substantial code duplication.

The asynchronous validation features of Silverlight 4, which have been incorporated into the Windows Phone SDK, decouple input validation from properties and provide a better solution where composite validation is required.

Furthermore, asynchronous validation is needed in situations such as validating input on a remote server, where asynchronous WCF service calls are performed.

Asynchronous and Composite Validation

Present since the Windows Phone 7.1 SDK is the INotifyDataErrorInfo interface, which is also present in Silverlight 4. This new API eliminates the need to rely on exceptions to indicate invalid property values. In addition, implementing INotifyDataErrorInfo makes it possible to evaluate the validity of a property on a secondary thread.

The INotifyDataErrorInfo interface contains three is used to determine whether the control contains validation errors. The GetErrors method returns all errors that are detected, and the ErrorsChanged event notifies listeners when an error has been added or removed from the set of known errors.

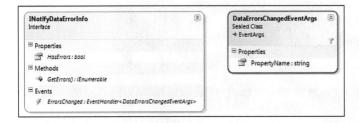

FIGURE 26.10   INotifyDataErrorInfo interface is used to monitor input validation errors.

To enable validation using the INotifyDataErrorInfo interface, the binding expression's NotifyOnValidationError property is set to true, as shown:

```
<TextBox Text="{Binding ValidatedString1, Mode=TwoWay,
                NotifyOnValidationError=True}" />
```

The next section looks at implementing INotifyDataErrorInfo so that it can be reused across your entire app.

A Reusable Implementation of the `NotifyDataErrorInfo` Interface

The `DataErrorNotifier` class in the downloadable sample code is a reusable implementation of the `INotifyDataErrorInfo` interface.

`DataErrorNotifier` makes implementing asynchronous validation easy. With the addition of a single validation method to your viewmodel, `DataErrorNotifier` manages the list of errors and takes care of raising data error events. Furthermore, validation can be restricted by registering only those properties that you want to be validated.

`DataErrorNotifier` is designed to validate classes that implement a custom `IValidateData` interface, such as the `ViewModelBase` class. The validation logic has been decoupled from the `ViewModelBase` class to be reusable for other types as well.

The `DataErrorNotifier` requires an instance of `IValidateData`. The `IValidateData` interface defines an asynchronous validation mechanism with a nonblocking `BeginValidate` method and an event to signal when validation is complete (see Figure 26.11).

26

FIGURE 26.11   `DataErrorNotifier` provides validation for the `ViewModelBase` class.

The `ViewModelBase` class implements `IValidateData`. `ViewModelBase` creates an instance of the `DataErrorNotifier` class and passes itself to the `DataErrorNotifier`'s constructor, as shown:

```
protected ViewModelBase()
{
    dataErrorNotifier = new DataErrorNotifier(this, this);
...
}
```

`DataErrorNotifier` subscribes to the viewmodel's `PropertyChanged` event. When the `PropertyChanged` event is raised, validation is performed automatically.

NOTE

If you want validation to be performed prior to the setting of the property's backing field, modify the `DataErrorNotifier` so that it subscribes to the `PropertyChanging` event of the viewmodel rather than its `PropertyChanged` event.

The `DataErrorNotifier` takes responsibility for the `INotifyDataErrorInfo` implementation. Ordinarily, a viewmodel calls only the `ViewModelBase`'s `AddValidationProperty` and `IsComplete` methods. Both the `ViewModelBase` class and the `DataErrorNotifier` implement `INotifyDataErrorInfo`. The `ViewModelBase` class, however, merely calls through to its `DataErrorNotifier` instance.

Leveraging the `DataErrorNotifier` Class

To register a property for validation in a viewmodel, the `AddValidationProperty` is called in the constructor of the viewmodel, as demonstrated in the following excerpt:

```
AddValidationProperty(() => ARequiredStringProperty);
```

`AddValidationProperty` causes the `DataErrorNotifier` to automatically attempt to validate the property when the property changes, or when the viewmodel is being validated in its entirety.

The lambda expression provides the `ViewModelBase` class with the means to resolve both the property and the name of the property. The `ViewModelBase.AddValidationProperty` method retrieves the name of the property and passes it and a `Func` to the `DataErrorNotifier`, as shown:

```
protected void AddValidationProperty(Expression<Func<object>> expression)
{
    PropertyInfo propertyInfo = PropertyUtility.GetPropertyInfo(expression);
    string name = propertyInfo.Name;
    Func<object> getter = (Func<object>)Delegate.CreateDelegate(
                              typeof(Func<object>),
                              this,
                              propertyInfo.GetGetMethod());

    dataErrorNotifier.AddValidationProperty(name, getter);
}
```

`DataErrorNotifier` stores the association between the property name and the `Func`, which allows the property to be retrieved by name during validation.

The `AddValidationProperty` method of the `DataErrorNotifier` is shown in the following excerpt:

```
public void AddValidationProperty(string name, Func<object> property)
{
```

```
    lock (propertyDictionaryLock)
    {
        propertyDictionary[name] = property;
    }
}
```

Provisioning for Asynchronous or Synchronous Validation

The validation infrastructure contained in the `ViewModelBase` and the `DataErrorNotifier` classes caters for both asynchronous and synchronous validation models. When using this system, validation code should reside in one of two overridable methods: `BeginValidation` or `GetPropertyErrors`.

`BeginValidation` uses an asynchronous event driven validation model, and `GetPropertyErrors` provides for a simpler synchronous model for when asynchronous processing is not required.

`DataValidationError` Class

When using either the synchronous or asynchronous validation models, validation errors are represented using a custom class named `DataValidationError`. `DataValidationError` has an `ErrorMessage` property of type string, and an `Id` property of type int. The purpose of the `Id` property is that it allows you to use the same error message for multiple fields.

Provisioning for Synchronous Validation

The `ViewModelBase.GetPropertyErrors` method allows your viewmodel to perform input validation using a simple synchronous approach. The `GetPropertyErrors` method is overridden to validate specific properties in your viewmodel. The method returns all errors for the specified property as an `IEnumerable<DataValidationError>`.

In the following example, the `GetPropertyErrors` method has been overridden in a viewmodel containing two properties, neither of which is allowed to be null or to consist of entirely whitespace:

```
protected override IEnumerable<DataValidationError> GetPropertyErrors(
    string propertyName, object value)
{
    if (!string.IsNullOrWhiteSpace((string)value))
    {
        yield break;
    }

    switch (propertyName)
    {
        case "ValidatedString1":
            yield return new DataValidationError(1,
                "ValidatedString1 is required.");
            break;
```

```
        case "ValidatedString2":
            yield return new DataValidationError(2,
                "ValidatedString2 is required.");
            break;
    }
    yield break;
}
```

If an exception is raised during the execution of this method, it is handled by the ViewModelBase class. Exception handling is discussed further in the next section.

Provisioning for Asynchronous Validation

The BeginValidation method of the ViewModelBase class is the main extensibility point for providing asynchronous validation. This method should be overridden in subclasses to perform composite validation or validation of property values using, for example, WCF services.

The ViewModelBase class implementation of the BeginValidation method calls the virtual GetPropertyErrors method, which as you saw in the preceding section, retrieves the list of errors for a specified property. See the following excerpt:

```
public virtual void BeginValidation(string memberName, object value)
{
    IEnumerable<DataValidationError> errors;
    try
    {
        errors = GetPropertyErrors(memberName, value);
    }
    catch (Exception ex)
    {
        OnValidationComplete(
            new ValidationCompleteEventArgs(memberName, ex));
        return;
    }
    OnValidationComplete(
            new ValidationCompleteEventArgs(memberName, errors));
}
```

The base implementation of the BeginValidation method executes synchronously, retrieving the list of errors and raising the ValidationComplete event.

> **NOTE**
>
> When the BeginValidation method has finished validating, it is imperative that the ValidationComplete event is raised; otherwise, the DataErrorNotifier will not raise

the `INotifyDataErrorInfo.ErrorsChanged` event, which prevents the UI from signaling that a validation error exists.

The following excerpt provides an example implementation of the `BeginValidation` method:

```
public override void BeginValidation(string memberName, object value)
{
    try
    {
        if (string.IsNullOrEmpty((string)value))
        {
            List<DataValidationError> errors
                = new List<DataValidationError>();
            DataValidationError error = null;
            switch (memberName)
            {
                case "ValidatedString1":
                    error = new DataValidationError(1,
                        "ValidatedString1 is required.");
                    break;
                case "ValidatedString2":
                    error = new DataValidationError(2,
                        "ValidatedString2 is required.");
                    break;
            }

            if (error != null)
            {
                errors.Add(error);
            }
            OnValidationComplete(
                new ValidationCompleteEventArgs(memberName, errors));
        }
        else
        {
            OnValidationComplete(
                new ValidationCompleteEventArgs(memberName));
        }
    }
    catch (Exception ex)
    {
        OnValidationComplete(
            new ValidationCompleteEventArgs(memberName, ex));
    }
}
```

26

The `ViewModelBase` class contains a string keyed `Dictionary` of errors for each property, which is of type `Dictionary<string, List<DataValidationError>>`.

Decoupling Validation

The `DataErrorNotifier` instance relies on an `IValidateData` object to perform the actual semantic validation of viewmodel property values. Thus, the strategy for validating the viewmodel can be decoupled from the viewmodel itself. In most cases, however, the viewmodel implements `IValidateData`.

Validating Properties as They Change

The `DataErrorNotifier` class subscribes to the viewmodel's `PropertyChanged` event so that when a property is changed, it is also validated. See the following excerpt:

```
public DataErrorNotifier(
    INotifyPropertyChanged owner, IValidateData validator)
{
    this.validator
            = ArgumentValidator.AssertNotNull(validator, "validator");
    ArgumentValidator.AssertNotNull(owner, "owner");

    validator.ValidationComplete += validator_ValidationComplete;
    owner.PropertyChanged += HandleOwnerPropertyChanged;
}


void HandleOwnerPropertyChanged(object sender, PropertyChangedEventArgs e)
{
    if (e == null || e.PropertyName == null)
    {
        return;
    }
    BeginGetPropertyErrorsFromValidator(e.PropertyName);
}
```

When a viewmodel property changes, a potentially asynchronous validation operation is commenced from the `BeginGetPropertyErrorsFromValidator` method, shown in the following excerpt:

```
void BeginGetPropertyErrorsFromValidator(string propertyName)
{
    Func<object> propertyFunc;
    lock (propertyDictionaryLock)
    {
        if (!propertyDictionary.TryGetValue(propertyName, out propertyFunc))
        {
            /* No property registered with that name. */
            return;
        }
    }
```

```
    }
    validator.BeginValidation(propertyName, propertyFunc());
}
```

The `BeginGetPropertyErrorsFromValidator` method performs the following tasks:

▶ The property `Func` is retrieved from the property `Dictionary`.

▶ The property value is retrieved by invoking the property `Func`.

▶ The `BeginValidation` method of the viewmodel (implementing `IValidateData`) is
called using the property name and the property value.

When the `IValidateData` finishes validating a property value, it raises the
`IValidateData.ValidationComplete` event. This event is handled by the
`HandleValidationComplete` method.

The first thing that the `HandleValidationComplete` method does is update the list of
validation errors for the specified property. It does this by calling the `SetPropertyErrors`
method, which attempts to retrieve the list of errors for that property. If the specified list
of errors is different from the existing list of known errors for that property, the list of
known errors is updated (or removed if empty) and the `ErrorsChanged` event is raised:

```
public void SetPropertyErrors(
    string propertyName, IEnumerable<DataValidationError> dataErrors)
{
    ArgumentValidator.AssertNotNullOrEmpty(propertyName, "propertyName");

    List<DataValidationError> list;
    bool raiseEvent = false;
    lock (errorsLock)
    {
        bool created = false;

        int paramErrorCount = dataErrors == null ? 0 : dataErrors.Count();
        if ((errorsField == null || errorsField.Count < 1)
            && paramErrorCount < 1)
        {
            return;
        }

        if (errorsField == null)
        {
            errorsField
                = new Dictionary<string, List<DataValidationError>>();
            created = true;
        }
        bool listFound = false;
```

26

```
    if (created ||
        !(listFound = errorsField.TryGetValue(propertyName, out list)))
    {
        list = new List<DataValidationError>();
    }

    if (paramErrorCount < 1)
    {
        if (listFound)
        {
            errorsField.Remove(propertyName);
            raiseEvent = true;
        }
    }
    else
    {
        var tempList = new List<DataValidationError>();
        foreach (var dataError in dataErrors)
        {
            if (created || list.SingleOrDefault(
                e => e.Id == dataError.Id) == null)
            {
                tempList.Add(dataError);
                raiseEvent = true;
            }
        }
        list.AddRange(tempList);
        errorsField[propertyName] = list;
    }
}

if (raiseEvent)
{
    OnErrorsChanged(propertyName);
}
}
```

The OnErrorsChanged method raises the ErrorsChanged event on the UI thread using the app's Dispatcher. An extension method is used to ensure that the method is invoked only if the thread is not the UI thread; otherwise, the delegate is called from the current thread.

```
protected virtual void OnErrorsChanged(string property)
{
    Dispatcher dispatcher = Deployment.Current.Dispatcher;
    dispatcher.InvokeIfRequired(
        delegate
        {
```

```
        ErrorsChanged.Raise(this,
            new DataErrorsChangedEventArgs(property));
    });
}
```

Asynchronous Validation of All Properties

As the user completes a form, individual properties are validated. To validate an entire form at once, the same approach is used; however, each property is validated, one by one, until all are validated, or until one is deemed invalid.

The IsComplete method of the DataErrorValidator attempts to validate each known property and accepts handlers that are invoked when one of the following three conditions is met:

▶ completeAction—The viewmodel is complete; that is, no properties have associated data-validation errors.

▶ incompleteAction—The viewmodel is incomplete; that is, one or more properties have an associated data-validation error.

▶ unknownAction—Determination of the viewmodel's completeness failed because an exception was raised.

To validate each property, the DataErrorValidator creates a list of all known property names, and as each property is validated, the property name is removed from the list, as shown in the following excerpt:

```
public void IsComplete(Action completeAction,
                       Action incompleteAction,
                       Action<Exception> unknownAction)
{
    this.completeAction = completeAction;
    this.incompleteAction = incompleteAction;
    this.unknownAction = unknownAction;

    try
    {
        if (!LockedOperations.TrySetTrue(
            ref isEvaluating, isEvaluatingLock))
        {
            return;
        }

        if (propertyDictionary == null)
        {
            if (completeAction != null)
            {
```

```
                    completeAction();
                }
                return;
            }


            lock (waitingForPropertiesLock)
            {
                waitingForProperties.Clear();
                foreach (KeyValuePair<string, Func<object>> pair
                                          in propertyDictionary)
                {
                    waitingForProperties.Add(pair.Key);
                }
            }
            foreach (KeyValuePair<string, Func<object>> pair
                in propertyDictionary)
            {
                validator.BeginValidation(pair.Key, pair.Value());
            }
        }
        catch (Exception ex)
        {
            isEvaluating = false;
            if (unknownAction != null)
            {
                unknownAction(ex);
            }
        }
    }
}
```

The `LockedOperations.TrySetTrue` method provides for thread safety when reading and setting the `isEvaluating` flag. If `isEvaluating` is already true, the call to the `IsComplete` method is ignored, as shown:

```
public static bool TrySetTrue(ref bool value, object valueLock)
{
    ArgumentValidator.AssertNotNull(valueLock, "valueLock");
    if (!value)
    {
        lock (valueLock)
        {
            if (!value)
            {
                value = true;
                return true;
            }
        }
```

```
            }
        }
        return false;
}
```

The `TrySetTrue` method reduces the amount of locking related code in the `IsComplete` method.

When the list of property names in the `IsComplete` method is empty, or an exception is raised, the evaluation of the `IsComplete` method is deemed to be complete.

At completion, one of the three `IsComplete` action arguments is invoked. If the `ValidationCompleteEventArgs` contains an `Exception`, the `unknownAction` is invoked. If there are any data validation errors for the property, the `incompleteAction` is invoked. If there are no properties left to validate, the `completeAction` is invoked. See the following excerpt:

```
void HandleValidationComplete(object sender, ValidationCompleteEventArgs e)
{
    try
    {
        if (e.Exception == null)
        {
            SetPropertyErrors(e.PropertyName, e.Errors);
        }
    }
    catch (Exception ex)
    {
        Debug.WriteLine("Unable to set property error." + ex);
    }

    if (!isEvaluating)
    {
        return;
    }

    lock (isEvaluatingLock)
    {
        if (!isEvaluating)
        {
            return;
        }

        try
        {
            bool finishedEvaluating;
            lock (waitingForPropertiesLock)
```

```
        {
            waitingForProperties.Remove(e.PropertyName);
            finishedEvaluating = waitingForProperties.Count < 1;
        }

        if (e.Exception != null)
        {
            isEvaluating = false;
            if (unknownAction != null)
            {
                unknownAction(e.Exception);
            }
        }
        if (e.Errors != null && e.Errors.Count() > 0)
        {
            isEvaluating = false;
            if (incompleteAction != null)
            {
                incompleteAction();
            }
        }

        if (finishedEvaluating)
        {
            bool success = isEvaluating;
            isEvaluating = false;
            if (success && completeAction != null)
            {
                completeAction();
            }
        }
    }
    catch (Exception ex)
    {
        Debug.WriteLine("Unable to validate property." + ex);
        isEvaluating = false;
    }
    }
}
```

An Example of Asynchronous Input Validation

The downloadable sample code contains a number of examples of asynchronous input validation. The simplest is located in the AsyncValidationViewModel class.

The `AsyncValidationView` contains two string properties that are required to be non-null or whitespace strings (see Figure 26.12).

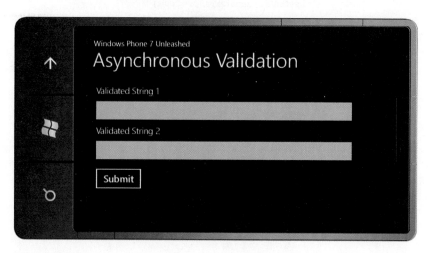

FIGURE 26.12   `AsyncValidationView` page.

When either of the two properties is set to an empty or whitespace string, a data validation error is created for that property. This validation occurs when the user modifies the text or when the Submit button is tapped (see Figure 26.13).

FIGURE 26.13   The Validated String 1 form field is deemed invalid.

The two `TextBox` controls are each bound to a property in the viewmodel, as shown in the following excerpt:

```
<StackPanel x:Name="ContentPanel" Grid.Row="1" Margin="12,60,12,0">
    <TextBlock Text="Validated String 1"
```

```
                Style="{StaticResource PhoneTextTitle3Style}" />
    <TextBox Text="{Binding ValidatedString1, Mode=TwoWay,
                            NotifyOnValidationError=True}"
                Style="{StaticResource ValidatingTextBoxStyle}" />
    <TextBlock Text="Validated String 2"
                Style="{StaticResource PhoneTextTitle3Style}" />
    <TextBox Text="{Binding ValidatedString2, Mode=TwoWay,
                            NotifyOnValidationError=True}"
                Style="{StaticResource ValidatingTextBoxStyle}" />
    <StackPanel Orientation="Horizontal">
        <Button Content="Submit"
            Command="{Binding SubmitCommand}"
            Width="144" Height="75" HorizontalAlignment="Left" />
        <controls:ValidationSummary />
    </StackPanel>
    <TextBlock Text="{Binding Message}"
                Style="{StaticResource PhoneTextNormalStyle}" />
</StackPanel>
```

The submit Button is bound to the viewmodel's SubmitCommand. The SubmitCommand is instantiated in the constructor of the AsyncValidationViewModel class, as shown in the following excerpt:

```
public AsyncValidationViewModel()
{
    AddValidationProperty(() => ValidatedString1);
    AddValidationProperty(() => ValidatedString2);

    submitCommand = new DelegateCommand(
        delegate
        {
            IsComplete(
                () => Message = "Data Submitted!",
                () => Message = string.Empty,
                obj => Message = "An error occured: " + obj.Message);
        });
}
```

When the button is pressed, the SubmitCommand calls the IsComplete method of the ViewModelBase class, which calls the DataErrorNotifier.IsComplete method with the same signature. Recall that the IsComplete method has the following three parameters:

▶ An Action to perform if there are no validation errors.

▶ An Action to perform if there are validation errors.

▶ A Func to perform if an exception is raised and the validation process fails.

The `IsComplete` method causes the overridden `BeginValidation` method of the `AsyncValidationViewModel` class to be called. Asynchronous behavior is simulated by calling a private `Validate` method using a thread from the `ThreadPool`. In a less trivial application, we could imagine that this call could be to a web service, for example.

```
public override void BeginValidation(string memberName, object value)
{
    try
    {
        /* Perform validation asynchronously. */
        ThreadPool.QueueUserWorkItem(state => Validate(memberName, value));
    }
    catch (Exception ex)
    {
        OnValidationComplete(
            new ValidationCompleteEventArgs(memberName, ex));
    }
}
```

As previously stated, it is imperative that the `ValidationComplete` event is raised no matter what the outcome of the validation activity. Therefore, the validation logic is wrapped in a try-catch block, so that if an exception occurs, the `ValidationComplete` event is still raised, as shown in the following excerpt:

```
void Validate(string propertyName, object value)
{
    try
    {
        IEnumerable<DataValidationError> errors
            = GetPropertyErrors(propertyName, value);
        if (errors != null && errors.Count() > 0)
        {
            OnValidationComplete(
                new ValidationCompleteEventArgs(propertyName, errors));
        }
        else
        {
            OnValidationComplete(
                new ValidationCompleteEventArgs(propertyName));
        }
    }
    catch (Exception ex)
    {
        OnValidationComplete(
            new ValidationCompleteEventArgs(propertyName, ex));
    }
}
```

26

If either of the viewmodel's string properties fails validation, a `DataValidationError` for the property is added to the list of validation errors for that property.

Detecting a Change of Data Context

The `FrameworkElement.DataContext` property is a fundamental part of the XAML data-binding system and allows an object to be associated with a top-level element in the visual tree and then inherited by descendants of that element.

Unfortunately, the Windows Phone SDK does not include a public event for detecting when the `DataContext` of a `FrameworkElement` is changed. As a workaround, I have included in the downloadable sample code a class named `DataContextChangedListener` that uses attached properties to emulate a `DataContextChanged` event, which allows you to receive notification when a `FrameworkElement`'s data context is changed (see Listing 26.4).

The `Subscribe` method of the `DataContextChangedListener` associates a `PropertyChangedCallback` delegate with a specified `FrameworkElement`. The delegate is invoked when a change to the `DataContextProperty` is detected.

The `HandleDataContextChanged` handler is called when the `FrameworkElement` object's `DataContext` is changed because changing the `DataContext` of the `FrameworkElement` causes all bindings for the `FrameworkElement` to be reevaluated.

The fact that the `DataContextProperty` is named DataContextProperty is arbitrary and has no effect on the association between the attached property and the `FrameworkElement.DataContext` property.

LISTING 26.4   `DataContextChangedListener` Class

```
public class DataContextChangedListener
{
    static readonly DependencyProperty DataContextProperty
        = DependencyProperty.RegisterAttached(
            "DataContextProperty",
            typeof(object),
            typeof(FrameworkElement),
            new PropertyMetadata(HandleDataContextChanged));

    static readonly DependencyProperty HandlersProperty
        = DependencyProperty.RegisterAttached(
            "HandlersProperty",
            typeof(PropertyChangedCallback),
            typeof(FrameworkElement),
            new PropertyMetadata(
                (object)((PropertyChangedCallback)(delegate { }))));
```

```
public static void Subscribe(
    FrameworkElement element, PropertyChangedCallback handler)
{
    ArgumentValidator.AssertNotNull(element, "element");
    ArgumentValidator.AssertNotNull(handler, "handler");

    PropertyChangedCallback handlers
        = (PropertyChangedCallback)element.GetValue(HandlersProperty);
    handlers += handler;

    element.SetValue(HandlersProperty, handlers);

    if (element.GetBindingExpression(DataContextProperty) == null)
    {
        element.SetBinding(DataContextProperty, new Binding());
    }
}

public static void Unsubscribe(
    FrameworkElement element, PropertyChangedCallback handler)
{
    ArgumentValidator.AssertNotNull(element, "element");
    ArgumentValidator.AssertNotNull(handler, "handler");

    PropertyChangedCallback handlers
        = (PropertyChangedCallback)element.GetValue(HandlersProperty);
    handlers -= handler;
    element.SetValue(HandlersProperty, handlers);
}

static void HandleDataContextChanged(
    DependencyObject d, DependencyPropertyChangedEventArgs e)
{
    FrameworkElement element = (FrameworkElement)d;
    PropertyChangedCallback handlers
        = (PropertyChangedCallback)element.GetValue(HandlersProperty);

    PropertyChangedCallback tempEvent = handlers;
    if (tempEvent != null)
    {
        tempEvent(d, e);
    }
}
}
```

26

The `ValidationSummary` control uses the `DataContextChangedListener` to subscribe to the `INotifyDataErrorInfo.ErrorsChanged` event of the viewmodel.

When the control is loaded, the control uses the static `DataContextChangedListener.Subscribe` method to add its `HandleDataContextChanged` method to the list of handlers.

If and when the handler is called, the control unsubscribes from the previous `INotifyDataErrorInfo` and subscribes to the new object's event. See the following excerpt:

```
void HandleLoaded(object sender, System.Windows.RoutedEventArgs e)
{
...
    DataContextChangedListener.Subscribe(this, HandleDataContextChanged);
}


void HandleDataContextChanged(
    DependencyObject d, DependencyPropertyChangedEventArgs e)
{
    /* Unsubscribe to previous notifier. */
    INotifyDataErrorInfo oldNotifier = e.OldValue as INotifyDataErrorInfo;
    if (oldNotifier != null)
    {
        oldNotifier.ErrorsChanged -= HandleErrorsChanged;
    }

    /* When the DataContext is an INotifyDataErrorInfo,
     * monitor it for errors. */
    INotifyDataErrorInfo notifier = DataContext as INotifyDataErrorInfo;
    if (notifier != null)
    {
        notifier.ErrorsChanged += HandleErrorsChanged;
    }
}
```

Hopefully, the `FrameworkElement.DataContextChanged` event will be made public in a later release of the Windows Phone SDK; in the meantime, however, the custom `DataContextChangedListener` is a simple solution that can be used wherever we need to respond to a change of an element's data context.

Adding `INotifyDataErrorInfo` Support to the `ValidationSummary` Control

Now that you have looked at the `INotifyDataErrorInfo` interface and at the inner workings of the custom validation system, let us examine how the `ValidationSummary` control has been extended to support the `INotifyDataErrorInfo` interface.

As you saw in the previous section, the `ValidationSummary` control monitors its data context for validation errors if the data context implements `INotifyDataErrorInfo`.

When the `INotifyDataErrorInfo.ErrorsChanged` event is raised by the data context, the control's `HandleErrorsChanged` handler is called (see Listing 26.5).

`ValidationSummary` maintains a dictionary of validation errors, which are keyed by the associated property name. The `HandleErrorsChanged` method retrieves the list of validation errors from the `INotifyDataErrorInfo` and combines the list with the list in its own dictionary. If no list exists for the particular property name, a new list is added to the dictionary.

LISTING 26.5   `ValidationSummary.HandleErrorsChanged` Method

```
void HandleErrorsChanged(object sender, DataErrorsChangedEventArgs args)
{
    INotifyDataErrorInfo notifier = sender as INotifyDataErrorInfo;
    if (notifier == null)
    {
        return;
    }

    string propertyName = args.PropertyName;
    if (string.IsNullOrEmpty(propertyName))
    {
        return;
    }

    IEnumerable notifierErrors = notifier.GetErrors(args.PropertyName);

    List<object> errorList;
    if (!errorLookup.TryGetValue(propertyName, out errorList))
    {
        errorList = new List<object>();
    }

    foreach (var error in errorList)
    {
        RemoveError(error);
    }

    errorList.Clear();

    foreach (var error in notifierErrors)
    {
        AddError(error);
    }
    errorLookup[propertyName] = errorList;

    foreach (var error in errorList)
```

```
    {
        AddError(error);
    }
}
```

The `ValidationSummary` control now has support for both the property setter validation approach and for the Silverlight 4 `INotifyDataErrorInfo` validation approach.

Incorporating Group Validation

In the previous example, you saw how the `ViewModelBase.IsComplete` method is used to trigger validation of a viewmodel. This section looks at extending the validation to set control-enabled states based on the presence of validation errors and at hiding validation errors until the user has had a chance to fill out the form.

Before proceeding, you may want to briefly review the section "Performing Group Validation" earlier in the chapter, and in particular Figure 26.7.

The `SendEmailViewModel` in the downloadable sample code is a more complex example of asynchronous input validation. In it, the `sendEmailCommand` is prevented from executing if it is already in execution or if the form is invalid.

When `SendEmailView` is first displayed, the Send button is enabled and no validation errors are displayed (see Figure 26.14).

FIGURE 26.14   `SendEmailView` page. The Send button is enabled and no validation errors are shown, even though the form is not complete.

When the Send button is tapped, the viewmodel is validated. If invalid, the Send button is disabled (see Figure 26.15).

FIGURE 26.15   `SendEmailView` page. The Send button is disabled after the form is deemed incomplete.

The Send button is bound to the viewmodel's `ICommand` named `SendEmailCommand`, as shown:

```
<Button Content="Send"
        Command="{Binding SendEmailCommand}" />
```

Evaluation of whether the command can execute depends on the following criteria:

▶ If the command is in execution, it cannot be executed.

▶ If an attempt to execute the command has not occurred before, it can be executed.

▶ If the viewmodel has validation errors, it cannot be executed.

`SendEmailCommand` is instantiated in the viewmodel constructor, as shown:

```
sendEmailCommand = new DelegateCommand(arg => SendEmail(),
                        arg => !sending && (!sendAttempted || !HasErrors));
```

The `SendEmail` method passes three Lambda expressions to the `ViewModelBase` class's `IsComplete` method (see Listing 26.6). The first action is performed if the form is deemed complete, in which case an `EmailComposeTask` is used to dispatch the email. The second action is performed if the form is not complete, and the third displays a warning message if an error is raised.

LISTING 26.6   `SendEmailViewModel.Send` **Method**

```
void SendEmail()
{
    if (sending)
    {
        return;
    }

    try
    {
        sending = sendAttempted = true;
        Message = string.Empty;
        RefreshCommands();
        IsComplete(() =>
                {
                    sending = false;
                    EmailComposeTaskAdapter task = getEmailTaskAdapter();
                    task.Body = body;
                    task.Cc = cc;
                    task.Subject = subject;
                    task.To = to;
                    task.Show();
                },
                () =>
                {
                    sending = false;
                    RefreshCommands();
                },
                obj =>
                {
                    sending = false;
                    RefreshCommands();
                    string errorMessage = obj != null
                                ? obj.Message : string.Empty;
                    Message = "Unable to send email: "
                                + errorMessage;
                });
    }
    catch (Exception ex)
```

```
    {
        sending = false;
        Message = "Unable to send email: " + ex.Message;
    }
}
```

A call to `RefreshCommands` raises the `CanExecuteChanged` event of the command, which in turn sets the `IsEnabled` property of the button:

```
void RefreshCommands()
{
    sendEmailCommand.RaiseCanExecuteChanged();
}
```

Summary

This chapter began by defining the two types of input validation: syntactic and semantic. Syntactic validation ensures that user input has the correct format and can be converted to the correct type, whereas semantic validation may entail more complex validation, such as the evaluation of business rules.

This chapter then looked at the Silverlight 3 property setter validation system, which is included in the Windows Phone SDK. You saw how this system relies on the raising of exceptions to indicate validation errors. Noncritical exceptions raised in property setters produce binding errors, which signal validation errors.

You saw how Windows Phone requires custom templates for enabling visualization of input validation errors, and you looked at using Expression Blend to copy and customize the way error-related visual states are displayed.

Finally, the chapter examined the Silverlight 4 validation system, which is also included in the Windows Phone SDK, and which enables asynchronous and composite input validation. You looked at setting control-enabled states based on the presence of validation errors, and at hiding validation errors until the user has had a chance to fill out the form.

26

CHAPTER 27

Communicating with Network Services

Network services have the potential to broaden your app's capabilities by connecting it to a vast collection of online resources. Many services such as Twitter and Facebook offer web APIs that allow your app to interact or even extend the services.

Windows Phone devices have low power mobile processors, which limit their processing power. By leveraging network services, your app can provide capabilities more akin to a desktop application.

This chapter begins by looking at the types of network services available on the phone. It then looks at monitoring network connectivity and at determining the type of network connection that the phone is using—Wi-Fi or cellular—enabling you to tailor the amount of data traffic your app uses accordingly.

The chapter then looks at the Open Data Protocol (OData) and how to create an app that consumes the eBay OData service. You see a useful custom component that allows your app to fetch data from a service as soon as the user scrolls to the end of a `ListBox`.

The chapter then looks at using the Simulation Dashboard to simulate real-world network conditions during development.

Finally, the chapter looks at the new Windows Phone 8 Data Sense feature. You learn how to reduce or halt your app's data usage when a user approaches or exceeds his or her data plan limit.

Network Service Technologies

Windows Phone provides various ways of consuming network services, including the following:

▶ **SOAP services**—SOAP stands for Simple Object Access Protocol. SOAP uses an XML format. In Windows Phone, SOAP services are usually consumed using Windows Communication Foundation (WCF).

▶ **REST services**—REST stands for Representational State Transfer. REST relies on HTTP and uses unique URLs to identify resource entities. Create Read Update Delete (CRUD) operations are performed using HTTP GET, POST, PUT, and DELETE. Various open-source projects are available for consuming REST services.

▶ **OData**—OData stands for Open Data Protocol. It is a web protocol for querying and updating data. OData is the main topic of this chapter.

▶ **Plain HTTP services**—Some services are provided using nonstandardized protocols, where HTTP GET requests are used to consume an API. For example, Google search can be queried using a URL, and the results can be returned in JSON.

Windows Phone apps can access these services directly, or in the case of WCF or OData, may use a proxy that is generated from the service's published metadata.

Visual Studio generates proxy classes for SOAP and OData services by selecting the Add Service Reference from the Project menu.

A network service can be hosted on your own server, or on the cloud. It may be a service that you have written in-house, or it could also be a third-party service, where you can query the service but may not have access to its source code.

Monitoring Network Connectivity

Although most phones have a data plan from a cellular network provider, a network connection will most likely not be available at all times. In fact, in some areas it can be difficult staying connected to a network. Therefore, it is imperative that your app is engineered to be resilient to network disruptions.

Furthermore, awareness of the type of network connection that the device is using allows you to tailor the volume of data traffic that it uses. When connected to a local area network via Wi-Fi or a USB cable, it may be acceptable for an app to download large data files. Conversely, depleting a user's cellular broadband connection by transferring a lot of data is probably not acceptable.

Connection Priorities

The Windows Phone OS automatically chooses a connection type based on the following ordered priorities:

▶ Network connection to a PC via a tethered connection

▶ Wi-Fi

▶ Mobile broadband

The Windows Phone OS favors a network connection via a PC above all other connection types. The phone periodically checks whether a higher priority connection is available and switches connections accordingly.

The API for determining the connection status of the device is located in the Microsoft. Phone.Net.NetworkInformation and System.Net.NetworkInformation namespaces. Within this API is an event for notification when a connection change occurs.

The `System.Net.NetworkInformation.NetworkInterface` class and the `System.Net.NetworkInformation.NetworkChange` class represent the non-phone-specific portion of the API, whereas the `Microsoft.Phone.Net.NetworkInformation.NetworkInterface` inherits from `System.Net.NetworkInformation.NetworkInterface` and is specific to the phone (see Figure 27.1).

FIGURE 27.1   Network connection related classes.

The `NetworkInterface.GetIsNetworkAvailable` method allows you to determine whether any network connection is available; however, there is one caveat (see the following note).

> **NOTE**
>
> `GetIsNetworkAvailable` is not always a *true* indicator of whether a useable network is available. A network connection is considered to be available if any network interface is marked "up" and is not a loopback or tunnel interface. There are cases where the phone may not be connected to a network, yet a network is still considered available, and `GetIsNetworkAvailable` returns true.

An alternative and albeit more reliable method for determining network availability is the `NetworkInterface.NetworkInterfaceType` property. While the `NetworkInterfaceType` enum includes many values, the phone implementation supports only the following five values:

▶ **None**—Indicates that no network connection is established.

▶ **MobileBroadbandCdma**—Indicates a connection to a CDMA cellular network.

▶ **MobileBroadbandGsm**—Indicates a connection to a GSM cellular network.

▶ **Ethernet**—Indicates a network connection is established via a PC. Ordinarily, this is done with a USB cable.

▶ **Wireless80211**—Indicates a Wi-Fi connection is established to a LAN.

To determine whether the phone is connected to a network, the NetworkInterfaceType property can be compared to the NetworkInterfaceType.None enum value, as shown:

```
bool connected = NetworkInterface.NetworkInterfaceType
                        != NetworkInterfaceType.None;
```

The NetworkInterfaceType.None value represents a state where the phone does not have Internet access. As Dolhai points out in an article available at http://www.codeproject.com/KB/windows-phone-7/ZuneDetectAndNetworking.aspx, under some circumstances, such as disconnecting the phone from an Ethernet connection, reading the NetworkInterfaceType property can block the calling thread for many seconds. It is advisable, therefore, to read the property from a background thread. In a moment you see how to do that using a custom class, but first let us briefly look at how to monitor changes to the network connection state.

Monitoring Connection Events

The NetworkChange.NetworkAddressChanged event is raised if the IP address of the phone changes, which typically happens when any of the following events occur:

▶ The device connects to, or disconnects from, a Wi-Fi or mobile network.

▶ The phone is linked to the PC via the Zune software or the Windows Phone Connect Tool.

▶ The phone is unlinked from the PC when either the Zune software or the Windows Phone Connect Tool is closed, or when the USB cable is disconnected.

> **NOTE**
>
> When linked to a PC with no Internet connection present (via the Zune software or Windows Phone Connect Tool), the phone device does not automatically switch to an available Wi-Fi connection.

When the phone switches connections, the NetworkAddressChanged event may be raised several times. This can be troublesome if your event handler performs some expensive task. To remedy this, the custom NetworkConnectionMonitor class, provided in the down-loadable sample code, uses Reactive Extensions (Rx) to sample the event so that, at most, only one NetworkAddressChanged event is raised each second (see Listing 27.1).

When the event is handled, the NetworkConnectionMonitor.Update method is called, which sets the network connection type and raises the NetworkConnectionMonitor.NetworkConnectionChanged event on the UI thread.

For more information on Rx, see Chapter 17, "Building Location Aware Apps."

LISTING 27.1 NetworkConnectionMonitor Class

```
public class NetworkConnectionMonitor : INetworkConnectionMonitor
{
    const int sampleRateMs = 1000;
    IDisposable subscription;

    public event EventHandler<EventArgs> NetworkConnectionChanged;
    public NetworkConnectionType NetworkConnectionType  { get; private set; }

    public bool Connected
    {
        get
        {
            return NetworkConnectionType != NetworkConnectionType.None;
        }
    }

    public NetworkConnectionMonitor()
    {
        Update();
        var observable
            = Observable.FromEvent<NetworkAddressChangedEventHandler, EventArgs>(
                handler => new NetworkAddressChangedEventHandler(handler),
                handler => NetworkChange.NetworkAddressChanged += handler,
                handler => NetworkChange.NetworkAddressChanged -= handler);

        IObservable<IEvent<EventArgs>> sampler
            = observable.Sample(TimeSpan.FromMilliseconds(sampleRateMs));

        subscription = sampler.ObserveOn(Scheduler.ThreadPool).Subscribe(
                                                    args => Update());
    }

    void Update()
    {
        switch (NetworkInterface.NetworkInterfaceType)
```

```
        {
            case NetworkInterfaceType.None:
                NetworkConnectionType = NetworkConnectionType.None;
                break;
            case NetworkInterfaceType.MobileBroadbandCdma:
            case NetworkInterfaceType.MobileBroadbandGsm:
                NetworkConnectionType = NetworkConnectionType.MobileBroadband;
                break;
            /* These values do not apply to Windows Phone. */
            case NetworkInterfaceType.AsymmetricDsl:
            case NetworkInterfaceType.Atm:
            /* Content omitted. */
            /* Phone values */
            case NetworkInterfaceType.Ethernet:
            case NetworkInterfaceType.Wireless80211:
            default:
                NetworkConnectionType = NetworkConnectionType.Lan;
                break;
        }
        Deployment.Current.Dispatcher.BeginInvoke(new Action(
            () => NetworkConnectionChanged.Raise(this, EventArgs.Empty)));
    }
}
```

The custom `NetworkConnectionMonitor` class does not expose a `NetworkInterfaceType` property, because only three values apply to the phone. Instead, it uses a custom enum type called `NetworkConnectionType`, which provides a simplified view on the type of connection, with the following three values:

▶ `None`—Indicates that no network connection is established

▶ `Lan`—Indicates that a connection to a local area network is established, and that the app can probably be more indulgent with the amount of data it transfers

▶ `MobileBroadband`—Indicates that the phone is using a cellular network, and that data usage should be used more sparingly, if at all

To use the `NetworkConnectionMonitor`, define it as a field in your class and subscribe to the `NetworkConnectionChanged` event, as shown:

```
readonly INetworkConnectionMonitor networkConnectionMonitor;

public YourViewModel()
{
    networkConnectionMonitor = new NetworkConnectionMonitor();
    networkConnectionMonitor.NetworkConnectionChanged
        += delegate
```

```
        {
            WebServiceAvailable = networkConnectionMonitor.Connected;
            CanPerformDownloadLargeFile
                = networkConnectionMonitor.NetworkConnectionType
                            == NetworkConnectionType.Lan;
        };
}
```

Alternatively, an implementation of the INetworkConnectionMonitor can be passed to the viewmodel, allowing it to be replaced with a mock for unit testing. This is demonstrated later in this chapter.

Introduction to OData

The example app for this section consumes live eBay data, which is exposed using the Open Data Protocol (OData). OData is a web protocol for querying and updating data. It defines operations on resources using HTTP verbs (PUT, POST, UPDATE, and DELETE), and it identifies those resources using a standard URI syntax. Data is transferred over HTTP using the AtomPub or JSON standards. For AtomPub, the OData protocol defines some conventions on the standard to support the exchange of query and schema information.

For in-depth information on the OData standard, visit http://odata.org.

A key advantage of the OData protocol is its accessibility by a broad range of clients. Client libraries are available for Windows Phone, iPhone, Silverlight, PHP, AJAX/Javascript, Ruby, and Java.

An OData service can be implemented on any server that supports HTTP. The .NET implementation is supported through WCF Data Services, which is a .NET Framework component that used to be known as ADO.Net Data Services (codename Astoria). WCF Data Services provides a framework for creating OData web services and includes a set of client libraries (one for the desktop CLR, and one for the Silverlight CLR) for building clients that consume OData feeds.

Services that expose their data using the OData protocol are referred to as OData producers, and clients that consume data exposed using the OData protocol are referred to as consumers. OData producers allow CRUD operations to be performed using query string parameters. The odata.org website provides a list of current producers and consumers. Among the producers, there are applications such as SharePoint 2010, Windows Azure Storage, and IBM WebSphere, as well as several live OData services such as the eBay data service, which is used in the sample app.

Consuming OData

The OData tools that accompany the Windows Phone SDK have been much improved since the first release of Windows Phone. In the first release, an external tool had to be downloaded and used to generate the OData service proxies. In addition, the LINQ interpreter on the phone did not support closures on local variables, which meant that using a variable inside a LINQ expression caused a runtime failure. That made LINQ to OData on the phone mostly unusable. This has since been rectified, and service proxies can now be generated using the Add Service Reference dialog.

Before you see how to create an OData consumer using LINQ, you should become familiar with the OData URI syntax.

OData URI Structure

A URI used by an OData consumer has up to three significant parts, as follows:

▶ A service root URI

▶ A resource path

▶ Query string options

An example of an OData URI is
http://ebayodata.cloudapp.net/Items?search=mobile&$top=5&$skip=5

The components of this URI are then broken down as follows:

▶ `http://ebayodata.cloudapp.net` is the service root.

▶ `/Items` is the resource path.

▶ `search=phone&$top=3&$skip=5` are the query string options.

If you use Internet Explorer (IE) to navigate to this URI, you should see something like Figure 27.2. The page shows real eBay items for sale. The query retrieves three items—the sixth, seventh, and eighth items from a search result set—that match the phrase *phone*. This was done using the query string parameters *search*, `$top`, and `$skip`.

IE has a built-in feed reader, which is enabled by default. A quick way to view the XML result is to right-click the page and select View Source. This is a nuisance when developing, however, and you may prefer to disable the feed reader instead.

To disable the feed reader within IE, complete the following steps:

1. Select the Tools menu.

2. Select the Internet Options submenu.

3. Select the Content tab.

4. Click the Settings button of the Feed and Web Slices section to present the Feed Settings dialog.

5. Uncheck the Turn on Feed Reading View option.

6. Click OK, closing all dialog boxes.

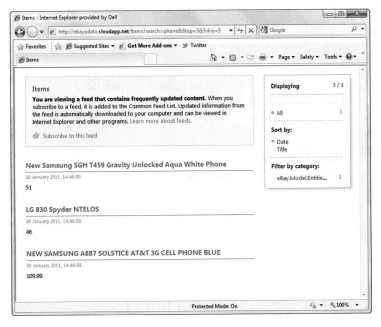

FIGURE 27.2   By default, IE presents the query result using its built-in feed reader.

After the feed reader has been switched off, the entire XML query result can be viewed with syntax highlighting, as shown in Figure 27.3.

FIGURE 27.3   Disabling the built-in feed reader allows you to view the XML.

The format of the XML is, in this case, an Atom feed. Some services are capable of supporting other formats, which can be specified using the $format query option.

Generating an OData Proxy

To generate the proxies for the eBay OData service, right-click the project node in the Visual Studio Solution Explorer and select Add Service Reference. The Add Service Reference is displayed, allowing you to enter the OData service URL (see Figure 27.4).

FIGURE 27.4   Add Service Reference dialog is used to generate the OData service proxies.

TIP

Changing the namespace of the generated service proxy and entity classes can be achieved by selecting Show All Files in the Visual Studio Solution Explorer and expanding the Service Reference node. Change the namespace by setting the Custom Tool Namespace property in the properties of the Reference.datasvcmap file using the Visual Studio properties pane.

OData Query Options

To retrieve data from an OData service, a URI is constructed that specifies the resources that you are interested in—for example, Products—and you restrict the items returned by the service using various query options.

The following are the three types of OData query string options:

▶ **System query options**—System query options are used to control the amount and order of the data that an OData service returns for the resource identified by the URI. The names of all System Query Options are prefixed with a "$" character. Not all system query options need to be supported by a producer. If not supported, the server should return an HTTP status code 405 (Method Not Allowed). The following is a summary list of OData system query options defined by the standard:

  ▶ `$orderby`—This option allows you to order the results of a query by an entity property. For example, to retrieve the list of eBay product categories, ordered by Name, the following query could be used: http://ebayodata.cloudapp.net/ Categories?$orderby=Name.

  ▶ `$top`—This option allows you to select the first N items from a result set, where N is a positive integer specified in the query. For example, the following query selects the first five items from the complete list of eBay items: http:// ebayodata.cloudapp.net/Items?$top=5.

  ▶ `$skip`—This option allows you to select items that occur after a particular index in the result set and is useful when performing paging. By default, an OData service usually limits the number of items returned at any one time. In the case of the eBay OData service, this limit is 500 items. The `$skip` option, in conjunction with the `$top` option, can be used to page through results.

  ▶ `$filter`—This option allows you to restrict the results to those matching the specified criteria. The `$filter` option supports various logical, arithmetic, and grouping operators, as well as a set of functions, such as `substringof`. See the OData website http://www.odata.org/developers/protocols/ uri-conventions#QueryStringOptions for more information on the `$filter` option.

  ▶ `$expand`—This option allows you to retrieve a graph of entities. For example, rather than retrieving the first three product categories and then the products within those three categories in another query, by using the `$expand` option you are able to retrieve them all at once. This is done as shown in the following example: http://services.odata.org/OData/OData.svc/ Categories?$top=3&$expand=Products.

The syntax of a `$expand` query option is a comma-separated list of navigation properties. Additionally, each navigation property can be followed by a forward slash and another navigation property to enable identifying a multilevel relationship.

  ▶ `$format`—This option allows you to specify the format of the response. Valid `$format` values include Atom, XML, and JSON. The `$format` value may also be set to a custom value specific to a particular OData service.

  ▶ `$select`—This option allows you to retrieve only the data that you are interested in and can be important for performance when working with OData on the phone. The value of a `$select` option is a comma-separated list of selection clauses. Each selection clause may be a property name, navigation property name, or the "*" character. To select only the names of the top five search

27

results for the phrase *phone*, the following query could be used: http://
ebayodata.cloudapp.net/Items?search=phone&$top=5&$select=Title.

`$inlinecount`—This option allows you to retrieve a count of the number of
items in a result set, along with the entity elements. When combined with a
`$top` option of 0 (specified by `&$top=0`), you can retrieve the number of items
in a set without having to go to the trouble of downloading unnecessary bytes.

▶ **Custom query options**—Custom query options are specific to the OData service
that uses them. They differ in that they are not prefixed by a $ symbol. The
following is an example of a custom query option, where *xname* is the parameter name, and *xvalue* is its value: http://services.odata.org/OData/OData.svc/
Products?xname=xvalue.

▶ **Service operation parameters**—A service operation is a function specific to the
particular OData service. Service operation parameters work much like custom query
options, where key/value pairs are provided to a custom function as arguments. For
example, a service operation exists on the OData sample website that retrieves all
products with a particular rating. The rating is specified using the *rating* service operation parameter, as shown: http://services.odata.org/OData/OData.svc/
GetProductsByRating?rating=5.

Using an OData Proxy

To query an OData producer, such as the eBay OData service, first create an instance of
the generated OData model class, using the service root URI, like so:

```
EBayData ebayData = new EBayData(new Uri("http://ebayodata.cloudapp.net/"));
```

We then create a `DataServiceCollection`, which is used to query the OData service asynchronously and to populate itself with the objects representing items in the response feed.
The `DataServiceCollection` type inherits from `ObservableCollection`, which means it
supports `INotifyCollectionChanged` out of the box, and it can be used directly within the
user interface.

To instantiate a `DataServiceCollection`, an OData model instance is passed to its
constructor, like so:

```
searchResult = new DataServiceCollection<Item>(ebayData);
```

Because the `DataServiceCollection` queries the OData producer asynchronously, we
subscribe to its `LoadCompleted` handler to be notified when the query has completed, as
shown in the following example:

```
searchResult.LoadCompleted
    += (sender, args) =>
    {
```

```
        if (args.Error != null)
        {
            /* Handle search error. */
        }
    };
```

Subscribing to the `LoadCompleted` event is, however, optional. Regardless of whether it is handled, if an error does not occur, the collection is populated automatically after the call completes.

A second URI is used to specify the resources and query options:

```
var itemsUri = new Uri("/Items?search=phone&$top=5&$select=Title",
    UriKind.Relative);
```

This second URI is then used to fetch the results, using the `LoadAsync` method of the `DataServiceCollection`:

```
searchResult.LoadAsync(itemsUri);
```

Alternatively, a `DataServiceQuery` can be created, which eliminates the manual creation of the request URI, as shown:

```
IQueryable<Item> serviceQuery
= ebayData.Items.AddQueryOption("search", "phone")
                .AddQueryOption("$top", 5);
```

With an `IQueryable<T>` the search results can be further restricted using LINQ to OData, as demonstrated in the following example:

```
serviceQuery = from item in serviceQuery
                where item.CurrentPrice > 100.0
                select item;

searchResult.LoadAsync(serviceQuery);
```

When the query completes, the `searchResult DataServiceCollection` is automatically populated with strongly typed objects representing the resource; in this case it produces eBay `Item` objects.

Although OData is a standard, OData services differ in their coverage of query options; all query options are not provided by all services. Be sure to read any relevant documentation for the OData service that you intend to consume in your app.

The full API documentation for the eBay OData service can be found at http://ebayodata.cloudapp.net/docs.

27

Building an eBay OData Consumer Application

This section creates an eBay search app that uses the eBay OData service to search for items and to present search results on a page. The section also looks at how to retrieve data on demand when the user scrolls to the bottom of the `ListBox`.

Creating an OData Wrapper

The previous section looked at querying an OData service using the OData model class. Although accessing the OData service model classes directly from a viewmodel is possible, it can make unit testing difficult because it relies on the actual OData producer.

In the sample for this chapter, an intermediary class called `EbayClient` performs all OData queries. `EbayClient` implements the custom `IEbayClient` interface, shown in the following excerpt:

```
public interface IEbayClient
{
    void SearchItemsAsync(string query,
                          int beginIndex = 0, int maxItems = 0);
    event EventHandler<SearchItemsCompleteEventArgs> SearchItemsComplete;
}
```

By using the `IEbayClient` interface and not a concrete implementation, we are able to substitute the `EbayClient` implementation for a mock type to enable testing of the user interface without needing to send data over the wire.

The `IEbayClient` interface is designed to be used asynchronously; the `SearchItemsAsync` method has a void return type, and an event is used to signal that the call has completed. When the search completes, the `SearchItemsComplete` method is raised using a custom extension method (see Listing 27.2).

The static `HttpUtility.UrlEncode` method transforms any special characters entered by the user into URL compatible characters. This prevents the user from injecting OData query options, or inadvertently causing the request to fail.

LISTING 27.2   `EbayClient` Class

```
public class EbayClient : IEbayClient
{
    DataServiceCollection<Item> searchResult;

    public void SearchItemsAsync(string query,
                                 int beginIndex = 0, int maxItems = 0)
    {
        EBayData ebayData
            = new EBayData(new Uri("http://ebayodata.cloudapp.net/"));

        searchResult = new DataServiceCollection<Item>(ebayData);
```

```
            searchResult.LoadCompleted
                += (sender, args) =>
                    {
                        if (args.Error != null)
                        {
                            SearchItemsComplete.Raise(this,
                                new SearchItemsCompleteEventArgs(
                                        null, query, args.Error));
                            return;
                        }
                        SearchItemsComplete.Raise(this,
                            new SearchItemsCompleteEventArgs(searchResult, query));
                    };
            string parameter = HttpUtility.UrlEncode(query);

            IQueryable<Item> serviceQuery
                = ebayData.Items.AddQueryOption("search", parameter)
                            .AddQueryOption("$skip", beginIndex)
                            .AddQueryOption("$top", maxItems);

            //serviceQuery = from item in serviceQuery
            //               where item.CurrentPrice > 100.0
            //               select item;

            searchResult.LoadAsync(serviceQuery);
        }


        public event EventHandler<SearchItemsCompleteEventArgs> SearchItemsComplete;
}
```

The `SearchItemsCompleteEventArgs` class extends the custom `ResultEventArgs`, which contains the result produced by the OData proxy, the type of which is defined by a generic parameter. An optional parameter allows it to supply an `Exception` instance if the call fails (see Listing 27.3).

LISTING 27.3   ResultEventArgs Class

```
public class ResultEventArgs<T> : EventArgs
{
    public T Result { get; private set; }
    public Exception Error { get; private set; }

    public ResultEventArgs(T result, Exception error = null)
    {
        Result = result;
```

```
        Error = error;
    }
}
```

The `SearchItemsCompleteEventArgs` adds a string `Query` property, which identifies the original query (see Listing 27.4).

LISTING 27.4   `SearchItemsCompleteEventArgs` Class

```
public class SearchItemsCompleteEventArgs
    : ResultEventArgs<ObservableCollection<Item>>
{
    public string Query { get; private set; }
    public SearchItemsCompleteEventArgs(
        ObservableCollection<Item> result, string query, Exception error = null)
        : base(result, error)
    {
        Query = query;
    }
}
```

The sample also comprises a view named `EbaySearchView` and its viewmodel: `EbaySearchViewModel`.

`EbaySearchViewModel` Class

The viewmodel uses the `IEbayClient` instance to query the eBay OData service. The viewmodel exposes two commands:

▶ `SearchCommand`—Triggered by entering text into a `TextBox` in the view, this command calls the `Search` method, which calls the `IEbayClient`'s `SearchItemsAsync` method.

▶ `FetchMoreDataCommand`—This command allows the search results to be paged.

The commands are initialized in the `EbaySearchViewModel` constructor, which is shown in the following excerpt:

```
public EbaySearchViewModel(
    Func<IEbayClient> getEbayClientFunc,
    INetworkConnectionMonitor networkConnectionMonitor)
{
    this.networkConnectionMonitor = ArgumentValidator.AssertNotNull(
                    networkConnectionMonitor, "networkConnectionMonitor");
    this.getEbayClientFunc = ArgumentValidator.AssertNotNull(
                        getEbayClientFunc, "getEbayClientFunc");
```

```
networkConnectionMonitor.NetworkConnectionChanged
    += (sender, args) => UpdateCommands();

SearchText = "star wars action figure";

searchCommand = new DelegateCommand<string>(
    query =>
    {
        if (!string.IsNullOrEmpty(query))
        {
            Search(query);
        }
    }, obj => networkConnectionMonitor.Connected);

fetchMoreDataCommand = new DelegateCommand(
    obj =>
    {
        if (!string.IsNullOrEmpty(lastQuery))
        {
            Search(lastQuery, true);
        }
    }, obj => networkConnectionMonitor.Connected);
}
```

The enabled state of each command depends on the `Connected` property of the `INetworkConnectionMonitor`. When the `NetworkConnectionChanged` event is raised, the viewmodel's `UpdateCommands` method is called, which calls the `RaiseCanExecuteChanged` method on each command, causing the `Enabled` state to be reevaluated:

```
void UpdateCommands()
{
    searchCommand.RaiseCanExecuteChanged();
    fetchMoreDataCommand.RaiseCanExecuteChanged();
}
```

The viewmodel's `Search` method uses a `Func` named `getEbayClientFunc` to retrieve an `IEbayClient` (see Listing 27.5). The `Search` method sets the viewmodel's `Busy` property to true, causing a `ProgressBar` in the view to be made visible.

To reduce the amount of data retrieved from the OData service, the number of records retrieved by the `IEbayClient` is restricted to 10.

LISTING 27.5   `EbaySearchViewModel.Search` Method and Related Members

```
const int chunkSize = 10;
string lastQuery;
```

```
bool appendResult;

void Search(string query, bool append = false)
{
    if (lastQuery == query && Busy)
    {
        return;
    }

    lastQuery = query;
    appendResult = append;

    IEbayClient ebayClient = getEbayClientFunc();
    ebayClient.SearchItemsComplete -= HandleEbayClientSearchItemsComplete;
    ebayClient.SearchItemsComplete += HandleEbayClientSearchItemsComplete;
    int beginIndex = appendResult ? Items.Count : 0;

    try
    {
        Busy = true;
        ebayClient.SearchItemsAsync(query, beginIndex, chunkSize);
    }
    catch (Exception ex)
    {
        Busy = false;
        Console.WriteLine("Unable to perform search." + ex);
        MessageService.ShowError("Unable to perform search.");
    }
}
```

If the call to SearchItemsAsync fails immediately, the ViewModelBase class's MessageService is used to present a dialog to the user.

For more information on the MessageService, see Chapter 2, "Fundamental Concepts in Windows Phone Development."

When the search completes, the HandleEbayClientSearchItemsComplete handler is called. Old requests are ignored. The method returns immediately if the search query does not match the last query (see Listing 27.6).

If the search was not a new search but a request to fetch the next page of the current search results, the results are added to the end of the Items collection.

LISTING 27.6   EbaySearchViewModel.HandleEbayClientSearchItemsComplete Method

```
void HandleEbayClientSearchItemsComplete(
    object sender, SearchItemsCompleteEventArgs args)
```

```
{
    /* Ignore old query results. */
    if (args.Query != lastQuery)
    {
        return;
    }

    Busy = false;
    if (args.Error == null)
    {
        if (args.Result.Count > 0)
        {
            if (appendResult)
            {
                foreach (var item in args.Result)
                {
                    Items.Add(item);
                }
            }
            else
            {
                Items = new ObservableCollection<Item>(args.Result);
            }
        }
        else
        {
            MessageService.ShowMessage("No match found.");
        }
    }
    else
    {
        MessageService.ShowError(
            "An error occured while attempting to search.");
    }
}
```

EbaySearchView Page

When the viewmodel is created within the view, it receives a `Func` that allows it to resolve the `EbayClient` (see Listing 27.7).

The view contains a `TextBox` to allow the user to enter a search query.

The view subscribes to the `KeyUp` event of the `TextBox`, which allows the app to detect when the user taps the Enter key on the Software Input Panel (SIP) and to execute the `viewmodel` object's `SearchCommand`.

LISTING 27.7   `EbaySearchView` Class

```
public partial class EbaySearchView : PhoneApplicationPage
{
    public EbaySearchView()
    {
        InitializeComponent();
        DataContext = new EbaySearchViewModel(
            () => new EbayClient(), new NetworkConnectionMonitor());
    }

    EbaySearchViewModel ViewModel
    {
        get
        {
            return (EbaySearchViewModel)DataContext;
        }
    }

    void TextBox_KeyUp(object sender, KeyEventArgs e)
    {
        if (e.Key == Key.Enter)
        {
            e.Handled = true;
            TextBox textBox = (TextBox)sender;
            this.Focus();
            ViewModel.SearchCommand.Execute(textBox.Text);
        }
    }
}
```

The view contains a `ListBox` for displaying search results (see Listing 27.8). The `ListBox` contains a custom attached property `ScrollViewerMonitor.AtEndCommand`, which automatically causes the `ListBox` to be populated with more records when the user scrolls to the end of the list. The `ScrollViewerMonitor` class is discussed in detail in the next section.

LISTING 27.8   EbaySearchView.xaml (excerpt)

```
<Grid x:Name="ContentPanel" Grid.Row="1">
    <Grid.RowDefinitions>
        <RowDefinition Height="Auto" />
        <RowDefinition Height="*" />
        <RowDefinition Height="Auto" />
    </Grid.RowDefinitions>
    <TextBox Text="{Binding SearchText}"
             KeyUp="TextBox_KeyUp" />
```

```
<ListBox Grid.Row="1"
    ItemsSource="{Binding Items}"
    u:ScrollViewerMonitor.AtEndCommand="{Binding FetchMoreDataCommand}">
    <ListBox.ItemTemplate>
        <DataTemplate>
            <Grid Margin="14,5,4,10">

                <!-- Content omitted. -->
                <Image Source="{Binding GalleryUrl}"
                    MaxWidth="100" MaxHeight="100"
                    Margin="0, 0, 10, 0"
                    Grid.RowSpan="4" />

                <TextBlock Text="{Binding Title}"
                        Grid.Column="1" Grid.ColumnSpan="3"
                        Style="{StaticResource PhoneTextSmallStyle}" />

                <TextBlock Text="current price:"
                        Grid.Row="1" Grid.Column="1"
                        HorizontalAlignment="Right" />
                <TextBlock Text="{Binding CurrentPrice,
                        Converter={StaticResource StringFormatConverter},
                        ConverterParameter=\{0:C\}}"
                        Grid.Row="1" Grid.Column="2"
                        Margin="10,0,0,0" />

                <TextBlock Text="time left:"
                        Grid.Row="2" Grid.Column="1"
                        HorizontalAlignment="Right" />
                <TextBlock Text="{Binding TimeLeftCustom}"
                        Grid.Row="2" Grid.Column="2"
                        Margin="10,0,0,0" />
                <HyperlinkButton NavigateUri="{Binding ViewItemUrl}"
                            Content="view"
                            TargetName="_blank"
                            Margin="0, 0, 10, 0"
                            Grid.Row="2" Grid.Column="3"
                            HorizontalAlignment="Left" />
            </Grid>
        </DataTemplate>
    </ListBox.ItemTemplate>
</ListBox>
<Grid Grid.Row="2"
    Visibility="{Binding Busy,
    Converter={StaticResource BooleanToVisibilityConverter}}">
    <Grid.RowDefinitions>
```

```
            <RowDefinition />
            <RowDefinition />
        </Grid.RowDefinitions>
        <TextBlock Text="Loading..."
                Style="{StaticResource LoadingStyle}"/>
        <ProgressBar IsIndeterminate="True"
                VerticalAlignment="Bottom"
                Grid.Row="1" />
    </Grid>
</Grid>
```

In the grid row beneath the `ListBox` there is another `Grid` containing a `TextBlock` and a `ProgressBar`. This grid becomes visible when the viewmodel's `Busy` property is true.

When text is entered into the search query `TextBlock`, and the SIP's Enter button is tapped, the viewmodel's `SearchCommand` is executed (see Figure 27.5).

FIGURE 27.5   The eBay search page.

The eBay logo is displayed using a `TextBlock` located in the title panel, with a `Run` for each letter of the eBay logo, as shown in the following excerpt:

```
<StackPanel Grid.Row="0" Style="{StaticResource PageTitlePanelStyle}">
    <TextBlock Text="Windows Phone Unleashed"
```

```
                Style="{StaticResource PhoneTextAppTitleStyle}" />
    <TextBlock Style="{StaticResource PhoneTextPageTitleStyle}"
            FontFamily="{StaticResource LogoFontFamily}">
    <Run Foreground="#ff0000">e</Run><Run Foreground="#000099">b</Run>
    <Run Foreground="#ffcc00">a</Run><Run Foreground="#99cc00">y</Run>
    <Run FontFamily="{StaticResource PhoneFontFamilyNormal}">search</Run>
    </TextBlock>
</StackPanel>
```

For more information on the `TextBlock` and `Run` classes, see Chapter 6, "Mastering Text Elements and Fonts."

The next section demonstrates how the viewmodel's `FetchMoreDataCommand` is executed when the user scrolls to the end of the list.

Fetching Data When the User Scrolls to the End of a List

Most phone users are concerned about network usage. Network traffic comes at a premium, and a user's perception of the quality of your app depends a lot on its responsiveness. When it comes to fetching data from a network service, it should be done in the most efficient way possible. Making the user wait while your app downloads a lot of data is a bad idea. Instead, data should be retrieved in bite-sized chunks.

I have created a `ScrollViewerMonitor` class that uses an attached property to monitor a `ListBox` and fetch data as the user needs it. You use it by adding an attached property to a control that contains a `ScrollViewer`, such as a `ListBox`, as shown in the following example:

```
<ListBox ItemsSource="{Binding Items}"
    u:ScrollViewerMonitor.AtEndCommand="{Binding FetchMoreDataCommand}" />
```

The `AtEndCommand` property specifies a command that is executed when the user scrolls to the end of the list.

The `ScrollViewerMonitor` works by retrieving the first child `ScrollViewer` control from its target (usually a `ListBox`). It then listens to its `VerticalOffset` property for changes. When a change occurs, and the `ScrollableHeight` of the `scrollViewer` is the same as the `VerticalOffset`, the `AtEndCommand` is executed (see Listing 27.9).

The `VerticalOffset` property is a dependency property, and to monitor it for changes I borrowed some of Pete Blois's code (http://blois.us/), which allows you to detect changes to any dependency property. This class is called `BindingListener` and is located in the downloadable sample code.

LISTING 27.9   `ScrollViewerMonitor` Class

```
public class ScrollViewerMonitor
{
    public static DependencyProperty AtEndCommandProperty
        = DependencyProperty.RegisterAttached(
            "AtEndCommand", typeof(ICommand),
            typeof(ScrollViewerMonitor),
            new PropertyMetadata(OnAtEndCommandChanged));

    public static ICommand GetAtEndCommand(DependencyObject obj)
    {
        return (ICommand)obj.GetValue(AtEndCommandProperty);
    }

    public static void SetAtEndCommand(DependencyObject obj, ICommand value)
    {
        obj.SetValue(AtEndCommandProperty, value);
    }

    public static void OnAtEndCommandChanged(
        DependencyObject d, DependencyPropertyChangedEventArgs e)
    {
        FrameworkElement element = (FrameworkElement)d;
        if (element != null)
        {
            element.Loaded -= element_Loaded;
            element.Loaded += element_Loaded;
        }
    }
    static void element_Loaded(object sender, RoutedEventArgs e)
    {
        FrameworkElement element = (FrameworkElement)sender;
        element.Loaded -= element_Loaded;
        ScrollViewer scrollViewer = FindChildOfType<ScrollViewer>(element);
        if (scrollViewer == null)
        {
            throw new InvalidOperationException("ScrollViewer not found.");
        }

        var listener = new DependencyPropertyListener();
        listener.Changed
            += delegate
                {
                    bool atBottom = scrollViewer.ScrollableHeight > 0
                                    && scrollViewer.VerticalOffset
```

```
                                            >= scrollViewer.ScrollableHeight;

                if (atBottom)
                {
                    ICommand atEnd = GetAtEndCommand(element);
                    if (atEnd != null)
                    {
                        atEnd.Execute(null);
                    }
                }
            };
        Binding binding = new Binding("VerticalOffset") {
                                        Source = scrollViewer };
        listener.Attach(scrollViewer, binding);
    }

    static T FindChildOfType<T>(DependencyObject root) where T : class
    {
        var queue = new Queue<DependencyObject>();
        queue.Enqueue(root);

        while (queue.Count > 0)
        {
            DependencyObject current = queue.Dequeue();
            int start = VisualTreeHelper.GetChildrenCount(current) - 1;
            for (int i = start; 0 <= i; i--)
            {
                var child = VisualTreeHelper.GetChild(current, i);
                var typedChild = child as T;
                if (typedChild != null)
                {
                    return typedChild;
                }
                queue.Enqueue(child);
            }
        }
        return null;
    }
}
```

The EbaySearchViewModel contains a FetchMoreDataCommand. When the user scrolls to the bottom of the list, the command is executed, which then sets a Busy flag and calls the network service asynchronously.

Extending OData Entity Classes

When adding a service reference to an OData service, the generated entities classes are made *partial* classes. This provides a useful extensibility point for extending the model, and for providing custom logic within entities themselves.

The `EbayModel.Item` class, for example, contains a `TimeLeft` property. This property is provided as a string. If it was of type `TimeSpan`, however, it would be easier to work with.

This section creates a new partial `Item` class and, within it, a `TimeSpan` property that converts the string value provided by the OData service into a `TimeSpan` value.

The following is an example of the format used by the `TimeLeft` string:

```
P0DT0H13M8S
```

The string contains tokens that indicate value positions for days, hours, minutes, and seconds. Unfortunately, this format is not compatible with the `TimeSpan.Parse` method. Therefore, we need to break up the string into its constituents parts. This can be done using a regular expression.

When you construct regular expressions, they can quickly become complex. Having a decent work bench for constructing them can make life easier. I really like the free regular expression tool called Expresso (www.ultrapico.com). Expresso allows you to specify sample text to see whether your regular expression produces the appropriate result (see Figure 27.6). It also includes other interfaces that assist in the construction of regular expressions.

FIGURE 27.6   Expresso, regular expression editor.

The regular expression to deconstruct the `TimeLeft` value can be plugged in to a new partial `Item` class (see Listing 27.10).

LISTING 27.10   Custom `Item` Class

```
public partial class Item
{
    public TimeSpan? TimeLeftCustom
    {
        get
        {
            return ConvertToTimeSpan(TimeLeft);
        }
    }

    TimeSpan? ConvertToTimeSpan(string timeLeft)
    {
        Regex regex  = new Regex(
            @"P(?<Days>\d+)DT(?<Hours>\d+)H(?<Minutes>\d+)M(?<Seconds>\d+)S");
        Match match = regex.Match(timeLeft);
        if (match.Success)
        {
            string timeSpanString = string.Format("{0}.{1}:{2}:{3}",
                match.Groups["Days"].Value,
                match.Groups["Hours"].Value,
                match.Groups["Minutes"].Value,
                match.Groups["Seconds"].Value);
            TimeSpan result;
            if (TimeSpan.TryParse(timeSpanString, out result))
            {
                return result;
            }
        }
        return null;
    }
}
```

The `TimeLeftCustom` property is now able to be used in the view, like any of the other `Item` class's properties.

Simulating Real-World Conditions with the Simulation Dashboard

As a developer, it is a common mistake to assume that an application will be used under the same conditions of that during development. With mobile development, this assumption is all the more erroneous. You should never assume that a phone is going to have an active Internet connection, nor that a connection will be able to support a fast data rate. If your app performs poorly or even fails when there is a slow or intermittent data connection, users are likely to give your app a poor rating on the Windows Phone Marketplace.

The Windows Phone SDK includes a tool called the Simulation Dashboard, which enables you to simulate a less-than-optimal data connection while debugging your app (see Figure 27.7).

FIGURE 27.7   Simulation Dashboard.

To open the Simulation Dashboard, in Visual Studio, select Simulation Dashboard from the Tools menu.

> **NOTE**
>
> When the launch project is set to a project that is not a type that runs as a standalone application—for example, a class library or a background agent—the menu option for the Simulation Dashboard is not available.

The Simulation Dashboard allows you to alter the network speed and signal strength of the data connection. You can also set the lock screen state, which is useful when testing apps that are enabled to run beneath the lock screen.

The Trigger Reminders button interrupts your app by presenting a reminder while you are debugging. This is useful for testing that your app is able to cope with deactivation.

Moderating Data Usage with Data Sense

Data usage can be costly when users exceed their data plan limits, or when the phone is using a roaming connection. Thus, it is important to consider the amount of data that your app transfers when not using a Wi-Fi connection.

New to Windows Phone 8 is the Data Sense feature that allows you to determine when users are over their data plan limits, and to discontinue data usage or to postpone tasks that transfer data until a Wi-Fi connection is available.

Data Sense allows users to specify their data plan limit. Data Sense monitors data usage in relation to the specified limit. With this information, your app can help users to save money by reducing data usage in some situations.

> **NOTE**
>
> Data Sense requires that a phone come installed with a Data Sense app, which is optional for mobile operators. As a result, users of your app might not have the Data Sense app on their phones. Without the app, a user is unable to enter the data limit.
>
> When a user's data limit is unknown, you can still use the Data Sense API to determine whether the phone is using a Wi-Fi connection or roaming. You cannot, however, use the Data Sense API to determine whether the phone is approaching the user's data limit, or if it is over.

Using the Data Sense API

Apps that make use of the Data Sense API require the ID_CAP_NETWORKING capability. Enable the capability by opening the WMAppManifest.xml file in design view and selecting the capability in the Capabilities tab.

The Data Sense API provides your app with the following three important pieces of information:

- ▶ Whether the phone is roaming
- ▶ If the user is approaching the limit of his or her data plan
- ▶ If the user has exceeded the limit of his or her data plan

If the phone is roaming or the user has exceeded the data plan limit, the cost of transferring data may be high. Your app should, therefore, either not transfer data or seek permission from the user to transfer data.

If the user is approaching the limit of the data plan, your app should minimize its data usage.

The source code for this section is located in the DataDrivenApps/DataSense directory of the WPUnleashed.Examples project in the downloadable sample code. The Data Sense API is located in the Windows.Networking.Connectivity namespace.

27

Listing 27.11 demonstrates how to retrieve a `ConnectionCost` object using the static `GetInternetConnectionProfile` method of `NetworkInformation` class. `ConnectionCost` includes the following four properties:

- ▶ `ApproachingDataLimit` (of type `bool`)

- ▶ `Roaming` (of type `bool`)

- ▶ `OverDataLimit` (of type `bool`)

- ▶ `NetworkCostType` (of type `NetworkCostType`)

LISTING 27.11   DataSenseViewModel.UpdateNetworkInformation Method

```
void UpdateNetworkInformation()
{
    ConnectionProfile connectionProfile
        = NetworkInformation.GetInternetConnectionProfile();
    ConnectionCost = connectionProfile.GetConnectionCost();

    if (connectionProfile.NetworkAdapter.IanaInterfaceType
            == (int)IanaInterfaceTypes.Wifi
        || connectionCost.NetworkCostType == NetworkCostType.Unrestricted)
    {
        /* Connection is a Wi-Fi connection.
         * Restricting data usage is not necessary. */
        DoNotTransferData = false;
        MinimizeUsage = false;
    }
    else
    {
        /* Data usage should be moderated. */

        if (connectionCost.Roaming || connectionCost.OverDataLimit)
        {
            DoNotTransferData = true;
        }

        if (connectionCost.ApproachingDataLimit)
        {
            MinimizeUsage = true;
        }
    }
}
```

The `ConnectionCost` object's `NetworkCostType` property can be one of the following values:

▶ Unknown

▶ Unrestricted

▶ Fixed

▶ Variable

If the value is `Unrestricted`, there is no need to limit data usage. If not `Unrestricted`, your app should take into account the other three properties of the `ConnectionCost` object.

If the user has not specified a data limit in the phone settings and the `NetworkCostType` is equal to Unknown, it is up to you to choose the best behavior for your app. When Unknown, the value of ApproachingDataLimit and OverDataLimit is false. The Roaming property returns an accurate value even when the NetworkCostType is Unknown.

> **NOTE**
>
> Unfortunately, you cannot use the Simulation Dashboard to test your Data Sense code by switching the network type from Wi-Fi to a cellular option. The Simulation Dashboard does not change the values of the properties that the Data Sense API uses.

Summary

This chapter began by looking at the types of network services available on the phone. It then looked at monitoring network connectivity. You saw how to determine the type of network connection that the phone is using: Wi-Fi or cellular, enabling you to tailor the amount of data traffic accordingly. You saw how `GetIsNetworkAvailable` is not a reliable means of determining the network connection state.

The chapter then looked at the Open Data Protocol (OData) and how to create an app that consumes the eBay OData service. You saw a useful custom component that allows your app to fetch data from a service as soon as the user scrolls to the end of a `ListBox`.

The chapter then looked at using the Simulation Dashboard to simulate real-world network conditions during development.

Finally, the chapter looked at the new Windows Phone 8 Data Sense feature. You learned how to reduce or halt your app's data usage when users approach or exceed their data plan limits.

27

Preserving App State and Settings

Preserving app state is one of the key challenges facing Windows Phone developers.

To capture and restore state that is maintained across application launches, Windows Phone provides a segregated storage area called the local folder. The local folder is a managed storage area where your app can read and write data; it is inaccessible to other apps.

> **NOTE**
>
> In the Windows Phone 7.1 OS, the local folder was known as isolated storage.

This chapter begins with a conceptual overview of the local folder and looks at managing files and directories within the data store. You see how to read and write files using the .NET Isolated Storage API, and you are introduced to the new Windows Storage API present in Windows Phone 8. You then explore the `IsolatedStorageSettings` class and see how it is used to automatically persist application settings.

The chapter then examines a custom state preservation system, which uses an attribute-based mechanism for preserving viewmodel property values automatically. You see that by decorating your viewmodel's properties with an attribute, the property's value can be preserved using binary serialization, either transiently using an OS managed `State` dictionary, or persistently in isolated storage.

Finally, you learn how the custom state preservation API is used to preserve fields and to inject logic during state operations.

Understanding Managed Storage

In Windows Phone, apps do not have direct access to the underlying file system and must instead use a managed storage API. This helps to prevent unauthorized access to files by other apps.

Managed storage for Windows Phone works in much the same way as isolated storage in Silverlight for the browser. There is, however, no quota imposed on how much data can be stored on the phone; you are limited only by the storage capacity of the device. There is also no user-specific storage area as there is for the browser; each app has only one local folder assigned to it when it is installed.

Although the relaxation of the storage quota may appear convenient, it comes with the added responsibility of respecting the needs of your users and not consuming space unnecessarily. Phone users generally like to install new apps, download media from the Internet, and sync media to the phone from a PC. This means that storage on the device can be filled up quickly.

When a Windows Phone has only 10% of storage space remaining, the user receives a notification. The user then has the option to delete pictures, music, and apps to recover the necessary storage space. Reaching this point is not favorable from the user's perspective.

To minimize the amount of isolated storage space that your app uses, adhere to the following points:

▶ If your application creates temporary files, delete them when they are no longer needed.

▶ Allow users to delete data that they have created.

▶ Consider using the cloud to store data when the phone is connected to a LAN.

▶ Trim application data periodically. For example, if your app caches a list of products, periodically remove items that have been in the list the longest.

> **NOTE**
>
> If an app is uninstalled, its local folder is deleted.
>
> When an app is updated in the Marketplace, its local folder is left untouched. It is your responsibility to ensure that any data saved in the local folder is transformed to be compatible with the new version of your application.

Besides being able to read and write files in the local folder, the isolated storage API also provides a managed dictionary for saving app settings (see Figure 28.1).

This managed dictionary is the `IsolatedStorageSettings` class, discussed later in the chapter.

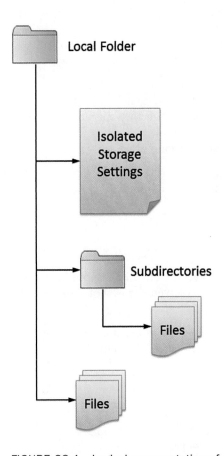

FIGURE 28.1   Logical representation of an application's isolated storage area.

28

Working with Files and Directories

With Windows Phone 8, now you can use two ways to work with files and directories in Windows Phone. The first is the .NET Isolated Storage API, and the second is the WinPRT Windows Storage API. The .NET Isolated Storage API is still fully supported and provides cross-platform compatibility with Silverlight. It also provides built-in support for application settings, which the WinPRT Windows Storage API does not. The WinPRT Windows Storage API is new to Windows Phone 8 and provides cross-platform compatibility with the Windows 8 WinRT Windows Storage API.

This section touches on both approaches, beginning with the .NET Isolated Storage API.

Introducing the .NET Isolated Storage API

The .NET isolated storage API uses the same stream-based model that is present in .NET for the desktop. The isolated storage API is located in the System.IO.IsolatedStorage namespace.

The IsolatedStorageFile class allows access to the virtual file system for reading and writing files, creating and deleting directories, and listing directory contents. The IsolatedStorageFile for an application can be retrieved using the static GetUserStoreForApplication method, as shown in the following example:

```
using (IsolatedStorageFile storageFile
        = IsolatedStorageFile.GetUserStoreForApplication())
{
...
}
```

IsolatedStorageFile implements IDisposable and should therefore be disposed of when it is no longer needed. Placing it within a using block is a convenient way of disposing of the object.

The class IsolatedStorageFile has a misleading name, because rather than representing a single file in isolated storage, it represents the virtual file system. The public members of the IsolatedStorageFile class are presented in Table 28.1.

TABLE 28.1 IsolatedStorageFile Methods for File Management

Name	Description
CreateDirectory	Creates a new folder in the virtual file system.
DeleteDirectory	Deletes a folder in the virtual file system.
DirectoryExists	Determines whether the specified path refers to an existing directory in the virtual file system.
GetDirectoryNames	Returns an array of strings, which are the directories in the root of an isolated store. This method includes an overload that allows you to locate directories and subdirectories using a search pattern. Within the search pattern, single-character ? and multicharacter * wildcards are supported.
CreateFile	Creates a file in the virtual file system, and returns an IsolatedStorageFileStream, which is used to write data to the file.
DeleteFile	Deletes a file in the virtual file system.
FileExists	Determines whether the specified path refers to an existing file in the isolated store.
GetFileNames	Enumerates files in isolated storage scope that match a given pattern. This method includes an overload that allows you to locate files using a search pattern. Within the search pattern, single-character ? and multicharacter * wildcards are supported.

Name	Description
OpenFile	Opens a named file and returns an `IsolatedStorageFileStream`, which is used to access the file. By providing various `FileMode`, `FileAccess`, and `FileShare` arguments, you can specify the kind of access you need to the file, such as reading or writing to the file, and appending or overwriting the file.

Reading and Writing Data to Isolated Storage

Chapter 7, "Employing Media and Web Elements," discussed storing web content to isolated storage. The following (slimmed down) example taken from that chapter tests for the existence of a directory called WebContent. If it does not exist, it is created. We then create a file named Webpage.html. If the file already exists, it is overwritten. We then write some HTML to the file, as shown:

```csharp
using (IsolatedStorageFile isolatedStorageFile
              = IsolatedStorageFile.GetUserStoreForApplication())
{
    if (!isolatedStorageFile.DirectoryExists("WebContent"))
    {
        isolatedStorageFile.CreateDirectory("WebContent");
    }

    using (IsolatedStorageFileStream isolatedStorageFileStream
        = isolatedStorageFile.OpenFile(
          @"WebContent\Webpage.html", FileMode.Create))
    {
        using (StreamWriter streamWriter
            = new StreamWriter(isolatedStorageFileStream))
        {
            streamWriter.Write(@"<html><head></head><body>
                <h2>Stored in Isolated Storage</h2></body></html>");
        }
    }
}
```

Using `FileMode.Create` in an `OpenFile` call is equivalent to requesting that if the file does not exist, `FileMode.CreateNew` should be used; otherwise, `FileMode.Truncate` should be used.

> **NOTE**
>
> The file system used by Windows Phone is TexFat and supports filenames that are no longer than 247 characters. Files placed into isolated storage sit in the apps install directory, which has a path resembling the following:
>
> \APPLICATIONS\INSTALL\45DC3711-8AF7-42BF-A749-6C491F2B427F\INSTALL

28

The length of this path minus the native path to this directory leaves approximately 161 characters. If you attempt to write a file whose path is longer, an `IsolatedStorageException` is raised.

After the file is written to isolated storage, it can be retrieved, as shown in the following example:

```
string html;

using (IsolatedStorageFile isolatedStorageFile
        = IsolatedStorageFile.GetUserStoreForApplication())
{
    using (IsolatedStorageFileStream isolatedStorageFileStream
            = isolatedStorageFile.OpenFile(
                @"WebContent\Webpage.html", FileMode.Open))
    {
        using (StreamReader streamReader
                = new StreamReader(isolatedStorageFileStream))
        {
            html = streamReader.ReadToEnd();
        }
    }
}
```

> **NOTE**
>
> Attempting to open a file using a `FileMode.Open` argument raises an exception if the file does not exist. `FileMode.OpenOrCreate` specifies that the operating system should open a file if it exists; otherwise, a new file should be created.

Serialization Performance Implications

When your app is transitioning from a nonrunning state to a running state, and vice versa, it is important that it completes all activities as quickly as possible. Being slow at startup or shutdown can make your app appear sluggish and poorly engineered. Furthermore, there is a limit of 10 seconds before an app's process is terminated when it is being closed or deactivated.

To improve performance, consider favoring binary serialization over other types of serialization, such as XML or JSON serialization.

Unlike interacting with the user interface, there is no requirement to perform isolated storage activities on the main thread. When loading state at startup, or while performing arbitrary CRUD operations, the use of a background thread can improve the responsiveness of your app during long-running storage operations.

> **TIP**
>
> To prevent locking the UI unnecessarily, if a storage operation takes more than 100 milliseconds to complete, move the operation to a background thread or switch to the WinPRT Windows Storage API, which provides awaitable methods for most IO operations.

Introducing the WinPRT Windows Storage API

The Windows Storage API resembles the Isolated Storage API with one key difference: the API is predominately asynchronous, with the majority of its methods being awaitable.

The Windows Storage API is located in the Windows.Storage namespace.

The StorageFolder and StorageFile classes underpin the Windows Storage API and represent folders and files within the local folder.

To retrieve the StorageFolder representing the local folder of your app, use the ApplicationData.Current.LocalFolder property. Observe the following method, which writes some text to a new file in the local folder:

```
async void SaveSampleFile()
{
    string assemblyName = Assembly.GetExecutingAssembly().FullName;
    assemblyName = assemblyName.Substring(
        0, assemblyName.IndexOf(",", StringComparison.Ordinal));

    string fileContent = string.Format(
        "This text was saved to a file at {0} from the assembly: {1}.",
        DateTime.Now, assemblyName);

    IStorageFolder folder = ApplicationData.Current.LocalFolder;
    IStorageFile file = await folder.CreateFileAsync(
                            fileName, CreationCollisionOption.ReplaceExisting);

    using (Stream stream = await file.OpenStreamForWriteAsync())
    {
        byte[] content = Encoding.UTF8.GetBytes(fileContent);
        await stream.WriteAsync(content, 0, content.Length);
    }
}
```

Creating a file is achieved using the IStorageFolder object's CreateFileAsync method. This method is awaitable, which means that you can perform the IO operation without blocking the UI thread.

The StorageFolder class implements IStorageFolder, and it is a good practice to use the interface API rather than the concrete class wherever possible.

28

As with the .NET Isolate Storage API, the Windows Storage API is stream based. You can see in the previous excerpt that writing bytes to the file is achieved using the awaitable `Stream.WriteAsync` method.

You look at performing other IO operations using the Windows Storage API in Chapter 30, "Auto-Launching with File and Protocol Associations."

Measuring the Amount of Available Free Space

The `AvailableFreeSpace` property of the `IsolatedStorageFile` allows you to determine the amount of space remaining on the device. This property returns a long value indicating the number of bytes remaining.

The `Quota` property, of the `IsolatedStorageFile` class serves no real purpose because no storage limit is imposed on Windows Phone apps.

Application Settings

Saving objects in persistent state is such a common task that the isolated storage API includes an `IDictionary<string, object>` class named `IsolateStorageSettings` that is automatically persisted to isolated storage when your app is closed or tombstoned. `IsolateStorageSettings` is a convenient way to store global application state (see Figure 28.2).

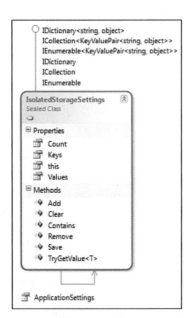

FIGURE 28.2   An app's `IsolatedStorageSettings` instance is retrieved using the `IsolatedStorageSettings.ApplicationSettings` property.

`IsolateStorageSettings` is a singleton, accessible via the `IsolatedStorageSettings.ApplicationSettings` property. The `ApplicationSettings` property can be used the same as you would any other `IDictionary`.

To place an object in persistent state, add a key/value pair to the collection, like so:

```
IsolatedStorageSettings.ApplicationSettings["Foo"] = "Bah";
```

To retrieve the item from persistent state, the following can be used:

```
string value = (string)IsolatedStorageSettings.ApplicationSettings["Foo"];
```

If it is uncertain whether an item exists in `ApplicationSettings`, use the `TryGetValue` method as shown:

```
string value;
if (!IsolatedStorageSettings.ApplicationSettings.TryGetValue("Foo",
                                                    out value))
{
    value = "Unknown";
}
```

The `Contains` method can also be used to test whether an item exists in the dictionary.

Serialization Requirements

Objects placed in `ApplicationSettings` have the same serialization requirements as transient application state (see Chapter 3, "Understanding the Application Execution Model"); data placed in `ApplicationSetting` must be a primitive type, a known serializable type (for example, `Decimal`), or be capable of being serialized using a `DataContractSerializer`. If an object is unable to be serialized, an exception is raised.

> **CAUTION**
>
> If even a single object in the `ApplicationSettings` raises an exception when the `IsolatedStorageSettings.Save` method is called, all settings are prevented from being saved.

When the user exits your app, Windows Phone automatically calls `Save` to preserve the `IsolatedStorageSettings` object so that it can be automatically reinstated when your application starts again.

Abstracting `IsolatedStorageSettings`

This section briefly touches on the topic of abstracting the `IsolatedStorageSettings` class. By providing a custom API for application settings, it decouples your code from the

28

.NET-specific `IsolatedStorageSettings` class and allows you to change the way settings are stored, thereby increasing the portability of your code.

The `IsolatedStorageSettings` class uses a `DataContractSerializer` that serializes objects using XML, which is significantly slower than, for example, a binary serializer.

In the Calcium project there exists an `ISettingsService` that includes methods to retrieve items from persistent storage. The Calcium settings API allows you to retrieve a value from isolated storage while supplying a default value, which is returned if no value exists, as shown in the following example:

```
var settingsService = Dependency.Resolve<ISettingsService>();
int exampleSetting = settingsService.GetSetting("Example Setting Key", 5);
```

The `GetSetting` method uses generics to return an object of the correct type, matching the default value's type.

To set a value, the `SetSetting` method is called like so:

```
settingsService.SetSetting("Example Setting Key", 2);
```

We do not delve deeper into the code in this chapter, but if you are interested in this topic, the source code is open source and freely available at http://calciumsdk.com.

Building an Automatic State Preservation System

App tombstoning presents a new challenge for developers moving to the Windows Phone platform. As the complexity of your app increases, so too does the task of preserving your app's transient and persistent state.

For this chapter, I have created an automatic state preservation system, which you are free to use. I intend to continue to refine and integrate it into the open source Calcium project.

The system presented in this section allows you to register properties for state preservation using a custom attribute. In addition, there is an API that uses lambda expressions for registering properties with nonpublic accessors and fields.

Using the system involves registering a property so that it is automatically saved and restored after tombstoning. This is done by decorating the property with the custom `Stateful` attribute, as shown in the following example:

```
[Stateful(ApplicationStateType.Persistent)]
public int SomeProperty { get; set; }
```

The `Stateful` attribute receives an `ApplicationStateType` value, which indicates the type of state persistency that the property requires. `ApplicationStateType` enum has the following two values:

▶ **Persistent**—State is saved to isolated storage.

▶ **Transient**—State is saved to the `PhoneApplicationService.Current.State`.

The attribute-based approach is the simplest way for preserving the state of a property. Yet, to register fields or inject custom logic, the `ViewModelBase` class also provides the methods shown in Table 28.2.

TABLE 28.2 `ViewModelBase` State Related Methods

Method Name	Description
RegisterStatefulProperty	Allows you to specify a property using a lambda expression and a type of application state that should be applied, either transient or persistent. Calling this method causes the property to be automatically saved and restored.
DeregisterStatefulProperty	Removes a property from the list of registered state properties.
RegisterState	Allows you to supply a `Func` for reading a value and an `Action` for writing a value. This method offers more flexibility than the `RegisterStatefulProperty` method and is suitable, for example, when a property does not have a public setter.
DeregisterState	Removes the set of delegates from the list of registered state delegates, identified by a string key.

The eBay Search example from the Chapter 27, "Communicating with Network Services," has been augmented to demonstrate the use of the state preservation system.

A `SearchCount` property has been added to the new `EbaySearchStateViewModel` (replacing the `EbaySearchViewModel`) to demonstrate the `State` attribute. This property is incremented each time a search takes place. It is preserved in isolated storage by using the `Stateful` attribute, as shown in the following excerpt:

```
[Stateful(ApplicationStateType.Persistent)]
public int SearchCount { get; set; }
```

When the viewmodel is instantiated, the `ViewModelBase` class identifies all properties that have been decorated with the attribute and registers them with a custom `ViewState` class.

Additionally, within the viewmodel's constructor there now exists various state registration statements. The first, shown in the following excerpt, registers the `SearchText` property for transient state preservation:

```
RegisterStatefulProperty(ApplicationStateType.Transient, () => SearchText);
```

A lambda expression is used to identify the property. As part of this call, the expression is deconstructed to determine the name of the property and to create the property accessor (get and set) delegates, which are used to retrieve and set the SearchText property during state preservation operations. If the app is deactivated, the SearchText property (and any other registered transient state properties) are placed in the PhoneApplicationService.State dictionary and reinstated if and when the app is reactivated.

In the following example, the Items collection is registered for transient state preservation:

```
RegisterStatefulProperty(
    ApplicationStateType.Transient, () => Items, x => Items = x);
```

Persisting an object to isolated storage works in the same way; however, we specify that the value is to be placed in persistent storage using the Persistent enum value, as shown:

```
RegisterStatefulProperty(
    ApplicationStateType.Persistent, () => SearchCount);
```

Customizing ViewModel State Preservation

A viewmodel has the opportunity to customize how its state is persisted by overriding the SaveState method from the ViewModelBase class, as shown:

```
public override void SaveState(
    IDictionary<string, object> persistentDictionary,
    IDictionary<string, object> transientDictionary)
{
    base.LoadState(persistentDictionary, transientDictionary);
    byte[] state = Serialize(items);
    transientDictionary[itemsStateKey] = state;
    transientDictionary[queryStateKey] = lastQuery;
}
```

The Serialize and Deserialize methods of the ViewModelBase class are able to convert an object to and from an array. The serialization mechanism is discussed in more detail in the next section.

Conversely, a viewmodel may restore its own state by overriding the LoadState method, as shown in the following example:

```
public override void LoadState(
    IDictionary<string, object> persistentDictionary,
    IDictionary<string, object> transientDictionary)
{
    base.SaveState(persistentDictionary, transientDictionary);
    object state;
    if (transientDictionary.TryGetValue(itemsStateKey, out state))
```

```
    {
        byte[] bytes = state as byte[];
        Items = Deserialize<ObservableCollection<Item>>(bytes);
    }

    if (transientDictionary.TryGetValue(queryStateKey, out state))
    {
        lastQuery = (string)state;
        SearchText = lastQuery;
    }
}
```

Automatic State Preservation Inner Workings

This section looks at how the state preservation system works behind the scenes. You see how properties decorated with the Stateful attribute are identified and how delegates for property accessors are created to store and retrieve property value. You also see how a custom ViewState class is used to load and save state via the ViewModelBase class.

The following sections are advanced in nature. Feel free to skip ahead. If you choose to use the custom state preservation system, you may return to this chapter at a later time.

Identifying Stateful ViewModels

The custom IStatePreservation interface is implemented by viewmodels that want to save and restore state. If a viewmodel implements IStatePreservation it has its LoadState or SaveState method called during page navigation.

LoadState and SaveState accept two parameters: a persistent state dictionary, which is normally the IsolatedStorageSettings.ApplicationSettings dictionary, and a transient state dictionary, which is normally the PhoneApplicationService state dictionary.

To coordinate this activity the custom StateManager class is used. When the application starts, the StateManager class subscribes to the relevant navigation events of the PhoneApplicationFrame, as shown:

```
public static void Initialize()
{
    PhoneApplicationService.Current.Deactivated += OnDeactivated;
    var frame = (PhoneApplicationFrame)Application.Current.RootVisual;
    frame.Navigating += OnNavigating;
    frame.Navigated += OnNavigated;
}
```

When navigating away from a page, the StateManager requests that the associated viewmodel save its state, if it implements IStatePreservation:

```
static void OnNavigating(object sender, NavigatingCancelEventArgs e)
```

28

```
{
    var frame = (PhoneApplicationFrame)Application.Current.RootVisual;
    var element = frame.Content as FrameworkElement;
    if (element != null)
    {
        IStatePreservation preserver
            = element.DataContext as IStatePreservation;
        if (preserver != null)
        {
            preserver.SaveState(
                IsolatedStorageSettings.ApplicationSettings,
                PhoneApplicationService.Current.State);
        }
    }
}
```

When navigating to a page, the `StateManager` requests that the viewmodel load its state:

```
static void OnNavigated(object sender, NavigationEventArgs e)
{
    var element = e.Content as FrameworkElement;
    if (element != null)
    {
        IStatePreservation statePreservation
            = element.DataContext as IStatePreservation;
        if (statePreservation != null)
        {
            statePreservation.LoadState(
                IsolatedStorageSettings.ApplicationSettings,
                PhoneApplicationService.Current.State);
        }
    }
}
```

It is not necessary to implement `IStatePreservation` on each viewmodel because the `ViewModelBase` class implements it. When the `ViewModelBase` class is instantiated, it locates all attributes decorated with the `StateFul` attribute and registers those properties with the custom `ViewState` class. The `ProperyInfo` class is used to create a delegate for both the get and set property accessors, as shown in the following excerpt:

```
void ReadStateAttributes()
{
    var properties = GetType().GetProperties();

    foreach (PropertyInfo propertyInfo in properties)
    {
```

```
            object[] attributes = propertyInfo.GetCustomAttributes(
                            typeof(StatefulAttribute), true);

            if (attributes.Length <= 0)
            {
                continue;
            }

            StatefulAttribute attribute
                = (StatefulAttribute)attributes[0];
            var persistenceType = attribute.StateType;

            if (!propertyInfo.CanRead || !propertyInfo.CanWrite)
            {
                throw new InvalidOperationException(string.Format(
                    "Property {0} must have a getter and a setter.",
                    propertyInfo.Name));
            }

            /* Prevents access to internal closure warning. */
            PropertyInfo info = propertyInfo;

            viewState.RegisterState(
                propertyInfo.Name,
                () => info.GetValue(this, null),
                obj => info.SetValue(this, obj, null),
                persistenceType);
        }
}
```

The `ViewState` class provides thread state access to two dictionaries: one for persistent state; the other for transient state. The `RegisterState` method places the `Func` and `Action` associated with the state into its respective dictionary, as shown:

```
public void RegisterState<T>(
    string stateKey,
    Func<T> getterFunc,
    Action<T> setterAction,
    ApplicationStateType stateType)
{
    ArgumentValidator.AssertNotNull(stateKey, "propertyName");
    ArgumentValidator.AssertNotNull(getterFunc, "propertyGetterFunc");
    ArgumentValidator.AssertNotNull(setterAction, "propertySetterAction");

    if (stateType == ApplicationStateType.Persistent)
    {
```

```
        lock (persistentStateLock)
        {
            persistentState[stateKey]
                = new Accessor<T>(getterFunc, setterAction);
        }
    }
    else
    {
        lock (transientStateLock)
        {
            transientState[stateKey]
                = new Accessor<T>(getterFunc, setterAction);
        }
    }
}
```

The nested Accessor class is a container for a Func and an Action and is usually populated with lambda expressions for the getter and setter of a viewmodel property. The following excerpt shows the nested Accessor class:

```
class Accessor<T> : IStateAccessor
{
    readonly Func<T> getter;
    readonly Action<T> setter;

    public Accessor(Func<T> getter, Action<T> setter)
    {
        this.getter = getter;
        this.setter = setter;
    }

    public object Value
    {
        get
        {
            return getter();
        }
        set
        {
            setter((T)value);
        }
    }
}
```

When the `StateManager` calls the `IStatePreservation.SaveState` method of the `ViewModelBase` instance, the `ViewModelBase` class calls the `ViewState` object's `SavePersistentState` and `SaveTransientState` methods, which are shown in the following excerpt:

```
public void SavePersistentState(IDictionary<string, object> stateDictionary)
{
    SaveState(stateDictionary, persistentState, persistentStateLock);
}

public void SaveTransientState(IDictionary<string, object> stateDictionary)
{
    SaveState(stateDictionary, transientState, transientStateLock);
}
```

The `ViewState.SaveState` method enumerates the `Accessor` objects in the specified `accessors` dictionary and resolves the value to be serialized using the `Accessor.Value` property. The value is serialized to a byte array, which is then stored in the specified state dictionary, as shown in the following excerpt:

```
void SaveState(
        IDictionary<string, object> stateDictionary,
        Dictionary<string, IStateAccessor> accessors,
        object propertiesLock)
{
    lock (propertiesLock)
    {
        foreach (KeyValuePair<string, IStateAccessor> pair in accessors)
        {
            string stateKey = pair.Key;
            IStateAccessor accessor = pair.Value;

            object accessorValue = accessor.Value;

            if (accessorValue == null)
            {
                stateDictionary.Remove(stateKey);
                continue;
            }

            byte[] bytes;
            try
            {
                bytes = Serialize(accessorValue);
            }
            catch (Exception ex)
```

28

```
        {
            stateDictionary[pair.Key] = null;
            Debug.Assert(false,
                        "Unable to serialize state value. " + ex);
            continue;
        }

        stateDictionary[stateKey] = bytes;
    }
  }
}
```

Using the Silverlight Serializer for Binary Serialization

Mike Talbot's Silverlight Serializer is used in the sample code to serialize objects. The Silverlight Serializer has better performance and is easier to use than the built-in `DataContractSerializer`.

See http://whydoidoit.com/silverlight-serialize for more information on the Silverlight Serializer.

When using the Silverlight Serializer, an object can be converted to and from a byte array without the need to decorate it with a myriad of `DataMember` attributes, as is necessary with the `DataContractSerializer`.

The `SilverlightSerializer` class is used in the custom `ViewState` class to serialize and deserialize viewmodel data, as shown in the following excerpt:

```
protected byte[] Serialize(object value)
{
    byte[] state = SilverlightSerializer.Serialize(value);
    return state;
}

protected T Deserialize<T>(byte[] data) where T : class
{
    T result = SilverlightSerializer.Deserialize<T>(data);
    return result;
}
```

Within the `ViewState` class, state restoration works in much the same way as state persistence, but in reverse. We enumerate over the `Accessor` objects and attempt to retrieve a corresponding state value from the state dictionary. This value is then converted from a byte array to an object using the `Deserialize` method, as shown in the following excerpt:

```
void LoadState(
        IDictionary<string, object> stateDictionary,
        Dictionary<string, IStateAccessor> accessors,
```

```
        object propertiesLock)
{
    lock (propertiesLock)
    {
        foreach (KeyValuePair<string, IStateAccessor> pair in accessors)
        {
            object stateValue;
            string stateKey = pair.Key;
            IStateAccessor accessor = pair.Value;

            if (!stateDictionary.TryGetValue(stateKey, out stateValue))
            {
                continue;
            }
            byte[] bytes = stateValue as byte[];

            if (bytes == null)
            {
                Debug.Assert(false, "state value is not a byte[]");
                continue;
            }

            object deserializedValue;
            try
            {
                deserializedValue = Deserialize(bytes);
            }
            catch (Exception ex)
            {
                string message = "Unable to deserialize bytes. " + ex;
                    ➥Debug.Assert(false, message);
                continue;
            }

            if (deserializedValue == null)
            {
                const string message
                    = "Deserialized object should not be null.";
                    ➥Debug.Assert(false, message);
                continue;
            }

            try
            {
                accessor.Value = deserializedValue;
            }
```

```
            catch (Exception ex)
            {
                Console.WriteLine("Unable to set state value. " + ex);
                continue;
            }
        }
    }
}
```

The ViewModelBase class includes various state registration methods that can be used instead of the State attribute to specify stateful properties. The RegisterStatefulProperty method, for example, allows you to specify a stateful property using a lambda expression, as shown in the following example:

```
RegisterStatefulProperty(ApplicationStateType.Transient, () => SearchText);
```

The RegisterStatefulProperty method has an optional setAction parameter, which allows you to provide an alternative handler for setting the value; this is useful for properties that lack a public set accessor. The RegisterStatefulProperty calls the overloaded private method by the same name, as shown:

```
protected void RegisterStatefulProperty<TProperty>(
    ApplicationStateType applicationStateType,
    Expression<Func<TProperty>> expression,
    Action<TProperty> setAction = null)
{
    RegisterStatefulProperty((name, getter, setter)
        => viewState.RegisterState(
                name, getter, setter, applicationStateType),
            expression, setAction);
}
```

The private RegisterStatefulProperty method retrieves the PropertyInfo instance for the expression (described in the next section) and uses it to create delegates for the property accessors. It then invokes the specified registerAction, which, in this case, is a call to viewState.RegisterState. The RegisterStatefulProperty method is shown in the following excerpt:

```
void RegisterStatefulProperty<T>(
    Action<string, Func<T>, Action<T>> registerAction,
    Expression<Func<T>> expression, Action<T> setAction = null)
{
    ArgumentValidator.AssertNotNull(registerAction, "registerAction");
    ArgumentValidator.AssertNotNull(expression, "expression");

    PropertyInfo propertyInfo = PropertyUtility.GetPropertyInfo(expression);
```

```
string name = propertyInfo.Name;
var propertyGetterFunc = propertyInfo.CreateGetter<T>(this);


if (setAction == null)
{
    try
    {
        setAction = propertyInfo.CreateSetter<T>(this);
    }
    catch (Exception ex)
    {
        string message = string.Format(
            "Unable to get setter for property '{0}' {1} ", name, ex);
        Console.WriteLine(message);
        Debug.Assert(false, message);
        return;
    }
}
registerAction(name, propertyGetterFunc, setAction);
}
```

Unwinding a Property Lambda Expression

Resolving a property's name and creating delegates for its get and set property accessors involves unwinding of the Lambda expression and retrieving the `PropertyInfo` instance. In the sample code, this is done using the custom `PropertyUtility.GetPropertyInfo` method, which retrieves the `PropertyInfo` instance from the expression's `Member` property, as shown:

```
public static PropertyInfo GetPropertyInfo<T>(Expression<Func<T>> expression)
{
    var memberExpression = expression.Body as MemberExpression;
    if (memberExpression == null)
    {
        throw new ArgumentException(
            "MemberExpression expected.", "expression");
    }

    if (memberExpression.Member == null)
    {
        throw new ArgumentException("Member should not be null.");
    }

    if (memberExpression.Member.MemberType != MemberTypes.Property)
    {
        throw new ArgumentException("Property expected.", "expression");
```

```
    }

    PropertyInfo propertyInfo = (PropertyInfo)memberExpression.Member;
    return propertyInfo;
}
```

Creating Property Accessor Delegates

When the `PropertyInfo` instance has been obtained, it is used to create a delegate for the get and set accessors. For this the `Delegate.CreateDelegate` method is used, via a custom `PropertyInfo` extension method called `CreateGetter`, in the `PropertyUtility` class. Within the `CreateGetter` method, the type argument, required by the `Delegate.CreateDelegate` method, is generated using the `Expression.GetFuncType` method. If the property is of type string, for example, a type representing a `Func<string>` is produced. See the following excerpt:

```
public static Func<TProperty> CreateGetter<TProperty>(
    this PropertyInfo propertyInfo, object owner)
{

    ArgumentValidator.AssertNotNull(propertyInfo, "propertyInfo");
    ArgumentValidator.AssertNotNull(owner, "owner");

    Type getterType = Expression.GetFuncType(
                    new[] { propertyInfo.PropertyType });

    object getter = Delegate.CreateDelegate(
                    getterType, owner, propertyInfo.GetGetMethod());

    return (Func<TProperty>)getter;
}
```

The `Expression.GetFuncType` method is also equivalent to the `Type` method `MakeGenericType`, which could have been used instead, like so:

```
Type getterType = typeof(Func<>).MakeGenericType(propertyInfo.PropertyType);
```

Creating a delegate for the set accessor means resolving the generic `Action` type in the same manner:

```
public static Action<TProperty> CreateSetter<TProperty>(
    this PropertyInfo propertyInfo, object owner)
{

    ArgumentValidator.AssertNotNull(propertyInfo, "propertyInfo");
    ArgumentValidator.AssertNotNull(owner, "owner");

    var propertyType = propertyInfo.PropertyType;
```

```
var setterType = Expression.GetActionType(new[] { propertyType });

Delegate setter = Delegate.CreateDelegate(
        setterType, owner, propertyInfo.GetSetMethod());

return (Action<TProperty>)setter;
}
```

These two methods provide the delegates that are retained by the `ViewState` class.

Summary

This chapter began with a conceptual overview of the local folder and looks at managing files and directories within the data store. You saw how to read and write files using the .NET Isolated Storage API, and you were introduced to the new Windows Storage API present in Windows Phone 8. You then explored the `IsolatedStorageSettings` class and saw how it is used to automatically persist application settings.

The chapter examined a custom state preservation system, which uses an attribute-based mechanism for preserving viewmodel property values automatically. You saw that by decorating your viewmodel's properties with an attribute, the property's value can be preserved using binary serialization, either transiently using an OS managed `State` dictionary or persistently in isolated storage.

Finally, you saw how the custom state preservation API is used to preserve fields and to inject logic during state operations.

28

CHAPTER 29

Storing App Data in a Local Database

For some apps, having to rely on a cloud service for storing application data is not practical. Some scenarios cry out for local storage of structured data on the phone.

With the Mango release of Windows Phone (7.5), Microsoft introduced a relational database system to the phone, allowing you to place a local database in either isolated storage or in your app's XAP file.

Windows Phone apps use LINQ to SQL for all database operations; LINQ to SQL is used to define the database schema and to select, insert, update, and delete data from the database. LINQ to SQL provides an object-oriented approach to working with relational data and is composed of an object model and a runtime. With LINQ to SQL, classes represent database tables, and foreign key relationships between tables are represented by aggregated collections.

This chapter begins with an overview of how local databases are deployed to the phone and discusses the main elements of LINQ to SQL.

The chapter then explores the code-first approach to data model creation and walks through a sample Twitter timeline viewer that caches data in a local database, during which you explore several facets of LINQ to SQL, including entity creation, change tracking, and entity multiplicity (one-to-many relationships).

The database-first approach to data model creation is then discussed. You see how to retrieve a local database file from isolated storage and how to use the SqlMetal tool to generate a data model from a database.

The chapter then takes a short deviation and examines a custom navigation service that allows navigation from a viewmodel without being coupled to the built-in navigation of the phone, which can increase the testability of your viewmodel classes.

The chapter then gets back on topic to examine a technique for observing LINQ to SQL queries using a custom log. You see how to upgrade a schema without losing data, and you learn how to use version numbering to provide incremental updates to your database schema.

Finally, you look at mapping inheritance hierarchies using LINQ to SQL and at concurrency and conflict detection when performing updates.

SQL Server Compact

The database used on the phone is based on SQL Server Compact Edition (SQL CE). SQL CE shares a common API with the other Microsoft SQL Server editions. Each SQL CE database resides in a single .sdf file, which can be up to 4GB in size. The .sdf file can be encrypted, using a password, with 128-bit encryption for data security.

NOTE

On Windows Phone, the database filename is required to use the .sdf file extension. A `NotSupportedException` is raised if you attempt to create a database with a name not ending in .sdf.

Deployment of Local Databases

Understanding how local databases can be deployed to the phone is important when determining the best approach for your app. This section looks behind the scenes at what happens when an app is installed on the phone, and at the two locations for local database deployment.

It so happens that a XAP file, which is produced when you build your project, is also a Zip file. When an app is installed on the phone, the *package manager* extracts the app's XAP file into an install directory (see Figure 29.1).

For more information on XAP files, see the section "Understanding the Role of XAP Files" in Chapter 2, "Fundamental Concepts in Windows Phone Development."

The install directory is read-only. An app is not able to add or remove items from its install directory, nor is it able to make any changes to any items in the directory.

During installation, the app is also assigned a data directory. The contents of this directory and all subdirectories are readable and writable by the app.

NOTE

An app's root directory and all contents therein are off-limits to any other app.

FIGURE 29.1   Install and Application Data directories.

A local database can be placed either in isolated storage or in the app's install directory by including it within the XAP. You see why the choice of where to place a local database is important in a moment.

An app's data directory is persistent, whereas its install directory is not. When publishing an update for your app on the Windows Phone Marketplace, the install directory of your app is replaced, but the data directory for your app remains intact.

Moreover, when placed in the install directory, a database is read-only. This suits certain scenarios, such as when you want to include structured reference data with your app, data that may change with each application update but that is not modifiable by the app itself. An example of this kind of data is a dictionary of word definitions.

The most common place for a database, however, is in isolated storage. When in isolated storage the database is readable and writable and is retained during an app update.

There are two common scenarios for deploying a database to isolated storage. The first is where your app has a complex domain model and you want to persist its state. Perhaps your app is a shopping cart or a to-do list. The second scenario is where you fetch a subset of reference data from the cloud, cache it locally, and combine it with user-specific data.

This chapter demonstrates each deployment option and focuses on using a local database as a cache by creating a Twitter app that downloads timeline information and caches it in a database so that it is available when the phone is offline.

29

LINQ to SQL on the Phone

Retrieval and storage of data in a local database is done entirely using LINQ to SQL, which provides object-relational mapping (ORM) capabilities, allowing you to use LINQ to communicate with a relational database. LINQ to SQL maps the object model, which you define by decorating entity classes with attributes, to a relational database. When your app runs, LINQ to SQL translates language-integrated queries into Transact-SQL and then sends the queries to the database for execution. When the database returns the results, LINQ to SQL translates the results back to objects.

When first learning of Microsoft's choice to go with LINQ to SQL in Windows Phone, I was somewhat dismayed that it was chosen over the Entity Framework. Yet, while the Entity Framework offers a more powerful API and set of tools, it is not optimized for mobile devices. I have since come to see LINQ to SQL as a good fit for the phone, because it offers a simple API for rapid data layer construction.

LINQ to SQL makes heavy use of the `System.Data.Linq.DataContext` class, which serves as a proxy to your database, allowing you to query the database via `Table` objects representing tables in the database (see Figure 29.2). Each `Table` member of a `DataContext` allows the storage and retrieval of entity objects; an instance of an entity represents a table row. Persisting changes to the local database is done using the `DataContext.SubmitChanges` method.

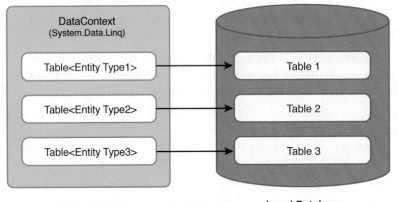

FIGURE 29.2   `DataContext` `Table` members are associated with database tables.

By default, `DataContext` also tracks changes to your entity objects so that you can easily push changes back to your database.

An entity is a POCO (Plain Old CLR Object), representing a domain object, and is decorated with a `System.Data.Linq.Mapping.Table` attribute. Other data related attributes, placed on and within each entity class, define the mapping between the object model and the schema of the database, and determine the structure of the database.

LINQ to SQL Platform Differences

Windows Phone supports most of the features of LINQ to SQL, apart from several notable absences present on other platforms and some additional features not seen in LINQ to SQL on other platforms. The following is a list of some of the most notable differences:

▶ LINQ to SQL on Windows Phone does not directly support the execution of Transact-SQL, which includes Data Definition Language (DDL) and Data Modeling Language (DML) statements.

▶ Local databases run in your app's process and not in a background process, as is the case with most desktop-based databases.

▶ A local database cannot be accessed by other apps; it lives in the sandboxed execution environment of your app.

▶ Transactions are not directly supported.

For more detailed information on the various API differences, see http://bit.ly/xQMxmm.

New features have also been added to LINQ to SQL, specifically for Windows Phone apps. These include support for multiple table indexes and the ability to programmatically alter the database schema (described later in this chapter).

Getting Started with Local Databases

Using LINQ to SQL in your phone app requires referencing the assembly `System.Data.Linq`, which is included in the Windows Phone Framework Class Library (FCL).

There are two commonly used approaches to the creation of an application's data model: code-first and database-first. Code-first entails writing your classes first, and then using those classes to generate the database. Conversely, database-first entails creating your database schema and then using a tool to generate an object model for interacting with the database. The database-first approach is discussed later in the chapter. For now, though, we concentrate on the code-first approach.

Code-First Data Model Creation

Code-first is the recommended approach for creating your data model in Windows Phone. It involves writing your classes and then generating your database using metadata contained in those classes.

Until now I have never been a fan of code-first when building desktop and client/server applications, because I saw how it can lead to a lack of attention being paid to the database schema—to its structure, constraints, and indexes. Yet, applied wisely, code-first offers some key advantages. One such advantage is that you do not break the application by forgetting to propagate a schema change to other developers on your team, because all changes to the schema are done via code metadata.

The following list outlines the steps for creating a data model and generating a database using the code-first approach and LINQ to SQL:

1. Manually create POCO classes representing your domain entities.

2. Create a class deriving from `DataContext`, with properties within the class representing tables within the database.

3. When instantiating your `DataContext`, provide a connection string with the location of your database file in isolated storage. The `DataContext` creates a database with the relationships defined in your data model.

After the database is in place, you are able to interact with the `DataContext` and the entity objects using LINQ to SQL.

The following section looks at each of these steps in detail, during the creation of a sample Twitter timeline viewer.

Sample Twitter Timeline Viewer

The principle example for this chapter is a Twitter timeline viewer that downloads the tweets of a specified Twitter user, caches them in a local database, and displays them on a page. The code for this example is located in the DataDrivenApps/TwitterExample directory of the WPUnleashed.Examples project.

The Twitter timeline viewer has a simple data model consisting of two entities representing a Twitter user and a tweet or `TimelineItem` (see Figure 29.3), and it demonstrates using a local database to cache cloud data.

FIGURE 29.3   A `TwitterUser` has many `TimelineItems`.

`TimelineItem` represents a status update (tweet) that contains information including the tweet text, the time the tweet occurred, and the user's id (see Listing 29.1). The `TwitterUser` class holds a collection, specifically an `EntitySet` of `TimelineItem` objects.

LISTING 29.1   `TimelineItem` Class (excerpt)

```
[Table]
public class TimelineItem : NotifyPropertyChangeBase
{
    string id;

    [Column(IsPrimaryKey = true)]
    public string Id
    {
```

```csharp
    get
    {
        return id;
    }
    set
    {
        Assign(ref id, value);
    }
}

string text;

[Column(DbType = "NVarChar(140)")]
public string Text
{
    get
    {
        return text;
    }
    set
    {
        Assign(ref text, value);
    }
}
DateTime? receivedTime;

[Column]
public DateTime? ReceivedTime
{
    get
    {
        return receivedTime;
    }
    set
    {
        Assign(ref receivedTime, value);
    }
}

string twitterUserId;

[Column(CanBeNull = false)]
public string TwitterUserId
{
    get
    {
```

```
            return twitterUserId;
        }
        set
        {
            Assign(ref twitterUserId, value);
        }
    }

    EntityRef<TwitterUser> user;

    [Association(Storage = "user",
                 ThisKey = "TwitterUserId",
                 IsForeignKey = true)]
    public TwitterUser TwitterUser
    {
        get
        {
            return user.Entity;
        }
        set
        {
            user.Entity = value;
        }
    }
}
```

To declare the TimelineItem class as representing a table in the database, it is decorated with a Table attribute. The TableAttribute class includes a Name property, which allows you to explicitly define the name of the database table. If it is not provided, the name of the class is used as the table name. For example, to override the TimelineItem table name to something else, the following could be used:

```
[Table(Name = "SomethingElse")]
public class TimelineItem : NotifyPropertyChangeBase
{ ... }
```

Using the Column Attribute

Each property of the TimelineItem is decorated with a Column attribute, which tells the DataContext that the property is stored in a column by the same name. As with TableAttribute, you can use its Name property to specify a different name for the column in the database.

ColumnAttribute includes various other properties described in the following sections.

IsPrimaryKey

`IsPrimaryKey` is used to designate the member or members of the entity class that compose the primary key of the table. Composite keys are also supported by supplying more than one property decorated with a `Column` attribute with `IsPrimaryKey` set to true.

At least one member of an entity class must be designated as the primary key, or else the entity is deemed to be read-only. If an attempt is made to create, update, or delete a read-only entity, an `InvalidOperationException` is raised.

AutoSync

`AutoSync` is used to specify whether the column is automatically synchronized from the value generated by the database on insert or update commands.

The following is a list of valid values for this property:

- ▶ `Default`

- ▶ `Always`

- ▶ `Never`

- ▶ `OnInsert`

- ▶ `OnUpdate`

If the column in your database provides a default value, set this property to `OnInsert`, `OnUpdate`, or `Always`.

CanBeNull

`CanBeNull` indicates whether a column can contain null values. This property is relevant when inserting data into the database, but not during the creation of the table.

> **NOTE**
>
> The `DataContext.CreateDatabase` method uses only the `ColumnAttribute.DbType` property, and not the `ColumnAttribute.CanBeNull` property when determining whether a column should allow null values. For this reason, you must specify whether a column can contain null values in the `DbType` property as well as setting `CanBeNull` to true.

If not specified, `CanBeNull` defaults to true if the member is a reference type; if the member is a value type, such as an `int`, then `CanBeNull` defaults to false.

DbType

`DbType` specifies the text that defines the column in a Transact-SQL create table statement. Using this property allows you to tailor a column data type to better match the data being stored in the column. If used correctly it can help to decrease the size of your database and may improve the speed of some queries.

For example, by not specifying the `DbType` of a string property, LINQ to SQL generates DDL for a column containing up to 4000 Unicode characters (*NVARCHAR(4000)*). If you,

29

however, know that a field will always contain values of relatively the same length (within two characters difference), then NCHAR can be faster and more space efficient for data, and it may pay dividends to specify it using `DbType`.

NOTE

SQL CE is a Unicode-only database, so you must use Unicode data types when assigning the `DbType` property. In particular, use NVARCHAR instead of VARCHAR, and NCHAR instead of CHAR.

Expression

`Expression` allows you to automatically populate a field using a SQL expression. Use this property to define a column as containing computed values when you use `DataContext.CreateDatabase` to generate your database.

For example, if you want to create a column defined in SQL as *InventoryValue AS UnitPrice * UnitsInStock*, use the following `Expression` string:

```
UnitPrice * UnitsInStock
```

NOTE

LINQ to SQL does not support computed columns as primary keys.

IsDbGenerated

Entity members with `IsDbGenerated` are synchronized immediately after the row of data, representing the entity, is inserted into the database. The entity member's value is set when `DataContext.SubmitChanges` completes.

IsDescriminator

`IsDescriminator` is used in conjunction with the `InheritanceMapping` attribute to provide an inheritance hierarchy in your data model. For more information, see the section "Mapping an Inheritance Hierarchy," later in this chapter.

IsVersion

`IsVersion` allows you to designate an entity class member to be used for optimistic concurrency control (OCC). This property is discussed in the later section "Concurrency."

UpdateCheck

`UpdateCheck` tells the data context when to detect change conflicts. This property is discussed in the later section "Concurrency."

Data Context Change Tracking

The dirty state of an entity is monitored by the data context. This is usually accomplished with change notifications, provided through the `INotifyPropertyChanging.PropertyChanging` and `INotifyPropertyChanged.PropertyChanged` events, raised in the property setters of the entity.

Combining the `PropertyChanged` and `PropertyChanging` events raising into every property setter can add up to a lot of plumbing code. Fortunately the `Assign` method, in the custom `ViewModelBase` class, used throughout this book, raises the events required for change tracking.

For more information on the property change notification, in relation to the `ViewModelBase` class, see Chapter 2.

For entities that do not implement `INotifyPropertyChanging`, LINQ to SQL maintains a copy of their values. When `DataContext.SubmitChanges` is called, the current and original values are compared to determine whether the object has changed.

> **TIP**
>
> To decrease the amount of memory used by your app, ensure that entity classes implement `INotifyPropertyChanged` and `INotifyPropertyChanging`.

`TwitterUser` Class

The `TwitterUser` class contains various properties, such as the screen name of the Twitter user. It also includes a collection of `TimelineItem` objects that are maintained using an `EntitySet`. An `EntitySet` provides for deferred loading and manages the relationship of the collection side of one-to-many relationships between entities.

The `TwitterUser` constructor initializes the `EntitySet`, specifying two handlers: one that is called when a `TimelineItem` is added to its collection; the other when a `TimelineItem` is removed (see Listing 29.2).

The `TwitterUser` class also uses the `Index` attribute, which tells the `DataContext` to create a database index for the secondary column ScreenName.

Indexes improve the speed of data retrieval operations by allowing the database engine to quickly locate a record. Without an index, potentially all rows in a table need to be scanned, an expensive O(n) operation.[1]

LISTING 29.2   `TwitterUser` Class (excerpt)

```
[Table]
[Index(Columns = "ScreenName")]
```

---

1. *O(n) describes algorithm complexity. For more information on Big O notation see http://en.wikipedia.org/wiki/Big_O_notation.*

29

```csharp
public class TwitterUser : NotifyPropertyChangeBase
{
    public TwitterUser()
    {
        timelineItems = new EntitySet<TimelineItem>(
                                AttachTimelineItem, DetachTimelineItems);
    }

    string id;

    [Column(IsPrimaryKey = true)]
    public string Id
    {
        get
        {
            return id;
        }
        set
        {
            Assign(ref id, value);
        }
    }
    string screenName;

    [Column]
    public string ScreenName
    {
        get
        {
            return screenName;
        }
        set
        {
            Assign(ref screenName, value);
        }
    }

... (ImageUrl and Description properties omitted)

    readonly EntitySet<TimelineItem> timelineItems;

    [Association(
        Storage = "timelineItems",
        OtherKey = "TwitterUserId")]
    public EntitySet<TimelineItem> TimelineItems
    {
```

```
        get
        {
            return timelineItems;
        }
        set
        {
            timelineItems.Assign(value);
        }
    }

    void AttachTimelineItem(TimelineItem entity)
    {
        OnPropertyChanging("TimelineItems", timelineItems, timelineItems);
        entity.TwitterUser = this;
        OnPropertyChanged("TimelineItems");
    }

    void DetachTimelineItems(TimelineItem entity)
    {
        OnPropertyChanging("TimelineItems", timelineItems, null);
        entity.TwitterUser = null;
        OnPropertyChanged("TimelineItems");
    }
}
```

The `PropertyChanging` event is raised manually before the assignment of the `TimelineItem.TwitterUser` property, and the `PropertyChanged` event is raised after it has been assigned. These calls indicate to the change tracking infrastructure that the `TwitterUser` object is dirty and differs from the stored value in the database.

Multiplicity and the `Association` Attribute

One-to-many entity relationships can be defined by decorating entity properties with `Association` attributes. Two entities participating in a one-to-many relationship with each other each use properties of the `Association` attribute to indicate on which side each resides.

One-to-many entity relationships are represented as foreign key relationships in the database.

The one-to-many relationship between `TwitterUser` and `TimelineItem` is defined with an `Association` attribute placed on the `TwitterUser` property of the `TimelineItem` class. The attribute declares that the `TwitterUserId` column of the `TimelineItem` table is a foreign key of the `TwitterUser` table. It also declares that the user field holds a reference (an `EntityRef`) to a `TwitterUser` object.

Conversely, on the many side of the relationship, the `TwitterUser` property of the `TimelineItem` declares that the `TwitterUserId` property holds the foreign key of the `TwitterUser`.

An `EntityRef` represents the one side of a one-to-many relationship, whereas an `EntitySet` is the reciprocal and represents the many side.

Twitter `DataContext`

The `TwitterDataContext` class is the proxy to the Twitter local database and includes two public `Table<TSource>` properties: `TwitterUsers` and `TimelineItems` (see Listing 29.3).

The assignment of the `DataContext.Log` property allows you to monitor the activities of the `DataContext` at runtime, and in particular, to observe the generated SQL as it is being sent to the database. This customized logging is examined later in the chapter.

The `GetTable` property of the `DataContext` class retrieves a `Table<TEntity>` object representing a table in the underlying database. `Table` objects can be queried using LINQ to SQL.

LISTING 29.3   `TwitterDataContext` Class

```
public class TwitterDataContext : DataContext
{
    public TwitterDataContext(string connection) : base(connection)
    {
        Log = new DebugStreamWriter();
    }

    public Table<TwitterUser> TwitterUsers
    {
        get
        {
            return GetTable<TwitterUser>();
        }
    }

    public Table<TimelineItem> TimelineItems
    {
        get
        {
            return GetTable<TimelineItem>();
        }
    }

}
```

The `Table<TEntity>` class allows you to perform CRUD (create, read, update, delete) operations on a table. For example, you can insert a row (representing an entity) into the underlying table using the `Table.InsertOnSubmit(TEntity entity)` method.

The `Table<TEntity>` class also allows you to attach a disconnected (or detached) entity to a new `DataContext`.

As an aside, the `DataContext` base class automatically initializes its public fields of type `Table<TEntity>`. By placing a public field in a `DataContext` derived class, such as the following, the field is automatically assigned when the `DataContext` is instantiated:

```
public Table<TwitterUser>;
```

Although this offers a way of exposing `Table` objects from your `DataContext` using less code, the use of public fields is not recommended because it breaks the convention that fields should have private visibility; nonprivate fields violate the encapsulation of the class and make the class less amenable to change.

Database Utilities

Whereas `DataContext` enables you to create and delete a database file, a custom class, called `DatabaseUtility`, is used to directly create and delete the database in isolated storage and to build the connection string for the database.

`TwitterDatabaseUtility` extends the `DatabaseUtility` class, providing the default database filename. `TwitterDatabaseUtility` is used in various locations to create a `DataContext` for the Twitter database.

`DatabaseUtility` includes an `InitializeDatabase` method that creates the isolated storage file for the database. When it is called, if the `wipe` parameter is true and the database already exists, it is deleted before being re-created. See the following excerpt:

```
public void InitializeDatabase(DataContext dataContext, bool wipe = false)
{
    ArgumentValidator.AssertNotNull(dataContext, "dataContext");

    if (localDatabaseMode != LocalDatabaseMode.ReadWrite
        && localDatabaseMode != LocalDatabaseMode.Exclusive)
    {
        return;
    }
```

29

```
    if (wipe && dataContext.DatabaseExists())
    {
        dataContext.DeleteDatabase();
    }

    if (!dataContext.DatabaseExists())
    {
        dataContext.CreateDatabase();
    }
}
```

Initialization of the local database occurs when the `Launching` event of the `PhoneApplicationService` is raised. For testing purposes, if a debugger is attached, the database is deleted so as to begin with a clean slate. The following excerpt shows the `Launching` event handler:

```
void Application_Launching(object sender, LaunchingEventArgs e)
{
    Debug.WriteLine("Application Launching");

    StateManager.Initialize();

    /* For the Twitter demo. */
    var twitterDatabaseUtility = new TwitterDatabaseUtility();
    bool wipeDatabase = Debugger.IsAttached;
    twitterDatabaseUtility.InitializeDatabase(wipeDatabase);
}
```

When the app is launched, the handler ensures that the database file is created in isolated storage.

Connection Strings

When instantiating a `DataContext`, a connection string must be supplied, indicating the location of the database file and an optional password. See the following example:

```
string connectionString
  = "Data Source='isostore:/DirectoryName/FileName.sdf';Password='password'";
DataContext dataContext = new DataContext(connectionString);
```

The Data Source parameter defines the location of the database file in isolated storage, and the Password parameter is used to access (or create) an encrypted database.

The *isostore* prefix of the Data Source value specifies that the file is located in isolated storage. By omitting the *isostore* prefix, it indicates that the file is located in the XAP file relative to its root directory. You see an example of using a database located in the XAP file later in the chapter.

Table 29.1 describes the database connection string parameters in more detail.

TABLE 29.1   Local Database Connection String Parameters for Windows Phone

Parameter	Description

`data source`
 alias:
 `datasource`
	The name of the database file. This is a required parameter.

`Password`
 aliases:
 `Pwd,`
 `database password,`
 `ssce:database password`
	A password that is used to encrypt a database or to access an already encrypted database. The string can be up to 40 characters in length.
	
	 When creating a database, if you specify a password, encryption is automatically enabled on the database. If you specify a blank password, the database is not encrypted.

`max buffer size`
 alias:
 `ssce:max buffer size`
	The largest amount of memory, in kilobytes, that a local database can use before it starts flushing changes to disk. If not specified, the default value is 384. The maximum value is 512.

`max database size`
 alias:
 `ssce:max database size`
	The maximum size of a local database, in megabytes. If not specified, the default value is 32. The maximum value is 512.

`Mode`
 aliases:
 `file mode`
 `ssce:mode`
	The locking mode to use when opening the database file. The following values are valid:
	
	 Read Write: Allows multiple contexts to open and modify the database. This is the default setting if the mode property is not specified.
	
	 Read Only: Allows you to open a read-only copy of the database. This value must be used when using a database located in your app's XAP file.
	
	 Exclusive: Prevents other contexts from opening or modifying the database.
	
	 Shared Read: Allows other contexts to read, but not modify, the database while you have it open.
	
	 Typically either *Read Write* or *Read* is used. Sometimes it can be beneficial for performance to use two distinct data contexts in an app—one that opens the database in *Read* only mode, and another, used less frequently for updates, which opens it in *Read Write* mode.

29

Parameter	Description
Culture Identifier	The culture code to use with the database. For example, en-US for United States English. For the full list of culture codes supported by Windows Phone, see http://bit.ly/yAsBuU. This property is ignored if used when connecting to an existing database.
Case Sensitive alias: CaseSensitive	A Boolean value that determines whether the database collation is case-sensitive. This must be set to true to enable case-sensitive collation or false for collation that is not case sensitive. If not specified, the default value is false. This property is ignored if used when connecting to an existing database.

NOTE

A database must be encrypted when it is created; a password cannot be used to encrypt the database after it has been created.

The `ConnectionString` property of the custom `DatabaseUtility` class constructs a connection string using its `DatabasePassword` property, its `DataSource` property, and the `localDatabaseMode` field represented as a custom enum value. See the following excerpt:

```
public string ConnectionString
{
    get
    {
        if (string.IsNullOrWhiteSpace(DatabasePassword))
        {
            return string.Format("Data Source='{0}';Mode={1}",
                DataSource, localDatabaseMode.ToConnectionStringValue());
        }
        return string.Format("Data Source='{0}';Password='{1}';Mode={2}",
                DataSource,
                DatabasePassword,
                localDatabaseMode.ToConnectionStringValue());
    }
}
```

The following excerpt shows the `LocalDatabaseMode` enum, which represents the four connection string `Mode` values that were listed in Table 29.1:

```csharp
public enum LocalDatabaseMode
{
    ReadWrite,
    ReadOnly,
    Exclusive,
    SharedRead
}
```

An extension method is used to convert an enum value to a valid `Mode` value. Using an enum, combined with an extension method for conversion, is an elegant alternative to loosely typed strings. The following excerpt shows the `ToConnectionStringValue` method:

```csharp
public static class LocalDatabaseModeExtensions
{
    public static string ToConnectionStringValue(
        this LocalDatabaseMode mode)
    {
        switch (mode)
        {
            case LocalDatabaseMode.ReadWrite:
                return "Read Write";
            case LocalDatabaseMode.ReadOnly:
                return "Read Only";
            case LocalDatabaseMode.Exclusive:
                return "Exclusive";
            case LocalDatabaseMode.SharedRead:
                return "Shared Read";
            default:
                throw new ArgumentException(
                    "Unknown mode: " + mode);
        }
    }
}
```

Connection Strings for XAP File Databases

To target a database file in your app's XAP file, do not include the `isostore` prefix in the Data Source segment of its connection string. The following example shows a connection string for an .sdf file located in a XAP file:

```csharp
string connectionString
    = "Data Source='/ProjectDirectoryName/FileName.sdf';Mode=Read Only";
DataContext dataContext = new DataContext(connectionString);
```

29

> **NOTE**
>
> The connection string for a database located in your XAP file must use the Mode of Read Only; otherwise, a `System.Data.SqlServerCe.SqlCeException` is raised when attempting to access the database, regardless of whether your query is only attempting to read, such as with a select operation.

The custom `DatabaseUtility` class takes care of building the connection string. A preprocessor directive in the `TwitterDatabaseUtility` class allows you to change the location of the Twitter database to the XAP file. If enabled, the `Read Only` mode parameter is automatically introduced into the connection string. Being in read-only mode, however, breaks the app, because the `TwitterService` needs to write to the database.

Leveraging a Custom Twitter Service

A custom Twitter service is used for all communication with the Twitter web API. The service also provides the capability to cache the results of calls to Twitter using a local database.

The viewmodel, which presents the Twitter timeline information, consumes the Twitter service using an `ITwitterService` interface.

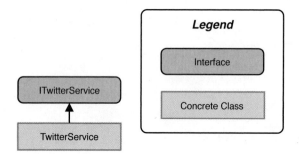

The `ITwitterService` contains two methods designed to execute asynchronously. They are as follows:

▶ GetTimeline(**string** screenName,
        Action<ResultEventArgs<TwitterUser>> completeAction)

▶ GetCachedTimeline(
        string screenName,
        Action<ResultEventArgs<TwitterUser>> completeAction)

A caller of either method provides an `Action` argument, which, on completion of the method, is invoked, notifying the caller of the result.

The `ResultEventArgs` class either contains the result produced by the operation or an `Exception` object. `ResultEventArgs` is presented in Chapter 27, "Communicating with Network Services."

`GetTimeline` uses the Twitter web API to retrieve a Twitter user's details and list of status updates. After a response is received from the Web, the result is converted into entity objects representing the Twitter user and the status updates (`TimelineItem` objects).

`GetCachedTimeline` is used to retrieve a `TwitterUser` from the database. This method does not produce a result until `GetTimeline` has successfully completed at least once, because until then no data has been placed in the database.

The default implementation of the `ITwitterService` is the `TwitterService` class. `TwitterService` relies on the `TwitterDatabaseUtility`. A `TwitterDataContext` is created when the `TwitterService` is instantiated; as shown:

```
public class TwitterService : ITwitterService
{
    readonly TwitterDatabaseUtility twitterDatabaseUtility
                                      = new TwitterDatabaseUtility();
    readonly TwitterDataContext dataContext;

    public TwitterService()
    {
        dataContext = twitterDatabaseUtility.CreateContext();
    }
...
}
```

The public `GetTimeline` method queues the Twitter call on a `ThreadPool` thread. To demonstrate population using the local database, the `ThreadPool` thread is made to wait for 3 seconds before calling the main `GetTimelineCore` method. If an exception is raised, the complete action is called, as shown:

```
public void GetTimeline(
    string screenName, Action<ResultEventArgs<TwitterUser>> completeAction)
{
    ArgumentValidator.AssertNotNullOrWhiteSpace(screenName, "userName");
    ArgumentValidator.AssertNotNull(completeAction, "completeAction");

    ThreadPool.QueueUserWorkItem(
        delegate
        {
            try
            {
                /*Wait for a moment to demonstrate the database retrieval.*/
                Wait(3000); /* Equivalent to Thread.Sleep(3000); */
                GetTimelineCore(screenName, completeAction);
```

```
            }
        catch (Exception ex)
        {
            Console.WriteLine(ex);
            completeAction(new ResultEventArgs<TwitterUser>(null, ex));
        }
    });
}
```

GetTimelineCore uses the Twitter web API (see Listing 29.4). A WebClient is used to dispatch an HTTP request to the site. When the call returns, it is handled within a lambda expression. The result of the call is an XML fragment, which we convert to an XElement using the XElement.Parse method.

The user information is then extracted from the root element, before building a list of TimelineItems. Finally, the data context is used to store the TwitterUser and its associated TimelineItems in the database.

LISTING 29.4   GetTimelineCore Method

```
void GetTimelineCore(
        string screenName, Action<ResultEventArgs<TwitterUser>> completeAction)
{
    WebClient twitterClient = new WebClient();
    twitterClient.DownloadStringCompleted
        += (o, args) =>
        {
            if (args.Error != null)
            {
                completeAction(
                        new ResultEventArgs<TwitterUser>(null, args.Error));
                return;
            }

            try
            {
                XElement rootElement = XElement.Parse(args.Result);

                XElement element = rootElement.Descendants("status").First();
                XElement userElement = element.Descendants("user").First();
                var twitterUser = new TwitterUser
                {
                    Id = userElement.Element("id").Value,
                    ScreenName = userElement.Element("screen_name").Value,
                    Description = userElement.Element("description").Value,
```

```
                ImageUrl = userElement.Element("profile_image_url").Value,
            };

        IEnumerable<TimelineItem> items = from statusElement
                        in rootElement.Descendants("status")
                select new TimelineItem
                {
                    Id = statusElement.Element("id").Value,
                    ReceivedTime = ConvertToDateTime(
                        statusElement.Element("created_at").Value),
                    Text = statusElement.Element("text").Value
                };
        TwitterUser storedUser = dataContext.TwitterUsers.Where(
            user => user.ScreenName == screenName).FirstOrDefault();

        if (storedUser != null)
        {
            dataContext.TimelineItems.DeleteAllOnSubmit(
                dataContext.TimelineItems.Where(
                    item => item.TwitterUserId == storedUser.Id));
            dataContext.TwitterUsers.DeleteOnSubmit(storedUser);
            dataContext.SubmitChanges();
        }

        twitterUser.TimelineItems.AddRange(items);
        dataContext.TwitterUsers.InsertOnSubmit(twitterUser);

        dataContext.SubmitChanges();

        completeAction(new ResultEventArgs<TwitterUser>(twitterUser));
    }
    catch (Exception ex)
    {
        Debug.WriteLine("Unable to get timeline. " + ex);
        completeAction(new ResultEventArgs<TwitterUser>(null, ex));
        return;
    }
};

twitterClient.DownloadStringAsync(new Uri(
    "http://api.twitter.com/1/statuses/user_timeline.xml?screen_name="
    + screenName));
}
```

29

After the Twitter web API has been queried and the result stored in the database, the cached data can be retrieved from the database. This allows the Twitter timeline information to remain viewable when no network connection is available.

> **NOTE**
>
> Changes to the entity model are not persisted to the database until `DataContext.SubmitChanges` is called. New entity objects that have been added to the data context are not inserted into the database until `SubmitChanges` is called, and entities that have been removed from the data context are not deleted from the database until `SubmitChanges` is called.

Retrieving the cached data from the local database is the task of the `TwitterService.GetCachedTimeline` method.

You see the same pattern applied as earlier; the principle `GetCachedTimelineCore` method is called from a `ThreadPool` thread, as shown:

```
public void GetCachedTimeline(
    string screenName, Action<ResultEventArgs<TwitterUser>> completeAction)
{
    ArgumentValidator.AssertNotNullOrWhiteSpace(screenName, "userName");
    ArgumentValidator.AssertNotNull(completeAction, "completeAction");

    ThreadPool.QueueUserWorkItem(
        delegate
        {
            try
            {
                GetCachedTimelineCore(screenName, completeAction);
            }
            catch (Exception ex)
            {
                Console.WriteLine(ex);
                completeAction(new ResultEventArgs<TwitterUser>(null, ex));
            }
        });
}
```

The `GetCachedTimelineCore` method uses the data context to retrieve the Twitter user with the specified screen name, shown in the following excerpt:

```
void GetCachedTimelineCore(
    string userName, Action<ResultEventArgs<TwitterUser>> completeAction)
{
    TwitterUser storedUser = dataContext.TwitterUsers.Where(
        user => user.ScreenName == userName).FirstOrDefault();
```

```
        completeAction(new ResultEventArgs<TwitterUser>(storedUser));
}
```

You saw how the `TwitterService` is able to retrieve live data from the Twitter web API and then cache it using a local database. Subsequent sections look at presenting this data to the user.

Gathering the User's Credentials with the Sign-In View

The `TwitterSignInView` and associated viewmodel provide the UI for gathering the user's Twitter credentials. The sample, however, does not require the user to sign in to Twitter, because we are merely retrieving the timeline for the user, and this does not require authentication.

A sign-in screen is included to provide the infrastructure to extend the app in the direction of being a fully blown Twitter app. It also provides a nice segue to demonstrate the custom `INavigationService`, which is discussed later in the chapter.

The `TwitterSignInViewModel` class contains properties for the user's Twitter credentials and a property that causes the password to be retained by the app (see Listing 29.5).

The viewmodel relies on the `ViewModelBase` class for state persistency. The `Username`, `Password`, and `RememberPassword` properties are each decorated with the custom `State` attribute so that they are persisted to isolated storage. For details on the custom state preservation system, see Chapter 28, "Preserving App State and Settings."

When executed, the viewmodel's `SignInCommand` is responsible for navigating to the `TwitterTimeline` page and for deregistering state preservation for the Password property if the user has indicated that the app should not remember the password.

The `Navigate` method and the custom navigation functionality are discussed later in this chapter.

LISTING 29.5   `TwitterSignInViewModel` Class

```
public class TwitterSignInViewModel : ViewModelBase
{
    public TwitterSignInViewModel()
    {
        signInCommand = new DelegateCommand(
            obj =>
            {
                if (!rememberPassword)
                {
                    DeregisterStatefulProperty(
                        ApplicationStateType.Persistent, () => Password);
                }
                Navigate("/TwitterTimeline/" + username);
```

```csharp
        });
    }

    string username;

    [Stateful(ApplicationStateType.Persistent)]
    public string Username
    {
        get
        {
            return username;
        }
        set
        {
            Assign(ref username, value);
        }
    }
    string password;

    [Stateful(ApplicationStateType.Persistent)]
    public string Password
    {
        get
        {
            return password;
        }
        set
        {
            Assign(ref password, value);
        }
    }
    readonly DelegateCommand signInCommand;

    public ICommand SignInCommand
    {
        get
        {
            return signInCommand;
        }
    }

    bool rememberPassword = true;

    [Stateful(ApplicationStateType.Persistent)]
    public bool RememberPassword
    {
```

```
        get
        {
            return rememberPassword;
        }
        set
        {
            Assign(ref rememberPassword, value);
        }
    }
}
```

Within the view's XAML, an `AppBarIconButton` is bound to the `SignInCommand`.

A `ToggleSwitch` from the Windows Phone Toolkit is used to set the `RememberPassword` property of the viewmodel. See the following excerpt:

```xaml
<Grid x:Name="LayoutRoot" Background="Transparent">
    <Grid.RowDefinitions>
        <RowDefinition Height="Auto"/>
        <RowDefinition Height="*"/>
    </Grid.RowDefinitions>

    <u:AppBar>
        <u:AppBarIconButton
            Command="{Binding SignInCommand}"
            Text="Sign In"
        IconUri="/Images/ApplicationBarIcons/ApplicationBar.Check.png" />
    </u:AppBar>

    <StackPanel Grid.Row="0" Style="{StaticResource PageTitlePanelStyle}">
        <TextBlock Text="Windows Phone Unleashed"
            Style="{StaticResource PhoneTextAppTitleStyle}" />
        <TextBlock Text="Twitter sign in"
            Style="{StaticResource PhoneTextPageTitleStyle}" />
    </StackPanel>

    <StackPanel x:Name="ContentPanel" Grid.Row="1"
            Margin="{StaticResource PhoneHorizontalMargin}">
        <TextBlock Text="username"
            Style="{StaticResource LabelTextIndentedStyle}" />
        <TextBox Text="{Binding Username, Mode=TwoWay}" />
        <TextBlock Text="password"
            Style="{StaticResource LabelTextIndentedStyle}" />
        <!--<PasswordBox Password="{Binding Password, Mode=TwoWay}" />-->
        <TextBox Text="not required in this example." IsReadOnly="True" />
        <toolkit:ToggleSwitch
```

29

```
                    IsChecked="{Binding RememberPassword, Mode=TwoWay}"
                            Header="Remember Password" />
        </StackPanel>

    </Grid>
```

Tapping the application bar button executes the `SignInCommand`, which causes the app to navigate to the timeline view page (see Figure 29.4).

FIGURE 29.4   Twitter sign-in page.

If the app happens to be tombstoned or exited, the state of the various controls is retained in persistent storage.

Tapping the `ApplicationBarIconButton` navigates the app to the timeline view page.

Viewing Tweets with the Timeline View

The timeline view presents a Twitter user's list of recent tweets (status updates). The `TwitterTimelineViewModel` class relies on the `ITwitterService` to retrieve the list of tweets.

`TwitterTimelineViewModel` contains several properties, which are described in the following list:

▶ **TimelineItems**—An `IEnumerable` of `TimelineItem` objects, which is populated using the `ITwitterService`. This list is bound to a `ListBox` control in the view.

▶ **ScreenName**—The Twitter screen name that was supplied by the user on the sign-in view.

▶ **ImageUrl**—The URL to the Twitter user's avatar. This is retrieved from the Twitter web API.

▶ **Message**—An arbitrary string used to supply feedback to the user during retrieval.

▶ **Busy**—A `bool` value indicating whether an asynchronous operation is under way.

The viewmodel also includes a command of type `DelegateCommand<string>` named `loadUserTimelineCommand`, which coordinates the retrieval of the list of status updates. `LoadUserTimelineCommand` receives a Twitter screen name, which is passed to the `ITwitterService`. See the following excerpt:

```
public class TwitterTimelineViewModel : ViewModelBase
{
    readonly ITwitterService twitterService;

    public TwitterTimelineViewModel(ITwitterService twitterService)
    {
        this.twitterService = ArgumentValidator.AssertNotNull(
                                twitterService, "twitterService");

        loadUserTimelineCommand = new DelegateCommand<string>(LoadTimeline);
    }
...
}
```

When the `LoadUserTimelineCommand` executes, the `LoadTimeline` method is called. This method first ensures that a Twitter screen name has been supplied; if not, it navigates back to the sign-in page.

The `ITwitterService.GetCachedTimeline` method executes asynchronously and attempts to retrieve the cached timeline from the local database. When it returns, the viewmodel is populated using the `HandleGetTimelineResult`. After attempting to restore the cached timeline, the `ITwitterService.GetTimeline` method is used to retrieve the latest data from the Twitter web API. See the following excerpt:

```
void LoadTimeline(string twitterScreenName)
{
    if (string.IsNullOrWhiteSpace(twitterScreenName))
    {
        var messageService = Dependency.Resolve<IMessageService>();
        messageService.ShowError("Please provide a twitter screen name.");

        var navigationService = Dependency.Resolve<INavigationService>();
        navigationService.GoBack();
        return;
    }

    if (twitterScreenName == screenName)
    {
```

```
        return;
    }

    Busy = true;

    try
    {
        Message = "Retrieving cached timeline from database.";

        twitterService.GetCachedTimeline(twitterScreenName,
            args =>
            {
                HandleGetTimelineResult(args);
                Message = "Retrieving real data from Twitter.";
                Busy = true;
                twitterService.GetTimeline(
                    twitterScreenName, HandleGetTimelineResult);
            });
    }
    catch (Exception ex)
    {
        Busy = false;
        Message = string.Format("Error retrieving items.");
        Console.WriteLine(ex);
    }
}
```

The `HandleGetTimelineResult` method is called twice, once for the cached items and then for the live Twitter data. The `Error` property of the `ResultEventArgs` is used to determine whether the call completed successfully, and if so, the viewmodel's properties are populated accordingly:

```
void HandleGetTimelineResult(ResultEventArgs<TwitterUser> e)
{
    Busy = false;

    if (e.Error != null)
    {
        Message = "Unable to retrieve timeline.";
        return;
    }

    if (e.Result == null)
    {
        Message = "No result";
        return;
```

```
    }

    Message = "Received result.";
    TimelineItems = e.Result.TimelineItems.ToList();
    ScreenName = e.Result.ScreenName;
    ImageUrl = e.Result.ImageUrl;
}
```

When the viewmodel is instantiated, in the view's code-beside class, it is passed a `TwitterService` object, as shown:

```
public TwitterTimelineView()
{
    InitializeComponent();
    DataContext = new TwitterTimelineViewModel(new TwitterService());
}
```

The view executes the `LoadUserTimelineCommand` in its `OnNavigatedTo` handler, as shown:

```
protected override void OnNavigatedTo(NavigationEventArgs e)
{
    base.OnNavigatedTo(e);

    string twitterName;
    if (NavigationContext.QueryString.TryGetValue("name", out twitterName))
    {
        ViewModel.LoadUserTimelineCommand.Execute(twitterName);
    }
}
```

The view XAML contains controls to display the Twitter timeline information, as well as the Twitter user information. A `ListBox` presents each `TimelineItem` using a `DataTemplate`, as shown in the following excerpt:

```
<Grid x:Name="ContentPanel" Grid.Row="1">
    <Grid.RowDefinitions>
        <RowDefinition Height="Auto" />
        <RowDefinition Height="*" />
        <RowDefinition Height="Auto" />
    </Grid.RowDefinitions>

    <Grid Margin="{StaticResource PhoneMargin}">
        <Grid.ColumnDefinitions>
            <ColumnDefinition Width="Auto" />
            <ColumnDefinition Width="*" />
        </Grid.ColumnDefinitions>
```

```xml
            <Image Source="{Binding ImageUrl}"
                    MaxWidth="60" MaxHeight="60" />
            <TextBlock Grid.Column="1" Text="{Binding ScreenName}"
                Style="{StaticResource PhoneTextExtraLargeStyle}" />
        </Grid>

        <ListBox Grid.Row="1"
            ItemsSource="{Binding TimelineItems}"
            Margin="{StaticResource PhoneHorizontalMargin}">
            <ListBox.ItemTemplate>
                <DataTemplate>
                    <Border CornerRadius="10"
                    BorderBrush="{StaticResource PhoneBorderBrush}"
                    BorderThickness="2"
                    Margin="14,5,4,10">
                        <Grid Margin="10">
                            <Grid.RowDefinitions>
                                <RowDefinition />
                                <RowDefinition />
                            </Grid.RowDefinitions>
                            <Grid.ColumnDefinitions>
                                <ColumnDefinition Width="100" />
                                <ColumnDefinition Width="*" />
                            </Grid.ColumnDefinitions>
                            <TextBlock
                                Text="{Binding ReceivedTime,
                                StringFormat='0:HH:mm:ss'}"
                                MaxWidth="100" />

                            <TextBlock Text="{Binding Text}"
                            Grid.Column="1"
                            TextWrapping="Wrap"
                            Style="{StaticResource PhoneTextSmallStyle}" />

                        </Grid>
                    </Border>
                </DataTemplate>
            </ListBox.ItemTemplate>
        </ListBox>
    </Grid>
```

A `ProgressIndicator` is used to monitor the `Busy` property of the viewmodel and to display the viewmodel's `Message` text, as shown:

```xml
<shell:SystemTray.ProgressIndicator>
```

```
<shell:ProgressIndicator IsIndeterminate="{Binding Busy}"
                         IsVisible="{Binding Busy}"
                         Text="{Binding Message}" />
</shell:SystemTray.ProgressIndicator>
```

When a result is received from the Twitter service, it is displayed in the view as shown in Figure 29.5.

FIGURE 29.5   `TwitterTimelineView` page.

Viewing a Local Database Schema

Visually exploring your database schema can help to reveal inadequacies in its structure. Missing indexes and foreign key relationships can be overlooked when relying solely on metadata in your code. In addition, having the capability to arbitrarily query your tables to see what is in your database can be useful during development.

Given that SQL CE database files usually reside in isolated storage, however, makes exploring the schema difficult.

This section looks at tools to retrieve your local database file from isolated storage and at using Visual Studio and SQL Server Management Studio to view the database on your desktop.

File Explorers for Isolated Storage

The Windows Phone SDK comes with a tool that allows you to read and write to your app's isolated storage area via the command line. The first part of this section examines the Isolated Storage Explorer present in the Windows Phone SDK. The second part examines a free alternative third-party explorer named WP7 Isolated Storage Explorer.

Windows Phone SDK Isolated Storage Explorer

Depending on your operating system, Isolated Storage Explorer is installed in one of following locations:

▶ Program Files\Microsoft SDKs\Windows Phone\v8.0\Tools\IsolatedStorageExplorerTool

▶ Program Files (x86)\Microsoft SDKs\Windows Phone\v8.0\Tools\IsolatedStorageExplorerTool

When using Isolated Storage Explorer, your app must be deployed to the device or emulator. The emulator or device must be running, but the app does not have to be running.

Isolated Storage Explorer uses the following syntax:

```
ISETool.exe <ts|rs|dir[:device-folder]> <xd|de> <Product GUID> [<desktop-path>]
```

Table 29.2 lists the command-line options for Isolated Storage Explorer.

TABLE 29.2   Isolated Storage Explorer Command-Line Options

Option	Description
ts	(Take snapshot) Copies the files and directories in isolated storage from the device or emulator to your computer.
rs	(Restore snapshot) Replaces the files and directories in isolated storage on the device or emulator with files and directories from your computer.
dir	Lists the files and directories in the specified directory of isolated storage. If a directory is not specified, the files and directories in the root are listed.
device-folder	Specifies the directory in isolated storage on the device or emulator that you want to target.
xd	Indicates to target the emulator.
de	Indicates to target a tethered device.
Product GUID	Specifies the ProductID from the WPAppManifest.xml file for the application you want to test.
desktop-path	Specifies the directory on your computer where isolated storage files are written to or copied from. A subdirectory named IsolatedStore is created in desktop-path when files are copied using the ts command. If the specified directory already exists, a ts command overwrites the contents of the directory with no warning.

Source: http://msdn.microsoft.com/en-us/library/hh286408(v=vs.92).aspx

To use the Isolated Storage Explorer, open a command window and navigate to the location of ISETool.exe. Retrieve the product GUID from the ProductID attribute of the App element in the project's WMAppManifest.xml file.

Listing the files and directories at the root directory of an app's isolated storage area can be done using the following command (replacing the GUID with your app's product GUID):

```
ISETool.exe dir xd 11111111-2222-3333-4444-555555555555
```

To copy all the files from isolated storage to your computer, use the following command:

```
ISETool.exe ts xd 11111111-2222-3333-4444-555555555555 "C:\Phone"
```

This command creates a directory on your computer named C:\Phone\IsolatedStore and copies the files and directories in isolated storage into the directory.

CAUTION

If the IsolatedStore directory exists and the copy command is performed, the contents of the IsolatedStore directory are overwritten without any warning.

Use the following command to replace all the files in isolated storage with files from your computer:

```
SETool.exe rs xd 11111111-2222-3333-4444-555555555555 "C:\Phone\IsolatedStore"
```

WP7 Isolated Storage Explorer

A useful alternative to the built-in Isolated Storage Explorer is the WP7 Isolated Storage Explorer, which can be found at http://wp7explorer.codeplex.com/. This open source tool can be used to retrieve a local database from isolated storage, and it works both on the emulator and a real device. The advantage of the WP7 Isolated Storage Explorer is that it comes with a GUI.

The tool can be used either as a standalone application or within Visual Studio and provides a dockable tool window that displays the contents of your app's isolated storage directory (see Figure 29.6).

WP7 Isolated Storage Explorer uses WCF service to communicate with your app.

FIGURE 29.6   WP7 Isolated Storage Explorer dockable window.

After installing the tool, to use it in your project, add a reference to the IsolatedStorageExplorer assembly, and then add some initialization code to your app's launching and activated events, as shown:

```
void Application_Launching(object sender, LaunchingEventArgs e)
{
    IsolatedStorageExplorer.Explorer.Start("localhost");
}

void Application_Activated(object sender, ActivatedEventArgs e)
{
    IsolatedStorageExplorer.Explorer.RestoreFromTombstone();
}
```

The capability to retrieve files from isolated storage and open them on your desktop is very useful, and being able to retrieve a local database from isolated storage means that it can then be loaded into Visual Studio or SQL Server Management Studio, allowing you to explore the schema and to verify the results of your mapping attributes. It is also possible to modify the structure of a database and use the SqlMetal tool to generate your data model, including its DataContext and entity classes. The database-first approach using SqlMetal is discussed in a later section.

Viewing and Modifying an SQL CE Database File

After an SQL CE file has been retrieved from isolated storage, it can be opened in an application such as Visual Studio or Microsoft SQL Server Management Studio.

To open an .sdf file in Visual Studio follow these steps:

1. Within Visual Studio, right-click the Data Connections node in the Server Explorer and select Add Connection. The Add Connection dialog is displayed (see Figure 29.7).

FIGURE 29.7   Visual Studio's Add Connection dialog.

2. Within the Add Connection dialog, set the Data Source to Microsoft SQL Server Compact 3.5.

3. Browse and locate the .sdf file using the Connection Properties section.

4. Select OK.

The Server Explorer pane allows you to explore and modify the database schema (see Figure 29.8) and to view table data by right-clicking a table node and selecting Show Table Data.

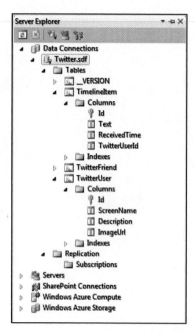

FIGURE 29.8   Server Explorer with the Twitter.sdf database connected.

The ability to visually explore your database schema is important during development. The next section looks at how to generate an entity model from a database using a database-first approach, allowing you to not only view the schema, but also to make changes to it.

Database-First Using SqlMetal

So far this chapter has focused on a code-first approach for generating a local database. To reiterate, code-first is the recommended approach for developing on the phone. The database-first approach, however, can also be used, although it is not fully supported.

SqlMetal is a command-line tool used to generate an entity model from a database. SqlMetal is not fully compatible with Windows Phone, because the code it generates does not compile until some minor alterations are made to it.

SqlMetal generates a `DataContext` derived class and entities representing database tables. Associations are inferred from the foreign key relationships in the database.

SqlMetal can be launched via a Visual Studio Command Prompt by selecting Microsoft Visual Studio 2010/Visual Studio Tools/Visual Studio Command Prompt (2010) in the Windows Start menu.

In the following example, the database file has been downloaded from isolated storage, using the WP7 Isolated Storage Explorer, and placed in a directory called

C:\Unleashed. SqlMetal is provided with the database path, the name code file to output, and the namespace in which to place all generated classes (ignore line breaks):

```
C:\Unleashed>SqlMetal C:\Unleashed\Twitter.sdf
            /code:C:\Unleashed\TwitterDataModel.cs
            /namespace:DanielVaughan.WPUnleashed.Examples
```

After the code file has been generated, it can be added to your project. But before it can be compiled, two constructors must be removed. The key to identifying the errant constructors is that they both accept an IDbConnection and resemble the methods shown in the following excerpt:

```
public Twitter(System.Data.IDbConnection connection)
    : base(connection, mappingSource)
{
    OnCreated();
}

public Twitter(
        System.Data.IDbConnection connection,
        System.Data.Linq.Mapping.MappingSource mappingSource) :
      base(connection, mappingSource)
{
    OnCreated();
}
```

An example of a generated code file is located in the downloadable sample code. The file is named TwitterDataModel_Generated_Unused.cs.

Deploying a Database to Isolated Storage

As stated earlier in this chapter, a local database is read-only when it is located in a XAP file. If you want to provide a prepopulated database that is writable from your app, the database must be copied by your app, from your XAP file, to isolated storage.

Like any other resource, such as an image file, an .sdf database file may be stored as content within your app's XAP file. The app then reads the database file as a Stream of bytes and writes the bytes to isolated storage. After the database has been copied to isolated storage, it is ready to be used by your app.

> **NOTE**
>
> To prevent the size of your project's assembly from being unnecessarily increased by the inclusion of a database file, set the file's Build Action to Content in the Visual Studio Properties pane. This decreases your app's startup time because it takes less time for the CLR to load a smaller assembly. It does not, however, affect your project's XAP file size.

Listing 29.6 shows the custom `IsolatedStorageUtility` class, whose `CopyApplicationResourceToIsolatedStorage` method locates an application resource and copies it as a stream to a specified location in isolated storage.

LISTING 29.6   `IsolatedStorageUtility` Class (excerpt)

```csharp
public class IsolatedStorageUtility : IIsolatedStorageUtility, ISettingsService
{
    public void CopyApplicationResourceToIsolatedStorage(
                        string inResourceName, string outFilename)
    {
        ArgumentValidator.AssertNotNull(inResourceName, "inResourceName");
        ArgumentValidator.AssertNotNullOrWhiteSpace(outFilename, "outFilename");

        Uri uri = new Uri(inResourceName, UriKind.Relative);

        string destination = outFilename;
        int separatorIndex = destination.LastIndexOf("/");
        if (separatorIndex == destination.Length - 1)
        {
            throw new InvalidOperationException(
                string.Format("Destination '{0}' should not end with '/'",
                            destination));
        }

        string directory = null;
        if (separatorIndex != -1)
        {
            directory = destination.Substring(0, separatorIndex);
        }
        using (Stream resourceStream = Application.GetResourceStream(uri).Stream)
        {
            using (IsolatedStorageFile isolatedStorageFile
                    = IsolatedStorageFile.GetUserStoreForApplication())
            {
                if (!string.IsNullOrWhiteSpace(directory)
                    && !isolatedStorageFile.DirectoryExists(directory))
                {
                    isolatedStorageFile.CreateDirectory(directory);
                }

                using (IsolatedStorageFileStream outStream
                    = isolatedStorageFile.OpenFile(
                                        destination, FileMode.Create))
                {
                    resourceStream.CopyTo(outStream);
```

```
                }
            }
        }
    }
    ...
}
```

A database file can then be copied from a XAP file to isolated storage in a single step:

```
IsolatedStorageUtility.CopyApplicationResourceToIsolatedStorage(
        "/Subdirectory/XapDatabase.sdf",
        "/Subdirectory/IsolatedStorageDatabase.sdf");
```

This can be seen in action in the unit test class named `IsolatedStorageUtilityTests`, located in the downloadable sample code (see Listing 29.7). The `CopyDatabaseToIsolatedStorage` test method copies an .sdf file to isolated storage and then verifies that the bytes of both files are equivalent.

The `CollectionAssert.AreEquivalent` method compares the members of both collections. If all members match, the assert succeeds. The `CollectionAssert` class is a part of the Windows Phone Toolkit Unit Testing Framework, discussed in Chapter 24, "Unit Testing Apps."

LISTING 29.7 `IsolatedStorageUtilityTests.CopyDatabaseToIsolatedStorage` **Method**

```
[TestMethod]
public void CopyDatabaseToIsolatedStorage()
{
    const string databaseName = "TestDatabase.sdf";
    IsolatedStorageUtility utility = new IsolatedStorageUtility();
    utility.CopyApplicationResourceToIsolatedStorage(databaseName, databaseName);

    Uri uri = new Uri(databaseName, UriKind.Relative);

    byte[] resourceBytes;

    using (Stream resourceStream = Application.GetResourceStream(uri).Stream)
    {
        resourceBytes = resourceStream.ReadAllBytes();
    }

    Assert.IsNotNull(resourceBytes, "Resource bytes in null");
    Assert.IsTrue(resourceBytes.Length > 0, "Resource bytes length <= 0.");

    using (IsolatedStorageFile isolatedStorageFile
                    = IsolatedStorageFile.GetUserStoreForApplication())
```

29

```
        {
            using (IsolatedStorageFileStream outStream
                = isolatedStorageFile.OpenFile(databaseName, FileMode.Open))
            {
                byte[] isolatedStorageBytes = outStream.ReadAllBytes();
                Assert.IsNotNull(isolatedStorageBytes);
                Assert.IsTrue(isolatedStorageBytes.Length > 0);

                CollectionAssert.AreEquivalent(resourceBytes, isolatedStorageBytes);
            }
        }
    }
}
```

Abstracting the Navigation Service

This section begins with a brief note about its inclusion. I did not intend to show the abstraction of the navigation service. When I began work on the sample for this chapter, however, and I reached the point of needing to navigate from the sign-in page to the timeline page, I felt that it would make for a nice demonstration of a custom testable navigation service.

The custom navigation service abstracts the navigation mechanism provided by the `System.Windows.Controls.Frame` component or the `System.Windows.Navigation.NavigationService` (available via the `NavigationService` property of the `Page` class).

A custom `INavigationService` interface is used to navigate in a UI technology agnostic manner, and it allows the class implementation of the interface to be replaced to enable unit testing of viewmodels. `INavigationService` contains the following three methods:

▶ `GoBack`—Navigates the application to the most recent entry in the back navigation history, or raises an exception if no entry exists

▶ `Navigate(Uri source)`—Navigates to the content specified by the uniform resource identifier (URI)

▶ `Navigate(string relativeUrl)`—Navigates to the content specified by the relative URL

Included in the downloadable sample code are two implementations of the `INavigationService`, which are also present and maintained in the open-source project Calcium (http://calciumsdk.net). The first implementation, named `NavigationServiceWrapper`, leverages the `System.Windows.Navigation.NavigationService` of a `Page`. The second implementation, named `FrameNavigationService`, relies on the phone app's root `Frame` (see Listing 29.8). The `FrameNavigationService` is the implementation used in the sample for this chapter; it is the recommended implementation for use on the phone.

LISTING 29.8 `FrameNavigationService` Class

```csharp
public class FrameNavigationService : INavigationService
{
    Frame frameUseProperty;

    Frame Frame
    {
        get
        {
            if (frameUseProperty == null)
            {
                frameUseProperty = (Frame)Application.Current.RootVisual;
            }
            return frameUseProperty;
        }
    }

    public FrameNavigationService(Frame frame)
    {
        frameUseProperty = ArgumentValidator.AssertNotNull(frame, "frame");
    }


    [InjectDependencies]
    public FrameNavigationService()
    {
        /* Intentionally left blank. */
    }

    public void GoBack()
    {
        Frame.GoBack();
    }
    public void Navigate(Uri source)
    {
        ArgumentValidator.AssertNotNull(source, "source");
        Frame.Navigate(source);
    }

    public void Navigate(string relativeUrl)
    {
        ArgumentValidator.AssertNotNull(relativeUrl, "relativeUrl");
        Frame.Navigate(new Uri(relativeUrl, UriKind.Relative));
    }
}
```

The `INavigationService` is placed in the IoC container in the `App` class's `InitializeContainer` method, as shown:

```
void InitializeContainer()
{
    SimpleContainer container = new SimpleContainer();
    container.InitializeServiceLocator();

    ...

    Dependency.Register<INavigationService, FrameNavigationService>(true);
}
```

The `InjectDependencies` attribute, on the `FrameNavigationService` parameterless constructor, indicates to the dependency injection system that it should use that particular constructor when instantiating the class.

In the Twitter timeline viewer sample for this chapter, the `TwitterSignInViewModel` class uses the `INavigationService` to navigate to the `TimelineView` page. `TwitterSignInViewModel` relies on a `UriMapping` to navigate to the page. The URI mapping is located in the App.xaml file of the project and causes the root frame of the app to direct to TwitterTimelineView.xaml whenever an attempt is made to navigate to a URI beginning with /TwitterTimeline/. See the following excerpt from the App.xaml file:

```
<phone:PhoneApplicationFrame.UriMapper>
    <navigation:UriMapper>
        <navigation:UriMapper.UriMappings>
            <navigation:UriMapping Uri="/TwitterTimeline/{name}"
                MappedUri="/DataDrivenApps/TwitterExample
                           /TwitterTimelineView.xaml?name={name}" />
        </navigation:UriMapper.UriMappings>
    </navigation:UriMapper>
</phone:PhoneApplicationFrame.UriMapper>
```

The screen name of the Twitter user is passed using a query string parameter called name.

By abstracting the `INavigationService` you increase the reusability of your viewmodel code, and it enables you to coordinate navigation via viewmodel logic. This alleviates the logic fragmentation that can occur when relying on the view to perform navigation.

Observing LINQ to SQL Queries with a Custom Log

LINQ to SQL allows you to capture the generated SQL as it is being sent to a local database. This can be achieved by creating a custom `TextWriter` that outputs to the Visual Studio console window using `Debug.WriteLine`. An instance of the custom `TextWriter` is assigned to the `Log` property of the `DataContext` class.

John Gallardo demonstrates how to do this on his blog at http://bit.ly/mJYY74. The custom `TextWriter`, called `DebugStreamWriter`, is shown in Listing 29.9.

LISTING 29.9   DebugStreamWriter Class

```csharp
public class DebugStreamWriter : TextWriter
{
    readonly int bufferSize = 256;
    readonly StringBuilder stringBuilder;

    public DebugStreamWriter(int bufferSize = 256)
    {
        this.bufferSize
            = ArgumentValidator.AssertGreaterThan(0, bufferSize, "bufferSize");
        stringBuilder = new StringBuilder(bufferSize);
    }

    public override Encoding Encoding
    {
        get
        {
            return Encoding.UTF8;
        }
    }

    public override void Write(char value)
    {
        stringBuilder.Append(value);
        if (stringBuilder.Length >= bufferSize)
        {
            Flush();
        }
    }

    public override void WriteLine(string value)
    {
        Flush();
        using (var reader = new StringReader(value))
        {
            string line;
            while ((line = reader.ReadLine()) != null)
            {
                Debug.WriteLine(line);
            }
        }
    }

    protected override void Dispose(bool disposing)
    {
```

29

```
        if (disposing)
        {
            Flush();
        }
    }

    public override void Flush()
    {
        if (stringBuilder.Length > 0)
        {
            Debug.WriteLine(stringBuilder);
            stringBuilder.Clear();
        }
    }
}
```

To send all LINQ to SQL logging output to the `DebugStreamWriter`, it is assigned to the `Log` property of the `DataContext` class. I have chosen to do this in the `TwitterDataContext` class, as shown:

```
public class TwitterDataContext : DataContext
{
    public TwitterDataContext(string connection) : base(connection)
    {
        Log = new DebugStreamWriter();
    }
    ...
}
```

With this in place, we are able to view the activity of the `DataContext` via the Visual Studio Output pane (see Figure 29.9).

Observing the generated SQL can help you gain an understanding of how LINQ to SQL works, as well as giving you the opportunity to optimize query complexity.

FIGURE 29.9   The Output pane displays the LINQ to SQL query.

Updating a Database Schema

It is almost inevitable that when updating your app, adding new features and so forth, you will want to make changes to your database schema. Fortunately, local database support on the phone includes the capability to perform additive changes to a database, such as adding tables, columns, indexes, or associations, while preserving the data in the database.

For more complex schema changes, however, such as dropping a column from a table, you need to create a new database and migrate the data to the new schema.

> **NOTE**
>
> Changes to your local database schema begin with changing the object model of the corresponding data context. Therefore, modify your entity classes first to reflect the desired state of the schema.

The `Microsoft.Phone.Data.Linq.DatabaseSchemaUpdater` class provides four schema alter-ing methods:

▶ `AddColumn<T>(string columnPropertyName)`

▶ `AddTable<T>()`

▶ AddIndex<T>(string indexName)

▶ AddAssociation<T>(string associationPropertyName)

The following sections discuss each of these methods in greater detail.

AddColumn

AddColumn allows you to add a new column to an existing table. For example, if you added a new property to the TwitterUser class to record the user's age, you would then need to use the DatabaseSchemaUpdater to create a new column to store the Age value. This could be achieved in the following manner:

```
using (DataContext dataContext
            = new TwitterDataContext("isostore:Twitter.sdf"))
{
    DatabaseSchemaUpdater updater
                = dataContext.CreateDatabaseSchemaUpdater();
    updater.AddColumn<TwitterUser>("Age");
    updater.Execute();
}
```

> **NOTE**
>
> The AddColumn method only allows columns to be added that can contain null values. Therefore, decorating a property with [Column(CanBeNull = false)] prevents the AddColumn method from succeeding and causes an SqlCeException to be raised when the DatabaseSchemaUpdater.Execute method is called.

The database does not change to reflect updates from the DatabaseSchemaUpdater until its Execute method is called, at which point all changes are submitted to the local database as a single transaction, which ensures the database maintains integrity if it is interrupted, such as when the user exits the app during an upgrade.

AddTable

Using the AddTable method allows you to create a new table for an entity class. On adding a new table, the DatabaseSchemaUpdater also applies the metadata associated with the entity class and creates any related indexes or foreign key constraints.

To add a new entity to the Twitter data model, we first create that entity and decorate it with Table and Column attributes. In the following example, the TwitterFriend class represents a Twitter user, who happens to be a contact of another Twitter user (see Listing 29.10). TwitterFriend contains an Id and a ScreenName property. In addition, an index is declared for the ScreenName property.

LISTING 29.10   `TwitterFriend` Class

```
[Table]
[Index(Columns = "ScreenName")]
public class TwitterFriend : NotifyPropertyChangeBase
{
    string id;

    [Column(IsPrimaryKey = true)]
    public string Id
    {
        get
        {
            return id;
        }
        set
        {
            Assign(ref id, value);
        }
    }

    string screenName;

    [Column]
    public string ScreenName
    {
        get
        {
            return screenName;
        }
        set
        {
            Assign(ref screenName, value);
        }
    }
}
```

The following code is used to upgrade the schema to include a new table for storing `TwitterFriend` data:

```
using (DataContext dataContext
            = new TwitterDataContext("isostore:Twitter.sdf"))
{
```

```
DatabaseSchemaUpdater updater
            = dataContext.CreateDatabaseSchemaUpdater();
updater.AddTable<TwitterFriend>();
updater.Execute();
}
```

It can be seen from Figure 29.10 that after execution, the Twitter database contains the new table, with a secondary index on the ScreenName column, as desired.

FIGURE 29.10   The TwitterFriend table has been added to the schema.

AddIndex

Suboptimal query performance is sometimes caused by table scans, where a query causes every row of a table to be examined. Depending on the kind of data in a column, bottlenecks of this nature can often be rectified by placing an index on the column.

The need for an index may be discovered after a table has been populated with a substantial number of records, and after an app has been published to the marketplace, or the need may arise with the introduction of a new feature that causes the table to be queried in a different way. In both cases, adding an index to an existing table is done by decorating the entity class with an Index attribute, and then by calling DatabaseSchemaUpdater.AddIndex.

For example, if we add an EmailAddress property to the TwitterFriend class, and later decide to add an index to improve query performance, we would first decorate the TwitterFriend class with an index attribute, like so:

```
[Index(Name = "EmailAddressIndex",
      Columns = "EmailAddress", IsUnique = true)]
public class TwitterFriend : NotifyPropertyChangeBase
{
...
}
```

After it is decorated with the `Index` attribute, the schema can be updated to include a new index for the column, as shown in the following excerpt:

```
using (DataContext dataContext
            = new TwitterDataContext("isostore:Twitter.sdf"))
{
    DatabaseSchemaUpdater updater
            = dataContext.CreateDatabaseSchemaUpdater();
    updater.AddIndex<TwitterFriend>("EmailAddressIndex");
    updater.Execute();
}
```

AddAssociation

`AddAssociation` allows you to add a one-to-many association between two entities. This method results in a foreign key constraint being added to the column that holds the primary key of the foreign table.

`AddAssociation` accepts a single parameter, `associationPropertyName`, which is the name of the entity member that holds the foreign key of another table.

To illustrate, if we were to add a new association between the `TwitterUser` and the `TimelineItem` classes that matches the existing association, we would first set about by adding a new property to the `TimelineItem` class to hold the id of a `TwitterUser`, like so:

```
[Table]
public class TimelineItem : NotifyPropertyChangeBase
{
    string twitterUser2Id;

    [Column]
    public string TwitterUser2Id
    {
        get
        {
            return twitterUser2Id;
        }
        set
        {
            Assign(ref twitterUser2Id, value);
        }
    }

    EntityRef<TwitterUser> user2;

    [Association(Storage = "user2", ThisKey = "TwitterUser2Id",
            IsForeignKey = true, Name = "FK_TwitterUser2")]
```

29

```
    public TwitterUser TwitterUser2
    {
        get
        {
            return user2.Entity;
        }
        set
        {
            user2.Entity = value;
        }
    }
...
}
```

TIP

Explicitly providing a name for the foreign key constraint avoids collisions with existing
constraint names, especially if similar associations have already been defined, as is the
case with our `TwitterUser` property.

On the other side, the *one* side of the association, we would create a new `EntitySet` property for the new `TimelineItem` children, as shown:

```
[Table]
[Index(Columns = "ScreenName")]
public class TwitterUser : NotifyPropertyChangeBase
{
    readonly EntitySet<TimelineItem> timelineItems2;

    [Association(
        Storage = "timelineItems2",
        OtherKey = "TwitterUserId")]
    public EntitySet<TimelineItem> TimelineItems2
    {
        get
        {
            return timelineItems2;
        }
        set
        {
            timelineItems2.Assign(value);
        }
    }
...
}
```

To materialize the association in the database, we would then perform the following updates:

```
using (TwitterDataContext dataContext
                = twitterDatabaseUtility.CreateContext())
{
    DatabaseSchemaUpdater updater
                = dataContext.CreateDatabaseSchemaUpdater();
    updater.AddColumn<TimelineItem>("TwitterUser2Id");
    updater.AddAssociation<TimelineItem>("TwitterUser2");
    updater.Execute();
}
```

Schema Versioning

The DatabaseSchemaUpdater class provides a DatabaseSchemaVersion property that allows you to programmatically distinguish between different versions of your database.

When a local database is created with the DataContext.CreateDatabase method, a table named _Version is automatically created. This table holds the current DatabaseSchemaVersion number.

In the following example, the database version is used to determine what needs to be done to update the schema to the current version:

```
using (TwitterDataContext dataContext
                = twitterDatabaseUtility.CreateContext())
{
    DatabaseSchemaUpdater updater
                = dataContext.CreateDatabaseSchemaUpdater();
    int databaseVersion = updater.DatabaseSchemaVersion;

    if (databaseVersion < 2)
    {
        updater.AddColumn<TwitterUser>("Homepage");
        updater.DatabaseSchemaVersion = 2;
        updater.Execute();
    }

    if (databaseVersion < 3)
    {
        updater.AddColumn<TwitterUser>("Birthday");
        updater.DatabaseSchemaVersion = 3;
        updater.Execute();
    }
}
```

29

TIP

As you make changes to your schema, take note of them. This eases the burden of writing schema versioning code later.

Mapping an Inheritance Hierarchy

So far in this chapter, you have seen how LINQ to SQL has been used to map entity classes to database tables, in a one-to-one fashion. There are times, however, when constraining an entity model to a flat hierarchy can feel too restrictive, and you may want to use inheritance in your entity model. This is possible with LINQ to SQL using single table inheritance.

When multiple classes of a hierarchy are stored within the same table, this is called *single table inheritance*. It works by dedicating a column within the table to represent the type of the particular entity class.

Although this approach decreases the level of normalization in a database, it can be an effective approach for entity classes that have a small degree of variation in their storage needs.

The following example creates an entity model representing bank accounts. These bank accounts objects are stored using a single table in a local database.

The example code for this section is located in the /DataDrivenApps / LinqToSqlInheritanceMapping directory of the WPUnleashed.Examples project in the downloadable sample code.

At the base of the class hierarchy is the `BankAccount` class, and deriving from this are the three classes: `SavingsAccount`, `CheckingAccount`, and `FixedDepositAccount` (see Figure 29.11).

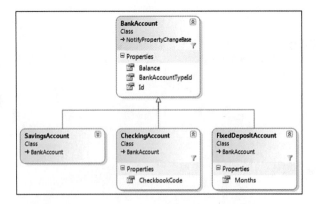

FIGURE 29.11   Bank account class hierarchy.

The two primary elements for mapping an inheritance hierarchy are the InheritanceMapping attribute and the Column attribute's IsDiscriminator property.

Listing 29.11 shows that the BankAccount class declares each of its derived types using the InheritanceMapping attribute. The Code property of the InheritanceMapping attribute is the unique column value representing the derived type. The BankAccountTypeId is decorated with a Column attribute that has its IsDescriminator property set to true, indicating that it corresponds to the InheritanceMapping attribute's Code property.

Thus, if an entity is a SavingsAccount, LINQ to SQL sets its BankAccountTypeId to 0. If the entity is a CheckingAccount, then BankAccountTypeId is set to 1. And so on.

LISTING 29.11   BankAccount Class

```
[Table]
[InheritanceMapping(Code = 0, Type = typeof(SavingsAccount), IsDefault = true)]
[InheritanceMapping(Code = 1, Type = typeof(CheckingAccount))]
[InheritanceMapping(Code = 2, Type = typeof(FixedDepositAccount))]
public class BankAccount : NotifyPropertyChangeBase
{
    int id;

    [Column(
        IsPrimaryKey = true,
        DbType = "INT IDENTITY NOT NULL",
        IsDbGenerated = true,
        UpdateCheck = UpdateCheck.Never)]
    public int Id
    {
        get
        {
            return id;
        }
        set
        {
            Assign(ref id, value);
        }
    }

    int bankAccountTypeId;

    [Column(DbType = "Int NOT NULL", IsDiscriminator = true)]
    public int BankAccountTypeId
    {
        get
        {
            return bankAccountTypeId;
```

```
        }
        set
        {
            Assign(ref bankAccountTypeId, value);
        }
    }
    decimal balance;

    [Column]
    public decimal Balance
    {
        get
        {
            return balance;
        }
        set
        {
            Assign(ref balance, value);
        }
    }
}
```

Only the base class is decorated with a `Table` attribute; entity subclasses are not. Members of the subclass that are to be stored in the database are decorated with a `Column` attribute (see Listing 29.12).

LISTING 29.12   `CheckingAccount` Class

```
[Index(Columns = "CheckbookCode")]
public class CheckingAccount : BankAccount
{
    string checkbookCode;

    [Column(DbType = "NCHAR(16)")]
    public string CheckbookCode
    {
        get
        {
            return checkbookCode;
        }
        set
        {
            Assign(ref checkbookCode, value);
        }
    }
}
```

The custom `BankingDataContext` class has a single `BankAccounts` property and is used in the same manner as the Twitter example earlier in this chapter (see Listing 29.13).

LISTING 29.13   `BankingDataContext` Class

```
public class BankingDataContext : DataContext
{
    public BankingDataContext(string connection) : base(connection)
    {
        Log = new DebugStreamWriter();
    }

    public Table<BankAccount> BankAccounts
    {
        get
        {
            return GetTable<BankAccount>();
        }
    }
}
```

The `BankingDataContextTests` class, in the WPUnleashed.Tests project, demonstrates storage and retrieval of various banking entity types. A custom `BankingDatabaseUtility` is used to initialize the database file. Two accounts are inserted into the database, and then are retrieved using LINQ to SQL. See the following excerpt:

```
[TestMethod]
[Tag("i1")]
public void ContextShouldReadAndWrite()
{
    using (BankingDataContext context = databaseUtility.CreateContext())
    {
        SavingsAccount savingsAccount = new SavingsAccount {Balance = 50};
        CheckingAccount checkingAccount = new CheckingAccount
                                    {
                                        Balance = 100,
                                        CheckbookCode = "12345"
                                    };
        context.BankAccounts.InsertAllOnSubmit(new List<BankAccount>
                                    {
                                        savingsAccount,
                                        checkingAccount
                                    });
        context.SubmitChanges();
    }
```

29

```
using (BankingDataContext context = databaseUtility.CreateContext())
{
    List<BankAccount> accounts = context.BankAccounts.ToList();
    Assert.IsTrue(accounts.Count > 2, "There should be two accounts.");

    IQueryable<SavingsAccount> savingsAccounts
        = context.BankAccounts.OfType<SavingsAccount>();
    Assert.IsTrue(savingsAccounts.Any());

    SavingsAccount account = savingsAccounts.First();
    Assert.IsTrue(account.Balance == 50, "Balance should be 50");
}
}
```

Having support for mapping inheritance hierarchies in LINQ to SQL is a tolerable way of bridging the object relational divide.

Concurrency

LINQ to SQL has built-in support for optimistic concurrency; an entity is able to be retrieved and used in more than one operation at a time. When an entity is retrieved from the database, and then updated, if changes by another party occur in the interim, they are identified and a conflict is detected.

The mechanism supporting this feature is configured using two `Column` attribute properties: `IsVersion` and `UpdateCheck`.

`IsVersion` allows you to designate an entity class member to be used for optimistic concurrency control (OCC). Before committing a change to an entity, the data context verifies that no other transaction has modified its data. If the check reveals conflicting modifications, the committing transaction rolls back and an exception is raised.

> **NOTE**
>
> `IsVersion` is not required for conflict detection. When not specified, however, the data context must retain copies of the entity's member values and must compare the original values with the database values to detect conflicts, which is not terribly efficient.

LINQ to SQL supports multitier applications by allowing entities to be attached to a `DataContext`. Such an entity may have been retrieved using a different `DataContext` instance, or deserialized after being sent over the wire from another tier via a web service.

In the following example, you see that by adding a version property to the `BankAccount` class (presented in the previous section), you can prevent conflicting changes from being written to the database. `BankAccount` now contains a `DateVersion` property of type `byte[]`:

```
byte[] dataVersion;
```

```
[Column(
    IsVersion = true,
    IsDbGenerated = true,
    UpdateCheck = UpdateCheck.Never)]
public byte[] DataVersion
{
    get
    {
        return dataVersion;
    }
    set
    {
        Assign(ref dataVersion, value);
    }
}
```

The `DataVersion` value is materialized as a ROWVERSION field in the database (see Figure 29.12). The ROWVERSION data type causes the table field to be automatically updated whenever a row update occurs.

FIGURE 29.12   By default, the version member is materialized as a ROWVERSION column.

The `BankingDataContextTests` class contains a test method for demonstrating conflict detection. It creates a `CheckingAccount`, called `beforeAccount`, and inserts it into the database.

It then retrieves the same account, this time in the scope of a new `BankingDataContext`, sets its `CheckbookCode` to a new value, and then updates the database.

Finally, it attaches the `beforeAccount` instance to a new `DataContext` and attempts to update the `CheckbookCode` to a new value. See the following excerpt:

```
[TestMethod]
[Tag("i2")]
[ExpectedException(typeof(ChangeConflictException))]
```

29

```
public void ContextShouldEnforceUpdateChecking()
{
    CheckingAccount beforeAccount;

    using (BankingDataContext context = databaseUtility.CreateContext())
    {
        beforeAccount = new CheckingAccount
                            {
                                Balance = 100,
                                CheckbookCode = "11111"
                            };
        context.BankAccounts.InsertOnSubmit(beforeAccount);
        context.SubmitChanges();
    }

    using (BankingDataContext context = databaseUtility.CreateContext())
    {
        CheckingAccount afterAccount
            = (CheckingAccount)context.BankAccounts.Where(
                        x => x.Id == beforeAccount.Id).First();
        afterAccount.CheckbookCode = "22222";
        context.SubmitChanges();
    }

    using (BankingDataContext context = databaseUtility.CreateContext())
    {
        context.BankAccounts.Attach(beforeAccount);
        beforeAccount.CheckbookCode = "33333";
        context.SubmitChanges();
    }
}
```

When `context.SubmitChanges` is called, a conflict is detected because the `afterAccount` object, representing the same account, was updated in the database in the interim. This raises a `ChangeConflictException` (see Figure 29.13), which is defined as an expected exception, using the `ExpectedException` test attribute shown in the previous excerpt.

Providing a dedicated version property within your entity classes is good practice when enabling conflict detection. When not used, the data context relies solely on the `Column` attribute's `UpdateCheck` property for inferring conflict detection behavior.

FIGURE 29.13 A `ChangeConflictException` is raised when a conflict is detected.

ColumnAttribute.UpdateCheck

`UpdateCheck` informs the data context when to verify that a member value in the database has not changed since it was retrieved. The following is the list of valid `UpdateCheck` values:

▶ `Always`

▶ `Never`

▶ `WhenChanged`

When performing an update without the existence of a dedicated version member, LINQ to SQL generates an UPDATE statement with a WHERE clause that includes the original column values. If the values do not match those in the database, no update occurs, and a conflict is detected, raising an exception.

The default value of `UpdateCheck` is `UpdateCheck.Always`. If set to `UpdateCheck.Always`, conflict detection occurs even if the entity's member value has not changed.

If the `UpdateCheck` attribute property is set to `UpdateCheck.Never`, the member does not participate in conflict detection. You can use this value to effectively switch off conflict detection for a particular member.

If the `UpdateCheck` attribute property is set to `UpdateCheck.WhenChanged`, conflict detection for the member occurs only if the value has changed in the entity object.

29

Summary

This chapter began with an overview of how local databases are deployed to Windows Phone.

The chapter explored the code-first approach to data model creation and walked through a sample Twitter timeline viewer that caches data in a local database, during which you explored several facets of LINQ to SQL including entity creation, change tracking, and entity multiplicity.

The chapter then looked at the database-first approach to data model creation. You saw how to retrieve a local database file from isolated storage and how to use the SqlMetal tool to generate a data model from a database.

The chapter then examined a custom navigation service that allows navigation from a viewmodel without reliance on the built-in navigation of the phone, which can increase the testability of viewmodel classes.

A technique for observing LINQ to SQL queries using a custom log was discussed. You saw how to upgrade a schema without losing data, and how to use version numbering to provide incremental updates to your database schema.

Finally, the chapter looked at mapping inheritance hierarchies using LINQ to SQL, and at concurrency and conflict detection.

CHAPTER 30

Auto-Launching with File and Protocol Associations

File and protocol associations are used to automatically launch your app when another app launches a specific file type or URI.

In previous versions of the Windows Phone OS, apps had no built-in way to communicate with other apps on the device, and no means to associate themselves with particular file types as is commonplace on the desktop.

Fortunately, the Windows Phone 8 SDK includes two new capabilities that allow your app to associate itself with files that have a specific file extension and to send messages to apps that have subscribed to a particular URI protocol, thus allowing the delegation of data handling responsibilities, sharing of data between apps, and inter-app communication.

This chapter begins with a brief introduction to file and protocol associations. It then looks at enabling file associations in your app, and you see how to register your app for handling file launch requests for specific file types. You explore two sample apps that demonstrate the concepts of registration and launching of file and protocol associations.

Finally, the chapter delves into protocol associations. You see how to register a protocol association, how to create a protocol association landing page, and how to send and receive protocol messages. You also look at programmatically launching built-in apps.

Understanding File and Protocol Associations

File and protocol associations allow you to delegate responsibility for handling a file or a message to another app. For example, when a Windows Phone app encounters a file type that it is not specifically designed to handle, it may ask the OS to launch the file. The OS then forwards the request to an app that is registered to work with that particular file type.

Both file and protocol associations function in the same way. File associations allow you to designate your app as a handler for a particular file type, and protocol associations allow you to designate your app as a handler for URIs that include a particular protocol prefix.

You register a file or protocol association for your app by following two steps:

▶ Adding a registration entry to your project's WMAppManifest.xml file

▶ Creating a landing page that is able to handle the incoming file or protocol launch

A Note About the Sample

The source code for this chapter can be found in the FileAndProtocolAssociations directory, in the downloadable sample code. In the sample, the FileAndProtocolAssociations solution contains two phone app projects that demonstrate registration and launching of a file type and protocol association. The WPUnleashed.FileAndProtocolAssociations project performs the registration when it is first run. The other project, WPUnleashed.AppThatLaunchesACustomFileType, demonstrates the effect of launching a file or protocol from another app deployed on the phone.

Auto-Launching with a File Extension Association

File associations allow your app to automatically launch when the user attempts to open a file of a particular type, or when another app requests the OS to open a file.

A file could come from a variety of sources including the following:

▶ An email attachment

▶ A link on a website via the phone's web browser

▶ A Near Field Communications (NFC) tag

▶ Another installed app

Registering a File Association

Registration of a file association is done in your app's WMAppManifest.xml file. To edit the WMAppManifest.xml file, in the Visual Studio Solution Explorer, right-click the WMAppManifest.xml file, and then select View Code.

A file association is specified with the `FileTypeAssociation` element. Listing 30.1 shows an excerpt from the WMAppManifest.xml file in the WPUnleashed.FileAndProtocolAssociations project.

The following elements are used to register a file association:

▶ **Extensions Element**—Contains `FileTypeAssociation` elements and other extension items such as `Protocol` extension elements, discussed later in this chapter.

▶ **FileTypeAssociation**—Defines a file association. You can register a maximum of 20 file associations for your app. The *Name* attribute is required and allows you to choose a friendly name for the association. The `TaskID` and `NavUriFragment` elements must be specified as shown.

▶ **Logos**—An optional element that provides a list of logo images used by built-in apps to indicate the type of file.

▶ **Logo**—An optional element that provides the path to a file in your app that is used to represent files with the extension type. There are three Logo types: small, medium, and large.

▶ **SupportedFileTypes**—Lists one or more file extensions that are associated with the file type. At most, 20 file extensions can be listed for the file type.

▶ **FileType**—Indicates the file extension for the file type. The file extension text should include the period (.) character.

NOTE

The `Extensions` element must immediately follow the `Tokens` element in the WMAppManifest.xml file.

In the sample, the file extension .unl has been chosen arbitrarily and is intended to represent the word "**unl**eashed." When the WPUnleashed.FileAndProtocolAssociations app is launched, the existence of the extension in the WMAppManifest.xml file causes the file association to be registered with the OS.

LISTING 30.1   WMAppManifest.xml `FileTypeAssociation` Element

```
<Extensions>

  <FileTypeAssociation Name="UnleashedFileType"
                       TaskID="_default"
                       NavUriFragment="fileToken=%s">
    <Logos>
      <Logo Size="small">UnleashedIcon33.png</Logo>
      <Logo Size="medium">UnleashedIcon69.png</Logo>
      <Logo Size="large">UnleashedIcon176.png</Logo>
    </Logos>
```

30

```
  <SupportedFileTypes>
    <FileType>.unl</FileType>
  </SupportedFileTypes>
</FileTypeAssociation>


  . . .


</Extensions>
```

You can define a set of logos (image files) that visually represent the file association of your app. These logos provide an integrated look to custom file types appearing in built-in apps.

Table 30.1 lists the three image sizes that can be defined for each file association.

TABLE 30.1   File Extension Logo Sizes

Logo Size	Dimensions	Where it is used
small	33×33 pixels	Email attachments
medium	69×69 pixels	Office Hub list view
large	176×176 pixels	Browser download

> **NOTE**
>
> Although the `Logo` element is optional in the WMAppManifest.xml file, if you do provide one or more `Logo` elements, you must provide all three.

Receiving a File Launch Request

By associating your app with a file extension, the Windows Phone OS sends requests to open any files of the registered type to your app. It does so by launching your app and providing a deep link URI that contains a file token—a guid that is used to retrieve a file from storage.

It is your app's responsibility to recognize the incoming file launch URI and redirect to a page that can handle the request.

Detecting a File Launch

When an app is the subject of a file association, it is launched and navigated to a URI beginning with this text: /FileTypeAssociation.

The value of a fileToken query string parameter is used to retrieve the file from storage. The following example shows a deep-link URI from a file launch:

```
/FileTypeAssociation?fileToken=54195f9-1de0-65d1-3f21-c533f1909a18
```

When your app is launched as a result of a file association, the app can use a URI mapping to redirect to a page designed to handle the launch request.

The App.xaml file in the WPUnleashed.FileAndProtocolAssociations project has a UriMapping for the /FileTypeAssociation URI that redirects to the FileView.xaml page, which is shown in the following excerpt:

```
<Application.RootVisual>
    <phone:PhoneApplicationFrame
        Navigated="CompleteInitializePhoneApplication"
        NavigationFailed="RootFrame_NavigationFailed">
        <phone:PhoneApplicationFrame.UriMapper>
            <navigation:UriMapper>
                <navigation:UriMapper.UriMappings>
                    <navigation:UriMapping Uri="/FileTypeAssociation"
                        MappedUri="/FileView.xaml" />
                    ...
                </navigation:UriMapper.UriMappings>
            </navigation:UriMapper>
        </phone:PhoneApplicationFrame.UriMapper>
    </phone:PhoneApplicationFrame>
</Application.RootVisual>
```

The fileToken query string parameter that is present in the incoming /FileTypeAssociation URI is automatically included during the mapping process.

> **TIP**
>
> An alternative to defining the URI mapping in the App.xaml file is to create a custom URI mapper as described in Chapter 31, "Extending the Search Experience." Creating a custom URI mapper allows you to programmatically determine the destination URI using factors other than the content of the deep-link URI.

The NavigationContext's QueryString property is an IDictionary<string, string>. It contains the fileToken parameter. The landing page's OnNavigatedTo method passes the dictionary to the viewmodel's Load method, as shown:

```
protected override void OnNavigatedTo(NavigationEventArgs e)
{
    base.OnNavigatedTo(e);

    ViewModel.Load(NavigationContext.QueryString);
}
```

30

Retrieving a Launched File

In the sample for this section, processing of the query string is performed by the FileViewModel in the WPUnleashed.FileAndProtocolAssociations project (see Listing 30.2).

The `fileToken` parameter that is passed to your app within the deep-link URI allows you to retrieve the file using the Windows Phone SDK's storage API.

The `SharedStorageAccessManager` retrieves the name of the file using the token and then copies the file to the app's private storage area where it can be freely accessed by the app.

The `SharedStorageAccessManager` is part of the WinPRT API. The class has two static methods, `GetSharedFileName` and `CopySharedFileAsync`, that are designed specifically for the scenario presented in this section.

> **NOTE**
>
> The new `Windows.Storage` API allows your app to store and retrieve files in your app's private storage area and is the WinPRT equivalent of the Silverlight Isolated Storage API that you may already be familiar with. See Chapter 28, "Preserving App State and Settings."

LISTING 30.2   `FileViewModel.Load` Method

```
public async Task Load(IDictionary<string, string> queryStringDictionary)
{
    string fileToken;

    if (!queryStringDictionary.TryGetValue("fileToken", out fileToken))
    {
        MessageService.ShowError(
            "Unable to locate the file token in the query string.");
        return;
    }

    string fileName = SharedStorageAccessManager.GetSharedFileName(fileToken);

    StorageFolder folder = ApplicationData.Current.LocalFolder;
    string tempFileName = "temp_" + fileName;
    IStorageFile file = await SharedStorageAccessManager.CopySharedFileAsync(
        folder, tempFileName, NameCollisionOption.ReplaceExisting, fileToken);

    ReadFile(file);
}
```

The viewmodel's `ReadFile` method uses more of the new WinRT API to retrieve the content of the file using the asynchronous `IStorageFile OpenAsync` method (see Listing 30.3). The string that is read from the file is set as the viewmodel's `FileContent` property.

LISTING 30.3 `FileViewModel.ReadFile` Method

```
async void ReadFile(IStorageFile file)
{
    string fileContent;

    using (IRandomAccessStream streamOpenedFile
                            = await file.OpenAsync(FileAccessMode.Read))
    {
        using (IInputStream inputStream = streamOpenedFile.GetInputStreamAt(0))
        {
            using (StreamReader reader
                        = new StreamReader(inputStream.AsStreamForRead()))
            {
                fileContent = await reader.ReadToEndAsync();
            }
        }
    }

    FileContent = fileContent;
}
```

The FileView.xaml page has a binding to the viewmodel's `FileContent` property, as shown:

```
<TextBlock Text="{Binding FileContent, StringFormat='"\{0\}"'}"
           TextWrapping="Wrap"
           Style="{StaticResource PhoneTextExtraLargeStyle}"/>
```

In the next section you look at launching a file from another app that is then displayed on the FileView page.

Launching a File

Any app can request that the OS launch a file. Launching a file is achieved using the `Windows.System.Launcher` class. The following excerpt from the MainPageViewModel retrieves a file stored in the app's private storage area and launches it using the Launcher's `LaunchFileAsync` method:

```
async Task LaunchFile()
{
    StorageFolder folder = ApplicationData.Current.LocalFolder;
    StorageFile file = await folder.GetFileAsync("Sample.unl");
    Launcher.LaunchFileAsync(file);
}
```

The path to the file must exist. If the file does not exist, a `FileNotFoundException` is raised.

The MainPageViewModel in the WPUnleashed.AppThatLaunchesACustomFileType project saves a sample file with the .unl extension (see Listing 30.4). The storage API is used to create a new file. A message is constructed, converted to bytes, and then written to the file using the Stream `WriteAsync` method.

LISTING 30.4   `MainPageViewModel.SaveSampleFile` Method

```
async void SaveSampleFile()
{
    string assemblyName = Assembly.GetExecutingAssembly().FullName;
    assemblyName = assemblyName.Substring(
        0, assemblyName.IndexOf(",", StringComparison.Ordinal));

    string fileContent = string.Format(
        "This text was saved to a file at {0} from the assembly: {1}.",
        DateTime.Now, assemblyName);

    IStorageFolder folder = ApplicationData.Current.LocalFolder;
    IStorageFile file = await folder.CreateFileAsync(
                            fileName, CreationCollisionOption.ReplaceExisting);

    using (Stream stream = await file.OpenStreamForWriteAsync())
    {
        byte[] content = Encoding.UTF8.GetBytes(fileContent);
        await stream.WriteAsync(content, 0, content.Length);
    }
}
```

> **NOTE**
>
> The sample's `MainPageViewModel` class is a linked file that is shared by both projects to reduce code duplication.

An `ICommand` named `launchFileCommand` calls the `LaunchFile` method, like so:

```
launchFileCommand = new DelegateCommand(obj => LaunchFile());
```

A button in the view is bound to the `LaunchFileCommand` property, as shown:

```
<Button Content="Launch File" Command="{Binding LaunchFileCommand}" />
```

Tapping the button causes the file to be loaded by the `LaunchFile` method, and the app is deactivated. The OS identifies the app that is registered to handle the .unl file extension and launches the WPUnleashed.FileAndProtocolAssociations app, which then navigates to the FileView.xaml page to display the file contents (see Figure 30.1).

FIGURE 30.1   The file content is displayed on the FileView.xaml page.

NOTE

Launching a file or a protocol from within the app that has the file or protocol registration produces slightly different life-cycle behavior. When launching from a different app, the app is deactivated (its `Deactivated` event is raised). When launching from the same app, the app is closed (its `Closed` event is raised) and then reopened to handle the launch request.

Reserved File Extensions

A small number of file extensions cannot be associated with your app. Table 30.2 lists the file extensions that are reserved for built-in apps, such as Office, and Table 30.3 lists file extensions that are reserved by the Windows Phone OS.

TABLE 30.2   File Types Reserved for Built-In Apps

.cer	.mp3	.pfx	.rtf
.docx/.doc	.p7b	.png	.xap
.jpg/.jpeg	.pem	.pptx/.ppt	.xlsx/.xls

30

TABLE 30.3   File Types Reserved for the Windows Phone OS

.ade	.dll	.mag	.msh2	.ps2xml	.tsk
.adp	.exe	.mam	.msh2xml	.psc1	.url
.app	.fxp	.maq	.mshxml	.psc2	.vb
.application	.gadget	.mar	.msi	.psm1	.vbe
.appref-ms	.grp	.mas	.msp	.pst	.vbp
.asp	.hlp	.mat	.mst	.pvw	.vbs
.bas	.hme	.mau	.msu	.py	.vhd
.bat	.hpj	.mav	.ops	.pyc	.vhdx
.cab	.hta	.maw	.pcd	.pyo	.vsmacros
.chm	.inf	.mcf	.pif	.rb	.vsw
.cmd	.ins	.mda	.pl	.rbw	.webpnp
.cnt	.isp	.mdb	.plg	.rdp	.ws
.com	.its	.mde	.plsc	.reg	.wsc
.cpf	.jar	.mdt	.prf	.rgu	.wsf
.cpl	.js	.mdw	.prg	.scf	.wsh
.crd	.jse	.mdz	.printerexport	.scr	.xaml
.crds	.ksh	.msc	.provxml	.shb	.xdp
.crt	.lnk	.msh	.ps1	.shs	.xip
.csh	.mad	.msh1	.ps1xml	.theme	.xnk
.der	.maf	.msh1xml	.ps2	.tmp	

How File and Protocol Associations Affect the User Experience

How the OS behaves in response to a file or protocol launch request is affected by whether a registered app exists for the request. If an installed app has a corresponding file or protocol registration, the OS immediately launches the app. If multiple installed apps are registered for the file or protocol, the user is given the choice on which app to launch.

If no installed app is registered for the file type or protocol, the user is offered the option of downloading one.

CAUTION

Do not register for a file or protocol association unless your app can perform a useful action with it. If your app causes the app menu to be shown too frequently, the user may choose to uninstall your app to avoid always having to select a choice.

Auto-Launching with a Protocol Association

A protocol association allows your app to be automatically launched when another app uses the `Windows.System.Launcher` API to launch a URI. The URI is prefixed with a protocol name that is associated with your app.

Registering for a Protocol Association

Registration of a protocol association is achieved using your app's WMAppManifest.xml file. To edit the WMAppManifest.xml file, in the Visual Studio Solution Explorer, right-click the WMAppManifest.xml file and then select View Code.

A protocol association is declared using a *Protocol* element, as shown in the following excerpt:

```
<Extensions>
  <Protocol Name="unleashed"
            NavUriFragment="encodedLaunchUri=%s" TaskID="_default" />
</Extensions>
```

The `Protocol` element includes the following three mandatory elements:

▶ **Name**—The prefix in your custom URI scheme. The value of Name must be a string between 3 and 39 characters in length and may contains numbers, lowercase letters, or a hyphen ('-').

▶ **NavUriFragment**—Must always be specified as `encodedLaunchuri=%s`

▶ **TaskID**—Must always be specified as `_default`

NOTE

A maximum of 10 protocol associations can be registered in an app.

Receiving a Protocol Launch Request

By associating your app with a particular protocol, the OS sends any launch requests that specify that protocol to your app. The OS does this by launching your app and providing a deep-link URI that may include actions encoded in the URI to be performed by your app.

It is your app's responsibility to recognize the incoming protocol request and redirect to a page that can handle it.

Detecting a Protocol Launch

The deep-link URI that is received by your app includes a query string parameter named `encodedLaunchUri`. The value of this parameter is the URL that was provided to the

30

`Windows.System.Launcher`. The value has two parts: a protocol name portion that comes before the colon character (:) and the payload message, which can be any text, formatted to suit the needs of your app.

For example, in the following URI, *unleashed* is the protocol name:

```
unleashed:AMessagePayloadWithSomeUsefulInformationEncoded
```

When your app is launched as a result of a protocol association, the app can use a URI mapping to redirect to a page designed to handle the launch request.

The App.xaml file in the WPUnleashed.FileAndProtocolAssociations has a UriMapping for the /Protocol URL that redirects to the ProtocolMessageView.xaml page. See the following excerpt:

```
<Application.RootVisual>
    <phone:PhoneApplicationFrame
        Navigated="CompleteInitializePhoneApplication"
        NavigationFailed="RootFrame_NavigationFailed">
        <phone:PhoneApplicationFrame.UriMapper>
            <navigation:UriMapper>
                <navigation:UriMapper.UriMappings>
                    <navigation:UriMapping Uri="/Protocol"
                        MappedUri="/ProtocolMessageView.xaml" />
                </navigation:UriMapper.UriMappings>
            </navigation:UriMapper>
        </phone:PhoneApplicationFrame.UriMapper>
    </phone:PhoneApplicationFrame>
</Application.RootVisual>
```

The entire protocol string, including the protocol name, is passed to the mapped page, ProtocolMessageView.xaml.

As you saw earlier with the FileView landing page, the ProtocolMessageView page passes the query string dictionary to its viewmodel during its `OnNavigateTo` method; as shown:

```
protected override void OnNavigatedTo(NavigationEventArgs e)
{
    base.OnNavigatedTo(e);

    ViewModel.Load(NavigationContext.QueryString);
}
```

The viewmodel's `Load` method attempts to retrieve the `encodedLaunchUri` query string parameter as shown in Listing 30.5. It then removes the protocol name and colon that prepends the string. The viewmodel's `Message` property is populated with the result.

LISTING 30.5   `ProtocolMessageViewModel.Load` **Method**

```
public async Task Load(IDictionary<string, string> queryStringDictionary)
{
    string encodedLaunchUrl;

    if (!queryStringDictionary.TryGetValue("encodedLaunchUri", out
        ➥encodedLaunchUrl))
    {
        MessageService.ShowError(
            "Unable to locate the encodedLaunchUri in the query string.");
        return;
    }

    int messageIndex = encodedLaunchUrl.IndexOf(":") + 1;
    if (messageIndex < 1)
    {
        MessageService.ShowError("Protocol message not found.");
        return;
    }

    string messageContent = encodedLaunchUrl.Substring(messageIndex);
    Message = messageContent;
}
```

With the protocol association in place and the landing page constructed, you now look at launching a protocol URI.

Launching a Protocol URI

Any app may request that the OS launch a protocol URI. This is achieved using the `Windows.System.Launcher` class.

The following excerpt from the MainPageViewModel constructs a URI by appending the protocol name with a custom message. The Launcher's `LaunchFileAsync` method is then called like so:

```
void LaunchProtocol()
{
    Launcher.LaunchUriAsync(new Uri("unleashed:" + protocolMessage));
}
```

The viewmodel contains a string property named `ProtocolMessage`, which allows the user to compose a message to be sent to a registered app for the protocol.

The view contains a `TextBox` that is bound to the `ProtocolMessage` property as shown:

```
<TextBox Text="{Binding ProtocolMessage, Mode=TwoWay}"
                    Width="250"/>
```

30

The viewmodel contains an `ICommand` named `launchProtocolCommand` that calls the `LaunchProtocol` method:

```
launchProtocolCommand
            = new DelegateCommand(obj => LaunchProtocol());
```

A `Button` in the view is bound to the `LaunchProtocolCommand` property:

```
<Button Content="Launch Protocol" Command="{Binding LaunchProtocolCommand}" />
```

Tapping the button causes the protocol URI to be constructed, and the app is deactivated. The OS dispatches the URI to the app that is registered to handle the *unleashed* protocol. The OS launches the WPUnleashed.FileAndProtocolAssociations, and the app navigates to the ProtocolMessageView.xaml page, which is displayed in Figure 30.2.

FIGURE 30.2   The protocol message is displayed by the ProtocolMessageView.xaml page.

Protocol associations allow your app to communicate with other apps on the device and allow the user to select the app that best suits his or her needs for handling a particular protocol message.

Reserved Protocol Names

Some reserved protocol names cannot be associated with your app. There are two types: those reserved for Windows Phone built-in apps, shown in Table 30.4, and those reserved for the Windows Phone OS, shown in Table 30.5.

Any attempt to register your app with a reserved protocol name is ignored. When a URI is launched, if it contains a protocol name that is reserved for a built-in app, only the built-in app is launched.

TABLE 30.4   Protocol Names Reserved for Built-In Apps

http	Tel
Onenote	Map
Mailto	Zune

TABLE 30.5   Protocol Names Reserved for the Operating System

Explorer.AssocActionId.BurnSelection	File	telnet
Explorer.AssocActionId.CloseSession	Iehistory	tn3270
Explorer.AssocActionId.EraseDisc	Ierss	Vbscript
Explorer.AssocActionId.ZipSelection	Javascript	windowsmediacenterapp
Explorer.AssocProtocol.search-ms	Jscript	windowsmediacenterssl
Explorer.BurnSelection	LDAP	windowsmediacenterweb
Explorer.CloseSession	Res	WMP11.AssocProtocol.MMS
Explorer.EraseDisc	rlogin	
Explorer.ZipSelection	StickyNotes	

Launching Built-In Apps

In addition to handling protocol requests, the `Windows.System.Launcher` class allows you to launch some of the phone's built-in apps. For example, the following demonstrates how to launch the built-in Wi-Fi settings app:

```
Launcher.LaunchUriAsync(new Uri("ms-settings-wifi:"));
```

Table 30.6 lists URIs that can be used to launch other built-in apps.

30

TABLE 30.6   URI Schemes for Launching Built-In Apps

URI Scheme	Description
http:[URL]	Launches the web browser and navigates to the specified URL.
mailto:[email address]	Launches the Email app and creates a new message with the specified email address on the To line. Note that the email is not sent until the user taps Send.
ms-settings-accounts:	Launches the Account Settings app.
ms-settings-airplanemode:	Launches the Airplane Mode Settings app.
ms-settings-bluetooth:	Launches the Bluetooth Settings app.
ms-settings-cellular:	Launches the Cellular Settings app.
ms-settings-emailandaccounts:	Launches the Email and Accounts settings app.
ms-settings-location:	Launches the Location Settings app.
ms-settings-lock:	Launches the Lock Screen settings app.
ms-settings-wifi:	Launches the Wi-Fi Settings app.
zune:navigate?appid=[app ID]	Launches the Windows Phone Store and shows the details page for the specified app.
zune:reviewapp	Launches the Store and shows the review page for the calling app.
zune:reviewapp?appid=[app ID]	Launches the Store and shows the review page for the specified app.
zune:search?[search parameter]=[value]	Launches the Store and searches for the specified content.
zune:search?keyword=[search keyword]&contenttype=app	Launches the Store and searches for apps by keyword.
zune:search?publisher=[publisher name]	Launches the Store and searches for items by publisher name.

Summary

This chapter began with a brief introduction to file and protocol associations. It then looked at enabling file associations in your app, and you saw how to register your app for handling file launch requests for specific file types. You explored two sample apps that demonstrate the concepts of registration and launching of file and protocol associations.

Finally, the chapter delved into protocol associations. You saw how to register a protocol association, how to create a protocol association landing page, and how to send and receive protocol messages. You also looked at programmatically launching built-in apps.

CHAPTER 31

Extending the Search Experience

Search Integration allows you to add your app to a list of predefined categories. When the user performs a search using the built-in Search app, if a search result falls into one of the categories, a link to your app is displayed. This functionality works even if your app is not installed on the device, allowing the user to install and launch the selected app directly from a search result.

Extending the search experience of the phone allows your app to add features that enrich the user's experience and extends your app's presence on the phone.

This chapter begins with an overview of search quick cards and outlines the steps to navigate from a search result to an app. It then looks at associating your app with predefined search categories, via the WMAppManifest.xml file and the Extras.xml file. It then demonstrates two ways for performing redirection within your app, via a search deep-link URI.

The chapter then looks at creating a simple landing page that displays quick card information.

Finally, the chapter looks at retrieving the search query when your app is launched directly from search results, via App Instant Answer.

The source code for this chapter can be found in the SearchExtensibility solution, in the downloadable sample code.

Understanding Quick Cards

When performing a search on the phone, the built-in Search app allows the user to view some results using a detailed view of the result, called a *quick card*. Quick cards are displayed using a Pivot control, and categories of information are grouped into pivot items. This information may include content such as photos, descriptions, ratings, reviews, and some item-specific data, such as price comparisons in the Product card or the duration of a movie in theaters in the Movie card.

In addition, the *apps* pivot item is a springboard for launching apps that have nominated themselves as applicable to the category of the search result.

Figure 31.1 shows the user path to launching an app from a search result listing. When the user enters Thai Food as search terms, a list of nearby restaurants is displayed in the *local* pivot item. Tapping a search result presents a quick card for that item. The quick card displays detailed information for the search result, which is presented in a pivot. When the user navigates to the *apps* pivot item, a list of apps is presented.

FIGURE 31.1   Launching an app from a search result's quick card.

Although apps do not have to be installed on the device to be presented on a quick card, those that are installed appear at the top of the list.

The particular information that a quick card contains depends on the search that is performed. The following lists the four classes of quick cards:

▶ Places

▶ Products

▶ Movies

▶ Events

Places are locations listed in the *local* pivot page of search results. Products are listed under the *products* heading in the *web* pivot item of search results. Movies that are playing in theaters are listed under the Movies Near... heading in the web pivot item of search results, and Events are listed on the see+do pivot item of Local Scout.

The next section describes how to add your app to list of apps on a quick card.

Configuring Your App for Search Integration

Adding your app to the list of apps on a quick card involves the following steps:

► Modification of the WMAppManifest.xml file

► Creation of an Extras.xml file

► Creation of a search-related landing page in your app

► Configuration of URI rerouting for the search landing page in your app

Configuring the Application Manifest

An app that nominates itself for search integration must define the list of Bing search categories that the app can handle. This is done via the app's WMAppManifest.xml file. Listing 31.1 shows an excerpt from the sample app's WMAppManifest.xml file.

Each Extension element uses the following four attributes to describe the extension:

► `ExtensionName`—Specifies the category of the search result. If Bing determines that a search result falls into the category, the quick card for the result will include a link to your app. See the source code for a complete list of search extension names.

► `ConsumerID`—Identifies that the extension is for extending search. All search extensions require the same value of 5B04B775-356B-4AA0-AAF8-6491FFEA5661.

► `TaskID`—Corresponds to the name of the default task that is specified in the Tasks element of the same file. Usually this value is _default.

► `ExtraFile`—The location of the Extras.xml file. The file must reside in a folder Extensions and be named Extras.xml.

LISTING 31.1   WMAppManifest.xml (excerpt)

```
<Deployment ...>
  <DefaultLanguage .../>
  <App ...>
    <IconPath IsRelative="true" IsResource="false">
        Assets\ApplicationIcon.png
    </IconPath>
    <Capabilities>
...
    </Capabilities>
    <Tasks>
      <DefaultTask  Name ="_default" NavigationPage="MainPage.xaml"/>
      <!--<DefaultTask Name="_default"
              NavigationPage="SearchExtras?PlaceName=Azteca Mexican
            ➥Restaurants&amp;
```

```
                    PlaceAddress=3040 148th Ave NE, Redmond, WA,
                    98052&amp;Category=Bing_Places_Food_and_Dining" />-->
    </Tasks>
    <Tokens>
      ...
    </Tokens>

    <Extensions>
      <!-- All product extensions. In your application,
              only declare extensions that are relevant. -->
      <Extension ExtensionName="Bing_Products_Arts_and_Crafts"
              ConsumerID="{5B04B775-356B-4AA0-AAF8-6491FFEA5661}"
                         ➥TaskID="_default"
              ExtraFile="Extensions\\Extras.xml" />
      <Extension ExtensionName="Bing_Products_Baby_and_Nursery"
              ConsumerID="{5B04B775-356B-4AA0-AAF8-6491FFEA5661}"
                         ➥TaskID="_default"
              ExtraFile="Extensions\\Extras.xml" />
      ...

      <!-- All place extensions. In your application,
                only declare extensions that are relevant. -->
      <Extension ExtensionName="Bing_Places_Arts_and_Entertainment"
              ConsumerID="{5B04B775-356B-4AA0-AAF8-6491FFEA5661}"
                         ➥TaskID="_default"
              ExtraFile="Extensions\\Extras.xml" />
      ...

      <!-- The movies extension. In your application,
                      only declare extensions that are relevant. -->
      <Extension ExtensionName="Bing_Movies"
              ConsumerID="{5B04B775-356B-4AA0-AAF8-6491FFEA5661}" TaskID="_default"
              ExtraFile="Extensions\\Extras.xml" />
    </Extensions>

    <ScreenResolutions>
...
    </ScreenResolutions>

  </App>
</Deployment>
```

31

During development, you can save time by simulating launching the app via the Search Experience. The `NavigationPage` property of the `DefaultTask` can be replaced during development. That way, you avoid having to perform a search every time you want to test your app.

By default, when you attempt to open the WMAppManifest.xml file, Visual Studio will open a GUI editor for the file. To edit the file using a text editor, right-click the file in the Solution Explorer and select View Code.

Limit your app to search extension names that the app is expressly designed to handle. Apps that misuse Search extensibility risk failing certification or being pulled from the Marketplace.

Customizing Captions via the Extras.xml File

Each `ExtensionName` value in the WMAppManifest.xml file is defined in an Extras.xml file. The Extras.xml file allows you to add custom captions for your app in the quick card, depending on the category of the search result; see Listing 31.2.

The Extras.xml file is composed of the following elements:

▶ `ExtrasInfo`—The root element.

▶ `AppTitle`—(Used only in Windows Phone OS 7.1). Contains the default and localized strings representing the title of the application as it will appear in the apps pivot page. Only one AppTitle element is allowed.

▶ `ConsumerID`—Must correspond to the search extensions value: 5B04B775-356B-4AA0-AAF8-6491FFEA5661.

▶ `ExtensionName`—The name of the extension associated with the caption specified in the `CaptionString` element. The extension listed here must also be listed in WMAppManifest.xml. Do not specify the same extension name in more than one `ExtensionInfo` element because it prevents your app from appearing on a quick card.

▶ `Default`—Specifies the default and localized caption strings for the caption associated with the extension in the `Extensions` element.

The `AppTitle` is relevant only to Windows Phone 7.1 apps and not Windows Phone 8 apps. For Windows Phone 7.1 apps, the `AppTitle` defines the title used in the app list. Conversely, for Windows Phone 8 apps, the title that is displayed is the value of the `Title` attribute of `App` element in the WMAppManifest.xml file.

LISTING 31.2   Extras.xml (excerpt)

```xml
<ExtrasInfo>

  <AppTitle>
    <default>WPUnleashed Search Extensibility</default>
    <fr-FR> WPUnleashed Extensibilité Recherche</fr-FR>
  </AppTitle>

  <!-- Search-related captions -->
  <Consumer ConsumerID="{5B04B775-356B-4AA0-AAF8-6491FFEA5661}">

    <!-- Products caption for all product categories -->
    <ExtensionInfo>
      <Extensions>
        <ExtensionName>Bing_Products_Arts_and_Crafts</ExtensionName>
        <ExtensionName>Bing_Products_Baby_and_Nursery</ExtensionName>
        <ExtensionName>Bing_Products_Beauty_and_Fragrance</ExtensionName>
        ...
      </Extensions>
      <CaptionString>
        <default>Product URI Details</default>
        <fr-FR>Détails du produit URI</fr-FR>
      </CaptionString>
    </ExtensionInfo>

    <!-- Places caption for place categories -->
    <ExtensionInfo>
      <Extensions>
        <ExtensionName>Bing_Places_Arts_and_Entertainment</ExtensionName>
        <ExtensionName>Bing_Places_Automotive_and_Vehicles</ExtensionName>
        <ExtensionName>Bing_Places_Business_to_Business</ExtensionName>
        <ExtensionName>Bing_Places_Computers_and_Technology</ExtensionName>
        <ExtensionName>Bing_Places_Education</ExtensionName>
        ...
      </Extensions>
      <CaptionString>
        <default>Place URI Details</default>
      </CaptionString>
    </ExtensionInfo>

    <!-- Movies caption for all movie cards -->
    <ExtensionInfo>
      <Extensions>
        <ExtensionName>Bing_Movies</ExtensionName>
      </Extensions>
```

```
    <CaptionString>
      <default>Movie URI Details</default>
    </CaptionString>
  </ExtensionInfo>

 </Consumer>
</ExtrasInfo>
```

> **NOTE**
>
> A maximum of 50 captions can be specified in the Extras.xml file, for a maximum of 50 `ExtensionInfo` elements. Each `ExtensionInfo` element may contain no more than one `ExtensionName` element. The same `CaptionString` element (having the same caption text) can be used in more than one `ExtensionInfo` element, but an extension specified in an `ExtensionName` element cannot appear multiple times.

> **NOTE**
>
> The Extras.xml file can contain localized strings, so it must be UTF-8 encoded. All strings must be present within the file; strings cannot be referenced from a resource file.

With the Extras.xml file in place, a landing page can be defined to handle launching your app from a quick card.

Defining a Quick Card Target Page

When an app is launched from a quick card, a deep-link URI is used to deliver information about the quick card to the app via query string parameters. All deep-link URIs for search extensibility follow the same format and do not include the name of your app page. You must redirect navigation from the quick card to the appropriate page in your app.

The following is an example of a deep-link search URI:

```
/SearchExtras?PlaceName=Azteca Mexican Restaurants&amp;PlaceAddress=3040 148th Ave
NE, Redmond, WA, 98052&amp;Category=Bing_Places_Food_and_Dining
```

Redirection to a dedicated landing page can be achieved in a couple of ways. The first is by defining a URI Mapping within the app's App.xaml file, as shown in the following excerpt:

```
<Application.Resources>
        <nav:UriMapper x:Key="UriMapper"
xmlns:nav="clr-namespace:System.Windows.Navigation;assembly=Microsoft.Phone">
            <nav:UriMapper.UriMappings>
                <nav:UriMapping Uri="/SearchExtras"
```

```
                              MappedUri="/SearchLandingView.xaml" />
              </nav:UriMapper.UriMappings>
          </nav:UriMapper>
      </Application.Resources>
```

In this example, the `UriMapper` is defined within the Application Resources. To make your app use the custom URI mapper, it must be assigned to the `RootFrame`'s `UriMapper` property, as demonstrated in the following excerpt from the App.xaml.cs file:

```
void InitializePhoneApplication()
{
    ...

    /* Assign the quick card URI-mapper class to the application frame. */
    RootFrame.UriMapper = (UriMapperBase)Resources["UriMapper"];
    ...
}
```

An alternative approach to configuring the `UriMapper` is to define the `UriMapper` within the `Application.RootVisual` element in the App.xaml. You can see how this is performed in the WPUnleashed.Example project of the WPUnleashed solution, in the MainExamples directory of the downloadable sample code.

Another approach to achieving redirection is by creating a custom URI Mapper class, as shown in Listing 31.3. Using a custom URI mapper gives you more flexibility in being able to redirect to different pages within your app depending, for example, on the Bing search category.

The `CustomUriMapper` class derives from `UriMapperBase` and handles all navigation requests. When a request for the /SearchExtras URI arrives, the `MapUri` method is called, which determines if the request originates from a quick card. A URI is created to handle each particular search category.

LISTING 31.3   `CustomUriMapper` Class

```
public class CustomUriMapper : UriMapperBase
{
    const string targetPageName = "SearchLandingView.xaml";

    public override Uri MapUri(Uri uri)
    {
        if (uri == null)
        {
            return null;
        }

        string url = uri.ToString();
```

```
    /* Parse the URI when launched from a Bing Search. */
    const string searchExtrasPath = "/SearchExtras";

    if (url.StartsWith(searchExtrasPath))
    {
        string queryString = url.Substring(searchExtrasPath.Length);
        /* Uri.Query is not available for relative URIs,
            * hence the extraction of the query string from the URL. */
        IDictionary<string, string> queryDictionary
            = HttpUtilityAdvanced.ParseQueryString(queryString);

        string category;
        if (queryDictionary.TryGetValue("Category", out category))
        {
            if (category.StartsWith("Bing_Products"))
            {
                /* Create a new URI for product cards. */
                return CreateProductCardUri(queryDictionary);
            }

            if (category.StartsWith("Bing_Places"))
            {
                /* Create a new URI for place cards. */
                return CreatePlaceCardUri(queryDictionary);
            }

            if (category.StartsWith("Bing_Movies"))
            {
                /* Create a new URI for movie cards. */
                return CreateMovieCardUri(queryDictionary);
            }
        }
    }

    /* Return the URI when it is not related to App Connect for Search. */
    return uri;
}

Uri CreateProductCardUri(IDictionary<string, string> queryDictionary)
{
    List<string> keys = new List<string> { "ProductName", "Category" };
    var result = CreateCardUri(queryDictionary, keys);
    return result;
}


Uri CreatePlaceCardUri(IDictionary<string, string> queryDictionary)
```

```csharp
{
    List<string> keys = new List<string>
        {
            "PlaceName", "PlaceLatitude", "PlaceLongitude", "PlaceAddress",
                "Category"
        };
    var result = CreateCardUri(queryDictionary, keys);
    return result;
}


Uri CreateMovieCardUri(IDictionary<string, string> queryDictionary)
{
    List<string> keys = new List<string> { "MovieName", "Category" };
    var result = CreateCardUri(queryDictionary, keys);
    return result;
}


Uri CreateCardUri(IDictionary<string, string> queryDictionary,
                ➥List<string> keys)
{
    StringBuilder sb = new StringBuilder();
    sb.Append('/');
    sb.Append(targetPageName);
    if (keys.Any())
    {
        sb.Append('?');
    }

    int keyCount = keys.Count;

    for (int i = 0; i < keyCount; i++)
    {
        string key = keys[i];

        string itemValue;
        queryDictionary.TryGetValue(key, out itemValue);
        sb.Append(key);
        sb.Append("=");
        sb.Append(itemValue);

        if (i < keyCount - 1)
        {
            sb.Append("&");
        }
    }
```

```
            return new Uri(sb.ToString(), UriKind.Relative);
    }
}
```

A custom class named HttpUtilityAdvanced is used to parse the URI query string into a dictionary of string key/value pairs. When using the desktop .NET framework, the HttpUtility class contains a method for parsing query strings. Unfortunately, no such method exists for this purpose in the Windows Phone SDK. I have created a class named HttpUtilityAdvanced to fill this gap. It is located in the downloadable sample code in the WPUnleashed project. The ParseQueryString method deconstructs the specified query string and returns a dictionary of the query string key and values. See Listing 31.4.

LISTING 31.4   HttpUtilityAdvanced Class

```
public class HttpUtilityAdvanced
{
    public static IDictionary<string, string> ParseQueryString(string queryString)
    {
        var parameterDictionary = new Dictionary<string,
                            string>(StringComparer.InvariantCultureIgnoreCase);

        int startIndex = queryString.IndexOf('?');
        string queryPart;
        if (startIndex > -1)
        {
            queryPart = queryString.Substring(startIndex + 1);
        }
        else
        {
            queryPart = queryString;
        }

        string[] strings = queryPart.Split('&');

        foreach (string queryItem in strings)
        {
            int equalsIndex = queryItem.IndexOf('=');
            if (equalsIndex >= 0)
            {
                string key
                    = HttpUtility.UrlDecode(queryItem.Substring(0, equalsIndex));
                string itemValue
                    = HttpUtility.UrlDecode(queryItem.Substring(equalsIndex + 1));

                parameterDictionary.Add(key, itemValue);
            }
```

```
        else
        {
            parameterDictionary.Add(queryItem, null);
        }
    }

    return parameterDictionary;
    }
}
```

The custom URI mapper can be assigned to the RootFrame's UriMapper, in the App.xaml.cs file, as shown in the following excerpt:

```
void InitializePhoneApplication()
{
    ...

    /* Assign the quick card URI-mapper class to the application frame. */
    RootFrame.UriMapper = new CustomUriMapper();
    ...
}
```

Creating a Landing Page to Display Quick Card Information

The landing page for the sample is the SearchLandingView.xaml page, whose viewmodel is the SearchLandingViewModel class; see Listing 31.5.

An ObservableCollection of query string parameters is populated via the LoadUriParameters when the page is navigated to. The custom ParameterInfo class contains two string properties: Key and Value.

LISTING 31.5 SearchLandingViewModel Class

```
class SearchLandingViewModel : ViewModelBase
{
    readonly ObservableCollection<ParameterInfo> parameters
        = new ObservableCollection<ParameterInfo>();

    public ObservableCollection<ParameterInfo> Parameters
    {
        get
        {
            return parameters;
        }
    }
```

```
    }

    public void LoadUriParameters(IDictionary<string, string> queryStringParameters)
    {
        parameters.Clear();

        foreach (KeyValuePair<string, string> pair in queryStringParameters)
        {
            parameters.Add(new ParameterInfo(pair.Key, pair.Value));
        }
    }
}
```

The view's `OnNavigatedTo` method passes the query string dictionary, which is retrieved from the `NavigationContext`, as shown in the following excerpt:

```
protected override void OnNavigatedTo(NavigationEventArgs e)
{
    base.OnNavigatedTo(e);

    ViewModel.LoadUriParameters(NavigationContext.QueryString);
}
```

The landing page has a `ListBox` that is bound to the viewmodel's `Parameters` property. Parameters are displayed using a `DataTemplate`, shown in the following excerpt:

```
<ListBox Margin="0,0,-12,0" ItemsSource="{Binding Parameters}" >
    <ListBox.ItemTemplate>
        <DataTemplate>
            <StackPanel>
                <TextBlock
                    Text="{Binding Key}"
                    TextWrapping="Wrap"
                    Style="{StaticResource PhoneTextLargeStyle}"/>
                <TextBlock
                    Text="{Binding Value}"
                    TextWrapping="Wrap"
                    Style="{StaticResource PhoneTextAccentStyle}"/>
            </StackPanel>
        </DataTemplate>
    </ListBox.ItemTemplate>
</ListBox>
```

App Instant Answer

In addition to quick card search integration, App Instant Answer displays links to Windows Phone apps directly within search results. Unlike quick card integration, no registration of extension details is required for an app to appear in search results.

If an app matches a search query, the built-in search app displays the app in the search results. Tapping the app in the search results launches the app. The search query is passed to the app using a launch URI query string parameter named `bing_query`. If your app is launched from App Instant Answer, you can parse the launch URI to determine the query that corresponds to the launch.

The following example shows a launch URI from an App Instant Answer (when the default navigation page is set to MainPage.xaml). In this example, the user was searching for "xbox games".

/MainPage.xaml?bing_query=xbox%20games

> **NOTE**
>
> Unlike quick card integration, all App Instant Answer launches navigate to the landing page of your app, as they would in a standard app launch. You cannot specify a different navigation target.

Summary

This chapter began with an overview of search quick cards and outlined the steps to navigate from a search result to an app. It then looked at associating your app with predefined search categories, via the WMAppManifest.xml file and the Extras.xml file. Next, it demonstrated two ways for performing redirection within your app, via a search deep-link URI.

The chapter then looked at creating a simple landing page that displays quick card information.

Finally, the chapter looked at retrieving the search query when your app is launched directly from search results, via App Instant Answer.

CHAPTER 32

Conducting Background Activities with Scheduled Actions

The need to perform background processing is not uncommon for Windows Phone apps. The transient nature of the app's life cycle makes performing some long-running or periodic tasks difficult.

One of Microsoft's goals with Windows Phone has been to solve the battery life limitations present on other phone platforms. One way that it first did this was to limit the number of apps that could run simultaneously to just one app. This meant that using a cloud service and push notification was the only way to simulate background processing.

Since the introduction of multitasking capabilities in the Windows Phone 7.5 (Mango) release, a limit of one foreground app in execution is still in place*, yet Microsoft introduced a new way to run part of your app in the background.

This chapter looks at the scheduled notification system, which consists of a useful set of classes for setting reminders and alarms, which are able to present a message to the user at a predetermined time regardless of whether your app is running in the foreground.

The chapter then examines the scheduled task system, which extends the principles underpinning the notification system and offers the capability to run your own code in the background. You see how to create a to-do list app, which leverages a local database and updates live tiles from a background agent.

*. There is one exception to this. Apps that register as a geographic location provider are able to continue running despite there being a different app running in the foreground. For more information, see Chapter 17, "Building Location Aware Apps."

Finally, the chapter delves into a more advanced topic that explains how to use a `Mutex` to provide safe access to resources shared by your foreground app and your background agent.

The source code for this chapter can be found in the BackgroundAgents.sln solution in the BackgroundAgents directory within the downloadable source code.

Background Tasks

Background tasks refer collectively to actions that are registered with the phone OS to run in the background, and that occupy the following four distinct areas of application functionality:

▶ Scheduled notifications

▶ Scheduled tasks

▶ Background file transfers

▶ Background audio

Of these, scheduled notifications are the simplest to use and understand. They are notifications that can be set from your app to display a message to the user at some time in the future.

Scheduled tasks allow you to register a class containing a method that is called periodically, even when your app is not running. They are multipurpose and offer the greatest utility for extending your app to perform background activities. Scheduled tasks may be used to perform some action periodically, such as querying a cloud service and updating a live tile, or they may be used to perform a less-frequent resource-intensive action, such as batch processing a set of images.

Transferring large files is difficult when your app may be tombstoned or closed at any time. The phone includes a background file transfer system that allows you to request a file to be downloaded from the Web to isolated storage, or uploaded from isolated storage to a cloud service.

Windows Phone devices generally offer a rich multimedia experience for users. Users today are frequently forgoing a dedicated audio device and turning instead to the phone to play audio. Windows Phone allows you to build an audio app that can respond to the phone's built-in play controls, even when your app is not running.

The following sections explore scheduled notification and scheduled tasks in detail. Background file transfers and background audio are discussed in subsequent chapters.

Scheduled Notifications

Sometimes an app may need to schedule a message to be displayed to the user at a future date. One way to achieve this, without relying on the user to have the app open to display the message, is to use a scheduled notification. Scheduled notifications present a dialog to the user at a predefined date and time that provides the user with the following three options:

▶ A snooze button allows the user to postpone the notification for several minutes. The snooze period can be set by the user when using a reminder.

▶ A dismiss button allows the user to close the notification.

▶ Tapping elsewhere within the notification dialog launches your app.

The Windows Phone notification system consists of two types of notifications: alarms and reminders. These provide a simple way to link back to your app and do not depend on your app being in the foreground. Figure 32.1 shows an alarm being displayed.

FIGURE 32.1   An `Alarm` may be snoozed or dismissed by the user.

> **NOTE**
>
> Tapping an alarm or reminder launches your app. If your app is in the foreground and the user taps the alarm, the alarm dialog is dismissed.

The two types of scheduled notifications are represented by the `Alarm` and `Reminder` classes. Both types may be set to be periodic, occurring every day, for example, or set to occur only once.

Registration of a notification is done using the `ScheduledActionService` class, which is demonstrated later in this section. `ScheduledActionService` handles the registration of both scheduled notifications and scheduled tasks.

> **NOTE**
>
> Although scheduled notifications offer an effective and easy way to link back to your app, there is a limit to how many can be registered by your app. This limit is 50

alarms and reminders in total. Attempting to register more than this number raises an
`InvalidOperationException`.

`Alarm` and `Reminder` classes are derived from the `ScheduleNotification` class, which
contain a `Content` property and a `Title` property that are displayed to the user (see
Figure 32.2).

> **NOTE**
>
> The `Title` property is supported only by the `Reminder` class and not by the `Alarm` class.
> `Alarm` overrides the `Title` property, and its setter raises a `NotSupportedException` if it
> is used. When the alarm notification is displayed, the title in the alarm dialog is always
> *Alarm*.

The most important distinction between alarms and reminders is that reminders allow you
to deep link to your app. This means that a URI can be associated with the reminder, so
that when the user taps the reminder, your app is launched to a specific page and you can
determine the course of action based on the URI's query string. While tapping an alarm
also launches the app, it does not provide an equivalent URI property.

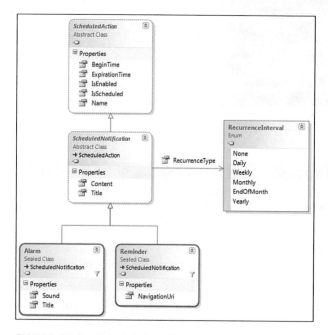

FIGURE 32.2   Scheduled notifications class diagram.

Another distinction between the `Alarm` and `Reminder` classes is that the `Alarm` class
includes a `Sound` property, which allows you to specify the sound file to play when an
alarm occurs, which the `Reminder` class does not.

The time and date of the notification are specified using the ScheduledAction.BeginTime property, which is of type DateTime. The date component of the BeginTime property is relevant only when using a RecurrenceType of None. RecurrenceType defines if, and for what period, scheduled notification should be periodically presented to the user. If the value is None (the default), the notification is raised only once.

When setting the BeginTime property of a notification, the value must fall after the current time or an InvalidOperationException ensues.

The ScheduledAction.ExpirationTime property is used to define the window for which the notification is raised; when the date and time on the phone occur after the ExpirationTime value, the notification schedule expires and the notification is no longer raised. If not specified, ExpirationTime is set to DateTime.MaxValue, resulting in it never expiring.

The following sections examine the use of each notification type in greater detail.

Alarm Registration

As previously stated, registering an alarm is done via the ScheduledActionService. When using the ScheduledActionService, each notification must be given a unique name, or an exception is raised when you try to add it to the service. In the following example, we avoid reregistering a notification by detecting whether a notification with the same name has already been registered. We then use the ScheduledActionService class's Add method to register the alarm, as shown:

```
Alarm alarm = new Alarm(alarmName)
{
    BeginTime = DateTime.Now.AddDays(1),
    Content = "A test alarm.",
    RecurrenceType = RecurrenceInterval.None,
    Sound = new Uri("/Sounds/Alarm.wma", UriKind.Relative),
};

if (ScheduledActionService.Find(alarm.Name) != null)
{
    ScheduledActionService.Remove(alarm.Name);
}

ScheduledActionService.Add(alarm);
```

The BeginTime property indicates when the alarm is due to occur. RecurrenceInterval.None specifies that the alarm is not recurring, which need not be specified because it is the default value.

The Alarm.wma audio file is located in the project and has its Build Action set to Content. When the alarm occurs, the audio file is played.

The Alarm class properties are examined in greater detail in the following section, where you explore the downloadable sample code for this section.

Alarm Sample

The sample code for this section includes a page that allows you to enter the details of a new alarm—including its name and begin time—and to set the alarm via an application bar button. The code is located in the Alarms directory of the WPUnleashed. BackgroundAgents project, in the BackgroundAgents solution.

Within the sample, the `AlarmViewModel` class contains various properties that correspond to the following properties of the `Alarm` class:

- ▶ **BeginTime**—A `DateTime` value indicating when the alarm should occur.

- ▶ **Name**—A unique string identifier for the alarm.

- ▶ **RecurrenceType**—A `RecurrenceInterval` enum value that specifies whether the alarm is a one-time alarm or that it should recur every day or month.

- ▶ **ExpirationTime**—When the alarm is a recurring alarm, this value indicates when the alarm is to be deemed no longer valid and removed by the OS.

- ▶ **Content**—A string that is presented in the alarm dialog when the alarm occurs.

- ▶ **Sound**—When the alarm occurs, a sound is played. This property is a relative URI to an audio file within the assembly, allowing you to change the default sound that is played to one of your choosing.

The viewmodel contains a single `ICommand` called `AlarmSetCommand`, which is initialized in the viewmodel's constructor, as shown:

```
public AlarmViewModel()
{
    alarmSetCommand = new DelegateCommand(obj => SetAlarm());
}
```

When executed, the command calls the `SetAlarm` method, which creates a new `Alarm` using the viewmodel's property values. The built-in `ScheduledActionService` is used to register the alarm, as shown in the following excerpt:

```
void SetAlarm()
{
    Alarm alarm = new Alarm(alarmName)
            {
                BeginTime = alarmBeginTime,
                ExpirationTime = alarmExpirationTime,
                Content = alarmContent,
                RecurrenceType = alarmRecurrenceType,
                Sound = alarmSound,
                /* Alarm does not support setting the Title. */
                // Title = alarmTitle
            };
```

```
if (ScheduledActionService.Find(alarm.Name) != null)
{
    ScheduledActionService.Remove(alarm.Name);
}

ScheduledActionService.Add(alarm);

MessageService.ShowMessage("alarm set");
}
```

The alarmSound field of the viewmodel is set to a Content resource located in the project's Sounds directory, as shown:

```
readonly Uri alarmSound = new Uri("/Sounds/Alarm.wma", UriKind.Relative);
```

Although nearly all of the viewmodel's properties are used merely as values for a new Alarm, one property, RecurrenceIntervals, allows the user to pick the recurrence type of the alarm using a Windows Phone Toolkit ListPicker in the view. The ListPicker is bound to the RecurrenceIntervals property of the viewmodel.

Population of the recurrenceIntervals backing field is done using the custom EnumUtility class, presented in Chapter 6, "Mastering Text Elements and Fonts." The CreateEnumValueList method retrieves the possible enum values using reflection. See the following excerpt:

```
readonly IEnumerable<RecurrenceInterval> recurrenceIntervals
                = EnumUtility.CreateEnumValueList<RecurrenceInterval>();

public IEnumerable<RecurrenceInterval> RecurrenceIntervals
{
    get
    {
        return recurrenceIntervals;
    }
}
```

By using reflection to retrieve the list of enum values, it means they do not have to be hard-coded into the viewmodel.

The view allows the user to set the properties of a new alarm. Windows Phone Toolkit TimePicker and DatePicker controls are used to set the beginning and expiration times of the alarm, as shown in the following excerpt:

```
<StackPanel Grid.Row="1" Margin="12,0,12,0">
    <TextBlock Text="name" />
    <TextBox Text="{Binding AlarmName, Mode=TwoWay}" />
    <TextBlock Text="content" />
```

```
<TextBox Text="{Binding AlarmContent, Mode=TwoWay}" />
<StackPanel Orientation="Horizontal">
    <StackPanel>
        <TextBlock Text="begin time" />
        <toolkit:TimePicker
            Value="{Binding AlarmBeginTime, Mode=TwoWay}" />
    </StackPanel>
    <StackPanel>
        <TextBlock Text="expires" />
        <toolkit:DatePicker
            Value="{Binding AlarmExpirationTime, Mode=TwoWay}" />
    </StackPanel>
</StackPanel>
<toolkit:ListPicker
    Header="recurrence interval"
    ItemsSource="{Binding RecurrenceIntervals}"
    SelectedItem="{Binding AlarmRecurrenceType, Mode=TwoWay}" />
</StackPanel>
```

The view also includes an `AppBar` with a button that is bound to the `AlarmSetCommand`, like so:

```
<u:AppBar>
    <u:AppBarIconButton
            Command="{Binding AlarmSetCommand}"
            Text="Set Alarm"
            IconUri="/Images/ApplicationBarIcons/Check.png" />
</u:AppBar>
```

The various viewmodel properties are initialized with default values. Figure 32.3 shows the set alarm view, which allows the user to enter the new alarm information.

When the set alarm button is tapped, the `AlarmSetCommand` is executed, registering the alarm with the OS. When the begin time for the alarm comes around, the alarm dialog is displayed to the user.

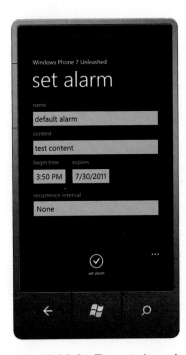

FIGURE 32.3   The set alarm view.

Reminder Registration

Reminder registration is done in much the same way as for `Alarm` objects. The reminder is instantiated and then registered with the `ScheduledActionService`. With reminders, however, you are able to provide a URI that allows you to deep link back to a particular page within the app, as shown in the following excerpt:

```
Reminder reminder = new Reminder("ReminderName")
    {
        BeginTime = DateTime.Now.AddMinutes(5),
        ExpirationTime = DateTime.Now.AddDays(5),
        Content = "Your daily reminder.",
        RecurrenceType = RecurrenceInterval.Daily,
        NavigationUri = new Uri("/ReminderView.xaml?Id=ReminderName",
                        UriKind.Relative),
        Title = reminderTitle
    };

if (ScheduledActionService.Find(reminder.Name) != null)
{
    ScheduledActionService.Remove(reminder.Name);
}

ScheduledActionService.Add(reminder);
```

The following section looks at creating a page that allows you to experiment with reminders.

Reminder Sample

The Reminder sample mirrors the alarm sample; however, the reminder sample demonstrates how to use the deep linking feature of reminders to allow editing of a reminder after it has been created.

The sample code for this section is located in the Reminders directory of the WPUnleashed.BackgroundAgents project in the BackgroundAgents solution.

Like the Alarm sample, the ReminderView page allows the user to enter the details of a new reminder and to set the reminder via an application bar button.

The ReminderViewModel class contains various properties that correspond to the Reminder class properties. Unlike the Alarm class, however, the Reminder class does not provide the ability to customize the sound effect of the notification.

The viewmodel contains two ICommand properties: one for registering a new reminder and the other for displaying an existing reminder after it has been navigated to via a deep link. The backing fields for both commands are initialized in the viewmodel constructor, like so:

```
public ReminderViewModel()
{
    reminderSetCommand = new DelegateCommand(obj => SetReminder());
    loadReminderCommand = new DelegateCommand<string>(LoadReminder);
}
```

When executed, the ReminderSet command calls the SetReminder method, which creates a new Reminder using the viewmodel's property values. In addition, we construct a Uri object that links back to the page if and when the user taps the reminder when it is displayed. See the following excerpt:

```
void SetReminder()
{
    const string reminderUrlFormat = "/Reminders/ReminderView.xaml?Id={0}";
    string navigationUrl = string.Format(reminderUrlFormat, ReminderName);
    Uri navigationUri = new Uri(navigationUrl, UriKind.Relative);
    Reminder reminder = new Reminder(ReminderName)
                    {
                        BeginTime = reminderBeginTime,
                        ExpirationTime = reminderExpirationTime,
                        Content = reminderContent,
                        RecurrenceType = reminderRecurrenceType,
                        NavigationUri = navigationUri,
                        Title = reminderTitle
                    };
```

```
if (ScheduledActionService.Find(reminder.Name) != null)
{
    ScheduledActionService.Remove(reminder.Name);
}
ScheduledActionService.Add(reminder);
MessageService.ShowMessage("reminder set");
}
```

When the `LoadReminderCommand` executes, the `LoadReminder` method is called with the command parameter, which should be the name of a registered `Reminder`. The `ScheduledActionService` is used to retrieve the `Reminder` by name. If it is located, the viewmodel's properties are populated with the `Reminder` values, as shown:

```
void LoadReminder(string name)
{
    Reminder reminder = ScheduledActionService.Find(name) as Reminder;
    if (reminder == null)
    {
        MessageService.ShowError("Reminder not found.");
        return;
    }
    ReminderBeginTime = reminder.BeginTime;
    ReminderContent = reminder.Content;
    ReminderName = reminder.Name;
    ReminderRecurrenceType = reminder.RecurrenceType;
    ReminderTitle = reminder.Title;
}
```

`LoadReminderCommand` is executed via the view's `OnNavigatedTo` method. When the user taps a reminder, the app starts with the `ReminderView` displayed. The `OnNavigatedTo` method extracts the `Reminder` name using a key exposed by the viewmodel (see Listing 32.1).

The command is prevented from being executed more than once using an `initialized` flag. `OnNavigatedTo` may be called more than once if the app was tombstoned or a back navigation took place.

LISTING 32.1   `ReminderView` Class

```
public partial class ReminderView : PhoneApplicationPage
{
    bool initialized;

    readonly ReminderViewModel viewModel;
    public ReminderView()
    {
```

```
        InitializeComponent();


        DataContext = viewModel = new ReminderViewModel();
    }


    protected override void OnNavigatedTo(NavigationEventArgs e)
    {
        base.OnNavigatedTo(e);


        if (initialized)
        {
            return;
        }
        initialized = true;


        string reminderId;
        if (NavigationContext.QueryString.TryGetValue(
                ReminderViewModel.IdQueryKey, out reminderId))
        {
            viewModel.LoadReminderCommand.Execute(reminderId);
        }
    }
}
```

The root grid within the view XAML contains a custom `AppBar` that includes an
`AppBarIconButton` bound to the `ReminderSetCommand`, like so:

```
<u:AppBar>
    <u:AppBarIconButton
                Command="{Binding ReminderSetCommand}"
                Text="Set"
                IconUri="/Images/ApplicationBarIcons/Check.png" />
</u:AppBar>
```

The view allows the user to set the properties of a new `Reminder` or to edit the properties
of an existing `Reminder`.

```
<StackPanel Grid.Row="1" Margin="12,0,12,0">
    <TextBlock Text="name" />
    <TextBox Text="{Binding ReminderName, Mode=TwoWay}" />
    <TextBlock Text="title" />
    <TextBox Text="{Binding ReminderTitle, Mode=TwoWay}" />
    <TextBlock Text="content" />
    <TextBox Text="{Binding ReminderContent, Mode=TwoWay}" />
    <StackPanel Orientation="Horizontal">
        <StackPanel>
```

```xml
            <TextBlock Text="begin time" />
            <toolkit:TimePicker
                Value="{Binding ReminderBeginTime, Mode=TwoWay}" />
        </StackPanel>
        <StackPanel>
            <TextBlock Text="expires" />
            <toolkit:DatePicker
                Value="{Binding ReminderExpirationTime, Mode=TwoWay}" />
        </StackPanel>
    </StackPanel>
    <toolkit:ListPicker
        Header="recurrence interval"
        ItemsSource="{Binding RecurrenceIntervals}"
        SelectedItem="{Binding ReminderRecurrenceType, Mode=TwoWay}" />
</StackPanel>
```

Figure 32.4 shows the set reminder view, which allows the user to enter the new reminder information.

FIGURE 32.4   Set Reminder view.

After the reminder has been set, and the begin time arrives, a dialog is presented to the user, displaying the reminder information (see Figure 32.5).

FIGURE 32.5   A reminder can be snoozed or dismissed by the user.

Tapping the reminder launches the app and automatically causes the app to navigate to the NavigateUri property of the Reminder, which allows the Reminder to be modified and reregistered.

Alarms and reminders offer a simple way to add notification support to your app. The next section looks at scheduled tasks and how they offer the capability to perform application logic in the background.

Scheduled Tasks

A scheduled task allows you to perform an activity in the background while your app is or is not running. A task can be used to query a cloud service and update the app's shell tiles, and it provides your users with the opportunity to respond to some event.

Scheduled tasks follow the same model as scheduled notifications, yet they add one other dimension: user-defined task agents. Whereas scheduled notifications rely solely on built-in task agents for presenting notification dialogs, with scheduled tasks, you define your own.

Like scheduled notifications, scheduled tasks are registered with the ScheduledActionService when your app is running. Registration causes your task agent to run in the background at an indeterminate time and in a separate process.

After a scheduled task is registered, it is persisted across reboots of the OS. The user can view and/or disable background tasks from the Settings screen by navigating to Settings/applications/background tasks (see Figure 32.6).

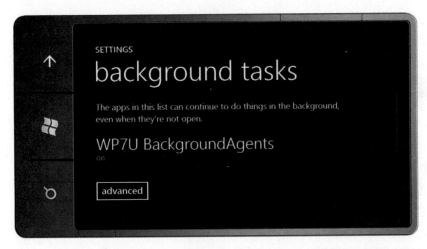

FIGURE 32.6   The user can disable scheduled tasks via the background tasks screen.

The scheduled task system consists of the following three components:

▶ A task registration service called `ScheduledActionService`, which is the same service used by the scheduled notification system (uses `Alarms` and `Reminders`).

▶ A background agent that derives from `ScheduledTaskAgent`, which is used to perform the background activity.

▶ The tasks themselves, which can be either of type `PeriodicTask` or `ResourceIntensiveTask`. Task objects allow you to pass information to your task agent from your app, determine how the task agent is executed, and when it expires.

Background Agent Types

Windows Phone supports three types of background agents: `ScheduledTaskAgent`, `AudioPlayerAgent`, and `AudioStreamingAgent` (see Figure 32.7).

Audio player agents are specialized agents used to retrieve audio files and coordinate the playback of background audio. `AudioPlayerAgent` and `AudioStreamingAgent` are explored in Chapter 34, "Coordinating Background Audio Playback."

`ScheduledTaskAgent` is an abstract class, which you subclass to provide your own logic to be performed whenever the OS chooses to invoke your agent. When invoked, the OS passes the registered task object to the task agent, which allows you to determine what kind of activity is to be performed.

ScheduledTaskAgents handle two kinds of tasks: periodic and resource intensive, which are represented by the PeriodicTask and ResourceIntensiveTask classes, respectively.

FIGURE 32.7   BackgroundAgent types.

> **NOTE**
>
> An app may have only one periodic task and/or one resource intensive task. If an attempt is made to register more than one of either type, an InvalidOperationException is raised.

Scheduled tasks are registered in the same manner as ScheduledNotification objects— with the ScheduledActionService. At an indeterminate time after registration, the operating system instantiates your task agent and passes it the scheduled task (see Figure 32.8). The agent performs any processing it needs to do in the background, and then signals that it has either completed its work or that it is unable to complete.

It is important to recognize the distinction between the roles of tasks and task agents. Tasks contain information that is passed to the task agent. Their purpose is to allow the ScheduledActionService to determine how and when to run the task agent. The task agent performs the background activity, and that is where you can place your code to be executed in the background.

PeriodicTask and ResourceIntensiveTask are analogous to the ScheduledNotification classes: Alarm and Reminder. ScheduledTask and ScheduledNotification both derive from ScheduledAction, which includes properties for the name and expiration date of the task (see Figure 32.9).

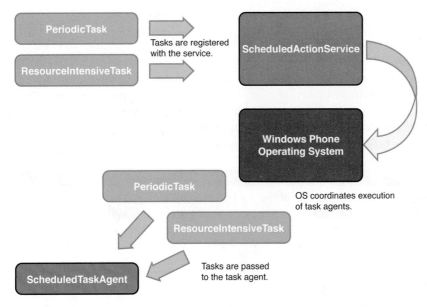

FIGURE 32.8   Periodic tasks are registered with the `ScheduledActionService`. The OS invokes the `ScheduledTaskAgent`, passing it the `PeriodicTask` object.

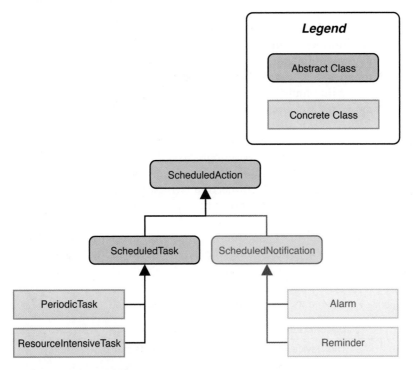

FIGURE 32.9   `ScheduledTask` is derived from `ScheduledAction`, the same base class for scheduled notifications.

The following sections examine the two `ScheduledTask` types, `PeriodicTask` and `ResourceIntensiveTask`, in greater detail.

Periodic Tasks

A periodic task is used to perform short operations and is allocated a 15-second window to complete its work. Periodic tasks run, at most, every 30 minutes. Typical scenarios for periodic tasks include performing small incremental data synchronization with a cloud service, using geographic location to track the location of the device, or polling a social network cloud service for new messages or status updates.

> **NOTE**
>
> When retrieving the geographic location of the device within a scheduled task (via a `GeoCoordinateWatcher`), a cached location value is used instead of real-time data. This helps to minimize the power consumption of background agents. It does, however, also introduce a lag for determining the location of the device, which may be problematic in some scenarios.

Periodic Task Invocation   There are no guarantees that a periodic task will ever run. To minimize resources, the phone OS launches all periodic tasks for all apps on the device at approximately the same time. This can mean that if a large number of periodic tasks are registered, not all will be invoked. Moreover, Battery Saver mode is an option that the user can enable on the device to indicate that battery life should be prioritized. If this mode is enabled, periodic agents may not run, even if the task interval has elapsed.

There is also a limit on the total number of periodic agents that can be scheduled on a device. This limit varies from device to device, but it can be as low as six. If this limit is approached, the user is warned that multiple background agents are running, and that it may cause faster battery consumption.

Resource Intensive Tasks   Resource intensive tasks (also known as *on idle* tasks) are allocated a substantially longer execution time than periodic tasks. Resource intensive tasks, however, run only when the phone meets a minimum set of requirements relating to processor activity, power source, and network connection type (see Table 32.1). This task is typically used to synchronize large amounts of data to the phone during periods of inactivity.

Resource intensive tasks typically run for a maximum of 10 minutes. The runtime is cut short, however, if one or more of the requirements that determine eligibility to launch are no longer met.

TABLE 32.1   Run Eligibility Requirements for Resource Intensive Tasks

Requirement	Description
External power	The device must be connected to an external power supply.
Non-cellular connection	The device must have a network connection over Wi-Fi or through a connection to a PC.

Requirement	Description
Minimum battery power	The device's battery power must be greater than 90%.
Device screen lock	The device's screen must be locked.
No active phone call	A phone call cannot be under way.

32

CAUTION

Due to the hefty requirements for resource intensive tasks, it is possible that a resource intensive task may never be launched. Be mindful of this when designing your app, and allow your foreground app to adapt to the absence of any processing that should have taken place in the background but did not.

Using Scheduled Tasks

Using scheduled tasks in your app involves creating an agent class and adding an XML fragment to your WMAppManifest.xml file. This process can be done manually or by using the Windows Phone Scheduled Task Agent project template that resides beneath the Windows Phone node of the Add New Project dialog (see Figure 32.10).

FIGURE 32.10   Adding a new Windows Phone Scheduled Task Agent project.

The benefit of using the project template to create a scheduled task agent is seen when you reference that project from your primary phone project; a required XML fragment is automatically placed in the WMAppManifest.xml file.

> **NOTE**
>
> Scheduled tasks have restricted capabilities, and some APIs are off-limits. Even if your scheduled task does not use any of the restricted APIs, the mere presence of code that does, in a referenced assembly, may cause your app to fail the Windows Phone Marketplace certification process. It is therefore wise to segregate your scheduled task in a separate project. If there is shared code between your foreground app and scheduled task projects, it can be placed in a third project and referenced by both.
>
> In the samples for this chapter, I have chosen to place the background agent code within the same project as the main application, purely for the sake of convenience.
>
> For more information on scheduled task limitations, see the section "Scheduled Task API Limitations" later in the chapter.

A secondary benefit that can arise from using a separate project for your agent is that it can help to minimize the size of the assembly that is loaded by the CLR when your agent is invoked, which may marginally improve the load time of your agent. The larger an assembly is, the longer it takes the CLR to load it.

The XML fragment placed in the WMAppManifest.xml file informs the OS of the agent class type so that it can be resolved and invoked. The XML fragment resembles the following:

```
<Tasks>
    <DefaultTask  Name ="_default" NavigationPage="MainPage.xaml"/>
    <ExtendedTask Name="BackgroundTask">
        <BackgroundServiceAgent Specifier="ScheduledTaskAgent"
                                Name="[An identifier]"
                                Source="[Assembly Name]"
                                Type="[Class Name]" />
    </ExtendedTask>
</Tasks>
```

Table 32.2 provides descriptions of the attributes of the `BackgroundServiceAgent` element.

TABLE 32.2   `BackgroundServiceAgent` Attributes

Attribute	Description
Specifier	Indicates the kind of agent and can be AudioPlayerAgent, AudioStreamingAgent, or ScheduledTaskAgent
Name	An arbitrary identifier for the agent
Source	The assembly in which the agent class resides
Type	The namespace qualified name of the agent class

> **NOTE**
>
> If an attribute of the `BackgroundServiceAgent` element is incorrect—for example, the type is unresolvable or the Specifier is not a known value—an `InvalidOperationException` is raised when the OS attempts to invoke the task agent, and not before.

Scheduled Task Agent

When using the Windows Phone Scheduled Task Agent project template, you begin with a class resembling the following:

```
public class ScheduledAgent : ScheduledTaskAgent
{
    protected override void OnInvoke(ScheduledTask task)
    {
        //TODO: Add code to perform your task in background

        NotifyComplete();
    }
}
```

Your agent's `OnInvoke` method is called by the OS. In this method, your app can determine the type of `ScheduledTask` that triggered the invocation of the agent and perform actions accordingly. The task passed to the `OnInvoke` method is either a `PeriodicTask` or a `ResourceIntensiveTask`. To branch according to the type of task, something like the following can be used:

```
if (task is PeriodicTask)
{
    ProcessPeriodicTask();
}
else
{
    ProcessResourceIntensiveTask();
}
```

The `NotifyComplete` method of the base class informs the background task system that your task has finished its activities and signals that it is okay for the process to be terminated.

> **NOTE**
>
> Call `NotifyComplete` only when your agent has finished everything it needs to do, or your agent may be terminated along with any child threads spawned along the way.

If your agent is unable to perform its work because of an unavailable resource—a cloud service, for example—call the `Abort` method instead of the `NotifyComplete` method. `Abort` has the same effect on task termination, but causes the task's `IsScheduled` property to be set to false, which can then be detected and dealt with appropriately by your foreground app. If `IsScheduled` is false, you know that `Abort` was called.

NOTE

To maximize the number of dormant applications, each scheduled task agent is limited to 6MB of RAM. If your agent exceeds that amount, the agent is terminated. Two consecutive violations result in schedule suspension.

Be mindful, however, that this limitation is not enforced while debugging.

The amount of memory available to your agent can be measured like so:

```
long usedBytes
        = Microsoft.Phone.Info.DeviceStatus.ApplicationCurrentMemoryUsage;
long limitBytes
        = Microsoft.Phone.Info.DeviceStatus.ApplicationMemoryUsageLimit;
if ((usedBytes + 1048576) < limitBytes) // 1 048 576 = 1 MB
{
    /* Do work with 1 MB. */
}
```

Scheduled Task Registration

Registering a task is achieved from your foreground app.

NOTE

`ScheduledAction` objects can be registered only when your app is in the foreground, and not from a background agent. Attempting to register `ScheduledAction` in a background agent raises an `InvalidOperationException`.

The following shows how to create a new `PeriodicTask`:

```
string taskName = "a unique name";
PeriodicTask periodicTask = new PeriodicTask(taskName)
    {
        /* Description is required. */
        Description = "A description for the task"
    };
```

All `ScheduledAction` objects added to the `ScheduledActionService` must be named uniquely. Therefore, you should test whether the task has already been added to the scheduled action service. The task may then be added to the service as shown:

```
if (ScheduledActionService.Find(taskName) != null)
{
    ScheduledActionService.Remove(taskName);
}
/* This can only be called when the application
 * is running in the foreground. */
ScheduledActionService.Add(periodicTask);
```

32

> **NOTE**
>
> Tasks expire after a maximum of 14 days. If the task's ExpirationTime property is not set, it defaults to 14 days.
>
> Tasks can be renewed by removing them, re-creating them, and then adding them back to the ScheduledActionService. However, this can be done only from a foreground app, which means that if the user does not launch your app, you have no way to prevent your tasks from expiring after the default expiration period of 14 days.

The next section looks at putting periodic tasks into action.

To-Do List Scheduled Task Sample

This section looks at creating a to-do list app that uses periodic tasks in conjunction with a scheduled task agent. The app allows the user to enter a to-do item, which is stored in a local database, and which can be pinned as a live tile on the start experience. We look at using a periodic task to update the status of the to-do item live tiles.

TodoItem

To-do items are represented by the TodoItem class, which contains three properties: Id, Description, and DueDate. DueDate is of type DateTime and indicates when the to-do item should be considered overdue. TodoItem objects are persisted using LINQ to SQL. The TodoItem class is decorated with a Table attribute, and its properties with Column attributes (see Listing 32.2).

LISTING 32.2   TodoItem Class

```
[Table]
public class TodoItem : NotifyPropertyChangeBase
{
    int id;

    [Column(
        IsPrimaryKey = true,
        DbType = "INT IDENTITY NOT NULL",
        IsDbGenerated = true,
        UpdateCheck = UpdateCheck.Never)]
```

```
public int Id
{
    get
    {
        return id;
    }
    set
    {
        Assign(ref id, value);
    }
}

string description;

[Column]
public string Description
{
    ...
}

DateTime dueDate;

[Column]
public DateTime DueDate
{
    ...
}
}
```

For more information on LINQ to SQL and using databases in Windows Phone, see Chapter 29, "Storing App Data in a Local Database."

We now look briefly at the app's data layer, before moving on to its viewmodels. Persistence of TodoItem objects is performed using a LINQ to SQL DataContext instance, and an intermediary service that decouples the data context from the app's viewmodels.

TodoDataContext

To retrieve and store TodoItem objects in a database, we use a custom DataContext class called TodoDataContext. This class allows TodoItem objects to be retrieved via its TodoItems property (see Listing 32.3).

LISTING 32.3   TodoDataContext Class

```
public class TodoDataContext : DataContext
{
    public TodoDataContext(string connection)
        : base(connection)
```

```
    {
    }

    public Table<TodoItem> TodoItems
    {
        get
        {
            return GetTable<TodoItem>();
        }
    }
}
```

In the sample app, viewmodels do not directly interact with the `TodoDataContext`, but perform all CRUD operations via a to-do service. This decouples the data context from the viewmodels, allowing you to replace the to-do service with an implementation that could, for example, use a cloud service rather than a local database. Decoupling the data context also means that you have the flexibility to unit test the code outside an emulator, perhaps on a build server.

TodoService

A custom service provides for all CRUD operations for the `TodoItem` objects. It serves as an intermediary between the LINQ to SQL `DataContext` for `TodoItems` and viewmodel logic.

When the `TodoService` is instantiated, a `TodoDataContext` is created. `TodoItem` objects can then be retrieved using the `GetTodoItem` method, shown in the following excerpt:

```
public TodoItem GetTodoItem(int itemId)
{
    TodoItem item = dataContext.TodoItems.Where(
                    todoItem => todoItem.Id == itemId).FirstOrDefault();

    if (item == null)
    {
        throw new KeyNotFoundException(
            string.Format("Item with key '{0}' was not found.", itemId));
    }

    return item;
}
```

Conversely, inserting a new `TodoItem` into the database is done using the service's `AddOrUpdateItem` method.

If the `TodoItem` has an `Id` that is less than 1, it indicates that the `TodoItem` does not already exist in the database. If greater than 0, it is indicative of an update. See the following excerpt:

```
public void AddOrUpdateItem(TodoItem todoItem)
{
    ArgumentValidator.AssertNotNull(todoItem, "todoItem");

    if (todoItem.Id <= 0)
    {
        dataContext.TodoItems.InsertOnSubmit(todoItem);
    }
    dataContext.SubmitChanges();
}
```

The third method of the `TodoService` worth noting is `GetTodoItems`, which retrieves all `TodoItem` objects via the `TodoItems` property of the data context, like so:

```
public IEnumerable<TodoItem> GetTodoItems()
{
    return dataContext.TodoItems;
}
```

As you see in a moment, `GetTodoItems` is used by the `TodoListViewModel`.

With the `TodoService` in place we now look at how the service is used by the app's view-models to display all to-do items and to create new to-do items.

TodoItemViewModel

The `TodoItemView` page retrieves all `TodoItem` objects for the user and displays them in a list. Its viewmodel relies on the to-do service being passed as a constructor argument.

Retrieving the `TodoItem` objects is performed in the viewmodel's `PopulateItems` method. The to-do service is used to retrieve the items, and then, using a LINQ expression, the items are grouped by the `TodoItem.DueDate` property. This allows the list to be bound to a `LongListSelector` in the view. See the following excerpt:

```
void PopulateItems()
{
    try
    {
        IEnumerable<TodoItem> items = todoService.GetTodoItems();

        IEnumerable<CustomGrouping<TodoItem>> groups
                = from todoItem in items
                  orderby todoItem.DueDate
                  group todoItem by todoItem.DueDate.Date
                  into grouping
                  select new CustomGrouping<TodoItem>(
                            new DateGroupingKey(grouping.Key),
                            grouping.AsEnumerable());
```

```
        GroupedTodoItems = groups.ToList();
    }
    catch (Exception ex)
    {
        Message = "Unable to retrieve items.";
        Console.WriteLine(ex);
    }
}
```

TodoItems are grouped using a custom class called DateGroupingKey, which allows us to provide some additional logic to the item groupings, namely an Overdue property (see Listing 32.4). This allows you to change the background for the grouping header to red if the to-do items in the group have due dates occurring in the past.

Alternatively, you may choose to use a value converter for determining whether the date is overdue. The example uses a custom key class, however, because it better encapsulates the date value and the logic for determining whether it is overdue.

LISTING 32.4   DateGroupingKey Class

```
public class DateGroupingKey
{
    public DateTime DateTime { get; private set; }

    public DateGroupingKey(DateTime dateTime)
    {
        DateTime = dateTime;
        Overdue = DateTime.Now > dateTime;
    }

    public bool Overdue { get; private set; }
}
```

The viewmodel's Load method commences population of the to-do items asynchronously, using a thread from the thread pool. This prevents blocking the UI thread during a potentially long-running operation.

A PeriodicTask is registered with the ScheduledActionService. If the PeriodicTask has already been registered, it is first removed. This resets the task's expiration date. See the following excerpt:

```
public void Load()
{
    ThreadPool.QueueUserWorkItem(delegate { PopulateItems(); });

    PeriodicTask periodicTask = new PeriodicTask(agentName)
    {
```

```
        Description = "Updates a tile.",
        ExpirationTime = DateTime.Now.AddDays(14)
    };

    if (ScheduledActionService.Find(agentName) != null)
    {
        ScheduledActionService.Remove(agentName);
    }

    /* This can only be called when the app
     * is running in the foreground. */
    ScheduledActionService.Add(periodicTask);
}
```

The `TodoListViewModel` constructor calls its `Load` method after initializing various
`ICommands` (see Listing 32.5). `NewItemCommand` uses the `ViewModelBase` class's `Navigate`
method to open the `TodoItemView` page. `EditItemCommand` also navigates to the
`TodoItemView` page, but passes the `Id` of the `TodoItem`, provided as a command argument.

LISTING 32.5   `TodoListViewModel` Constructor

```
public TodoListViewModel(
    ITodoService todoService, IDeviceProperties deviceProperties)
{
    this.todoService = ArgumentValidator.AssertNotNull(
                                    todoService, "todoService");
    this.deviceProperties = ArgumentValidator.AssertNotNull(
                    deviceProperties, "deviceProperties");

    editItemCommand = new DelegateCommand<int>(
        todoItemId => Navigate(todoItemViewUrl + "?TodoItemId=" + todoItemId));

    testAgentCommand = new DelegateCommand(
                        obj => ScheduledActionService.LaunchForTest(
                            agentName, TimeSpan.Zero));

    backupDatabaseCommand = new DelegateCommand(obj => BackupDatabase());

    restoreDatabaseCommand = new DelegateCommand(obj => RestoreDatabase());
    Load();
}
```

`BackupDatabaseCommand` and `RestoreDatabaseCommand` are discussed later in this chapter.

Debugging Scheduled Tasks

Debugging a task agent is done by calling the `ScheduledActionService.LaunchForTest` method. Calling `LaunchForTest` is a way of forcing the OS to run your task agent. `LaunchForTest` accepts two parameters: the name of the scheduled task and a `TimeSpan` that indicates the delay before the task agent is invoked. By specifying `TimeSpan.Zero`, the task agent is invoked immediately.

With the `TestAgentCommand` wired up to the UI, you can instruct the OS to launch the task agent, allowing you to step into the task agent's `OnInvoke` method. The task agent for the sample is discussed later in this section.

The viewmodel relies on a custom `IDeviceProperties` interface, which allows the viewmodel to retrieve the Windows Live anonymous ID. Windows Live anonymous IDs are discussed further in Chapter 33, "Performing Background File Transfers."

`TodoListView` XAML

The `TodoListView` XAML contains a `LongListSelector` that is bound to the `GroupedTodoItems` property of the viewmodel (see Listing 32.6). The `LongListSelector`'s `ItemTemplate` uses a `TextBlock` to display the `Description` property of each `TodoItem`. When the user taps the description, the `EditItemCommand` is executed, and the `Id` of the `TodoItem` is passed as a command parameter. This is done using the custom commanding infrastructure, introduced in Chapter 8, "Taming the Application Bar."

The `LongListSelector`'s `GroupHeaderTemplate` contains a `Border` whose background is determined by the `Overdue` property of the group key, which is a `DateGroupingKey` instance.

LISTING 32.6   TodoListView.xaml (excerpt)

```xml
<StackPanel x:Name="ContentPanel" Grid.Row="1" Margin="12,0,12,0">
    <phone:LongListSelector
            ItemsSource="{Binding GroupedTodoItems}"
            IsGroupingEnabled="True"
            Background="Transparent"
            Height="600">
        <phone:LongListSelector.ItemTemplate>
            <DataTemplate>
                <StackPanel Orientation="Horizontal">
                    <TextBlock Text="{Binding Description}"
                        Margin="12,10,0,10"
                        Style="{StaticResource PhoneTextLargeStyle}"
                        c:Commanding.Event="Tap"
                        c:Commanding.Command="{Binding DataContext.EditItemCommand,
                                              ElementName=page}"
                        c:Commanding.CommandParameter="{Binding Id}" />
                </StackPanel>
            </DataTemplate>
        </phone:LongListSelector.ItemTemplate>
```

```
        <phone:LongListSelector.GroupHeaderTemplate>
            <DataTemplate>
                <Border Background="Transparent">
                    <Border Background="{Binding Key.Overdue,
                        Converter={StaticResource BooleanToBrushConverter}}"
                            Padding="5"
                            HorizontalAlignment="Left"
                            Margin="0,10,0,0">
                        <TextBlock
                            Text="{Binding Key.DateTime, StringFormat=\{0:d\}}"
                            Foreground="{StaticResource PhoneForegroundBrush}"
                            Style="{StaticResource PhoneTextLargeStyle}"
                            VerticalAlignment="Bottom" />
                    </Border>
                </Border>
            </DataTemplate>
        </phone:LongListSelector.GroupHeaderTemplate>
    </phone:LongListSelector>
</StackPanel>
```

The custom `BooleanToBrushConverter` is used to transform the `Overdue` property of type `bool` to a brush. For more information about the `BooleanToBrushConverter`, see Chapter 9, "Enriching the User Experience with the Windows Phone Toolkit Controls."

The `BooleanToBrushConverter` is defined as a page resource as shown:

```
<phone:PhoneApplicationPage.Resources>
    <ValueConverters:BooleanToBrushConverter
            x:Name="BooleanToBrushConverter"
            BrushIfTrue="Red"
            BrushIfFalse="Blue" />
</phone:PhoneApplicationPage.Resources>
```

Overdue groups are shown with a red header, and regular groups have a blue header (see Figure 32.11).

The custom `AppBar` for the page includes an `AppBarHyperlinkButton`, which takes the user to the `TodoItemView` page and allows the user to create a new to-do item. The other view-model commands are bound to `AppBarMenuItems`, as shown:

```
<u:AppBar>
    <u:AppBarHyperlinkButton
            NavigateUri="/TodoList/TodoItemView.xaml"
            Text="New"
            IconUri="/Images/ApplicationBarIcons/Add.png" />
    <u:AppBar.MenuItems>
        <u:AppBarMenuItem
```

```
                Command="{Binding BackupDatabaseCommand}"
                Text="Backup" />
        <u:AppBarMenuItem
                Command="{Binding RestoreDatabaseCommand}"
                Text="Restore" />
        <u:AppBarMenuItem
                Command="{Binding TestAgentCommand}"
                Text="test agent" />
    </u:AppBar.MenuItems>
</u:AppBar>
```

FIGURE 32.11   To-do items are grouped according to when they are due to expire.

You have seen how the list of to-do items is displayed; the next section examines how new to-do items are created.

TodoItemView and ViewModel

The `TodoItemView` allows the user to perform the following three tasks:

▶ Create a new todo item

▶ Update an existing todo item

▶ Delete a todo item

The `TodoItemViewModel` constructor receives the `ITodoService`, initializes commands, and registers persistent state, as shown:

```
public TodoItemViewModel(ITodoService todoService)
{
    this.todoService = ArgumentValidator.AssertNotNull(
                                    todoService, "todoService");
```

```
saveCommand = new DelegateCommand<bool>(SaveItem);
loadItemCommand = new DelegateCommand<int>(LoadItem);
deleteCommand = new DelegateCommand(obj => DeleteItem());
RegisterStatefulProperty(ApplicationStateType.Transient,
                            () => TodoDescription);
RegisterStatefulProperty(ApplicationStateType.Transient,
                            () => TodoDueDate);
}
```

The viewmodel contains a `Description` property and a `DueDate` property, which coincide with the properties of the `TodoItem` class. When the `SaveCommand` is executed, the `SaveItem` method is called. `SaveItem` uses the `ITodoService` to persist the `TodoItem` to the database, and to optionally create a live tile representing the to-do item.

Creating the To-Do Item Shell Tile

To create a shell tile, you must pass a `StandardTileData` instance to the static `ShellTile.Create` method. Because this is performed in several places in the sample, the code for creating the `StandardTileData` has been placed into a class called `TodoTileDataCreator` (see Listing 32.7). This class uses the to-do item's due date to determine the numeric icon shown on the tile. If it exceeds 99 days, it is not shown. The tile has a foreground and a background image, and shows the description and due date of the to-do item.

LISTING 32.7   `TodoTileDataCreator` Class

```
public static class TodoTileDataCreator
{
    public static StandardTileData CreateTile(
        string todoItemDescription, DateTime dueDate)
    {
        /* The Count property of the tile data is set
         * to the number of days remaining.
         * It must be between 0 and 99 inclusively. */
        int daysUntilDue = 0;
        bool overdue = DateTime.Now > dueDate;
        if (!overdue)
        {
            int temp = (int)(DateTime.Now - dueDate).TotalDays;
            if (temp < 100)
            {
                daysUntilDue = temp;
            }
        }

        const string tilesDirectory = "/TodoList/Images/Tiles/";
```

```
        string backgroundUrl = overdue
                            ? tilesDirectory + "Overdue.jpg"
                            : tilesDirectory + "Ok.jpg";

        StandardTileData tileData = new StandardTileData
            {
                Title = todoItemDescription,
                BackgroundImage = new Uri(backgroundUrl, UriKind.Relative),
                Count = overdue ? 0 : daysUntilDue,

                BackTitle = dueDate.ToShortDateString(),
                BackContent = todoItemDescription,
                BackBackgroundImage = new Uri(
                    tilesDirectory + "Background.jpg", UriKind.Relative)
            };

        return tileData;
    }
}
```

Saving a To-Do Item

Saving an item involves instantiating a new item and sending it to the ITodoService to be stored in the database (see Listing 32.8).

If a shell tile is created for the to-do item, the NavigationUri of the tile is set to the TodoItemView page, and the Id of the TodoItem is placed in the query string of the URI, so that by tapping the tile, the user is brought back to the TodoItemView page, which allows editing or deletion of the to-do item.

> **NOTE**
>
> Calling ShellTile.Create immediately deactivates your app.

The final task of the SaveItem method is to navigate the user back to the TodoItemList page.

LISTING 32.8   TodoItemViewModel SaveItem Method

```
void SaveItem(bool createTile)
{
    if (string.IsNullOrWhiteSpace(todoDescription))
    {
        MessageService.ShowError("Please enter a description.",
                                 "Required Field Missing");
        return;
    }
```

```csharp
    if (todoItem == null)
    {
        todoItem = new TodoItem();
    }

    todoItem.Description = todoDescription;
    todoItem.DueDate = todoDueDate;

    todoService.AddOrUpdateItem(todoItem);
    StandardTileData tileData = TodoTileDataCreator.CreateTile(
                                todoItem.Description, todoItem.DueDate);

    string url = string.Format("/TodoList/TodoItemView.xaml?{0}={1}",
                                TaskScheduler.TodoItemIdQueryKey,
                                todoItem.Id);

    if (createTile)
    {
        /* Creating a shell tile takes the user to the start experience. */
        ShellTile.Create(new Uri(url, UriKind.Relative), tileData);
    }
    else
    {
        ShellTile shellTile = ShellTile.ActiveTiles.Where(
          tile => tile.NavigationUri.ToString()
                        .Contains(url)).FirstOrDefault();

        if (shellTile != null)
        {
            shellTile.Update(tileData);
        }
        Navigate(todoListUrl);

    }
}
```

Editing an Existing To-Do Item

The TodoItemViewModel can be in one of two modes: creation mode or edit mode. Either a new item is to be created, or an existing to-do item is being edited. This is indicated to the view using a VisualState property, which is of type string. By default, the view-model is in creation mode. When the user taps a to-do shell tile, or a to-do item on the TodoListView page, the view is placed in edit mode.

If in edit mode, the viewmodel's LoadItem method is used to retrieve the TodoItem with the specified Id from the ITodoService. The viewmodel's TodoDescription and

`TodoDueDate` are populated using the retrieved item's values, as shown in the following excerpt:

```
TodoItem todoItem;

void LoadItem(int itemId)
{
    try
    {
        todoItem = todoService.GetTodoItem(itemId);
    }
    catch (KeyNotFoundException)
    {
        MessageService.ShowError("Item not found.");
    }

    TodoDescription = todoItem.Description;
    TodoDueDate = todoItem.DueDate;

    VisualState = "Update";
}
```

As you see later in this section, the `VisualState` property is used by the `TodoItemView` page to hide or reveal elements on the page.

When in edit mode, the user also has the ability to delete the to-do item. The `DeleteItem` method uses the `ITodoService` to perform the data operation. Any shell tiles whose `NavigationUri` contains the query string corresponding to the to-do item are also removed. See the following excerpt:

```
void DeleteItem()
{
    if (todoItem == null)
    {
        throw new InvalidOperationException("Not in edit mode.");
    }

    todoService.RemoveTodoItem(todoItem);

    string tileQueryString = string.Format("{0}={1}",
                                    TaskScheduler.TodoItemIdQueryKey,
                                    todoItem.Id);
    ShellTile tile = ShellTile.ActiveTiles.FirstOrDefault(
        x => x.NavigationUri.ToString().Contains(tileQueryString));
    if (tile != null)
    {
        tile.Delete();
    }
```

```
        Navigate(todoListUrl);
}
```

The `TodoItemView` page uses the IoC container to resolve the `ITodoService` instance. If it has not been defined in the container, a `TodoService` is instantiated.

For more information on Inversion of Control and IoC containers, see Chapter 24, "Unit Testing Apps."

The following excerpt shows the `TodoItemView` constructor and fields:

```
readonly TodoItemViewModel viewModel;
bool initialized;

public TodoItemView()
{
    InitializeComponent();

    var todoService = Dependency.Resolve<ITodoService, TodoService>();
    DataContext = viewModel = new TodoItemViewModel(todoService);
}
```

The `Id` of the `TodoItem` is passed as a query string parameter, which causes the view to be placed in edit mode. This is determined in the `OnNavigatedTo` method of the view. If the `TodoItem Id` has been supplied, the viewmodel's `LoadItemCommand` is executed.

When the `LoadItemCommand` completes, the visual state of the view is updated according to the `VisualState` property of the viewmodel, as shown in the following excerpt:

```
protected override void OnNavigatedTo(NavigationEventArgs e)
{
    base.OnNavigatedTo(e);

    if (initialized)
    {
        return;
    }
    initialized = true;

    string itemId;
    if (NavigationContext.QueryString.TryGetValue("TodoItemId", out itemId))
    {
        /* Custom commanding infrastructure performs automatic conversion
         * from a string to an int. */
        viewModel.LoadItemCommand.Execute(itemId);
    }
    VisualStateManager.GoToState(this, viewModel.VisualState, true);
}
```

The `TodoItemView` page contains a `TextBox` to edit the viewmodel's `TodoDescription` property and a Windows Phone Toolkit `DatePicker` to edit the `TodoDueDate` property.

To force the `TextBox` to update the viewmodel when the text changes, the custom `UpdateSourceTriggerExtender` is used. This prevents changes to the description from being missed if the user taps an application bar item without first tapping elsewhere on the page to lose focus. See the following excerpt:

```xml
<StackPanel x:Name="ContentPanel" Grid.Row="1" Margin="12,0,12,0">
    <TextBlock Text="description"
               Style="{StaticResource PhoneTextNormalStyle}" />
    <!-- UpdateSourceTriggerExtended causes the value
         to be updated in the viewmodel as soon as the text changes. -->
    <TextBox Text="{Binding TodoDescription, Mode=TwoWay}"
             u:UpdateSourceTriggerExtender.UpdateSourceOnTextChanged="True" />
    <TextBlock Text="due"
               Style="{StaticResource PhoneTextNormalStyle}" />
    <toolkit:DatePicker Value="{Binding TodoDueDate, Mode=TwoWay}" />
</StackPanel>
```

For more information on the `UpdateSourceTriggerExtender`, see Chapter 26, "Validating User Input."

The view contains an `AppBar` with an `AppBarHyperlinkButton` that links back to the `TodoListView` page and `AppBarIconButtons` that are bound to the various viewmodel commands, as shown:

```xml
<u:AppBar>
    <u:AppBarHyperlinkButton
                NavigateUri="/TodoList/TodoListView.xaml"
                Text="Items"
                IconUri="/Images/ApplicationBarIcons/List.png" />
    <u:AppBarIconButton
                x:Name="Button_Delete"
                Command="{Binding DeleteCommand}"
                Text="Delete"
                IconUri="/Images/ApplicationBarIcons/Delete.png" />
    <u:AppBarIconButton
                Command="{Binding SaveCommand}"
                CommandParameter="False"
                Text="Save"
                IconUri="/Images/ApplicationBarIcons/Save.png" />
    <u:AppBarIconButton
                Command="{Binding SaveCommand}"
                CommandParameter="True"
                Text="Save &amp; Pin"
                IconUri="/Images/ApplicationBarIcons/AddTile.png" />
</u:AppBar>
```

The visibility of the Delete button is determined by the `VisualState` property of the view-model. When the `VisualState` property is equal to Update, the Delete button is shown; if equal to Create, it is collapsed (see Figure 32.12). See the sample code if you are interested in the visual state group XAML.

FIGURE 32.12   Creating a new to-do item.

When tapping the Save & Pin button, the app is deactivated and the tile is displayed on the Start Experience (see Figure 32.13).

Tapping the tile returns the user to the `TodoItemView`, where the item can be edited or deleted.

FIGURE 32.13   To-do item shell tile is displayed on the Start Experience.

When the tile is overdue, a different image is displayed. Changing the properties of the tile can be done from your foreground app or from a background agent, which is demonstrated in the following section.

Updating Tiles Using a Scheduled Task Agent

The background agent for the sample is the `TaskScheduler` class, which is a subclass of the `ScheduledTaskAgent` class. `TaskScheduler` is registered using the WMAppManifest.xml file.

As you saw earlier, a periodic task is registered in the `TodoItemViewModel` class. This causes the `TaskScheduler.OnInvoke` method to be called periodically. The `OnInvoke` method determines what kind of task is being launched by the OS, either periodic or resource intensive. For the to-do sample, it is always a periodic task (see Listing 32.9).

LISTING 32.9   `TaskScheduler` `OnInvoke` Method (excerpt)

```
protected override void OnInvoke(ScheduledTask task)
{
    /* Detect if the task is periodic or resource intensive. */
    if (task is PeriodicTask)
    {
        ProcessPeriodicTask();
    }
    else
    {
        ProcessResourceIntensiveTask();
    }
...
    NotifyComplete();
}
```

The main purpose of the `TaskScheduler` is to refresh the shell tiles on the Start Experience, updating the overdue status and changing the background image as required (see Listing 32.10).

The `ProcessPeriodicTask` method retrieves all tiles for the app containing the to-do item query string parameter. Each tile is processed by extracting the `Id` of the to-do item, and then by retrieving the actual `TodoItem` object using the to-do service. A new `StandardTileData` object is created for the `TodoItem` using the `TodoTileDataCreator`, and the tile is updated.

LISTING 32.10   `TaskScheduler` `ProcessPeriodicTask` Method

```
void ProcessPeriodicTask()
{
    TodoService todoService = new TodoService();

    string queryWithEquals = TodoItemIdQueryKey + "=";
```

```
IEnumerable<ShellTile> tiles = ShellTile.ActiveTiles.Where(
        tile => tile.NavigationUri.ToString().Contains(queryWithEquals));

foreach (var tile in tiles)
{
    /* NavigationUri.Query raises an exception on relative URIs. */
    Dictionary<string, string> queryPairs
        = UrlUtility.ParseQueryString(tile.NavigationUri.ToString());
    string idString = queryPairs[TodoItemIdQueryKey];
    int todoItemId;
    if (!int.TryParse(idString, out todoItemId))
    {
        Debug.Assert(false, "Invalid id " + idString);
        continue;
    }

    TodoItem todoItem;
    if (!todoService.TryGetTodoItem(todoItemId, out todoItem))
    {
        Debug.Assert(false, "Unknown item " + idString);
        continue;
    }

    StandardTileData tileData = TodoTileDataCreator.CreateTile(
                                    todoItem.Description,
                                    todoItem.DueDate);
    tile.Update(tileData);
}
}
```

Using a scheduled task agent to update shell tiles provides the means to engage with your users even when your app is not running. It should be remembered, however, that there is no guarantee that a scheduled task will run; therefore, it is wise not to depend solely on a background task for activities critical to the proper functioning of your app. Indeed, updating of shell tiles should also be done within your foreground app, which is not done in the sample.

Scheduled Task API Limitations

Scheduled task agents do not have access to the entire set of APIs that foreground apps do. There is a set of APIs that are off-limits, and using an API from the set either raises an UnauthorizedAccessException at runtime or causes the app to fail certification during submission to the Windows Phone Marketplace. For the list of unsupported APIs, see Table 32.3.

TABLE 32.3   Scheduled Task Agent Unsupported APIs

Namespace	Unsupported API
Microsoft.Devices	Camera
Microsoft.Devices	VibrateController
Microsoft.Devices	NowPlaying
Microsoft.Devices.Radio	All APIs in this namespace are unsupported
Microsoft.Devices.Sensors	All APIs in this namespace are unsupported
Microsoft.Phone.BackgroundAudio	BackgroundAudioPlayer
Microsoft.Phone.BackgroundTransfer	Add(BackgroundTransferRequest)
Microsoft.Phone.Controls	WebBrowser
Microsoft.Phone.Info	IsKeyboardDeployed
Microsoft.Phone.Notification	All APIs in this namespace are unsupported
Microsoft.Phone.Scheduler	Add(ScheduledAction)
Microsoft.Phone.Shell	All APIs are unsupported except the following: ShellToast method of ShellToast class Update(ShellTileData) method of ShellTile class Delete() method of ShellTile class
Microsoft.Phone.Tasks	All APIs in this namespace are unsupported
Microsoft.Xna*	All APIs in all XNA Framework namespaces are unsupported
System.Windows	MessageBox
System.Windows	Clipboard
System.Windows.Controls	MediaElement
System.Windows.Controls	MultiScaleImage
System.Windows.Media	LicenseAcquirer
System.Windows.Media	A/V Capture
System.Windows.Navigation	All APIs in this namespace are unsupported

Source: http://msdn.microsoft.com/en-us/library/hh202962(v=VS.92).aspx

One noteworthy limitation is the inability to display visual elements from a background agent. You see a workaround in the next section.

Providing Feedback to the User from an Agent

On occasion, your background agent may want to notify the user of some event. This is not possible using custom UI nor with a MessageBox.

A solution is to use a shell toast, which can provide immediate feedback to the user. A toast notification can be presented from within your task agent like so:

```
protected override void OnInvoke(ScheduledTask task)
{
    ShellToast toast = new ShellToast
                    {
                        Title = "Windows Phone Unleashed",
                        Content = "Task Scheduler running..."
                    };
    toast.Show();

    /* ... */
}
```

If the user taps the toast notification, your app is launched in the foreground. By setting the `NavigationUri` property for the `ShellToast`, you can also provide a deep link with a query string, as was demonstrated for the to-do item shell tiles.

Using a `Mutex` to Access Common Resources Safely

Your app's task agent may be invoked even when your app is in the foreground. It is, therefore, important to ensure that simultaneous access to shared resources, such as files in isolated storage, is controlled and performed safely.

A `System.Threading.Mutex` can be employed to synchronize critical sections of code—code that accesses a common resource—within your primary app and your background agent. A `Mutex` is a synchronization primitive. It is similar to the `Monitor` class, but with a scope that allows you to achieve interprocess synchronization, enabling you to synchronize across your foreground app and your background agent.

Unlike Silverlight for the browser, a `Mutex` instance in Windows Phone must be named, and the scope of a `Mutex` is limited to your primary app and its background agent.

> **NOTE**
>
> A `Mutex` cannot be used to synchronize different apps, nor as a conduit for interapp communication.

Listing 32.11 shows an excerpt from the `CommonResourceExample` class in the downloadable sample code that demonstrates how to read and write to a file in isolated storage in a safe manner, while preventing another thread, such as from your background agent, from accessing the file simultaneously.

When the `ReplaceFileContents` method is called, `WaitOne` is called on the `Mutex`, which blocks if the `Mutex` is owned by another thread in your foreground app or a background agent. If not owned, or when released by another thread, the contents of a file are read, and then overwritten with a new content string. The result is returned to the caller. By using a `Mutex`, the result is guaranteed to be the content of the file immediately prior to writing the new content.

LISTING 32.11   CommonResourceExample Class (excerpt)

```
public class CommonResourceExample
{
    static readonly Mutex mutex = new Mutex(false, "CommonResourceExample");
    static readonly string fileName = "CommonResourceExample.txt";

    public string ReplaceFileContents(string fileContent)
    {
        try
        {
            mutex.WaitOne();
            string result = ReadFileCore();
            WriteFileCore(fileContent);
            return result;
        }
        finally
        {
            mutex.ReleaseMutex();
        }
    }
    void WriteFileCore(string fileContent)
    {
        using (IsolatedStorageFile isolatedStorageFile
                    = IsolatedStorageFile.GetUserStoreForApplication())
        {
            using (IsolatedStorageFileStream outStream
                    = isolatedStorageFile.OpenFile(
                            fileName, FileMode.Create))
            {
                using (StreamWriter writer = new StreamWriter(outStream))
                {
                    writer.Write(fileContent);
                }
            }
        }
    }

    string ReadFileCore()
    {
        using (IsolatedStorageFile isolatedStorageFile
                    = IsolatedStorageFile.GetUserStoreForApplication())
        {
            if (!isolatedStorageFile.FileExists(fileName))
            {
                return string.Empty;
```

```
        }

        using (IsolatedStorageFileStream inStream
                = isolatedStorageFile.OpenFile(
                    fileName, FileMode.Open))
        {
            using (StreamReader reader = new StreamReader(inStream))
            {
                return reader.ReadToEnd();
            }
        }
    }
}
```

It is important to ensure that your `Mutex` is released upon exiting from a critical section. This is done by wrapping the section in a try/finally block. If your foreground app or your background agent terminates while owning a mutex, the state of the mutex is set to signaled and the next waiting thread gets ownership.

To test whether the `Mutex` is owned, you can specify a timeout parameter to the `WaitOne` method (see Listing 32.12). This is an effective way to prevent your task agent from being terminated because it is blocked on a `WaitOne` call. Recall that a `PeriodicTask` has a maximum 15 seconds of execution time.

LISTING 32.12   Using `WaitOne` to Determine Whether a `Mutex` Is Owned

```
bool mutexAcquired = false;
try
{
    mutexAcquired = mutex.WaitOne(10000);
    if (mutexAcquired)
    {
        /* Access common resource here. */
        Debug.WriteLine("mutex entered.");
    }
}
finally
{
    if (mutexAcquired)
    {
        mutex.ReleaseMutex();
    }
}

if (!mutexAcquired)
{
```

```
    /* Unable to acquire ownership of mutex. */
    Debug.WriteLine("mutex timed out.");
}
```

TIP

To test whether a `Mutex` is owned, without blocking the calling thread, use a timeout value of 0 when calling `WaitOne`.

`Mutex` provides an effective way to synchronize critical sections of code and can assist in avoiding race conditions and other concurrency issues when accessing shared resources.

Summary

This chapter looked at the scheduled notification system, which consists of a useful set of classes for setting reminders and alarms that can present a message to the user at a predetermined time, whether or not your app is running in the foreground.

It then examined the scheduled task system, which extends the principles underpinning the notification system and offers the capability to run your own code in the background. You saw how to create a to-do list app, which leverages a local database and updates live tiles from a background agent.

Finally, the chapter explained how to use a `Mutex` to provide safe access to resources shared by your foreground app and your background agent.

The next chapter continues with the to-do list app and demonstrates how to use a background transfer service to back up the to-do database to a cloud service.

32

Performing Background File Transfers

When developing a phone app, your app may need to transfer files to or from a remote server. In some cases your app may not be able to continue without having a certain file on hand. But in other cases, the file may not be required immediately and can be downloaded asynchronously using a background file transfer. Candidates for these kinds of file transfers include downloading large files (for example, music and video files) or backing up an app's local database.

Transferring files from a foreground app can be problematic because of the transient nature of an app's run cycle; if your app is tombstoned or terminated, any file transfers under way are interrupted. Background file transfers allow your app to download or upload files asynchronously and remain active even if your app is terminated while still allowing your app to monitor the progress of the transfer.

The previous chapter looked at background actions and how a to-do list app uses a local database to store to-do item information. This chapter continues with the to-do list sample, and you see how to back up and restore the to-do list local database using a background transfer request. The chapter examines how to leverage the URL routing features of ASP.NET to pass arguments to a WCF service via a background transfer request, and you see how to retrieve the user's Windows Live anonymous ID. Finally the chapter looks at monitoring a background transfer using a progress indicator.

Background Transfer Requests

Transfer requests are represented by the `BackgroundTransferRequest` class. The

`BackgroundTransferService` maintains a queue of background requests and is used to submit new background requests, remove requests from the queue, and retrieve active requests.

Submitting a background request can be done by creating an instance of the `BackgroundTransferRequest` class, specifying the request end points, and then adding the request to the `BackgroundTransferService`. The following excerpt shows a transfer request that downloads a file from a remote server to a location in isolated storage:

```
BackgroundTransferRequest request
    = new BackgroundTransferRequest(remoteUri, localUri)
    {
        TransferPreferences = TransferPreferences.AllowBattery,
        Method = "Get",
    };

BackgroundTransferService.Add(request);
```

> **NOTE**
>
> An app can have at most five requests queued at a given time. Attempting to add more than five raises an `InvalidOperationException`. It is the responsibility of the app to remove requests from the queue by using the `BackgroundTransferService.Remove` method after requests have completed.

By default, background transfer requests occur only when the device has a Wi-Fi connection and is connected to external power. By using the `TransferPreferences` property of the `BackgroundTransferRequest` class, you can override this behavior so that transfers occur when one or both of these conditions are not met. Table 33.1 describes the available `TransferPreferences` values.

> **NOTE**
>
> Setting the `TransferPreferences` property does not guarantee that transfers will occur under the preferred conditions. If the battery level is critical, for example, background transfers are suspended regardless of the `TransferPreferences` value.

TABLE 33.1 `TransferPreferences` Enum

Enumeration Value	Description
None	Allows transfers only when the device is using external power and has a Wi-Fi connection. This is the default setting.
AllowCellular	Allows transfers when the device is connected to external power and has a Wi-Fi or cellular connection.

Enumeration Value	Description
AllowBattery	Allows transfers when there is a Wi-Fi connection and the device is using battery or external power.
AllowCellularAndBattery	Allows transfers when the device is using battery or external power and has a Wi-Fi or cellular connection.

CAUTION

Transferring files when the phone does not have a Wi-Fi connection can unduly consume the user's data plan. In addition, transferring files without an external power connection can rapidly drain the phone's battery. Both cases can potentially result in a poor experience for the user; therefore, it is recommended to leave the default value of TransferPresences as None.

BackgroundTransferRequest is bidirectional, allowing you to transfer files from and to the phone device. The BackgroundTransferRequest API is peculiar in that it determines the direction of the request based on which of its two constructors is used, and whether its UploadLocation property has been set. The constructor to use when performing a download (from a remote server to isolated storage) has two parameters: the remote URI and the local (destination) URI. To perform an upload (from isolated storage to a remote server), its single parameter constructor is used in conjunction with its UploadLocation property. The following excerpt demonstrates the creation of an upload transfer request:

```
Uri remoteUri = new Uri(remoteUrl, UriKind.Absolute);

BackgroundTransferRequest request
    = new BackgroundTransferRequest(remoteUri)
        {
            Method = "POST",
            UploadLocation = new Uri(uploadPath, UriKind.Relative)
        };

BackgroundTransferService.Add(request);
```

By default, BackgroundTransferRequest uses the HTTP method GET.

NOTE

If you are performing an upload and fail to set the method to POST, an ArgumentNullException is raised because the BackgroundTransferRequest mistakes your request for a download and complains that the download URI was not supplied. Conversely, if Method is set to anything other than GET, BackgroundTransferRequest assumes the transfer is an upload and raises an ArgumentNullException if UploadLocation is not specified.

It is another peculiar aspect of the API that an `ArgumentNullException` is raised rather than an `InvalidOperationException`.

A parameter indicating the direction and nature of the transfer would, in my view, make the `BackgroundTransferRequest` easier to use.

`BackgroundTransferRequest` provides the following two events for monitoring the progress and status of a background transfer:

▶ `TransferProgressChanged`

▶ `TransferStatusChanged`

Both events pass a `BackgroundTransferEventArgs` object that provides nothing apart from a reference to the associated `BackgroundTransferRequest`.

The `TransferProgressChanged` event, as its name implies, allows you to track the amount of data that has been transferred. The following excerpt shows a `TransferProgressChanged` event handler that determines the current progress of a transfer as a value between 0 and 1:

```
void HandleTransferProgressChanged(object sender,
                                   BackgroundTransferEventArgs e)
{
    if (e.Request.BytesSent > 0)
    {
        Progress = (double)e.Request.TotalBytesToSend / e.Request.BytesSent;
    }
    else
    {
        Progress = 0;
    }
}
```

The `TransferStatusChanged` event allows you to monitor the critical events of the transfer request and enables you to determine, for example, when the transfer has completed and whether an error has occurred, as shown:

```
void HandleTransferStatusChanged(object sender,
                                 BackgroundTransferEventArgs e)
{
    if (e.Request.TransferStatus == TransferStatus.Completed)
    {
        BackgroundTransferService.Remove(e.Request);

        if (e.Request.TransferError != null)
        {
```

```
        /* Handle the error. */
        return;
      }
    }
  }
}
```

The `Request.TransferStatus` property identifies the request's current state. Table 33.2 describes each `TransferStatus` enum value.

TABLE 33.2 `TransferStatus` Enumeration

Enumeration Value	Description
None	The request has not yet been queued. This is the default value before the request is submitted to the `BackgroundTransferService`.
Transferring	The requested file is currently being transferred.
Waiting	The request is waiting in the background transfer service queue. This status can indicate that the request is queued and waiting for previous transfers to complete or that the service is retrying the request due to a network error.
WaitingForWiFi	The request is waiting in the background transfer service queue for a Wi-Fi connection.
WaitingForExternalPower	The request is waiting in the background transfer service queue for external power to be connected.
WaitingForExternalPower-DueToBatterySaverMode	The request is waiting for the device to be connected to external power because the user has enabled Battery Saver mode on the device.
WaitingForNonVoiceBlockingNetwork	The background transfer service does not run when the device is on a nonsimultaneous voice and data network, including 2G, EDGE, and standard GPRS. This status indicates the service is waiting for a supported network connection.
Paused	The request has been paused and waiting in the background transfer service queue.
Completed	The request has completed. This means that the request is no longer actionable by the background transfer service regardless of whether the transfer was completed successfully. To confirm that a transfer was successful, confirm that the `TransferError` property is null.

33

Enumeration Value	Description
Unknown	The background transfer service could not retrieve the request status from the service. In this state, a `BackgroundTransferRequest` object is no longer useable. You may attempt to retrieve a new instance using the `Find(string)` method.

The role of the `TransferStatusChanged` event is discussed in greater detail later in the chapter.

Handling App Termination and Resubscription to Transfer Events

When a `BackgroundTransferRequest` has been added to the `BackgroundTransferService`, you can store the value of the request's `RequestId` property in isolated storage. This enables you to retrieve the request later if your app is terminated, and to continue monitoring the progress of your background request by resubscribing to the request's `TransferStatusChanged` and `TransferProgressChanged` events.

The `BackgroundTransferService.Find` method is used to retrieve an existing request, like so:

```
BackgroundTransferRequest request
        = BackgroundTransferService.Find("request id string");
if (request != null)
{
    request.TransferStatusChanged += HandleUploadTransferStatusChanged;
    request.TransferProgressChanged += HandleTransferProgressChanged;
}
```

Background File Transfer Sample Code

The sample for this chapter continues from where we left off in Chapter 32, "Conducting Background Activities with Scheduled Actions." This chapter looks at backing up the to-do items database to a remote server using WCF.

Within the BackgroundAgents solution in the downloadable sample code is a project named WPUnleashed.BackgroundAgents.Web. This project exposes a WCF service named BackupService, which allows the phone app to save files to the Backups directory on the server by way of its `SaveFile` method (see Listing 33.1). The `SaveFile` method accepts a Stream, which is written to a file on the server. The unique ID of the user is also sent to the server to allow correct retrieval of the file at a later time.

LISTING 33.1   `BackupService` Class

```
[ServiceBehavior(InstanceContextMode = InstanceContextMode.PerCall)]
[AspNetCompatibilityRequirements(
```

```
                RequirementsMode = AspNetCompatibilityRequirementsMode.Allowed)]
public class BackupService : IBackupService
{
    public void SaveFile(string userId, string fileName, Stream fileStream)
    {
        string location = string.Format(
                            @"~\Backups\{0}_{1}", userId, fileName);
        var filepath = HttpContext.Current.Server.MapPath(location);
        using (Stream outputStream = File.OpenWrite(filepath))
        {
            CopyStream(fileStream, outputStream);
        }
    }

    static void CopyStream(Stream input, Stream output)
    {
        var buffer = new byte[8 * 1024];
        int streamLength;

        while ((streamLength = input.Read(buffer, 0, buffer.Length)) > 0)
        {
            output.Write(buffer, 0, streamLength);
        }
    }
}
```

There is no retrieval method in the WCF service because an ordinary HTTP GET request is used to download the file.

The WPUnleashed.BackgroundAgents contains a web reference to the WPUnleashed.BackgroundAgents.Web project, and the service is consumed within the TodoListViewModel class.

Using URL Rerouting with a WCF Service

The Web Application project uses URL rerouting to allow the BackgroundTransferRequest to pass the user ID and filename to the service via the URL.

The routing system on the server is initialized in the RegisterRoutes method of the Global class in the Web Application project. The URL routing APIs reside in the System.Web.Routing namespace. A new ServiceRoute is added to the RouteTable, so that when a request for the URL BackupService arrives, the built-in WebServiceHostFactory creates an instance of the BackupService class to service the request. See the following excerpt:

```
public class Global : System.Web.HttpApplication
{
    protected void Application_Start(object sender, EventArgs e)
```

```
    {
        RegisterRoutes();
    }

    void RegisterRoutes()
    {
        RouteTable.Routes.Add(new ServiceRoute(
            "BackupService", new WebServiceHostFactory(),
            typeof(BackupService)));
    }
    ...
}
```

The service interface for the backup service defines a `UriTemplate` that maps the incoming request URL, which includes the user ID and filename, to the `SaveFile` method parameters. This means that we are able to translate the incoming URL and forward the call to the service method. See the following:

```
[ServiceContract(Namespace = "http://danielvaughan.org")]
public interface IBackupService
{
    [OperationContract, WebInvoke(
        Method = "POST", UriTemplate = "UploadFile/{userId}/{fileName}")]
    void SaveFile(string userId, string fileName, Stream fileStream);
}
```

URL rerouting is an elegant way of providing a WCF service with extra information, such as the user's ID, while still remaining compatible with the `BackgroundTransferRequest` and its simple `Uri` `UploadLocation` property.

Retrieving the User's Windows Live Anonymous ID

To associate a database file on the server with the user of the device, the app retrieves the user's Windows Live anonymous ID from the `Microsoft.Phone.Info.UserExtendedProperties` class. The Windows Live anonymous ID is a representation of the user's Windows Live ID that does not include any user identifiable information. When a user activates a device, he must provide a Windows Live ID. The Windows Live anonymous ID lets you identify the user by his Windows Live account, without actually seeing his details, and there is no way to correlate the anonymous ID with the Windows Live ID.

When retrieving the anonymous ID from `UserExtendedProperties` by way of the ANID2 key value (see Listing 33.2), the resulting string is the hashed representation of the anonymous ID.

> **NOTE**
>
> New to Windows Phone 8 is the ANID2 property that is a hashed version of the Windows Phone 7.5 ANID property. ANID2 is hashed with your publisher ID to ensure that different publishers cannot track users across different apps. You can no longer use the ANID property to retrieve the Windows Live anonymous ID in Windows Phone 8. ANID can be accessed only from Windows Phone OS 7.0 and Windows Phone OS 7.1 apps that use the Microsoft Advertising SDK for Windows Phone.

LISTING 33.2   DeviceProperties Class

```csharp
public class DeviceProperties : IDeviceProperties
{
    /// <summary>
    /// Gets the windows live anonymous ID.
    /// This method requires ID_CAP_IDENTITY_USER
    //  to be present in the capabilities of the WMAppManifest.
    /// </summary>
    /// <returns>The string id for the user.</returns>
    static string GetWindowsLiveAnonymousId()
    {
        object result;
        UserExtendedProperties.TryGetValue("ANID2", out result);

        return result != null ? result.ToString() : null;
    }

    string windowsLiveAnonymousId;

    public string WindowsLiveAnonymousId
    {
        get
        {
            return windowsLiveAnonymousId
                ?? (windowsLiveAnonymousId = GetWindowsLiveAnonymousId());
        }
    }
}
```

> **TIP**
>
> It is better to associate data with the user of the device rather than the device itself. By relying on the ID of the user, rather than the ID of the device, you can provide a greater level of assurance that if the phone changes ownership, the new user of the phone will not have access to previous owner's data.

Retrieving the anonymous ID from the `UserExtendedProperties` does not work on the emulator. For testing purposes, the `IDeviceProperties` implementation can be swapped with a mock implementation that retrieves a predefined anonymous ID.

TodoListViewModel

The `TodoListViewModel` constructor accepts an `IDeviceProperties` instance and an `ITodoService` instance, which, as you saw in Chapter 32, is used for storage and retrieval of to-do items. See the following excerpt:

```
public TodoListViewModel(
    ITodoService todoService, IDeviceProperties deviceProperties)
{
...
    backupDatabaseCommand = new DelegateCommand(obj => BackupDatabase());
    restoreDatabaseCommand = new DelegateCommand(obj => RestoreDatabase());

    Load();
}
```

The viewmodel contains a method that leverages the `IDeviceProperties` instance to create a unique ID to use to identify itself to calls to a WCF service.

```
string GetUserId()
{
    string id = deviceProperties.WindowsLiveAnonymousId;
    if (string.IsNullOrWhiteSpace(id))
    {
        id = "Emulator";
    }
    return id;
}
```

The anonymous ID is passed to the WCF service when backing up the local database file and used as part of the URL when restoring it.

Backing Up the Local Database

To transfer the local database to the server, it must first be copied to a directory in isolated storage. This prevents the file from being modified by the SQL CE engine while the transfer is under way. The viewmodel's `BackupDatabase` method creates a temporary directory and then copies the local .sdf database file to the directory, as shown:

```
string uploadUrl = "http://localhost:60182/BackupService/UploadFile/";
const string localDatabaseName = "Todo.sdf";
const string transferDirectory = "/shared/transfers";

string uploadPath = transferDirectory + "/" + localDatabaseName;
using (IsolatedStorageFile isolatedStorageFile
```

```
                        = IsolatedStorageFile.GetUserStoreForApplication())
{
    if (!isolatedStorageFile.FileExists(localDatabaseName))
    {
        throw new InvalidOperationException(
            "Database file does not exist in isolated storage.");
    }
    if (!isolatedStorageFile.DirectoryExists(transferDirectory))
    {
        isolatedStorageFile.CreateDirectory(transferDirectory);
    }
    isolatedStorageFile.CopyFile(localDatabaseName, uploadPath, true);
}
```

The `BackupDatabase` method then constructs a destination URL for the upload. The
remote URL is constructed using the base URL of the upload file path on the server. This
URL is rerouted when it arrives at the server, and its segments are passed as arguments to
the `SaveFile` WCF service method. See the following excerpt:

```
string deviceId = GetUserId();
string remoteUrl = string.Format("{0}{1}/{2}",
                                 uploadUrl,
                                 deviceId,
                                 localDatabaseName);

Uri remoteUri = new Uri(remoteUrl, UriKind.Absolute);
```

A `BackgroundTransferRequest` is constructed, which causes the file to be uploaded to the
server. Uploads use the HTTP POST method, as shown:

```
BackgroundTransferRequest request
    = new BackgroundTransferRequest(remoteUri)
        {
            TransferPreferences = TransferPreferences.AllowBattery,
            Method = "POST",
            UploadLocation = new Uri(uploadPath, UriKind.Relative)
        };
```

To monitor the progress of the transfer request, while the app is running in the foreground, we subscribe to the `TransferStatusChanged` and the `TransferProgressChanged`
events. The transfer request is then added to the `BackgroundTransferService`, which
queues the upload. See the following:

```
request.TransferStatusChanged += HandleUploadTransferStatusChanged;
request.TransferProgressChanged += HandleUploadTransferProgressChanged;

BackgroundTransferService.Add(request);
```

```
Message = "Backing up data to cloud.";
ProgressVisible = true;
```

When the viewmodel's `ProgressVisible` property is set to true, it causes a progress indicator to be displayed in the view. This occurs via a custom `ProgressIndicatorProxy` class, first discussed in Chapter 5, "Using Content Controls, Items Controls, and Range Controls." In addition, the progress indicator also displays the progress of the operation via the viewmodel's `Progress` property. The `Progress` property is updated whenever the `TransferProgressChanged` event is raised, as shown:

```
void HandleTransferProgressChanged(
        object sender, BackgroundTransferEventArgs e)
{
    if (e.Request.BytesSent > 0)
    {
        Progress = (double)e.Request.TotalBytesToSend / e.Request.BytesSent;
    }
    else
    {
        Progress = 0;
    }
}
```

When the request's `TransferStatusChanged` event is raised, if the request has completed, it is removed from the `BackgroundTransferStatus`, and the progress indicator is hidden.

> **NOTE**
>
> A `TransferStatus` of Completed does not necessarily mean that the transfer completed successfully, but rather that the operation has ended for whatever reason. It is therefore critical to test for the presence of an error contained in the `Request.TransferError` property.

The `ViewModelBase` class's `MessageService` is used to display the result to the user, as shown:

```
void HandleUploadTransferStatusChanged(
        object sender, BackgroundTransferEventArgs e)
{
    if (e.Request.TransferStatus == TransferStatus.Completed)
    {
        BackgroundTransferService.Remove(e.Request);

        ProgressVisible = false;
```

```
    if (e.Request.TransferError != null)
    {
        MessageService.ShowError("An error occured during backup.");
    }
    else
    {
        MessageService.ShowMessage("Backup successful.");
    }
}
}
```

After the local database file has been transferred to the server, the user can nominate to restore the database from the backup.

Restoring the Local Database

Restoring the local database involves submitting a background transfer request to download the previously uploaded file from the server. The file is downloaded to a temporary location in isolated storage, the existing local database is disconnected, and its file is replaced.

The RestoreDatabase method begins by creating a temporary directory where the downloaded .sdf file can be placed by the BackgroundTransferService:

```
const string downloadPath = transferDirectory + "/" + localDatabaseName;

using (IsolatedStorageFile isolatedStorageFile
            = IsolatedStorageFile.GetUserStoreForApplication())
{
    if (!isolatedStorageFile.DirectoryExists(transferDirectory))
    {
        isolatedStorageFile.CreateDirectory(transferDirectory);
    }
}
```

It then creates two Uri objects specifying the location of the .sdf file on the remote server, and the file's destination location in isolated storage, as shown:

```
string deviceId = GetUserId();

string remoteUrl = string.Format("{0}{1}_{2}",
                                downloadUrl,
                                deviceId,
                                localDatabaseName);
Uri remoteUri = new Uri(remoteUrl, UriKind.Absolute);
Uri localUri = new Uri(downloadPath, UriKind.Relative);
```

The BackgroundTransferRequest is constructed using the two Uri objects. The default HTTP method Get is used because we are downloading the file to the device. See the following excerpt:

```
BackgroundTransferRequest request
    = new BackgroundTransferRequest(remoteUri, localUri)
    {
        TransferPreferences = TransferPreferences.AllowBattery,
    };
```

Finally, we subscribe to the transfer request's status changed and progress changed events, and the request is added to the BackgroundTransferService. The progress indicator is displayed, and it is updated as the progress of the background transfer changes:

```
request.TransferStatusChanged += HandleDownloadTransferStatusChanged;
request.TransferProgressChanged += HandleDownloadTransferProgressChanged;

BackgroundTransferService.Add(request);
Message = "Restoring data from cloud.";
Progress = 0;
ProgressVisible = true;
```

When the background transfer completes, the TransferStatusChanged event handler is called (see Listing 33.3). The downloaded file is copied to the location of the local database, which replaces the existing file. The ITodoService.Initialize method re-creates the connection to the database, and the viewmodel's GroupedTodoItems are re-created via a call to PopulateItems.

LISTING 33.3   HandleDownloadTransferStatusChanged Method

```
void HandleDownloadTransferStatusChanged(object sender,
                                         BackgroundTransferEventArgs e)
{
    if (e.Request.TransferStatus == TransferStatus.Completed)
    {
        BackgroundTransferService.Remove(e.Request);

        ProgressVisible = false;

        if (e.Request.TransferError != null)
        {
```

```
        MessageService.ShowError("An error occured during restore.");
        return;
    }

    try
    {
        using (IsolatedStorageFile isolatedStorageFile
                    = IsolatedStorageFile.GetUserStoreForApplication())
        {
            string downloadedFile
                    = e.Request.DownloadLocation.OriginalString;
            isolatedStorageFile.CopyFile(downloadedFile,
                                    localDatabaseName, true);
        }

        todoService.Initialize();

        ClearPinnedItems();
        PopulateItems();
    }
    catch (Exception ex)
    {
        MessageService.ShowError("An error occured during restore.");
        return;
    }

    MessageService.ShowMessage("Restore successful.");
    }
}
```

Backup and restore operations are actuated by application bar menu items in the view. The view's AppBar menu items are bound to the BackupDatabaseCommand and the RestoreDatabaseCommand (see Figure 33.1).

FIGURE 33.1   The `TodoListView` provides menu items for backing up and restoring the local database, and a progress indicator that shows the progress of the background transfer request.

Using a `BackgroundTransferRequest` is an effective way to back up your apps' data because it does not rely on your foreground app being active. Be mindful, however, that the `BackgroundTransferService` does not guarantee that a transfer request will be serviced.

Summary

In this chapter you saw how to back up and restore the to-do list database using a background transfer request. The chapter examined how to leverage the URL routing features of ASP.NET to pass arguments to a WCF service via a background transfer request, and you saw how to retrieve the user's Windows Live anonymous ID. Finally, the chapter looked at monitoring a background transfer using a progress indicator.

CHAPTER 34

Coordinating Background Audio Playback

W indows Phone allows you to create apps that respond to the Universal Volume Control (UVC) on the phone and, in conjunction with an onscreen menu, coordinate the playback of audio, even when your app is not running in the foreground.

This chapter begins with an overview of the background audio player and shows how it is used to control the playback of local or remote audio files. You look at how audio file information is represented by the `AudioTrack` class and examine the role of background audio agents, which are used to coordinate audio playback while your app is not running in the foreground.

The chapter then demonstrates how to build a UI that leverages the background audio agent for controlling playback while your app is in the foreground.

Finally, the chapter examines audio streaming agents and how they are used to provide custom streaming and decoding of audio files. You see how a custom audio streaming agent can be employed to play audio directly from an assembly resource, something that is not possible using the built-in streaming and decoding system of the phone.

Background Agent Recap

In Chapter 32, "Conducting Background Activities with Scheduled Actions," you learned that Windows Phone supports the following three types of `BackgroundAgents`:

▶ `ScheduledTaskAgent`

▶ `AudioPlayerAgent`

▶ `AudioStreamingAgent`

Background agents are classes invoked by the OS at certain times to carry out activities in the background (from another process) while your app may not be running in the foreground.

This chapter examines the last two agent types: `AudioPlayerAgent` and `AudioStreamingAgent`.

Background Audio Overview

The following compose the three main classes used for background audio, which are explored in this chapter:

▶ `BackgroundAudioPlayer`

▶ `AudioPlayerAgent`

▶ `AudioStreamingAgent`

`BackgroundAudioPlayer` is a class that allows you to specify an audio file for playback and to carry out playback activities such as play, pause, fast-forward, and rewind. `BackgroundAudioPlayer` allows you to specify track information, such as the title of the track and its location. The built-in playback capabilities of the `BackgroundAudioPlayer` allow audio files to be streamed from either a remote server, or locally, from isolated storage.

Out of the box, `BackgroundAudioPlayer` supports playback formats such as MP3, WMA, and WAV. For a complete list of supported audio formats, see http://bit.ly/pnnT8C. `BackgroundAudioPlayer` offers little in the way of coordinating the playback of a list of audio tracks. This is the task of the `AudioPlayerAgent`.

`AudioPlayerAgent` classes are specialized agents used to retrieve audio files and coordinate the playback of background audio via the `BackgroundAudioPlayer`. `AudioPlayerAgent` provides a number of method callbacks that are automatically called by the OS based on user actions.

An `AudioStreamingAgent` can be used to customize how audio data is procured by your `BackgroundAudioPlayer`. You can supplant the `BackgroundAudioPlayer`'s media sourcing capabilities by providing your own logic to download and decode an audio file.

Background Audio Player

The `BackgroundAudioPlayer` class implements the singleton pattern. The single instance of the `BackgroundAudioPlayer` is accessed in your foreground app via its static `Instance` property, as shown:

```
BackgroundAudioPlayer.Instance.Track
    = new AudioTrack(
            new Uri("http://example.com/Audio.mp3", UriKind.Absolute),
            "Track Name", "Artist", "Album", null);
BackgroundAudioPlayer.Instance.Play();
```

The behavior of the `BackgroundAudioPlayer` changes depending on whether it is being used in your foreground app or from an `AudioPlayerAgent`. When the `BackgroundAudioPlayer` is used in your foreground app, all calls are relayed to your `AudioPlayerAgent`. When used from an `AudioPlayerAgent`, the `BackgroundAudioPlayer` affects the playback of audio directly. Without an `AudioPlayerAgent`, the `BackgroundAudioPlayer` does nothing.

This dual behavior can be best understood by looking at the internal workings of the `BackgroundAudioPlayer`. The `BackgroundAudioPlayer` is a proxy that relies on a native implementation of an internal `IAudioPlaybackManager` interface. When the `BackgroundAudioPlayer` is used in your foreground app, the `IAudioPlaybackManager` relays all audio requests to the app's `AudioPlayerAgent`. Conversely, when used from your `AudioPlayerAgent`, the `IAudioPlaybackManager` uses the native audio playback system instead.

`BackgroundAudioPlayer` contains several public methods that allow you to control the playback of audio (see Table 34.1).

TABLE 34.1   `BackgroundAudioPlayer` Audio Playback Related Methods

Method Name	Description
FastForward	Starts fast-forwarding through the current `AudioTrack`
Pause	Pauses playback at the current position
Play	Plays or resumes the current `AudioTrack` at its current position
Rewind	Starts rewinding through the current `AudioTrack`
SkipNext	Skips to the next track
SkipPrevious	Skips to the previous track
Stop	Stops and resets media to be played from the beginning

`BackgroundAudioPlayer` contains several public audio playback-related properties, which are shown in Table 34.2.

TABLE 34.2   `BackgroundAudioPlayer` Audio Playback-Related Properties

Property Name	Description
BufferingProgress	A double value representing the amount of buffering that is completed for the media content. This property is most relevant for streaming remote audio files.
CanPause	A `bool` value indicating whether the media can be paused when the `Pause` method is called.
CanSeek	A `bool` value indicating whether the media can be repositioned by setting the value of the `Position` property.
Error	The last `Exception` object, if any, to have occurred while playing the current `AudioTrack`.
PlayerState	Gets the current `PlayState` of the player.

Property Name	Description
Position	Gets or sets the current position within the current `AudioTrack`.
Track	Gets or sets the current audio track, whether it is playing or not.
Volume	The media's volume represented on a linear scale between 0 and 1. The default is 0.85.

`BackgroundAudioPlayer` contains a principle event, `PlayStateChanged`, which is used to detect, for example, when a track begins playing.

New in Windows Phone 8 is the capability to retrieve the current play state and preceding play state from the `PlayStateChangedEventArgs`. For compatibility with Windows Phone 7.1 OS, the signature of the `PlayStateChanged` event has not changed in the Windows Phone SDK. Therefore, to retrieve the play states, you must cast the `EventArgs` argument to a `PlayStateChangedEventArgs` object, as shown in the following example:

```
void HandlePlayStateChanged(object sender, EventArgs e)
{
    /* New in Windows Phone 8, the current and previous playstate
     * can be retrieved using the PlayStateChangedEventArgs. */
    PlayStateChangedEventArgs args = (PlayStateChangedEventArgs)e;
    PlayState currentPlayState = args.CurrentPlayState;
    PlayState previousPlayState = args.IntermediatePlayState;
    ...
}
```

You see later in the chapter how this event can be used to hide and show UI elements based on the current state of the player.

Representing Audio Files with the `AudioTrack` Class

The `AudioTrack` class includes information about the location of an audio file, as well as track metadata, such as the track's title. Table 34.3 describes each of the `AudioTrack` properties.

TABLE 34.3 `AudioTrack` Properties

Property Name	Description
Album	The `string` name of the track's album.
AlbumArt	A `Uri` indicating the location of an image showing the album cover. Once set, this value can be used to show the album cover in your foreground app.
Artist	The `string` name of the artist.
Duration	A `TimeSpan` representing the length of the track.

Property Name	Description
PlayerControls	A Flags enum value that determines which playback controls are enabled in the system user interface. The current phone OS (7.5) supports All, None, SkipNext, SkipPrevious, and Pause. This property allows you to disable the next, previous, or pause buttons on the audio menu when the user presses the UVC.
Source	The URI path to the track.
Tag	An arbitrary string associated with this track, used to store application-specific state.
Title	Text to display as the track's title.

AudioTrack implements IEditableObject to enable batching of property change requests. After an AudioTrack object has been instantiated, it cannot be changed without putting it in edit mode first. AudioTrack uses an IAudioTrack backing field, which links the managed AudioTrack object to the native audio system via Com Interop. To make changes to an AudioTrack object, its BeginEdit method must be called. When all changes have been made, EndEdit should be called. This commits the property changes to the OS via the native IAudioTrack object.

Creating a Custom Audio Player Agent

An audio player agent can be created by selecting the Windows Phone Audio Playback Agent project type from the Visual Studio New Project dialog (see Figure 34.1). This produces a new project that includes a class that derives from AudioPlayerAgent.

FIGURE 34.1   Visual Studio Windows Phone agent projects.

When you link to an Audio Player Agent project from your main project, a `BackgroundServiceAgent` task definition is added to your main project's WMAppManifest.xml file, resembling the following:

```xml
<Tasks>
  <DefaultTask  Name="_default" NavigationPage="MainPage.xaml"/>
  <ExtendedTask Name="BackgroundTask">
      <BackgroundServiceAgent Specifier="AudioPlayerAgent"
          Name="<Unique name within the app>"
          Source="<Assembly>"
          Type="<Namespace.Class>" />
  </ExtendedTask>
</Tasks>
```

It is not necessary to use Visual Studio's Audio Player Agent project template to create a custom background audio agent. You can create the class and add the task definition to the WMAppManifest.xml file manually if you so choose.

AudioPlayerAgent Sample

The custom audio player agent for this section includes a simple playlist, which includes both locally stored and remote audio files. The class is called BackgroundAudioPlayerAgent, and it is located in the WPUnleashed.BackgroundAudio project, within the BackgroundAudio solution in the downloadable sample code.

A static list of audio tracks defines the playlist, shown in the following excerpt:

```csharp
static readonly List<AudioTrack> playList
    = new List<AudioTrack>
        {
            new AudioTrack(new Uri("AudioFiles/Audio01.wma",
                              UriKind.Relative),
                          "Ringtone 1",              // title
                          "Windows Phone",           // artist
                          "Windows Phone Ringtones", // album
                          null),
            /* ... */

            /* A remote URI. */
            new AudioTrack(new Uri("http://example.com/track.mp3",
                              UriKind.Absolute),
                          "Episode 29",
                          "Windows Phone Radio",
                          "Windows Phone Radio Podcast",
                          null)
        };
```

> **TIP**
>
> `AudioPlayerAgents` remain active during playback. This allows the creation of dynamic playlists. During playback, you could retrieve a playlist on a background thread from a remote server.

If providing playback of local media files, the files must be copied to isolated storage before they can be played by the background audio player. The `IIsolatedStorageUtility` is a custom interface that abstracts access to isolated storage. It is used by the `BackgroundAudioPlayerAgent` to detect whether the media files have already been written to isolated storage; if not, it is used to copy the sample files. The downloadable sample code contains all the code for the `IIsolatedStorageUtility` and its default implementation `IsolatedStorageUtility`. See the following excerpt:

```
internal static void CopyAudioToIsolatedStorage(
    IIsolatedStorageUtility isolatedStorageUtility)
{
    ArgumentValidator.AssertNotNull(
        isolatedStorageUtility, "isolatedStorageUtility");
    /* If a file exists, do not copy. */
    if (isolatedStorageUtility.FileExists("AudioFiles/Audio01.wma"))
    {
        return;
    }

    string[] files = new[] { "Audio01.wma", "Audio02.wma", "Audio03.wma" };

    var sourceToDestinations = from file in files
                    let path = "AudioFiles/" + file
                    select new KeyValuePair<string, string>(path, path);

    isolatedStorageUtility.CopyApplicationResourcesToIsolatedStorage(
                                        sourceToDestinations);
}
```

The custom `BackgroundAudioPlayerAgent` keeps track of the current track number using a static `int` field. This is made possible because, unlike its `ScheduledTaskAgent` counterpart, the process for an `AudioPlayerAgent` is not terminated when `NotifyComplete` is called.

The track number field is used to select the correct track to play when the user requests the previous or next track, as shown:

```
void PlayNextTrack(BackgroundAudioPlayer player)
{
    if (++trackNumber >= playList.Count)
    {
        trackNumber = 0;
    }
```

```
    PlayTrack(player);
}


void PlayPreviousTrack(BackgroundAudioPlayer player)
{
    if (--trackNumber < 0)
    {
        trackNumber = playList.Count - 1;
    }

    PlayTrack(player);
}
```

A `PlayTrack` method is used to toggle the play state of the `BackgroundAudioPlayer`, as shown:

```
void PlayTrack(BackgroundAudioPlayer player)
{
    if (player.PlayerState == PlayState.Paused)
    {
        player.Play();
    }
    else
    {
        player.Track = playList[trackNumber];
    }
}
```

During playback, when the `BackgroundAudioPlayer.Track` property is set, the track does not begin immediate playback, but rather the `BackgroundAudioPlayer` is placed into a `TrackReady` state, and the `AudioPlayerAgent.OnPlayStateChanged` method is called. You see how this fits together in a moment.

AudioPlayerAgent **Virtual Methods**

`AudioPlayerAgent` has the following three virtual methods that can be overridden in your implementation:

- ▶ OnPlayStateChanged
- ▶ OnUserAction
- ▶ OnError

The following sections explore each method in detail.

AudioPlayerAgent.OnPlayStateChanged

`OnPlayStateChanged` enables you to respond to changes in the playback state of an audio track. For example, it allows you to transition the play state of a track once it has completed downloading or to move to the next track when a track finishes, as shown in the following excerpt:

```
protected override void OnPlayStateChanged(
    BackgroundAudioPlayer player, AudioTrack track, PlayState playState)
{
    switch (playState)
    {
        case PlayState.TrackReady:
            /* The track to play is set in the PlayTrack method. */
            player.Play();
            break;

        case PlayState.TrackEnded:
            PlayNextTrack(player);
            break;
    }

    NotifyComplete();
}
```

Table 34.4 describes the `PlayState` enum values that can be handled in the `OnPlayStateChanged` method.

TABLE 34.4   `PlayState` Enum

Enum Value	Description
BufferingStarted	The current track has started buffering.
BufferingStopped	The current track has stopped buffering.
Error	An error occurred.
FastForwarding	The current track is fast-forwarding.
Paused	Playback for the app is paused.
Playing	This app is currently playing a track.
Rewinding	The current track is rewinding.
Shutdown	The app has shut down.
Stopped	No playback is occurring in this application.
TrackEnded	The last track has ended and the app is currently changing tracks.
TrackReady	The current track is ready for playback.
Unknown	The current `Microsoft.Phone.BackgroundAudio.PlayState` is indeterminate. For example, a new `Microsoft.Phone.BackgroundAudio.AudioTrack` has been set, but playback has not been initiated.

NOTE

Whereas the `OnPlayStateChanged` method is used to respond to playback state changes, the `OnError` method is called when an error occurs during playback, and not `OnPlayStateChanged`.

AudioPlayerAgent.OnUserAction

The name of the `OnUserAction` method is somewhat misleading. The task of the `OnUserAction` method is to handle `BackgroundAudioPlayer` actions that occur in your foreground app.

Two actions cause the `AudioPlayerAgent.OnUserAction` method to be called. The first action occurs when the user presses the Universal Volume Control (UVC), and an onscreen menu is displayed allowing the user to play, pause, and skip forward and backward between tracks (see Figure 34.2). User actions do not directly affect the `BackgroundAudioPlayer`, but rather your `AudioPlayerAgent` is responsible for manipulating the player via the `OnUserAction` method.

FIGURE 34.2   Tapping the onscreen menu background launches your app.

The second action occurs when your app is in the foreground and it calls one of the playback related methods on the `BackgroundAudioPlayer.Instance` object, such as `Play`. This type of action may or may not have been directed by the user.

TIP

The volume up and volume down buttons and the play/pause button of the UVC can be simulated in the Windows Phone emulator using the F9, F10, and F11 keys, respectively.

Although a function key simulates pressing the play/pause button, the play/pause button is not a required hardware button on Windows Phone devices and therefore may not be present on every device.

OnUserAction is passed a UserAction enum value that allows you to determine the behavior of the audio player agent. In some cases, the player can be put into action immediately. See the following excerpt:

```
protected override void OnUserAction(
    BackgroundAudioPlayer player, AudioTrack track, UserAction action,
    object param)
{
    /* User actions can be initiated from the main application
     * or from the UVC (Universal Volume Control). */
    switch (action)
    {
        case UserAction.Play:
            PlayTrack(player);
            break;

        case UserAction.Pause:
            player.Pause();
            break;

        case UserAction.SkipPrevious:
            PlayPreviousTrack(player);
            break;

        case UserAction.SkipNext:
            PlayNextTrack(player);
            break;

        case UserAction.Stop:
            player.Stop();
            break;
    }

    NotifyComplete();
}
```

Table 34.5 lists the UserAction enum values that can be handled in the OnUserAction method.

> **NOTE**
>
> The param object argument, of the OnUserAction method, is used only with the action argument UserAction.Seek, in which case the param argument is a TimeSpan that indicates the requested track position.

34

TABLE 34.5   `UserAction` Enum

Enum Value	Description
FastForward	Fast-forward the current track.
Pause	Pause playback.
Play	Play or resume playback.
Rewind	Rewind the current track.
Seek	Seek to a position within the current track.
SkipNext	Skip to the next track.
SkipPrevious	Skip to the previous track.
Stop	Stop playback.

AudioPlayerAgent.OnError

OnError is called when an Exception is raised during playback of an audio track. The method is generally called when the agent encounters a connection error when downloading an audio file from a remote server and offers the opportunity to transition to a different track, one that is potentially stored locally if the error is due to an absence of network connectivity.

In the following excerpt you see that when an error is determined to be fatal, the Abort method is called, signaling to the OS that playback should be disabled. The method implementation is identical to the base class implementation and need not be implemented if you do not want to provide explicit error handling:

```
protected override void OnError(BackgroundAudioPlayer player,
                                AudioTrack track,
                                Exception error, bool isFatal)
{
    if (isFatal)
    {
        Abort();
    }
    else
    {
        NotifyComplete();
    }
}
```

Controlling Background Audio from Your Foreground App

Most apps employing background audio are going to want to provide an enhanced interface within the foreground app for controlling playback and displaying track information. This section looks at the MainPage and associated classes of the WPUnleashed.BackgroundAudio project. The page allows the user to play audio via the

BackgroundAudioPlayer class. It provides application bar buttons for play and pause, stop, rewind, and forward, and several fields for displaying the current track information.

> **NOTE**
>
> It is a Windows Phone Marketplace certification requirement that when the user is already playing background music on the phone when your app is launched, your app must ask the user for consent to stop playing or to adjust the background music. This prompt must occur each time the app launches, unless there is an opt-in setting provided to the user, and the user has used this setting to opt in.

A Testable BackgroundAudioPlayer

The BackgroundAudioPlayer class is inherently difficult to use in unit tests because of the cross-process interaction with the AudioPlayerAgent and its dependence on native phone components. For this reason I have provided a wrapper called BackgroundAudioPlayerProxy, which implements a custom IBackgroundAudioPlayer interface. In addition, a second implementation, MockBackgroundAudioPlayer, allows you to test whether your code called the background audio player as expected; it allows you to test, for example, whether your code attempted to play a track.

The code for IBackgroundAudioPlayer and its associated class implementations is not shown in this chapter because it is lengthy, and the methods, properties, and events of the IBackgroundAudioPlayer coincide with those of the built-in BackgroundAudioPlayer. You can, however, find the code in the downloadable sample code for the book.

MainPageViewModel

The viewmodel is declared as a field of the MainPage, as shown:

```
readonly MainPageViewModel viewModel = new MainPageViewModel(
                                    new BackgroundAudioPlayerProxy(),
                                    new IsolatedStorageUtility());
```

The MainPageViewModel class constructor accepts an IBackgroundAudioPlayer as well as an IIsolatedStorageUtility instance (see Listing 34.1). A subscription to the PlayStateChanged event of the background audio player allows the viewmodel to update various properties whenever the play state changes.

The viewmodel contains five commands for controlling the BackgroundAudioPlayer while the app is in the foreground, which provide for playing, pausing, stopping, and skipping between tracks.

The viewmodel's Refresh method is called to update the viewmodel, which relies on the state of the BackgroundAudioPlayer. A Timer is used to monitor the progress of the track while it is being played.

34

LISTING 34.1   `MainPageViewModel` Constructor

```
public MainPageViewModel(
    IBackgroundAudioPlayer backgroundAudioPlayer,
    IIsolatedStorageUtility isolatedStorageUtility)
{
    player = ArgumentValidator.AssertNotNull(
                backgroundAudioPlayer, "backgroundAudioPlayer");
    ArgumentValidator.AssertNotNull(
                isolatedStorageUtility, "isolatedStorageUtility");

    player.PlayStateChanged += HandlePlayStateChanged;
    BackgroundAudioPlayerAgent.CopyAudioToIsolatedStorage(isolatedStorageUtility);

    playCommand = new DelegateCommand(obj => player.Play());
    pauseCommand = new DelegateCommand(obj => player.Pause());
    stopCommand = new DelegateCommand(obj => player.Stop());
    previousTrackCommand = new DelegateCommand(obj => player.SkipPrevious());
    nextTrackCommand = new DelegateCommand(obj => player.SkipNext());

    Refresh(false);

    timer = new Timer(HandleTimerTick, null, 3000, 1000);
}
```

The viewmodel's `TrackArtist` and `TrackTitle` properties reflect the `Artist` and `Title` properties of the current `AudioTrack`.

The viewmodel's `VisualState` property, which is of type `string`, determines the visual state of the view, and the visibility of various application bar buttons. The `VisualState` value is set to the `PlayerState` property of the `BackgroundAudioPlayer`, as shown:

```
void Refresh(bool setVisualState = true)
{
    switch (player.PlayerState)
    {
        case PlayState.Playing:
            CanPause = true;
            TrackArtist = player.Track.Artist;
            TrackTitle = player.Track.Title;
            break;
        case PlayState.Paused:
            CanPause = false;
            break;
    }

    BufferingProgress = player.BufferingProgress;
```

```
if (setVisualState)
{
    VisualState = player.PlayerState.ToString("G");
}

if (player.Error != null)
{
    MessageService.ShowError("A problem occured:" + player.Error);
}
}
```

When the viewmodel's `VisualState` property changes, the view responds by refreshing the `VisualStateManager` state. This is performed from the `MainPage` constructor, as shown:

```
public MainPage()
{
    InitializeComponent();

    DataContext = viewModel;

    viewModel.PropertyChanged
        += (sender, args) =>
            {
                if (args.PropertyName == "VisualState")
                {
                    SetVisualState();
                }
            };
}
```

The view's custom `AppBar` includes icon buttons bound to the viewmodel's commands, as shown:

```
<u:AppBar>
    <u:AppBarIconButton
            Command="{Binding PreviousTrackCommand}"
            Text="Previous"
            IconUri="/Images/ApplicationBarIcons/Previous.png" />

    <!-- A toggle button is used rather than visual state to avoid
         repopulating the app bar when the user taps play or pause. -->
    <u:AppBarToggleButton
            x:Name="Button_Play"
            Command1="{Binding PlayCommand}"
            Text1="Play"
            Icon1Uri="/Images/ApplicationBarIcons/Play.png"
```

```
        Command2="{Binding PauseCommand}"
        Text2="Pause"
        Icon2Uri="/Images/ApplicationBarIcons/Pause.png"
        Toggled="{Binding CanPause}"/>

<u:AppBarIconButton
        x:Name="Button_Stop"
        Command="{Binding StopCommand}"
        Text="Stop"
        IconUri="/Images/ApplicationBarIcons/Stop.png" />

<u:AppBarIconButton
        Command="{Binding NextTrackCommand}"
        Text="Previous"
        IconUri="/Images/ApplicationBarIcons/Next.png" />
</u:AppBar>
```

The viewmodel's `ViewState` property determines the visibility of each button. The XAML that defines the `VisualStateGroups` is not shown, but if you are interested, see the downloadable sample code.

Two `TextBlock` controls are used to display the viewmodel's `TrackArtist` and `TrackTitle` properties, like so:

```
<TextBlock Text="{Binding TrackArtist}"
        Style="{StaticResource PhoneTextTitle3Style}"
        TextWrapping="Wrap" />
<TextBlock Text="{Binding TrackTitle}"
        Style="{StaticResource PhoneTextTitle2Style}"
        TextWrapping="Wrap" />
```

Whenever the track changes, these fields are updated according to the new track.

Monitoring Playback Progress

The viewmodel contains a `Position` property that reflects the progress of the current `AudioTrack`. Because the `BackgroundAudioPlayer` does not have facility to monitor the progress of a track directly, the viewmodel uses a `Timer` to periodically raise a property changed event for the `Position` property. The tick handler is shown in the following excerpt:

```
void HandleTimerTick(object state)
{
    if (player.PlayerState == PlayState.Playing)
    {
        OnPropertyChanged(() => Position);
    }
}
```

When a `Position` property change is detected in the view, it prompts a `Slider` control to reread the property. The `Position` get accessor calculates the position value, which is returned as a value between 0 and 1, as shown:

```
public double Position
{
    get
    {
        if (player.Track == null || player.Track.Duration.TotalSeconds < 1)
        {
            return 0;
        }
        double result = player.Position.TotalSeconds
                            / player.Track.Duration.TotalSeconds;
        return result;
    }
    set
    {
        if (player.Track != null)
        {
            double newSeconds = player.Track.Duration.TotalSeconds * value;
            TimeSpan newPosition = TimeSpan.FromSeconds(newSeconds);
            player.Position = newPosition;
        }
        OnPropertyChanged(() => Position);
    }
}
```

Raising a property changed event for the `Position` property causes the `Slider`, which is bound to the property, to be updated. The `Slider` is defined like so:

```
<Slider Value="{Binding Position, Mode=TwoWay}" Minimum="0" Maximum="1" />
```

Figure 34.3 shows the `MainPage` with the slider indicating the progress of the current track and the application bar icon buttons for controlling playback.

Numerous possibilities exist for extending an app such as this. For example, it could be extended to include a view for the playlist or an image for the album art—the sky's the limit!

34

FIGURE 34.3   A user interface to control the `BackgroundAudioPlayer` from a foreground app.

Audio Streaming Agents

Audio streaming agents allow you to customize how audio files are downloaded and decoded by your app, and they enable you to support live streaming scenarios not natively supported by the phone.

An audio streaming agent can be created in the same manner as an audio player agent, by using the "Windows Phone Audio Streaming Agent" Visual Studio project template (shown previously in Figure 34.1).

The Visual Studio project template produces a class that derives from `AudioStreamingAgent`. The agent must then be registered with your main project's WMAppManifest.xml file, which is done automatically when linking to an Audio Streaming Agent project. The XML definition can be seen alongside the `AudioPlayerAgent`, as shown:

```
<Tasks>
  <DefaultTask  Name="_default" NavigationPage="MainPage.xaml"/>
    <ExtendedTask Name="BackgroundTask">
        <BackgroundServiceAgent Specifier="AudioPlayerAgent"
            Name="<Unique name within the app>"
            Source="<Assembly>"
            Type="<Namespace.Class>" />
        <BackgroundServiceAgent Specifier="AudioStreamingAgent"
            Name="<Unique name within the app>"
```

```
            Source="<Assembly>"
            Type="<Namespace.Class>" />
    </ExtendedTask>
</Tasks>
```

Registering a custom `AudioStreamingAgent` does not disable the built-in streaming and decoding of the phone. The OS determines whether to use the built-in audio streaming, or your custom `AudioStreamingAgent`, based on the `AudioTrack`'s `Source` property, each time a new `AudioTrack` is played. To have your custom `AudioStreamingAgent` called for a particular track, assign the `Source` property of the `AudioTrack` to null, as shown in the following excerpt:

```
new AudioTrack(null, /* Uri is null so that it is sent
                      * to the AudioStreamingAgent
                      * called AssemblyAudioStreamingAgent. */
                      "Assembly Track!",
                      "Acquired using AudioStreamingAgent",
                      "Unleashed",
                      null,
                      "AudioFiles/Audio04.mp3", // Tag parameter.
                      EnabledPlayerControls.All),
```

If the `Uri` is not null, the OS performs all streaming and decoding. By using this technique, you can use a combination of both the inbuilt streaming and decoding for some tracks, and custom streaming and decoding for others.

The `AudioTrack` class contains a `Tag` property, which can be used to pass information to an `AudioStreamingAgent`. Notice from the previous excerpt that this property is set to the relative path of an audio file resource. You see, in the next section, how this value is used to resolve an audio file resource from the current assembly.

`AudioStreamingAgent` contains a virtual method named `OnBeginStreaming`, which is overridden to handle streaming and decoding of an audio track. The method has two parameters: the `AudioTrack` and an `AudioStreamer`. The `AudioStreamer` allows you to attach your own `MediaStreamSource`. `MediaStreamSource` provides you with direct access to APIs for manipulating encoded elementary audio and video streams. It enables you to implement your own mechanism for processing the contents of a media file, enabling support beyond the native built-in media formats.

Creating a custom `MediaStreamSource` is a large topic and one that is outside the scope of this book. A good starting point for learning about the `MediaStreamSource` is the MSDN ManagedMediaHelpers project located at http://archive.msdn.microsoft.com/ManagedMediaHelpers.

Although this section does not cover `MediaStreamSource` in detail, it does, however, look at applying a specialized `MediaStreamSource` from the ManagedMediaHelpers project to enable the playback of audio files that are located in an app's assembly, something that is not supported by the phone's built-in streaming and decoding system.

Using a `MediaStreamSource` to Play Back an Assembly Resource

The built-in streaming and decoding system on the phone only supports playback of local audio files when they are located in isolated storage. This section looks at enabling the direct playback of audio files located within an app assembly.

The code for this section resides in the `AssemblyAudioStreamingAgent` class of the WPUnleashed.BackgroundAudio project in the downloadable sample code. `AssemblyAudioStreamingAgent` is a subclass of `AudioStreamingAgent` and overrides the base type's `OnBeginStreaming` method (see Listing 34.2). The custom `IsolatedStorageUtility` is used to retrieve the byte stream for an audio file, whose location is specified by the `AudioTrack.Tag` property. An `Mp3MediaStreamSource`, from the `ManagedMediaHelpers` library, is created using the stream. The `Mp3MediaStreamSource` is then assigned to the `AudioStreamer`, which then relies on the `Mp3MediaStreamSource` to provide format-independent audio data.

LISTING 34.2   `AssemblyAudioStreamingAgent.OnBeginStreaming` Method

```
protected override void OnBeginStreaming(AudioTrack track, AudioStreamer streamer)
{
    IsolatedStorageUtility utility = new IsolatedStorageUtility();
    Uri uri = new Uri(track.Tag, UriKind.Relative);
    Stream stream = utility.GetApplicationResourceStream(uri);
    Mp3MediaStreamSource mediaStreamSource
            = new Mp3MediaStreamSource(stream, stream.Length);
    streamer.SetSource(mediaStreamSource);

    /* Not to be called. */
    //NotifyComplete();
}
```

> **NOTE**
>
> Do not call `NotifyComplete` within the `OnBeginStreaming` method. Doing so causes the process running the `AudioStreamingAgent` to be terminated, which halts playback of the file.

Having the capability to provide your own custom streaming means that you can support other third-party services or retrieve files from, for example, a WCF service, which is not supported natively by the OS.

Listing 34.3 demonstrates how to use a `WebRequest` to manually stream an audio file from the Web.

LISTING 34.3 `OnBeginStreaming` **Method with** `WebRequest`

```
protected override void OnBeginStreaming(AudioTrack track, AudioStreamer streamer)
{
    HttpWebRequest request
            = WebRequest.CreateHttp("http://localhost:4864/Audio.mp3");
    request.AllowReadStreamBuffering = true;
    request.BeginGetResponse(asyncResult =>
        {
            HttpWebResponse response
                = request.EndGetResponse(asyncResult) as HttpWebResponse;
            if (response != null)
            {
                Stream stream = response.GetResponseStream();
                mediaStreamSource = new Mp3MediaStreamSource(
                                        stream, response.ContentLength);
                streamer.SetSource(mediaStreamSource);
            }
        }, null);
}
```

Although not something you will need every day, audio streaming agents provide the means to overcome any limitations imposed by the built-in streaming and decoding system on the phone.

Summary

This chapter began with an overview of the background audio player and showed how it is used to control the playback of local or remote audio files. You looked at how audio file information is represented by the `AudioTrack` class and examined the role of background audio agents, which are used to coordinate audio playback while your app is not running in the foreground. You saw that when used in the foreground, a `BackgroundAudioPlayer` forwards all calls to the registered `AudioPlayerAgent`. Conversely, when a `BackgroundAudioPlayer` is used in an `AudioPlayerAgent`, it directly affects playback on the device.

The chapter then demonstrated how to build a UI that leverages the background audio agent, for controlling playback while your app is in the foreground.

Finally, the chapter examined audio streaming agents, and you saw how they are used to provide custom streaming and decoding of audio files. You also saw how a custom audio streaming agent can be employed to play audio directly from an assembly resource, something not possible using the built-in streaming and decoding system of the phone.

Bibliography

Chapter 2, "Fundamental Concepts in Windows Phone Development"

"Model-View-ViewModel," http://en.wikipedia.org/wiki/Model_View_ViewModel.

Smith, Josh, "WPF Apps with the Model-View-ViewModel Design Pattern," http://msdn.microsoft.com/en-us/magazine/dd419663.aspx.

Chapter 3, "Understanding the Application Execution Model"

Rodriguez, Jaime, "Running a Windows Phone Application under the Lock Screen," http://blogs.msdn.com/b/jaimer/archive/2010/11/01/running-a-windows-phoneapplication-under-the-lock-screen.aspx.

Chapter 7, "Employing Media and Web Elements"

Rodriguez, Jaime, "A deepzoom primer (explained and coded)," http://blogs.msdn.com/b/jaimer/archive/2008/03/31/a-deepzoom-primer-explained-and-coded.aspx.

Chapter 9, "Enriching the User Experience with the Windows Phone Toolkit Controls," and Chapter 16, "Sensing Motion and Attitude"

Sampson, Nigel, "Using LoopingSelector from the Silverlight Toolkit," http://compiledexperience.com/blog/posts/using-loopingselector-from-the-silverlight-toolkit.

Chapter 11, "Creating Expansive and Engaging Apps with the Pivot and Panorama"

Vaughan, Katka, "Netflix Browser for Windows Phone 7—Part 1," http://www.codeproject.com/KB/windows-phone-7/NetflixBrowser.aspx.

Chapter 26, "Validating User Input"

"Understanding Validation in Silverlight," *AJ's blog*, http://ajdotnet.wordpress.com/2010/02/28/understanding-validation-in-silverlight.

Chapter 27, "Communicating with Network Services"

Dolhaig, "Zune Detection and Network Awareness," *The Code Project*, http://www.codeproject.com/KB/windows-phone-7/ZuneDetectAndNetworking.aspx.

Index

A

How can we make this index more useful? Email us at indexes@samspublishing.com

C

D

G

H

I

M

O

P

How can we make this index more useful? Email us at indexes@samspublishing.com

U

W